A FIRST LOOK AT
COMMUNICATION
THEORY

TENTH EDITION

EM GRIFFIN

ANDREW LEDBETTER

GLENN SPARKS

A FIRST LOOK AT
COMMUNICATION THEORY

TENTH EDITION

EM GRIFFIN

Wheaton College

ANDREW LEDBETTER

Texas Christian University

GLENN SPARKS

Purdue University

McGraw Hill Education

A FIRST LOOK AT COMMUNICATION THEORY, TENTH EDITION

Published by McGraw-Hill Education, 2 Penn Plaza, New York, NY 10121. Copyright © 2019 by McGraw-Hill Education. All rights reserved. Printed in the United States of America. Previous editions © 2015, 2012, and 2009. No part of this publication may be reproduced or distributed in any form or by any means, or stored in a database or retrieval system, without the prior written consent of McGraw-Hill Education, including, but not limited to, in any network or other electronic storage or transmission, or broadcast for distance learning.

Some ancillaries, including electronic and print components, may not be available to customers outside the United States.

This book is printed on acid-free paper.

1 2 3 4 5 6 QVS 22 21 20 19 18

ISBN 978-1-259-91378-5
MHID 1-259-91378-3

Portfolio Manager: *Jamie Laferrera*
Product Developer: *Alexander Preiss*
Marketing Manager: *Meredith Leo*
Content Project Manager: *Maria McGreal*
Buyer: *Laura Fuller*
Design: *Lumina Datamatics, Inc.*
Content Licensing Specialist: *Lori Slattery*
Cover Image: *©McGraw-Hill Education*
Compositor: *Lumina Datamatics, Inc.*

All credits appearing on page or at the end of the book are considered to be an extension of the copyright page.

Library of Congress Cataloging-in-Publication Data

Cataloging-in-Publication Data has been requested from the Library of Congress.

The Internet addresses listed in the text were accurate at the time of publication. The inclusion of a website does not indicate an endorsement by the authors or McGraw-Hill Education, and McGraw-Hill Education does not guarantee the accuracy of the information presented at these sites.

mheducation.com/highered

ABOUT THE AUTHORS

Em Griffin is Professor Emeritus of Communication at Wheaton College in Illinois, where he taught for more than 35 years and was chosen Teacher of the Year. In 2016, he was awarded the Wallace A. Bacon Lifetime Teaching Excellence Award from the National Communication Association. He received his M.A. and Ph.D. in communication from Northwestern University; his research interest is in the development of close friendships. Em is the author of three applied communication books: *The Mind Changers* (persuasion), *Getting Together* (group dynamics), and *Making Friends* (close relationships). Throughout his life, Em has served as an active volunteer in four nonprofit organizations—Young Life (high school youth), Opportunity International (microfinance services for women in poverty), Chicago Center for Conflict Resolution (mediation), and his church. Em's wife, Jean, is an artist and a musician. They've been married for more than 50 years and have two adult children, Jim and Sharon, and six grandchildren—all deeply involved in baseball or hockey. You can reach Em at em.griffin@wheaton.edu.

Andrew Ledbetter is an Associate Professor of Communication Studies at Texas Christian University. He received his M.A. and Ph.D. in communication studies from the University of Kansas. His research addresses how people use communication technology to maintain family and other interpersonal relationships. Andrew has published more than 50 articles and book chapters, and he has received recognition for teaching excellence from both the National Communication Association and Central States Communication Association. His wife, Jessica, is a former attorney who is pursuing a doctorate in higher education administration at Texas Christian University. With their daughters, Sydney and Kira, they enjoy involvement in their church, playing board and card games, running, reading, cooking, and following the TCU Horned Frogs and Kansas Jayhawks. You can reach Andrew at a.ledbetter@tcu.edu, visit his blog at www.andrewledbetter.com, or follow him on Twitter via @dr_ledbetter.

Glenn Sparks is a professor in the Brian Lamb School of Communication at Purdue University in Indiana, where he has taught for 32 years and won the highest undergraduate teaching award given by the College of Liberal Arts. He received his Ph.D. in communication arts from the University of Wisconsin-Madison. Glenn is the author of *Media Effects Research: A Basic Overview* and a personal memoir, *Rolling in Dough: Lessons I Learned in a Doughnut Shop*. He's co-author of *Refrigerator Rights: Our Crucial Need for Close Connection*. Glenn is an avid sports fan and an aspiring theremin player. He is married to Cheri, who is also a Ph.D. and lecturer in the Brian Lamb School of Communication at Purdue. They have three adult children, David, Erin, and Jordan, and four grandchildren, Caleb, Joshua, Autumn, and Benjamin. You can reach Glenn at gsparks@purdue.edu.

DEDICATION

We dedicate this book to our wives, Jeanie, Jessica, and Cheri, who encouraged us to work together, celebrated with us when the process went well, and comforted us when it didn't. Just as they lovingly supported us in this project, we commit to being there for them in what they feel called to do.

Em, Andrew, Glenn

CONTENTS

PREFACE FOR INSTRUCTORS

If you're already familiar with *A First Look at Communication Theory* and understand the approach, organization, and main features of the book, you may want to jump ahead to the "Major Changes in the Tenth Edition" section. For those who are new to the text, reading the entire preface will give you a good grasp of what you and your students can expect.

A Balanced Approach to Theory Selection. We've written *A First Look* for students who have no background in communication theory. It's designed for undergraduates enrolled in an entry-level course, regardless of the students' classification. The trend in the field is to offer students a broad introduction to theory relatively early in their program. But if a department chooses to offer its first theory course on the junior or senior level, the course will still be the students' first comprehensive look at theory, so the book will meet them where they are.

Our goal in this text is to present 32 communication theories in a clear and interesting way. After reading about a given theory, students should understand the theory, know the research that supports it, see useful applications in their lives, and be aware of the theory's possible flaws. We hope readers will discover relationships among theories located across the communication landscape—a clear indication that they grasp what they're reading. But that kind of integrative thinking only takes place when students first comprehend what a theorist claims.

With the help of more than 400 instructors, we've selected a range of theories that reflect the diversity within the discipline. Some theories are proven candidates for a Communication Theory Hall of Fame. For example, Aristotle's analysis of logical, emotional, and ethical appeals continues to set the agenda for many public speaking courses. Mead's symbolic interactionism is formative for interpretive theorists who are dealing with language, thought, meaning, self-concept, or the effect of society upon the individual. Berger's uncertainty reduction theory was the first objective theory to be crafted by a social scientist trained in the field. And no student of mediated communication should be ignorant of Gerbner's cultivation theory, which explains why heavy television viewing cultivates fear of a mean and scary world.

It would be shortsighted, however, to limit the selection to the classics of communication. Some of the discipline's most creative approaches are its newest. For example, Sandra Petronio's theory of communication privacy management undergirds much of the research conducted in the field of health communication. Leslie Baxter's theory of relational dialectics offers insight into the ongoing tensions inherent in personal relationships. Robert McPhee's communicative constitution of organizations describes how the principle of social construction works in an organizational context. And, like almost all social media theorizing, Caroline Haythornthwaite's media multiplexity theory is still being tested and refined.

Organizational Plan of the Book. Each chapter introduces a single theory in 10 to 15 pages. We've found that most undergraduates think in terms of discrete packets of information, so the concentrated coverage gives them a chance to focus their thoughts while reading a single chapter. This way, students can gain an in-depth understanding of important theories instead of acquiring only a vague familiarity with a jumble of related ideas. The one-chapter–one-theory arrangement also gives teachers the opportunity to skip theories or rearrange the order of presentation without tearing apart the fabric of the text.

The first four chapters provide a framework for understanding the theories to come. The opening chapter, "Launching Your Study of Communication Theory," presents working definitions of both *theory* and *communication*, and also prepares students for the arrangement of the chapters and the features within them. Chapter 2, "Talk About Theory," lays the groundwork for understanding the differences between objective and interpretive theories. Chapter 3, "Weighing the Words," presents two sets of criteria for determining a good objective or interpretive theory. Based on Robert Craig's (University of Colorado) conception, Chapter 4, "Mapping the Territory," introduces seven traditions within the field of communication theory.

Following this integrative framework, we feature 32 theories in 32 self-contained chapters. Each theory is discussed within the context of a communication topic: interpersonal messages, relationship development, relationship maintenance, influence, group communication, organizational communication, public rhetoric, media and culture, media effects, gender and communication, or intercultural communication. These communication context sections usually cover three theories. Each section's two-page introduction outlines a crucial issue that theorists working in this area address. The placement of theories in familiar contexts helps students recognize that theories are answers to questions they've been asking all along. The final chapter, "Common Threads in Comm Theories," offers students a novel form of integration that will help them discern order in the tapestry of communication theory that might otherwise seem chaotic.

Because all theory and practice has value implications, we briefly explore a dozen ethical principles throughout the book. Consistent with the focus of this text, each principle is the central tenet of a specific ethical theory. Other disciplines may ignore these thorny issues, but to discuss communication as a process that is untouched by questions of good and bad, right and wrong, or questions of character would be to disregard an ongoing concern in our field.

Features of Each Chapter. Most people think in pictures. Students will have a rough time understanding a theory unless they apply its explanations and interpretations to concrete situations. Many chapters offer an extended example to illustrate the "truth" a theory proposes. We encourage readers to try out ideas by visualizing a first meeting of freshman roommates, trying to persuade other students to support a zero-tolerance policy on driving after drinking, considering the turbulent marriage of a prophet and a prostitute, and many others. We also use two speeches of President Barack Obama, and scenes from *Mad Men, The Office, The Help*, and *Thank You for Smoking* to illustrate principles of the theories. The case studies in chapters follow the pedagogical principle of explaining what students don't yet know in terms of ideas and images that are already within their experience.

Some theories are tightly linked with an extensive research project. For example, the impact of cognitive dissonance theory was greatly spurred by Festinger's surprising finding in his now classic $1/$20 experiment. And Orbe's co-cultural theory emerged when he conducted intensive focus groups with members of the LGBTQ community, African American men, and people with physical disabilities. When such exemplars exist, we describe the research in detail so that students can learn from and appreciate the benefits of grounding theory in systematic observation. In this way, readers of *A First Look* are led through a variety of research designs and data analyses.

Students will encounter the names of Baxter, Berger, Bormann, Burgoon, Burke, Deetz, Fisher, Giles, Kramarae, Orbe, Pacanowsky, Pearce, Ting-Toomey, Walther, Wood, and many others in later communication courses. We therefore make a concerted effort to link theory and theorist. By pairing a particular theory with its originator, we try to promote both recall and respect for a given scholar's effort.

The text of each chapter concludes with a section that critiques the theory. This represents a hard look at the ideas presented in light of the criteria for a good theory outlined in Chapter 3. Some theorists have suggested that we are "friends" of their theory. We appreciate that because we want to present all of the theories in a constructive way. But after we summarize a theory's strengths, we then discuss its weaknesses, unanswered questions, and possible errors that remain. We try to stimulate a "That makes sense, and yet I wonder . . ." response among students.

We include a short list of thought questions at the end of each chapter. Labeled "Questions to Sharpen Your Focus," these probes encourage students to make connections among ideas in the chapter and also to apply the theory to their everyday communication experience. As part of this feature, words printed in italics remind students of the key terms of a given theory.

Each chapter ends with a short list of annotated readings entitled "A Second Look." The heading refers to resources for students who are interested in a theory and want to go further than a 10- to 15-page introduction allows. The top item is the resource we recommend as the starting point for further study. The other listings identify places to look for material about each of the major issues raised in the chapter. The format is designed to offer practical encouragement and guidance for further study without overwhelming the novice with multiple citations. The sources of quotations and citations of evidence are listed in an "Endnotes" section at the end of the book.

We think instructors and students alike will get a good chuckle out of the cartoons we've selected for each chapter. The art's main function, however, is to illustrate significant points in the text. As in other editions, we're committed to using quality cartoon art from *The New Yorker* and comic strips such as "Calvin and Hobbes" and "Dilbert." Perceptive cartoonists are modern-day prophets—their humor serves the education process well when it slips through mental barriers or attitudinal defenses that didactic prose can't penetrate.

A co-authored book always faces the challenge of being consistent in style and voice across chapters. This has been less of a problem for us because of our history together. Andrew Ledbetter and Glenn Sparks continue to be co-authors and equal partners with Em. Both men are highly recognized scholars in their field—Andrew in online communication and family communication, Glenn in media effects and interpersonal communication. Glenn was a student in Em's first persuasion course at Wheaton; Andrew aced one of the last communication theory classes Em taught before he retired from full-time teaching. Despite differences in our ages of more than 40 years, the three of us are close friends and colleagues who have published together before. Each of us vets and edits what the other two write and offers advice on what to cover. We're convinced that this interactive process ensures students will read up-to-date information presented in the same style that has characterized the book throughout the previous nine editions.

While no author considers his or her style ponderous or dull, we believe we've presented the theories in a clear and lively fashion. Accuracy alone does not communicate. We've tried to remain faithful to the vocabulary each theorist uses so that the student can consider the theory in the author's own terms, but we also translate technical language into more familiar words. Students and reviewers cite readability and interest as particular strengths of the text. We encourage you to sample a chapter so you can decide for yourself.

In 13 of the chapters, you'll see photographs of the theorists who appear in "Conversations with Communication Theorists," eight-minute video clips of our discussions together. The text that accompanies each picture previews intriguing comments the theorists made so students can watch the interview with a specific purpose in mind. These videos are available at *www.afirstlook.com*, our authors' website averaging 50,000 log-ins a month. On that site you will also find auto-graded quizzes, chapter outlines, theory abstracts, web links, an archive of theory chapters no longer in the text, and a list of feature film scenes illustrating specific theories. In a password-protected section of the site, instructors can see suggestions for classroom discussion and activities, recommendations for further theory resources, chapter-by-chapter changes from the previous edition, and a chart of theory coverage in other communication theory texts.

Along with many of these resources, an Instructor's Manual, test bank, and lecture slides are available through McGraw-Hill Connect. Connect, McGraw-Hill Education's integrated assignment and assessment platform, also offers SmartBook for the new edition, which is the first adaptive reading experience proven to improve grades and help students study more effectively. Additional information about Connect is available at the end of this preface.

Major Changes in the Tenth Edition. Responding to instructors' desire to offer students more than one social media theory, we're introducing Caroline Haythornthwaite's media multiplexity theory, which explores the mix of media that people use to connect with each other and the strength of their relational bond. We've also added Mark Orbe's co-cultural theory, which is based on extensive phenomenological research among the LGBTQ community, people with physical disabilities, and African American men. The theory plots their patterns of communication with those in the dominant culture based on their desire to stay separate from, seek accommodation from, or assimilate into that culture. To make room for these theories, we've moved our treatment of Watzlawick's interactional view and Philipsen's speech codes theory to the archive at *www.afirstlook.com*, where full chapters can be easily accessed if you desire to assign them to your students.

We've made a concerted effort to update and replace examples that no longer have the explanatory power or appeal they did when introduced in previous editions. We've also worked hard to sharpen the end-of-chapter Critique sections, and in almost all chapters we base our comments on the six criteria for a good interpretive or scientific theory outlined in Chapter 3. Half the chapters in the book have undergone major additions, deletions, or alterations. Here's a sample:

- Our revised critique of *social information processing theory* cites MIT professor Sherry Turkle's challenge to Walther's basic claim that anything we do face-to-face can be done just as well or better online. She claims smartphones are drastically reducing our ability for conversation, intimacy, and empathy.

- *Relational dialectics theory* has now been fully updated to center on Baxter's second version of the theory, which draws heavily on the thinking of Mikhail Bakhtin. We have replaced the fictional film *Bend It Like Beckham* with examples drawn from real-life research on family communication.

- *Social judgment theory* is now illustrated with the issue of gun control rather than airline safety.

- The *narrative paradigm* is used as a lens to consider the coherence and fidelity of a story about the turbulent marriage between a prophet and a prostitute.

- *Media ecology* now includes a section on the relationship between Marshall McLuhan's theory and his strong religious faith. It then answers the question of why he didn't speak out against behavioral changes in society that he considered immoral.

- *Dramatism* has been rearranged to foreground Burke's thoughts about language, guilt– redemption, and identification. Building from this background, we then introduce the dramatistic pentad, applying it to comprehend reactions to an Obama campaign speech.

- *Cultural studies* now includes Larry Frey's appeal for communicative activism for social justice. This is the only ethical reflection in the book highlighting an ethicist currently active in the field of communication.

- *Agenda-setting theory* now includes the recently introduced third level, whereby the media tell us how issues connect to each other. The chapter also describes the process of melding agendas into communities.

- *Standpoint theory* now more clearly differentiates between the concepts of *social location* and *standpoint*. The critique section also mentions intersectionality as an extension and challenge to feminist thinking.

- Based on updated research, the presentation of *face-negotiation theory* has been simplified. Em concludes the chapter with a story about how knowledge of the theory helped him mediate a bitter conflict at a mosque.

McGraw-Hill Education also offers a robust custom publishing program, Create, that you may want to consider. Create enables you to build a book with only the chapters you need, and arrange them in the order you'll teach them. There's also the option of adding materials you prepare or using chapters from other McGraw-Hill books or resources from their library. When you build a Create book, you will receive a complimentary print review copy in just a few days or a complimentary eBook via email in about one hour.

Acknowledgments. We gratefully acknowledge the wisdom and counsel of many generous scholars whose intellectual capital is embedded in every page you'll read. Over the last 30 years, more than a thousand communication scholars have gone out of their way to make the book better. People who have made direct contributions to this edition include Ron Adler, Santa Barbara City College; Ryan Bisel, University of Oklahoma; Sarah Bunting, Ayurveda; Judee Burgoon, University of Arizona; Sandy Callaghan, Texas Christian University; Ken Chase, Wheaton College; Jeff Child, Kent State University; Stan Deetz, University of Colorado; Sandy French, Radford University; Darin Garard, Santa Barbara City College; Howard Giles, University of California, Santa Barbara; Caroline Haythornthwaite, Syracuse University; Arthur Jensen, Syracuse University; Gang Luo, Ohio University; Bree McEwan, DePaul University; Marty Medhurst, Baylor University; Julia Moore, University of Utah; Mark Orbe, Western Michigan University; Doug Osman, Purdue University; Kim Pearce, CMM Institute for Personal and Social Evolution; Sandra Petronio, University of Indiana–Purdue University Indianapolis; Russ Proctor, Northern Kentucky University; Doug Pruim, Purdue University; Art Ramirez, University of South Florida; Erin Ruppel, University of Wisconsin–Milwaukee; Jordan Soliz, University of Nebraska–Lincoln; Samuel Hardman Taylor, Cornell University; Jessica Vitak, University of Maryland; Deborah Whitt, Wayne State College; Steve Wilson, Purdue University; Paul Witt, Texas Christian University; Julia Wood, University of North Carolina; Robert Woods Jr., Spring Arbor University. Without their help, this edition would be less accurate and certainly less interesting.

Em has great appreciation for Sharon Porteous, a recent Wheaton graduate who served as his research assistant and assembled the comprehensive index that contains thousands of entries—a task no one should do more than once in life.

We are grateful to all the women and men at McGraw-Hill who have been indispensable in making this edition possible: Alex Preiss, Product Developer; Jamie Laferrera, Portfolio Manager; David Patterson, Managing Director; Lori Slattery, Content Licensing Specialist; and Joyce Berendes, Senior Content Licensing Manager. We are greatly appreciate the work of Melissa Sacco, Associate Development Program Director and Sudheer Purushothaman, Project Manager at Lumina Datamatics.

We've been fortunate to work closely with a group of outside contractors who have worked in concert for the last four editions. Jenn Meyer, a commercial computer artist, created and revised figures on 24-hour notice; Judy Brody achieved the impossible by making the extensive and complicated permissions process palatable; Robyn Tellefsen, freelance writer and editor, was Em's student research assistant for the fourth edition of the book, proofreader for three editions, and copy editor for the last two. She also edited a book Glenn wrote. Robyn is quite familiar with communication theory and is someone whose edits we trust implicitly. Thus, the book your students read is better than the one we wrote. Stu Johnson has been the steady webmaster of *www.afirstlook.com* since its inception, creating multiple digital paths for users to find what they want and quickly short-circuiting glitches when they occur. And Amy Keating, for whom Andrew served as graduate advisor at TCU, graciously volunteers to respond to the almost daily requests for passwords to enter the instructors-only section of *www.afirstlook.com*. It's a wonderful team and we're incredibly fortunate to have their skills and friendship.

We offer a special word of appreciation to Emily Langan, who is a central member of our team. Emily is Em's former student who now teaches the courses he taught at Wheaton. This edition is Emily's fifth as author of the ever-evolving Instructor's Manual that is famous among communication theory instructors.

Em recalls the time when he first introduced Emily at a National Communication Association short course on teaching communication theory. The participants stood and applauded. Now she's the lead instructor of that course, where she introduces Em. The three of us are grateful for her wisdom, dedication, creativity, and friendship.

Em Griffin
Andrew Ledbetter
Glenn Sparks

connect®

McGraw-Hill Connect® is a highly reliable, easy-to-use homework and learning management solution that utilizes learning science and award-winning adaptive tools to improve student results.

Homework and Adaptive Learning

- Connect's assignments help students contextualize what they've learned through application, so they can better understand the material and think critically.
- Connect will create a personalized study path customized to individual student needs through SmartBook®.
- SmartBook helps students study more efficiently by delivering an interactive reading experience through adaptive highlighting and review.

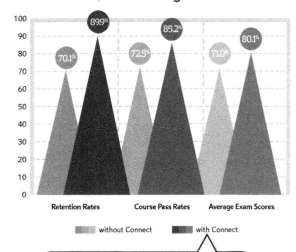

Connect's Impact on Retention Rates, Pass Rates, and Average Exam Scores

Retention Rates: 70.1% without Connect, 89.9% with Connect
Course Pass Rates: 72.5% without Connect, 85.2% with Connect
Average Exam Scores: 71.0% without Connect, 80.1% with Connect

without Connect   with Connect

Using **Connect** improves retention rates by **19.8%**, passing rates by **12.7%, and** exam scores by **9.1%.**

Over **7 billion questions** have been answered, making McGraw-Hill Education products more intelligent, reliable, and precise.

73% of instructors who use **Connect** require it; instructor satisfaction **increases** by 28% when **Connect** is required.

Quality Content and Learning Resources

- Connect content is authored by the world's best subject matter experts, and is available to your class through a simple and intuitive interface.
- The Connect eBook makes it easy for students to access their reading material on smartphones and tablets. They can study on the go and don't need internet access to use the eBook as a reference, with full functionality.
- Multimedia content such as videos, simulations, and games drive student engagement and critical thinking skills.

Robust Analytics and Reporting

©Hero Images/Getty Images

- Connect Insight® generates easy-to-read reports on individual students, the class as a whole, and on specific assignments.

- The Connect Insight dashboard delivers data on performance, study behavior, and effort. Instructors can quickly identify students who struggle and focus on material that the class has yet to master.

- Connect automatically grades assignments and quizzes, providing easy-to-read reports on individual and class performance.

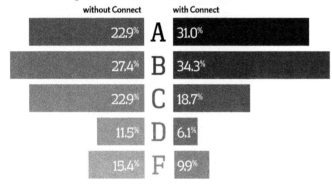

Impact on Final Course Grade Distribution

without Connect		with Connect
22.9%	A	31.0%
27.4%	B	34.3%
22.9%	C	18.7%
11.5%	D	6.1%
15.4%	F	9.9%

More students earn **As** and **Bs** when they use **Connect**.

Trusted Service and Support

- Connect integrates with your LMS to provide single sign-on and automatic syncing of grades. Integration with Blackboard®, D2L®, and Canvas also provides automatic syncing of the course calendar and assignment-level linking.

- Connect offers comprehensive service, support, and training throughout every phase of your implementation.

- If you're looking for some guidance on how to use Connect, or want to learn tips and tricks from super users, you can find tutorials as you work. Our Digital Faculty Consultants and Student Ambassadors offer insight into how to achieve the results you want with Connect.

www.mheducation.com/connect

DIVISION ONE

Overview

Launching Your Study of Communication Theory

This is a book about theories—communication theories. After that statement you may already be stifling a yawn. Many college students, after all, regard theory as obscure, dull, and irrelevant. People outside the classroom are even less charitable. An aircraft mechanic once chided a professor: "You academic types are all alike. Your heads are crammed so full of theory, you wouldn't know which end of a socket wrench to grab. Any plane you touched would crash and burn. All Ph.D. stands for is 'piled higher and deeper.'"

The mechanic could be right. Yet it's ironic that even in the process of knocking theory, he resorts to his own theory of cognitive overload to explain what he sees as the mechanical stupidity of scholars. As authors of this book, we appreciate his desire to make sense of his world. Here's a man who spends a hunk of his life making sure that planes stay safely in the air until pilots are ready to land. When we really care about something, we should seek to answer the *why* and *what if* questions that always emerge. That was the message Em heard from University of Arizona communication theorist Judee Burgoon when he talked with her in our series of interviews, *Conversations with Communication Theorists.*[1] If we care about the fascinating subject of communication, she suggested, we've got to "do theory."

WHAT IS A THEORY AND WHAT DOES IT DO?

In previous editions we used *theory* as "an umbrella term for all careful, systematic, and self-conscious discussion and analysis of communication phenomena," a definition offered by the late University of Minnesota communication professor Ernest Bormann.[2] We like this definition because it's general enough to cover the diverse theories presented in this book. Yet the description is so broad that it doesn't give us any direction on how we might construct a theory, nor does it offer a way to figure out when thoughts or statements about communication haven't attained that status. If we call any idea a "theory," does saying it's so make it so?

In Em's discussion with Judee Burgoon, she suggested that a theory is nothing more than a "set of systematic hunches about the way things operate."[3] Since Burgoon is one of the most frequently cited scholars in the communication discipline, he was intrigued by her unexpected use of the nontechnical term *hunch*. Would it

"It's just a theory, but perhaps it's their opposable thumbs that makes them crazy."
©Charles Barsotti/The New Yorker Collection/The Cartoon Bank

therefore be legitimate to entitle the book you're reading *Communication Hunches?* She assured Em that it would, quickly adding that they should be "informed hunches." So for Burgoon, a theory consists of *a set of systematic, informed hunches about the way things work.* In the rest of this section, we'll examine the three key features of Burgoon's notion of a theory. First, we'll focus on the idea that theory consists of a *set of hunches.* But a set of hunches is only a starting point. Second, we'll discuss what it means to say that those hunches have to be *informed.* Last, we'll highlight the notion that the hunches have to be *systematic.* Let's look briefly at the meaning of each of these core concepts of theory.

A Set of Hunches

If a theory is a set of hunches, it means we aren't yet sure we have the answer. When there's no puzzle to be solved or the explanation is obvious, there's no need to develop a theory. Theories always involve an element of speculation, or conjecture. Being a theorist is risky business because theories go beyond accepted wisdom. Once you become a theorist, you probably hope that all thinking people will eventually embrace the trial balloon you've launched. When you first float your theory, however, it's definitely in the hunch category.

By referring to a plural "set of hunches" rather than a single "hunch," Burgoon makes it clear that a theory is not just one inspired thought or an isolated idea. The dog in the cartoon above may be quite sure that all humans are crazy. But, despite what the pup says, that isolated conviction isn't really a theory. To become one, it would have to go further. For example, good theories define their key terms, so we might ask how the dog defines "crazy." Perhaps the hound would say he thinks his owner is crazy because she shows no interest in eating puppy chow and insists that

Theory
A set of systematic, informed hunches about the way things work.

her dogs stay off the furniture. That definition may be debatable, but at least it begins to flesh out the dog's initial hunch. A theory will also give some indication of scope. Are some humans crazier than others? Apes and giant pandas have opposable thumbs too. Are they just as crazy? Theory construction involves multiple hunches.

Informed Hunches

For Burgoon, it's not enough to think carefully about an idea; a theorist's hunches should be *informed.* Working on a hunch that opposable thumbs make people crazy, the canine theorist could go check it out. Before developing a theory, there are articles to read, people to talk to, actions to observe, or experiments to run, all of which can cast light on the subject. At the very least, theorists should be familiar with alternative explanations and interpretations of the types of phenomena they are studying. (Little doggie, could it be that animals who bark at passing cars are actually the crazy ones?)

Pepperdine University emeritus communication professor Fred Casmir's description of theory parallels Burgoon's call for multiple informed hunches:

> Theories are sometimes defined as guesses—but significantly as "educated" guesses. Theories are not merely based on vague impressions nor are they accidental by-products of life. Theories tend to result when their creators have prepared themselves to discover something in their environment, which triggers the process of theory construction.[4]

Hunches That Are Systematic

Most scholars reserve the term *theory* for an *integrated system* of concepts. A theory not only lays out multiple ideas, but also specifies the relationships among them. In common parlance, it connects the dots. The links among the informed hunches are clearly drawn so that a pattern emerges.

The dog's hunch definitely doesn't rise to this standard. It's a one-shot claim that isn't part of a conceptual framework. Yes, he suggests there's some connection between opposable thumbs and craziness, but the connecting word *that* in the cartoon doesn't really show the relationship between humans' insane behavior and their anatomy. To do that, the puppy theorist could speculate about the nature of opposable thumbs. They lead humans to eat with their hands rather than with their mouths buried in a dish, and to shake hands when they greet instead of smelling each other. (Everyone knows that smelling is believing.) Humans also use their hands to grasp tools and build machines that sever their connection to the natural world. No other creature on earth does that. If the hound can explain how opposable thumbs lead humans to an artificial view of reality, he's on his way to integrating his thoughts into a coherent whole. As you read about any theory covered in this book, you have a right to expect a set of *systematic,* informed hunches.

Images of Theory

In response to the question *What is a theory?* we've presented a verbal definition. Many students are visual learners as well and would appreciate a concrete image that helps us understand what a theory is and does. So we'll present three metaphors that we find helpful, but will also note how an overreliance on these representations of theory might lead us astray.

Theories as Nets: Philosopher of science Karl Popper said that "theories are nets cast to catch what we call 'the world'. . . . We endeavor to make the mesh ever finer and finer."[5] This metaphor highlights the ongoing labor of the theorist as a type of deep-sea angler. For serious scholars, theories are the tools of the trade. The term *the world* can be interpreted as everything that goes on under the sun—thus requiring a *grand* theory that applies to all communication, all the time. Conversely, catching the world could be construed as calling for numerous *special* theories—different kinds of small nets to capture distinct types of communication in local situations. But either way, the quest for finer-meshed nets is somewhat disturbing because the study of communication is about people rather than schools of fish. The idea that theories could be woven so tightly that they'd snag everything humans think, say, or do seems naive. The possibility also raises questions about our freedom to choose some actions and reject others.

Theories as Lenses: Many scholars see their theoretical constructions as similar to the lens of a camera or a pair of glasses, as opposed to a mirror that accurately reflects the world out there. The lens imagery highlights the idea that theories shape our perception by focusing attention on some features of communication while ignoring other features, or at least pushing them into the background. Two theorists could analyze the same communication event—an argument, perhaps—and, depending on the lens each uses, one theorist may view the speech act as a breakdown of communication or the breakup of a relationship, while the other theorist will see it as democracy in action. A danger of the lens metaphor is that we might regard what is seen through the glass as so dependent on the theoretical stance of the viewer that we abandon any attempt to discern what is real or true.

Theories as Maps: A good map helps us understand unfamiliar terrain. It's designed with a purpose. Road maps explain how to get from point A to point B. Political maps show boundaries between states and nations. Climate maps reveal whether a place is hot or cold. Within this analogy, a communication theory is a kind of map that's designed to help you navigate some part of the topography of human relationships. In a sense, this book of theories is like a scenic atlas that pulls together 32 must-see locations. However, we must remember that the map is not the territory.[6] Like a still photograph, no theory can fully portray the richness of interaction between people that is constantly changing, always varied, and inevitably more complicated than what any theory can chart. As a person intrigued with communication, aren't you glad it's this way?

WHAT IS COMMUNICATION?

So far we've discussed *theory,* but what about *communication*? What is it, exactly? To ask this question is to invite controversy and raise expectations for clarity that can't be met. When it comes to defining what it is we study, there's little discipline in the discipline. Frank Dance, the University of Denver scholar credited with publishing the first comprehensive book on communication theory, cataloged more than 120 definitions of *communication*—and that was 50 years ago.[7] Communication scholars have suggested many more since then, yet no single definition has risen to the top and become the standard within the field of communication.

At the conclusion of his study, Dance suggested that we're "trying to make the concept of communication do too much work for us."[8] Other communication theorists agree, noting that when the term is used to describe almost every kind of human interaction, it's seriously overburdened. Michigan Tech University communication professor Jennifer Slack brings a splash of reality to attempts to draw definitive lines around what our theories and research cover. She declares that "there is no single, absolute essence of communication that adequately explains the phenomena we study. Such a definition does not exist; neither is it merely awaiting the next brightest communication scholar to nail it down once and for all."[9]

Despite the pitfalls of trying to define *communication* in an all-inclusive way, it seems to us that students who are willing to spend a big chunk of their college education studying communication deserve a description of what it is they're looking at. Rather than giving the final word on what human activities can be legitimately referred to as *communication,* this designation would highlight the essential features of communication that shouldn't be missed. So for starters, we offer this working definition:

> *Communication is the relational process of creating and interpreting messages that elicit a response.*

Communication
The relational process of creating and interpreting messages that elicit a response.

To the extent that there is redeeming value in this statement, it lies in drawing your attention to five features of communication that you'll run across repeatedly as you read about the theories in the field. We'll flesh out these concepts in the rest of this section.

1. Messages

Messages are at the core of communication study. University of Colorado emeritus communication professor Robert Craig says that communication involves "talking and listening, writing and reading, performing and witnessing, or, more generally, doing anything that involves 'messages' in any medium or situation."[10]

When academic areas such as psychology, sociology, anthropology, political science, literature, and philosophy deal with human symbolic activity, they intersect with the study of communication. The visual image of this intersection of interests has prompted some to refer to communication as a *crossroads discipline.* The difference is that communication scholars are parked at the junction focusing on messages, while other disciplines are just passing through on their way to other destinations. All the theories covered in this book deal specifically with messages.

Text
A record of a message that can be analyzed by others (e.g., a book, film, photograph, or any transcript or recording of a speech or broadcast).

Communication theorists use the word *text* as a synonym for a message that can be studied, regardless of the medium. This book is a text. So is a verbatim transcript of a conversation with your instructor, a recorded presidential news conference, a silent YouTube video, or a Justin Bieber song. To illustrate the following four parts of the definition, suppose you received this cryptic text message from a close friend: "Pat and I spent the night together." You immediately know that the name Pat refers to the person with whom you have an ongoing romantic relationship. An analysis of this text and the context surrounding its transmission provides a useful case study for examining the essential features of communication.

2. Creation of Messages

This phrase in the working definition of communication indicates that the content and form of a text are usually *constructed, invented, planned, crafted, constituted, selected,* or *adopted* by the communicator. Each of these terms is used in at least one of the theories in this book, and they all imply that the communicator is making a conscious choice of message form and substance. For whatever reason, your friend sent a text message rather than meeting face-to-face, calling you on the phone, sending an email, or writing a note. Your friend also chose the seven words that were transmitted to your cell phone. There is a long history of textual analysis in the field of communication, wherein the rhetorical critic looks for clues in the message to discern the motivation and strategy of the person who created the message.

There are, of course, many times when we speak, write, or gesture in seemingly mindless ways—activities that are like driving on cruise control. These are preprogrammed responses that were selected earlier and stored for later use. In like manner, our repertoire of stock phrases such as *thank you, no problem, whatever,* or a string of swear words were chosen sometime in the past to express our feelings, and over time have become habitual responses. Only when we become more mindful of the nature and impact of our messages will we have the ability to alter them. That's why consciousness-raising is a goal of several theories in this book—each one seeks to increase our communication choices.

3. Interpretation of Messages

Messages do not interpret themselves. The meaning that a message holds for the creators and receivers doesn't reside in the words that are spoken, written, or acted out. Many communication scholars believe that *words don't mean things, people mean things.* Symbolic interactionist Herbert Blumer stated the implication of this claim: "Humans act toward people or things on the basis of the meanings they assign to those people or things."[11]

What is the meaning of your friend's text message? Does "spent the night together" mean *talking until all hours? Pulling an all-night study session? Sleeping on the sofa? Making love?* If it's the latter, how would your friend characterize their sexual liaison? *Recreational sex? A chance hookup? Friends with benefits? Developing a close relationship? Falling in love? The start of a long-term commitment?* Perhaps of more importance to you, how does Pat view it? What emotional meaning is behind the message for each of them? *Satisfaction? Disappointment? Surprise? The morning-after-the-night-before blahs? Gratefulness? Guilt? Ecstasy?* And finally, what does receiving this message through a digital channel mean for you, your friendship, and your relationship with Pat? None of these answers are in the message. Words and other symbols are *polysemic*—they're open to multiple interpretations.

Polysemic
A quality of symbols that means they're open to multiple interpretations.

4. A Relational Process

The Greek philosopher Heraclitus observed that "one cannot step into the same river twice."[12] These words illustrate the widespread acceptance among communication scholars that communication is a *process*. Much like a river, the flow of communication is always in flux, never completely the same, and can only be described with reference to what went before and what is yet to come. This means that the text message "Pat and I spent the night together" is not the whole story. You'll probably contact both your friend and Pat to ask clarifying questions. As they are answered or avoided, you'll interpret the message in a different way. That's because communication is a process, not a freeze-frame snapshot.

In the opening lines of her essay "Communication as Relationality," University of Georgia rhetorical theorist Celeste Condit suggests that the communication process is more about relationships than it is about content.

> Communication is a process of relating. This means it is not primarily or essentially a process of transferring information or of disseminating or circulating signs (though these things can be identified as happening within the process of relating).[13]

Communication is a relational process not only because it takes place between two or more persons, but also because it affects the nature of the connections among those people. It's obvious that the text message you received will influence the triangle of relationships among you, Pat, and your (former?) friend. But this is true in other forms of mediated communication as well. Television viewers and moviegoers have emotional responses to people they see on-screen. And as businesses are discovering, even the impersonal recorded announcement that "this call may be monitored for quality assurance purposes" has an impact on how we regard their corporate persona.

5. Messages That Elicit a Response

This final component of communication deals with the effect of the message on people who receive it. At the end of his groundbreaking book on communication theory, Dance concludes, " 'Communication,' in its broadest interpretation, may be defined as the eliciting of a response."[14] If a message fails to stimulate any cognitive, emotional, or behavioral reaction, it seems pointless to refer to it as *communication*. We often refer to such situations as a message "falling on deaf ears" or the other person "turning a blind eye."

Picture a mother driving her 10-year-old son home from school. He's strapped in the seat behind her playing *Subway Surfers* on his tablet, equipped with earbuds. His mother asks if he has any homework. Is that communication? Not if he doesn't hear the question or see her lips moving. What if he isn't wired for sound and hears her voice? It depends. If he's glued to the screen and totally engrossed in avoiding subway cars, he may literally tune her out—still no communication.

Suppose, however, the boy hears her words and feels *bad* that he has homework, *sad* that his mom's so nosy, *mad* that she broke his game-playing concentration, or *glad* that he finished the assignment during class. Although these are internal feelings that his mother may miss, each response would have been triggered by Mom's question and would therefore qualify as communication—even if he doesn't reply. And of course, any vocal response, even a noncommittal grunt, indicates that some form of communication has occurred.

In like manner, surely you would respond to your friend's cryptic message about the night spent with Pat—even if you give your friend "the silent treatment." In fact, the text seems to have been crafted and sent to provoke a response. How closely your thoughts, feelings, words, or actions would match what your friend expected or intended is another matter. Successful or not, the whole situation surrounding the text and context of the message fits the working definition of communication that we hope will help you frame your study of communication theory: *Communication is the relational process of creating and interpreting messages that elicit a response.*

AN ARRANGEMENT OF IDEAS TO AID COMPREHENSION

Now that you have a basic understanding of what a communication theory is, knowing how we've structured the book and arranged the theories can help you grasp their content. After this chapter, there are three more chapters in the "Overview" division that will help you compare and contrast theories—think of these chapters as a bird's-eye view of the communication theory terrain. In Chapter 2, co-author Glenn Sparks and another leading communication scholar analyze a highly acclaimed TV ad in order to illustrate how half the theories in the book are based on *objective* assumptions, while the other half are constructed using an *interpretive* set of principles. Chapter 3 presents criteria for judging both kinds of theories so you can make an informed evaluation of a theory's worth rather than relying solely on your gut reaction. Finally, Chapter 4 describes seven traditions of communication theory and research. When you know the family tree of a theory, you can explain why it has a strong affinity with some theories but doesn't speak the same language as others.

Following this overview, there are 32 chapters that run 10–15 pages apiece, each concentrating on a single theory. We think you'll find that the one-chapter, one-theory format is user-friendly because it gives you a chance to focus on a single theory at a time. This way, they won't all blur together in your mind. These chapters are arranged into four major divisions, according to the primary communication context they address. The theories in Division Two, "Interpersonal Communication," consider one-on-one interaction. Division Three, "Group and Public Communication," deals with face-to-face involvement in collective settings. Division Four, "Mass Communication," pulls together theories that explore electronic and print media. Division Five, "Cultural Context," delves into systems of shared meaning that are so all-encompassing we often fail to realize their impact upon us.

These four divisions are based on the fact that theories are tentative answers to questions that occur to people as they mull over practical problems in specific situations. It therefore makes sense to group them according to the different communication settings that usually prompt those questions. This organizational plan is like having four separately indexed file cabinets. Although there is no natural progression from one division to another, the plan provides a convenient way to classify and retrieve the 32 theories.

Finally, Division Six, "Integration," seeks to distill core ideas that are common to a number of theories. Ideas have power, and each theory is driven by one or more ideas that may be shared by other theories from different communication contexts. For example, in each of the four context divisions, there's at least one theory committed to the force of narrative. They each declare that people respond to stories and dramatic imagery with which they can identify. Reading about key concepts that cut across multiple theories wouldn't mean much to you now, but after you become familiar with a number of communication theories, it can be an eye-opening experience that also helps you review what you've learned.

CHAPTER FEATURES TO ENLIVEN THEORY

In many of the chapters ahead, we use an extended example from life on a college campus, a well-known communication event, or the conversations of characters in movies, books, or TV shows. The main purpose of these illustrations is to provide a mind's-eye picture of how the theory works. The imagery will also make the basic thrust of the theory easier to recall. But if you can think of a situation in your own life where the theory is relevant, that personal application will make it doubly interesting and memorable for you.

You might also want to see how others put the theories into practice. With our students' permission, we've weaved in their accounts of application for almost all the theories featured in the text. We're intrigued by the rich connections these students make—ones we wouldn't have thought of on our own. Some students draw on scenes from short stories, novels, or movies. To see an annotated list of feature film scenes that illustrate the theories, go to the book's website, www.afirstlook. com, and under Theory Resources, click on Suggested Movie Clips.

As co-authors of this book, the three of us (Em, Andrew, and Glenn) will draw upon our life experiences as well. We've been professional colleagues for years and are close friends, so we'd like that warmth to extend to readers by writing in a direct, personal voice. In the first four chapters, we've written using words like *we* and *our*. We want you to know the basic commitments we share collectively as communication scholars. For each of the remaining chapters on specific theories, one of us took the lead in preparing the content. These chapters use *I, my,* and *me* when referring to individual thoughts or stories from our lives. Since Em was the original and sole author of the book for many years, many examples come from his life. So unless you see a reference in a chapter that Andrew or Glenn is sharing his own ideas, feelings, or experiences, you can assume that the "I" refers to Em. We don't use personal references in every chapter, but when we do, we want you to know whose voice you're "hearing."

We also make a consistent effort to link each theory with its creator(s). It takes both wisdom and courage to successfully plant a theoretical flag. In a process similar to the childhood game king-of-the-hill, as soon as a theorist constructs a theory of communication, critics try to pull it down. That's OK, because the value of a theory is discerned by survival in the rough-and-tumble world of competitive ideas. For this reason we always include a section in theory chapters labeled "Critique." Theorists who prevail deserve to have their names associated with their creations.

There is a second reason for tying a theory to its author. Many of you will do further study in communication, and a mastery of names like Deetz, Giles, Walther, Baxter, Berger, and Burke will allow you to enter into the dialogue without being at a disadvantage. Ignoring the names of theorists could prove to be false economy in the long run.

Don't overlook the three features at the end of each chapter. The "Questions to Sharpen Your Focus" will help you mull over key points of the theory. They can be answered by pulling together information from this text and from the text of your life. The italicized words in each question highlight terms you need to know in order to understand the theory. Whenever you see a picture of the theorist, it's captured from one of our *Conversations with Communication Theorists* and shown alongside a brief description of what we talked about. You can view these 6- to 8-minute interviews at www.afirstlook.com. And the feature entitled "A Second Look" offers an annotated bibliography of resources should you desire to know more about the theory. You'll find it a good place to start if you are writing a research paper on the theory or are intrigued with a particular aspect of it.

You've already seen the last feature we'll mention. In every chapter we include a cartoon for your learning and enjoyment. Cartoonists are often modern-day prophets. Their incisive wit can illustrate a feature of the theory in a way that's more instructive and memorable than a few extra paragraphs would be. In addition to enjoying their humor, you can use the cartoons as minitests of comprehension. Unlike our comments on the dog theorizing about opposable thumbs earlier in this chapter, we usually don't refer to the art or the caption that goes with it. So if you can't figure out why a particular cartoon appears where it does, make a renewed effort to grasp the theorist's ideas.

Some students are afraid to try. Like travelers whose eyes glaze over at the sight of a road map, they have a phobia about theories that seek to explain human intentions and behavior. We sympathize with their qualms and misgivings, but find that the theories in this book haven't dehydrated life or made it more confusing. On the contrary, they add clarity and provide a sense of competence as we communicate with others. We hope they do that for you as well.

Every so often a student will ask one of us, "Do you really think about communication theory when you're talking to someone?" Our answer is "Yes, but not all the time." Like everyone else, we often speak on autopilot—words, phrases, sentences, descriptions roll off the tongue without conscious thought. Old habits die hard. But when we're in a new setting or the conversational stakes are high, we start to think strategically. And that's when the applied wisdom of theories that fit the situation comes to mind. By midterm, many of our students discover they're thinking that way as well. That's our wish for you as you launch your study of communication theory.

QUESTIONS TO SHARPEN YOUR FOCUS

1. Suppose you share the aircraft mechanic's suspicion that scholars who create theories would be all thumbs working on a plane's wings or engine. What would it take to transform your *hunch* into a *theory?*

2. Which *metaphor* of theory do you find most helpful—theory as a *net,* a *lens,* or a *map?* Can you think of another image that you could use to explain to a friend what this course is about?

3. Suppose you want to study the effects of yawns during intimate conversations. Would your research be addressing *communication* as we've defined it (the *relational process of creating and interpreting messages to elicit a response*)? If not, how would you change the definition to make it include your interest?

4. You come to this course with a vast array of communication experiences in *interpersonal, group and public, mass media,* and *intercultural contexts.* What are the communication *questions* you want to answer, *puzzles* you want to solve, or *problems* you want to fix?

A SECOND LOOK

Recommended resource: Gregory Shepherd, Jeffrey St. John, and Ted Striphas (eds.), *Communication as . . . Perspectives on Theory,* Sage, Thousand Oaks, CA, 2006.

Diverse definitions of communication: Frank E. X. Dance, "The Concept of Communication," *Journal of Communication,* Vol. 20, 1970, pp. 201-210.

Brief history of communication theory since the early 1990s: Barbie Zelizer, "Making Communication Theory Matter," *Communication Theory,* Vol. 26, No. 4, 2015, pp. 410–415.

Theories of communication as practical: Joann Keyton, Ryan S. Bisel, and Raymond Ozley, "Recasting the Link Between Applied and Theory Research: Using Applied Findings to Advance Communication Theory Development," *Communication Theory,* Vol. 19, No. 2, 2009, pp. 146–160.

Multidimensional view of theory: James A. Anderson and Geoffrey Baym, "Philosophies and Philosophic Issues in Communication, 1995–2004," *Journal of Communication,* Vol. 54, 2004, pp. 589–615.

To access 50-word summaries of theories
featured in the book, see Appendix A or click on
Theory Overview under Theory Resources at
www.afirstlook.com.

Talk About Theory

I met Glenn Sparks and Marty Medhurst during my first year teaching at Wheaton College. Glenn and Marty were friends who signed up for my undergraduate persuasion course. As students, both men were interested in broadcast media. After graduating from Wheaton, each went on for a master's degree at Northern Illinois University. Each then earned a doctorate at a different university, and both are now nationally recognized communication scholars. Marty is on the faculty at Baylor University; Glenn is at Purdue University and is a co-author of this book.

Despite their similar backgrounds and interests, Glenn and Marty are quite different in their approaches to communication. Glenn calls himself a *behavioral scientist,* while Marty refers to himself as a *rhetorician.* Glenn's training was in empirical research; Marty was schooled in rhetorical theory and criticism. Glenn conducts experiments; Marty interprets texts.

Behavioral scientist
A scholar who applies the scientific method to describe, predict, and explain recurring forms of human behavior.

Rhetorician
A scholar who studies the ways in which symbolic forms can be used to identify with people, or to persuade them toward a certain point of view.

To understand the theories ahead, you need to first grasp the crucial differences between the objective and interpretive approaches to communication. As a way to introduce the distinctions, I asked Glenn and Marty to bring their scholarship to bear on a television commercial that first aired during Super Bowl XLVII, the game where the lights went out. It's a stealth ad for beer that doesn't show booze on a beach, men in a bar flirting with a waitress serving brew, or a guy tapping a keg yelling, "Party all night!" These are typical images that turn off a significant portion of viewers who see them as silly, distasteful, or unethical. That's because those ads appear to promote the dangerous practice of binge drinking among young adults as a way to gain acceptance or get a buzz. Instead, this ad portrays the bond that develops between a shaggy-hooved Clydesdale horse and his young trainer.[1]

TWO COMMUNICATION SCHOLARS VIEW A HEARTWARMING AD

Using no dialogue or voice-over, the Super Bowl commercial tells a visual story in 60 seconds. We see scenes of the newborn foal, his trainer asleep in the sick colt's stall, horseplay between them as the animal gains stature, and the fully grown horse running free alongside the trainer's truck. When it's time for this magnificent animal to become part of a working team of Clydesdales promoting beer, the trainer leads him into the company's horse van and gazes wistfully as it disappears down the road.

Three years later, the man discovers the Clydesdales will be in a Chicago parade and drives to the city to reconnect with his horse. He smiles with pride as the horse prances by, but blinders keep the animal from seeing him. As the trainer walks sadly back to his truck, the harness is removed and the horse catches a glimpse of him. The final shots show the Clydesdale galloping down the street to catch up with his human friend, who then buries his face in the horse's mane as they are reunited.

Since the sponsor spent $7 million to air this one-minute commercial—and more than that to film it—its marketing department obviously believed that featuring this huge draft horse would sell huge amounts of draft beer. There's no doubt that most critics and viewers liked the ad. Former *Advertising Age* analyst Ken Wheaton concluded, "Weepy, sentimental, nostalgic. I don't care. This is everything I want from a Budweiser Super Bowl spot."[2] Yet as you'll see, social scientist Glenn and rhetorical critic Marty take different theoretical approaches as they analyze the intent of the ad and how it works.

Glenn: An Objective Approach

After the 2013 Super Bowl ended, a research company announced that the Clydesdale ad was the year's commercial winner.[3] The researchers tracked 400 viewers who used a mobile app to express their feelings during the broadcast. The extent of viewers' enthusiasm for the Clydesdale ad was on par with what they felt when their favorite team scored a touchdown. Social scientists wonder why the commercial produced such positive sentiment and whether it resulted in action. They want to explain and predict human behavior.

Objective approach
The assumption that truth is singular and is accessible through unbiased sensory observation; committed to uncovering cause-and-effect relationships.

How do scientists satisfy these interests? After observing behavior, we identify or construct a theory that offers insight into what we've observed. In this case, advertising guru Tony Schwartz' *resonance principle of communication* is a promising theoretical idea.[4] Although Schwartz passed away in 2008, his theory lives on.

According to Schwartz, successful persuasive messages evoke past experiences that create *resonance* between the message content and a person's thoughts or feelings. Schwartz believed that resonance leads to persuasion. It's not *arguments* that persuade people as much as it is *memories* of personal experiences triggered by the message.

The heartwarming story of a worker dedicated to a horse he loves may tap into viewers' deep memories of their own devotion to animals they once nurtured. The emotional scene at the end of the ad might stir reminiscence of your pet's excitement when you would return home or the tremendous relief at being reunited with one you thought lost. Once these good feelings are evoked, Schwartz believed people associate them with the advertised product. For beer drinkers, those good feelings may lead to more sales. For viewers who see drinking beer as a health risk, the good feelings may lead to positive thoughts about a company that seems to care not only about selling beer, but also about taking good care of those splendid Clydesdales. In this case, persuasion may be measured both in beer sales and positive thoughts about Budweiser—a company well aware that its success may lead to alcohol abuse among consumers and a bad corporate reputation.

Theories need to be validated. For scientists, it's not enough to identify a theory that seems to apply to the situation. We want an objective test to find out if a theory is faulty. For example, I'd want to discover if commercials that trigger warm emotional memories are better than other ads at selling products or generating good feelings toward the sponsor. Testing audience response is a crucial scientific enterprise. Even though a theory might sound plausible, we can't be sure it's valid until it's been tested. In science, theory and research walk hand in hand.

Marty: An Interpretive Approach

There is more going on here than a simple reunion of man and horse. The entire ad is structured by an archetypal mythic pattern of birth-death-rebirth. Archetypal myths are those that draw upon a universal experience—what psychoanalyst Carl Jung called the "collective unconscious."[5] Deep within the mental makeup of all human beings is the archetype of the birth-death-rebirth cycle. The use of such archetypes, according to rhetorical theorist Michael Osborn, touches off "depth responses" that emotionally resonate at the core of our being.[6] The ad activates these emotions by incorporating the form of the cycle within a mini-narrative.

We first see the newborn colt in the barn as the breeder feeds him, strokes his coat, and even sleeps next to him in the stall. Birth naturally leads to growth, as we watch the colt mature before our eyes. But just as this Clydesdale grows to full stature, the Budweiser 18-wheeler arrives to take away the treasured horse. Symbolically, this is a death because it represents an absence or void. What once was is no more. Then, three years later, the breeder and his horse are reunited in an act of rebirth. The former relationship, which had been shattered by the symbolic death, is now restored with the reunion of man and horse.

It is significant that the passage of time is three years. Just as Christians believe Jesus lay in the tomb for three days before his resurrection, so the horse is gone for three years before he reappears. But once he re-emerges, it is as though he never left. That which was lost has been found. The emotions evoked by this ad are strong because we are dealing with life and death, with loss and restoration. All of us unconsciously long for a reunion with those people or things in our lives that have been most important to us. Even the music—"Landslide" by Fleetwood Mac—underscores the archetypal pattern, as it speaks of love, loss, change, and being afraid. Fear of death is a primordial human instinct. It is only through a rebirth that we can reclaim what time and change have taken from us.

The ad subtly suggests that Budweiser beer is our constant mainstay. Life changes and losses happen, but Bud never changes, never disappears. We see that in the shots of the beer bottle on the breeder's table as he reads about the upcoming parade in Chicago. Bud is portrayed as our companion and our comforter, something that will be with us through the dark nights of separation and loss.

Interpretive approach
The linguistic work of assigning meaning or value to communicative texts; assumes that multiple meanings or truths are possible.

OBJECTIVE OR INTERPRETIVE WORLDVIEWS: SORTING OUT THE LABELS

Although both of these scholars focus on the warm feelings viewers have when seeing the Budweiser Clydesdale ad, Glenn's and Marty's approaches to communication study clearly differ in starting point, method, and conclusion. Glenn is a social *scientist* who works hard to be *objective*. When we refer to theorists and researchers like Glenn throughout the book, we'll use the terms *scientist* and *objective scholar* interchangeably. Marty is a *rhetorical critic* who does *interpretive* study. Here the labels get tricky.

While it's true that all rhetorical critics do interpretive analysis, not all interpretive scholars are rhetoricians. Most (including Marty) are *humanists* who study what it's like to be another person in a specific time and place. But a growing number of postmodern communication theorists reject that tradition. These interpretive scholars refer to themselves with a bewildering variety of brand names: social constructionists, critical theorists, hermeneuticists, post-structuralists, deconstructivists, phenomenologists, cultural studies researchers,

Humanistic scholarship
Study of what it's like to be another person in a specific time and place; assumes there are few important panhuman similarities.

and social action theorists, as well as combinations of these terms. Writing from this postmodernist perspective, University of Utah theorist James Anderson observes:

> With this very large number of interpretive communities, names are contentious, border patrol is hopeless and crossovers continuous. Members, however, often see real differences.[7]

All of these scholars, including Marty, do interpretive analysis—scholarship concerned with meaning—yet there's no common term like *scientist* that includes them all. So from this point on we'll use the designation *interpretive scholars* or the noun form *interpreters* to refer to the entire group, and use *rhetoricians, humanists, postmodernists,* or *critical scholars* only when singling out a particular subgroup.

The separate worldviews of interpretive scholars and scientists reflect contrasting assumptions about ways of arriving at knowledge, the core of human nature, questions of value, and the purpose of theory. The rest of this chapter sketches out these differences.

WAYS OF KNOWING: DISCOVERING TRUTH OR CREATING MULTIPLE REALITIES?

How do we know what we know, if we know it at all? This is the central question addressed by a branch of philosophy known as *epistemology*. You may have been in school for a dozen-plus years, read assignments, written papers, and taken tests without ever delving into the issue *What is truth?* With or without in-depth study of the issue, however, we all inevitably make assumptions about the nature of knowledge.

Epistemology
The study of the origin, nature, method, and limits of knowledge.

Scientists assume that Truth is singular. They see a single, timeless reality "out there" that's not dependent on local conditions. It's waiting to be discovered through the five senses of sight, sound, touch, taste, and smell. Since the raw sensory data of the world is accessible to any competent observer, science seeks to be bias-free, with no ax to grind. The evidence speaks for itself. As Galileo observed, anyone could see through his telescope. Of course, no one person can know it all, so individual researchers pool their findings and build a collective body of knowledge about how the world works.

Scientists consider good theories to be those that are faithful representations of the way the world really is. Of the metaphors introduced in Chapter 1, they like the image of theory as a mirror that reflects reality, or a net that captures part of it. Objective theorists are confident that once a principle is discovered and validated, it will continue to hold true as long as conditions remain relatively the same. That's why Glenn believes the theory of resonance can explain why other media messages succeed or fail.

Interpretive scholars seek truth as well, but many interpreters regard that truth as socially constructed through communication. They believe language creates social realities that are always in flux rather than revealing or representing fixed principles or relationships in a world that doesn't change. Knowledge is always viewed from a particular standpoint. A word, a gesture, or an act may have constancy within a given community, but it's dangerous to assume that interpretations can cross lines of time and space.

Texts never interpret themselves. Most of these scholars, in fact, hold that truth is largely subjective—that meaning is highly interpretive. But rhetorical critics like

Marty are not relativists, arbitrarily assigning meaning on a whim. They do maintain, however, that objectivity is a myth; we can never entirely separate the knower from the known.

Convinced that meaning is in the mind rather than in the verbal sign, interpreters are comfortable with the notion that a text may have multiple meanings. Rhetorical critics are successful when they get others to view a text through their interpretive lens—to adopt a new perspective on the world. For example, did Marty convince you that the Budweiser ad draws upon a deep-seated pattern of birth-death-rebirth ingrained in all of us? As Anderson notes, "Truth is a struggle, not a status."[8]

HUMAN NATURE: DETERMINISM OR FREE WILL?

One of the great philosophical debates throughout history revolves around the question of human choice.[9] Hard-line *determinists* claim that every move we make is the result of heredity ("biology is destiny") and environment ("pleasure stamps in, pain stamps out"). On the other hand, free-will purists insist that every human act is ultimately voluntary ("I am the master of my fate: I am the captain of my soul"[10]). Although few communication theorists are comfortable with either extreme, most tend to line up on one side or the other. Scientists stress the forces that shape human behavior; interpretive scholars focus on conscious choices made by individuals.

Determinism
The assumption that behavior is caused by heredity and environment.

The difference between these two views of human nature inevitably creeps into the language people use to explain what they do. Individuals who feel like puppets on strings say, "I *had* to . . . ," whereas people who feel they pull their own strings say, "I *decided* to. . . ." The first group speaks in a passive voice: "I was distracted from studying by the argument at the next table." The second group speaks in an active voice: "I stopped studying to listen to the argument at the next table."

In the same way, the language of scholarship often reflects theorists' views of human nature. Behavioral scientists usually describe human conduct as occurring *because of* forces outside the individual's awareness. Their causal explanations tend not to include appeals to mental reasoning or conscious choice. They usually describe behavior as the response to a prior stimulus. Schwartz' theory of resonance posits that messages triggering emotional memories from our past will inevitably affect us. We *will* be swayed by an ad that strikes a responsive chord.

In contrast, interpretive scholars tend to use explanatory phrases such as *in order to* and *so that* because they attribute a person's action to conscious intent. Their word selection suggests that people are free agents who could decide to respond differently under an identical set of circumstances. Marty, for example, uses the language of voluntary *action* rather than knee-jerk *behavior* when he writes, "It is only through a rebirth that we can reclaim what time and change have taken from us." If someone *reclaims* what was lost, it is an act of volition. The trainer decided to go to Chicago. Others who felt loss might not. The consistent interpreter doesn't ask why this man made that choice. As Anderson explains, "True choice demands to be its own cause and its own explanation."[11]

Human choice is problematic for the behavioral scientist because as individual freedom goes up, predictability of behavior goes down. Conversely, the roots of humanism are threatened by a highly restricted view of human choice. In an impassioned plea, British author C. S. Lewis exposes the paradox of stripping away people's freedom and yet expecting them to exercise responsible choice:

> In a sort of ghastly simplicity we remove the organ and expect of them virtue and enterprise. We laugh at honor and are shocked to find traitors in our midst. We castrate and bid the geldings be fruitful.[12]

Lewis assumes that significant decisions are value laden; interpretive scholars would agree.

THE HIGHEST VALUE: OBJECTIVITY OR EMANCIPATION?

When we talk about values, we're discussing priorities, questions of relative worth.[13] Values are the traffic lights of our lives that guide what we think, feel, and do. The professional values of communication theorists reflect the commitments they've made concerning knowledge and human nature. Since most social scientists hold to a distinction between the "knower" and the "known," they place value on objectivity that's not biased by ideological commitments. Because humanists and others in the interpretive camp believe that the ability to choose is what separates humanity from the rest of creation, they value scholarship that expands the range of free choice.

As a behavioral scientist, Glenn works hard to maintain his objectivity. He is a man with strong moral and spiritual convictions, and these may influence the topics he studies. But he doesn't want his personal values to distort reality or confuse what *is* with what he thinks *ought to be*. As you can see from Glenn's call for

Empirical evidence
Data collected through direct observation.

objective testing, he is frustrated when theorists offer no *empirical evidence* for their claims or don't even suggest a way in which their ideas could be validated by an independent observer. He is even more upset when he hears of researchers who fudge the findings of their studies to shore up questionable hypotheses. Glenn shares the research values of Harvard sociologist George Homans—to let the evidence speak for itself: "When nature, however stretched out on the rack, still has a chance to say 'no'—then the subject is science."[14]

Marty is aware of his own ideology and is not afraid to bring his values to bear upon a communication text and come under scrutiny. He doesn't take an overtly critical stance toward advertising or the capitalist system. But his insight of Bud framed as a constant companion and comforter gives us the resource to laugh at the irony of hugging a bottle of beer whenever we feel lonely or a sense of loss.

Critical interpreters value socially relevant research that seeks to liberate people from oppression of any sort—economic, political, religious, emotional, or any other. They decry the detached stance of scientists who refuse to take responsibility for the results of their work. Whatever the pursuit—a Manhattan Project to split the atom, a Human Genome Project to map human genes, or a class project to analyze the effectiveness of an ad—critical interpreters insist that knowledge is never neutral. "There is no safe harbor in which researchers can avoid the power structure."[15]

Emancipation
Liberation from any form of political, economic, racial, religious, or sexual oppression; empowerment.

In the heading for this section, we've contrasted the primary values of scientific and interpretive scholars by using the labels *objectivity* and *emancipation*. University of Colorado emeritus communication professor Stan Deetz frames the issue somewhat differently. He says that every general communication theory has two priorities—*effectiveness* and *participation*.[16] Effectiveness is concerned with successfully communicating information, ideas, and meaning to others. It also includes persuasion. Participation is concerned with increasing the possibility that all points of view will affect collective decisions and individuals being open to new ideas. It also encourages difference, opposition, and independence. The value question is *Which concern has higher priority?* Objective theorists usually foreground effectiveness and relegate participation to the background. Interpretive theorists tend to focus on participation and downplay effectiveness.

PURPOSE OF THEORY: UNIVERSAL LAWS OR INTERPRETIVE GUIDES?

Even if Glenn and Marty could agree on the nature of knowledge, the extent of human autonomy, and the ultimate values of scholarship, their words would still sound strange to each other because they use distinct vocabularies to accomplish different goals. As a behavioral scientist, Glenn is working to pin down universal laws of human behavior that cover a variety of situations. As a rhetorical critic, Marty strives to interpret a particular communication text in a specific context.

If these two scholars were engaged in fashion design rather than research design, Glenn would probably tailor a coat suitable for many occasions that covers everybody well—one size fits all. Marty might apply principles of fashion design to style a coat that makes an individual statement for a single client—a one-of-a-kind, custom creation. Glenn adopts a theory and then tests it to see if it covers everyone. Marty uses theory to make sense of unique communication events.

Since theory testing is the basic activity of the behavioral scientist, Glenn starts with a hunch about how the world works—perhaps the idea that stories are more persuasive than arguments. He then crafts a tightly worded hypothesis that temporarily commits him to a specific prediction. As an empiricist, he can never completely "prove" that he has made the right gamble; he can only show in test after test that his behavioral bet pays off. If repeated studies uphold his hypothesis, he can more confidently predict which media ads will be effective, explain why, and make recommendations on how practitioners can craft messages that stir up memories.

The interpretive scholar explores the web of meaning that constitutes human existence. When Marty creates scholarship, he isn't trying to prove theory. However, he sometimes uses the work of rhetorical theorists like Michael Osborn to inform his interpretation of the aural and visual texts of people's lives. Robert Ivie, former editor of the *Quarterly Journal of Speech,* suggests that rhetorical critics ought to use theory this way:

> We cannot conduct rhetorical criticism of social reality without benefit of a guiding rhetorical theory that tells us generally what to look for in social practice, what to make of it, and whether to consider it significant.[17]

OBJECTIVE OR INTERPRETIVE: WHY IS IT IMPORTANT?

Why is it important to grasp the differences between objective and interpretive scholarship? The first answer is because you can't fully understand a theory if you aren't familiar with its underlying assumptions about *truth, human nature,* the *purpose of the theory,* and its *values.* If you're clueless, things can get confusing fast. It's like the time my wife, Jeanie, and I were walking around the Art Institute of Chicago, enjoying the work of French impressionists who painted realistic scenes that I could recognize. Then I wandered into a room dedicated to abstract expressionism. The paintings seemed bizarre and made no sense to me. I was bewildered and somewhat disdainful until Jeanie, who is an artist, explained the goals these painters had and the techniques they used to achieve them. So too with interpretive and objective communication theories. Right now you are probably more familiar and comfortable with one approach than you are with the other. But when you understand what each type of theorist is about, your comfort zone will expand and your confusion will diminish.

There's another reason to master these *metatheoretical* differences. After exposure to a dozen or more theories, you may find that they begin to blur together in your mind. Classifying them as scientific or interpretive is a good way to keep them straight. It's somewhat like sorting 52 cards into suits—spades, hearts, diamonds, and clubs. In most sophisticated card games, the distinction is crucial. By the end of this course you could have up to 32 cards in your deck of communication theories. Being able to sort them in multiple combinations is a good way to show yourself and your professor that you've mastered the material. When you can compare and contrast theories on the basis of their interpretive or objective worldview, you've begun an integration that's more impressive than rote memorization.

Metatheory
Theory about theory; the stated or inherent assumptions made when creating a theory.

Understanding these objective/interpretive choice points can also help you decide the direction you want to take in your remaining course work. Some concentrations in the field of communication tend to have either a scientific or an interpretive bias. For example, all the theories we present in the relationship development, influence, and media effects sections of the book are proposed by objective scholars. Conversely, most of the theories we cover in the public rhetoric, media and culture, organizational communication, and gender and communication sections are interpretive. You'll want to see if this is true at your school before you choose the specific route you'll take.

Finally, theorists in both camps hope you'll care because each group believes that its brand of work holds promise for improving relationships and society. The scientist is convinced that knowing the truth about how communication works will give us a clearer picture of social reality. The interpreter is equally sure that unearthing communicator motivation and hidden ideologies will improve society by increasing free choice and discouraging unjust practices.

If you think you have a good grasp of how objective and interpretive theories differ, continue on to Chapters 3 and 4. But if you'd like to see an example of what each type of theory looks like, you might flip ahead to *Expectancy Violations Theory* (Chapter 7) and *Relational Dialectics Theory* (Chapter 11). Both are interpersonal theories—the former highly objective and the latter highly interpretive. As you read each chapter, try to spot the differences between their approaches to ways of knowing, human nature, values, and the purpose of theory.

PLOTTING THEORIES ON AN OBJECTIVE-INTERPRETIVE SCALE

In this chapter I've introduced four important areas of difference between objective and interpretive communication scholars and the theories they create. Once you understand how they differ, it will be helpful for you to realize that not all theorists fall neatly into one category or the other. Many have a foot in both camps. It's more accurate to picture the *objective* and *interpretive* labels as anchoring the ends of a continuum, with theorists spread out along the scale.

Objective _____ **Interpretive**

Figure 2-1 displays our evaluation of where each theory we feature fits on an objective-interpretive continuum. For easier reference to positions on the scale, we've numbered the five columns at the bottom of the chart. In placing a theory, we've tried to factor in choices the theorists have made about ways of knowing, human nature, what they value most, and the purpose of theory. We've consulted a number of scholars in the field to get their "read" on appropriate placements. They didn't always agree, but in most cases the discussion has sharpened our understanding of theory and the issues to be considered in the process of creating one. What we learned is reflected in the chapters ahead.

Of course, the position of each dot won't make much sense to you until you've read about the theory. But by looking at the pattern of distribution, you can see that roughly half the theories have an objective orientation, while the other half reflect an interpretive commitment. This 50-50 split matches the mix of scholarship we see in the field. When talking about relationships among the theories and the common assumptions made by a group of theorists, your instructor may frequently refer back to this chart. So for easy reference, we reproduce the appropriate "slice" of the chart on the first page of each chapter.

Now that you have an idea of the differences between objective and interpretive theories, you may wonder whether some of these theories are better than others. We think so. Chapter 3, "Weighing the Words," offers a set of six standards you can use to judge the quality of objective theories, and a half dozen alternative criteria to discern the worth of interpretive theories. By applying the appropriate criteria, you can see if you agree with our evaluations.

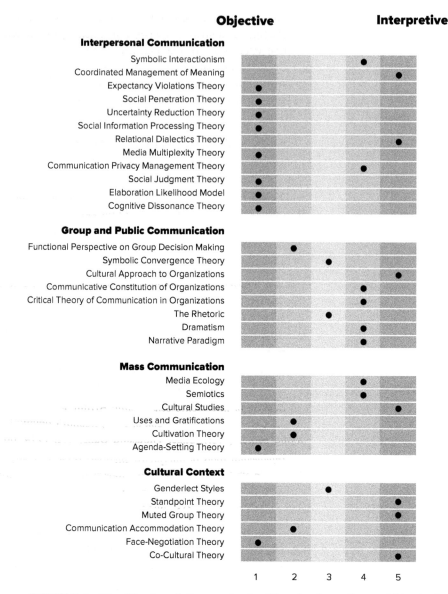

FIGURE 2–1   Classification of Communication Theories According to Objective/Interpretive Worldview

QUESTIONS TO SHARPEN YOUR FOCUS

1. Compare Glenn Sparks' and Marty Medhurst's approaches to the Clydesdale commercial. Which analysis makes the most sense to you? Why?

2. How do scientists and interpretive scholars differ in their answers to the question *What is truth?* Which perspective do you find more satisfying?

3. How do you account for the wide-ranging diversity among types of interpretive theories (*rhetorical, critical, humanistic, postmodern,* etc.) compared to the relative uniformity of objective theories?

4. Think of the communication classes you've taken. Did an *objective* or *interpretive* orientation undergird each course? Was this due more to the nature of the subject matter or to the professor's point of view?

A SECOND LOOK

Recommended resource: James A. Anderson and Geoffrey Baym, "Philosophies and Philosophic Issues in Communication 1995-2004," *Journal of Communication,* Vol. 54, 2004, pp. 589-615.

Metatheoretical overview: James A. Anderson, *Communication Theory: Epistemological Foundations,* Guilford, New York, 1996, pp. 13-77.

Metatheory: Robert T. Craig, "Metatheory," in *Encyclopedia of Communication Theory,* Sage, Los Angeles, CA, 2009, pp. 657-661.

Contemporary scientific scholarship: Charles Berger, Michael Roloff, and David Roskos-Ewoldsen (eds.), *Handbook of Communication Science,* 2nd ed., Sage, Los Angeles, CA, 2010.

Contemporary rhetorical scholarship: Sonja Foss, Karen Foss, and Robert Trapp, *Contemporary Perspectives on Rhetoric,* 3rd ed., Waveland, Prospect Heights, IL, 2000.

Defense of empirical scholarship: Robert Bostrom and Lewis Donohew, "The Case for Empiricism: Clarifying Fundamental Issues in Communication Theory," *Communication Monographs,* Vol. 59, 1992, pp. 109-129.

Defense of interpretive scholarship: Arthur Bochner, "Perspectives on Inquiry II: Theories and Stories," in *Handbook of Interpersonal Communication,* 2nd ed., Mark Knapp and Gerald Miller (eds.), Sage, Thousand Oaks, CA, 1994, pp. 21-41.

Intellectual roots of interpretive theories: Isaac E. Catt, "The Two Sciences of Communication in Philosophical Context," *Review of Communication,* Vol. 14, 2014, pp. 201-228.

Scientific research: Glenn Sparks, *Media Effects Research: A Basic Overview,* 4th ed., Wadsworth, Belmont, CA, 2013.

Rhetorical analysis: Martin J. Medhurst, "George W. Bush at Goree Island: American Slavery and the Rhetoric of Redemption," *Quarterly Journal of Speech,* Vol. 96, 2010, pp. 257-277.

Weighing the Words

In Chapter 2 we looked at two distinct approaches to communication theory—objective and interpretive. Because the work of social scientists and interpreters is so different, they often have trouble understanding and valuing their counterparts' scholarship. This workplace tension parallels the struggle between Democrats and Republicans. Members of both political parties study the same financial reports, projected statistics, and potential solutions for fixing the nation's economic woes. Nevertheless, when it comes to proposing a plan of action, the two parties are often miles apart. The distance is usually due to the different assumptions each party uses to guide its thinking. Their philosophies can be so divergent that significant agreement seems nearly impossible, and meaningful compromise an unrealistic option.

In politics, when it gets down to the nitty-gritty of adopting specific proposals and passing concrete laws, the partisan bickering can make the conversation tense. The same can be said of the disputes that are common between objective and interpretive communication scholars. Differences in ways of knowing, views of human nature, values, goals of theory building, and research methods seem to lead to tension and misunderstanding.

Friendly attitudes between empiricists and interpreters can be hard to come by when each group insists on applying its own standards of judgment to the work of the other group. As a first-time reader of communication theory, you could easily get sucked into making the same mistake. If you've had training in the scientific method and judge the value of every communication theory by whether it predicts human behavior, you'll be tempted to reject 50 percent of the theories presented in this book. On the other hand, if you've been steeped in the humanities and expect every theory to help unmask the meaning of a text, you'll be inclined to dismiss the other half.

Regardless of which approach you favor, not all objective or interpretive communication theories are equally good. For each type, some are better than others. Like family members trying to decide which pizza to order, you'll want a way to separate the good, the bad, and the nasty. Since we've included theories originating in the social sciences as well as the humanities, you need to have two separate lenses through which to view their respective claims. This chapter offers that pair of bifocals. We hope by the time you finish you'll be on friendly terms with the separate criteria that behavioral scientists and a wide range of interpretive scholars use to weigh the words of their colleagues. We'll start with the standards that social scientists use to judge the worth of objective theories, and then turn to the criteria that interpretive scholars employ to evaluate their communication theories.

WHAT MAKES AN OBJECTIVE THEORY GOOD?

An objective theory is credible when it fulfills the twin objectives of scientific knowledge. The theory *predicts* some future outcome, and it *explains* the reasons for that outcome. Social scientists of all kinds agree on four additional criteria a theory must meet to be good—*relative simplicity, testability, practical utility,* and *quantifiable research.* As we discuss these standards, we will use the terms *objective* and *scientific* interchangeably.

Scientific Standard 1: Prediction of Future Events

A good objective theory predicts what will happen. Prediction is possible only when we are dealing with things we can see, hear, touch, smell, and taste over and over again. As we repeatedly notice the same things happening in similar situations, we begin to speak of invariable patterns or universal laws. In the realm of the physical sciences, we are seldom embarrassed. Objects don't have a choice about how to respond to a stimulus. The sun can't choose to rise in the west instead of the east.

The social sciences are another matter. Although theories of human behavior often cast their predictions with confidence, a good measure of humility on the part of the theorist is advisable. Even the best theory may only be able to speak about people in general, rather than about specific individuals—and these only in terms of probability and tendencies, not absolute certainty.

What do good scientific communication theories forecast? Some predict that a specific type of communication triggers a particular response. (Mutual self-disclosure creates interpersonal intimacy.) Other theories predict that people will use different types of communication depending upon some pre-existing factor. (People avoid messages that they think will be disagreeable so they won't experience cognitive dissonance.) These claims may or may not be true, but you should regard the scientific theories presented in this book as valuable to the extent that theorists are willing to make confident predictions about communication behavior.

Scientific Standard 2: Explanation of the Data

A good objective theory explains an event or human behavior. Philosopher of science Abraham Kaplan said that theory is a way of making sense out of a disturbing situation.[1] An objective theory should bring clarity to an otherwise jumbled state of affairs; it should draw order out of chaos.

A good social science theory describes the process, focuses our attention on what's crucial, and helps us ignore that which makes little difference. But it also goes beyond raw data and explains *why.* When Willie Sutton was asked why he robbed banks, urban legend says the Depression-era bandit replied, "Because that's where the money is." It's a great line, but as a theory of motivation, it lacks explanatory power. There's nothing in the words that casts light on the internal processes or environmental forces that led Sutton to crack a safe while others tried to crack the stock market.

Sometimes a communication theory can sound great, but upon closer inspection it doesn't explain much. Years ago, researchers discovered that by having people answer a few key questions about the emotions they felt prior to giving a speech, they could predict which people would be the most nervous or apprehensive during the talk itself. A theory based on the research claimed that *communication apprehension* was a trait only some people possess. The theory had great predictive power in identifying nervous public speakers, but it lacked a good explanation for why some people became nervous and others didn't.[2] It merely suggested that nervous speakers possessed the trait of communication apprehension.

You can probably sense that this circular thinking leaves something to be desired. How do people acquire the trait? Are they born with it? Can they get rid of it through some type of intervention? Over the past few decades, theorists have grappled with the question of how well "trait" theories explain behavior.[3] If the rationale behind why people engage in certain behaviors is simply *That's the kind of people they are,* objective scholars won't be happy with the theory's explanatory power. As a student of communication theory, you shouldn't be either. When you evaluate an objective theory, keep in mind that the *reason* something happens becomes as important as the fact that it does.

Scientific Standard 3: Relative Simplicity

A good objective theory is as simple as possible—no more complex than it has to be. Several decades ago a cartoonist named Rube Goldberg made people laugh by sketching plans for complicated machines that performed simple tasks. His "better mousetrap" went through a sequence of 15 mechanical steps that were triggered by turning a crank and ended with a bird cage dropping over a cheese-eating mouse.

Goldberg's designs were funny because the machines were so needlessly convoluted. They violated the scientific principle called Occam's razor, so named because philosopher William of Occam implored theorists to "shave off" any assumptions, variables, or concepts that aren't necessary to explain what's going on.[4] When you've concentrated on a subject for a long time, it's easy to get caught up in the grandeur of a theoretical construction. Yet the *rule of parsimony*—another label for the same principle—states that given two plausible explanations for the same event, we should accept the less complex version. Theoretical physicist Albert Einstein put it this way: "Any intelligent fool can make things bigger and more complex. . . . It takes a touch of genius—and a lot of courage—to move in the opposite direction."[5]

**Rule of parsimony
(Occam's razor)**
Given two plausible explanations for the same event, we should accept the simpler version.

Einstein practiced what he preached. His elegant formula ($E = mc^2$) explains the relationships among energy, mass, time, and the speed of light using just three terms, and history credits him with more than a touch of genius. But relative simplicity doesn't necessarily mean *easy to understand.* Trained physicists admit they're still struggling to fully comprehend the theory of relativity. That theory is parsimonious not because it's a no-brainer, but because it doesn't carry the extraneous baggage rival theories carry as they try to explain why time stands still when you approach the speed of light.

Scientific Standard 4: Hypotheses That Can Be Tested

A good objective theory is testable. If a prediction is wrong, there ought to be a way to demonstrate the error. Karl Popper called this requirement *falsifiability,* and saw it as the defining feature of scientific theory.[6] But some theories are so loosely stated that it's impossible to imagine empirical results that could disprove their hypotheses. And if there is no way to prove a theory false, then any claim that it's true seems hollow. A boyhood example may help illustrate this point.

When I was 12 years old, I had a friend named Mike. We spent many hours shooting baskets in his driveway. The backboard was mounted on an old-fashioned, single-car garage with double doors that opened outward like the doors on a cabinet. In order to avoid crashing into them on a drive for a layup, we'd open the doors during play. But since the doors would only swing through a 90-degree arc, they extended about 4 feet onto the court along the baseline.

One day Mike announced that he'd developed a "never-miss" shot. He took the ball at the top of the free-throw circle, drove toward the basket, then cut to the right corner. When he got to the baseline, he took a fade-away jump shot, blindly arcing the ball over the top of the big door. I was greatly impressed as the ball swished through the net. When he boasted that he never missed, I challenged him to do it again, which he did. But his third shot was an air ball—it completely missed the rim.

Before I could make the kind of bratty comment junior high school boys tend to make, he quickly told me that the attempt had not been his never-miss shot. He claimed to have slipped as he cut to the right and therefore jumped from the wrong place. Grabbing the ball, he drove behind the door again and launched a blind arcing shot. Swish. *That,* he assured me, was his never-miss shot.

I knew something was wrong. I soon figured out that any missed attempt was, by definition, not the ballyhooed never-miss shot. When the ball went in, however, Mike heralded the success as added evidence of 100 percent accuracy. I now know that I could have called his bluff by removing the net from the basket so he couldn't hear whether the shot went through. This would have forced him to declare from behind the door whether the attempt was of the never-miss variety. But as long as I played by his rules, there was no way to disprove his claim.

Unfortunately, some theories are stated in a way that makes it impossible to prove them false. They shy away from the put-up-or-shut-up standard—they aren't testable. If it isn't possible to gather clear evidence that goes against a theory's claims, then it's also impossible to collect evidence that clearly supports those claims.

Falsifiability
The requirement that a scientific theory be stated in such a way that it can be tested and disproved if it is indeed wrong.

Scientific Standard 5: Practical Utility

Over time, a good objective theory is useful. Since an oft-cited goal of social science is to help people have more control over their daily lives, people facing the types of thorny social situations that the theory addresses should be able to benefit from its wisdom. This requirement is consistent with social psychologist Kurt Lewin's claim that there is nothing as practical as a good theory. A theory that communication practitioners find helpful may not be more valid than one to which few folks turn for guidance, but because of its influence, it may prove more valuable.

As you read about theories crafted from an objective perspective, let usefulness be one measure of their worth. A word of caution, however: Most of us can be a bit lazy or shortsighted, having a tendency to consider unimportant anything that's hard to grasp or can't be applied to our lives right now. Before considering a theory irrelevant, make certain you understand it and consider how others have made use of its insight. We'll try to do our part by presenting each theory as clearly as possible and suggesting potential applications. Perhaps you'll be even more interested in how other students have found a theory useful in their lives. That's why we've included a student-written application in almost all of the 32 chapters that feature a specific theory. Of course, theories that only apply to students' behavior aren't as practical as theories that apply across different groups of people. The wider the scope of a theory's application, the greater its practical utility.

Scientific Standard 6: Quantitative Research

As the heading suggests, scientists tend to appeal to *numbers* as they gather evidence to support their theories. Almost all scientific research depends on a *comparison of differences*—this group compared to that group, this treatment as opposed to that treatment, these results versus those results. Since objective theorists aim to mirror reality, it makes sense for them to measure and report what they discover in precise numerical terms rather than in linguistic terms, which are open to interpretation. Enlightenment philosopher David Hume insisted on the superiority of quantitative methods over qualitative research:

> If we take in our hand any volume . . . let us ask: Does it contain any abstract reasoning concerning quantity or number? No. Does it contain any experimental reasoning concerning the matter of fact or existence? No. Commit it then to the flames, for it can contain nothing but sophistry and illusion.[7]

Given the radical nature of Hume's over-the-top pronouncement, we can wryly imagine the English philosopher making daily trips to a used bookstore for fuel to heat his home in winter. But the idea that numbers are more reliable than words does run deep in the scientific community. More than other quantitative methods, objective theorists use *experiments* and *surveys* to test their predictions.

Experiments. Working under the assumption that human behavior is not random, an experimenter tries to establish a cause-and-effect relationship by systematically manipulating one factor (the independent variable) in a tightly controlled situation to learn its effect on another factor (the dependent variable). A laboratory experiment would be an appropriate way to answer the question, *Does greater perceived attitude similarity lead to increased interpersonal attraction?* The experimenter might first identify a range of attitudes held by the participating subjects and then systematically alter the attitude information provided about an experimental confederate—someone in cahoots with the experimenter—before they met. A similarity-causes-attraction hypothesis would be supported if the subjects whose attitudes meshed with what they thought the confederate believed ended up liking that person better than did those who thought they were quite different from the confederate.[8]

Experiment
A research method that manipulates a variable in a tightly controlled situation in order to find out if it has the predicted effect.

"Are you just pissing and moaning, or can you verify what you're saying with data?"

©Edward Koren/The New Yorker Collection/The Cartoon Bank

Survey
A research method that uses questionnaires and structured interviews to collect self-reported data that reflects what respondents think, feel, or intend to do.

Surveys. Whether using questionnaires or structured interviews, survey researchers rely on self-reported data to discover people's past behavior and what they now think, feel, or intend to do. For example, media-effects researchers have used survey methodology to answer the research question, *Do people who watch a high amount of dramatic violence on television hold an exaggerated belief that the world is a mean and scary place?* They asked the number of hours a day the respondents watched TV and then gave a series of forced-choice options that tapped into respondents' perceived odds of becoming a victim of violence. The researchers discovered a positive relationship between the amount of viewing and the amount of fear.[9]

Although the presence of a correlation doesn't necessarily imply a causal relationship, it keeps that possibility alive. It's also the case that if a survey shows two variables *aren't* correlated, that's a powerful clue that one of the variables *isn't* a cause of the other. A survey can save valuable time that would otherwise be needed to establish cause-and-effect by conducting an experiment. In addition to the clues they provide about causal relationships, surveys are often the most convenient way to discover what people are thinking, feeling, and intending to do—the key components of our attitudes.

WHAT MAKES AN INTERPRETIVE THEORY GOOD?

Unlike scientists, interpretive scholars don't have a six-point set of agreed-upon criteria for evaluating their theories. But, even though there is no universally approved model, rhetoricians, critical theorists, and other interpreters repeatedly urge that interpretive theories should accomplish some or all of the following functions: *identify values, create understanding, inspire aesthetic appreciation, stimulate agreement, reform society,* and *conduct qualitative research*. The rest of this chapter examines these oft-mentioned ideals.

Interpretive Standard 1: Clarification of Values

A good interpretive theory brings people's values into the open. The theorist actively seeks to acknowledge, identify, or unmask the ideology behind the message under scrutiny.

Interpretive theorists should also be willing to reveal their own ethical commitments. As Webster University dean of communications Eric Rothenbuhler states, "Theoretical positions have moral implications, and when we teach them, advocate their use by others, or promote policies based upon them they have moral consequences."[10] Of course, not all interpretive scholars occupy the same moral ground, but there are core values most of them share. For example, humanists usually place a premium on individual liberty. Klaus Krippendorff of the Annenberg School for Communication at the University of Pennsylvania wants to make sure that scholars' drive for personal freedom extends to the people they study. His *ethical imperative* directs the theorist to "grant others that occur in your construction the same autonomy you practice constructing them."[11] When theorists follow this rule, scholarly monologue gives way to collegial dialogue. In this way, people have a say in what's said about them. This kind of communal assessment requires reporting multiple voices rather than relying on one or two informants.

Ethical imperative
Grant others that occur in your construction the same autonomy you practice constructing them.

Some interpretive scholars value equality as highly as they do freedom. This commitment leads to continual examination of the power relationships inherent in all communication. Critical theorists, in particular, insist that scholars can no longer remain ethically detached from the people they are studying or from the political and economic implications of their work. For critical theorists, "There is no safe harbor in which researchers can avoid the power structure."[12]

Interpretive Standard 2: New Understanding of People

Interpretive scholarship is good when it offers fresh insight into the human condition. Rhetorical critics, ethnographers, and other humanistic researchers seek to gain new understanding by analyzing the activity they regard as uniquely human—symbolic interaction. As opposed to social science theorists who attempt to identify communication patterns common to all people, an interpretive scholar typically examines a one-of-a-kind speech community that exhibits a specific language style. By analyzing this group's communication practice, the researcher hopes to develop an understanding of local knowledge or members' unique rules for interaction. Interpretive theories are tools to aid this search for situated meaning.

Some critics fear that by relying on rhetorical theory, we will read our preconceived ideas into the text rather than letting the words speak for themselves. They suggest that there are times when we should "just say no" to theory. But University of Minnesota communication theorist Ernest Bormann noted that rhetorical theory works best when it suggests universal patterns of symbol-using: "A powerful explanatory structure is what makes a work of humanistic scholarship live on through time."[13]

Bormann's claim is akin to the behavioral scientist's insistence that theory explains why people do what they do. But the two notions are somewhat different.

Self-referential imperative
Include yourself as a constituent of your own construction.

Science wants an objective explanation; humanism desires subjective understanding. Krippendorff urges us to recognize that we, as theorists, are both the cause and the consequence of what we observe. His *self-referential imperative* for building theory states, "Include yourself as a constituent of your own construction."[14]

Interpretive Standard 3: Aesthetic Appeal

The way a theorist presents ideas can capture the imagination of a reader just as much as the wisdom and originality of the theory he or she has created. As with any type of communication, both content and style make a difference. Objective theorists are constrained by the standard format for acceptable scientific writing—propositions, hypotheses, operationalized constructs, and the like. But interpretive theorists have more room for creativity, so aesthetic appeal becomes an issue. Although the elegance of a theory is in the eye of the beholder, clarity and artistry seem to be the two qualities needed to satisfy this aesthetic requirement.

No matter how great the insights the theory contains, if the essay describing them is disorganized, overwritten, or opaque, the theorist's ideas will come across murky rather than clear. A student of mine who fought through a theorist's monograph filled with esoteric jargon likened the experience to "scuba diving in fudge."

According to University of Pittsburgh professor Barbara Warnick, a rhetorical critic can fill one or more of four roles—artist, analyst, audience, and advocate.[15] As an artist, the critic's job is to spark appreciation. Along with clarity, it's another way to construct an interpretive theory with aesthetic appeal. By artfully incorporating imagery, metaphor, illustration, and story into the core of the theory, the theorist can make his or her creation come alive for others. We can't illustrate all of these artful devices in a single paragraph, but many students of rhetoric are moved by the way University of Wisconsin rhetorical critic Edwin Black summed up his analysis of Lincoln's Gettysburg address:

> The Gettysburg Address is, finally and inevitably, a projection of Lincoln himself, of his discretion, of his modesty on an occasion which invited him to don the mantle of the prophet, of his meticulous measure of how far he ought to go, of the assurance of his self-knowledge: his impeccable discernment of his own competence, his flawless sense of its depth and its limits. As an actor in history and a force in the world, Lincoln does not hesitate to comprehend history and the world. But he never presumes to cast his mind beyond human dimensions. He does not recite divine intentions; he does not issue cosmic judgments. He knows, to the bottom, what he knows. Of the rest, he is silent.[16]

Interpretive Standard 4: Community of Agreement

We can identify a good interpretive theory by the amount of support it generates within a community of scholars who are interested and knowledgeable about the same type of communication. Interpretation of meaning is subjective, but whether the interpreter's case is reasonable or totally off the wall is ultimately decided by others in the field. Their acceptance or rejection is an objective fact that helps verify or vilify a theorist's ideas.

Sometimes interpretive theorists present a controversial thesis to an audience restricted to true believers—those who already agree with the author's position. But an interpretive theory can't meet the community of agreement standard unless it becomes the subject of widespread analysis. For example, former National

Communication Association president David Zarefsky warns that rhetorical validity can be established only when a work is debated in the broad marketplace of ideas. For this Northwestern University rhetorical critic, sound arguments differ from unsound ones in that "sound arguments are addressed to the general audience of critical readers, not just to the adherents of a particular 'school' or perspective. . . . They open their own reasoning process to scrutiny."[17]

John Stewart is the editor of *Bridges Not Walls,* a collection of humanistic articles on interpersonal communication. As the book has progressed through 11 editions, Stewart's judgment to keep, drop, or add a theoretical work has been made possible by the fact that interpretive scholarship is "not a solitary enterprise carried out in a vacuum." It is instead, he says, "the effort of a community of scholars who routinely subject their findings to the scrutiny of editors, referees, and readers."[18]

Interpretive Standard 5: Reform of Society

A good interpretive theory often generates change. Some interpretive scholars, but by no means all, aren't content merely to interpret the intended meanings of a text. Contrary to the notion that we can dismiss calls for social justice or emancipation as *mere rhetoric,* critical interpreters are reformers who can have an impact on society. They want to expose and publicly resist the ideology that permeates the accepted wisdom of a culture. Kenneth Gergen, a Swarthmore College social psychologist, states that theory has the capacity to challenge the guiding assumptions of the culture, to raise fundamental questions regarding contemporary social life, to foster reconsideration of that which is "taken for granted," and thereby to generate fresh alternatives for social action.[19]

Along with many interpretive scholars, *critical theorists* tend to reject any notion of permanent truth or meaning. They see society's economic, political, social, religious, and educational institutions as socially constructed by unjust communication practices that create or perpetuate gross imbalances of power. The aim of their scholarship is to unmask these communication practices in an attempt to stimulate change. To traditional thinkers, their activity looks like a few angry children in kindergarten knocking over other kids' blocks, but they are intentionally using theory to carve out a space where people without power can be heard. For example, a critical theorist working from a Marxist, feminist, or postmodern perspective might craft a theory to support an alternative interpretation of the Golden Rule, namely, *He who has the gold, rules.* The theorist would then apply this reinterpretation to a specific practice, perhaps the publishing and pricing of required textbooks such as the one you're reading. To the extent that the theory stimulates students to rethink, respond, and react to this "free-market" process, it is a good interpretive theory.

Critical theorists
Scholars who use theory to reveal unjust communication practices that create or perpetuate an imbalance of power.

Interpretive Standard 6: Qualitative Research

While scientists use *numbers* to support their theories, interpretive scholars use *words.* That's the basic difference between quantitative and qualitative research. As the editors of the *Handbook of Qualitative Research* describe the process, "Qualitative researchers study things in their natural settings, attempting to make sense of, or to interpret, phenomena in terms of the meaning people bring to them."[20] A focus on meaning and significance is consistent with the maxim that once hung on the wall of Einstein's Princeton University office:[21]

> Not everything that can be counted counts, and
> not everything that counts can be counted.

The interpretive scholar's qualitative tools include open-ended interviews, focus groups, visual texts, artifacts, and introspection. But *textual analysis* and *ethnography* are the two methods most often used to study how humans use signs and symbols to create and infer meaning.

Textual Analysis. The aim of *textual analysis* is to describe and interpret the characteristics of a message. Communication theorists use this term to refer to the intensive study of a single message grounded in a humanistic perspective.

Textual analysis
A research method that describes and interprets the characteristics of any text.

Rhetorical criticism is the most common form of textual research in the communication discipline. For example, rhetorical critics have asked, *What does Martin Luther King's choice of language in his "I Have a Dream" speech on the Washington mall reveal about his strategic intent?* They've then undertaken a close reading of the text and context of that famous speech and concluded that King was trying to simultaneously appeal to multiple audiences without alienating any of them.[22]

Ethnography. The late Princeton anthropologist Clifford Geertz said that *ethnography* is "not an experimental science in search of law, but an interpretive [approach] in search of meaning."[23] As a sensitive observer of the human scene, Geertz was loath to impose his way of thinking onto a society's construction of reality. He wanted his theory of communication grounded in the meanings that people within a culture share. Getting it right means seeing it from their point of view.

Ethnography
A method of participant observation designed to help a researcher experience a culture's complex web of meaning.

When Stan Musial—one of the greatest baseball players in history—passed away in 2013 at the age of 92, his many admirers took the opportunity to share their memories. One story that circulated revealed that Musial was an amateur ethnographer. After baseball was desegregated in 1945, Musial noticed a group of black players on his all-star team congregating in the back corner of the dugout to play poker. In an effort to start dialogue, foster team spirit, and begin friendships, Musial cautiously approached the table and sat down. He felt like he had entered another world. In order to befriend his black teammates, he had to learn their group rituals, linguistic expressions, and cultural experiences that were all unfamiliar to him. His task was even more difficult because he didn't know the first thing about poker. Gradually, through listening and making careful mental notes, Musial began to understand his teammates and see the game of baseball through their eyes instead of his. That's ethnography.[24]

CONTESTED TURF AND COMMON GROUND AMONG THEORISTS

Throughout this chapter we have urged using separate measures for weighing the merits of objective and interpretive theories. That's because the two sets of criteria reflect the divergent mindsets of scientists and interpretive scholars as outlined in Chapter 2. Perhaps the field of personality assessment offers a way to understand how deeply these differences run. Some of you have taken the Myers-Briggs Type Indicator, a test that measures individual preferences on four bipolar scales. The *sensing-intuition* scale shows how people perceive or acquire information—how they seek to find out about things. As you read through the descriptions of *sensing* and *intuition* below, consider how closely they reflect the contrast of objective and interpretive epistemology—different ways of knowing.[25]

Sensing. One way to "find out" is to use your sensing function. Your eyes, ears, and other senses tell you what is actually there and actually happening, both inside and outside of yourself. Sensing is especially useful for appreciating the realities of a situation.

Intuition. The other way to "find out" is through intuition, which reveals the meanings, relationships, and possibilities that go beyond the information from your senses. Intuition looks at the big picture and tries to grasp the essential patterns.

These are differences that make a difference. It's hard to imagine two theorists becoming intellectual soul mates if each discounts or disdains the other's starting point, method, and conclusion. Does that mean they can't be friends? Not necessarily. There are at least three reasons for guarded optimism.

A firm foundation for their friendship would be a mutual respect for each other's curiosity about the communication process and a recognition that they are both bringing the very best of their intellect to bear on what they study. A second basis for mutual appreciation would be an understanding that the strong point of science is a rigorous comparison of multiple messages or groups, while the forte of humanism is its imaginative, in-depth analysis of a single message or group. Anthropologist Gregory Bateson described *rigor* and *imagination* as the two great contraries of the mind. He wrote that either "by itself is lethal. Rigor alone is paralytic death, but imagination alone is insanity."[26]

A third reason for mutual appreciation can be seen in a side-by-side comparison of the two sets of criteria in Figure 3–1. The chart suggests that the standards set by scientists and the evaluative criteria used by interpretive theorists share some similarities. Work down through the chart line-by-line and note a bit of overlap for each pair of terms. Here are the points of contact we see:

1. Both *prediction* and *value clarification* look to the future. The first suggests what *will* happen, the second, what *ought* to happen.

2. An *explanation* of communication behavior can lead to further *understanding* of people's motivation.

3. For many students of theory, *simplicity* has an *aesthetic appeal.*

4. *Testing hypotheses* is a way of achieving a *community of agreement.*

5. What could be more *practical* than a theory that *reforms* unjust practices?

6. Both *quantitative research* and *qualitative research* reflect a commitment to learn more about communication.

Identifying reasons for mutual appreciation doesn't guarantee such esteem will actually develop. Republicans and Democrats have a common goal to bring about a more perfect union, but it's often difficult to see anything more than political

Scientific Theory	Interpretive Theory
Prediction of Future	Clarification of Values
Explanation of Data	Understanding of People
Relative Simplicity	Aesthetic Appeal
Testable Hypothesis	Community of Agreement
Practical Utility	Reform of Society
Quantitative Research	Qualitative Research

FIGURE 3–1   Summary of Criteria for Evaluating Communication Theory

gridlock when members of the two parties get together. Similarly, when objective and interpretive theorists work in the same academic department, tensions can run high. At the very least, the two scholarly communities should have a familiarity with each other's work. That's one reason we've elected to present both objective and interpretive theories in this book.

You'll find that we usually refer to these requirements for good theory in the critique sections at the end of each chapter. As you might expect, the 32 theories stack up rather well—otherwise we wouldn't have picked them in the first place. But constructing theory is difficult, and most theories have an Achilles' heel that makes them vulnerable to criticism. All of the theorists readily admit a need for fine-tuning their work, and some even call for major overhauls. We encourage you to weigh their words by the standards you think are important before reading the critique at the end of each chapter.

QUESTIONS TO SHARPEN YOUR FOCUS

1. How can we call a scientific theory good if it is *capable of being proved wrong?*

2. How can we decide when a *rhetorical critic* provides a *reasonable interpretation?*

3. All theories involve trade-offs; no theory can meet every standard of quality equally well. Of the 12 *criteria* discussed, which two or three are most important to you? Which one is least important?

4. Do you think objective scholars have any room in their approach for *intuition?* If so, how might that work? Do interpretive scholars have any space for *sensing?*

A SECOND LOOK

Scientific evaluation: Steven Chaffee, "Thinking About Theory," in *An Integrated Approach to Communication Theory and Research,* 2nd ed., Don Stacks and Michael Salwen (eds.), Routledge, NY, 2009, pp. 13–29.

Interpretive evaluation: Klaus Krippendorff, "On the Ethics of Constructing Communication," in *Rethinking Communication: Vol. 1,* Brenda Dervin, Lawrence Grossberg, Barbara O'Keefe, and Ellen Wartella (eds.), Sage, Newbury Park, CA, 1989, pp. 66–96.

Progress in scientific research: Franklin Boster, "On Making Progress in Communication," *Human Communication Research,* Vol. 28, 2002, pp. 473–490.

Quantitative theory: Michael Beatty, "Thinking Quantitatively," in Stacks and Salwen, pp. 30–39.

Qualitative theory: James A. Anderson, "Thinking Qualitatively," in Stacks and Salwen, pp. 40–58.

Quantitative methods: Franklin Boster and John Sherry, "Alternative Methodological Approaches to Communication Science," in *The Handbook of Communication Science,* 2nd ed., Charles Berger, Michael Roloff, and David Roskos-Ewoldsen (eds.), Sage, Los Angeles, CA, 2010, pp. 55–71.

Qualitative methods: Norman K. Denzin and Yvonna S. Lincoln, *Collecting and Interpreting Qualitative Materials,* 4th ed. Sage, Thousand Oaks, CA, 2013.

To view a chapter-by-chapter list of changes from the previous edition, click on Changes under Theory Resources at *www.afirstlook.com.*

Mapping the Territory

(Seven Traditions in the Field of Communication Theory)

In Chapter 1, we presented working definitions for the concepts of *communication* and *theory*. In Chapters 2 and 3, we outlined the basic differences between objective and interpretive communication theories. These distinctions should help bring order out of chaos when your study of theory seems confusing. And it may seem confusing. University of Colorado emeritus communication professor Robert Craig describes the field of communication theory as awash with hundreds of unrelated theories that differ in starting point, method, and conclusion. He suggests that our field of study resembles "a pest control device called the Roach Motel that used to be advertised on TV: Theories check in, but they never check out."[1]

Plus, classifying that diverse collection of theories isn't easy. Perhaps it's a bit like trying to sort out all the different types of aliens in the *Star Wars* universe. One guide to the series doesn't even try to group them—it just lists 143 different species in alphabetical order.[2] That wouldn't be much help to Rey as she walks into the diverse crowd at Maz Kanata's cantina in *The Force Awakens,* wondering which of the crazy creatures she can trust. Likewise, a laundry list of theories wouldn't help you much in your quest to understand communication. You need a way to organize, contrast, and compare the theories you'll encounter.

Craig thinks *practical application* is a great starting point for developing such a tool. If you're like many communication majors, you'd like your study of communication to help build a career, maintain close relationships, and change the world for the better. That kind of real-world impact excites Craig, too. He's convinced that our search for different types of theory should be grounded where real people grapple with everyday problems and practices of communication. Craig explains that "all communication theories are relevant to a common practical lifeworld in which *communication* is already a richly meaningful term."[3] Communication theory is the systematic and thoughtful response of communication scholars to questions posed as humans interact with one another—the best thinking within a practical discipline.[4]

Craig thinks we can chart the *field of communication theory* if we take a look at the actual approaches researchers use to study communication problems. He identifies seven established traditions of communication theory that include most, if not all, of what theorists have done. These already established traditions offer "distinct, alternative vocabularies" that describe different "ways of conceptualizing communication problems and practices."[5] This means that scholars within a given tradition talk comfortably with one another but might have trouble understanding those who work in other camps. As Craig suggests, we shouldn't try to smooth over these between-group disagreements. Theorists argue because they have something important to argue about.

In the rest of the chapter we'll outline the seven traditions Craig describes. Taken together, they reveal the breadth and diversity of the field of communication theory. The classifications will also help you understand why some theories share common ground, while others have conflicting goals and assumptions. As we introduce each tradition, we'll highlight how its advocates tend to define communication. We'll then provide an example of research that the tradition has inspired.[6] Since we find that the topic of friendship is of great interest to most college students—and to us—for each tradition we'll feature a research study that demonstrates how that tradition approaches this type of close relationship. At the end of each section, we'll recap by identifying the practical question the research study aimed to solve and why the tradition helped the researchers answer it.

THE SOCIO-PSYCHOLOGICAL TRADITION

Communication as Interaction and Influence

The socio-psychological tradition epitomizes the scientific or objective perspective described in Chapter 2. Scholars in this tradition believe there are communication truths that can be discovered by careful, systematic observation. They look for cause-and-effect relationships that will predict the results when people communicate. When searching for universal laws of communication, they try to focus on what *is* without being biased by their personal view of what *ought to be*. As social scientists, they heed the warning of the skeptical newspaper editor: "You think your mother loves you? Check it out—at least two sources." For communication theorists in the socio-psychological tradition, checking it out usually means quantitatively measuring variables in a series of surveys or controlled experiments. That's what the three of us did when we wanted to understand what predicts friendship that lasts over the long haul.

While teaching at a small liberal arts college where he had the opportunity to be personally involved in the lives of his students, Em always wondered if there was a way to predict which college friendships would survive and thrive after graduation. As someone trained in the socio-psychological tradition, he began a longitudinal study—a series of surveys taken at multiple points in time, spanning two decades.[7] Em asked 45 pairs of best friends to respond to questions about their relationship, such as (1) when they became close friends, (2) the similarity of their academic majors, and (3) the extent to which they avoided discussing awkward topics. He also (4) assessed their self-disclosure to each other and (5) measured their communication efficiency by watching them play two rounds of the cooperative word game *Password.* Would any of these measures forecast who would be friends forever?

In order to find an answer, Em needed a reliable and valid measure of relational closeness. He invited Glenn to help create one. Based on social psychologist Harold Kelley's interactional theory, which suggests that close relationships are characterized by "strength, frequency, diversity, and duration," Glenn and Em developed a composite measure that assessed these properties.[8] For example, they gauged *relative strength* by asking the pair how many friends they feel closer to than their college best friend.

Nineteen years after the initial study, Andrew helped locate the study participants and asked them to respond to this measure of relational closeness. We weren't surprised that participants with a longer history as best friends when they came to the study were most likely to remain close two decades later. Of more interest to us as communication scholars, those with similar academic majors and those with better scores on the *Password* game also remained close.[9] Remember that participants' choice of major and the *Password* game occurred about two decades earlier, yet these factors still predicted friendship long after college. It appears that communicating on the same wavelength and sharing common academic interests is a boon to long-lasting friendship. Maybe it's no surprise, then, that working together on this research project solidified our friendship with each other. Eventually, that friendship led to the three of us joining together to write the book you're reading now.

Recap: The practical question we sought to answer was, "what predicts friendship that lasts over time?" We approached this question from the socio-psychological tradition because it's designed to identify cause-and-effect patterns.

THE CYBERNETIC TRADITION

Communication as a System of Information Processing

MIT scientist Norbert Wiener coined the word *cybernetics* to describe the field of artificial intelligence.[10] The term is a transliteration of the Greek word for "steersman" or "governor," and it illustrates the way feedback makes information processing possible in our heads and on our laptops. During World War II, Wiener developed an anti-aircraft firing system that adjusted future trajectory by taking into account the results of past performance. His concept of feedback anchored the cybernetic tradition, which regards communication as the link connecting the separate parts of any system, such as a computer system, a family system, or a media system. Theorists in the cybernetic tradition seek to answer such questions as, *How does the system work? What could change it?* and *How can we get the bugs out?*

Cybernetics
The study of information processing, feedback, and control in communication systems.

University of Washington communication professor Malcolm Parks studies personal relationships by asking both partners to describe their social network. In one major study of college students' same-sex friendships, he separately asked each partner to prepare a list of his or her closest relationships, including four family members and eight non-family ties.[11] In almost all cases, the eight people who weren't family were other friends or romantic partners rather than co-workers, coaches, or teachers. Parks then had the two friends trade lists and asked questions that probed their relationship with the key people in their *friend's* social network. These included:

1. Prior contact: Which people did you know before you met your friend?
2. Range of contact: How many of them have you now met face-to-face?
3. Communication: How often do you communicate with each of them?
4. Liking: How much do you like or dislike each of the ones you know?
5. Support: To what extent does each of them support your friendship?
6. Support: To what extent does *your own* network support your friendship?

Note that the first four questions establish the links within and between the friends' social networks. Both support questions reveal the feedback friends receive from these support systems.

Using a number of traditional measures that assess personal relationships, Parks measured the amount of *communication* between the friends, the *closeness* of their relationship, and their *commitment* to see it continue. When he compared these three measures to the quantity and quality of links to their friend's social network, the results were striking. Friends who had multiple and positive interactions with their partner's social networks had more communication with, closeness to, and commitment toward their partner than friends who had little involvement and felt little support from these folks. Friendships don't exist in a vacuum; they are embedded in a network that processes social information.

Recap: The practical question Parks sought to answer was, "how are friendships shaped by other people that the friends know?" He approached this question from the cybernetic tradition because it's designed to understand how information flows through social networks.

THE RHETORICAL TRADITION

Communication as Artful Public Address

Rhetoric
The art of using all available means of persuasion, focusing on lines of argument, organization of ideas, language use, and delivery in public speaking.

Whether speaking to a crowd, congregation, legislature, or jury, public speakers have sought practical advice on how to best present their case. Well into the twentieth century, the rhetorical theory and advice from Plato, Aristotle, Cicero, Quintilian, and other Greco-Roman rhetors served as the main source of wisdom about public speaking. There are a half dozen features that characterize this influential tradition of rhetorical communication:

- A conviction that speech distinguishes humans from other animals. Cicero suggested that only oral communication had the power to lead humanity out of its brutish existence and establish communities with rights of citizenship.[12]

- A confidence that public address delivered in a democratic forum is a more effective way to solve political problems than rule by decree or force. Within this tradition, the phrase *mere rhetoric* is a contradiction in terms.

- A setting in which a single speaker attempts to influence multiple listeners through persuasive discourse. Effective communication requires audience adaptation.

- Oratorical training as the cornerstone of a leader's education. Speakers learn to deliver strong arguments in powerful voices that carry to the edge of a crowd.

- An emphasis on the power and beauty of language to move people emotionally and stir them to action. Rhetoric is more art than science.

- Oral public persuasion as the province of males. A key feature of the women's movement has been the struggle for the right to speak in public.

Readers of Aristotle's *The Rhetoric* may be surprised to find a systematic analysis of friendship. He defines a friend as "one who loves and is loved in return."[13] The Greek word for this kind of love is *philia,* as in Philadelphia (the city of brotherly love). Aristotle then catalogs more than 20 personal qualities that make people attractive to us as friends: they are pleasant to deal with, share our interests, and show that they are "not inclined to leave [us] in the lurch."[14] Saint John's University philosopher Eugene Garver concluded that Aristotle didn't analyze friendship as a way to help Greek citizens develop close relationships.[15] Instead, he wanted to instruct orators on how to make their case seem more probable. If by word and deed a speaker appears friendly, listeners will be more open to the message.

Rochester Institute of Technology rhetorician Keith Jenkins found that friendly spirit of goodwill in his analysis of Barack Obama's 2008 campaign rhetoric. Obama frequently laced his policy arguments with personal stories of people he had met. Jenkins thinks this rhetorical strategy created a sense of community and an atmosphere of trust: "Whether he referred to ordinary Americans on the south side of Chicago or 'brothers, sisters, nieces, nephews, uncles and cousins, of every race and every hue, scattered across three continents' . . . his audience got a sense that Obama understood their experiences in America. Such a connection gave Obama the authority to speak to the problems of all Americans."[16]

Perhaps you're uncomfortable with the idea of using friendship as a means to achieve other goals, such as an election victory. Aristotle had no such qualms. Rhetoric is the discovery of *all* available means of persuasion.

Recap: The practical question Jenkins sought to answer was, "How did Obama persuade people by appealing to close relationships?" He approached this question from the rhetorical tradition because it's designed to understand how language changes the minds of others.

THE SEMIOTIC TRADITION

Communication as the Process of Sharing Meaning Through Signs

Semiotics
The study of verbal and nonverbal signs that can stand for something else, and how their interpretation impacts society.

Symbols
Arbitrary words and nonverbal signs that bear no natural connection with the things they describe; their meaning is learned within a given culture.

Semiotics is the study of signs. A *sign* is anything that can stand for something else. High body temperature is a <u>sign</u> of infection. Birds flying south <u>sign</u>al the coming of winter. An arrow de<u>sign</u>ates which direction to go.

Words are also signs, but of a special kind. They are *symbols*. Unlike the examples just cited, words are arbitrary symbols that have no inherent meaning, no natural connection with the things they describe. For example, there's nothing in the sound of the word *share* or anything visual in the letters *h-u-g* that signifies a good friendship. One could just as easily coin the term *snarf* or *clag* to symbolize a close relationship between friends. The same thing is true for nonverbal symbols like *winks* or *waves*.

Cambridge University literary critic I. A. Richards railed against the semantic trap that he labeled "the proper meaning superstition"—the mistaken belief that words have a precise definition.[17] For Richards and other semiologists, meaning doesn't reside in words or other symbols; meaning resides in people. Most theorists grounded in the semiotic tradition are trying to explain and reduce the misunderstanding created by the use of ambiguous symbols.

Metropolitan State University of Denver communication professor Michael Monsour recognized that the word *intimacy* used in the context of friendship might mean different things to different people, and the disparity could lead to confusion. So he asked 164 communication students what they meant by intimacy when used in reference to their same-sex and their opposite-sex friends. Roughly two-thirds of the respondents were female, two-thirds were single, and two-thirds were under the age of 30. Participants offered 27 distinct interpretations of intimacy between friends, and the number of meanings suggested by each respondent ranged from 1–5, with an average of two different meanings per person.[18]

Seven meanings were mentioned often enough to include them in the final results. Self-disclosure was by far the meaning of intimacy mentioned most. In rank order of frequency, the seven interpretations were:

1. Self-disclosure: Revelations about self that the friend didn't know
2. Emotional expressiveness: Closeness, warmth, affection, and caring
3. Physical contact: Nonsexual touch
4. Trust: Confidence that the other is reliable
5. Unconditional support: Being there for the other in good times and bad
6. Sexual contact: Overt sexual activity
7. Activities: Doing things together of a nonsexual nature

The content and order of the top five interpretations of intimacy held relatively constant for both opposite-sex and same-sex friendships. The notable deviations were that a few more men in opposite-sex friendships thought of intimacy as sexual contact, but in same-sex relationships characterized intimacy as activities together. For Monsour, the major contribution of this study is that for friends in both kinds of relationships, the word *intimacy* is multidimensional—a polysemic linguistic sign. A symbol like this can easily be misunderstood. Yet if two of the students in Monsour's study referred to intimacy in a conversation, with a few exceptions, it's likely they'd understand what the other was talking about.

Recap: The practical question Monsour sought to answer was, "What does the word *intimacy* mean to people in the context of friendship?" He approached this question from the semiotic tradition because it's designed to understand how the meanings of symbols change between people and across time.

THE SOCIO-CULTURAL TRADITION

Communication as the Creation and Enactment of Social Reality

The socio-cultural tradition is based on the premise that as people talk, they produce and reproduce culture. Most of us assume that words reflect what actually exists. However, theorists in this tradition suggest that the process often works the other way around. Our view of reality is strongly shaped by the language we use.

University of Chicago linguist Edward Sapir and his student Benjamin Lee Whorf were pioneers in the socio-cultural tradition. The Sapir–Whorf hypothesis of linguistic relativity states that the structure of a culture's language shapes what people think and do.[19] "The 'real world' is to a large extent unconsciously built upon the language habits of the group."[20] Their theory of linguistic relativity counters the assumption that words merely act as neutral vehicles to carry meaning. Language actually structures our perception of reality.

Sapir–Whorf hypothesis of linguistic relativity
The claim that the structure of a language shapes what people think and do; the social construction of reality.

Contemporary socio-cultural theorists grant even more power to language. They claim it is through the process of communication that "reality is produced, maintained, repaired, and transformed."[21] Or, stated in the active voice, *persons-in-conversation co-construct their own social worlds.*[22] When these worlds collide, the socio-cultural tradition offers help in bridging the culture gap that exists between "us" and "them."

Patricia Sias, a communication professor at the University of Arizona, takes a socio-cultural approach when studying friendships that form and dissolve in organizational settings. She writes that "relationships are not entities external to the relationship partners, but are mental creations that depend on communication for their existence and form. . . . If relationships are constituted in communication they are also *changed* through communication."[23] Sias uses a social construction lens through which to view deteriorating friendships in the workplace.

Sias located 25 people in a variety of jobs who were willing to talk about their failing workplace friendships. Some relationships were between peer co-workers, others between a supervisor and a subordinate. All the workers spontaneously told stories about their deteriorating friendship that revealed how communication between the two co-workers had changed. Although the friendships went sour for a variety of reasons—personality problems, distracting life events, conflicting expectations, betrayal, and promotion—the *way* the friendships dissolved was remarkably similar. Almost all workers told stories of using indirect communication to change the relationship.

While their friendships were deteriorating, the former friends still had to talk with each other in order to accomplish their work. But these co-workers stopped eating lunch together and socializing outside the office. While on the job they avoided personal topics and almost never talked about the declining state of their relationship. Even seemingly safe topics such as sports or movies were no longer discussed; small talk and watercooler chitchat disappeared.

Although linguistic connection was sparse, nonverbal communication spoke loudly. The workers who talked with Sias recalled the lack of eye contact, snappy or condescending tones of voice, and physically backing away from the other. Ideally, social construction research in the office would capture the real-time communication of co-workers, but that would require a video-recorded account of office conversations when the friendship was in the process of deteriorating—a high hurdle for Sias to clear. Nevertheless, her participants' accounts indicate communication practices that eroded formerly stable friendships.

Recap: The practical question Sias sought to answer was, "What communication practices shape deteriorating workplace friendships?" She approached this question from the socio-cultural tradition because it's designed to understand how communication creates social realities.

THE CRITICAL TRADITION

Communication as a Reflective Challenge to Unjust Discourse

The term *critical theory* comes from the work of a group of German scholars known as the "Frankfurt School" because they were part of the independent Institute for Social Research at Frankfurt University. Originally set up to test the ideas of Karl Marx, the Frankfurt School rejected the economic determinism of orthodox Marxism yet carried on the Marxist tradition of critiquing society.

What types of communication practice and research are critical theorists *against?* Although there is no single set of abuses that all of them denounce, critical theorists consistently challenge three features of contemporary society:

1. *The control of language to perpetuate power imbalances.* Critical theorists condemn any use of words that inhibits emancipation.

2. *Blind reliance on the scientific method and uncritical acceptance of empirical findings.* Critical theorists are suspicious of empirical work that scientists say is ideologically free, because science is not the value-free pursuit of knowledge it claims to be.

Culture industries
Entertainment businesses that reproduce the dominant ideology of a culture and distract people from recognizing unjust distribution of power within society (e.g., film, television, music, and advertising).

3. *The role of mass media in dulling sensitivity to repression.* Critical theorists see the "culture industries" of television, film, music, and print media as reproducing the dominant ideology of a culture and distracting people from recognizing the unjust distribution of power within society.

For example, Southwestern University communication professor Davi Johnson Thornton began her investigation of interracial friendship by watching the TV show *Psych.* The USA Network detective comedy focuses on the interracial friendship between a white cop (Shawn) and a black cop (Gus) in the Santa Barbara police department. At first glance, TV portrayals of close interracial friendships might seem like a good thing. Thornton isn't so sure. Her critical analysis of the show argues that its particular portrayal of black–white friendship might actually reinforce racism rather than work against it.

Thornton began her work by watching each episode of the show's first four seasons several times. After talking with other people familiar with the show, she selected specific instances that illustrate the show's approach to interracial humor. Overall, she concluded that the comedy "encourages a lighthearted, breezy attitude toward race and racism."[24] Much of the show's comedy mocks those who take race too seriously, like the embarrassed club bouncer who commits a racial gaffe when speaking with Gus and Shawn. Within the trust and acceptance of their friendship, the cop buddies seem to have no need for such "political correctness." In fact, Shawn often makes casual jokes about Gus' black identity (his favorite nickname for Gus is "Chocolate"). However, Thornton notes this "privilege-to-mock" runs only one direction, as Gus rarely pokes fun at Shawn's whiteness.[25]

Most friendships are characterized by an equality of power, and the casual viewer probably perceives Gus and Shawn's friendship that way. Yet in portraying the cozy comfort of a warm friendship, Thornton thinks the show simultaneously ignores the political and historical power differences so frequently attached to race. When European Americans view the show, she's concerned it will subtly encourage them to believe that "mainstream (middle-class, white) culture can accommodate diversity without serious threat to the privileges of whiteness."[26] Although her investigation focuses on *Psych,* she thinks other interracial comedies (re)produce such ideologies as well.

Recap: The practical question Thornton sought to answer was, "What ideologies of interracial friendship are produced through the TV show *Psych*?" She approached this question from the critical tradition because it's designed to critique how language and the mass media perpetuate unjust differences in power.

THE PHENOMENOLOGICAL TRADITION

Communication as the Experience of Self and Others Through Dialogue

Phenomenology
Intentional analysis of everyday experience from the standpoint of the person who is living it; explores the possibility of understanding the experience of self and others.

Although *phenomenology* is an imposing philosophical term, it basically refers to the intentional analysis of everyday life from the standpoint of the person who is living it. Thus, the phenomenological tradition places great emphasis on people's perception and their interpretation of their own experience. For the phenomenologist, an individual's story is more important, and more authoritative, than any research hypothesis or communication axiom. As psychologist Carl Rogers asserted, "Neither the Bible nor the prophets—neither Freud nor research—neither the revelations of God nor man—can take precedence over my own direct experience."[27]

The problem, of course, is that no two people have the same life story. Since we cannot experience another person's experience, we tend to talk past each other and then lament, "Nobody understands what it's like to be me." Thus, theorists who work within the phenomenological tradition seek to answer two questions: *Why is it so hard to establish and sustain authentic human relationships?* and *How can this problem be overcome?*

Ohio University communication professor Bill Rawlins works within this tradition as he studies friendship by taking an in-depth look at the actual conversations between friends. In his book *The Compass of Friendship: Narratives, Identities, and Dialogues,* he devotes an entire chapter to a 90-minute recorded conversation between Chris and Karen, two women who agree they've been friends for "30 years and counting."[28] Rawlins provided no guidelines or instructions. The women only know that he is interested in their friendship. After an hour of recounting stories about shared experiences, Chris brings up Karen's slow retreat into silence the past winter. Obviously bothered by losing contact, Chris continues . . .

> CHRIS: And I thought, "Well that's okay; everybody has these times when they feel this way." But I feel like you should *alert* people that *care* about you [laughs] to the fact that this is what is goin' on—
>
> KAREN: [laughs] Yeah . . .
>
> CHRIS: "I'm going into my cave. See ya in the spring," or whatever. Or "I don't wish to have anything, writing or any communications for a while. Not to worry. Adios. Bye to everybody. Hasta la vista or whatever."
>
> KAREN: Yeah.
>
> CHRIS: Or something, because I [pause], I [pause], I . . .
>
> KAREN: You were worried.[29]

The dialogue above is less than a minute of the women's conversation, yet it provides a rich resource for Rawlins' insight into their friendship. Chris says to herself at the time that such feelings are commonplace and "OK." Even so, she believes that Karen "should *alert* people that *care* about you to the fact that this is going on. . . ." They both laugh at this paradoxical recommendation that Karen communicate to significant others that she does not intend to communicate with them. Chris rehearses two voices for Karen here: a humorous one that trades on a hibernation metaphor, and then a more serious, explicit statement with Spanish flourishes at the end that seem to add a comical flavor. As Karen affirms this idea, however, Chris surrenders her comic tone and makes the frank request, "Or something," haltingly trying to offer her reasons, "I [pause], I [pause], I . . . ," which Karen completes for her: "You were worried." In short, Karen again recognizes the emotional basis of Chris' concerns and legitimates Chris' suggested policy for communicating social withdrawal.[30]

Rawlins' reconstruction of this segment reveals how *he* experiences the women's friendship. After reading his interpretation of the entire conversation, the women independently tell him that he was "right on" and had "nailed it."[31] That's because he paid attention to *their* interpretation of their experience.

Recap: The practical question Rawlins sought to answer was, "How do people create mutual understanding in their friendships?" He approached this question from the phenomenological tradition because it's designed to probe how people develop authentic human relationships.

FENCING THE FIELD OF COMMUNICATION THEORY

The seven traditions have deep roots in the field of communication theory. Team loyalties run strong, so theorists, researchers, and practitioners working within one tradition sometimes hear criticism from those in other traditions. In addition to whatever arguments each group might muster to defend their choice, they can also claim "squatters' rights" because scholars who went before had already established the right to occupy that portion of land. Taking the real estate metaphor seriously, in Figure 4-1 we've charted the seven traditions as equal-area parcels of territory that collectively make up the larger field of study. A few explanations are in order.

First, it's important to realize that the location of each tradition on the map is far from random. Our rationale for placing them where they are is based on the distinction between objective and interpretive theories outlined in Chapters 2 and 3. Craig generally agrees this basic continuum differentiates the traditions.[32] According to the scientific assumptions presented in Chapter 2, the socio-psychological tradition is the most objective, and so it occupies the far left position on the map—solidly rooted in objective territory. Moving across the map from left to right, the traditions become more interpretive and less objective. Some students wonder why rhetoric is rated more objective than semiotics. It's because rhetoricians have traditionally regarded what language refers to as "real," whereas semiologists perceive the relationship between a word and its referent as more tenuous. We see the phenomenological tradition as the most subjective of the seven traditions, and so it occupies the position farthest to the right—firmly grounded in interpretive territory. The order of presentation in this chapter followed a gradual shift from objective to interpretive concerns.

Second, some theories are hybrids that arise from multiple traditions. Scholars working in adjacent territories usually have an easier time appreciating each other's work. On the map they share a common border. Professionally, they are closer together in their basic assumptions. Even more remarkable are theories that draw on vastly different traditions. This sometimes happens when scholars follow Craig's admonition to use communication theory to answer practical questions. For example, cultivation theory (Chapter 29) asks how television influences people,

FIGURE 4-1   A Survey Map of Traditions in the Field of Communication Theory

particularly when they view violence. To answer that question, cultivation theorists have used the socio-psychological tradition to search for cause-and-effect associations between TV viewing and beliefs about the world. They've also drawn from the socio-cultural tradition to understand why the culture of Hollywood glorifies violence. Using both traditions provides a rich answer to the theory's practical question.

Pragmatism
An applied approach to knowledge; the philosophy that true understanding of an idea or situation has practical implications for action.

Finally, Craig doesn't think the seven charted traditions represent a complete map of the communication theory realm. He later suggested the possibility of a *pragmatist tradition*—one that "orients to practical problems, and evaluates ideas according to their usefulness rather than by an absolute standard of truth."[33] It would be a location where he sees his own work fitting in well. Likewise, one of Craig's students recently described a *spiritual tradition* devoted to understanding how people talk about transcendent truth.[34] Craig's openness to considering new territories leads us to offer a candidate of our own: the *ethical tradition.*

THE ETHICAL TRADITION

Communication as People of Character Interacting in Just and Beneficial Ways

More than many academic disciplines, the field of communication has been concerned with ethical responsibility. Since the time of Plato and Aristotle, communication scholars have grappled with the obligations that go along with the opportunities we have to communicate. Contemporary discussions of morality are increasingly beleaguered by the rise of ethical relativism.[35] Yet despite the postmodern challenge to all claims of Truth, at the turn of the century, the National Communication Association (NCA) adopted a "Credo for Ethical Communication."[36] If you read the credo (Appendix C), you'll find that its nine statements exist on the cusp of difficult questions about communication and ethics: *Is it always our duty to be honest? What limits, if any, should exist on freedom of expression? When does persuasion cross the line into intimidation and coercion?*

These are difficult questions to answer, and some scholars might suggest they have no place in a communication theory text. But to deal with human intercourse as a mechanical process separate from values would be like discussing sexual intercourse under ground rules that prohibit any reference to love. And within the ethical tradition, communication theorists do offer answers to these questions.

Craig has responded to our proposed ethical tradition by noting that, to define it fully, we'd have to explain how it compares to every other tradition.[37] Unfortunately, we don't have space to do that here. Still, we can at least ponder where the ethical tradition might fit on the map in Figure 4–1. Recall that many interpretive theories are concerned with questions of value (what *ought to be*; see Chapter 2). Also, one standard for evaluating an interpretive theory is whether it reforms society (see Chapter 3). Compared to their objective cousins, then, interpretive scholars seem to have an easier time speaking about ethical concerns. At the same time, many ethical theorists argue for universal moral standards to which everyone is accountable. So although the ethical tradition probably fits best toward the interpretive side of the map, the tradition's border may cross over into objective territory.

What might friendship research look like from the ethical tradition? The final chapter of Bill Rawlins' book *The Compass of Friendship* suggests what a friendship aligned with a moral compass looks like. The friends negotiate their relationship voluntarily, care about each other's well-being, respect each other as equals, and

engage in ongoing learning about each other.[38] But some objective scholars care
about ethical communication, too. Andrew's TCU friend and colleague Paul Witt
would agree. His "Communication and Character" course examines honesty, compassion, courage, patience, and humility—important ingredients for ethical friendships. Rawlins is an interpretive scholar; Witt is an objective scholar. Witt speaks
from the socio-psychological tradition, and Rawlins from the phenomenological. We
think both speak from the ethical tradition, too.

That kind of dialogue between traditions excites Craig. He urges us not to think
of the traditions as "inert containers" that seal ideas off from each other.[39] Rather,
the discipline of communication moves forward as each tradition challenges and

refines the others. The ethical tradition encourages every other tradition to consider what is right or wrong, what is good or bad, and who is virtuous or evil. Therefore, throughout this book, we've encapsuled the thoughts of some influential ethical theorists into 13 summary statements. Each of these *ethical reflections* appears in this book alongside a theory with which it naturally resonates.

With or without our addition of an ethical tradition, Craig's framework can help make sense of the great diversity in the field of communication theory. As you read about a theory in the section on media effects, remember that it may have the same ancestry as a theory you studied earlier in the section on relationship development. On the top of the first page of the next 32 chapters, we'll tie each theory to one or more traditions. Hopefully this label will make it easier for you to understand why the theorist has made certain choices. The labels are signposts that will help you navigate the world of communication theory.

QUESTIONS TO SHARPEN YOUR FOCUS

1. Communication departments rarely have a faculty representing all seven traditions. In order to create specialties and minimize conflict, some recruit from just one or two. What tradition(s) seems well-represented in your department?

2. Suppose you and your best friend have recently been on an emotional roller coaster. Which of the seven highlighted *definitions of communication* offers the most promise of helping you achieve a stable relationship? Why?

3. The map in Figure 4–1 represents seven traditions in the field of communication theory. In which region do you feel most at home? What other areas would you like to explore? Where would you be uncomfortable? Why?

4. Think of a time when you had to decide whether to lie or tell the truth. How did you decide what was the right thing to do? Overall, when is lying right and when is it wrong? How do you know?

A SECOND LOOK

Recommended resource: Robert T. Craig, "Communication Theory as a Field," *Communication Theory,* Vol. 9, 1999, pp. 119–161.

16-year review: Robert T. Craig, "The Constitutive Metamodel: A 16-Year Review," *Communication Theory,* Vol. 25, 2015, pp. 356–374.

Anthology of primary resources for each tradition: Heidi L. Muller and Robert T. Craig (eds.), *Theorizing Communication: Readings Across Traditions,* Sage, Los Angeles, CA, 2007.

Socio-psychological tradition: Carl Hovland, Irving Janis, and Harold Kelley, *Communication and Persuasion,* Yale University, New Haven, CT, 1953, pp. 1–55.

Cybernetic tradition: Norbert Wiener, *The Human Use of Human Beings,* Avon, New York, 1967, pp. 23–100.

Rhetorical tradition: Thomas M. Conley, *Rhetoric in the European Tradition,* Longman, New York, 1990, pp. 1–52.

Semiotic tradition: C. K. Ogden and I. A. Richards, *The Meaning of Meaning,* Harcourt, Brace & World, New York, 1946, pp. 1–23.

Socio-cultural tradition: Benjamin Lee Whorf, "The Relation of Habitual Thought and Behaviour to Language," in *Language, Culture, and Personality: Essays in Memory of Edward Sapir,* University of Utah, Salt Lake City, UT, 1941, pp. 123–149.

Critical tradition: Raymond Morrow with David Brown, *Critical Theory and Methodology,* Sage, Thousand Oaks, CA, 1994, pp. 3–34, 85–112.

Phenomenological tradition: Carl Rogers, "The Characteristics of a Helping Relationship," in *On Becoming a Person,* Houghton Mifflin, Boston, MA, 1961, pp. 39–58.

Ethical tradition: Richard L. Johannesen, "Communication Ethics: Centrality, Trends, and Controversies," in *Communication Yearbook 25,* William B. Gudykunst (ed.), Lawrence Erlbaum, Mahwah, NJ, 2001, pp. 201–235.

Alternative formulation of the seven traditions: François Cooren, "Communication Theory at the Center: Ventriloquism and the Communicative Constitution of Reality," *Journal of Communication,* Vol. 62, 2012, pp. 1–20.

Critique of Craig's model and his response: David Myers, "A Pox on All Compromises: Reply to Craig (1999)," and Robert T. Craig, "Minding My Metamodel, Mending Myers," *Communication Theory,* Vol. 11, 2001, pp. 218–230, 231–240.

To access outlines for all 37 chapters,
click on Chapter Outline under
Theory Resources at *www.afirstlook.com.*

DIVISION TWO

Interpersonal Communication

Communication theorists often use the image of a game to describe interpersonal communication. Various scholars refer to *language games, rules of the game, game-like behavior,* and even *game theory.* I'll use three specific game metaphors to illustrate what interpersonal communication *is,* and what it *is not.*[1]

Communication as Bowling   The bowling model of message delivery is likely the most widely held view of communication. I think that's unfortunate.

This model sees the bowler as the sender, who delivers the ball, which is the message. As it rolls down the lane (the channel), clutter on the boards (noise) may deflect the ball (the message). Yet if it is aimed well, the ball strikes the passive pins (the target audience) with a predictable effect.

In this one-way model of communication, the speaker (bowler) must take care to select a precisely crafted message (ball) and practice diligently to deliver it the same way every time. Of course, that makes sense only if target listeners are static, interchangeable pins waiting to be bowled over by our words—which they aren't. Communication theory that emphasizes message content to the neglect of relational factors simply isn't realistic. Real-life interpersonal communication is sometimes confusing, often unpredictable, and always involves more than just the speaker's action. This realization has led some observers to propose an interactive model for interpersonal communication.

Communication as Ping-Pong   Unlike bowling, Ping-Pong is not a solo game. This fact alone makes it a better analogy for interpersonal communication. One party puts the conversational ball in play, and the other gets into position to receive. It takes more concentration and skill to receive than to serve because while the speaker (server) knows where the message is going, the listener (receiver) doesn't. Like a verbal or nonverbal message, the ball may appear straightforward yet have a deceptive spin.

Ping-Pong is a back-and-forth game; players switch roles continuously. One moment the person holding the paddle is an initiator; the next second the same player is a responder, gauging the effectiveness of his or her shot by the way the ball comes back. The repeated adjustment essential for good play closely parallels the feedback process described in a number of interpersonal communication theories. There are, however, two inherent flaws in the table-tennis analogy.

The first defect is that the game is played with one ball, which at any point in time is headed in a single direction. A true model of interpersonal encounters would have people sending and receiving multiple balls at the same time. The other problem is that table tennis is a competitive game—there's a winner and a loser. In successful dialogue, both people win.

Communication as Charades   The game of charades best captures the simultaneous and collaborative nature of interpersonal communication. A charade is neither an action, like bowling a strike, nor an interaction, like a rally in Ping-Pong. It's a *transaction.*

Charades is a mutual game; the actual play is cooperative. One member draws a title or slogan from a batch of possibilities and then tries to act it out visually for teammates in a silent minidrama. The goal is to get at least one partner to say the exact words that are on the slip of paper. Of course, the actor is prohibited from talking out loud.

Suppose you drew the saying "God helps those who help themselves." For *God* you might try folding your hands and gazing upward. For *helps* you could act out offering a helping hand or giving a leg-up boost over a fence. By pointing at a number of real or imaginary people you may elicit a response of *them,* and by this point a partner may shout out, "God helps those who help themselves." Success.

Like charades, interpersonal communication is a mutual, ongoing process of sending, receiving, and adapting verbal and nonverbal messages with another person to create and alter the images in both our minds. Communication between us begins when there is some overlap between two images, and is effective to the extent that overlap increases. But even if our mental pictures are congruent, communication will be partial as long as we interpret them differently. The idea that "God helps those who help themselves" could strike one person as a hollow promise, while the other might regard it as a divine stamp of approval for hard work.

The three theories in this section reject a simplistic, one-way bowling analogy and an interactive Ping-Pong model of interpersonal communication. Instead, they view interpersonal communication in a way more akin to charades—a complex transaction in which overlapping messages simultaneously affect and are affected by the other person and multiple other factors.

a screen and the responses we receive through social media as playing a big part in shaping the content of that inner dialogue.[22] Those mental conversations are important because:

> The generalized other is an organized set of information that the individual carries in her or his head about what the general expectation and attitudes of the social group are. We refer to this generalized other whenever we try to figure out how to behave or how to evaluate our behavior in a social situation. We take the position of the generalized other and assign meaning to ourselves and our actions.[23]

Unlike most sociologists, Mead saw society as consisting of individual actors who make their own choices—society-in-the-making rather than society-by-previous-design.[24] Yet these individuals align their actions with what others are doing to form education systems, health care systems, legal systems, economic systems, and all the other societal institutions in which they take part. It is unclear from *Mind, Self, and Society* whether Mead regarded the *generalized other* as (1) an overarching looking-glass self that we put together from the reflections we see in everyone we know or (2) the institutional expectations, rules of the game, or accepted practices within society that influence every conversation that takes place in people's minds. Either way, the generalized other shapes how we think and interact within the community.

Generalized other
The composite mental image a person has of his or her self based on societal expectations and responses.

To summarize, there is no "me" at birth. The "me" is formed only through continual symbolic interaction—first with family, next with playmates, then in institutions such as schools. As the generalized other develops, this imaginary composite person becomes the conversational partner in an ongoing mental dialogue. In this way, kids participate in their own socialization. The child gradually acquires the roles of those in the surrounding community. Mead would have us think of the "me" as the organized society within the individual.

But society does not always speak in a single, consistent voice. The application log of Andrew's student Cody strikingly reveals how a person's generalized other can change in a short period of time when a single group holds sway.

> I joined the military at age 18 and in three hellish months of basic training witnessed firsthand how the Army used language to create a new reality and alter my self-concept. I was told to stand in line and "shut my mouth." My orders were to follow orders. I was not to ask why, or question the judgment of my leaders. As one of my drill sergeants so eloquently stated, "You were not issued an opinion." All of the sergeants made us repeat mantras such as "BLOOD, BLOOD, BLOOD, MAKES THE GREEN GRASS GROW" and "Two in the chest, one in the head, KILL, KILL, KILL."
>
> The Army created a new social reality. The drill sergeants were the models for what we as soldiers were to become. They would recite tales of killing like normal men would recall catching a touchdown pass in high school. I was told over and over, "Killing is what we do; it is a privilege. You all will learn to do so efficiently and without remorse." Only through killing the enemy could we neutralize any threat our republic deemed dangerous.
>
> Where previously I thought of killing as a practice reserved for villains and tyrants, I came to see it as not only acceptable but something worthy of praise. I thirsted for the opportunity to prove myself worthy of the task; I longed to belong to the hall of hallowed combat vets. When my father looked me in the eyes and my drill sergeant shook my hand at my graduation from Basic Combat Training, I

knew that I had changed. I was able to define myself by what others expected and the way others treated me. In Mead's terms, I had become a new "me." I later served as a drill sergeant.

A SAMPLER OF APPLIED SYMBOLIC INTERACTION

Since Mead believed that a theory is valuable to the extent that it is useful, I've pulled together six separate applications of symbolic interactionism. Not only will this provide a taste of the practical insights the theory has generated, it will give you a chance to review some of the theoretical ideas covered in the chapter.

Creating Reality. Shakespeare wrote, "All the world's a stage, and all the men and women merely players."[25] In his book *The Presentation of Self in Everyday Life*, University of California, Berkeley, sociologist Erving Goffman described social interaction as a dramaturgical performance.[26] Consistent with that character-in-a-play metaphor, Goffman claimed that we are all involved in a constant negotiation with others to publicly define our identity and the nature of the situation. He warned that "the impression of reality fostered by a performance is a delicate, fragile thing that can be shattered by minor mishaps."[27] His colleague Joan Emerson outlines the cooperative effort required to sustain the definition of a gynecological exam as a routine medical procedure.[28] The doctor and nurse enact their roles in a medical setting to assure patients that "everything is normal, no one is embarrassed, no one is thinking in sexual terms." The audience of one is reassured only when the actors give a consistent performance.

Meaning-ful Research. Mead advocated research through participant observation, a form of ethnography in which researchers systematically set out to share in the lives of the people they study. The participant observer adopts the stance of an interested—yet ignorant—visitor who listens carefully to what people say in order to discover how they interpret their world. Mead had little sympathy for tightly controlled behavioral experiments or checklist surveys. The results might be quantifiable, but the lifeless numbers are void of the meaning the experience had for the person. Mead would have liked the wrangler who said that the only way to understand horses is to smell like a horse, eat from a trough, and sleep in a stall. That's participant observation.

Participant observation
A method of adopting the stance of an ignorant yet interested visitor who carefully notes what people say and do in order to discover how they interpret their world.

Generalized Other. The sobering short story "Cipher in the Snow" tells the true account of a boy who is treated as a nonentity by his parents, his teachers, and other children. Their negative responses gradually reduce him to what they perceive him to be—nothing. He eventually collapses and dies in a snowbank for no apparent reason. The interactionist would describe his death as symbolic manslaughter.[29] This sad outcome brings to mind the 2012 Sandy Hook school massacre and many other events where a single shooter turns a gun on a group of people and then commits suicide. In the bloody aftermath, the authorities discover that the killer was a detached soul who lived a life of social isolation and alienation after years of verbal and nonverbal put-downs. Interactionists might call this symbolic destruction.

Naming. Here's a partial list of epithets I heard in public places over a one-year period; they were all spoken in a demeaning voice: *dummy, ugly, slob, fag, nigger, retard, fundamentalist, liberal, Neanderthal, slut, liar.* Sticks and stones can break my bones, but names can *really* hurt me. Name-calling can be devastating because the labels force us to view ourselves in a warped mirror. The grotesque images aren't easily dismissed.

Self-Fulfilling Prophecy. One implication of the looking-glass-self hypothesis is that each of us has a significant impact on how others view themselves. That kind of interpersonal power is often referred to as *self-fulfilling prophecy*, the tendency for our expectations to evoke responses in others that confirm what we originally anticipated. The process is nicely summed up by Eliza Doolittle, a woman from the gutter in George Bernard Shaw's play *Pygmalion,*the inspiration for the musical *My Fair Lady:* "The difference between a lady and a flower girl is not how she behaves, but how she's treated."[30]

Symbol Manipulation. Saul Alinsky was a product of the "Chicago School" of sociology at a time when Mead was having his greatest influence. Similar to Barack Obama, Alinsky became a community organizer in Chicago when he finished grad school, and applied what he learned to empower the urban poor. For example, in the early 1960s he helped found The Woodlawn Organization (TWO) to oppose his alma mater's complicity in substandard neighborhood housing. He searched for a symbol that would galvanize Woodlawn residents into united action and stir the sympathies of other Chicago residents. He had previously described his technique for selecting a symbolic issue:

> You start with the people, their traditions, their prejudices, their habits, their attitudes and all of those other circumstances that make up their lives. It should always be remembered that a real organization of the people . . . must be rooted in the experiences of the people themselves.[31]

Alinsky found his symbol in the rats that infested the squalid apartments. TWO's rallying cry became "Rats as big as cats." Not only did the city start to crack down on slum landlords, but for the first time Woodlawn residents gained a sense of identity, pride, and political clout.

ETHICAL REFLECTION: LEVINAS' RESPONSIVE "I"

European Jewish philosopher Emmanuel Levinas agreed with Mead that the self is socially constructed. He stated that "without the Other, there is no 'I.'"[32] (Note that Levinas used the term "*I*" to refer to what Mead called the *self*—the "I" and the "me.") But there's a striking difference between how the two theorists thought this construction project takes place. Mead contended that the looking-glass self develops through the way *others respond to us;* Levinas insisted that the identity of our "I" is formed by the way *we respond to others.*

Levinas used the term *ethical echo* to designate the responsibility he believed we all have to take care of each other. That ethical echo has existed since the beginning of human history and is summed up in the words, "I am my brother's keeper." The way each of us meets that obligation shapes our "I." Levinas said that every time we gaze at *the face of the Other,* we are reminded of our caretaking responsibility. Thus, each person's face is a signpost pointing to the panhuman ethical requirement to actively care for all people. Since the "I" finds its identity in responding to and caring for the Other, not allowing the humanity of that face to register puts our identity at risk.

Self-fulfilling prophecy
The tendency for our expectations to evoke responses that confirm what we originally anticipated.

Responsive "I"
The self created by the way we respond to others.

Ethical echo
The reminder that we are responsible for taking care of each other; "I am my brother's keeper."

Levinas was clear about the burden that comes with looking at the face of the Other:

Face of the "Other"
A human signpost that points to our ethical obligation to care for the Other before we care for self.

My world is ruptured, my contentment interrupted. I am already obligated. Here is an appeal from which there is no escape, a responsibility, a state of being hostage. It is looking into the face of the Other that reveals the call to a responsibility that is before any beginning, decision or initiative on my part. . . . I am responsible for the Other without waiting for reciprocity, [even if I were] to die for it. Reciprocity is *his* affair.[33]

Duquesne University communication ethicist Ron Arnett regards Levinas as the premier ethical voice of the twentieth century. Arnett acknowledges that urging others to adopt a responsive "I" ethical standard is not an easy sell in this post-modern age, with its quest for comfort and self-actualization.[34] Yet Levinas noted that even in his dark hours as a prisoner in a World War II German concentration camp, he found joy in embracing the human responsibility of being for the Other before oneself. To the extent that we follow Levinas' lead, Arnett suggests our interpersonal communication will be characterized more by listening than telling.[35]

CRITIQUE: SETTING THE GOLD STANDARD FOR FOUR INTERPRETIVE CRITERIA

If we view theories as "testable explanations of directly or indirectly observable social regularities, Mead's ideas are seriously flawed."[36] That's the judgment of Indiana University sociologist Sheldon Stryker, and I agree. If we treat symbolic interactionism as an objective theory that must meet scientific standards of prediction and testability, it's a poor theory. But Mead's work was highly interpretive and deserves to be evaluated on the six criteria for good interpretive theories offered in Chapter 3, "Weighing the Words."

Let's start with *clarification of values,* which Mead did exceedingly well. Drawing upon William James, John Dewey, and other pragmatists, Mead proclaimed that humans are free to make meaningful choices on how to act when facing problems. In his critique, Stryker reveals, "What fascinated me as an undergraduate and graduate student was in part the dignity accorded humans by seeing them as important determiners of their lives rather than the pure product of conditioning."[37] Of course, this freedom and dignity are dependent upon our ability to communicate.

Certainly Mead offered a marvelous new *understanding of people* by showing how humans socially construct their concept of self as well as the way society influences—yet doesn't dictate—that construction project. We also can gain a new appreciation of human diversity from the extensive, theory-based *ethnographic research* describing individuals in similar situations responding in strikingly different ways.

Both the theory and the theorist have more than satisfied a fourth interpretive requirement for a good theory—the emergence of a *community of agreement.* The once-radical Mead–Cooley looking-glass-self hypothesis has now become a truism in the field of sociology.[38] Mead, a philosopher who saw communication as the most human thing people do, has been called "America's greatest sociological thinker."[39] Even if the text you use in your interpersonal communication course doesn't mention the theorist or the theory by name, you can spot Mead's pervasive influence by the way the book treats the topic of self-concept.

Symbolic interactionism doesn't meet the other two criteria for an interpretive theory nearly as well as the four discussed above. Given Mead's personal efforts to help the displaced and distressed amid urban industrialization, it's puzzling that his theory doesn't call for *reform of society*. His theory says little about power, domination, or emotion[40]—realities that a community organizer deals with every day.

In contrast to *aesthetic appeal,* most readers of *Mind, Self, and Society* get bogged down in the baffling array of ideas Mead tried to cover. The theory's fluid boundaries, vague concepts, and undisciplined approach don't lend themselves to an elegant summary. There are no *CliffsNotes* for this one. Perhaps Mead was precise when he presented his ideas in class, but their exact meaning became blurred in the years before his students compiled the manuscript. Whatever the explanation, the theory suffers from a lack of clarity.

A final note: Symbolic interactionism may also suffer from overstatement. Mead repeatedly declared that our capacity for language—the ability to use and interpret abstract symbols—is what distinguishes humans from other animals. My former graduate assistant is the mother of a son who has a permanent peripheral nerve disorder. His eyes, ears, and other sense receptors work fine, but the messages they send get scrambled on the way to his brain. Doctors say that he is, and always will be, unable to talk or interact with others on a symbolic level. After reading an early draft of this chapter, my assistant asked, "So this means that Caleb is less than human?" Her haunting question serves as a caution to any theorist who claims to have captured the essence of humanity.

QUESTIONS TO SHARPEN YOUR FOCUS

1. Blumer's three core *premises of symbolic interactionism* deal with *meaning, language,* and *thinking.* According to Blumer, which comes first? Can you make a case for an alternative sequence?

2. What do interactionists believe are the crucial differences between *human beings* and *animals?* What would you add to or subtract from the list?

3. As Mead used the terms, are the *looking-glass self,* the *objective self,* a person's "*me,*" and the *generalized other* all referring to the same thing? Why or why not?

4. Think of a time in your life when your self-concept changed in a significant way. Do you think the shift occurred because *others viewed you differently* or because *you treated others differently?* Could Mead and Levinas both be right?

A SECOND LOOK

Recommended resource: Larry T. Reynolds and Nancy J. Herman-Kinney (eds.), *Handbook of Symbolic Interactionism,* AltaMira, Walnut Creek, CA, 2003:

Gil Musolf, "The Chicago School," pp. 91–117.

Bernard Meltzer, "Mind," pp. 253–266.

Andrew Weigert and Viktor Gecas, "Self," pp. 267–288.

Michael Katovich and David Maines, "Society," pp. 289–306.

Primary source: George Herbert Mead, *Mind, Self, and Society,* University of Chicago, Chicago, IL, 1934.

Development of Mead's ideas: Herbert Blumer, *Symbolic Interactionism,* Prentice Hall, Englewood Cliffs, NJ, 1969, pp. 1–89.

Summary statement: Herbert Blumer, "Symbolic Interaction: An Approach to Human Communication," in *Approaches to Human Communication,* Richard W. Budd and Brent Ruben (eds.), Spartan Books, New York, 1972, pp. 401–419.

Basic concepts of symbolic interactionism: John Hewitt, *Self and Society: A Symbolic Interactionist Social Psychology,* 10th ed., Allyn and Bacon, Boston, MA, 2006, pp. 36–81.

The self as a social construction: Susan Harter, "Symbolic Interactionism Revisited: Potential Liabilities for the Self Constructed in the Crucible of Interpersonal Relationships," *Merrill-Palmer Quarterly,* Vol. 45, 1999, pp. 677–703.

Looking-glass self–a research review: David Lundgren, "Social Feedback and Self-Appraisals: Current Status of the Mead–Cooley Hypothesis," *Symbolic Interaction,* Vol. 27, 2004, pp. 267–286.

Generalized other: Clare Holdsworth and David Morgan, "Revisiting the Generalized Other: An Exploration," *Sociology,* Vol. 41, 2007, pp. 401–417.

Theory application: Jodi O'Brien (ed.), *The Production of Reality,* 6th ed., Sage, Los Angeles, CA, 2017.

Levinas' responsive "I": Ronald C. Arnett, "The Responsive 'I': Levinas' Derivative Argument," *Argumentation and Advocacy,* Vol. 40, 2003, pp. 39–50.

Critique: Peter Hull, "Structuring Symbolic Interaction: Communication and Power," *Communication Yearbook 4,* Dan Nimmo (ed.), Transaction Books, New Brunswick, NJ, 1980, pp. 49–60.

Critique: Sheldon Stryker, "From Mead to a Structural Symbolic Interactionism and Beyond," *Annual Review of Sociology,* Vol. 34, 2008, p. 18.

For self-scoring quizzes for this and all other chapters, click on
Self-Help Quizzes under Theory Resources at
www.afirstlook.com.

Coordinated Management of Meaning (CMM)

of W. Barnett Pearce & Vernon Cronen

Transmission model
Picturing communication as a transfer of meaning by a source sending a message through a channel to a receiver.

Barnett Pearce and Vernon Cronen regret the fact that most communication theorists and practitioners hold to a *transmission model* of communication. This model depicts a source that sends a message through a channel to one or more receivers.

Source → Message → Channel → Receiver

In this model, communication is considered successful to the extent that a high-fidelity version of the message gets through the channel and the receiver's interpretation of it closely matches what the sender meant. People who picture communication this way tend to focus either on the message content or on what each party is thinking, but CMM says they lose sight of the pattern of communication and what that pattern creates.

Pearce, a communication professor at the Fielding Graduate Institute before his death in 2010, and Cronen (University of North Carolina Wilmington) would undoubtedly extend their critique to the definition of communication we offered in Chapter 1. We suggested that *communication is the relational process of creating and interpreting messages that elicit a response.* What's wrong with this description? Although the two theorists would appreciate our concern for relationship and response, they would note that our definition continues to treat communication as merely a means of exchanging ideas. They'd say that our definition looks *through* communication rather than directly *at* it. It renders the ongoing process invisible.

Communication as constitutive
A force that shapes all our ideas, relationships, and our whole social environment.

In contrast, Pearce and Cronen offer the *coordinated management of meaning* (CMM) as a theory that looks directly at the communication process and what it's doing. They believe communication is a *constitutive force* that shapes all our ideas, relationships, and our whole social environment. Because that process is complicated, the theory offers multiple insights into what communication is creating and a number of tools for changing our communication patterns. So we can grasp the essentials of the theory without being overwhelmed, Kimberly Pearce, Barnett's wife and president of the CMM Institute for Personal and Social Evolution, boils down CMM into four claims about communication.

FIRST CLAIM: OUR COMMUNICATION CREATES OUR SOCIAL WORLDS

Communication perspective
An ongoing focus on how communication makes our social worlds.

Kim Pearce starts with what we've just covered and then adds what communication does: "Communication is not just a tool for exchanging ideas and information.... It 'makes' selves, relationships, organizations, communities, cultures, etc. This is what I've referred to as taking the *communication perspective.*"[1]

Selves, relationships, organizations, communities, and cultures are the "stuff" that makes up our social worlds. For CMM theorists, our social worlds are not something we find or discover. Instead, we create them. For most of his professional life, Barnett Pearce summed up this core concept of the theory by asserting that *persons-in-conversation co-construct their own social realities and are simultaneously shaped by the worlds they create.*[2]

Artist M. C. Escher's lithograph *Bond of Union* strikingly illustrates the core claims of CMM. It depicts a spiraling ribbon of tape that shapes the heads of two people and joins them together. The figures seem to be floating in space amid dozens of small globes. Unfortunately, I can't reproduce the art in this chapter, so I urge you to enter "Escher, Bond of Union" into your search engine so you can examine this vivid model of how persons-in-conversation are making the social worlds of which they are a part. I see three parallels between the picture and the theory.

First, Escher's art foregrounds interpersonal communication as the primary activity that's going on in the social universe. This squares with CMM's claim that *the experience of persons-in-conversation is the primary social process of human life.*[3] Barnett Pearce said this idea runs counter to the prevailing intellectual view of "communication as an odorless, colorless vehicle of thought that is interesting or important only when it is done poorly or breaks down."[4] He saw the ribbon in Escher's drawing as representing patterns of communication that literally form who the persons-in-conversation are and create their relationship. Their conversation does something to them quite apart from the issue they're discussing.

Second, the figures in the lithograph are bound together regardless of what they are talking about. This reflects Barnett Pearce's belief that the way people communicate is often more important than the content of what they say. The mood and manner that persons-in-conversation adopt play a large role in the process of social construction. He pointed out that the faces in *Bond of Union* have no substance; they consist in the twists and turns of the spiraling ribbon:

> Were the ribbon straightened or tied in another shape, there would be no loss of matter, but the faces would no longer exist. This image works for us as a model of the way the process of communication (the ribbon) creates the events and objects of our social worlds (the faces), not by its substance but by its form.[5]

Third, the endless ribbon in *Bond of Union* loops back to *re*form both persons-in-conversation. If Escher's figures were in conflict, each person would be wise to ask, "If I win this argument, what kind of person will I become?" Barnett Pearce said it's the same for us. Our actions are reflexively reproduced as the interaction continues; any action we take will bounce back and affect us. That's also true with the social worlds we create. Pearce wrote, "When we communicate, we are not just talking about the world, we are literally participating in the creation of the social universe."[6] And, like the figures in the lithograph, we then have to live in it. Like it or not, our communication has an afterlife.

Social constructionists
Curious participants in a pluralistic world who believe that persons-in-conversation co-construct their own social realities and are simultaneously shaped by the worlds they create.

These ideas identify CMM theorists and practitioners as *social constructionists—* curious participants in a pluralistic world. Barnett Pearce said they are *curious* because they think it's folly to profess certainty when dealing with individuals acting out their lives under ever-changing conditions. They are *participants* rather than spectators because they seek to be actively involved in what they study. They live in a *pluralistic world* because they assume that people make multiple truths rather than find a singular Truth.[7] So Escher's *Bond of Union* is an apt representation of persons-in-conversation even when one or both parties are CMM advocates.

SECOND CLAIM: THE STORIES WE TELL DIFFER FROM THE STORIES WE LIVE

Coherence

The process of making and managing meaning by telling stories.

CMM uses the term *story* to refer to much of what we say when we talk with others about our social worlds—ourselves, others, relationships, organizations, or the larger community. Pearce and Cronen claim that communication is a two-sided process of *stories told* and *stories lived*.[8] Stories told are tales we tell ourselves and others in order to make sense of the world around us and our place in it. CMM calls this process *coherence,* the making and managing of meaning. Stories lived are the ongoing patterns of interaction we enact as we seek to mesh our lives with others around us. CMM calls this effort *coordinating our actions together.* Pearce and Cronen labeled their theory *coordinated management of meaning* to encompass both types of stories.

Stories Told: Making and Managing Meaning

The stories we tell or hear are never as simple as they seem. Take, for example, the story that appeared in my inbox a month before my high school reunion. Decades earlier, the writer (Bea) and I had been in the same 7th and 8th grade class where we engaged in what I would describe as mild flirtation. Here's what I read:

> I'm writing because I still think about the mystery of you not speaking to me all the way through high school. You may not even remember that you ignored me, but I do. What did I do to make you so angry? My mother always wondered if someone had said something to you about me that wasn't true. I just never knew. I would feel better if we could say "hello" at least at the gathering.

This seems to be a rather straightforward tale of a young girl who felt bad when a guy ignored her. If so, you might expect a *that-was-years-ago* reaction, a *get-a-life* response, or a quick click on *delete.* Pearce and Cronen suggest, however, that there's

"And what's the story behind the story?"
©Arnie Levin/The New Yorker Collection/The Cartoon Bank

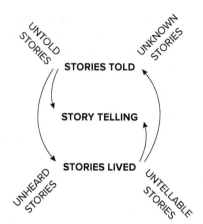

FIGURE 6-1 CMM's LUUUUTT Model

always much more to stories told that could enrich or alter their meaning. Emphasizing that CMM is a practical theory, they offer a number of analytical tools to help the listener consider alternative or additional interpretations. When I got this message from Bea, I used their LUUUUTT model pictured in Figure 6-1 to help me expand the story and possibly narrow the disparity between her account of me in the distant past and the stories each of us might want to live now.

LUUUUTT is an acronym to label the seven types of stories identified in the model.[9] The focus of the model depicts the tension between our stories lived and our stories told. That tension can be increased or decreased by the manner in which the stories are presented. The four descriptions of nonobvious stories radiating toward the corners remind us there's always more to the situation that we aren't aware of. Barnett and Kim Pearce use the term *mystery* to cover everything relevant that is not, or cannot, be said. As I reread Bea's message, I tried to imagine what each of those seven interrelated stories in the LUUUUTT model might be.

1. **L**ived stories—*what we actually did or are doing.* I have no reason to doubt Bea's claim. Although I can't recall intentionally avoiding conversation with her in high school, neither do I have a mental image of us talking together, even though we were both cast members in the school play. In contrast, I know we chatted in junior high.

2. **U**nknown stories—*information that's missing.* Bea's mother suggested that I was turned off by lies I heard about her daughter. Not so. But the multiple possibilities that Bea imagined and couldn't discount would surely be distressing.

3. **U**ntold stories—*what we choose not to say.* There was nothing in Bea's message about the attention I paid to her in junior high or anger she might have felt at the abrupt change in my behavior. Nor did she say anything about her current life.

4. **U**nheard stories—*what we say that isn't heard or acknowledged.* Did Bea try to reach out to me during those four years of silence and, if so, did I snub her? To ignore her email now would add insult to injury.

5. **U**ntellable stories—*stories that are forbidden or too painful for us to tell.* It would be the height of arrogance on my part to think that I had the power to ruin Bea's life back then. Yet I did wonder what she couldn't say.

6. Story **T**elling—*the manner in which we communicate.* "Why" questions often impute blame, but the tone of Bea's message struck me as a mix of curiosity, sadness, courage, and an honest effort to clear the air before the class reunion.

the bifurcation points in the midst of tough discussions and have the desire and skill to craft a response on the fly that would make better social worlds. If the current crop of more than 200,000 undergraduate communication majors developed that mindset and ability, he was convinced we could make a radically different social world.[19]

FOURTH CLAIM: GET THE PATTERN RIGHT, CREATE BETTER SOCIAL WORLDS

CMM advocates—people who take a communication perspective—see this fourth claim as an accurate and reassuring prediction. But they also regard the statement as a prescription—that we have an obligation or moral responsibility to use CMM insights and models to create the best social worlds possible.

What do these best social worlds look like? Barnett Pearce admitted he couldn't be specific because each situation is different. He also feared that those who have a precise image of what the ideal social world should be will try to compel others to live within their vision and end up making things worse.[20] But throughout their most recent publications on CMM, Barnett and Kim Pearce describe better social worlds as replete with *caring, compassion, love,* and *grace* among its inhabitants—not the stated goal of most communication theories.[21] And Kim Pearce stresses that these are not just internal emotional experiences. Rather, they are "a way of being with others that makes a space for something new to emerge."[22]

This interpersonal goal of CMM raises a serious question for students of communication. What characteristics or abilities does it take for a person to create conversational patterns that will change the social world for the better? The theorists' answer is that one does not need to be a saint, a genius, or an orator. The communicator, however, must be *mindful*.[23]

Mindfulness

The presence or awareness of what participants are making in the midst of their own conversation.

Mindfulness is a presence or awareness of what participants are making in the midst of their conversation. It's paying less attention to what they are talking about and focusing on what they are *doing* and *becoming*. Mindful participants don't speak on mental automatic pilot or cognitive cruise control. They are participant observers willing to step back and look for places in the conversational flow where they can say or do something that will make the situation better for everyone involved. For example, are you willing and able to be mindful when

> . . . talking to your roommate about the mess in your apartment?
> . . . responding to your mom's phone plea to spend spring break at home?
> . . . listening to your teammates complain about the coach?
> . . . replying to a sarcastic comment on Facebook?
> . . . dealing with a demanding customer at your minimum-wage McJob?
> . . . fending off unwelcome advances during a Friday night pub crawl?

To the extent that your answer is *yes,* CMM claims you have the capacity to make better social worlds.

Once the mindful communicator spots a bifurcation point in a pattern of communication that's deteriorating, what should he or she say? Barnett Pearce found it helpful to respond to challenging or boorish statements with phrases that showed curiosity rather than offense.[24] *Tell me more about that. What else was going on at the time? What experiences have led you to that position? Why don't people understand?* Those familiar with Hebrew wisdom literature will recognize the parallel with Proverbs 15:1, "A gentle answer turns away wrath."

Even a single word like *yes* can change the direction of the conversational pattern. In her autobiography, *Bossypants,* actress, comedian, writer, and producer Tina Fey offers "The Rules of Improvisation That Will Change Your Life . . ."

> The first rule of improvisation is AGREE. Always agree and SAY YES. When you're improvising, this means you are required to agree with whatever your partner has created. So if we're improvising and I say, "Freeze, I have a gun," and you say, "That's not a gun. It's your finger. You're pointing your finger at me," our improvised scene has ground to a halt. But if I say, "Freeze, I have a gun!" and you say, "The gun I gave you for Christmas. You bastard!" then we have started a scene because we have AGREED that my finger is in fact a Christmas gun.
>
> Now, obviously in real life you're not always going to agree with everything everyone says. But the Rule of Agreement reminds you to respect what your partner has created and to at least start from an open-minded place. Start with a YES and see where it takes you.
>
> As an improviser, I always find it jarring when I meet someone in real life whose first answer is no. "No we can't do that." "No that's not in the budget . . ." What kind of way is that to live?[25]

For an overall remedy to unsatisfactory or destructive patterns of interaction, CMM theorists advocate *dialogue*, a specific form of communication that they believe will create a social world where we can live with dignity, honor, joy, and love.[26] Although the term is used in multiple ways within our discipline, Barnett and Kim Pearce have adopted the perspective of Jewish philosopher Martin Buber.

Dialogic communication
Conversation in which parties remain in the tension between holding their own perspective while being profoundly open to the other.

For Buber, dialogue "involves remaining in the tension between holding our own perspective while being profoundly open to the other."[27] This of course takes "courage because it means giving up a person-position of clarity, certainty, or moral/intellectual superiority."[28] We might actually learn something new that will change what we think, or even who we are.[29] The following ethical reflection expands on Buber's concept of dialogue.

ETHICAL REFLECTION: MARTIN BUBER'S DIALOGIC ETHICS

Martin Buber was a German Jewish philosopher and theologian who immigrated to Palestine before World War II and died in 1965. His ethical approach focuses on relationships between people rather than on moral codes of conduct. "In the beginning is the relation," Buber wrote. "The relation is the cradle of actual life."[30]

Buber contrasted two types of relationships—*I-It* versus *I-Thou.* In an I-It relationship we treat the other person as a thing to be used, an object to be manipulated. Created by monologue, an I-It relationship lacks mutuality. Parties come together as individuals intent on creating only an impression. Deceit is a way to maintain appearances.

In an I-Thou relationship we regard our partner as the very one we are. We see the other as created in the image of God and resolve to treat him or her as a valued end rather than a means to our own end. This implies that we will seek to experience the relationship as it appears to the other person. Buber said we can do this only through dialogue.

For Buber, *dialogue* was a synonym for ethical communication. Dialogue is mutuality in conversation that creates the *Between*, through which we help each other to be more human. Dialogue is not only a morally appropriate act, but it is also a way

Narrow ridge
A metaphor of I-Thou living in the dialogic tension between ethical relativism and rigid absolutism.

to discover what is ethical in our relationship. It thus requires self-disclosure to, confirmation of, and vulnerability with the other person.

Buber used the image of the *narrow ridge* to illustrate the tension of dialogic living. On one side of the moral path is the gulf of relativism, where there are no standards. On the other side is the plateau of absolutism, where rules are etched in stone:

> On the far side of the subjective, on this side of the objective, on the narrow ridge, where I and Thou meet, there is the realm of the Between.[31]

Duquesne University communication ethicist Ron Arnett notes that "living the narrow-ridge philosophy requires a life of personal and interpersonal concern, which is likely to generate a more complicated existence than that of the egoist or the selfless martyr."[32] Despite that tension, many interpersonal theorists and practitioners have carved out ethical positions similar to Buber's philosophy. Consistent with CMM's foundational belief that persons-in-conversation co-construct their own social realities, Barnett and Kim Pearce are attracted to Buber's core belief that dialogue is a joint achievement that cannot be produced on demand, but occurs among people who seek it and are prepared for it.

CRITIQUE: HIGHLY PRACTICAL AS IT MOVES FROM CONFUSION TO CLARITY

Because CMM is an interpretive theory, I'll apply the six criteria suggested in Chapter 3 as I did when evaluating Mead's theory of *symbolic interactionism* in the previous chapter.

New understanding of people. By offering such diagnostic tools as the serpentine and LUUUUTT models of communication, CMM promotes a deeper *understanding of people* and of the social worlds they create through their conversation. Those models are just two of the tools the theorists offer. Students who want to have a greater understanding of the "making" of social worlds will find the daisy model, the hierarchical model, unwanted repetitive patterns, and strange loops equally helpful.

Clarification of values. Unlike many theories which seek only to describe communication patterns, CMM theorists and the researchers they inspire make it clear that their aim is to make better social worlds. Barnett and Kim Pearce promote values of curiosity, caring, compassion, mindfulness, gratitude, grace, and love. They have invited us to join them in an ongoing effort to enact these qualities in our stories told and stories lived. Some objective theorists may personally share these values, but believe a communication theory holding out the promise of making *better social worlds* should describe that goal in terms of specific behaviors and outcomes.

Community of agreement. Although many objective theorists dismiss CMM because of its social constructionist assumptions, CMM has generated widespread interest and *acceptance within the community* of interpretive communication scholars. For example, when Robert Craig proposed that a pragmatic tradition be added to his original list of seven traditions of communication theory (see Chapter 4), he cited CMM as the exemplar of a practical theory.[33]

Reform of society. If changing destructive patterns of communication in whole communities strikes you as a bit of a stretch, you should know that pursuit of this goal is why Barnett and Kim Pearce founded the Public Dialogue Consortium and the CMM Institute.[34] (Visit www.cmminstitute.net for updates, research, and applications.) Not only have many associates signed on to the cause, but they've also demonstrated that a dialogic form of communication is "learnable, teachable, and contagious."[35]

Qualitative research. CMM scholars and practitioners use a wide range of qualitative research methods—textual and narrative analyses, case studies, interviews, participant observation, ethnography, and collaborative action research.[36] It's not clear that this research has spawned new theoretical development,[37] but these studies have definitely helped practitioners apply CMM models of communication in novel ways.

Aesthetic appeal. Despite meeting the previous five criteria with ease, lack of clarity has seriously limited CMM's wider use. The theory has a reputation of being a confusing mix of ideas that are hard to pin down because they're expressed in convoluted language. In 2001, when Barnett Pearce asked those who use CMM in their teaching, training, counseling, and consulting what changes or additions they thought should be made to the theory, the most frequent plea was for user-friendly explanations expressed in easy-to-understand terms. The following story from the field underscores why this call for clarity is so crucial:

> My counseling trainees often find CMM ideas exciting, but its language daunting or too full of jargon. Some trainees connect with the ideas but most feel intimidated by the language and the concepts—diminished in some way or excluded! One trainee sat in a posture of physically cringing because she did not understand. This was a competent woman who had successfully completed counselor training three years ago and was doing a "refresher" with us. I don't think she found it too refreshing at that moment. CMM ideas would be more useful if they were available in everyday language—perhaps via examples and storytelling.[38]

I've tried to heed this advice while writing about CMM. Hopefully, you haven't cringed. But in order to reduce the wince factor, I've had to leave out many of the valued terms, tools, and models that are the working vocabulary of this complex theory. I've been guided by Kim Pearce's new book, *Compassionate Communicating Because Moments Matter,* where she lays out the essentials of CMM in the way the advocate requested.[39] This little volume, which is my recommended resource, is a clear statement of CMM's four core claims. In user-friendly language, Kim illustrates them with stories from her work and life together with her husband, Barnett. CMM's aesthetic appeal is on the rise.

QUESTIONS TO SHARPEN YOUR FOCUS

1. *Social constructionists* see themselves as curious participants in a pluralistic world. Are you willing to live with uncertainty, abandon a detached perspective, and not insist on a singular view of Truth so that you can join them?

2. Can you provide a rationale for placing this chapter on CMM immediately after the chapter on *symbolic interactionism?*

3. CMM suggests that we can take part in joint action without a common understanding—*coordination* without a shared *coherence.* Can you think of examples from your own life?

4. Can you recall an important conversation in which you may have helped create a better social world? Were you *mindful* of what you were making, and did you spot a *bifurcation point* where you could change the *pattern of conversation?*

CONVERSATIONS

View this segment online at www.afirstlook.com.

As you watch my conversation with Barnett Pearce, you might think of us as the persons-in-conversation pictured in Escher's *Bond of Union.* What kind of social world do you see us creating as we talk? I like to think that our conversation displays a few examples of dialogic communication. If so, was Pearce right in thinking you'll find this kind of talk contagious? At one point I repeat my "Questions to Sharpen Your Focus" query about how social constructionists must give up claims of certainty, objectivity, and Truth. I then ask if that's a fair question. See if you agree with Pearce's response and the reason he gives.

A SECOND LOOK

Recommended resource: Kimberly Pearce, *Compassionate Communicating Because Moments Matter: Poetry, Prose, and Practices,* Lulu, 2012, www.lulu.com.

Brief overview: W. Barnett Pearce, "The Coordinated Management of Meaning (CMM)," in *Theorizing About Intercultural Communication,* William Gudykunst (ed.), Sage, Thousand Oaks, CA, 2004, pp. 35-54.

Comprehensive statement: W. Barnett Pearce, *Making Social Worlds: A Communication Perspective,* Blackwell, Malden, MA, 2008.

Original statement: W. Barnett Pearce and Vernon E. Cronen, *Communication, Action, and Meaning: The Creation of Social Realities,* Praeger, New York, 1980; also www.cios.org/www/opentext.htm.

Evolution of the theory: W. Barnett Pearce, "Evolution and Transformation: A Brief History of CMM and a Meditation on What Using It Does to Us," in *The Reflective, Facilitative, and Interpretive Practice of the Coordinated Management of Meaning: Making Lives, Making Meaning,* Catherine Creede, Beth Fisher-Yoshida, and Placida Gallegos (eds.), Fairleigh Dickinson, Madison, NJ, 2012, pp. 1-21.

Social construction: W. Barnett Pearce, "Communication as Social Construction: Reclaiming Our Birthright," in *Socially Constructing Communication,* Gloria J. Galanes and Wendy Leeds-Hurwitz (eds.), Hampton, Cresskill, NJ, 2009, pp. 33-56.

Making meaning and coordinating actions: W. Barnett Pearce, *Communication and the Human Condition,* Southern Illinois University, Carbondale, IL, 1989, pp. 32-87.

Intellectual heritage: Vernon E. Cronen, "Coordinated Management of Meaning: The Consequentiality of Communication and the Recapturing of Experience," in *The Consequentiality of Communication,* Stuart Sigman (ed.), Lawrence Erlbaum, Hillsdale, NJ, 1995, pp. 17-65.

Peacemaking: W. Barnett Pearce and Stephen W. Littlejohn, *Moral Conflict: When Social Worlds Collide,* Sage, Thousand Oaks, CA, 1997.

Dialogic communication: W. Barnett Pearce and Kimberly A. Pearce, "Combining Passions and Abilities: Toward Dialogic Virtuosity," *Southern Communication Journal,* Vol. 65, 2000, pp. 161-175.

Buber's dialogic ethics: Martin Buber, *I and Thou,* 2nd ed., R. G. Smith (trans.), Scribner, New York, 1958.

Research review of CMM: J. Kevin Barge and W. Barnett Pearce, "A Reconnaissance of CMM Research," *Human Systems,* Vol. 15, 2004, pp. 13–32.

CMM as a practical theory: J. Kevin Barge, "Articulating CMM as a Practical Theory," *Human Systems,* Vol. 15, 2004, pp. 193–204.

To access scenes from feature films that illustrate
CMM and other theories, click on Suggested
Movie Clips under Theory Resources at
www.afirstlook.com.

Expectancy Violations Theory

of Judee Burgoon

Early in my teaching career, I was walking back to my office, puzzling over classroom conversations with four students. All four had made requests. Why, I wondered, had I readily agreed to two requests but just as quickly turned down two others? Each of the four students had spoken to me individually during the class break. Andre wanted my endorsement for a graduate scholarship, and Dawn invited me to eat lunch with her the next day. I said yes to both of them. Belinda asked me to help her on a term paper for a class with another professor, and Charlie encouraged me to play water polo that night with guys from his house, something I had done before. I said no to those requests.

Sitting down at my desk, I idly flipped through the pages of *Human Communication Research (HCR),* a behavioral science journal that had arrived in the morning mail. I was still mulling over my uneven response to the students when my eyes zeroed in on an article entitled "A Communication Model of Personal Space Violations."[1] "That's it," I blurted out to our surprised department secretary. I suddenly realized that in each case, my response to the student may have been influenced by the conversational distance between us.

I mentally pictured the four students making their requests—each from a distance that struck me as inappropriate in one way or another. Andre was literally in my face, less than a foot away. Belinda's 2-foot interval invaded my personal space, but not as much. Charlie stood about 7 feet away—just outside the range I would have expected for a let's-get-together-and-have-some-fun-that-has-nothing-to-do-with-school type of conversation. Dawn offered her luncheon invitation from across the room. At the time, each of these interactions had seemed somewhat strange. Now I realized that all four students had violated my expectation of an appropriate interpersonal distance.

Because I describe my impressions and reactions to these students, I've changed their names, and replaced them with names that start with the letters *A, B, C,* and *D* to represent the increasing distance between us when we spoke. (Andre was the closest; Dawn, the farthest away.) Figure 7-1 plots the intervals relative to my expectations.

FIGURE 7-1   Expectancy Violations in a Classroom Setting

Judee Burgoon, a communication scholar at the University of Arizona, wrote the journal article that stimulated my thinking. The article was a follow-up piece on the *nonverbal expectancy violations model* she had introduced in *HCR* two years earlier. Since my own dissertation research focused on interpersonal distance, I knew firsthand how little social science theory existed at that time to guide researchers studying nonverbal communication. I was therefore excited to see Burgoon offering a sophisticated theory of personal space. The fact that she was teaching in a communication department and had published her work in a communication journal was value added. I eagerly read Burgoon's description of her nonverbal expectancy violations model to see whether it could account for my mixed response to the various conversational distances chosen by the four students.

PERSONAL SPACE EXPECTATIONS: CONFORM OR DEVIATE?

Personal space
The invisible, variable volume of space surrounding an individual that defines that individual's preferred distance from others.

Burgoon defined *personal space* as the "invisible, variable volume of space surrounding an individual that defines that individual's preferred distance from others."[2] She claimed that the size and shape of our personal space depend on our cultural norms and individual preferences, but our space always reflects a compromise between the conflicting approach–avoidance needs that we as humans have for affiliation and privacy.

The idea of personal space wasn't original with Burgoon. In the 1960s, Illinois Institute of Technology anthropologist Edward Hall coined the term *proxemics* to refer to the study of people's use of space as a special elaboration of culture.[3] He entitled his book *The Hidden Dimension* because he was convinced that most spatial interpretation is outside our awareness. He claimed that Americans have four proxemic zones, which nicely correspond with the four interpersonal distances selected by my students:

Proxemics
The study of people's use of space as a special elaboration of culture.

1. Intimate distance: 0 to 18 inches (Andre)
2. Personal distance: 18 inches to 4 feet (Belinda)
3. Social distance: 4 to 12 feet (Charlie)
4. Public distance: 12 to 25 feet (Dawn)

Hall's book is filled with examples of "ugly Americans" who were insensitive to the spatial customs of other cultures. He strongly recommended that in order to be effective, we learn to adjust our nonverbal behavior to conform to the communication rules of our partner. We shouldn't cross a distance boundary uninvited.

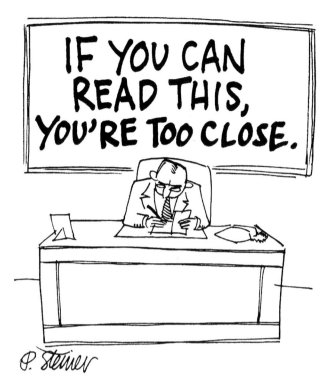

Cartoon by Peter Steiner. Reprinted with permission.

Burgoon's nonverbal expectancy violations model offered a counterpoint to Hall's advice. She didn't argue with the idea that people have definite expectations about how close others should come. In fact, she would explain Hall's proxemics classification as based on well-established American norms, plus his own experience. But contrary to popular go-along-to-get-along wisdom, Burgoon suggested that there are times when it's best to break the rules. She believed that under some circumstances, violating social norms and personal expectations is "a superior strategy to conformity."[4]

AN APPLIED TEST OF THE ORIGINAL MODEL

Whether knowingly or not, each of the four students making a request deviated from my proxemic expectation. How well did Burgoon's initial model predict my responses to these four different violations? Not very well. To help you capture the flavor of Burgoon's early speculation and recognize how far her current theory has come, I'll outline what the model predicted my responses would be and, in each case, compare that forecast to what I actually did.

Threat threshold
The hypothetical outer boundary of intimate space; a breach by an uninvited other occasions fight or flight.

Andre. According to Burgoon's early model, Andre made a mistake when he crossed my invisible *threat threshold* and spoke with me at an intimate eyeball-to-eyeball distance. The physical and psychological discomfort I'd feel would hurt his cause. But the model missed on that prediction, since I wrote the recommendation later that day.

Belinda. In the follow-up article I read that day, Burgoon suggested that noticeable deviations from what we expect cause us to experience a heightened state of arousal. She wasn't necessarily referring to the heart-pounding, sweaty-palms reaction that drives us to fight or flight. Instead, she pictured violations stimulating us to mentally review the nature of our relationship with the person who acted in a curious way. That would be good news for Belinda if I thought of her as a highly rewarding person. But every comment she made in class seemed to me a direct challenge, dripping with sarcasm. Just as Burgoon predicted, the narrow, 2-foot gap Belinda chose focused my attention on our rocky relationship, and I declined her request for help in another course. Score one for the nonverbal expectancy violations model.

Charlie. Charlie was a nice guy who cared more about having a good time than he did about studies. He knew I'd played water polo in college, but he may not have realized that his casual attitude toward the class was a constant reminder that I wasn't as good a teacher as I wanted to be. In her 1978 *HRC* article, Burgoon wrote that a person with "punishing power" (like Charlie) would do best to observe proxemic conventions or, better yet, stand slightly farther away than expected. Without ever hearing Burgoon's advice, Charlie did it right. He backed off to a distance of 7 feet—just outside the range of interaction I anticipated. Even so, I declined his offer to swim with the guys.

Dawn. According to this nonverbal expectancy violations model, Dawn blew it. Because she was an attractive communicator, a warm, close approach would have been a pleasant surprise. Her decision to issue an invitation from across the room, however, would seem to guarantee a poor response. The farther she backed off, the worse the effect would be. There's only one problem with this analysis: Dawn and I had lunch together in the student union the following day.

Although my initial intuition was that Burgoon's theory would explain my reaction to the students' requests, the theoretical scoreboard failed to offer strong support for my hunch. It read:

> Nonverbal expectancy violations model: **1**
> Unpredicted random behavior: **3**

Burgoon's initial controlled experiments didn't fare much better. But where I was ready to dismiss the whole model as flawed, she was unwilling to abandon *expectancy violation* as a key concept in human interaction. At the end of her journal article she hinted that some of her basic assumptions might need to be tested and reevaluated.[5]

Of course, that was then; this is now. For four decades, Judee Burgoon and her students have crafted a series of sophisticated laboratory experiments and field studies to discover and explain the effects of expectancy violations. One of the reasons I chose to write about her theory is that the current version is an excellent example of ideas continually revised as a result of empirical disconfirmation. As she has demonstrated, in science, failure can lead to success.

A CONVOLUTED MODEL BECOMES AN ELEGANT THEORY

When applied to theories, the term *elegant* suggests "gracefully concise and simple; admirably succinct."[6] That's what expectancy violations theory has become. Burgoon has dropped concepts that were central in earlier versions but never panned out.

Early on, for example, she abandoned the idea of a "threat threshold." Even though that hypothetical boundary made intuitive sense, repeated experimentation failed to confirm its existence.

Arousal, relational
A heightened state of awareness, orienting response, or mental alertness that stimulates a review of the relationship.

Burgoon's retreat from *arousal* as an explanatory mechanism has been more gradual. She originally stated that people felt physiologically aroused when their proxemic expectations were violated. Later she softened the concept to "an orienting response" or a mental "alertness" that focuses attention on the violator. She now views arousal as a side effect of a partner's deviation and no longer considers it a necessary link between expectancy violation and communication outcomes such as attraction, credibility, persuasion, and involvement.

By removing extraneous features, Burgoon has streamlined her model. By extending its scope, she has produced a complete theory. Her original nonverbal expectancy violations model was concerned only with spatial violations—a rather narrow focus. But by the mid-1980s, Burgoon concluded that proxemic behavior is part of an interconnected system of nonlinguistic cues. It no longer made sense to study interpersonal distance in isolation. She began to apply the model to a host of other nonverbal variables—facial expression, eye contact, touch, and body lean, for example. Burgoon continues to expand the range of expectancy violations. While not losing interest in nonverbal communication, she now applies the theory to what's said in emotional, marital, and intercultural communication as well. Consistent with this broad sweep, she has dropped the *nonverbal* qualifier and refers to her theory as "expectancy violations theory," or EVT. From this point on, so will I.

What does EVT predict? Burgoon sums up her empirically driven conclusions in a single paragraph. I hope my long narrative of the theory's development will help you appreciate the 40 years of work that lie behind these simple lines.

> Expectancies exert significant influence on people's interaction patterns, on their impressions of one another, and on the outcomes of their interactions. Violations of expectations in turn may arouse and distract their recipients, shifting greater attention to the violator and the meaning of the violation itself. People who can assume that they are well regarded by their audience are safer engaging in violations and more likely to profit from doing so than are those who are poorly regarded. When the violation act is one that is likely to be ambiguous in its meaning or to carry multiple interpretations that are not uniformly positive or negative, then the reward valence of the communicator can be especially significant in moderating interpretations, evaluations, and subsequent outcomes. . . . In other cases, violations have relatively consensual meanings and valences associated with them, so that engaging in them produces similar effects for positive- and negative-valenced communicators.[7]

CORE CONCEPTS OF EVT

A close reading of Burgoon's summary suggests that EVT offers a "soft determinism" rather than hard-core universal laws (see Chapter 2). The qualifying terms *may, more likely, can be,* and *relatively* reflect her belief that too many factors affect communication to ever allow us to discover simple cause-and-effect relationships. She does, however, hope to show a link among surprising interpersonal behavior and attraction, credibility, influence, and involvement. These are the potential outcomes of expectancy violation that Burgoon and her students explore. In order for us to appreciate the connection, we need to understand three core concepts of EVT: *expectancy, violation valence,* and *communicator reward valence.* I'll illustrate these three variables by referring back to my students' proxemic behavior and to another form of nonverbal communication—touch.

Expectancy

When I was a kid, my mother frequently gave notice that she *expected* me to be on my best behavior. I considered her words to be a wish or a warning, but that's not how Burgoon uses the word. She and her colleagues "prefer to reserve the term *expectancy* for what is predicted to occur rather than what is desired."[8] In other words, expectancy is like a forecast. Figure 7-1 shows that I anticipated conversations with students to take place at a distance of 2½ to 6 feet. How did this expectation arise? Burgoon suggests that I processed the context, type of relationship, and characteristics of the others automatically in my mind in order to gauge what they might do.

Context begins with cultural norms. Three feet is too close in England or Germany yet too far removed in Saudi Arabia, where you can't trust people who won't let you smell their breath. Context also includes the setting of the conversation. A classroom environment dictates a greater speaking distance than would be appropriate for a private chat in my office.

Relationship factors include similarity, familiarity, liking, and relative status. In one study, Burgoon discovered that people of all ages and stations in life anticipate that lower-status people will keep their distance. Because of our age difference and teacher–student relationship, I was more surprised by Andre's and Belinda's invasion of my personal space than I was by Charlie's and Dawn's remote location.

Communicator characteristics include all of the age/sex/place-of-birth demographic facts requested on applications, but they also include personal features that may affect expectation even more—physical appearance, personality, and communication style. Dawn's warm smile was a counterpoint to Belinda's caustic comments. Given this difference, I would have assumed that Dawn would be the one to draw close and Belinda the one to keep her distance. That's why I was especially curious when each woman's spatial "transgression" was the opposite of what I would have predicted.

We can do a similar analysis of my expectation for touch in that classroom situation. Edward Hall claimed that the United States is a "noncontact culture," so I wouldn't anticipate touch during the course of normal conversation.[9] Does this mean that Latin American or Southern European "contact cultures" wouldn't have tight expectations for nonverbal interaction? By no means. Burgoon is convinced that all cultures have a similar *structure* of expected communication behavior, but that the *content* of those expectations can differ markedly from culture to culture. Touch is fraught with meaning in every society, but the who, when, where, and how of touching are a matter of culture-specific standards and customs.

As a male in a role relationship, it never occurred to me that students might make physical contact while voicing their requests. If it had, Dawn would have been the likely candidate. But at her chosen distance of 25 feet, she'd need to be a bionic woman to reach me. As it was, I would have been shocked if she'd violated my expectation and walked over to give me a hug. (As a lead-in to the next two sections, note that I didn't say I would have been disturbed, distressed, or disgusted.)

Violation Valence

The term *violation valence* refers to the positive or negative value we place on a specific unexpected behavior, regardless of who does it. Do we find the act itself pleasing or distressing, and to what extent? With her commitment to the scientific method, Burgoon may have borrowed the concept of valence from chemistry, where the valence of a substance is indicated by a number and its sign (+3 or −2, for example). The term *net worth* from the field of accounting seems to capture the same idea.

We usually give others a bit of wiggle room to deviate from what we regard as standard operating procedure. But once we deal with someone who acts outside the range of expected behavior, we switch into evaluation mode. According to Burgoon, we first try to interpret the meaning of the violation, and then figure out whether we like it.

The meaning of some violations is easy to spot. As a case in point, no one would agonize over how to interpret a purposeful poke in the eye with a sharp stick. It's a hostile act, and if it happened to us, we'd be livid. Many nonverbal behaviors are that straightforward. For example, moderate to prolonged eye contact in Western cultures usually communicates awareness, interest, affection, and trust. A level gaze is welcome; shifty eyes are not. With the exception of a riveting stare, we value eye contact. Even Emerson, a man of letters, wrote, "The eyes of men converse as much as their tongues, with the advantage that the ocular dialect needs no dictionary. . . ."[10]

When a behavior has a socially recognized meaning, communicators can usually figure out whether to go beyond what others expect. If the valence is negative, do less than expected. If the valence is positive, go further. Burgoon validated this advice when she studied the effect of expectancy on marital satisfaction.[11] She questioned people about how much intimate communication they expected from their partner compared to how much focused conversation they actually got. Not surprisingly, intimacy was ranked as positive. Partners who received about as much intimacy as they expected were moderately satisfied with their marriages. But people were highly satisfied with their marriages when they had more good talks with their husbands or wives than they originally thought they would.

Many expectancy violations are equivocal, however. They're open to multiple interpretations. For example, the meaning of unexpected touch can be puzzling. Is it a mark of total involvement in the conversation, a sign of warmth and affection, a display of dominance, or a sexual move? Distance violations can also be confusing. Andre isn't from the Middle East, so why was he standing so close? I don't bark or bite, so why did Dawn issue her invitation from across the room? According to EVT, it's at times like these that we consider the reward valence of the communicator as well as the valence of the violation.

Before we look at the way communicator reward valence fits into the theory, you should know that Burgoon has found few nonverbal behaviors that are ambiguous when seen in a larger context. A touch on the arm might be enigmatic in isolation, but when experienced along with close proximity, forward body lean, a direct gaze, facial animation, and verbal fluency, almost everyone interprets the physical contact as a sign of high involvement in the conversation.[12] Or consider actor Eric Idle's words and nonverbal manner in a *Monty Python* sketch. He punctuates his question about Terry Gilliam's wife with a burlesque wink, a leering tone of voice, and gestures to accompany his words: "Nudge nudge. Know what I mean?

Violation valence

The perceived positive or negative value assigned to a breach of expectations, regardless of who the violator is.

Say no more . . . know what I mean?"[13] Taken alone, an exaggerated wink or a dig with the elbow might have many possible meanings, but as part of a coordinated routine, both gestures clearly transform a questionable remark into a lewd comment.

There are times, however, when nonverbal expectancy violations are quite confusing. The personal space deviations of my students are cases in point. Perhaps I just wasn't sensitive enough to pick up the cues that would help me make sense of their proxemic violations. But when the meaning of an action is unclear, EVT says we interpret the violation in light of how the violator can affect our lives.

Communicator Reward Valence

EVT is not the only theory that describes the tendency to size up other people in terms of the potential rewards they have to offer. *Social penetration theory* suggests that we live in an interpersonal economy in which we all "take stock" of the relational value of others we meet (see Chapter 8). The questions *What can you do for me?* and *What can you do to me?* often cross our minds. Burgoon is not a cynic, but she thinks the issue of reward potential moves from the background to the foreground of our minds when someone violates our expectation and there's no social consensus on the meaning of the act. She uses the term *communicator reward valence* to label the results of our mental audit of likely gains and losses.

The reward valence of a communicator is the sum of the positive and negative attributes the person brings to the encounter plus the potential he or she has to reward or punish in the future. The resulting perception is usually a mix of good and bad and falls somewhere on a scale between those two poles. I'll illustrate communicator characteristics that Burgoon frequently mentions by reviewing one feature of each student that I thought about immediately after their perplexing spatial violations.

Andre was a brilliant student. Although writing recommendations is low on my list of fun things to do, I would bask in reflected glory if he were accepted into a top graduate program.

Belinda had a razor-sharp mind and a tongue to match. I'd already felt the sting of her verbal barbs and thought that thinly veiled criticism in the future was a distinct possibility.

Charlie was the opposite of Andre—seldom in class and never prepared. I try to be evenhanded with everyone who signs up for my classes, but in Charlie's case I had to struggle not to take his casual attitude toward the course as a personal snub.

Dawn was a beautiful young woman with a warm smile. I felt great pleasure when she openly announced that I was her favorite teacher.

My views of Andre, Belinda, Charlie, and Dawn probably say more about me than they do about the four students. I'm not particularly proud of my stereotyped assessments, but apparently I have plenty of company in the criteria I used. Burgoon notes that the features that impressed me also weigh heavily with others when they compute a reward valence for someone who is violating their expectations. Status, ability, and good looks are standard "goodies" that enhance the other person's reward potential. The thrust of the conversation is even more important. Most of us value words that communicate acceptance, liking, appreciation, and trust. We're turned off by talk that conveys disinterest, disapproval, distrust, and rejection.

Why does Burgoon think the expectancy violator's power to reward or punish is so crucial? Because puzzling violations force victims to search the social context for clues to their meaning.[14] Thus, an ambiguous violation embedded in a host of

Communicator reward valence
The sum of positive and negative attributes brought to the encounter plus the potential to reward or punish in the future.

relationally warm signals takes on a positive cast. An equivocal violation from a punishing communicator stiffens our resistance.

Now that I've outlined EVT's three core concepts, you may be wondering which is more important when an unexpected violation occurs—the violation valence or the communicator reward valence? All things being equal, Burgoon says the nature of the violation will influence the response it triggers more than the reward potential of the one who did it. This is especially true if the surprising behavior on its own would be considered by the other as very positive or very negative—wonderful or disgusting no matter who did it.

On the other hand, communicator reward valence may loom large when it's especially strong either way. An unexpected handshake from a total creep might produce a shudder, and even a small sign of disinterest from a potential romantic partner might break your heart. Also, when the unexpected act itself is seen as ambiguous or relatively neutral, communicator reward valence can make the difference. In that case, a highly attractive or powerful violator will get a positive response. But an unexpected questionable statement or action coming from someone who has little to offer and low credibility will get a negative reaction. And for cases of expectancy violations that aren't clear-cut, it's harder to predict the outcome.[15]

So when you want to inform, persuade, or draw closer to someone, what takeaway does EVT offer? If you aren't sure the violation you're considering is the kind the other would welcome, or you think you have little to offer that he or she might want, then stifle your deviant tendencies and do your best to conform to expectations. But if you think the other won't automatically be offended by what you're planning and are sure he or she regards you as a rewarding person, go for it. If your analysis is correct, the expectancy violation you're considering is likely to produce a favorable response.

INTERACTION ADAPTATION—ADJUSTING EXPECTATIONS

Interaction adaptation theory
A systematic analysis of how people adjust their approach when another's behavior doesn't align with what's needed, anticipated, or preferred.

Interaction position
A person's initial stance toward an interaction as determined by a blend of personal requirements, expectations, and desires (RED).

Burgoon has recognized that "EVT does not fully account for the overwhelming prevalence of reciprocity that has been found in interpersonal interactions"[16] (see Chapter 9). She regards this shortcoming as particularly troubling. So she has reassessed EVT's single-sided view of unexpected communication and now favors a dyadic model of adaptation. That's because she views conversations as more akin to duets than solos. Interpersonal interactions involve synchronized actions rather than unilateral moves. Along with her former students Lesa Stern and Leesa Dillman, she has crafted *interaction adaptation theory (IAT)* as an extension and expansion of EVT.[17]

Burgoon states that human beings are predisposed to adapt to each other. That's often necessary, she says, because another person's actions may not square with the thoughts and feelings we bring to the interaction. She sees this initial *interaction position* as made up of three factors: requirements, expectations, and desires. *Requirements (R)* are the outcomes that fulfill our basic needs to survive, be safe, belong, and have a sense of self-worth. These are the panhuman motivations that Abraham Maslow outlined in his famous hierarchy of needs.[18] As opposed to requirements that represent what we need to happen, *expectations (E)* are what we think really will happen. Finally, *desires (D)* are what we personally would like to see happen. These RED factors coalesce or meld into our interaction position of what's needed, anticipated, and preferred. I'll continue to use touch behavior to show how Burgoon uses this composite mindset to predict how we adjust to another person's behavior.

In her course application log, Lindi briefly describes a roommate's unanticipated interaction with a casual friend:

> At the end of last year my roommate was hanging out with a bunch of our friends late at night and one of the guys started playing with her hair and continued to do so for the rest of the night. This unexpected violation of her personal space surprised her, but turned out to be a very pleasant experience. She was forced then to reevaluate their relationship. Even though they didn't develop a romantic relationship, this violation brought them closer together and helped them redefine their friendship.

Although details are sparse, it's possible to approximate the roommate's interactional position at the start of the evening. Her willingness to spend the night hanging around with a group of friends suggests she has a high need or requirement for affiliation and belongingness (R). Given her surprise at the guy fiddling with her hair, we can assume that this ongoing touch was definitely not the behavioral norm of the group, nor what she expected based on his past behavior (E). Yet her pleasure with this fellow's continual touch indicates that she had a strong desire for this kind of personal attention from him (D). Her initial interaction position would therefore be a mixture of what she needed, expected, and preferred.

With the help of hindsight, we can see that the valence of the guy playing with her hair was more positive than her interaction position. According to IAT, the pattern of response would therefore be one of reciprocity or convergence. *Reciprocity* would mean that she then ran her fingers through his hair. There's no hint that this happened. Yet since the whole group of friends could monitor her response, it's unlikely he would have continued with this form of touch unless she encouraged him with a smile or words indicating pleasure. That would be convergence.

Reciprocity
A strong human tendency to respond to another's action with similar behavior.

If, on the other hand, the valence she assigned to him messing with her hair was more negative than her interaction position, Burgoon predicts some form of compensation or divergent behavior. She might lean away from him, excuse herself to comb her hair, or simply look at him and say, "Cut it out." Unlike EVT, IAT addresses how people adjust their behavior when others violate their expectations. There's obviously more to IAT than I've been able to present, but hopefully this brief sketch lets you see that for Burgoon, one theory leads to another.

CRITIQUE: A WELL-REGARDED WORK IN PROGRESS

I have a friend who fixes my all-terrain cycle whenever I bend it or break it. "What do you think?" I ask Bill. "Can it be repaired?" His response is always the same: "Man made it. Man can fix it!"

Judee Burgoon shows the same resolve as she seeks to adjust and redesign an expectancy violations model that never quite works as well in practice as its theoretical blueprint says it should. Almost every empirical test she runs seems to yield mixed results. For example, her early work on physical contact suggested that touch violations were often ambiguous. However, a sophisticated experiment she ran in 1992 showed that unexpected touch in a problem-solving situation was almost always welcomed as a positive violation, regardless of the status, gender, or attractiveness of the violator.

Do repeated failures to predict outcomes when a person stands far away, moves in too close, or reaches out to touch someone imply that Burgoon ought to trade in her expectancy violations theory for a new model? Does IAT render EVT obsolete? From my perspective, the answer is no.

While we might wish for *predictions* that prove more reliable than a long-range weather forecast, a review of expectancy violations research suggests EVT may have reached that point. For example, a comparative empirical study tested how well three leading theories predict interpersonal responses to nonverbal immediacy—close proximity, touch, direct gaze, direct body orientation, and forward lean.[19] None of the theories proved to be right all the time, but EVT did better than the other two.

The fact that other researchers employ the theory to understand expectancy violations that occur when using digital technology suggests EVT is a valuable resource. Perhaps you've experienced an awkward moment when a close friend pulled out a cell phone in the midst of an intimate conversation and started playing a game or responding to a text. Communication researchers Aimee Miller-Ott (Illinois State University) and Lynne Kelly (University of Hartford) discovered that most people consider cell phone usage during an intimate interaction a violation of their expectations. It's not a pleasant surprise, and some who are bothered will make a comment to try to halt the multitasking behavior. In contrast, they found that friends who are just "hanging out" together aren't violating expectations if they use their phones during casual conversation.[20]

Burgoon's expectancy violations theory continues to meet the other five criteria of a good scientific theory as presented in Chapter 3. Her theory advances a reasonable *explanation* for the effects of expectancy violations during communication. The explanation she offers is *relatively simple* and has actually become less complex over time. The theory has *testable hypotheses* that the theorist is willing to adjust when her *quantitative research* doesn't support the prediction. Finally, the model offers *practical advice* on how to better achieve important communication goals of increased credibility, influence, and attraction. And based on what the revised EVT predicts, the scoreboard for my responses to the proxemic violations of Andre, Belinda, Charlie, and Dawn shows four hits and no misses.

QUESTIONS TO SHARPEN YOUR FOCUS

1. What *proxemic* advice would you give to communicators who believe they are seen as *unrewarding?*

2. EVT suggests that *violation valence* is especially important when it's clearly positive or negative. What verbal or nonverbal expectancy violations would be confusing to you even when experienced in context?

3. Using the concepts of *expectancy, violation valence,* and *communicator reward valence,* can you explain how the final version of EVT accurately predicts Em's response to the four requests made by Andre, Belinda, Charlie, and Dawn?

4. EVT and coordinated management of meaning (see Chapter 6) hold divergent views about *ways of knowing, human nature,* and *communication research.* Can you spot the different assumptions?

CONVERSATIONS

View this segment online at
www.afirstlook.com.

A few minutes into my discussion with Judee Burgoon, you'll notice that one of us violates a communication expectation of the other. See if you think the violation is accidental or strategic. How does this event affect the rest of the conversation? Burgoon's love of theory is apparent throughout the segment. Do you think her enthusiasm is bolstered by a view of theories as systematic hunches rather than timeless principles chiseled in stone? As a scientist, Burgoon believes that much of human behavior is genetically programmed, yet she insists communication is also a choice-driven, strategic behavior. As you watch, decide whether you think these beliefs are compatible.

A SECOND LOOK

Recommended resource: Judee K. Burgoon and Jerold Hale, "Nonverbal Expectancy Violations: Model Elaboration and Application to Immediacy Behaviors," *Communication Monographs,* Vol. 55, 1988, pp. 58–79.

Original model: Judee K. Burgoon, "A Communication Model of Personal Space Violations: Explication and an Initial Test," *Human Communication Research,* Vol. 4, 1978, pp. 129–142.

Expectancy: Judee K. Burgoon and Beth A. LePoire, "Effects of Communication Expectancies, Actual Communication, and Expectancy Disconfirmation on Evaluations of Communicators and Their Communication Behavior," *Human Communication Research,* Vol. 20, 1993, pp. 67–96.

Communicator reward valence: Judee K. Burgoon, "Relational Message Interpretations of Touch, Conversational Distance, and Posture," *Journal of Nonverbal Behavior,* Vol. 15, 1991, pp. 233–259.

Extension of the theory: Walid A. Afifi and Judee K. Burgoon, "The Impact of Violations on Uncertainty and the Consequences for Attractiveness," *Human Communication Research,* Vol. 26, 2000, pp. 203–233.

Cultural violations: Judee K. Burgoon and Amy Ebesu Hubbard, "Cross-Cultural and Intercultural Applications of Expectancy Violations Theory and Interaction Adaptation Theory," in *Theorizing About Intercultural Communication,* William B. Gudykunst (ed.), Sage, Thousand Oaks, CA, 2004, pp. 149–171.

Interaction adaptation theory: Judee K. Burgoon, Lesa Stern, and Leesa Dillman, *Interpersonal Adaptation: Dyadic Interaction Patterns,* Cambridge University, Cambridge, 1995.

Interaction adaptation theory application: Keri K. Stephens, Marian L. Houser, and Renee L. Cowan, "R U Able to Meat Me: The Impact of Students' Overly Casual Email Messages to Instructors," *Communication Education,* Vol. 58, 2009, pp. 303–326.

Explanation and comparison of EVT and IAT: Cindy H. White, "Expectancy Violations Theory and Interaction Adaptation Theory: From Expectations to Adaptation," in *Engaging Theories in Interpersonal Communication: Multiple Perspectives,* Leslie A. Baxter and Dawn O. Braithwaite (eds.), Sage, Thousand Oaks, CA, 2008, pp. 189–202.

Critique: Peter A. Andersen, Laura K. Guerrero, David B. Buller, and Peter F. Jorgensen, "An Empirical Comparison of Three Theories of Nonverbal Immediacy Exchange," *Human Communication Research,* Vol. 24, 1998, pp. 501–535.

Think about your closest personal relationship. Is it one of "strong, frequent and diverse interdependence that lasts over a considerable period of time?"[1] That's how UCLA psychologist Harold Kelley and eight co-authors defined the concept of close relationship. Though their definition could apply to parties who don't even like each other, most theorists reserve the term *close* for relationships that include a positive bond—usually romantic, friend, and family. All three types of intimacy can provide enjoyment, trust, sharing of confidences, respect, mutual assistance, and spontaneity.[2] The question is, *How do we develop a close relationship?*

Two distinct approaches have dominated the theory and practice of relational development. One *experiential approach* is typified by humanistic psychologist Carl Rogers. Based upon his years of nondirective counseling, Rogers described three necessary and sufficient conditions for relationship growth. When partners perceived (1) congruence; (2) unconditional positive regard; and (3) empathic understanding of each other, they could and would draw closer.[3]

Congruence is the match or fit between an individual's inner feelings and outer display. The congruent person is genuine, real, integrated, whole, transparent. The noncongruent person tries to impress, plays a role, puts up a front, hides behind a facade. "In my relationship with persons," Rogers wrote, "I've found that it does not help, in the long run, to act as though I was something I was not."[4]

Unconditional positive regard is an attitude of acceptance that isn't contingent upon performance. Rogers asked, "Can I let myself experience positive attitudes toward this other person—attitudes of warmth, caring, liking, interest, and respect?"[5] When the answer was *yes,* both he and his clients matured as human beings. They also liked each other.

Empathic understanding is the caring skill of temporarily laying aside our views and values and entering into another's world without prejudice. It is an active process of seeking to hear the other's thoughts, feelings, tones, and meanings as if they were our own. Rogers thought it was a waste of time to be suspicious or to wonder, *What does she really mean?* He believed that we help people most when we accept what they say at face value. We should assume that they describe their world as it really appears to them.

Rogerian ideas have permeated the textbooks and teaching of interpersonal communication.[6] The topics of self-disclosure, nonverbal warmth, empathic listening, and trust are mainstays of an introductory course.

The other approach assumes that relationship behavior is shaped by the *rewards and costs of interaction.* In 1992, University of Chicago economist Gary Becker won the Nobel Prize in economics on the basis of his application of supply-and-demand market models to predict the behavior of everyday living, including love and marriage.[7] News commentators expressed skepticism that matters of the heart could be reduced to cold numbers, but the economic metaphor has dominated social science discussions of interpersonal attraction and behavior for more than half a century. It's also the approach of popular dating websites like eHarmony, where customers complete a questionnaire that matches them to "singles who have been prescreened on 29 Dimensions of Compatibility: scientific predictors of long-term relationship success."[8] Like such dating services, the basic assumption of many relational theorists is that people interact with others in a way that maximizes their personal benefits and minimizes their personal costs.

Numerous parallels exist between the stock market and relationship market:

Law of supply and demand. A rare, desirable characteristic commands higher value on the exchange.

Courting a buyer. Most parties in the market prepare a prospectus that highlights their assets and downplays their liabilities.

Laissez-faire rules. Let the buyer beware. All's fair in love and war. It's a jungle out there.

Investors and traders. Investors commit for the long haul; traders try to make an overnight killing.

Even from these brief summaries, you can tell that a humanistic model of relational development is quite different from an economic model of social exchange. Yet both models affect each of the theories presented in this section.

All three theories regard communication as the means by which people can draw close to one another. Each considers instant intimacy a myth; relationships take time to develop and they don't always proceed on a straight-line trajectory toward that goal. In fact, most relationships never even get close. Yet some people do have deep, satisfying, long-lasting relationships. Why do they develop close ties when others don't? Each of the theories in this section offers an answer.

Social Penetration Theory

of Irwin Altman & Dalmas Taylor

A friend in need is a friend indeed.
Neither a borrower nor a lender be.

A soft answer turns away wrath.
Don't get mad, get even.

To know him is to love him.
Familiarity breeds contempt.

Proverbs are the wisdom of the ages boiled down into short, easy-to-remember phrases. There are probably more maxims about interpersonal relationships than about any other topic. But are these truisms dependable? As we can see in the pairings above, the advice they give often seems contradictory.

Consider the plight of Pete, a freshman at a residential college, as he enters the dorm to meet his roommate face-to-face for the first time. Pete has just waved goodbye to his folks and already feels pangs of loneliness as he thinks of his girlfriend back home. He worries how she'll feel about him when he goes home at Thanksgiving. Will she illustrate the reliability of the adage "absence makes the heart grow fonder," or will "out of sight, out of mind" be a better way to describe the next few months?

Pete finds his room and immediately spots the familiar shape of a lacrosse stick. He's initially encouraged by what appears to be a common interest, but he also can't forget that his roommate's Facebook profile expressed enthusiasm for several candidates on the opposite end of the political spectrum from Pete. Will "birds of a feather flock together" hold true in their relationship, or will "opposites attract" better describe their interaction?

Just then Jon, his roommate, comes in. For a few minutes they trade the stock phrases that give them a chance to size up each other. Something in Pete makes him want to tell Jon how much he misses his girlfriend, but a deeper sense of what is an appropriate topic of conversation when first meeting someone prevents him from sharing his feelings. On a subconscious level, perhaps even a conscious one, Pete is torn between acting on the adage "misery loves company" or on the more macho "big boys don't cry."

Pete obviously needs something more than pithy proverbs to help him understand relational dynamics. More than two decades before Pete was born, social psychologists Irwin Altman and Dalmas Taylor proposed a *social penetration process* that explains how relational closeness develops. Altman is distinguished professor emeritus of psychology at the University of Utah, and Taylor, now deceased, was provost and professor of psychology at Lincoln University in Pennsylvania. They predicted that Pete and Jon would end up best friends only if they proceeded in a "gradual and orderly fashion from superficial to intimate levels of exchange as a function of both immediate and forecast outcomes."[1] In order to capture the process, we first have to understand the complexity of people.

Social penetration
The process of developing deeper intimacy with another person through mutual self-disclosure and other forms of vulnerability.

PERSONALITY STRUCTURE: A MULTILAYERED ONION

Altman and Taylor compared people to onions. This isn't a commentary on the human capacity to offend. Like the self-description that the ogre in *Shrek* shares with his donkey sidekick in the original film, it's a depiction of the multilayered *structure* of personality. Peel the outer skin from an onion, and you'll find another beneath it. Remove that layer and you'll expose a third, and so on. Pete's outer layer is his public self that's accessible to anyone who cares to look. The outer layer includes a myriad of details that certainly help describe who he is but are held in common with others at the school. On the surface, people see a tall, 18-year-old male business major from Michigan who lifts weights and gets lots of texts from friends back home. If Jon can look beneath the surface, he'll discover the semiprivate attitudes that Pete reveals only to some people. Pete is sympathetic to liberal social causes, deeply religious, and prejudiced against people who are overweight.

Personality structure
Onion-like layers of beliefs and feelings about self, others, and the world; deeper layers are more vulnerable, protected, and central to self-image.

Pete's inner core is made up of his values, self-concept, unresolved conflicts, and deeply felt emotions—things he'd never dream of posting on social media. This is his unique private domain, which is invisible to the world but has a significant impact on the areas of his life that are closer to the surface. Perhaps not even his girlfriend or parents know his most closely guarded secrets about himself.

CLOSENESS THROUGH SELF-DISCLOSURE

Pete becomes accessible to others as he relaxes the tight boundaries that protect him and makes himself vulnerable. This can be a scary process, but Altman and Taylor believed it's only by allowing Jon to penetrate well below the surface that Pete can truly draw close to his roommate. Nonverbal paths to closeness include mock roughhousing, eye contact, and smiling. But the main route to deep social penetration is through verbal *self-disclosure.*

Self-disclosure
The voluntary sharing of personal history, preferences, attitudes, feelings, values, secrets, etc., with another person; transparency.

Figure 8-1 illustrates a wedge being pulled into an onion. It's as if a strong magnetic force were drawing it toward the center. The depth of penetration represents the degree of personal disclosure. To get to the center, the wedge must first cut through the outer layers. Altman and Taylor claimed that on the surface level this kind of biographical information exchange takes place easily, perhaps at the first meeting. But they pictured the layers of onion skin tougher and more tightly wrapped as the wedge nears the center.

Recall that Pete is hesitant to share his longing for his girlfriend with Jon. If he admits these feelings, he's opening himself up for some heavy-handed kidding or emotional blackmail. In addition, once the wedge has penetrated deeply, it will have cut a passage through which it can return again and again with little resistance.

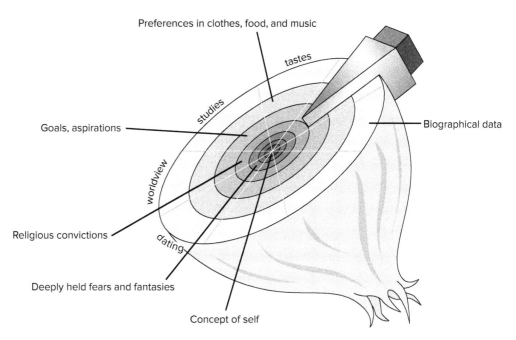

FIGURE 8-1   Penetration of Pete's Personality Structure

Future privacy will be difficult. Realizing both of these factors, Pete may be extra cautious about exposing his true feelings. Perhaps he'll fence off this part of his life for the whole school term. According to social penetration theory, a permanent guard would limit the closeness these two young men can achieve.

THE DEPTH AND BREADTH OF SELF-DISCLOSURE

Depth of penetration
The degree of disclosure in a specific area of an individual's life.

The *depth of penetration* is the degree of intimacy. Although Altman and Taylor's penetration analogy strikes some readers as sexual, this was not their intent. The analogy applies equally to intimacy in friendship and romance. Figure 8-1 diagrams the closeness Jon gains if he and Pete become friends during the year. In their framework of social penetration theory, Altman and Taylor outlined four observations about the process that will bring Pete and Jon to this point:

1. *Peripheral items are exchanged sooner and more frequently than private information.* When the sharp edge of the wedge has barely reached the intimate area, the thicker part has cut a wide path through the outer rings. The relationship is still at a relatively impersonal level ("big boys don't cry"). When University of Connecticut communication professor Arthur VanLear analyzed the content of conversations in developing relationships he discovered that 14 percent of talk revealed nothing about the speaker, 65 percent dwelled on public items, 19 percent shared semiprivate details, and only 2 percent disclosed intimate confidences.[2] Further penetration will bring Pete to the point where he can share deeper feelings ("misery loves company").

2. *Self-disclosure is reciprocal, especially in the early stages of relationship development.* The theory predicts new acquaintances like Pete and Jon will reach roughly equal levels of openness, but it doesn't explain why. Pete's vulnerability could make him seem more trustworthy, or perhaps his initial openness will make transparency seem more attractive. The young men might

also feel a need for emotional equity, so a disclosure by Pete will leave Jon feeling uneasy until he's balanced the account with his own payment—a give-and-take exchange in which each party is sharing deeper levels of feeling with the other. Whatever the reason, social penetration theory asserts a *law of reciprocity*.

Law of reciprocity
A paced and orderly process in which openness in one person leads to openness in the other; "You tell me your dream; I'll tell you mine."

3. *Penetration is rapid at the start, but slows down quickly as the tightly wrapped inner layers are reached.* Instant intimacy is a myth. Not only is there internal resistance to quick forays into the soul, but there are societal norms against telling too much too fast. Most relationships stall before a stable, intimate exchange is established. For this reason, these relationships fade or die easily after a separation or slight strain. Comfortable sharing of positive and negative reactions is rare. When it is achieved, relationships become more important to both parties, more meaningful, and more enduring. However, the rate at which we draw close may also have something to do with how we present our disclosures to the other person.

Three psychologists from the University of Arkansas (Denise Beike, Nicole Brandon, and Holly Cole) summarize the results of eight recent studies that show the powerful relational impact of sharing autobiographical memories. These personal narratives tend to contain a carefully structured story, deeper emotion, and greater detail than other shared information. The studies suggest that if Pete tells Jon the story of how he met his girlfriend instead of simply sharing his deep feelings for her, the guys will draw closer than they otherwise would. That's because storytelling alerts Jon that Pete is inviting him into the intimacy of his experiential world, not just sharing cold, neutral facts about his life. The researchers regard such autobiographical memories as a quick path to stronger bonds.[3]

4. *Depenetration is a gradual process of layer-by-layer withdrawal.* A warm friendship between Pete and Jon will deteriorate if they begin to close off areas of their lives that had previously been opened. Relational retreat is a sort of taking back of what has already been exchanged in the building of a relationship. Altman and Taylor compared the process to a movie shown in reverse. Surface talk still goes on long after deep disclosure is avoided. Relationships are likely to terminate not in an explosive flash of anger, but in a gradual cooling off of enjoyment and care.

While depth is crucial to the process of social penetration, *breadth* is equally important. Note that in Figure 8-1 I have segmented the onion much like an orange to represent how Pete's life is cut into different areas—dating, studies, and so forth. It's quite possible for Pete to be candid about every intimate detail of his romance yet remain secretive about his father's alcoholism or his own minor dyslexia. Because only one area is accessed, the relationship depicted in the onion drawing is typical of a summer romance—depth without breadth. Of course, breadth without depth describes the typical "Hi, how are you?" casual friendship. A model of true intimacy would show multiple wedges inserted deeply into every area.

Breadth of penetration
The range of areas in an individual's life over which disclosure takes place.

REGULATING CLOSENESS ON THE BASIS OF REWARDS AND COSTS

Will Pete and Jon become good friends? To answer that question, Altman and Taylor borrowed ideas from *social exchange theory*, developed by psychologists John Thibaut (University of North Carolina at Chapel Hill) and Harold Kelley

(University of California, Los Angeles).[4] If you want to know more about social exchange theory, I encourage you to visit www.afirstlook.com to read a chapter on the theory from a previous edition of this book. Here, I'll focus on the ideas from the theory that Altman and Taylor found useful for understanding the process of self-disclosure.

Investors choose where to put their money in the stock market. College freshmen like Pete and Jon choose where to put their time in friendships. Social exchange theory claims we make both decisions in similar ways. Whether finance or friendship, we want a good return on our investment, so we do a cost–benefit analysis beforehand. For the financial investor, that might involve combing the pages of *The Wall Street Journal* for tips about which stocks might increase in value. Pete and Jon don't have a newspaper with that kind of expert interpersonal advice, so instead they'll think about whether they'll enjoy interacting in the future. Right after their first encounter, Pete will sort out the pluses and minuses of friendship with Jon, computing a bottom-line index of relational satisfaction. Jon will do the same regarding Pete. If the perceived mutual benefits outweigh the costs of greater vulnerability, the process of social penetration will proceed.

Social exchange theory identifies three key components of this mental calculation: relational outcome, relational satisfaction, and relational stability. Altman and Taylor agreed these factors are important, and therefore included them in social penetration theory. I'll describe each of the three concepts below.

Relational Outcome: Rewards Minus Costs

Thibaut and Kelley suggested that people try to predict the *outcome* of an interaction before it takes place. Thus, when Pete first meets his roommate, he mentally gauges the potential rewards and costs of friendship with Jon. He perceives a number of benefits. As a newcomer to campus, Pete strongly desires someone to talk to, eat with, and just hang out with when he's not in class or studying. His roommate's interest in lacrosse, easy laugh, and laid-back style make Jon an attractive candidate.

Pete is also aware that there's a potential downside to getting to know each other better. If he reveals some of his inner life, his roommate may scoff at his faith in God or ridicule his liberal "do-gooder" values. Pete isn't ashamed of his convictions, but he hates to argue, and he regards the risk of conflict as real. Factoring in all the likely pluses and minuses, reaching out in friendship to Jon strikes Pete as net positive, so he makes the first move.

The idea of totaling potential benefits and losses to determine behavior isn't new. Since the nineteenth century, when philosopher John Stuart Mill first stated his principle of utility,[5] there's been a compelling logic to the *minimax principle of human behavior*. The minimax principle claims that people seek to maximize their benefits and minimize their costs. Thus, the higher we rate a relational outcome, the more attractive we find the behavior that might make it happen.

Social exchange theorists assume that we can accurately gauge the payoffs of a variety of interactions and that we have the good sense to choose the action that will provide the best result. Altman and Taylor weren't sure that we always base such decisions on reliable information, but that's not the issue. What mattered to them is that we decide to open up with another person using the perceived benefit-minus-cost outcome.

Social exchange
Relationship behavior and status regulated by both parties' evaluations of perceived rewards and costs of interaction with each other.

Outcome
The perceived rewards minus the costs of interpersonal interaction.

Minimax principle of human behavior
People seek to maximize their benefits and minimize their costs.

Lee, a former student of Em's, shared how he calculated cost–benefit ratios in one of his friendships. For him, self-disclosure has a higher emotional cost than it does for the average person:

> Self-disclosure makes me uncomfortable. However, the medium of music makes me a bit more comfortable and my desire to write a good song forces me to open up in ways I wouldn't otherwise. For example, I wrote a song for my friend John's birthday party where I put together a series of verses that commemorated all the things in the last year that John and I shared or thought were funny. John and I still had a relatively superficial relationship at that point, but I think by showing that I cared through the song, another layer of the onion was peeled away.

Early in a relationship, we tend to see physical appearance, similar backgrounds, and mutual agreement as benefits ("birds of a feather flock together"). Disagreement and deviance from the norm are negatives. But as the relationship changes, so does the nature of interaction that friends find rewarding. Deeper friendships thrive on common values and spoken appreciation, and we can even enjoy surface diversity ("opposites attract").

If Pete sees much more benefit than cost in a relationship with Jon, he'll start to reveal more of who he is. If the negatives outweigh the positives, he'll try to avoid contact with Jon as much as possible. Even though they're stuck together physically in the same dorm room, a negative assessment could cause him to hold back emotionally for the rest of the year.

Gauging Relational Satisfaction—The Comparison Level (CL)

Evaluating outcomes is a tricky business. Even if we mentally convert intangible benefits and costs into a bottom-line measure of overall effect, its psychological impact upon us may vary. A relational result has meaning only when we contrast it with other real or imagined possibilities. Social exchange theory offers two standards of comparison that Pete and others use to evaluate their interpersonal outcomes. The first point of reference deals with relative *satisfaction*—how happy or sad an interpersonal outcome makes a participant feel. Thibaut and Kelley called this the *comparison level*.

Comparison level (CL)
The threshold above which an interpersonal outcome seems attractive; a standard for relational satisfaction.

A person's comparison level (CL) is the threshold above which an outcome seems attractive. Suppose, for example, that Pete is looking forward to his regular Sunday night FaceTime chat with his girlfriend. Since they usually talk for about a half hour, 30 minutes is Pete's comparison level for what makes a pleasing conversation. If he's not in a hurry, a 45-minute conversation will seem especially gratifying, while a 15-minute chat would be quite disappointing. Of course, the length of the call is only one factor that affects Pete's positive or negative feelings when he hangs up. He has also developed expectations for the topics they'll discuss, his girlfriend's tone of voice, and the warmth of her words when she says goodbye. These are benchmarks Pete uses to gauge his relative satisfaction with the interaction.

To a big extent, our relational history establishes our CLs for friendship, romance, and family ties. We judge the value of a relationship by comparing it to the baseline of past experience. If Pete had little history of close friendship in high school, a relationship with Jon would look quite attractive. If, on the other hand, he's accustomed to being part of a close-knit group of intimate friends, hanging out with Jon could pale by comparison.

"I've done the numbers, and I will marry you."
©William Hamilton/The New Yorker Collection/The Cartoon Bank

Sequence plays a large part in evaluating a relationship. The result from each interaction is stored in the individual's memory. Experiences that take place early in a relationship can have a huge impact because they make up a large proportion of the total relational history. One unpleasant experience out of 10 is merely troublesome, but 1 out of 2 can end a relationship before it really begins. Trends are also important. If Pete first senses coolness from Jon yet later feels warmth and approval, the shift might raise Jon's attractiveness to a level higher than it would be if Pete had perceived positive vibes from the very beginning.

Gauging Relational Stability—The Comparison Level of Alternatives (CL_{alt})

Comparison level of alternatives (CL_{alt})
The best outcome available in other relationships; a standard for relational stability.

Thibaut and Kelley suggested that there is a second standard by which we evaluate the outcomes we receive. They called it the *comparison level of alternatives (CL_{alt})*. Don't let the similarity of the names confuse you—CL and CL_{alt} are two entirely different concepts. CL is your overall standard for a specific type of relationship, and it remains fairly stable over time. In contrast, CL_{alt} represents your evaluation of other relational options at the moment. For Pete, it's the result of thinking about his interactions with other people in his dorm. As he considers whether to invest his limited time in getting to know Jon, he'll ask, *Would my relational payoffs be better with another person?* His CL_{alt} is his *best available alternative* to a friendship with Jon. If CL_{alt} is less than Pete's current outcomes, his friendship with Jon will be *stable*. But if more attractive friendship possibilities become available, or roommate squabbles drive his outcomes below the established CL_{alt}, the instability of their friendship will increase.

Taken together, CL and CL_{alt} explain why some people remain in relationships that aren't satisfying. For example, social workers describe the plight of a physically abused wife as "high cost, low reward." Despite her anguish, she feels trapped in the terrible situation because being alone in the world appears even worse. As dreadful as her outcomes are, she can't imagine a better alternative. She won't leave until she perceives an outside alternative that promises a better life. Her relationship is very unsatisfying because her outcomes are far below her CL, but also quite stable because her outcomes are above her CL_{alt}.

The relative values of outcome, CL, and CL_{alt} go a long way in determining whether a person is willing to become vulnerable in order to have a deeper relationship. The optimum situation is when both parties find

$$\text{Outcome} > CL_{alt} > CL$$

Using Pete as an example, this notation shows that he forecasts a friendship with Jon that will be more than *satisfying*. The tie with Jon will be *stable* because there's no other relationship on campus that is more attractive. Yet Pete won't feel trapped, because he has other satisfying options available should this one turn sour. We see, therefore, that social exchange theory explains why Pete is primed for social penetration. If Jon's calculations are similar, the roommates will begin the process of mutual vulnerability that Altman and Taylor described, and reciprocal self-disclosure will draw them close.

ETHICAL REFLECTION: EPICURUS' ETHICAL EGOISM

The minimax principle that undergirds social exchange theory—and therefore social penetration theory as well—is also referred to as *psychological egoism*. The term reflects many social scientists' conviction that all of us are motivated by self-interest. Unlike most social scientists who limit their study to what *is* rather than what *ought* to be, *ethical egoists* claim we *should* act selfishly. It's right and it's good for us to look out for number one.

Ethical egoism
The belief that individuals should live their lives so as to maximize their own pleasure and minimize their own pain.

Epicurus, a Greek philosopher who wrote a few years after Aristotle's death, defined the good life as getting as much pleasure as possible: "I spit on the noble and its idle admirers when it contains no element of pleasure."[6] Although his position is often associated with the adage "Eat, drink, and be merry," Epicurus actually emphasized the passive pleasures of friendship and good digestion, and above all, the absence of pain. He cautioned that "no pleasure is in itself evil, but the things which produce certain pleasures entail annoyances many times greater than the pleasures themselves."[7] The Greek philosopher put lying in that category. He said the wise person is prepared to lie if there is no risk of detection, but since we can never be certain our falsehoods won't be discovered, he didn't recommend deception.

A few other philosophers have echoed the Epicurean call for selfish concern. Thomas Hobbes described life as "nasty, brutish and short" and advocated political trade-offs that would gain a measure of security. Adam Smith, the spiritual father of capitalism, advised every person to seek his or her own profit. Friedrich Nietzsche announced the death of God and stated that the noble soul has reverence for itself. Egoist writer Ayn Rand dedicated her novel *The Fountainhead* to "the exultation of man's self-esteem and the sacredness of his happiness on earth."[8] Of course, the moral advice of Epicurus, Hobbes, Nietzsche, and Rand may be suspect. If their counsel consistently reflects their beliefs, their words are spoken for their own benefit, not ours.

Uncertainty Reduction Theory

of Charles Berger

No matter how close two people eventually become, they always begin as strangers. Let's say you've just taken a job as a driver for a delivery service over the winter break. After talking with the other drivers, you conclude that your income and peace of mind will depend on working out a good relationship with Heather, the radio dispatcher. All you know for sure about Heather is her attachment to Hannah, a 100-pound Labrador retriever that never lets Heather out of her sight. The veteran drivers joke that it's hard to tell the difference between the voices of Heather and Hannah over the radio. With some qualms you make arrangements to meet Heather (and Hannah) over coffee and donuts before your first day of work. You really have no idea what to expect.

Chuck Berger believes it's natural to have doubts about our ability to predict the outcome of initial encounters. Berger, professor emeritus of communication at the University of California, Davis, notes that "the beginnings of personal relationships are fraught with uncertainties."[1] Unlike social penetration theory, which tries to forecast the future of a relationship on the basis of projected rewards and costs (see Chapter 8), Berger's uncertainty reduction theory (URT) focuses on how human communication is used to gain knowledge and create understanding.

> Central to the present theory is the assumption that when strangers meet, their primary concern is one of uncertainty reduction or increasing predictability about the behavior of both themselves and others in the interaction.[2]

Interpersonal ignorance is not bliss; it's frustrating! Berger contends that our drive to reduce uncertainty about new acquaintances gets a boost from any of three prior conditions:[3]

1. *Anticipation of future interaction:* We know we will see them again.
2. *Incentive value:* They have something we want.
3. *Deviance:* They act in a weird way.

Heather hooks you on all three counts. You know you're going to be dealing with her for the next few weeks, she can make or break you financially according to the routes she assigns, and she has this strange attachment to Hannah. According to Berger, when you add these three factors to your natural curiosity, you'll *really* want to solve the puzzle of who she is.

Berger believes our main purpose in talking to people is to "make sense" of our interpersonal world. That's why you're having breakfast with a stranger and her dog. If you brought your own hound to the meeting, chances are the two dogs would circle and sniff each other, trying to get some idea of what their counterpart was like. Humans are no different; we're just a bit more subtle, using symbols instead of smells to reach our conclusions.

UNCERTAINTY REDUCTION: TO PREDICT AND EXPLAIN

Attribution theory
A systematic explanation of how people draw inferences about the character of others based on observed behavior.

Berger focuses on predictability, which he sees as the opposite of uncertainty: "As the ability of persons to predict which alternative or alternatives are likely to occur next decreases, uncertainty increases."[4] He owes a debt to Fritz Heider's view of people as intuitive psychologists. Heider, the father of *attribution theory,* believed we constantly draw inferences about why people do what they do.[5] We need to predict *and* explain. If Heather's going to bark at you on the radio, you want to understand why.

Berger notes that there are at least two kinds of uncertainty you face as you set out for your first meeting with Heather. Because you aren't sure how you should

"What say we find another way to say hello?"
©Peter Steiner/The New Yorker Collection/The Cartoon Bank

act, one kind of uncertainty deals with *behavioral* questions. Should you shake hands? Who pays for the donuts? Do you pet the dog? Often there are accepted procedural protocols to ease the stress that behavioral uncertainty can cause. Good manners go beyond common sense.

A second kind of uncertainty focuses on *cognitive* questions aimed at discovering who the other person is as a unique individual. What does Heather like about her job? What makes her glad, sad, or mad? Does she have other friends, or does she lavish all her attention on Hannah? When you first meet a person, your mind may conjure up a wild mix of potential traits and characteristics. Reducing cognitive uncertainty means acquiring information that allows you to discard many of these possibilities. That's the kind of uncertainty reduction Berger's theory addresses—cognitive rather than behavioral uncertainty.

Uncertainty reduction
Increased knowledge of what kind of person another is, which provides an improved forecast of how a future interaction will turn out.

AN AXIOMATIC THEORY: CERTAINTY ABOUT UNCERTAINTY

Berger proposes a series of axioms to explain the connection between his central concept of uncertainty and eight key variables of relationship development: *verbal communication, nonverbal warmth, information seeking, self-disclosure, reciprocity, similarity, liking,* and *shared networks.*[6] *Axioms* are traditionally regarded as self-evident truths that require no additional proof. (All people are created equal. The shortest distance between two points is a straight line. What goes up must come down.) Here are Berger's eight truths about initial uncertainty.

Axiom
A self-evident truth that requires no additional proof.

> *Axiom 1, Verbal Communication:* Given the high level of uncertainty present when people meet for the first time, as the amount of verbal communication between them increases, the level of uncertainty for each person will decrease. As uncertainty is further reduced, the amount of verbal communication will increase.

When you first sit down with Heather, the conversation will be halting and somewhat stilted. But as words begin to flow, you'll discover things about each other that make you feel more confident in each other's presence. When your comfort level rises, the pace of the conversation will pick up.

> *Axiom 2, Nonverbal Warmth:* As nonverbal warmth increases, uncertainty levels will decrease in an initial interaction situation. In addition, decreases in uncertainty level will cause increases in nonverbal warmth.

When initial stiffness gives way to head nods and tentative smiles, you'll have a better idea of who Heather is. This assurance leads to further signs of warmth, such as prolonged eye contact, forward body lean, and pleasant tone of voice.

> *Axiom 3, Information Seeking:* High levels of uncertainty cause increases in information-seeking behavior. As uncertainty levels decline, information-seeking behavior decreases.

What is it about Heather that prompted the other drivers to warn you not to start off on the wrong foot? You simply have no idea. Like a bug with its antennae twitching, you carefully monitor what she says and how she acts in order to gather clues about her personality. But you become less vigilant after she explains that her pet peeve is drivers who complain about their assignments on the radio. Whether or not you think her irritation is justified, you begin to relax because you have a better idea of how to stay on her good side.

Axiom 4, Self-Disclosure: High levels of uncertainty in a relationship cause decreases in the intimacy level of communication content. Low levels of uncertainty produce high levels of intimacy.

Like Altman and Taylor (see Chapter 8), Berger equates intimacy of communication with depth of self-disclosure. Demographic data revealing that Heather was raised in Toledo and that you are a communication major are relatively nonintimate. They typify the opening gambits of new acquaintances who are still feeling each other out. But Heather's comment that she feels more loyalty from Hannah than from any person she knows is a gutsy admission that raises the intimacy level of the conversation to a new plane. Most people wait to express attitudes, values, and feelings until they have a good idea what the listener's response will be.

Axiom 5, Reciprocity: High levels of uncertainty produce high rates of reciprocity. Low levels of uncertainty produce low levels of reciprocity.

Self-disclosure research confirms the notion that people tend to mete out the personal details of their lives at a rate that closely matches their partner's willingness to share intimate information.[7] That's reciprocity. Reciprocal vulnerability is especially important in the early stages of a relationship. The issue seems to be one of power. When knowledge of each other is minimal, we're careful not to let the other person one-up us by being the exclusive holder of potentially embarrassing information. But when we already know some of the ups and downs of a person's life, an even flow of information seems less crucial. Berger would not anticipate long monologues at your first get-together with Heather; future meetings might be a different story.

Axiom 6, Similarity: Similarities between persons reduce uncertainty, while dissimilarities produce increases in uncertainty.

The more points of contact you establish with Heather, the more you'll feel you understand her inside and out. If you're a dog lover, the two of you will click. If, however, you're partial to purring kittens, Heather's devotion to this servile beast might cause you to wonder if you'll ever be able to figure out what makes her tick.

Axiom 7, Liking: Increases in uncertainty level produce decreases in liking; decreases in uncertainty produce increases in liking.

This axiom suggests that the more you find out about Heather, the more you'll appreciate who she is. It directly contradicts the cynical opinion that "familiarity breeds contempt" and affirms instead the relational maxim that "to know her is to love her."

Axiom 8, Shared Networks: Shared communication networks reduce uncertainty, while lack of shared networks increases uncertainty.

This axiom was not part of Berger's original theory, but his ideas triggered extensive research by other communication scholars who soon moved uncertainty reduction theory beyond the confines of two strangers meeting for the first time. Berger applauds this extension: "The broadening of the theory's scope suggests the potential usefulness of reconceptualizing and extending the original formulation."[8] For example, Malcolm Parks (University of Washington) and Mara Adelman (Seattle University) discovered that men and women who communicate more often with their romantic partners' family and friends have less uncertainty about the person they love than do those whose relationships exist in relative isolation.[9] Networking couples also tend to stay together. On the basis of these findings, Berger incorporated this axiom into his formal design.

THEOREMS: THE LOGICAL FORCE OF UNCERTAINTY AXIOMS

Once we grant the validity of the eight axioms, it makes sense to pair two of them together to produce additional insight into relational dynamics. The combined axioms yield an inevitable conclusion when inserted into the well-known pattern of deductive logic:

Theorem
A proposition that logically and necessarily follows from two axioms.

$$\text{If } A = B$$
$$\text{and } B = C$$
$$\text{then } A = C$$

Berger does this for all possible combinations, thereby generating 28 theorems—for example:

If similarity reduces uncertainty (axiom 6)
and reduced uncertainty increases liking (axiom 7)
then similarity and liking are positively related (theorem 21)

In this case, the result isn't exactly earthshaking. The connection between similarity and liking is a long-established finding in research on interpersonal attraction.[10] When viewed as a whole, however, these 28 logical extensions sketch out a rather comprehensive theory of interpersonal development—all based on the importance of reducing uncertainty in human interaction.

Instead of listing all 28 theorems, I've plotted the relationships they predict in Figure 9-1. The chart reads like a mileage table you might find in a road atlas.

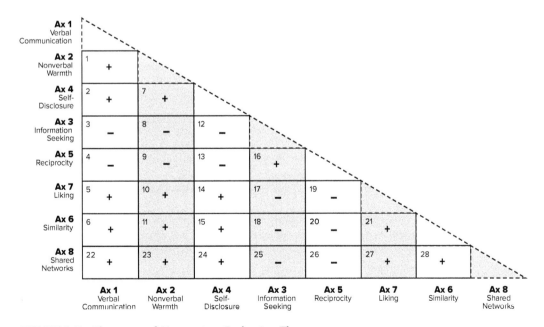

FIGURE 9-1 Theorems of Uncertainty Reduction Theory
Based on Berger and Calabrese, "Some Explorations in Initial Interaction and Beyond"

Select one axiom along the bottom and another down the side. The intersection between the two shows the number of Berger's theorem and the type of correlation it asserts. A plus sign (+) shows that the two interpersonal variables rise or fall together. A minus sign (−) indicates that as one increases, the other decreases. Will the warmth of Heather's nonverbal communication increase as the intimacy of her self-disclosure deepens? Theorem 7 says it will. Suppose you grow fond of Heather as a friend. Will you seek to find out more about her? Theorem 17 makes the surprising prediction that you won't (more on this later).

Recall from Malcolm Parks' research that good friends who have overlapping social networks communicate more frequently with each other than those who don't have those connections (see the cybernetic tradition in Chapter 4). You and Heather aren't good friends, but suppose you unexpectedly discover that her parents and your folks attend the same church service and sometimes play cards together. Does URT predict you'll be talking with each other more in the future than you otherwise would? Check the intersection between axioms 1 and 8 on the chart for Berger's prediction.

MESSAGE PLANS TO COPE WITH UNCERTAIN RESPONSES

Berger believes most social interaction is goal-driven; we have reasons for saying what we say. So after developing the core axioms and theorems of uncertainty reduction theory, he devoted his attention to explaining *how* we communicate to reduce uncertainty. Berger labeled his work "A Plan-Based Theory of Strategic Communication" because he was convinced we continually construct cognitive plans to guide our communication.[11] According to Berger, "*plans* are mental representations of action sequences that may be used to achieve goals."[12] Figure 9–2 offers a possible example of a strategic plan for your breakfast with Heather.

Your main reason for getting together with the dispatcher is to maximize your income over the holidays. Your overall strategy to reach that goal is to build a good working relationship with Heather, since she assigns the routes. The term *overall* is appropriate because Berger claims plans are "hierarchically organized with abstract action representations at the top of the hierarchy and progressively more concrete

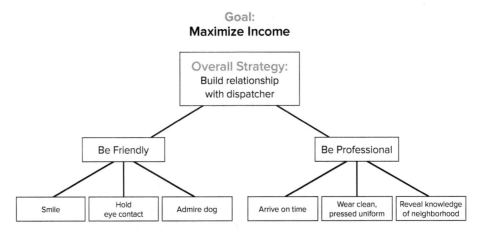

FIGURE 9-2   A Hierarchical Plan of Goal-Directed Communication

representations toward the bottom."[13] In order to build that relationship, you intend to converse in a *friendly* and *professional* manner. In this case, friendly means smiling, holding eye contact when she speaks, and admiring her dog. You'll show professionalism by arriving on time; wearing a clean, pressed uniform; and revealing knowledge of the neighborhood.

If you switch strategies at the top—seeking pity for a poor, struggling college student just starting out in life, for example—the alteration will cascade down the hierarchy, requiring changes in many of the behaviors below. Thus, a top-down revision of an action plan requires great amounts of cognitive capacity.

Even if you think carefully about your plan, Berger claims you can't be sure you'll reach your goal. You may have a great plan but execute it poorly. Heather may interpret words you meant one way to mean something else. Or she may have her own goals and plans that will inevitably thwart yours. Berger has come to the conclusion that uncertainty is central to *all* social interaction: "The probability of perfect communication is zero."[14] Thus he asks, "How do individuals cope with the inevitable uncertainties they must face when constructing messages?"[15] The following strategies are some of his answers.

Seeking Information. Uncertainty reduction theorists have outlined four approaches we can use to reduce uncertainty. Using a *passive strategy,* we unobtrusively observe others from a distance. This fly-on-the-wall tactic works best when we spot others reacting to people in informal, or "backstage," settings. (The strategy sounds like normal "scoping" behavior on any college campus.) Unless Heather lives in your neighborhood or hangs out in the same places, you might not have an opportunity to simply observe her behavior.

In an *active strategy,* we ask a third party for information. We realize that our mutual acquaintance will probably give a somewhat slanted view, but most of us have confidence in our ability to filter out the bias and gain valuable information. Regarding Heather, you've already used the active strategy by asking other drivers for their opinions about her.

With an *interactive strategy,* we talk face-to-face with the other person and ask specific questions—just what you're planning to do with Heather. This is the quickest route to reducing uncertainty, but continual probing in social settings begins to take on the feel of a cross-examination or the third degree. Our own self-disclosure offers an alternative way to elicit information from others without seeming to pry. By being transparent, we create a safe atmosphere for others to respond in kind—something the "law of reciprocity" suggests they will do (see Chapter 8).

When I (Andrew) told my 5-year-old daughter I was working on this chapter, I asked what she thought was the best way to find information about someone. Her answer demonstrates she's a child of the 21st century: "Check on Facebook!" Clearly she'd already learned the *extractive strategy* of searching for information online. Although this method was not part of Berger's original three uncertainty reduction strategies, Art Ramirez (University of South Florida) believes the Internet creates a new way for us to reduce uncertainty. Sometimes a name is all that's necessary to search for blogs, archived newspaper articles, tweets, and more—an unobtrusive process that's something like "conducting a personalized background check."[16] If you discover Heather writes a blog about her dog, you might reduce a lot of uncertainty even before you meet.

Passive strategy

Impression formation by observing a person interacting with others.

Active strategy

Impression formation by asking a third party about a person.

Interactive strategy

Impression formation through face-to-face discussion with a person.

Extractive strategy

Impression formation by searching the Internet for information about a person.

Choosing Plan Complexity. The complexity of a message plan is measured in two ways—the level of detail the plan includes and the number of contingency plans prepared in case the original one doesn't work. If it's crucial that you make top dollar in your holiday delivery job, you're likely to draw upon a plan from memory or create a new one far more complex than the sample shown in Figure 9–2. You're also likely to have a fallback plan in case the first one fails. On the other hand, you don't know much about Heather's goals or feelings, and high uncertainty argues for a less complex plan that you can adjust in the moment, once you get a feel for who she is and what she wants. This simpler approach is preferred for another reason. Enacting a complex plan takes so much cognitive effort that there's usually a deterioration in verbal and nonverbal fluency, with a resultant loss in credibility. Jeff, a student athlete, used an interactive strategy that has low complexity:

> I thought of URT this afternoon in the trainer's room where I again made eye contact with a girl I'd never met. We were the only two people in the room and I realized I needed a plan of action. I quickly ran through several strategies to reduce uncertainty. I chose a tried-and-true icebreaker line: "Hi, I know I've seen you around a ton of times, but I don't think I've ever met you. What's your name?" I hoped for the best, but prepared for a negative reaction. My contingency plan was to simply end the attempt at conversation and seem preoccupied with my treatment. Fortunately she responded with a look of relief, her name, and then a smile. Let the conversation begin. As Berger said, "Uncertainty is central to all social interaction." It sure makes life interesting.

Hedging. The possibility of plan failure suggests the wisdom of providing ways for both parties to save face when at least one of them has miscalculated. Berger catalogs a series of planned hedges that allow a somewhat gracious retreat. For instance, you may be quite certain about what you want to accomplish in your meeting with Heather, yet choose words that are *ambiguous* so as not to tip your hand before you find out more about her. You might also choose to be vague in order to avoid the embarrassment that would come from her refusing your specific request for preferred treatment in route assignment. *Humor* can provide the same way out. You could blatantly propose to use a portion of the saved time and good tips that come from prime assignments to stop at the butcher shop for a juicy bone for Hannah—but make the offer in a joking tone of voice. If Heather takes offense, you can respond, "Hey, I was just kidding."

The Hierarchy Hypothesis. What happens to action choices when plans are frustrated? Berger's *hierarchy hypothesis* asserts that "when individuals are thwarted in their attempts to achieve goals, their first tendency is to alter lower level elements of their message."[17] For example, when it's obvious the person we're talking to has failed to grasp what we're saying, our inclination is to repeat the same message—but this time louder. The tactic seldom works, but it takes less mental effort than altering strategic features higher up in the action plan. Berger describes people as "cognitive misers" who would rather try a quick fix than expend the effort to repair faulty plans.[18] There's no doubt that in-the-moment modifications are taxing, but when the issue is important, the chance to be effective makes it worth the effort. An additional hedge against failure is to practice in front of a friend who will critique your action plan before you put it into effect.[19] As a Hebrew proverb warns, "Without counsel, plans go wrong."[20]

Plan complexity
A characteristic of a message plan based on the level of detail it provides and the number of contingencies it covers.

Hedging
Use of strategic ambiguity and humor to provide a way for both parties to save face when a message fails to achieve its goal.

Hierarchy hypothesis
The prediction that when people are thwarted in their attempts to achieve goals, their first tendency is to alter lower-level elements of their message.

REDUCING UNCERTAINTY IN ONGOING RELATIONSHIPS: RELATIONAL TURBULENCE THEORY

Berger developed uncertainty reduction theory to explain first-time encounters. Can uncertainty also wreak havoc in ongoing relationships? Leanne Knobloch at the University of Illinois believes the answer is yes, although the type of uncertainty differs from what we experience with new acquaintances. After the get-to-know-you phase has passed, we're unlikely to wonder about someone's age, hobbies, or hometown. Instead, uncertainty in close relationships arises from whether we're sure about our own thoughts *(Am I really in love?),* those of the other person *(Does he really enjoy spending time together?),* and the future of the relationship *(Are we headed for a breakup?).*[21] Since Knobloch's work has focused on romantic relationships, I'll describe such *relational uncertainty* in that context, although we can experience uncertainty with friends and family, too.

Relational uncertainty
Doubts about our own thoughts, the thoughts of the other person, or the future of the relationship.

Like the common cold, romantic partners might "catch" relational uncertainty at any time. But just as colds occur more often in cooler weather and enclosed spaces, some life circumstances tend to generate relational uncertainty. Knobloch's initial research focused on romantic couples' transition from casual to serious dating—a time when couples negotiate what the relationship means and whether it's likely to continue.[22] Not only can this phase produce feelings of uncertainty, but couples also experience *partner interference* as they learn to coordinate their individual goals, plans, and activities in ways that don't annoy each other. The learning process isn't always smooth.

Partner interference
Occurs when a relational partner hinders goals, plans, and activities.

Knobloch believes uncertainty leads close partners to experience *relational turbulence.* If you've flown in an airplane, you've probably felt the bumps and lurches caused by turbulent air. Knobloch thinks that's a good metaphor for partners facing uncertainty and interference:

Relational turbulence
Negative emotions arising from perceived problems in a close relationship.

> When an aircraft encounters a dramatic change in weather conditions, passengers feel turbulence as the plane is jostled, jerked, and jolted erratically. Similarly, when a [couple] undergoes a period of transition that alters the climate of the relationship, partners experience turbulence as sudden intense reactions to their circumstances. Just as turbulence during a flight may make passengers [reconsider] their safety, fear a crash, or grip their seat, turbulence in a relationship may make partners ruminate about hurt, cry over jealousy, or scream during conflict.[23]

In times of relational turbulence, we're likely to feel unsettling emotions like anger, sadness, and fear. It's a bumpy emotional ride that makes us more *reactive,* or sensitive, to our partner's actions. Let's say your dating partner asks you to pick up a candy bar while you're at the store. If you forget, your partner might be bothered but probably won't make a big deal about the brief lapse in memory. When couples are already experiencing relational turbulence, however, the same gaffe could ignite a ridiculously big argument. Over time, turbulence leads to even more uncertainty and interference, which then creates more turbulence—a vicious cycle that threatens the health of the relationship.

Knobloch's research supports relational turbulence theory across many types of romantic relationships, ranging from couples facing clinical depression[24] to military spouses returning from deployment.[25] Her research suggests direct attempts to reduce uncertainty (such as the interactive strategy) may help resolve relational turbulence. She believes we're most likely to talk directly when the relationship has high intimacy and equal power. The talk still may produce pain, but intimacy and power equality provide stability in the face of relational turbulence.[26] And in the end, good things happen when a couple navigates turbulent waters together: "When partners use difficult experiences as a springboard for clarifying relational involvement or patterns of interdependence, they can improve the foundations of their relationship."[27]

CRITIQUE: NAGGING DOUBTS ABOUT UNCERTAINTY

Within the communication discipline, Berger's uncertainty reduction theory was an early prototype of what an objective theory should be, and it continues to inspire a new generation of scholars today. His theory makes specific *testable predictions,* and offers the human need to reduce interpersonal uncertainty as the engine that drives its axioms. Although combining the axioms generates a slew of theorems, they are straightforward, logically consistent, and *simple to understand.* As for *practical utility,* readers interested in promoting interpersonal ties can regard the linkages the theorems describe as a blueprint for constructing solid relationships. Subsequent survey and experimental *quantitative research* supports most of URT's axioms and has expanded the scope of the theory to cover development of established relationships. There are, however, continuing questions about Berger's reliance on the concept of *uncertainty* and his assumption that we're motivated to reduce it.

A dozen years after publishing the theory, Berger admitted his original statement contained "some propositions of dubious validity."[28] Critics quickly point to theorem 17, which predicts that the more you like people, the less you'll seek information about them.

> Frankly, it is not clear why information-seeking would decrease as liking increased other than being required by deductive inference from the axiomatic structure of uncertainty reduction theory. In fact, it seems more reasonable to suggest that persons will seek information about and from those they like rather than those they dislike.[29]

That's the blunt assessment of Kathy Kellermann, who originally participated in Berger's research program. We might be willing to dismiss this apparent error as only one glitch out of 28 theorems, but the tight logical structure that is the genius of the theory doesn't give us that option. Theorem 17 is dictated by axioms 3 and 7. If the theorem is wrong, one of the axioms is suspect. Kellermann targets the motivational assumption of axiom 3 as the problem.

Axiom 3 assumes that lack of information triggers a search for knowledge. But as Kellermann and Rodney Reynolds at California Lutheran University discovered when they studied motivation to reduce uncertainty in more than a thousand students at 10 universities, "wanting knowledge rather than lacking knowledge is what promotes information-seeking in initial encounters with others."[30] The distinction is illustrated by the story of a teacher who asked a boy, "What's the difference between *ignorance* and *apathy?*" The student replied, "I don't know, and I don't care." (He was right.) Kellermann and Reynolds also failed to find that anticipated future interaction, incentive value, or deviance gave any motivational kick to information seeking, as Berger claimed they would.

Another attack on the theory comes from Michael Sunnafrank at the University of Minnesota Duluth. He challenges Berger's claim that uncertainty reduction is the key to understanding early encounters. Consistent with Altman and Taylor's social

Predicted outcome value
A forecast of future benefits and costs of interaction based on limited experience with the other.

penetration theory (see Chapter 8) is Sunnafrank's insistence that the early course of a relationship is guided by its *predicted outcome value (POV)*.[31] He's convinced that the primary goal of our initial interaction with another is maximizing our relational outcomes rather than finding out who he or she is. If this is true, you'll be more concerned with establishing a smooth working relationship with Heather at your initial meeting than you will be in figuring out why she does what she does.

Who's right—Berger or Sunnafrank? Berger thinks there's no contest. He maintains that any predictions you make about the rewards and costs of working with Heather are only as good as the quality of your current knowledge. To the extent that you are uncertain of how an action will affect the relationship, predicted outcome value has no meaning. Walid Afifi (University of California, Santa Barbara) thinks *both* theories are too narrow.[32] In his *theory of motivated information management,* he suggests we're most motivated to reduce anxiety rather than uncertainty. So when uncertainty doesn't make us feel anxious, we won't seek to reduce it—like a couple enjoying the mystery of a date planned by one person for the other. As relational dialectics theory suggests, complete certainty is complete boredom (see Chapter 11).

Even though the validity of Berger's theory is in question, his analysis of initial interaction is a major contribution to communication scholarship. Berger notes that "the field of communication has been suffering and continues to suffer from an intellectual trade deficit with respect to related disciplines; the field imports much more than it exports."[33] Uncertainty reduction theory was an early attempt by a scholar trained within the discipline to reverse that trend. His success at stimulating critical thinking among his peers can be seen in the fact that every scholar cited in this chapter has been a member of a communication faculty.

Although some of Berger's axioms may not perfectly reflect the acquaintance process, his focus on the issue of reducing uncertainty is at the heart of communication inquiry. Appealing for further dialogue and modification rather than wholesale rejection of the theory, Berger asks:

> What could be more basic to the study of communication than the propositions that (1) adaptation is essential for survival, (2) adaptation is only possible through the reduction of uncertainty, and (3) uncertainty can be both reduced and produced by communicative activity?[34]

It's a sound rhetorical question.

QUESTIONS TO SHARPEN YOUR FOCUS

1. An *axiom* is a self-evident truth. Which one of Berger's axioms seems least self-evident to you?

2. Check out *theorem 13* in Figure 9-1. Does the predicted relationship between *self-disclosure* and *reciprocity* match the forecast of social penetration theory?

3. Which *uncertainty management strategy* would you use when scoping out a new professor? Group project member? Roommate? Romantic interest? If your answers differ across these relationships, why is that so?

4. When are you most likely to feel *relational turbulence* in your close relationships? Does anything other than *partner interference* or *relational uncertainty* help explain why you experience a bumpy emotional ride?

CONVERSATIONS

View this segment online at
www.afirstlook.com.

Chuck Berger would not be surprised if you were confused by the mid-chapter switch from axioms of uncertainty reduction to plan-based strategic communication. In his conversation with Em, he describes why he originally viewed the two lines of research as separate but now sees them as tightly linked. Many students find this interview especially fascinating because of Berger's strongly stated opinions. For example, he dismisses CMM's idea of co-creation of social reality (see Chapter 6) because it offers a "total amnesia model." He also criticizes social scientists who purposely create ambiguity so that they can never be proved wrong. Berger's explicit and forthright statements show he's willing to take that risk.

A SECOND LOOK

Recommended resource: Leanne K. Knobloch, "Uncertainty Reduction Theory," in *Engaging Theories in Interpersonal Communication: Multiple Perspectives,* Leslie A. Baxter and Dawn O. Braithwaite (eds.), Sage, Thousand Oaks, CA, 2008, pp. 133–144.

Original statement: Charles R. Berger and Richard Calabrese, "Some Explorations in Initial Interaction and Beyond: Toward a Developmental Theory of Interpersonal Communication," *Human Communication Research,* Vol. 1, 1975, pp. 99–112.

Comparison with other uncertainty theories: Walid A. Afifi, "Uncertainty and Information Management in Interpersonal Contexts," in *New Directions in Interpersonal Communication Research,* Sandi W. Smith and Steven R. Wilson (eds.), Sage, Thousand Oaks, CA, 2010, pp. 94–114.

Uncertainty reduction and online dating: Jennifer L. Gibbs, Nicole B. Ellison, and Chih-Hui Lai, "First Comes Love, Then Comes Google: An Investigation of Uncertainty Reduction Strategies and Self-Disclosure in Online Dating," *Communication Research,* Vol. 38, 2011, pp. 70–100.

Goals and plans in message production: Charles R. Berger, "Message Production Skill in Social Interaction," in *Handbook of Communication and Social Interaction Skills,* John O. Greene and Brant R. Burleson (eds.), Lawrence Erlbaum, Mahwah, NJ, 2003, pp. 257–290.

Uncertainty reduction in close relationships: Leanne K. Knobloch and Denise H. Solomon, "Information Seeking Beyond Initial Interaction: Negotiating Relational Uncertainty Within Close Relationships," *Human Communication Research,* Vol. 28, 2002, pp. 243–257.

Relational turbulence and military couples: Leanne K. Knobloch and Jennifer A. Theiss, "Experiences of U.S. Military Couples During the Post-Deployment Transition: Applying the Relational Turbulence Model," *Journal of Social and Personal Relationships,* Vol. 29, 2012, pp. 423–450.

Critique of axiom 3: Kathy Kellermann and Rodney Reynolds, "When Ignorance Is Bliss: The Role of Motivation to Reduce Uncertainty in Uncertainty Reduction Theory," *Human Communication Research,* Vol. 17, 1990, pp. 5–75.

Predicted outcome value theory: Artemio Ramirez Jr., Michael Sunnafrank, and Ryan Goei, "Predicted Outcome Value Theory in Ongoing Relationships," *Communication Monographs,* Vol. 77, 2010, pp. 27–50.

To access a chapter on reducing uncertainty when communicating
across cultures, click on Anxiety/Uncertainty Management Theory
in Archive under Theory Resources at
www.afirstlook.com.

Social Information Processing Theory

of Joseph Walther

As depicted in the award-winning movie *The Social Network*, in 2003 Mark Zuckerberg created "Facemash"—a website allowing Harvard students to compare the physical attractiveness of their female peers.[1] Although Harvard's administration quickly shut down Facemash and nearly expelled Zuckerberg, Facemash soon led to Facebook, launching the era of social media.

According to a Pew Research Center survey, 76 percent of online adults use social networking sites.[2] Young and middle-aged adults are particularly avid users, but even 35 percent of adults over 65 use social media. What's the appeal? A separate Pew study suggests much of the motivation is social—commenting on another person's post is the most frequent daily Facebook activity.[3] And although Facebook remains the most popular social media site on the planet, visually-oriented platforms like Snapchat and Instagram have become very popular among younger users.[4]

From telephone to smartphone, rapid changes in communication technology over the past several decades have frustrated communication scholars seeking to understand what all of this means for interpersonal relationships. Amid this flood of cyber-innovation, social information processing (SIP) theory has stood the test of time. Building on theories that explain interpersonal communication offline, Joe Walther (University of California, Santa Barbara) initially developed SIP to understand how online communication shapes the development of interpersonal and group relationships. Can people really form a meaningful connection when their only point of contact is through a computer?

When Walther developed SIP in the early 1990s, the prevailing answer to that question was *no*—and many people remain skeptical of online intimacy today. But he argues that given the opportunity for a sufficient exchange of social messages and subsequent relational growth, *as goes face-to-face communication, so goes online communication.* His experiments suggest that people can indeed form relationships online that are just as satisfying—in fact, sometimes even more satisfying—than their offline interactions.

ONLINE VERSUS FACE-TO-FACE: A SIP INSTEAD OF A GULP

Michelle is one of my (Andrew) wife's close college friends. I didn't meet her until we moved to my first full-time job in Ohio, where Michelle lived just two hours away. It was close enough to eat dinner together a few times, but far enough that we didn't see her often. By the time she moved overseas, I'd discovered a bit about her from our handful of meals, such as her Tennessee roots and passion for studying chemistry. I enjoyed those face-to-face meetings, but still felt like I had a lot more to learn about her before I could consider her a good friend. Since our future communication would be through Facebook, I wasn't sure how our friendship would progress when she moved away. Could we form a friendship that would be as close as if we lived in the same city? According to Walther's SIP, the answer is yes.

Walther labeled his theory *social information processing* because he believes relationships grow only to the extent that parties first gain information about each other and use that information to form interpersonal impressions of who they are. In taking this view, SIP theory is consistent with *social penetration theory* and *uncertainty reduction theory* (see Chapters 8 and 9), which both assume that as we gain information about others, our affinity for them grows as well. The diagram below depicts this process of getting to know another person. It's a chain of events that occurs regardless of the medium we're using to communicate: we get information, we form an impression, and then the relationship grows. SIP focuses on how the first link of the chain looks a bit different when communicating online. Throughout this chapter, I'll use the term "online communication" to refer to mediated messages through email, social media, cell phones, and other technological channels. Although we can use these technologies to communicate with images and video, SIP focuses on online communication that is textual.

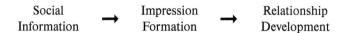

Social Information → Impression Formation → Relationship Development

Impression formation
The composite mental image one person forms of another; often associated with affinity.

Cues filtered out
Interpretation of online communication that regards lack of nonverbal cues as a fatal flaw for relationship development.

Flaming
Hostile online language that creates a toxic climate for relationship development and growth.

Before SIP, many communication theorists shared a *cues filtered out* interpretation of online messages. They believed the lack of nonverbal cues would disrupt the process of gaining information and forming an impression.[5] Communicators would have little clue as to their relative status. Norms for interaction wouldn't be clear. People would become more self-absorbed and less inhibited, leading to *flaming*—hostile language that zings its target and creates a toxic climate for relationship development and growth. If you've ever visited the comments section of a news story or YouTube video, you've seen such bitter communication.

Walther acknowledges online communication can be like that—impersonal and cold. But sometimes, so is face-to-face communication. At other times, face-to-face communication is warm and wonderful, and Walther believes online communication can be, too. He doesn't think the loss of nonverbal cues is necessarily fatal or even injurious to a well-defined impression of the other or the relational development it triggers.

Walther highlights two features of online communication that provide a rationale for SIP theory and give me hope for long-distance relational closeness with Michelle.[6] First, *verbal cues* can effectively compensate for missing nonverbal cues when exchanging social information. Second, online communicators need *extended time* to produce the same amount of impression formation and relationship development as face-to-face communicators, especially when the online channel is primarily text-based.

The lack of nonverbal cues leads to subtle changes in the steps of getting to know each other, but people can achieve the same level of closeness with some more time and effort. I'll explain what both of these features mean for me, Michelle, and anyone who wants to build and maintain a meaningful relationship online.

VERBAL CUES OF AFFINITY REPLACE NONVERBAL CUES

When I first met Michelle face-to-face, we had a range of nonverbal cues available to form impressions of each other. When she moved to England, we began connecting exclusively through Facebook, and those cues disappeared. Through many forms of social media, people can't pick up each other's tone of voice or rate of speech. A photo provides only a static image of physical context, facial expression, body position, and appearance. Although video chat transmits eye contact and gestures, we still can't shake hands or hug. According to the cues filtered out interpretation, all this should mean interpersonal disaster.

Inconsistent messages Messages in which the verbal and nonverbal content don't match.

Traditional wisdom about nonverbal communication would agree. Perhaps you've heard the adage that nonverbal cues carry 93 percent of a message's meaning. That statistic comes from UCLA psychologist Albert Mehrabian's research on *inconsistent messages,* or messages where the verbal and nonverbal content don't match.[7] Say you ask a friend what she thinks of a class, and she replies, "It's really great," while frowning, rolling her eyes, and speaking in monotone. Her verbal claim that it's a wonderful class clashes with her nonverbal hints that it isn't. In Mehrabian's research, people gave nonverbal cues more weight when interpreting such inconsistent messages. Of course, not all messages feature such inconsistencies, and emotion is only part of our communication behavior. Nonverbal cues become less powerful when they don't conflict with the verbal message or when we're conveying facts.[8] Nevertheless, when nonverbal cues go absent, perhaps emotional understanding does as well.

Walther doesn't think that's the case. He believes we can replace nonverbal cues with verbal messages that convey the same meaning. Because human beings are so powerfully driven to build connections with others, we find clever ways to make up for the lack of nonverbal information. The human need for affiliation overcomes the limited nature of the medium. For example, the average American teenager sends and receives 30 text messages per day, or about 900 a month.[9] Like Walther, teens seem to believe that a steady stream of short messages can quench their thirst for social information, even without the nonverbal cues that typically signal friendship or romantic attraction.

This ability to convert nonverbal cues into verbal meaning isn't new. Prior to electronic communication, people developed pen-pal relationships by discovering similarities and expressing affection through the written word alone. Long-distance romantic relationships thrived as the casual exchange of friendly notes progressed to a stream of passionate love letters. During World War II, postal letters so powerfully boosted soldier morale that the US government launched a campaign encouraging citizens to write to loved ones serving abroad. When the mass of letters became too expensive to transport, a technology known as *v-mail* reduced letters to small pieces of film that were expanded to readable size upon reaching soldiers.[10] History supports SIP's claim that people creatively adapt their communication to connect across cue-limited media.

Experimental Support for a Counterintuitive Idea

The examples of teen texters and soldiers abroad suggest that people can express affinity just as well through text as when face-to-face. But as a communication theorist steeped in the socio-psychological tradition, Walther isn't content to rely on such anecdotes to support his theory. Over the course of the past two decades, he's performed numerous controlled experiments to put his ideas to the test. After reading my description of the following study, see if you can identify how it provides evidence that humans are creative communicators, able to use text-only channels to convey a level of relational warmth that can equal face-to-face communication.[11]

Walther asked 28 pairs of students who didn't know each other to discuss moral dilemmas—a communication task used in many previous experiments. Half the pairs talked face-to-face, while the other half communicated online. In both cases, one member of each pair was a student accomplice—someone the researchers recruited ahead of time. Half of these confederates were asked to communicate in a friendly, positive way, while the other half were told to act unfriendly. During the experiment, video cameras recorded the face-to-face conversations from behind a one-way mirror, and all computer messages were saved. Afterward, trained raters categorized the different ways confederates communicated both verbal and nonverbal emotion. The naive participants rated their partners on the degree of affection expressed during the discussion.

Results of the experiment indicated that the method of communication made no difference in the emotional tone perceived by naive participants. Any discrepancy in warmth was due to the intention of each confederate—nice confederates successfully conveyed warmth, and grouchy confederates were perceived as mean. What verbal behaviors did confederates use online to show they were friendly? As you might expect, self-disclosure, praise, and statements of affection topped the list. These are core strategies of making an impression by reducing uncertainty and drawing close through social penetration.

Of course, face-to-face confederates could have used these same verbal behaviors—and indeed, some of them did. But, similar to Mehrabian's findings on inconsistent messages, *what* confederates said when physically present seemed insignificant compared to *how* they showed it nonverbally. Confederates primarily relied on facial expression, eye contact, tone of voice, body position, and other nonverbal cues to convey how they felt about their partners.[12]

For you, these findings suggest you might be able to convey just as much warmth through a series of text messages as you could through a face-to-face conversation, FaceTime talk, or series of Snapchat pictures. But compared to those visually-oriented channels, building warmth over texting might take longer.

EXTENDED TIME: THE CRUCIAL VARIABLE IN ONLINE COMMUNICATION

According to Walther, online communicators need a lot of time to build close connections. The SIP acronym suggests a liquid analogy that can help us understand Walther's thinking.[13] Suppose someone hands you a 12-ounce glass of water, cola, or beer—whatever drink you find refreshing. You could hoist the glass and chug the contents in a matter of seconds. That big gulp is similar to being face-to-face with someone you've just met and want to know better. For just a few hours of face-to-face meetings in Ohio over the course of two years, Michelle and I had this large amount of social information available.

But what if you had to drink your beverage through a straw—one *sip* at a time? You'd still be able to drain the entire 12 ounces, but it would take much longer. That's the situation for online communicators who are thirsty for social information. They end up with the same quantity and quality of interpersonal knowledge, but it accumulates at a slower rate.

Over an extended period, the issue is not the *amount* of social information that can be conveyed online; rather, it's the *rate* at which that information mounts up. Because typing is slower than talking, text-based messages take longer to compose. How much longer? Walther finds that messages spoken in person might take about four times longer to say online.[14] This four-to-one time differential explains why many early experiments seemed to show that online communication is task-oriented and impersonal. In the experiment described above, Walther compared 10 minutes of face-to-face time with 40 minutes of online talk. There was no difference in partner affinity between the two modes.

As a senior Nielsen executive notes, "Despite the almost unlimited nature of what you can do on the Web, nearly half of U.S. online time is spent on three activities—social networking, playing games and e-mailing."[15] Perhaps the additional time necessary to convey an impression explains why people invest so much time in online socializing. Along those lines, Walther advises online users to make up for the rate difference by sending messages more often. Not only does this practice help impression formation in personal relationships, but it's also reassuring to virtual group partners who naturally wonder who their colleagues are, what they're thinking, and if they're going to do the work they've promised.

I've found this to make a critical difference in my friendship with Michelle. For a long time, we each updated our Facebook status at least once a day. Without those updates, I doubt our friendship would've grown much closer. Over time, our Facebook conversations have ranged from political debates to discussions about Asian cuisine. I now consider her a good friend, and although I'm sure we could have built the same depth of friendship more quickly face-to-face, Facebook messages have worked just fine over a longer period of time.

Anticipated future interaction
A way of extending psychological time; the likelihood of future interaction motivates online communicators to develop a relationship.

Two other time factors can contribute to intimacy on the Internet. One of them is *anticipated future interaction*. Recall that Chuck Berger claims our drive to reduce uncertainty about someone we've just met gets an added boost when we think we're going to see each other again (see Chapter 9). Through his empirical research, Walther has discovered that members of an online conference or task group start to trade relational messages when they are scheduled for multiple meetings. It's as if the "shadow of the future" motivates them to encounter others on a personal level.[16]

Chronemics
The study of people's systematic handling of time in their interaction with others.

The other factor is *chronemics,* which is the label nonverbal researchers use to describe how people perceive, use, and respond to issues of time in their interaction with others. Unlike other nonverbal cues, no form of online communication can completely filter out time. A recipient can note the time of day a message was sent and then gauge the elapsed time until the reply. Does this knowledge really affect a relationship? Walther's work inspired me to investigate how college students evaluate email reply rate between friends. In the study, participants read an email message and a reply to that message. The text of the email exchange was the same for each participant, but the time stamp varied randomly. The study revealed that replying quickly (such as within an hour) yielded the most positive impressions, with some evidence that women are more attuned to reply rate than are men.[17] So if you want to convey a positive impression, a fast reply is probably best.

You now have the basic predictions of social information processing theory. SIP claims that online communicators can get to know each other and develop a mutual affinity by using the medium's available cues to manage relational development. The process will probably take longer than face-to-face bonding, but there's no reason to believe the relationship will be any less personal. Given enough time, as goes face-to-face, so goes online communication. After offering a similar summary, Walther asks, "Is this the best that one can hope to attain when communicating electronically—the mere potential for intimacy where time permits?"[18] His answer is no—sometimes, online talk actually surpasses the quality of relational communication that's available when parties communicate face-to-face. Walther's hyperpersonal perspective explains how this works.

HYPERPERSONAL PERSPECTIVE: CLOSER ONLINE THAN IN PERSON

Hyperpersonal perspective
The claim that online relationships are often more intimate than those developed when partners are physically together.

Walther uses the term *hyperpersonal* to label online relationships that are more intimate than if partners were physically together. Under the familiar *sender-receiver-channel-feedback* categories, he classifies four types of media effects that occur precisely because communicators aren't face-to-face and don't have a full range of nonverbal cues available. In an interview with fellow online researcher Nicole Ellison at the University of Michigan, Walther explained how these four characteristics shape the nature of online dating—a method more than 59 percent of Americans believe is a good way to find a significant other.[19] I'll draw on his insights as I explain the four elements of the hyperpersonal perspective.

Sender: Selective Self-Presentation

Selective self-presentation
An online positive portrayal without fear of contradiction, which enables people to create an overwhelmingly favorable impression.

Walther claims that through *selective self-presentation,* people who meet online have an opportunity to make and sustain an overwhelmingly positive impression. That's because they can write about their most attractive traits, accomplishments, and actions without fear of contradiction from their physical appearance, their inconsistent actions, or the objections of third parties who know their dark side. As a relationship develops, they can carefully edit the breadth and depth of their self-disclosure to conform to their cyber image, without worrying that nonverbal leakage will shatter their projected persona.

For dating site users, Walther notes that "selective self-presentation is a process that is probably very much involved in how people put together the profile" because they want people to find them attractive.[20] Jeff Hancock (Stanford University) believes the viewer of the profile sees it as a promise—and if online self-presentation differs too much from offline reality, potential partners will feel like that promise was broken.[21]

Receiver: Overattribution of Similarity

Attribution
A perceptual process whereby we observe what people do and then try to figure out what they're really like.

Attribution is a perceptual process whereby we observe what people do and then try to figure out what they're really like. Our basic interpretive bias is to assume that the specific action we see reflects the personality of the person who did it. People who *do* things like that *are* like that. But when it comes to reading a text message or tweet, we have very little to go on. Our only basis for judgment is the verbal behavior of the person who sent the message. Yet Walther says the absence of other cues doesn't keep us from jumping to conclusions. On the contrary, someone viewing an online dating profile will tend to overattribute the information on the profile and create an idealized image of the owner.

"I can't wait to see what you're like online."
©Paul Noth/The New Yorker Collection/The Cartoon Bank

My student Taylor described how a new boyfriend's Facebook and text messages helped her build a positive impression of him:

> Joseph Walther claims that communicators use whatever cues are available to form an impression, and I could tell by the frequency with which my boyfriend talked about his family and music that those were two things he really cared about. Because he was always on Facebook and quickly responded to my texts, I knew he was just as excited to talk to me as I was to talk to him, and his insightful questions meant he really was interested in who I was as a person.

Channel: Communicating on Your Own Time

Many forms of interpersonal communication require that parties synchronize their schedules in order to talk with each other. Although face-to-face, phone, and Skype conversations offer a sense of immediacy, co-presence is achieved at a high price. One partner's desire to communicate often comes at a bad time for the other. Parties can make a date to talk, of course, but locking in a time for communication raises expectations for significance that may be hard to meet.

Asynchronous channel
A nonsimultaneous medium of communication that each individual can use when he or she desires.

In contrast, many forms of online communication are *asynchronous* channels of communication, meaning that parties can use them nonsimultaneously—at different times. With time constraints relaxed, texters, tweeters, Snapchatters, and others are free to write and post when they are able to do so, knowing that recipients will view the message at a convenient time. That's a big plus, especially when they are communicating across time zones or their waking hours are out of sync. Even within the same time zone, online communication helps busy people maximize their time, as Glenn's daughter Jordan describes when explaining how she and her husband met through online dating: "How do you get a date when you know about four people in town and have to spend most of your 'free' time studying or working? We were both totally alone in a new city and had precious few avenues to meet people who shared our values. This is what led us to seek romance on the Internet."

Walther notes an added benefit of nonsimultaneous online communication: "In asynchronous interaction one may plan, contemplate, and edit one's comments more mindfully and deliberatively than one can in more spontaneous, simultaneous talk."[22] Across some social media, such careful editing is kind of the point—think of the many filters available on Instagram. Editing may also be a tremendous advantage when dealing with touchy issues, misunderstandings, or conflict between parties.

Feedback: Self-Fulfilling Prophecy

Self-fulfilling prophecy is the tendency for a person's expectation of others to evoke a response from them that confirms what he or she anticipated. Believing it's so can make it so. This process creates hyperpersonal relationships only if online parties first form highly favorable impressions of each other. When an online romantic relationship doesn't work out, daters might use that feedback to further revise their profiles with an eye toward better self-presentation. Then the process starts again—*senders* self-select what they reveal, *receivers* create an idealized image of their partner, and the *channel* lets users express themselves the way they want, when they want. What's not to like?

Beyond online dating, Walther suggests hyperpersonal communication may improve relationships between groups with a strong history of tension and conflict, such as Israeli Jews and Palestinian Muslims. As Walther asks, "When the turban and the yarmulke need not be visible during interactions, can [similarities] be made more [meaningful] than differences?"[23] One test in the Israeli education system suggests the answer can be yes, as one Jewish student reported after spending more than a year communicating online in a multicultural course: "This coming year, I will begin teaching . . . and when I use the word 'Arab' in my class, it will sound different than it would have before the course."[24] Walther also points to similar successful online interaction between hostile groups in Northern Ireland.[25]

Of course, online communication itself isn't a magical cure for intergroup hostility. To ease tensions, Walther recommends focusing on common tasks rather than group differences, allowing plenty of time for communication, and exclusively using text-only channels.[26] If that last suggestion surprises you, remember Walther's claim that fewer nonverbal cues means more positive sender self-presentation and receiver attribution. Walther hopes hyperpersonal effects might change the attitudes of hostile groups toward each other—changes that could persist even when they later meet face-to-face.

Self-fulfilling prophecy
The tendency for a person's expectation of others to evoke a response from them that confirms what was originally anticipated.

THE WARRANTING VALUE OF INFORMATION: WHAT TO TRUST?

Hyperpersonal effects aren't likely to occur when people don't trust each other. And in the sometimes rough-and-tumble world of social media, distrust is a real possibility. So Walther and his colleagues have examined how people evaluate the credibility of others through social media.

One thing that sets social media apart is the ability to add information to other people's pages—other users can supplement, or even contradict, the account owner's claims. On Instagram, such added information might be a comment on a picture; on Facebook, friends can tag other users in status updates and videos; on LinkedIn, people can vouch for the work skills of colleagues. These and other social media sites display two types of information—that controlled by the profile owner and that beyond the owner's direct control. Walther believes this is a difference that truly makes a difference in how social media users process information.

As an example, let's say you view a new classmate's Facebook profile for the first time. The classmate describes herself as "quiet and studious," lists her interests as "reading philosophy" and "playing solitaire," and is part of a group titled "I'd rather stay in and read a good book." Yet many of her friends' comments describe her as "the life of the party," with tags on photos of her socializing with large groups of people. If you think these messages contradict each other, who are you likely to believe—your classmate or her friends? Answering this question is at the heart of Walther's investigation of the *warranting value* of personal information, or what he describes as "the perceived validity of information presented online with respect to illuminating someone's offline characteristics."[27] For both Walther and scholars of debate, the word "warrant" has a similar meaning to the word "reason": If the information we're reading has warranting value, then it gives us reason to believe the information is true.

Warranting value
Reason to believe that information is accurate, typically because the target of the information cannot manipulate it easily.

If communicating online is like sipping through a straw, SIP has assumed that "all water passing through the [straw] is the same sort of water."[28] But now Walther believes social media lets users sip two different kinds of liquid at the same time. Like email messages, whose content is under the sole control of the sender, information posted by a profile owner is *low warrant information* because he or she can manipulate it with ease. Walther argues that we may not trust this information: "Because online impressions are controllable, they are often suspect."[29] Since the profile owner can't as easily manipulate what's posted by friends, we're more likely to accept such *high warrant information* as true. As Walther notes, this happens offline, too: You might believe a classmate who says he'll work hard with you on a group project, but you'll probably give even greater weight to the testimony of his lab partner last term. For the purpose of impression formation, low warrant information is like a sip of grape juice, but high warrant information is like a taste of fine wine.

Walther and his colleagues have tested warranting value through a series of experiments, with participants randomly assigned to view different versions of fake Facebook profiles. These experiments confirm that people trust high warrant information. In one study, the content of friends' posts altered evaluations of the profile owner's credibility and social attractiveness.[30] Another experiment directly compared low and high warrant information, finding that friends' comments overrode the profile owner's claims when forming impressions of physical attractiveness and extraversion.[31] These studies suggest that, unlike an email or text message, interpersonal information on social media comes from both the self and other site users. An outside observer won't give those two sources equal weight.

CRITIQUE: A GOOD OBJECTIVE THEORY IN NEED OF UPDATE

Because technology changes so rapidly, it's difficult to craft and defend enduring theories of online communication. Just as theorists begin to understand one technology, along comes the next.[32] Yet in this train of high-tech innovation, SIP remains popular among communication scholars because it stacks up well against all the criteria for a good social science theory (see Chapter 3). It offers specific, *quantitatively testable hypotheses* about a *relatively simple* set of variables. It clearly *explains* differences and similarities between face-to-face and online communication. The theory *predicts* communication behavior across media that didn't even exist when the theory was born, and SIP's advice is *useful* to many, ranging from spatially separated soul mates to international business partners.

However, the invention of smartphones and the subsequent explosion of social media may reduce the scope and validity of Walther's theory. Both the promise and the problem with mobile phones is that they are just that—mobile. We can, and do, take them with us all the time. Because of their easy portability, we can be linked and liked by hundreds of people wherever we go, 24/7. That's the upside, which seems consistent with Walther's quantitative research findings that given enough time, any positive relational development that can occur during face-to-face communication can be achieved (if not exceeded) through online communication.

In contrast, the qualitative research of Sherry Turkle, professor of science, technology, and society at MIT, suggests the connectivity provided by mobile phones has unanticipated consequences that Walther hasn't addressed in the two decades since he crafted his theory. She cautions that "those little devices in our pockets are so psychologically powerful that they don't only change what we do, they change who we are."[33] The technology and apps on a smartphone are engineered to hold our attention. Even though we hold to the fantasy that we can focus on whatever we want, in reality many of us are virtually glued to what's on the screen. We take our phones wherever we go and are loath to turn them off. Turkle admits she even sleeps with her phone by the pillow.[34] She's convinced this continuous distraction deflects us from that which makes us truly human—conversation, intimacy, and empathy.

Conversation. Turkle's primary concern is that our phones pull us away from face-to-face conversations with others. Late-night television host Stephen Colbert wanted to explore this trade-off with Turkle when she was a guest on *The Colbert Report*. Knowingly or not, he used Walther's liquid analogy when he asked, "Don't all these little tweets, these little sips of online connection, add up to one big gulp of real conversation?"[35] She responded with an emphatic, "No."

After a decade of interviews, focus groups, and analysis of online and offline communication, Turkle claims that for those brought up with Facebook, Twitter, Snapchat, WhatsApp, and other smartphone social apps, face-to-face conversation is becoming a lost art. Her highly regarded book *Reclaiming Conversation: The Power of Talk in a Digital Age* offers scores of examples how conversation is not only disappearing, but is intentionally avoided by those brought up in the digital age.[36] As one teenager described lunch-table talk to Turkle, "With my friends, it's no conversation, or conversation about what's on your phone."[37]

Intimacy. In their increasing flight from conversation, people who log on to social media constantly give up the possibility of closeness or intimacy with a special few in order to make weak connections with hundreds of "friends." Also, social media offers the opportunity to wait, calculate, and edit our self-presentation. Users can craft an onstage performance that seems flawless. But according to *social penetration theory,* vulnerability—not perceived perfection—is the path that leads to intimacy (see Chapter 8).

Referring to in-person romantic relationships, comedian Chris Rock suggested we send our "representatives" rather than our true self on a first date. Over time, our representatives can't do the job and "we" start to show up. We're vulnerable, and that's where the relational work takes place.[38] It's through such conversations that authentic and intimate relationships emerge. This calls into question Walther's basic claim that online and offline communication can be equivalent given enough time.

Empathy. Turkle believes the ability to feel what others feel is developed through face-to-face conversations, not through social media. When online, it's easy to ignore, swipe left, or blow off a person we don't like. She cites a study that discovered a 40 percent decrease on standard tests of empathy among college students since the rise of social media.[39] Of course, face-to-face conversations can be messy; sometimes we may say the wrong thing or need to apologize. But Turkle insists it's only through conversations with humanizing eye contact that we learn how to empathize with others.[40]

While Walther doesn't address the impact of smartphones, Turkle claims they give "the false sense of demanding little and giving a lot."[41] She thinks a phone in a hand or placed on a table—even when turned off—can tug us away from thoughtfully discussing, genuinely loving, or actively listening. The devices that allow us to talk to people everywhere may hinder our ability to connect with those who are right here, right now. The digital world has changed since Walther launched SIP.

QUESTIONS TO SHARPEN YOUR FOCUS

1. *SIP* proposes that online communication conveys relational information just as well as face-to-face communication, with only one difference. What is that difference?

2. Recall a time when you felt particularly drawn to another person when communicating through social media. Why did you feel drawn to this person? Does the presence (or absence) of verbal cues or extended time explain your attraction?

3. The *hyperpersonal perspective* suggests that the effects of *sender, receiver, channel,* and *feedback* promote greater intimacy. Which factor do you think has the greatest relational impact? Which has the least?

4. Most research on the *warranting principle* focuses on Facebook. What low- and high-warrant information is available on Twitter? Instagram? Snapchat? LinkedIn? On which site is it easiest to craft a trustworthy persona, and why?

CONVERSATIONS

View this segment online at www.afirstlook.com.

Most of Em's conversation with Joe Walther centers on users who have a great affinity for the Internet. Granted, they can develop strong impressions of others online, but does true intimacy require face-to-face communication? Are heavy Internet users more in love with the medium than with their partners? Can those who are socially shy develop better relationships through the computer? What code of ethical online behavior would Walther suggest? Walther offers advice to online communicators who want to meet in person. He also discusses the scope of SIP and how building theory is a risky business.

A SECOND LOOK

Recommended resource: Joseph B. Walther, "Social Information Processing Theory: Impressions and Relationship Development Online," in *Engaging Theories in Interpersonal Communication: Multiple Perspectives* (2nd ed.), Dawn O. Braithwaite and Paul Schrodt (eds.), Sage, Thousand Oaks, CA, 2015, pp. 417–428.

Original statement: Joseph B. Walther, "Interpersonal Effects in Computer-Mediated Interaction: A Relational Perspective," *Communication Research,* Vol. 19, 1992, pp. 52–90.

Hyperpersonal perspective: Joseph B. Walther, "Computer-Mediated Communication: Impersonal, Interpersonal, and Hyperpersonal Interaction," *Communication Research,* Vol. 23, 1996, pp. 3–43.

Overview of major online communication theories: Joseph B. Walther, "Theories of Computer-Mediated Communication and Interpersonal Relations," in *The Handbook of Interpersonal Communication,* 4th ed., Mark L. Knapp and John A. Daly (eds.), Sage, Thousand Oaks, CA, 2011, pp. 443–479.

Testing hyperpersonal communication: L. Crystal Jiang, Natalie N. Bazarova, and Jeffrey T. Hancock, "The Disclosure–Intimacy Link in Computer-Mediated Communication: An Attributional Extension of the Hyperpersonal Model," *Human Communication Research,* Vol. 37, 2011, pp. 58–77.

Verbal cues of affection in online communication: Joseph B. Walther, Tracy Loh, and Laura Granka, "The Interchange of Verbal and Nonverbal Cues in Computer-Mediated and Face-to-Face Affinity," *Journal of Language and Social Psychology,* Vol. 24, 2005, pp. 36–65.

Time effects in online communication: Joseph B. Walther, "Time Effects in Computer-Mediated Groups: Past, Present, and Future," in *Distributed Work,* Pamela J. Hinds and Sara Kiesler (eds.), MIT, Cambridge, MA, 2002, pp. 235–257.

Warranting: Joseph B. Walther, Brandon Van Der Heide, Lauren M. Hamel, and Hillary C. Shulman, "Self-Generated Versus Other-Generated Statements and Impressions in Computer-Mediated Communication: A Test of Warranting Theory Using Facebook," *Communication Research,* Vol. 36, 2009, pp. 229–253.

Online communication and group conflict: Joseph B. Walther, "Computer-Mediated Communication and Virtual Groups: Applications to Interethnic Conflict," *Journal of Applied Communication Research,* Vol. 37, 2009, pp. 225–238.

Online dating: Catalina L. Toma, Jeffrey T. Hancock, and Nicole B. Ellison, "Separating Fact from Fiction: Deceptive Self-Presentation in Online Dating Profiles," *Personality and Social Psychology Bulletin,* Vol. 34, 2008, pp. 1023–1036.

For self-scoring quizzes for this and all other chapters, click on
Self-Help Quizzes under Theory Resources at
www.afirstlook.com

The term *maintenance* may call to mind an auto repair shop where workers with oil-stained coveralls and grease under their fingernails struggle to service or fix a well-worn engine. The work is hard, the conditions are messy, and the repair requires mechanics who have a good idea what they're doing.

This image of rugged work is appropriate when thinking about the ongoing effort required to maintain a close relationship. Forming a relational bond is often easier than sustaining it. The beginning stages of intimacy provoke excitement at discovering another human being who sees the world as we do, with the added touch of wonder that the person we like likes us as well. As the relationship becomes more established, however, irritating habits, conflict, jealousy, and boredom can be the friction that threatens to pull the engine apart. The owner's manual of a new "Intimacy" should warn that periodic maintenance is necessary for friends, romantic partners, and even blood relatives to make it for the long haul.

Of course, personal relationships aren't inanimate machines with interchangeable parts that can be adjusted with a wrench. Expanding the *maintenance* metaphor to living organisms underscores the importance of individualized attention in relational health. Humanist communication writer John Stewart refers to a pair's personal relationship as a "spiritual child," born as the result of their coming together.[1] His analogy stresses that a relationship requires continual care and nurture for sustained growth. Stewart thinks it's impossible to totally kill a relationship as long as one of the "parents" is still alive. Yet when people ignore or abuse the spiritual children they've created, the results are stunted or maimed relationships.

What does a healthy relationship look like? Through an extensive research program on relationship maintenance, Dan Canary (University of Utah) and Laura Stafford (Bowling Green State University) conclude that long-term satisfying relationships have at least four characteristics—*liking, trust, commitment,* and *control mutuality.*[2] The first three seem like old relational friends, but control mutuality is a less familiar concept. According to Canary and Stafford, it is "the degree to which partners agree about which of them should decide relational goals and behavioral routines."[3] They may have an egalitarian relationship, or perhaps one person regularly defers to the other but is genuinely happy to do so. Either way, they could each embrace the following statement: *Both of us are satisfied with the way we handle decisions.*

Stafford and Canary surveyed 662 people involved in extended romantic relationships to find out what maintenance behaviors promoted liking, trust, commitment, and control mutuality. They discovered five interpersonal actions that contribute to long-term relational satisfaction:[4]

Positivity—Cheerful, courteous talk; avoiding criticism.

Openness—Self-disclosure and frank talk about their relationship.

Assurances—Affirming talk about the future of their relationship.

Networking—Spending time together with mutual friends and family.

Sharing tasks—Working together on routine jobs, chores, and assignments.

Researchers have found that friends and family members use these maintenance behaviors, too.[5] But why do we maintain some relationships and not others? Scholars have suggested two possible answers. First, the *exchange-oriented* perspective appeals to social exchange theory (see Chapter 9). Theorists in this tradition, including Canary and Stafford, believe we maintain relationships when costs and rewards are distributed fairly between partners. In contrast, the *communally oriented* perspective argues that maintenance doesn't involve such economic calculations. Theorists in that tradition think we maintain relationships not because we calculate a favorable cost-reward payoff, but rather because we see the other person as part of who we are.[6]

I (Andrew) conducted a study comparing the exchange and communal explanations. The results weren't simple—although communal orientation was the strongest predictor of couples' maintenance communication, cost–reward ratio was a significant predictor as well.[7] How could rewards and costs matter to partners, yet also *not* matter to them? It's a theoretical puzzle that shows relationships defy easy explanations.

The three theories in this section agree that balancing relational needs is more complex than balancing tires. Relational dialectics theory and communication privacy management theory both claim that relational maintenance consists of intricate dialogue about *me, you,* and *we.* Sometimes that dialogue involves struggle, confusion, and frustration. Media multiplexity theory examines how people juggle the multiple communication channels that serve as the roadways for 21st-century relational maintenance. Although maintaining relationships is tricky, these theorists agree that smooth-running, long-lasting relationships are worth the effort.

Relational Dialectics Theory

of Leslie Baxter & Mikhail Bakhtin

When you hit the "play" button on your favorite music streaming service, the song you hear will probably say something about relationships. Perhaps you'll hear Adele sing about lost love and old regrets in her hit single "Hello." If you're a country fan, you might hear Florida Georgia Line and Luke Bryan rejoice in the wild freedom of young friendship in "This Is How We Roll." Or you might hear Taylor Swift's "Blank Space," a wry ballad about how she moves from one tumultuous affair to another—a narrative with even more meaning when you know that her previous hits have chronicled love stories with several celebrity boyfriends.

Talk about relationships fills Netflix, too. Shows like *Parks and Recreation* and *The Big Bang Theory* celebrate enduring bonds among a group of friends (as did the aptly named *Friends* a decade before). Romantic comedy movies feature a similar discourse of relational connection, while *The Break-Up* emphasizes a competing account of freedom after a relationship ends. And from the exploits of the Kardashians to the plural marriages of *Sister Wives,* reality shows feature relationship stories that seem bizarre compared to the experiences of our family and friends.

Of course, family and friends engage in their own relationship talk, too. A parent tells you to spend less time socializing with friends. A friend urges you to blow off your parents. Students in your theory course gossip about a budding classroom romance. And there's a good chance your instructor has already chimed in with interpersonal advice of his or her own. Whether from people we know or the media we consume, we cannot escape this flood of relational talk.

Thus, when it's your turn to speak about relationships, University of Iowa emeritus professor Leslie Baxter believes your messages will flow from the discourses you've already heard. Her theory of relational dialectics treats such talk as the essence of close ties. The first time Baxter conducted a series of in-depth interviews, she quickly abandoned any hope of discovering scientific laws that neatly ordered the experiences of family, friends, and lovers. She saw no law of gravitational pull to predict interpersonal attraction, no coefficient of friction that would explain human conflict. Instead, she found people giving voice to competing discourses about their relationships.

By focusing on talk, Baxter separates relational dialectics theory from many of the other interpersonal theories in this book. Unsurprisingly, theories arising from the socio-*psychological* approach emphasize what goes on inside the mind: Uncertainty drives people to reduce it (Berger). The desire for intimacy causes self-disclosure (Altman and Taylor). Impression management online generates relationship development (Walther).

Baxter takes a different approach. Relational dialectics isn't being of two minds—the cognitive dilemma within the head of an individual who is grappling with conflicting desires. The term also isn't describing a struggle between two people. Rather, *relational dialectics* is about struggle between discourses, and these unceasing struggles are "located in the relationship between parties, produced and reproduced through the parties' joint communicative activity."[1] And despite the fact that we tend to think of struggle and competition as detrimental to intimate relationships, Baxter believes good things emerge from competing discourses. That's fortunate, because she also believes we can't avoid relational dialectics no matter how hard we try.

Relational dialectics
The dynamic and unceasing struggle between discourses about interpersonal relationships.

DISCOURSES THAT CREATE MEANING

Discourse
A set of propositions that cohere around a given object of meaning.

The central concept of relational dialectics theory is *discourse,* or "a set of propositions that cohere around a given object of meaning."[2] To picture how discourses shape the meaning of everyday objects, Baxter asks us to think about an apple.[3] Some discourses about apples emphasize health: after all, "An apple a day keeps the doctor away." But when baked with sugar and a buttery crust, the discourse of apples and health encounters competing discourses about the dangers of eating too much dessert. Other discourses question the practices that produce apples, urging us to buy apples that are organic and locally sourced. When you visit the store to buy those natural apples, the sticker price might invoke discourses you've heard about saving money. Which of these discourses best defines the apple? Baxter would say all of the above, and more: "The meaning of *apple* is pretty complex."[4] And if Granny Smiths are tough to figure out, interpersonal relationships present an even juicier challenge.

To help make sense of the world of discourse, Baxter draws heavily on the thinking of twentieth-century Russian intellectual Mikhail Bakhtin. He lived during the Soviet Union's Stalinist regime and experienced its brutal oppression of academics who dared to defy the dictator. Given the totalitarian government under which he suffered, it's no surprise that Bakhtin's philosophy criticized *monologue*—a mode of talking that emphasizes one official discourse and silences all others. Thus, he rejected an alternative Marxist version of dialectics—popular with Soviet thinkers at the time—that claimed all dialectical struggles reach an inevitable monologue of final resolution. In counterpoint, Bakhtin embraced *dialogue* as "a process in which unity and difference, in some form, are at play, both with and against one another."[5] We might envision Bakhtin's dialogue as a rambunctious town hall meeting where different voices vie for acceptance.

Monologue
Dominant talk that silences competing voices.

Dialogue
Multiple voices; talk where unity and difference play with and against one another.

In contrast to that public sphere of government, much of Bakhtin's scholarship considered how dialectics play out in popular fictional novels. He argued that a good book demonstrates dialogue in action. That might sound strange; after all, how could a story written by a single author be anything but a monologue? Bad literature may feature only the heavy-handed voice of a preachy author, but Bakhtin believed good literature bubbles with multiple characters voicing multiple perspectives. He upheld Dostoyevsky's work as a great example of dialogic fiction. But if you haven't tackled *The Brothers Karamazov,* you might picture the diverse voices of wise Dumbledore, sly Snape, bookish Hermione, and half-crazy Luna. As their voices affirm, intersect, and sometimes challenge each other, the meanings of the *Harry Potter* books emerge.

Baxter thinks the same spirit of dialogism animates interpersonal relationships. From that conviction, she's examined many types of ties, including friends, co-workers, and lovers. But for the remainder of the chapter, I'll primarily draw on examples from family relationships. Although Baxter believes discourses create any interpersonal connection, much of the recent research using the theory has investigated the family. Perhaps that's because many families feature a diverse cast of characters and discourses that rival any novel.

CAUGHT IN A CHAIN OF UTTERANCES

CMM theorists (see Chapter 6) believe what two people say in the moment is only part of the story. Baxter agrees. Talk reverberates with words spoken before, words yet to come, and words that speakers may never dare to voice. CMM theorists refer to these words as stories woven together. Baxter calls them *utterances* linked together in a *chain.* Adherents of both theories believe it's all very messy, and that's part of the fun of understanding it all.

Utterance chains
The central building blocks of meaning making, where utterances are linked to competing discourses near and far away, already spoken and not.

When I was a student, my (Andrew's) friend Bethany once told me about her mother's utterance: "It's your choice whether you want to come home during school break or not." Mom's meaning might sound straightforward: She's letting her daughter decide what to do. Baxter cautions against that hasty conclusion because the utterance exists in a chain that includes things the mother–daughter pair has said in the past and responses they anticipate in the future.

To understand Bethany's mom's utterance, Baxter insists we consider discourses on two dimensions. The first dimension categorizes discourses by *who speaks them: nearby* (or *proximal*) discourses that occur between the mother and daughter versus *distant* discourses spoken by other people, such as third parties and people in the broader culture. The second dimension categorizes discourses by *time: already-spoken* discourses in the past versus *not-yet-spoken* discourses anticipated in the future. Together, these intersect to form four "links" in the utterance chain that create the utterance's meaning. Considering these links might suggest why my friend voiced frustration about her mother's offer.

- *Nearby already-spoken* discourses are the relationship's history. Bethany might tell herself, *She's always talked about how she values my freedom, and she didn't object when I switched to a major she didn't like. On the other hand, last year she said I could decide whether to come home for break, but then she ripped into me when I went camping with friends instead.*

- *Nearby not-yet-spoken* discourses involve anticipated conversations with the other person in the future: *Maybe she learned from last year and won't nag me if I stay on campus. But if I don't go home now, I bet she'll demand that I come home during spring break.*

- *Distant already-spoken* discourses are past comments by those outside the relationship. These include cultural ideologies, such as those heard in the pop culture examples that began this chapter. Speaking from the ideology of individualism, Bethany might say to herself, *It's your choice; go home only if it makes you happy.* A collectivistic discourse might counter, *You should think about what your family really wants, too.* A religious discourse might command, *Honor your mother and father.* An academic discourse might declare, *Ignore your friends AND your family. Spend break in the library so you can raise your GPA.*

- *Distant not-yet-spoken* discourses imagine the evaluation of someone outside the relationship in the future. Her boyfriend might be such a third party: *If I do go home, my boyfriend will think I'm a wimp who can't stand up to my mom.* So is extended family: *If I don't go home, my aunts, uncles, and cousins will think I'm selfish.* Bakhtin was particularly interested in the future evaluation of a *superaddressee* whose moral authority is beyond question: "God, absolute truth, the court of dispassionate human conscience, the people, the court of history . . ."[6] If Bethany considers the ethical consequences of her choice, she's considering this superaddressee.

Superaddressee
An utterance's future audience whose moral authority is beyond question.

It's no wonder my friend had trouble deciding what to do. Among the competing discourses, at least one thread ties them together: Should Bethany honor her *connection* to her mother or her own individual *autonomy*? No matter what Bethany and her mom decide, the struggle between discourses of integration and discourses of separation will continue in their relationship. For Bakhtin and Baxter, this isn't bad news. They believe dialectical tension provides an opportunity to work out ways to mutually embrace the conflict between unity with and differentiation from each other. This competition between connection and autonomy appears again and again in relational dialectics research. So do two other discursive struggles.

THREE COMMON DIALECTICS THAT SHAPE RELATIONSHIPS

An uncountable number of discourses flow into our minds and out from our lips. And since these discourses often emerge from the cultural background, they don't occur at random. As Bakhtin put it, almost never are we "biblical Adams, dealing only with virgin and still unnamed objects, giving them names for the first time."[7] Rather, as we discuss supportive parents, clingy boyfriends, and know-it-all classmates, we echo discourses about relationships that we've heard before and expect to hear again.

Across hundreds of interviews about close ties, Baxter heard people voice three recurring themes: *integration–separation, stability–change,* and *expression–nonexpression.* In her first iteration of the theory, she called these *contradictions.* She no longer prefers that word because it may tempt people to think she's talking about psychological conflict between different desires (such as wanting connection versus wanting freedom). Baxter thinks we have such internal motivations, but because she takes communication seriously, she thinks cultural discourses create and shape them. So to make it clear she isn't talking about conflict between needs or between people, Baxter refers to these themes as *discursive struggles* or *competing discourses.*

Discursive struggles
Two or more discourses compete for dominance over meaning.

Internal dialectics
Discursive struggles played out within a relationship.

External dialectics
Discursive struggles played out between a couple and their community.

These oppositional pairs are listed on the left side of Figure 11–1. The terms within the chart label these discursive struggles as they address two different contexts. The Internal Dialectic column describes the three dialectics as they shape the relationship between two people. The External Dialectic column describes the dialectics as they create the relationship between two people and the community around them. Baxter would be disappointed if you think Figure 11–1 represents an exhaustive list of competing discourses. Accordingly, the ragged edge at the bottom of the figure suggests that these opposing forces are just the start of a much longer

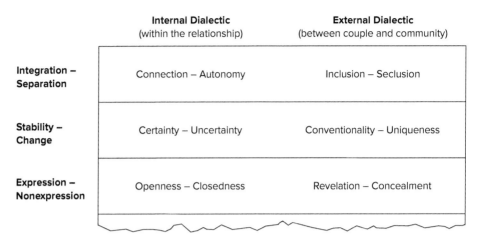

FIGURE 11-1   Typical Dialectical Tensions Experienced by Relational Partners
Based on Baxter and Montgomery, *Relating: Dialogues and Dialectics*

list of discursive struggles spoken by people as they jointly author their relationships in real time and space. As I describe these themes, you might try to think of when you've heard them voiced in popular media or by people you know.

Integration and Separation

Within any given relationship, Baxter regards the discursive struggle between connection and autonomy as foundational. If one side wins this *me-we* tug-of-war, the relationship loses:

> No relationship can exist by definition unless the parties sacrifice some individual autonomy. However, too much connection paradoxically destroys the relationship because the individual identities become lost.[8]

Integration–separation
A set of discursive struggles regarding independence versus interdependence; freedom versus intimacy.

The struggle between integration and separation shapes all relationships, but children and parents may especially struggle with this dialectic during the college years. Children invoke the discourse of *autonomy* when they stress their growing adult independence. In the next breath, though, they may emphasize their desire for ongoing *connection* with their parents. One dialectical study found college-aged daughters voicing this stay-away-close struggle. As one daughter said, "Sometimes the advice that I ask for, I do ask for it but what I receive is a little more dictatorial than I'm looking for."[9]

The discourses of integration and separation also address a pair's *inclusion* with and *seclusion* from other people in their social network. University of South Dakota researcher Carolyn Prentice heard both discourses when interviewing newly married couples and their in-laws. One bride described her desire for continuing inclusion with her parents: "My family's close and we'd always talked about when I got married, you know, my husband would come on our vacations . . ."[10] Her talk implied her husband's nearby already-spoken utterances: He'd expressed a desire to spend time with his family of origin, too. Couples also spoke about how they wanted time alone as a newly-married couple—a discourse sometimes marginalized by their in-laws' dominant discourse of inclusion.

Stability and Change

Many cultural discourses emphasize *certainty* in the family: We reward obedient children, applaud responsible teenagers, and condemn deadbeat parents. At the same time, other discourses revel in *uncertainty:* We plan surprise parties, go out to eat on a whim, and even arrange a spur-of-the-moment weekend getaway. Without the spice of variety to season our time together, relationships becomes bland, boring, and, ultimately, emotionally dead.

Stability-change
A set of discursive struggles regarding routine versus spontaneity; traditional versus novel.

Speaking of which, few topics produce as much uncertain discourse in families as death. Shortly after the passing of famed singer Prince, the press reported that he did not leave a will.[11] Some expressed astonishment that such a wealthy celebrity wouldn't have one. My wife wasn't surprised. When she was an attorney, she found people avoided such estate planning. A will and an advance directive aren't just legal documents—they're part of a distant already-spoken discourse that acknowledges the certainty of death. This discourse of certainty struggles with other talk that values uncertainty. As one participant put it in a dialectical study of end-of-life conversations, "I didn't want to believe she was terminally ill. I wonder if I didn't call more because I didn't want to have it confirmed that she was getting worse."[12]

The external version of certainty-uncertainty is conventionality-uniqueness. Discourses of conventionality consider how a relationship is similar to other relationships, while discourses of uniqueness emphasize difference. Baxter heard both discourses when she interviewed married couples who had renewed their vows. One woman stressed how the renewal ceremony communicated distant already-spoken discourses about the value of marriage: "It was important for our children to see

"Would you guys mind if I slept alone for a change?"
©by Don Orehek, reproduced by permission.

Communication Privacy Management Theory

of Sandra Petronio

Altman and Taylor's *social penetration theory* focused on self-disclosure as the primary way to develop close relationships (see Chapter 8). Yet Altman eventually concluded that openness is only part of the story. As Baxter observed, we also speak about our desire for privacy (see Chapter 11). Suppose you visit your school's health center because you're concerned about abnormal bleeding or a suspicious lump below the belt. Upon careful examination, the doctor says you might have cervical or testicular cancer; exploratory surgery will be necessary. While not life-threatening if caught in time, it is cancer, and you fear it could put at risk your ability to have children. Who will you tell right away—an immediate family member, a romantic partner, a good friend, maybe all three, or perhaps none of them?

Sandra Petronio, a communication professor at Indiana University–Purdue University Indianapolis, agrees with Altman that revealing this private information might strengthen your relationships with significant people in your life. The disclosure would also give them a chance to offer you comfort and perhaps help you figure out a course of action to deal with the disturbing diagnosis. However, disclosing your medical condition could stress your relationships if it turns out that people can't handle your scary and potentially embarrassing news, or if they carelessly post about it on social media. And even if people you confide in respond well, sharing confidential information always reduces your privacy.

Petronio sees *communication privacy management theory* (CPM) as a description of a privacy management system that contains three main parts. The first part of the system, *privacy ownership,* contains our privacy boundaries that encompass information we have but others don't know. Privacy boundaries can range from thin and porous filters to thick, impenetrable barriers that shield deep, dark secrets.

Privacy boundaries
A metaphor to show how people think of the borders between private and public information.

Privacy control, the second part of the system, involves our decision to share private information with another person. Petronio considers this the engine of privacy management. Decisions to share information or relinquish some control also reshape the boundaries contained in the privacy ownership part of the system.

Privacy turbulence, the third part of the privacy management system, comes into play when managing private information doesn't go the way we expect.[1] Perhaps your friend revealed your secret after you laid down a strict-confidence rule. The decisions you make in the aftermath of the breach are directed at reducing turbulence. Having a mental image of these three parts of the privacy management system is helpful in understanding the five core principles of Petronio's CPM.[2] The first four principles deal with issues of privacy ownership and control; the fifth involves privacy turbulence—the turmoil that erupts when rules are broken. The principles are:

1. People believe they own and have a right to control their private information.
2. People control their private information through the use of personal privacy rules.
3. When others are told or discover a person's private information, they become co-owners of that information.
4. Co-owners of private information need to negotiate mutually agreeable privacy rules about telling others.
5. When co-owners of private information don't effectively negotiate and follow mutually held privacy rules, boundary turbulence is the likely result.

Although these five statements seem deceptively simple, the management processes they describe are often quite complex. In the rest of the chapter I'll unpack the mental considerations and communication behaviors that each principle summarizes. The evidence for their validity comes from more than 100 research studies over a wide range of situations where there's a dialectical tension between privacy and disclosure. Since Petronio's own research has cut across interpersonal, family, online, and health communication contexts, I'll continue to use a variety of medical issues to illustrate how people manage their private information.

1. OWNERSHIP AND CONTROL OF PRIVATE INFORMATION

People believe they own and have a right to control their private information.

Private information
The content of potential disclosures; information that can be owned.

Instead of talking about *self-disclosure,* as many relational theorists do, Petronio refers to the *disclosure of private information.* There are four reasons she favors this term. In the first place, a lot of the private information we tell others isn't about ourselves. The revelation may be about other people or convey news of an impersonal nature. Another reason she avoids the self-disclosure label is that it's usually associated with interpersonal intimacy. For example, all three theories in the Relationship Development section assume that self-disclosure is a primary way to develop close personal ties (see Chapters 8–10). Yet Petronio notes that there are many other motives for disclosing private information.[3] For example, we could desire to relieve a burden, prevent a wrong, make an impression, gain control, or simply enjoy self-expression.

A third reason Petronio chooses to talk about the disclosure of private information is that the phrase has a neutral connotation, as opposed to self-disclosure, which has a positive feel. The outcome of disclosing private information may turn out well, but as bartenders and hairdressers can attest, it might be unwelcome—a real downer. Finally, while the term *self-disclosure* focuses on the unilateral act of the discloser, Petronio's preferred description directs attention to the content of what's said and how the confidant handles this now-not-so-private information. In that sense she thinks it's a more complete communication theory than prior approaches to self-disclosure.

How do we regard the private information we manage? The first principle of communication privacy management theory is quite clear: We see it as ours; we believe it belongs to us. Whether that perception is accurate isn't the issue. Our conviction is so strong that Petronio defines *privacy* as "the feeling one has the right to own private information."[4] You may feel that way about your overall GPA or even the grade you get in this course.

Privacy
The feeling that one has the right to own private information.

Ownership conveys rights as well as obligations. Privacy bolsters our sense of autonomy and makes us feel less vulnerable. That's the upside. But Petronio also suggests that ownership of private information can be a liability. She claims that when we are privy to something others don't know, we understand we are responsible for that information and will be held accountable for how we handle it. That's why we seek to control who else gets to know.

Within the context of medical privacy, probably no group faces more pressure for disclosure than those who have an observable stigma. For example, complete strangers often ask intrusive questions of those who are paralyzed that they wouldn't think of asking a nondisabled person. In a research study entitled "Just How Much Did That Wheelchair Cost?" University of Nebraska communication professor Dawn Braithwaite reports how people with physical disabilities manage their privacy boundaries. She found that in most cases, people who have paraplegia will answer a question if they deem it appropriate to the discussion or if it's posed by a kid. But if they think the question comes out of sheer nosiness or morbid curiosity, they avoid answering or respond with anger. One person confined to a wheelchair admitted, "I'm not beyond rolling over toes, really. I have been in situations where . . . there's really no other alternative."[5]

The people Braithwaite interviewed obviously believe they own their private information, and they actively work to maintain control of what, when, and with whom it is shared. The first principle of CPM says that's true for all of us. Our sense of ownership motivates us to create boundaries that will control the spread of what we know. The second principle of CPM addresses how thick those boundaries might be.

2. RULES FOR CONCEALING AND REVEALING

People control their private information through the use of personal privacy rules.

Rule-based theory
A theory that assumes we can best understand people's freely chosen actions if we study the system of rules they use to interpret and manage their lives.

Petronio refers to communication privacy management theory as a *rule-based theory*.[6] An easy way to grasp what she means is to remember that people usually have rules for managing their private information. When Petronio spots a pattern of disclosure within a group of people and these folks offer similar explanations for their actions, she articulates the internalized rules that appear to guide their decisions. These rules are guides for interpretation rather than ironclad laws. Yet in practice, they help people feel they have control over their private information.

CPM maintains that five factors play into the way we develop our own privacy rules: *culture, gender, motivation, context,* and *risk–benefit ratios*. These foundational criteria are evident in a study Petronio conducted among children and adolescents who reported that they were victims of sexual abuse.[7] After gaining permission from their parents, Petronio asked 38 victims between the ages of 7 and 18 to describe how they made the decision to tell someone what had happened. I'll draw upon her findings to illustrate the five constants in rule-making for privacy.

Culture. Cultures differ on the value of openness and disclosure. The United States is a patchwork of many co-cultures, but Petronio notes that, in general, US citizens are highly individualistic. This means they have a bias toward locking doors, keeping secrets, and preserving privacy. Regarding victims of sexual abuse, there's no firm evidence among Anglos, Hispanics, African Americans, or Asians that one group is more at risk than the others. But other researchers have found a difference when it comes to who suffers in silence. Presumably because of the Asian emphasis on submissiveness, obedience, family loyalty, and sex-talk taboos, Asian American children who are sexually abused are less likely than other kids to tell their mothers.[8]

Gender. Popular wisdom suggests that women disclose more than men, yet research on this issue is mixed at best. What is clear, however, is that both men and women more easily reveal private information to a woman than to a man.[9] This may be especially true when a young girl is sexually abused by an older man. As one female victim explained why she chose to tell her mother, "She's my mom and she's a grown-up, you know, and she's a girl."[10]

Motivation. Petronio emphasizes attraction and liking as interpersonal motives that can loosen privacy boundaries that could not otherwise be breached. That's certainly the case when a sexual perpetrator has sworn the victim to secrecy under threat of dire consequences. Some victims lowered their barriers and provided access when they felt the additional force of reciprocity. As one girl reported, "A sudden bond formed between [us by] her saying, you know, 'I was molested' and knowing that all of a sudden I wasn't all by myself. . . . I could trust her because I knew that she could feel the scariness. . . ."[11] In 2017, the #MeToo movement provided that sense of reciprocity as survivors posted their stories on social media.

Context. Traumatic events can temporarily or permanently disrupt the influence of culture, gender, and motivation when people craft their rules for privacy. Petronio has in mind the diagnosis of AIDS, the suicide or murder of a loved one, the loss of a limb, physical paralysis, experiencing the carnage of war or natural disaster, and sexual abuse as a child. Any of these events can generate privacy boundaries that are initially impenetrable. The sufferer first struggles to cope; talk may come later. The abused children who spoke to Petronio often shared what it took for them to feel secure before they were willing to be open about their experience. The abuser had to be away from the home or out of the car and doors had to be locked, with just the abused child and confidant together. Disclosure usually came while doing ordinary things together such as cooking, washing dishes, watching TV, or shopping. These mundane activities, which require no eye contact, seemed to offer the child a sense of normalcy and control that made a very abnormal conversation possible.

Risk–benefit ratio. Think back to the mental calculations that social exchange theory claims we make before deciding how we'll act (see Chapter 8). We add up the benefits and subtract the costs of each option in order to do what we think will have the best outcome. Risk–benefit ratios do the math for revealing as well as concealing private information. Typical benefits for revealing are relief from stress, gaining social support, drawing closer to the person we tell, and the chance to influence others. Realistic risks are embarrassment, rejection, diminished power, and everyone finding out our secret. All of these benefits and risks can come into play when sexually abused children adopt a rule that will guide their decision to speak out or keep silent. Because the stakes are high and it's so hard for them to know what response they'll get, kids sometimes use partial disclosure to test the waters before fully diving in. For example, one girl in Petronio's study said to her mother, "Mom, I've got to tell you something. He's been walking around the house with no clothes on."[12] When the mother showed that she believed her daughter, the girl then told her what her stepfather had done.

3. DISCLOSURE CREATES A CONFIDANT AND CO-OWNER

When others are told or discover a person's private information, they become co-owners of that information.

Collective privacy boundary
An intersection of personal privacy boundaries of co-owners of private information, all of whom are responsible for the information.

Sandra Petronio argues that a person can't just consider self in deciding whether to conceal or reveal. The act of disclosing private information creates a confidant and draws that person into a *collective privacy boundary,* whether willingly or reluctantly.

What does co-ownership mean? First, the discloser must realize that the personal privacy boundary encompassing the information has morphed into a collective boundary that seldom shrinks back to being solely personal. That would only be possible if the confidant were to die or suffer loss of memory. Once you let the cat out of the bag, it's hard to stuff him back in. Thus, those who own private information should consider carefully before sharing it with others. Second, as co-owners, people tend to feel a sense of responsibility for the information. That doesn't mean, however, that they perceive an equal responsibility. For example, the original owner may still feel like the sole titleholder and assume others will follow his or her lead when access to the information is an issue. Despite this perception, "once the

©Eric Lewis/The New Yorker Collection/The Cartoon Bank

information is known, others 'in the know' may have their own interpretation of how the information should be managed."[13] Finally, those who had the information foisted upon them may be much more casual about protecting it than those who sought it.

Communication professors Paige Toller (University of Nebraska Omaha) and Chad McBride (Creighton University) explored the complexities of co-owning private information within families. Specifically, they studied how parents manage privacy boundaries with their children when a family member dies or has a terminal illness.[14] Based on their interviews, they found that parents usually wanted to share information about a family member's death or illness with a young child in the interest of being open and honest. On the other hand, they often withheld information out of concern for the child's emotional welfare. They also concealed the news because they were afraid that their children might not make the most responsible judgments as co-owners of the information. Parents who choose to share sensitive information with a young child often discover that their own privacy boundary may be thick, but the child's is paper-thin or nonexistent.

4. COORDINATING MUTUAL PRIVACY BOUNDARIES

Co-owners of private information need to negotiate mutually agreeable privacy rules about telling others.

Mutual privacy boundary
A synchronized collective privacy boundary that co-owners share because they have negotiated common privacy rules.

This pivotal fourth principle of CPM is where Petronio moves from being descriptive to prescriptive. With the first three principles she's been mapping out how people handle their private information—they think they own it and they control it (Principle 1) through the use of privacy rules (Principle 2). If they disclose some of that private information, the recipients become co-owners of a patch of common informational territory, which entails rights as well as responsibilities (Principle 3). Principle 4 assumes that the privacy boundaries that co-owners place around this particular piece of information won't necessarily look the same. But Petronio thinks that for the sake of relational harmony they ought to be congruent, so this principle is a plea for co-owners to negotiate *mutual privacy boundaries*—collective boundaries that people shape together. Or, using the map metaphor, she urges parties to collaboratively draw the same borders around their common piece of informational real estate. If you receive private information from someone, Petronio believes it's best to think of yourself as a good steward or protective guardian over that information. This way, there's less chance of disagreement about how the information gets handled. Just as good real estate stewards protect the property entrusted to them, good stewards over private information are on guard to protect that information from falling into the wrong hands.

The overall process of co-managing collective boundaries that Petronio envisions isn't simple. These negotiations focus on *boundary ownership, boundary linkage,* and *boundary permeability*. In order to illustrate what's involved in coordinating boundary management rules, I'll use the privacy/disclosure issue that's received the most attention from health communication practitioners and scholars—HIV status.

Consider the plight of Nate, who goes to see his doctor because of a persistent fever and swollen glands. After running a series of tests, the doctor regretfully informs Nate that he's HIV positive. She assures Nate that this isn't a death sentence. With the advent of antiretroviral therapy, Nate may never have to experience the worsening, telltale symptoms of AIDS. But the news comes as a real blow. When he was in college, Nate engaged in risky sexual behavior that his wife,

Becky, knows nothing about. He's embarrassed and dreads telling her. Yet even if his state didn't have a mandatory partner notification program, he feels morally bound to tell her—if for no other reason than she needs to be tested and protected from his infection. He believes Becky will "stand by her man," but fears rejection from anyone else who hears about his condition. He doesn't want his extended family, friends, or co-workers to find out. But once he tells Becky, she may have different ideas about who else should hear and how much they should be told. For the sake of their relationship, Petronio believes they need to synchronize their privacy rules.

You might be wondering about the question of timing. Should Nate try to get Becky to agree about who she can or can't share the news with *before* he drops the bombshell, or does he need to share the news first and trust that *afterward* they can reach an agreement on how to handle the information? Petronio isn't too concerned about the timing. Whether the rules are worked out before or after the information is shared, she thinks Nate and Becky's relationship will be healthier *whenever* they reach a mutual agreement about how to handle the private information.

Boundary Ownership—Who Should Decide?

Boundary ownership
The rights and responsibilities that co-owners of private information have to control its spread.

Deliberate confidant
A recipient who sought out private information.

Reluctant confidant
A co-owner of private information who did not seek it nor want it.

Not all *boundary ownership* is 50–50. So when a secret is shared, how do people decide who calls the shots? Petronio thinks it might depend on how the recipient found the private information in the first place.[15] The *deliberate confidant* intentionally seeks private information. Sometimes they do so in order to help others out. For example, doctors, counselors, attorneys, and clergy solicit personal information only after they assure clients they have a privacy policy that severely limits their right to reveal the information to others. At other times, deliberate confidants are just nosy. As a general rule of thumb, the more eager people are to take on the role of confidant, the less control they have over what they hear.

Conversely, a *reluctant confidant* doesn't want the disclosure, doesn't expect it, and may find the revealed information an unwelcome burden. Picture the hapless airplane traveler who must listen to his or her seatmate's life story. This sort of reluctant confidant usually doesn't feel a strong obligation to follow the privacy guidelines of the discloser. If the reluctant recipient comes across the information by accident, he or she will be even less likely to cede control of revealing/concealing to the original owner. So if someone comes across our private thoughts jotted in a journal or encoded in an email, those thoughts could become quite public.

As for Becky, her role as Nate's confidant probably shifts when he makes his startling revelation. She didn't initiate this health conversation and, like many long-term partners, she may at first listen with half an ear out of a sense of obligation. But once he drops the bombshell, she will be all ears and deliberately probe for more details.

Shareholder
A confidant fully committed to handling private information according to the original owner's privacy rules.

Stakeholder
A confidant who deserves access and control regarding private information and the rules for sharing it.

How then will Becky and Nate negotiate how they share the health information moving forward? As the original owner, Nate might feel he has a greater stake in how the information should be handled. He may even believe he should have total control of how it's used. If Becky agrees that Nate has the right to call the shots, Petronio refers to her as a *shareholder* who is "fully vested in keeping the information according to the original owner's privacy rules."[16]

But given the impact of Nate's disclosure, Becky might believe she should be a *stakeholder*: someone who deserves access and control.[17] As with two business partners who jointly manage their bank account data, Becky could feel she deserves an equal say regarding health information about her sexual partner. Given Becky's probable fear, hurt, and anger that Nate never told her of his possible exposure to HIV, we might expect her to follow her own privacy rules rather than be constrained by his. If she later discovers that Nate has infected her with HIV, his rules will be history.

Boundary Linkage—Who Else Gets to Know?

Boundary linkage

An alliance formed by co-owners of private information as to who else should be able to know.

Boundary linkage is the process of the confidant being linked into the privacy boundary of the person who revealed the information. When Nate discloses his HIV status to Becky, she'll share at least some responsibility for what happens with that information in the future. As for Nate, his privacy boundary will morph into an expanded, joint boundary of a different shape. He clearly wants his condition to remain the couple's secret, but will that happen?

The major consideration in boundary linkage is the nature of the pair's relationship. When the revealer and recipient have a close, trusting relationship, there's a good chance the recipient will deal with the new information the way the discloser wants. But even though Nate and Becky would both say they've had five years of a loving marriage, news that her husband is HIV positive is likely to rock Becky's world. Her first question will probably be, *How did this happen?* And she won't be satisfied with a vague answer. As Nate reveals a sexual past that he always felt he alone owned, Becky's trust in him may take a big hit. From her perspective, she had a right to know about anything that could so profoundly affect her life and their relationship. She might indeed be committed to stay with Nate "in sickness and in health as long as we both shall live," but that doesn't mean she'll agree to a shroud of secrecy.

If the couple follows Petronio's advice to negotiate who else gets to know, they might bring up the following considerations, each of which is supported by research on the privacy and disclosure of HIV status.[18] Becky might insist that she can't live with the stress of keeping Nate's infection secret; she's willing to keep her father in the dark but needs to tell her mother. She also wants the ongoing social support of at least one close friend who knows what she's living with and can help her cope.

For his part, Nate voices his fear of the prejudice that he knows people living with HIV encounter.[19] When people find out he has HIV, he's apt to lose his job, his buddies, and the respect of others. He can't possibly tell his folks about the diagnosis because they know nothing of his sexual past. Nate imagines his shocked father bemoaning, "I can't even think about this," and then slamming the door on him forever. As for Becky telling her mother, he's seen her close-knit family in action. If his mother-in-law finds out, he's sure the rest of the family will know by the end of the day. At this point, Nate and Becky aren't even close to agreeing on who else can know what they know.

Boundary Permeability—How Much Information Can Flow?

Boundary permeability

The extent to which a boundary permits private information to flow to third parties.

Boundary permeability refers to the degree that privacy boundaries are porous. Some boundaries are protected by ironclad rules, with those in the know sworn to secrecy. These barriers are impervious to penetration. Petronio refers to such informational barriers as *closed, thick,* or *stretched tight.* Often that information is quarantined because public revelation would be highly embarrassing for those in the inner circle.

At the other extreme, some boundaries are quite porous. Petronio describes them as *open, thin,* or *loosely held.* Information permeates them easily. As barriers to disclosure, they are a facade. To the extent that privacy rules are supposed to check the flow of insider information, they are honored in the breach. As the movie *Mean Girls* illustrates, some confidences are meant to be spread.

Permeability is a matter of degree. Many privacy rules are crafted to be filters, letting some private information seep through, while other related facts are closely guarded. You may wonder how this could apply to Nate and Becky's situation. Isn't HIV infection like pregnancy—an either/or thing? Biologically, yes, but Petronio describes a number of ways that disclosure could be partial. For example, Nate might talk about movies that sympathetically portray people living with AIDS, enthusing about the Oscar-winning performance of Sean Penn in *Milk.* Or, similar to the sexually abused children Petronio interviewed, he could drop hints about his condition and watch for signs that others would handle further disclosure well. Along that line, some LGBTQ people living with HIV reveal their sexual orientation to others first, later speaking of their HIV status only if the response to the first disclosure is nonjudgmental. As with boundary linkage and boundary ownership, collaborative boundary permeability doesn't happen by accident.

If Nate and Becky can't find a way to coordinate their different views on boundary ownership, they're almost guaranteeing a turbulent future. The fifth principle describes what that might look like.

5. BOUNDARY TURBULENCE—RELATIONSHIPS AT RISK

When co-owners of private information don't effectively negotiate and follow mutually held privacy rules, boundary turbulence is the likely result.

Boundary turbulence
Disruption of privacy management and relational trust that occurs when collective privacy boundaries aren't synchronized.

When boundary coordination fails, turbulence is the result. Petronio uses the metaphor of *boundary turbulence* to refer to "disruptions in the way that co-owners control and regulate the flow of private information to third parties."[20] She likes to describe turbulence with a boat metaphor. Imagine sitting in a sailboat on a placid lake. A speedboat passes by and creates a wake that smacks the side of your boat and rocks it back and forth. Similarly, boundary turbulence can rock your relationships with the havoc it creates. According to Petronio, just as you might seek to steady the boat's rocking while hanging on to keep your balance, people will react to turbulence in an attempt to regulate the disturbed relationships left in its wake.

Petronio lists a variety of factors that can lead to boundary turbulence, which I'll lump into three categories—fuzzy boundaries, intentional breaches, and mistakes.[21] I'll illustrate the first two from research she's conducted on family and friends as health care advocates—the triangular interactions that occur when patients bring someone with them to their doctor appointments.[22]

Fuzzy Boundaries

Petronio has found that patients and the advocates they bring with them have rarely discussed what can and can't be revealed—typical of many interactions where private information is shared. She places the onus on the friend or family member: "Curiously, these informal advocates did not appear to confer with the patient before entering the medical situation to find out when or if the advocate should disclose private medical information."[23] Having no recognized mutual boundaries and only a vague idea of the patient's expectations, advocates resort to using their own privacy rules to guide what they say. The result is turbulence and a patient who is often embarrassed or unhappy.

In like manner, doctor-patient confidentiality can be compromised. As one doctor admitted, "When the patient is accompanied by a friend or relative, we're often unclear about that companion's function in the interview."[24] From a legal standpoint, once the patient invites someone else into the mix, the physician no longer has to be concerned about confidentiality. But the patient may be shocked when the companion hears the doctor reveal alarming test results, refer to a previous embarrassing medical condition, or offer a depressing prognosis.

Intentional Breaches

Sometimes those who are now in the know understand that the original owner will be horrified if they blab the secret, yet they reveal it anyway. They may do so to purposely hurt the original owner, or simply because breaking the confidence works to their personal advantage. A painful romantic breakup is the classic case when the spurned partner lashes out by revealing intimate details that make the other look bad. Petronio didn't run across disloyal breaches in her study of unofficial health advocates, but she did discover intentional boundary crossings when advocates faced a *confidentiality dilemma*. These occurred when patients said things to their doctor that advocates knew weren't true or avoided revealing embarrassing medical information that advocates knew was important for the physician to know.

Confidentiality dilemma
The tragic moral choice confidants face when they must breach a collective privacy boundary in order to promote the original owner's welfare.

Petronio cites the example of a man who tells his cardiologist that he quit smoking after his heart surgery. His daughter who's present is in a quandary. She could respect her father's privacy but by her silence put his health at risk. Or she could violate family privacy rules by revealing his continued smoking so that the doctor can make an informed medical decision. She faces a tragic moral choice where whatever she does is wrong. Petronio found that advocates placed in this position opt for health over privacy, and speculates, "Perhaps in cases when safety or well-being is at stake, privacy issues seem less significant for those trying to help."[25] In support of this interpretation, she notes that one man poignantly explained why he breached his wife's privacy boundary—*because I did not want my wife to die.*

Mistakes

Not all boundary and relational turbulence comes from privacy rules out of sync or the intentional breach of boundaries. Sometimes people create turmoil by making mistakes, such as letting secrets slip out when their guard is down or simply forgetting who might have access to the information. Many college social media users have attempted to scrub a piece of information they posted for their friends without thinking about the fact that future employers could also see the post. Other users make errors of judgment by discussing private information in the public arena of many Facebook friends. Another kind of mistake is a *miscalculation in timing.* Doctors and nurses have been known to phone people in the middle of the workday to tell them they have cancer. There's no good way to deliver that devastating news. But to do it at a time when the person may be interacting with co-workers takes away the chance to process the stark reality in private.

David's application log suggests that it may not make much difference whether a barrier breach is a mistake or intentional. The harm is done and the relationship suffers.

> When I was a freshman I had just broken up with my longtime girlfriend and it was affecting my play on the football field. The quarterback coach called me into his office and asked me what was wrong. As I didn't have anyone else to confide in, I told him the situation. I expected our privacy boundaries to be ruled by player–coach confidentiality. However, that same day at practice, he created boundary turbulence after I threw a bad pass. He asked me if I was "thinking about my girlfriend taking body shots off frat boys while doing keg stands." He said this in front of everyone. I can't say if it was an intentional breach or a mistake, but I now refuse to disclose any of my private information to that man.

CRITIQUE: KEEN DIAGNOSIS, GOOD PRESCRIPTION, CURE IN PROGRESS?

CPM nicely fulfills five of the six criteria for a good interpretive theory. Petronio painstakingly maps out the different ways people handle private information and discerns why they make the choices they do. This *understanding of people* is furthered by the *qualitative research* she and other communication scholars conduct to expand their knowledge of privacy management. Typically their research takes the form of open-ended interviews such as those Petronio conducted with sexually abused children, but Petronio also draws on the results of quantitative research to support the theory's conclusions. This extensive research and the fact that CPM provides a needed focus on privacy, where there was previously a theoretical void, has created a *community of agreement* on the worth of the theory among communication scholars. That community even extends to objective scholars—a rare thing for an interpretive theory. In medical terms, CPM provides an astute diagnosis of the use and abuse of privacy rules.

As for *clarification of values,* CPM presents privacy as valuable in its own right, not relationally inferior to openness, transparency, or self-disclosure. Additionally, Petronio upholds mutually coordinated privacy rules as the best way to establish effective boundaries that protect co-owned private information. It's a bit of a stretch to say the theory calls for a radical *reform of society* the way some critical theories do, but Petronio clearly believes that healthy relationships within a community depend on trust and that they'll be less at risk when people follow her research-based prescription for the prevention of turbulence.

The interpretive criterion that CPM does not meet well is *aesthetic appeal,* which is a matter of both style and clarity. Petronio's organizational style is one of arranging insights into multiple lists that result in a confusing array of classifications. Clarity is a problem as well. For example, in Principle 4 and throughout much of her writing, Petronio indicates that people who co-own private information should negotiate mutual privacy rules. Yet in another summary version of CPM, Petronio seems to directly contradict this principle. She writes, "As co-owners, the recipients have a responsibility to care for the information in the way that the original owner desires."[26] That sounds more like acquiescence or submission than negotiation. It's also confusing, as is Petronio's frequent use of qualifiers such as *may be, tend to be, possibly, perhaps,* and *sometimes.*

Petronio is aware of these problems. In her 40 years of work with the theory, she has acknowledged its ambiguities[27] and repackaged concepts for improved clarity. Her efforts have made writing this chapter easier.[28] In 2013, an entire issue of the *Journal of Family Communication* was devoted to CPM. In a preview to the issue's articles, Petronio provided a brief status report on the theory, noting the trend in CPM research to make "theoretical refinements."[29] We hope this trend continues and results in more clarity and less ambiguity.

Two gaps in the theory coverage bear mentioning. Petronio writes convincingly about the value of co-owner negotiation and how quickly trust can be lost when privacy rules are breached.[30] Yet she doesn't offer insight on how to conduct those negotiations, nor does she describe after-the-fact remedies for the mistrust that boundary turbulence stirs up. CPM needs to be expanded to suggest *how* to effectively negotiate mutual boundaries, and to offer *ways and means* to settle the turbulence that occurs when collective privacy boundaries are violated.

For years, Petronio has acknowledged that CPM is a work in progress. In 2004 she instructed readers to "please stand by,"[31] and in her 2013 report she encouraged us to "stay tuned."[32] For some time, she's been working on a new book about CPM that she promises will address the aforementioned thorny issues. Hopefully, after the next revision appears, there will be less need for a "new and improved" version of CPM.

QUESTIONS TO SHARPEN YOUR FOCUS

1. In Principle 2, Petronio cites five foundational criteria that affect our *personal privacy rules*. Which factor most shapes the rules you adopt? Is there one factor that seems to include or trump the other four? Do you think any factors should be added to the list?

2. Petronio says that *ownership* and *control of private information* don't always go together. Can you imagine a situation where you are the sole owner of a secret yet have no control over its disclosure or discovery?

3. CPM states that those who are privy to private information can avoid *boundary turbulence* by *negotiating mutual privacy rules*. Why do you think many *disclosers* and their *confidants* fail to have this discussion?

4. You want to share a secret with a friend but fear embarrassment. How would CPM explain this situation? How about *social penetration theory? Relational dialectics theory?* Where do the theories agree and disagree?

CONVERSATIONS

View this segment online at www.afirstlook.com.

In her conversation with Glenn, Sandra Petronio says that people believe they own and control their private information. When information is shared, it's crucial for the original owner to set expectations and negotiate with the co-owner as to how that information ought to be managed. When those expectations are violated or aren't negotiated at all, turbulence results. Petronio reflects on how turbulence can sometimes lead to complete privacy breakdowns, and how difficult it can be to manage relationships after that occurs. She also shares what she thinks is missing from the theory.

A SECOND LOOK

Recommended resource: Sandra Petronio, *Boundaries of Privacy: Dialectics of Discourse,* State University of New York, Albany, NY, 2002.

Summary statement: Sandra Petronio and Wesley T. Durham, "Communication Privacy Management Theory: Significance for Interpersonal Communication," in *Engaging Theories in Interpersonal Communication: Multiple Perspectives,* 2nd ed., Dawn O. Braithwaite and Paul Schrodt (eds.), Sage, Thousand Oaks, CA, 2015, pp. 335–347.

Current state of the art: Special Issue on Communication Privacy Management Theory, *Journal of Family Communication,* Vol. 13, 2013, pp. 1–75.

Five principles of CPM applied: Ashley Duggan and Sandra Petronio, "When Your Child Is in Crisis: Navigating Medical Needs with Issues of Privacy Management," in *Parent and Children Communicating with Society,* Thomas J. Socha (ed.), Routledge, New York, 2009, pp. 117–132.

Initial version: Sandra Petronio, "Communication Boundary Management: A Theoretical Model of Managing Disclosure of Private Information Between Married Couples," *Communication Theory,* Vol. 1, 1991, pp. 311–335.

Research review on secrecy: Sandra Petronio (ed.), *Balancing the Secrets of Private Disclosure,* Lawrence Erlbaum, Mahwah, NJ, 2000.

Development of CPM: Sandra Petronio, "Road to Developing Communication Privacy Management Theory: Narrative in Process, Please Stand By," *Journal of Family Communication,* Vol. 4, 2004, pp. 193–207.

Confidants: Sandra Petronio and Jennifer Reierson, "Regulating the Privacy of Confidentiality: Grasping the Complexities through Communication Privacy Management Theory," in *Uncertainty, Information Management, and Disclosure Decisions: Theories and Applications,* Tamara D. Afifi and Walid A. Afifi (eds.), Routledge, New York, 2009, pp. 365–383.

CPM and social media: Jeffrey T. Child, Angela R. Duck, Laura A. Andrews, Maria Butauski, and Sandra Petronio, "Young Adults' Management of Privacy on Facebook with Multiple Generations of Family Members," *Journal of Family Communication,* Vol. 15, 2015, pp. 349–367.

Media Multiplexity Theory

of Caroline Haythornthwaite

As I write this, it's the day after my (Andrew's) birthday. Yesterday I watched the Facebook timeline birthday posts roll in from family and colleagues, from casual acquaintances and valued friends. One of those friends is Bree McEwan, a professor of computer-mediated communication at DePaul University. Her message was different from the standard "happy birthday" greeting. She wrote, "Hope you receive lots of well wishes through lots of channels!" To most people, her message sounds outright weird. It could make sense that the more *people* who wish me a happy birthday, the happier birthday I will have. But what would the number of communication *channels* have to do with that?

At any rate, her hope was realized. My birthday was a multimedia experience:

- When I woke in the morning, I found cards on the table from my wife and kids.
- During the morning church service, my friend Heath tapped me on the shoulder from the pew behind and said, "Happy birthday."
- My Aunt Karmen sang me a happy birthday voicemail.
- My college friend Ashley emailed to tell me how much she appreciates me.
- My former students Kaitlin and Sam texted me their birthday messages.

By my count, I received birthday greetings through at least six communication channels. And that's hardly an exhaustive list of the media available to me. You can probably think of several other options, including Instagram, Snapchat, Skype, and Twitter. Given the pace at which new social media websites and apps appear, I wouldn't be surprised if you're using a technology that hasn't even emerged as of this writing.

McEwan is part of a growing group of scholars who examine the multiple channels we use to maintain our interpersonal relationships. So am I. Much of our work builds from that of Syracuse University professor Caroline Haythornthwaite. She is the chief theorist behind media multiplexity theory, which originally took a cybernetic approach to understanding how and why we use different communication channels (see Chapter 4). The theory claims that our social networks powerfully influence the media we use, including why we might choose one medium over another to wish someone a happy birthday. Perhaps even more important, the theory calls attention to the *number* of media we use with an interpersonal partner. Media multiplexity scholars are convinced of one simple fact: *The stronger the relational tie we have with a person, the more media we will use with that person.* In an age when we have more communication channels available than at any other time in human history, media multiplexity theory makes a timely claim.

MAPPING OUR SOCIAL NETWORKS

In Chapter 1, we suggested that a good theory is a kind of map. Like cities and the roads linking them, a theory shows us the connections between different concepts and ideas. Scholars in the cybernetic tradition think we can also map out what our relationships look like in a social network. Long before the era of Facebook and Snapchat, social scientists were developing such maps of interpersonal connections among groups of people. Media multiplexity theory stands on the shoulders of that work.

I've drawn one such map in Figure 13-1. The map features Cailin, Lisa, and Mandy—former students in my social media and personal relationships course. All three were bright, eager students whose contributions made the class enjoyable. They also didn't know each other well before the course. Therefore, I've drawn the connections among them with a dotted line. Social network scholars call this kind of bond a *weak tie*. It's weak because acquaintances, classmates, and distant relatives don't consume much of our time or energy. We know them, but we aren't emotionally close.

In contrast, *strong ties* such as romantic partners, immediate family, and BFFs (best friends forever) demand that we make a significant investment in the relationship. They're a major commitment. Moving day is a test of friendship—close friends show up to hoist the heavy, awkward couch while less-invested friends find any excuse to stay home. Sociologist Mark Granovetter offered a more formal definition of *tie strength,* claiming it's a "combination of the amount of time, the emotional intensity, the intimacy (mutual confidence), and the reciprocal services" exchanged in the relationship.[1] Therefore tie strength is on a continuum, and some ties fall somewhere between the weak and strong extremes. Nevertheless, scholars in this

Weak tie

A relationship involving a small investment of time and emotional energy, such as an acquaintance.

Strong tie

A relationship involving a large investment of time and emotional energy, such as a very close friend.

Tie strength

The degree of connection between people, determined by amount of time spent together, emotional intensity and intimacy, and willingness to exchange resources.

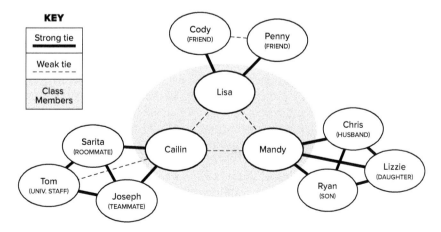

FIGURE 13-1 A Social Network Map

tradition often focus on ties that are clearly strong or weak. On the social network map in Figure 13-1, solid lines depict strong ties. You'll notice Mandy has a tight network of such ties. That's because Chris is her husband, and Ryan and Lizzie are their children. In contrast, Lisa's map includes two strong ties that are her close friends, but those friends don't know each other well.

The map gives an at-a-glance view of their social network. It shows who's connected, who's not, and a rough picture of the state of their relationships. Yes, there's more going on beyond the map; they know other people who aren't depicted here. And no, the map doesn't tell us every detail about these ties. Phenomenologists might urge us to interview Cailin and Sarita to more fully comprehend the uniqueness of the roomies' bond. But for cybernetic theorists, that's not the point. Instead, they want to understand how the structure of a network shapes the flow of information and resources between people. Their visual approach helps them figure that out.

WHEN ARE STRONG TIES WEAK, AND WHEN ARE WEAK TIES STRONG?

If you're like most people, you're probably thinking *strong ties = good* and *weak ties = not so good* (or maybe even *bad*). After all, who doesn't prefer hanging out with a close friend over an acquaintance that's barely known? With strong ties, we experience acceptance, intimacy, and enjoyment. Close friends are the folks who stick by us through the tough times and, if Mead is correct, our strong ties shape our identity (see Chapter 5). They also give us a sense of purpose—we couldn't imagine life without them.

In the late 1960s, Stanford sociologist Mark Granovetter claimed he wasn't so sure that strong ties are always better than weak ties. He affirmed the importance of close relationships for understanding our identity, but noted that strong ties feature a major weakness: They're redundant when it comes to accessing information and resources. Because we spend so much time with our strong ties, there's a good chance we know their strong ties, too. For example, Facebook tells me that my wife—who is, without question, my strongest tie—shares over 300 friends with me. That's a big chunk of my social network and a big chunk of hers. When I need new information, as I did when seeking a real estate agent before our move to Texas, Granovetter thinks it isn't ideal to ask a strong tie. That person generally has access to the same people and information we do. Indeed, when I asked my wife for her thoughts on how to find a real estate agent in a different time zone, she was just as lost as I was.

So I asked for help on Facebook, and I quickly received several leads. In the end, one of my former students contacted her sister, who contacted a friend, who happened to know a great agent in Fort Worth. Yes, my former student's sister's friend's agent saved the day—a connection made through people I didn't even know. It's like the "Six Degrees of Kevin Bacon" game that tries to link Hollywood actors to the *Footloose, Apollo 13,* and *X-Men: First Class* star. According to Granovetter, such quick and uncanny access to diverse information is one strength of weak ties. That's why career consultants emphasize the power of networking when searching for a job—in fact, LinkedIn is built for that purpose. Granovetter obviously didn't have Facebook or LinkedIn when he wrote in the 1960s. But even without those technological megaphones to shout at our acquaintances, he observed that weak ties meet needs that strong ties often can't.

Among weak ties, *bridging ties* serve a particularly powerful role. They're the ties that connect one strong tie group to another. In Figure 13-1, you'll see that

Bridging ties
Weak tie relationships that enable information and resources to pass between groups of people.

each student serves as a bridging tie between her individual networks. So if Cody mentions to Lisa that he needs a good mechanic, she might remember Mandy's husband Chris worked as one. Like the chain of folks who helped find my realtor, Mandy and Lisa's classmate connection serves as the bridge between people who don't know each other—a bridge over which information and resources can flow.

Granovetter wrote his treatise on tie strength while still a student and gave it the ironic title "The Strength of Weak Ties." However, he struggled to find a journal that would publish it. One scholar called his work "somewhat elementary," and another chided, "It is wasteful and quarrelsome to perpetuate ill-delineated arguments."[2] When the *American Journal of Sociology* took a chance and published the paper, Granovetter got the last laugh—the treatise now ranks among the 10 most influential articles in all of the social sciences.[3] It has inspired many scholars, including Haythornthwaite, who found his explanation of strong and weak ties particularly helpful for understanding the channels that sustain them.

MEDIA MULTIPLEXITY: TIE STRENGTH INVOLVES THE CHANNELS WE USE

So far, I've used Cailin, Mandy, and Lisa's relationship map to demonstrate strong and weak ties (see Figure 13-1). Given that they met in class, it's an example that resonates with the focus of Haythornthwaite's initial media multiplexity research. She also sought to create maps of relationships in education contexts. Unlike the face-to-face classroom of my former students, though, she was particularly interested in courses that take place online—often with students located far apart from one another. Such courses typically rely on a variety of communication media. Her initial research focused on email, instant messaging, telephone, and web-based communication. If she conducted the study today, she'd probably include text messaging, video chat, and social media.

At first, Haythornthwaite wanted to understand how online learners adapt to the computer-mediated environment: "What happens to such relationships when face-to-face contact is unavailable or severely limited? How do pairs maintain personal relationships at a distance and via computer-mediated communication?"[4] Those are good, practical questions, and they overlap territory mapped out by other theories (such as Walther's social information processing theory; see Chapter 10). But Haythornthwaite's findings soon drove her into unexplored terrain: "Asking 'who talks to whom about what and via which media' revealed the unexpected result that more strongly tied pairs make use of more of the available media, a phenomenon I have termed *media multiplexity*."[5] In other words, whether a pair chose email, instant messaging, or some other medium didn't matter much—at least as far as the strength of their relationship. Instead, what differentiated strong ties from weak ties was the *number* of media the pair employed. Greater tie strength seemed to drive greater numbers of media used.

Media multiplexity
Strongly tied pairs use more media to sustain their relationships than do weakly tied pairs.

Returning to the network map of my students, you'll notice that Cailin and Mandy are weakly tied. Thus, media multiplexity theory predicts they will communicate through only a few channels. Their relationship could depend entirely on the time they have to talk in class. If they become closer friends, the theory predicts they'll add more media. Perhaps they'll exchange phone numbers. Maybe they'll schedule a weekly lunch date. Note that even though both lunch and class occur face-to-face, Haythornthwaite thinks they're different enough contexts to count as different media. As the women become closer, they add more media; at the same time, as they add more media, they might become closer. That pattern suggests

©Harry Bliss/The New Yorker Collection/The Cartoon Bank

they're on the way to changing their weak tie into something stronger. Weak ties are uncomplicated and don't need many channels to sustain them. Strong ties require more media to orchestrate their varied and interdependent connection.

Although Haythornthwaite initially observed media multiplexity in educational and organizational groups, scholars in the socio-psychological tradition soon took her ideas and applied them to interpersonal contexts. For example, one study found multiplexity among members of a music-based social networking site—using more media predicted closer friendship.[6] Likewise, Art Ramirez (University of South Florida) studied people who reconnected with old friends through Facebook.[7] About 20 percent of his sample didn't add any further media after reconnecting, and those relationships were at greater risk for losing contact again. Those who expanded their channel use beyond the social media site were much more likely to maintain the reconnected relationship.

So that's the basic claim of media multiplexity theory: *Tie strength drives use of multiple media.* Haythornthwaite and other scholars have built from that central idea, logically tracing the consequences of the media/tie strength link. Here, I'll summarize three claims that demonstrate how Haythornthwaite's unexpected finding has grown into an insightful new theory.

Claim #1: Communication Content Differs by Tie Strength, Not by Medium

Earlier theories of communication technology suggested some channels can't effectively facilitate the ambiguous messages common in close relationships. Media multiplexity and social information processing (SIP) agree that those earlier theories weren't quite right—people can and do maintain close ties online. Where SIP and media multiplexity diverge is the logic for that belief. SIP researchers have been most interested in the getting-to-know-you phase of relationship initiation, and they've pointed to the need for extended time during it. Media multiplexity theorists have been more interested in the maintenance of ongoing relationships, and they've pointed to the nature of the interpersonal tie itself.

In her research, Haythornthwaite has found that the medium partners use doesn't change the topic of their talk. I've seen this in action with my co-authors, Em and Glenn. They're both hockey buffs. I confess that I'm not—I'm more familiar with the Mario Brothers than I am with the career of Mario Lemieux. Whether talking on a conference call, participating in a group email conversation, or meeting for dinner at a conference, I know there's a decent chance Em and Glenn will bring up hockey as a topic of conversation. As you can read in Chapter 28, Em got Glenn into hockey in the first place. Their close friendship drives their talk about the sport. Frankly, if the Blackhawks are serious contenders for the Stanley Cup, I'm convinced Em and Glenn would find a way to communicate about it—even if they could only use Morse code.

However, subsequent research adds at least one significant caveat to the claim that content differs by tie and not by medium. University of Illinois professor John Caughlin noted that media multiplexity theory has much to say on *what* media interpersonal partners use, but not *how* they link all those media together. He found that some people believe "the shift from one mode of communication to another . . . [is] awkward, uncomfortable, and intimidating."[8] Those who felt such discomfort also experienced relational dissatisfaction. When people constrained certain topics to certain channels, that choice produced dissatisfaction, too. Thus it may not be quite right to say that partners *never* choose different media for different content, but rather that they may pay a relational price for that kind of segmentation.

Claim #2: The Hierarchy of Media Use Depends on Group Norms

In Cailin, Lisa, and Mandy's social networking site class, we primarily communicated face-to-face. That's kind of ironic in a course entitled "Social Media and Interpersonal Relationships," so I also required students to communicate through Twitter. Students earned points by tweeting at least once per week about something relevant to the class. Face-to-face class time and Twitter served as our public channels where everybody communicated with everyone else. But I also know some students communicated more privately with each other through other media.

According to multiplexity scholars, this allocation of different channels for different kinds of ties creates a *hierarchy of media use expectations*. In such a hierarchy, members of the group use some media to communicate with all relational ties, whether weak or strong, as we did with face-to-face class time and Twitter. These are public, out-in-the-open communicative spaces. But pairs with a strong tie often feel they need more private channels to sustain their relationship. It seemed like some class members used email and text messaging for those purposes.

Hierarchy of media use expectations
Group norms that guide which media are used with all ties and which are reserved for strong ties.

Haythornthwaite would be quick to point out that there's nothing sacred about the face-to-face/Twitter/email/texting hierarchy observed in my classroom. I could have required my students to post on Facebook or Instagram instead. Other types of groups might turn to texting for weak ties and reserve face-to-face chats for strong ones. Although the way they allocate media differs from group to group, the fact that groups allocate media by tie strength—and do so based on social norms—exists in any set of people.

It's one thing when a professor or supervisor says, "You must use this medium to communicate." That's a common fact of organizational life. But what about the freer world of interpersonal relationships, where norms for media use aren't explicit? My colleague Samuel Hardman Taylor investigated this question in the context of extended family members.[9] He asked participants what would happen if a family member violated their expectations—say, if Uncle Ken started texting, or Cousin Suzi stopped phoning. Supporting expectancy violations theory (see Chapter 7), participants did indeed perceive such changes as violations of their expectations.

Their evaluations were especially strong when they enjoyed communicating with the relative. For example, it's a real loss if lovable Aunt Kristen leaves Instagram, but not so bad if it's weird Uncle Bill. If Aunt Kristen then texts us unexpectedly, we'll be delighted, while Uncle Bill's out-of-the-blue text message might seem creepy. These results demonstrate that media use expectations shape interpersonal groups as well as organizational ones. They also support Haythornthwaite's next claim: Adding and subtracting access to a medium changes the shape of our interpersonal ties, sometimes powerfully.

Claim #3: Adding and Subtracting Media Access Influences Weak Ties

When Facebook launched in 2004, it was like an earthquake in the college social scene. At first, only those with email addresses from specific universities could join. Over time Facebook loosened those rules, and as more and more people signed up, users made new acquaintances and reconnected with old friends.

Latent tie
The technical possibility of connection between two people who don't currently have a relationship.

Haythornthwaite would say that the launch of Facebook created *latent ties,* or "connection[s] available technically, even if not yet activated socially."[10] If you're on Facebook, you have a latent tie with every user of the site who isn't already your friend. Once you friend someone—say, a middle school classmate—and he or she accepts your request, you've converted that latent tie into a weak tie. If you start chatting and the person becomes a close friend, you've then developed a strong tie—and if the theory is right, your communication has probably spilled beyond Facebook.

What if your middle school friend gives up Facebook for Lent, or you take a more permanent break from social media? Or what if Facebook CEO Mark Zuckerberg decides to shut down the site? How would the loss of Facebook influence your friendship? Haythornthwaite thinks that depends on the strength of your tie. If you have a weak tie, Facebook's demise might exert a powerful influence on your friendship. After all, weak ties tend to communicate through a limited number of media. If a weak tie only uses two media, losing one cuts their communication opportunities in half. So if Facebook is your only channel, you might lose contact completely—unless you take the initiative to connect some other way.

On the flip side, Haythornthwaite thinks strong ties are relatively unaffected by the loss of a medium. For example, I am Facebook friends with my college pal Erin, but if we lost Facebook, we would still have email, texting, phone calls, and our ongoing game of "Words with Friends." Because strong ties tend to communicate through several media, they have built-in redundancy that can withstand the loss of a channel. In her application of the theory, my student Jessica reflected on how her overseas move impacted her ties:

> When I moved away from Texas for a teaching job in South Korea, I had to rely completely on media to communicate with my friends and family back home. My sister, Victoria, and I have always been very close. As time passed, I began to feel

disconnected with many friends whom I was used to spending time with face-to-face. That wasn't the case with Victoria. We found that Skype was the easiest way to call and text. We navigated around the 14-hour time difference by posting on each other's Facebook timelines, emailing, and sending pins on Pinterest. These messages ranged from inside humor to inspirational quotes. When I finally got a Korean phone number, Victoria was the first one to text me just because she could. It felt like the more communication channels we shared, the easier it was to still spend quality sister time together.

Overall, then, "a central thesis of MMT is that . . . changes to the media landscape alter strong ties only minimally, but may change the nature of weak ties considerably."[11] Note the word *changes* in that quote. Thus far I've mostly described the loss of a medium, yet the addition of a medium also exerts a greater effect on weak ties than on strong ties. If your extended family starts an ongoing group text conversation, it might strengthen your connection with the cousin you only see once a year at the family reunion. But it probably doesn't change your relationship with the cousin you also Snapchat, share Instagram photos, and FaceTime once a week.

What does this mean for Cailin, Mandy, and Lisa? Face-to-face class time is a medium, and by creating that course, I also created latent ties among all the communication majors eligible to take it. When these three students enrolled in and attended the class, they converted those latent ties to weak ties. If they become close friends, they will expand their friendships to other media, and after the class ends, their relationships will continue. But if class time is the only medium supporting their ties, those friendships will probably go dormant when the semester is done.

ARE MEDIA USE AND TIE STRENGTH ALWAYS ASSOCIATED WITH EACH OTHER?

I've just described three claims of the theory: (1) the content of communication differs by tie strength rather than medium, (2) group norms and the desire for privacy shape which media we use with strong and weak ties, and (3) changes in the media environment influence weak ties more than strong ties. Notice that all these claims build on the foundation of media multiplexity theory, which is the belief that strong ties use more media than do weak ties. As you'd expect for an objective theory steeped in both the cybernetic and socio-psychological traditions, scholars haven't taken this for granted; they've gathered evidence to support that crucial belief. At the same time, their empirical detective work has found that the tie strength/media use link may depend on some other ingredients. If those factors aren't present, tie strength and media use may not be so tightly linked—if they're linked at all. My own research has investigated the role of *medium enjoyment*.

Medium enjoyment
A preference for a specific medium, driven by the belief that it is fun and convenient.

It's no secret that I'm a fan of Facebook. I enjoy scrolling through my news feed and I update my status message almost every day. In contrast, I'm not much of a phone talker. I'll chat with people I know really well, but spending hours socializing on the phone isn't my idea of a good time. I also appreciate the convenience of text messaging, but when it comes to Twitter, I have a "meh" attitude (that character limit is a toughie). As I reflect on the different media available, I have no trouble identifying those I enjoy using and those I don't. Your preferences may not be the same as mine, but I'm certain you have opinions about communication media, too.

In one study, I sought to understand how those preferences might influence media multiplexity.[12] More than 400 college students took a survey about a relationship with an extended family member of their choice. I also asked them to choose one of six media they might use to contact that relative: voice telephone, text messaging, public social media, video chat, email, or instant messaging. Participants then completed quantitative scales that assessed how much they used this medium with the relative, how much they enjoyed the medium overall, and how close they felt to the relative (an important component of tie strength).

Not surprisingly, students who enjoyed the medium were more likely to use it with the relative. Supporting the fundamental prediction of media multiplexity theory, those who used the medium frequently also felt closer to their relative. However, upon closer investigation, I discovered that basic association depended on how much they enjoyed the medium. For those who really enjoyed the medium, frequency of use strongly predicted closeness with the relative. When students said they didn't enjoy the medium, frequency of use didn't predict closeness at all.

Why did this pattern emerge? I suspect it may have something to do with the preferences of *both* people in the relationship—the student and the extended family member. Even if your attitude toward the phone is negative like mine, you may nevertheless use it because you know Grandma really appreciates a call now and then. Accommodating to the other person's preferences may be a nice gesture that the other person appreciates (see Chapter 34), but if my research is right, it may not increase *your* perception of tie strength. As the study concluded, "Effective media choice does not match medium to message so much as medium to person." Socially savvy people take the media preferences of both individuals into account. Indeed, other research suggests patterns of multiplexity depend not just on enjoyment, but also on a person's level of communication competence.[13] Although Haythornthwaite didn't initially theorize about individual traits like enjoyment and social skill, her recent work on users of mapping software has shown that such factors motivate media use.[14] This kind of expansion testifies that media multiplexity theory is a flexible work in progress.

CRITIQUE: STRONG ON SIMPLICITY, WEAK ON EXPLANATION AND PREDICTION

Media multiplexity theory is the youngest theory in this book, yet it has gained a sizable following among scholars within and outside the communication discipline. It's a case of the right theory appearing at the right time. In 2002, Walther called for theory aimed at understanding the multimodal nature of interpersonal relationships; in the next few years, the development of Facebook, Twitter, and smartphones heightened this need even further. Media multiplexity theory emerged around the same time, and as I've written elsewhere, "To date, [the theory] represents the most comprehensive and systematic attempt to explain how the multimodality of social life influences, and is influenced by, the characteristics of interpersonal relationships."[15]

One of the theory's greatest strengths is its *relative simplicity.* Its claims revolve around one straightforward, empirical fact: Strong ties tend to use more media than do weak ties. From that easy-to-grasp idea, the theory traces the implications that logically follow for relationships and groups. These hypotheses are *testable,* and as scholars have conducted *quantitative research,* the numbers have tended to support the theory's claims. In the bewildering jungle of media options for interpersonal communication, media multiplexity theory is blazing a straight, simple, and sometimes even elegant trail.

Where the theory falters is its *explanation of the data*. It suffers from a vexing chicken-and-egg question: Which comes first, increased media use or tie strength? Haythornthwaite seems to emphasize that tie strength drives channel expansion. Yet at other times she acknowledges that increased communication probably strengthens the tie. We can observe that tie strength and media use tend to go up and down together. But because several studies have relied on survey data taken at a single point in time, it's almost impossible to determine what causes what. I've argued before that both probably cause each other over time in a cycle, but until we have solid experimental research or a good observational study conducted over a period of time, that's just speculation.[16] Such research could enhance the theory's ability to *predict future events*. For objective scholars, explanation and prediction are vital criteria. As the theory matures, I hope multiplexity scholars will find ways to clarify the crucial tie strength/media use link.

Despite the need for better prediction and explanation, the theory has demonstrated its *practical utility*. Ramirez used media multiplexity to explain how people can effectively rekindle old friendships on social media.[17] Another study concluded that "media multiplexity matters" when trying to understand how those suffering from eating disorders seek online and offline support.[18] Knowledge of the theory may also help relief organizations use multiple media effectively after a disaster.[19] And media multiplexity theory might help students like Cailin, Mandy, and Lisa understand how they can marshal media to meet their relational goals. If recent history is any indication, questions about how to effectively use multiple media won't go away. As media multiplexity theory grows, I hope it continues to seek practical answers to such questions.

QUESTIONS TO SHARPEN YOUR FOCUS

1. Draw a map of part of your social network. For whom are you a *strong tie?* A *weak tie?* When have you seen a weak tie provide strong benefits for you? For the other person?

2. Make a list of two or three strong ties and note the media you use with each. Now do the same for two or three weak ties. Which media do you tend to allocate to each type of tie? Why? What groups in your life shape these *media use expectations?*

3. Imagine you were to lose your cell phone for a week. How would this change your social life? Which relationships, if any, would be strongly affected? Which, if any, wouldn't be affected at all?

4. Identify one *communication medium you enjoy* and one you don't. Reflect on why that's the case. Do your attitudes toward these media have more to do with the characteristics of the media themselves or with how people you know tend to use them?

A SECOND LOOK

Recommended resource: Caroline Haythornthwaite, "Social Networks and Internet Connectivity Effects," *Information, Communication & Society,* Vol. 8, 2005, pp. 125–147.

Original statement: Caroline Haythornthwaite and Barry Wellman, "Work, Friendship, and Media Use for Information Exchange in a Networked Organization," *Journal of the American Society for Information Science,* Vol. 49, 1998, pp. 1101–1114.

Summary and review: Andrew M. Ledbetter, "Media Multiplexity Theory: Technology Use and Interpersonal Tie Strength" in *Engaging Theories in Interpersonal Communication: Multiple Perspectives,* 2nd ed., Dawn O. Braithwaite and Paul Schrodt (eds.), Sage, Thousand Oaks, CA, 2015, pp. 357–370.

High school cliques and multiplexity: Katrien Van Cleemput, "Friendship Type, Clique Formation and the Everyday Use of Communication in a Peer Group," *Information, Communication & Society,* Vol. 15, 2012, pp. 1258–1277.

Facebook relationship maintenance and multiplexity: Victoria S. Sosik and Natalya N. Bazarova, "Relational Maintenance on Social Network Sites: How Facebook Communication Predicts Relational Escalation," *Computers in Human Behavior,* Vol. 35, 2014, pp. 124–131.

Friendship, distance, and multiplexity: Andrew M. Ledbetter, "Patterns of Media Use and Multiplexity: Associations with Sex, Geographic Distance and Friendship Interdependence," *New Media & Society,* Vol. 11, 2009, pp. 1187–1208.

Family and multiplexity: Jennifer Schon, "'Dad Doesn't Text': Examining How Parents' Use of Information Communication Technologies Influences Satisfaction Among Emerging Adult Children," *Emerging Adulthood,* Vol. 2, 2014, pp. 304–312.

Online gaming and multiplexity: Emese Domahidi, Ruth Festl, and Thorsten Quandt, "To Dwell Among Gamers: Investigating the Relationship Between Social Online Game Use and Gaming-Related Friendships," *Computers in Human Behavior,* Vol. 35, 2014, pp. 107–115.

Political participation and multiplexity: Yuli P. Hsieh and Meng-Hao Li, "Online Political Participation, Civic Talk, and Media Multiplexity: How Taiwanese Citizens Express Political Opinions on the Web," *Information, Communication & Society,* Vol. 17, 2013, pp. 26–44.

Motives for media use: Jen Eden and Alice E. Veksler, "Relational Maintenance in the Digital Age: Implicit Rules and Multiple Modalities," *Communication Quarterly,* Vol. 64, 2016, pp. 119–144.

Influence

Getting a person to play a role in an unfamiliar situation can be a powerful method of influence. To explore its effectiveness, Yale social psychologists Irving Janis and Leon Mann surveyed students at a women's college to find out their attitudes and behavior toward smoking—a practice quite resistant to change.[1] They later asked many who smoked to take part in a role play that supposedly assessed their acting ability. Each woman was to take the role of a patient who had gone to the doctor because of a continual cough. She was now back in his office to get the results of a battery of tests the doctor had ordered. She had no script to follow and could respond to the other actor in whatever way she desired.[2]

One researcher then ushered her into a room that was decked out with a scale, sterilizer, fluorescent light for reading X-rays, and a medical school diploma on the wall. The room even smelled of disinfectant. The second experimenter wore a white lab coat with a stethoscope around his neck. Speaking in an authoritative tone of voice, the "doctor" came right to the point. Her chest X-ray gave a positive indication of lung cancer and the diagnosis was confirmed by lab tests. Without question, this condition had developed over a long time. He then paused to let the young woman respond. Often she would say that she'd been smoking too much. Most students eventually asked what they could do.

The doctor wasn't optimistic: "We need to operate immediately. Can you be prepared to check into the hospital tomorrow afternoon?" The surgery only had a 50-50 chance of success of stopping the cancer's spread. At this point the mini-drama could go in a number of directions. The student might express fear for her life, anguish over broken plans for graduation, hesitancy over what to tell her parents or fiancé, anger at God, or disbelief that it was happening to her. No matter how the dialogue went, the young woman got caught up in the situation and emotionally involved with the link between smoking and cancer.

Janis and Mann waited two weeks for the effects of the role play to take hold and then rechecked attitudes toward cigarette smoking. They found that role-play students expressed less favorable opinions toward smoking than they had before. They also discovered that the average cigarettes-per-day habit had dropped from 24 (more than a pack a day) to 14—a dramatic decrease in actual smoking behavior. The attitudes of smokers in the control group who didn't have the role-play experience remained the same as before. So did their 24 cigarettes-per-day habit.

Relapse is common when smokers try to cut back or quit cold turkey. Many find the force of nicotine addiction, cigarette advertising, and friends who smoke hard to resist. Yet after eight months the slippage was slight. On average, those who participated in the emotional role play lit up 15 times a day—only one cigarette more.

Why is role play so effective in this case? In their book, *New Techniques of Persuasion,* Gerald Miller (Michigan State University) and Michael Burgoon (University of Arizona) suggested three possibilities. Role play makes for *immediacy.* The cigarette–cancer connection becomes more real to the smoker when she can't get the image of the doctor delivering bad news out of her mind. There's also *personal involvement.* The smoker can no longer stand aloof from the threat of cancer when she's actively stating her fears to the doctor. Finally, Miller and Burgoon suggested we consider the effect of *nonverbal messages,* such as the doctor pointing to the patient's X-ray. "The impact of this simple behavioral sequence may well transcend the effects of an extended medical lecture on the dangers of cigarette smoking."[3]

We've recounted this experiment because it illustrates and measures what influence theorists, researchers, and many practitioners value. Will a persuasive approach change people's inner attitudes—their beliefs, their emotional response, and what they intend to do? Will that shift in attitude be matched by a change in actual behavior? Are these changes so deep-seated they will resist forces that tend to draw them back into old patterns of thinking and behavior? And will they last over time? The three theories that follow suggest different routes to this kind of effective interpersonal influence and, most important, explain why they work.

Social Judgment Theory

of Muzafer Sherif

Ryan and David are college roommates and friends. Like many students, they don't talk much about politics, but they've had a number of conversations about an issue that sharply divides them—gun control. I've listed 11 comments made during their wide-ranging discussions. Read through these opinions and consider the diversity of viewpoints they represent.

a. You must pass a mandatory background check to buy a gun.

b. A handgun in the home makes it a safer place.

c. Except for law enforcement, guns should be outlawed.

d. All gun ownership is protected by the Second Amendment.

e. Hunting rifles have a legitimate purpose.

f. Allowing citizens to buy assault weapons is crazy.

g. Any regulation will lead to the government taking away all guns.

h. US citizens should be allowed to carry concealed weapons.

i. Courses on handling guns would make the country safer.

j. The more guns out there, the more violence and death.

k. It takes a good guy with a gun to stop a bad guy with a gun.

Take a few minutes to mark your reactions to these statements. If you follow each instruction before jumping ahead to the next one, you'll have a chance to experience what social judgment theory predicts.

1. To begin, read through the items again and underline the single statement that most closely represents your point of view.

2. Now look and see whether any other items seem reasonable. Circle the letters in front of those acceptable statements.

3. Reread the remaining statements and cross out the letters in front of any that are objectionable to you. After you cross out these unreasonable ideas, you may have marked all 11 statements one way or another. It's also possible that you'll leave some items unmarked.

THREE LATITUDES: ACCEPTANCE, REJECTION, AND NONCOMMITMENT

Social judgment-involvement
Perception and evaluation of an idea by comparing it with current attitudes.

I've just taken you on paper through what social judgment theory says happens in our heads. We hear a message and immediately judge where it should be placed on the attitude scale in our minds. According to the late Muzafer Sherif, a social psychologist at the University of Oklahoma, this subconscious sorting of ideas occurs at the instant of perception. We weigh every new idea by comparing it with our present point of view. He called his analysis of attitudes the *social judgment-involvement approach,* but most scholars refer to it simply as *social judgment theory.*

Sherif believed that the three responses you made on the previous page are necessary to determine your attitude toward gun control, or any other attitude structure. In all probability you circled a range of statements that seemed reasonable to you and crossed out a number of opinions you couldn't accept. That's why Sherif would see your attitude as a *latitude* rather than any single statement you underlined. He wrote that an "individual's stand is not represented adequately as a point along a continuum. Different persons espousing the same position may differ considerably in their tolerance around this point."[1]

Latitude of acceptance
The range of ideas that a person sees as reasonable or worthy of consideration.

Latitude of rejection
The range of ideas that a person sees as unreasonable or objectionable.

Latitude of noncommitment
The range of ideas that a person sees as neither acceptable nor objectionable.

He saw an attitude as an amalgam of three zones. The first zone is called the *latitude of acceptance.* It's made up of the item you underlined and any others you circled as acceptable. A second zone is the *latitude of rejection.* It consists of the opinions you crossed out as objectionable. The leftover statements, if any, define the *latitude of noncommitment.* These were the items you found neither objectionable nor acceptable. They're akin to marking *undecided* or *no opinion* on a traditional attitude survey. Sherif said we need to know the location and width of each of these interrelated latitudes in order to describe a person's attitude structure.

David comes from a family where guns are a way of life. Some of his fondest childhood memories are of hunting with his father and target practice at a shooting range with his uncle's pistol. He'd like to share these experiences with Ryan, but so far his friend has balked at having anything to do with guns. Ryan says because guns put so many people at risk, there should be strict laws about their purchase and use. David would like to convince Ryan that guns are safe, great sport, and provide ultimate security in an increasingly violent world. If he can do that, maybe Ryan would back off on his desire for more government regulation.

Social judgment theory recommends David try to figure out the location and breadth of Ryan's three latitudes before further discussion. Figure 14-1 shows where Ryan places those 11 statements along the mental yardstick he uses to gauge gun safety. As you will discover in the next few pages, if David has a good idea of this cognitive map, he'll have a much better chance of crafting a message that will persuade Ryan to be more optimistic about firearms.

EGO-INVOLVEMENT: HOW MUCH DO YOU CARE?

There's one other thing about Ryan's attitude structure that David needs to know—how important the issue of gun safety is to Ryan. Sherif called this *ego-involvement.* Ego-involvement refers to how central an issue is in our lives. Does it have personal significance? How important is it to us?[2] In Figure 14-1, I've used an anchor to represent the position that most closely represents Ryan's commitment—the more guns floating around in society, the greater the number of people who will be shot and killed.[3] Sherif said that's what our favored position does: It anchors all our other thoughts about the topic.

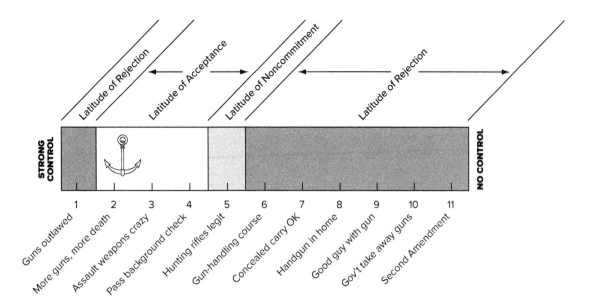

FIGURE 14–1 Ryan's Cognitive Map Regarding Gun Control

If gun control were only a casual concern for Ryan, it would be fitting to represent his stance with a small anchor that could easily be dragged to a new position. That might be the case for someone who didn't own a gun, never fired a bullet, and had no personal contact with anyone who had been threatened or shot with a gun. But that's not Ryan. In high school he volunteered with a dozen other students to tutor inner-city kids in reading and math. They each were paired with the same boy or girl every week, but got to know the other kids through the games they'd play after study. Halfway through the semester, a boy named Cleon whom Ryan joked around with each week was shot and killed in a drive-by shooting. Ryan thinks about Cleon a lot.

Closer to home but less tragic, Ryan's grandfather shot himself in the leg while loading a pistol. Lots of blood, but no permanent damage. Within the family it's become an ongoing joke, but in light of the massacres in Sandy Hook, San Bernardino, Orlando, and Las Vegas, Ryan is acutely aware of the damage a gun can cause. Others may experience only passing concern, their low ego-involvement represented with a small anchor, but Ryan's ego-involvement runs deep.

Ego-involvement
The importance or centrality of an issue to a person's life, often demonstrated by membership in a group with a known stand.

People who hold extreme opinions on either side of an issue almost always care deeply. While it's possible to feel passionate about middle-of-the-road positions, social judgment researchers find that large attitude anchors are usually located toward the ends of the scale. Extreme positions and high ego-involvement go together. That's why religion, sex, and politics are traditionally taboo topics in the wardroom of a US Navy ship at sea. When passions run deep, radical opinions are common and there's little tolerance for diversity.

Steven Spielberg's film *Lincoln* illustrates Sherif's concepts of ego-involvement and attitudes as latitudes.[4] Against the advice of his cabinet, the president pushes Congress to pass a constitutional amendment abolishing slavery. A *yes* vote falls somewhere within each Republican's latitude of acceptance. But to get the needed two-thirds majority, Lincoln needs to switch the votes of 20 Democrats, whose party publicly opposes the amendment. Abolition appears to fall within their latitude of rejection.

Yet Lincoln's men see a window of opportunity. Leaving Congress are 39 lame-duck Democrats who now have weaker party ties. With that lower ego-involvement, these 39 men may have a wider latitude of noncommitment toward the amendment and could be encouraged to *abstain* rather than vote *no*. Some might be swayed to broaden their latitude of acceptance, making a *yes* vote possible. The film shows Lincoln's political operatives in the House balcony noting which Democrats are sweating or at least not cheering when their leaders lambast the amendment. The aides then use Lincoln's popularity, moral arguments, job offers, threats, and bribes to induce latitude change. The amendment passes and slavery is abolished by a two-vote margin.

Everything I've presented up to this point deals with the way social judgment theory describes the cognitive *structure* of a person's attitude. We now turn to the two-step mental *process* that Sherif said is triggered when a person hears or reads a message. Ryan will first evaluate the content of any message from David about gun control to see where it falls vis-à-vis his own position—how far it is from his anchor. That's the *judgment* phase of social judgment theory. In the second stage of the process, Ryan will adjust his anchored attitude toward or away from the message he's just encountered. The next two sections explain the way Sherif said the two stages of this influence process work.

JUDGING THE MESSAGE: CONTRAST AND ASSIMILATION ERRORS

Sherif claimed that we use our own anchored attitude as a comparison point when we hear a discrepant message. He believed there's a parallel between systematic biases in the judgments we make in the physical world and the way we determine other people's attitudes. The last time I taught social judgment theory in class, I set up three pails of water to illustrate this principle. Even though the contents looked the same, the temperature of the water in the left bucket was just above freezing, the water in the right bucket was just below scalding, and the water in the middle bucket was lukewarm. A student volunteered to plunge her left hand into the left bucket and her right hand into the right bucket at the same time. Twenty seconds was about all she could take. I then asked her to plunge both hands into the middle bucket and judge the temperature of the water. Of course, this produced a baffling experience, because her left hand told her the water was hot, while her right hand sent a message that it was cold.

Contrast

A perceptual error whereby people judge messages that fall within their latitude of rejection as farther from their anchor than they really are.

Sherif hypothesized a similar *contrast* effect when people who are hot for an idea hear a message on the topic that doesn't have the same fire. Judged by their standard, even warm messages feel cold. Sherif's original *social judgment-involvement* label nicely captures the idea of a link between ego-involvement and perception. Since highly committed people tend to have large latitudes of rejection, any message that falls within that range will be perceived by them as more discrepant from their anchor than it really is. The message is mentally pushed away to a position that is farther out—not within the latitude of acceptance. So the hearers don't have to deal with it as a viable option.

All of this is bad news for David if he tries to lower Ryan's resistance to gun ownership using a direct approach:

Look, criminals can always get a gun. If that person wants to harm you on the street or in a bar, he'll think twice under a concealed carry law, because he can never be sure you won't pull a gun on him. And if that guy breaks into your house to rob you or terrorize your family, you're the last line of defense. You'd better be armed. The only way to stop a bad guy with a gun is for the good guys to have guns.

On a gun control scale where 1 represents a total ban on gun ownership and 11 means no regulation at all, David may intend his words to register at 7, 8, or 9 in Ryan's mind. But because these words fall within Ryan's latitude of rejection, he will hear them as farther away from his latitude of acceptance than they really are—perhaps at 9, 10, or 11—and think David is out of his mind.

Contrast is a perceptual distortion that leads to polarization of ideas. But according to Sherif, it happens only when a message falls within the latitude of rejection. *Assimilation* is the opposite error in judgment. It's the rubberband effect that draws an idea toward the hearer's anchor so it seems that he and the speaker share the same opinion. Assimilation takes place when a message falls within the latitude of acceptance. For example, suppose David says he's pleased the NRA won't oppose a law mandating a buyer background check using a federal database. That surprising statement would seem to be at a 4 on the gun control scale, but the theory suggests Ryan will hear it as more similar to his anchoring attitude than it really is, perhaps at a 3.

Assimilation
A perceptual error whereby people judge messages that fall within their latitude of acceptance as less discrepant from their anchor than they really are.

Sherif was unclear about how people judge a message that falls within their latitude of noncommitment. Most interpreters assume that a perceptual bias won't kick in and that the message will be heard roughly as intended.

DISCREPANCY AND ATTITUDE CHANGE

Judging how close or how far a message is from our own anchored position is the first stage of attitude change. Shifting our anchor in response is the second. Sherif thought that both stages of the influence process usually take place below the level of consciousness.

According to his theory, once we've judged a new message to be within our latitude of acceptance, we will adjust our attitude somewhat to accommodate the new input. The persuasive effect will be positive but partial. We won't travel the whole distance, but there will be some measurable movement toward the speaker's perceived position. How much movement? Sherif wasn't specific, but he did claim that *the greater the discrepancy, the more hearers will adjust their attitudes.* Thus, the message that persuades the most is the one that is most discrepant from the listener's position yet falls within his or her *latitude of acceptance* or *latitude of noncommitment.*

If we've judged a message to be within our *latitude of rejection,* we will also adjust our attitude, but in this case *away from* what we think the speaker is advocating. Since people who are highly ego-involved in a topic have a broad range of rejection, most messages aimed to persuade them are in danger of actually driving them further away. This predicted *boomerang effect* suggests that people are often *driven* rather than *drawn* to the attitude positions they occupy.

Boomerang effect
Attitude change in the opposite direction of what the message advocates; listeners driven away from rather than drawn to an idea.

The mental processes Sherif described are automatic. He reduced interpersonal influence to the issue of the distance between the message and the hearer's position:

> Stripped to its bare essential, the problem of attitude change is the problem of the degree of discrepancy from communication and the felt necessity of coping with the discrepancy.[5]

So the only space for volition in social judgment theory is the choice of alternative messages available to the person who's trying to persuade.

PRACTICAL ADVICE FOR THE PERSUADER

Sherif would have advised David to avoid the gun-lover quips that appear on bumper stickers: *Guns don't kill people, people kill people* and *Have you hugged your gun today?* They will just push Ryan deeper into his anti-firearms stance. To make sure his words have a positive effect, David should select a message that falls at the near edge of Ryan's latitude of acceptance, which the "background check" statement does. Even when the perceptual process of assimilation kicks in, Ryan will still judge David's message to be somewhat discrepant from his own point of view and shift his attitude slightly in that direction. Or David might try a somewhat riskier strategy to produce a greater attitude shift by saying something that falls within Ryan's latitude of noncommitment:

> Ryan, we've been friends for a long time. I know you hate guns in general and I understand some of the reasons why. I also know that basketball is a big chunk of your life. The sport of hunting is a big chunk of mine. I get the same thrill bagging

"I'm happy to say that my final judgment of a case is almost always consistent with my prejudgment of the case."

©Dana Fradon/The New Yorker Collection/The Cartoon Bank

A SECOND LOOK

Recommended resources: Daniel J. O'Keefe, "Social Judgment Theory," in *Persuasion: Theory and Research,* Sage, Los Angeles, CA, 2016, pp. 19-34; Donald Granberg, "Social Judgment Theory," in *Communication Yearbook 6,* Michael Burgoon (ed.), Sage, Beverly Hills, CA, 1982, pp. 304-329; Daniel J. O'Keefe, "Social Judgment Theory," in *Persuasion: Theory and Research,* Sage, Newbury Park, CA, 1990, pp. 29-44.

Original conception: Muzafer Sherif and Carl Hovland, *Social Judgment: Assimilation and Contrast Effects in Communication and Attitude Change,* Yale University, New Haven, CT, 1961.

Further development: Carolyn Sherif, Muzafer Sherif, and Roger Nebergall, *Attitude and Attitude Change: The Social Judgment-Involvement Approach,* W. B. Saunders, Philadelphia, PA, 1965.

Attitudes as latitudes: Kenneth Sereno and Edward Bodaken, "Ego-Involvement and Attitude Change: Toward a Reconceptualization of Persuasive Effect," *Speech Monographs,* Vol. 39, 1972, pp. 151-158.

Ego-involvement: William W. Wilmot, "Ego-Involvement: A Confusing Variable in Speech Communication Research," *Quarterly Journal of Speech,* Vol. 57, 1971, pp. 429-436.

Assimilation and contrast: Alison Ledgerwood and Shelly Chaiken, "Priming Us and Them: Automatic Assimilation and Contrast in Group Attitudes," *Journal of Personality and Social Psychology,* Vol. 93, 2007, pp. 940-956.

Message discrepancy: Stan Kaplowitz and Edward Fink, "Message Discrepancy and Persuasion," in *Progress in Communication Sciences: Advances in Persuasion, Vol. 13,* George Barnett and Frank Boster (eds.), Ablex, Greenwich, CT, 1997, pp. 75-106.

Boomerang effect: Hilobumi Sakaki, "Experimental Studies of Boomerang Effects Following Persuasive Communication," *Psychologia,* Vol. 27, No. 2, 1984, pp. 84-88.

Sleep study: Stephen Bochner and Chester Insko, "Communicator Discrepancy, Source Credibility and Opinion Change," *Journal of Personality and Social Psychology,* Vol. 4, 1966, pp. 614-621.

Changing social norms for drinking on campus: Sandi Smith, Charles Atkin et al., "A Social Judgment Theory Approach to Conducting Formative Research in a Social Norms Campaign," *Communication Theory,* Vol. 16, 2006, pp. 141-152.

Critique: Hee Sun Park, Timothy Levine, Catherine Y. K. Waterman, Tierney Oregon, and Sarah Forager, "The Effects of Argument Quality and Involvement Type on Attitude Formation and Attitude Change," *Human Communication Research,* Vol. 33, 2007, pp. 81-102.

Elaboration Likelihood Model

of Richard Petty & John Cacioppo

Like a number of women whose children are out of the home, Rita Francisco has gone back to college. Her program isn't an aimless sampling of classes to fill empty hours—she has enrolled in every course that will help her become a more persuasive advocate. Rita is a woman on a mission.

Rita's teenage daughter was killed when the car she was riding in smashed into a stone wall. After drinking three cans of beer at a party, the girl's 18-year-old boyfriend lost control on a curve while driving 80 miles per hour. Rita's son walks with a permanent limp as a result of injuries sustained when a high school girl plowed through the parking lot of a 7-Eleven on a Friday night. When the county prosecutor obtained a driving under the influence (DUI) conviction, it only fueled Rita's resolve to get young drinking drivers off the road. She has become active with Mothers Against Drunk Driving and works to convince anyone who will listen that zero-tolerance laws, which make it illegal for drivers under the age of 21 to have *any* measurable amount of alcohol in their system, should be strictly enforced. Rita also wants to persuade others that young adults caught driving with more than 0.02 percent blood alcohol content should automatically lose their driver's licenses until they are 21.

This is a tough sell on most college campuses. While her classmates can appreciate the tragic reasons underlying her fervor, few subscribe to what they believe is a drastic solution. As a nontraditional, older student, Rita realizes her younger classmates could easily dismiss her campaign as the ranting of a distraught parent. She's determined to develop the most effective persuasive strategy possible and wonders if she would have the most success by presenting well-reasoned arguments for enforcing zero-tolerance laws. Then again, couldn't she sway students more by lining up highly credible people to endorse her proposal?

THE CENTRAL AND PERIPHERAL ROUTES TO PERSUASION

Central route

Message elaboration; the path of cognitive processing that involves scrutiny of message content.

Message elaboration

The extent to which a person carefully thinks about issue-relevant arguments contained in a persuasive communication.

Peripheral route

A mental shortcut process that accepts or rejects a message based on irrelevant cues as opposed to actively thinking about the issue.

Ohio State psychologist Richard Petty thinks Rita is asking the right questions. He conducted his PhD dissertation study using the topic of teenage driving to test the relative effectiveness of strong-message arguments and high source credibility. He found that the results varied depending on which of two mental routes to attitude change a listener happened to use. Petty labeled the two cognitive processes the *central route* and the *peripheral route*. He sees the distinction as helpful in reconciling much of the conflicting data of persuasion research. Along with his University of Chicago colleague John Cacioppo, he launched an intensive program of study to discover the best way for a persuader to activate each route.

The central route involves *message elaboration*. Elaboration is "the extent to which a person carefully thinks about issue-relevant arguments contained in a persuasive communication."[1] In an attempt to process new information rationally, people using the central route carefully scrutinize the ideas, try to figure out if they have true merit, and mull over their implications. Similar to Berger's characterization of strategic message plans, elaboration requires high levels of cognitive effort (see Chapter 9).

The peripheral route offers a mental shortcut to accepting or rejecting a message "without any active thinking about the attributes of the issue or the object of consideration."[2] Instead of doing extensive cognitive work, recipients rely on a variety of cues that allow them to make quick decisions. Robert Cialdini of Arizona State University lists six cues that trigger a programmed response.[3] These cues allow people hearing a persuasive appeal to fly the peripheral route on automatic pilot:

1. Reciprocation—"You owe me."
2. Consistency—"We've always done it that way."
3. Social proof—"Everybody's doing it."
4. Liking—"Love me, love my ideas."
5. Authority—"Just because I say so."
6. Scarcity—"Quick, before they're all gone."

Figure 15-1 shows a simplified version of Petty and Cacioppo's elaboration likelihood model (ELM) as it applies to Rita's situation. Although their model's twin-route metaphor seems to suggest two mutually exclusive paths to persuasion, the theorists stress that the central route and the peripheral route are poles on a cognitive processing continuum that shows the degree of mental effort a person exerts when evaluating a message.[4] The elaboration scale at the top represents effortful scrutiny of arguments on the left-hand side and mindless reliance on non-content cues on the right. Most messages receive middle-ground attention between these poles, but there's always a trade-off. The more Rita's listeners work to discern the merits of strict zero-tolerance enforcement, the less they'll be influenced by peripheral factors such as their friends' scoffing laughter at her suggestion. Conversely, the more her hearers are affected by content-irrelevant factors such as Rita's age, accent, or appearance, the less they will be affected by her ideas. We'll work down the model one level at a time in order to understand Petty and Cacioppo's predictions about the likelihood of Rita's message being scrutinized by students at her college.

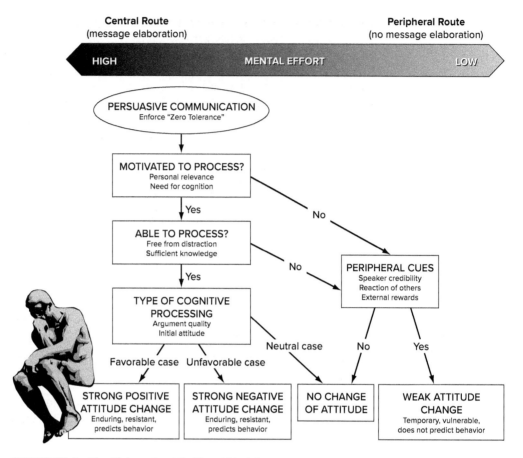

FIGURE 15-1   The Elaboration Likelihood Model

Based on Petty and Cacioppo, "The Elaboration Likelihood Model of Persuasion"

MOTIVATION FOR ELABORATION: IS IT WORTH THE EFFORT?

Petty and Cacioppo assume that people are motivated to hold correct attitudes. The authors admit we aren't always logical, but they think we make a good effort not to kid ourselves in our search for truth. We want to maintain reasonable positions.

But a person can examine only a limited number of ideas. We are exposed to so many persuasive messages that we would experience a tremendous information overload if we tried to interact with every variant idea we heard or read about. The only way to solve this problem is by being "lazy" toward most issues in life. Petty and Cacioppo claim we have a large-mesh mental filter that allows items we regard as less important to flow through without being carefully processed. But statements about things that are personally relevant get trapped and tested. In the terminology of social judgment theory (see Chapter 14), we're motivated to elaborate only ideas with which we are highly ego-involved.

There are few things in life more important to young Americans than the right to drive. A license is the closest thing our society has to an adolescent rite of passage; for some it is a passport to freedom. It seems unlikely, therefore, that students would regard Rita's zero-tolerance proposal as trivial. Yet threatening the loss of license may have less personal relevance to students who don't drink, or to those who already make sure they don't drive when they drink. And if students over 21 aren't worried about who's driving on the road, they too may feel that Rita's proposal has little to do with them. So ELM's authors would regard teenage students who drive after drinking a few beers as especially motivated to grapple with arguments about automatic driver's license suspension.

Petty and Cacioppo maintain that as long as people have a personal stake in accepting or rejecting an idea, they will be much more influenced by what a message says than by the characteristics of the person who says it. But when a topic is no longer relevant, it gets sidetracked to the periphery of the mind, where credibility cues take on greater importance. Without the motivation of personal relevance, there probably will be little elaboration.

The theorists do recognize, however, that some people have a need for cognitive clarity, regardless of the issue. In fact, they've developed a *Need for Cognition Scale* to identify individuals who are most likely to carefully consider message arguments.[5] Four of the items state:

Need for cognition
Desire for cognitive clarity; an enjoyment of thinking through ideas even when they aren't personally relevant.

I really enjoy a task that involves coming up with new solutions to problems.

I prefer my life to be filled with puzzles that I must solve.

I like tasks that require little thought once I've learned them.

Thinking is not my idea of fun.

If you substantially agree with the first two statements and take issue with the last two, Petty and Cacioppo would anticipate that you'd be a person who works through many of the ideas and arguments you hear.

ABILITY FOR ELABORATION: CAN THEY DO IT?

Once people have shown an inclination to think about the content of a message (motivation), the next issue is whether they are *able* to do so. Since Rita's immediate audience consists of young men and women who have duly impressed a college admissions officer with their ability to think, you would imagine that the question of ability would be moot. But issue-relevant thinking (elaboration) takes more than intelligence. It also requires concentration.

Distraction disrupts elaboration. Rita's classmates will be hard-pressed to think about her point of view if it's expressed amid the din of a student union snack bar where you can't hear yourself think. Or perhaps she presents her solution for highway safety when students are trying to concentrate on something else—Snapchat pictures on a cell phone, an upcoming exam, or a mental replay of the winning shot in an intramural basketball game.

Rita may face the same challenge as television advertisers who have only the fleeting attention of viewers. Like them, Rita can use repetition to ensure that her main point comes across, but too much commotion will short-circuit a reasoned consideration of the message, no matter how much repetition is used. In that case, students will use the peripheral route and judge the message by cues that indicate whether Rita is a competent and trustworthy person.

TYPE OF ELABORATION: OBJECTIVE VERSUS BIASED THINKING

As you can see from the downward flow in the central path of their model (Figure 15-1), Petty and Cacioppo believe motivation and ability strongly increase the likelihood that a message will be elaborated in the minds of listeners. Yet as social judgment theory suggests, they may not process the information in a fair and objective manner. Rita might have the undivided attention of students who care deeply about the right to drive, but discover that they've already built up an organized structure of knowledge concerning the issue.

When Rita claims that the alcohol-related fatal crash rate for young drivers is double that of drivers over 21, a student may counter with the fact that teenagers drive twice as many miles and are therefore just as safe as adults. Whether or not the statistics are true or the argument is valid isn't the issue. The point is that those who have already thought a lot about drinking and driving safety will probably have made up their minds and be biased in the way they process Rita's message.

Biased elaboration
Top-down thinking in which predetermined conclusions color the supporting data.

Petty and Cacioppo refer to *biased elaboration* as top-down thinking in which a predetermined conclusion colors the supporting data underneath. They contrast this with *objective elaboration,* or bottom-up thinking, which lets facts speak for themselves. Biased elaboration merely bolsters previous ideas.

Objective elaboration
Bottom-up thinking in which facts are scrutinized without bias; seeking truth wherever it might lead.

Perhaps you've seen a picture of Rodin's famous statue *The Thinker,* a man sitting with his head propped in one hand. If the thinker already has a set of beliefs to contemplate, Petty and Cacioppo's research shows that additional thought will merely fix them in stone. Rita shouldn't assume that audience elaboration will always help her cause; it depends on whether it's biased elaboration or objective elaboration. It also depends on the quality of her arguments.

ELABORATED ARGUMENTS: STRONG, WEAK, AND NEUTRAL

If Rita manages to win an unbiased hearing from students at her school, Petty and Cacioppo say her cause will rise or fall on the perceived strength of her arguments. The two theorists have no absolute standard for what distinguishes a cogent argument from one that's specious. They simply define a strong message as one that generates favorable thoughts when it's heard and scrutinized.

Strong arguments
Claims that generate favorable thoughts when examined.

Petty and Cacioppo predict that thoughtful consideration of *strong arguments* will produce major shifts in attitude in the direction desired by the persuader. Suppose Rita states the following:

> According to the Centers for Disease Control and Prevention, 1 in 10 high schoolers drive under the influence of alcohol, and young drivers are 17 times more likely to die from a crash when they're drunk.[6]

This evidence could give students cause for pause. They may not be comfortable with the facts, but some of them might find the statistics compelling and a reason to reconsider their stance. According to ELM, the enhanced thinking of those who respond favorably will cause their change in position to *persist over time, resist counterpersuasion,* and *predict future behavior*—the "triple crown" of interpersonal influence.

However, persuasive attempts that are processed through the central route can have dramatically negative effects as well. If, despite her strong convictions, Rita isn't able to come up with a strong argument for changing the current law, her persuasive attempt might actually backfire. For example, suppose she makes this argument:

When underage drinkers are arrested for violating zero-tolerance rules of the road, automatic suspension of their licenses would allow the secretary of state's office to reduce its backlog of work. This would give government officials time to check driving records so that they could keep dangerous motorists off the road in advance.

This weak argument will probably offend the sensibilities of those who think about it. Most people don't care about government workload, and they don't want officials snooping in their driving records without cause. Rather than compelling listeners to enlist in Rita's campaign, the argument will only give them a reason to oppose her point of view more vigorously. The elaborated idea will cause a boomerang effect that will last over time, defy other efforts to change it, and affect subsequent behavior. These are the same significant effects that the elaborated strong argument produces, but in the opposite direction.

Rita's ideas could also produce an ambivalent reaction. Listeners who carefully examine her argument may end up feeling neither pro nor con toward her evidence. Their neutral or mixed response obviously means they won't change their attitudes as a result of processing through the central route. For them, thinking about the pros and cons of the issue reinforces their original attitudes, whatever they may be.

PERIPHERAL CUES: AN ALTERNATIVE ROUTE OF INFLUENCE

Although the majority of this chapter has dealt with the central cognitive route to attitude change, most messages are processed on the less effortful peripheral path. Signposts along the way direct the hearer to favor or oppose the persuader's point of view without ever engaging in what Petty and Cacioppo call "issue-relevant thinking."[7] There is no inner dialogue about the merits of the proposal.

As explained earlier, the hearer who uses the peripheral route relies on a variety of cues as an aid in reaching a quick decision. The most obvious cues are tangible rewards linked to agreement with the advocate's position. Food, sex, and money are traditional inducements to change. I once overheard the conclusion of a transaction between a young man and a college senior who was trying to persuade him to donate blood in order to fulfill her class assignment. "OK, it's agreed," she said. "You give blood for me today, and I'll have you over to my place for dinner tomorrow night." Although this type of social exchange has been going on for centuries, Petty and Cacioppo would still describe it as peripheral. Public compliance to the request for blood? Yes. Private acceptance of its importance? Not likely.

Source credibility
Audience perception of the message source's expertise, character, and dynamism; typically a peripheral cue.

For many students of persuasion, *source credibility* is the most interesting cue on the peripheral route. Four decades of research confirm that people who are likable and have expertise on the issue in question can have a persuasive impact regardless of what arguments they present. Rita's appearance, manner of talking, and background credentials will speak so loudly that some students won't really hear what she says. Which students? According to Petty and Cacioppo, those students who are unmotivated or unable to scrutinize her message and therefore switch to the peripheral path.

Listeners who believe that Rita's twin tragedies have given her wisdom beyond their own will shift to a position more sympathetic to her point of view. The same holds true for those who see her as pleasant and warm. But there are students who will regard her grammatical mistakes as a sign of ignorance, or they'll be turned

"In the interest of streamlining the judicial process, we'll skip the evidence and go directly to sentencing."

©J.B. Handelsman/The New Yorker Collection/The Cartoon Bank

off by a maternal manner that reminds them of a lecture from mom. These peripheral route critics will become more skeptical of Rita's position. Note that attitude change on this outside track can be either positive or negative, but it lacks the robust persistence, invulnerability, and link to behavior we see in change that comes from message elaboration.

Nicely illustrating the fragility of peripheral route change, Holly wrote the following entry in her application log:

In his short story "Salvation," Langston Hughes recounts his childhood experience at a religious revival in his town. For days the old ladies of the church had been praying for the conversion of all the "little lambs" of the congregation. After working the congregation to a fever pitch, the preacher gave an altar call aimed at the children, and one after another they cried and went forward to be saved from hell. The author and his friend didn't feel anything, but after what seemed like forever, his friend went up so all the hubbub would finally stop. Langston knew that his friend hadn't really been converted, but since God didn't smite him for lying, he figured it would be safe for him to fake it as well, which he did. When the revival was over, the congregation calmed down and everyone went home praising the Lord. Langston says that was the day he stopped believing in God.

The preacher relied on peripheral cues. Langston went forward because of the expectation of authority figures, heightened emotion, and conformity pressure. But there was no elaboration of the message, no grappling with the issue, and certainly no encounter with God. The result of this peripheral route processing was as ELM predicts—his "salvation" didn't even last through the night.

PUSHING THE LIMITS OF PERIPHERAL POWER

In 1991, basketball superstar Magic Johnson held a candid press conference to announce that he had tested positive for HIV. At the time, such a diagnosis seemed like a death sentence; the story dominated network news coverage for days. University of South Florida psychologists Louis Penner and Barbara Fritzsche had just completed a study showing that many people had little sympathy for those who had contracted AIDS through sexual transmission. When asked to volunteer a few hours to help someone with AIDS stay in school, a little more than half of the women and none of the men in the study volunteered. Penner and Fritzsche extended their study when they heard of Magic Johnson's illness.[8] They wondered if the virus that had infected this popular figure—and his pledge to become an advocate for people living with HIV and AIDS—would cause students to react more positively toward people with AIDS.

For a while it did. The week after Johnson's announcement, 80 percent of the men offered assistance. That number tapered off to 30 percent, however, within a few months. The proportion of women offering help dipped below 40 percent in the same period. Penner and Fritzsche observed that people didn't grapple with the substance of Magic Johnson's message; rather, they paid attention to the man presenting it. Consistent with ELM's main thesis, the researchers concluded that "changes that occur because of 'peripheral cues' such as . . . being a well liked celebrity are less permanent than those that occur because of the substantive content of the persuasion attempt."[9]

Penner and Fritzsche could have added that the effects of star performer endorsements are subject to the sharp ups and downs of celebrity status. For example, Jared Fogle became famous as the spokesperson for Subway after he lost 200 pounds on a diet of Subway sandwiches. But his wholesome, healthy image was tarnished when he pleaded guilty to distributing child pornography and having illicit sexual contact with a minor.[10] Subway promptly terminated its contract with Fogle.

Although most ELM research has measured the effects of peripheral cues by studying credibility, a speaker's competence or character could also be a stimulus for effortful message elaboration. For example, the high regard that millions of sports fans had for Magic Johnson might for the first time have made it possible to scrutinize proposals for the prevention and treatment of AIDS without a moral stigma biasing each idea. Or the fact that Johnson's magic wasn't strong enough to repel HIV might cause someone to think deeply, "If it happened to a guy like Magic, it could happen to me." Even though Figure 15-1 identifies *speaker credibility, reaction of others,* and *external rewards* as variables that promote mindless acceptance via the peripheral route, Petty and Cacioppo emphasize that it's impossible to compile a list of cues that are strictly peripheral.[11]

Younghan Lee of Mississippi State University and Jakeun Koo at the University of Massachusetts agree there are times when source credibility is processed through the central route rather than functioning as a peripheral cue. This is particularly true when there's a close match between an advertised product that consumers really care about and the expertise of the star presenter. For example, if retired NFL quarterback Peyton Manning endorsed a specific brand of athletic shoes, his appearance in the ad would be processed by football players as a major argument in favor of buying that brand—central route processing. But for nonathletes who couldn't care less, their attitude toward the shoes would simply be a function of their more superficial feelings about Peyton Manning—peripheral route processing.[12]

When Rita ponders her persuasive strategy, she is aware that even the mood of the person listening to her message might play a role as a peripheral cue. She assumes that her classmate Sam will be a more sympathetic audience if she can present her ideas when he's in a good mood. And she's right, as long as Sam processes her message through the peripheral route without thinking too hard about what she's saying. His positive outlook prompts him to see her proposal in a favorable light.

Yet if Sam is somewhat willing and able to work through her arguments (moderate elaboration), his upbeat mood could actually turn out to be a disadvantage. He was feeling up, but he becomes depressed when he thinks about the death and disfigurement Rita describes. The loss of warm feelings could bias him against Rita's arguments. Petty suggests that Sam might process her arguments more objectively if his original mood matches the downbeat nature of Rita's experience.[13] Many variables like *perceived credibility* and the *mood of the listener* can act as peripheral cues. Yet if one of them motivates listeners to scrutinize the message or affects their evaluation of arguments, it no longer serves as a no-brainer. There is no variable that's always a shortcut on the peripheral route.

CHOOSING A ROUTE: PRACTICAL ADVICE FOR THE PERSUADER

Petty and Cacioppo's advice for Rita (and the rest of us) is clear. She needs to determine the likelihood that her listeners will give their undivided attention to evaluating her proposal. If it appears that they have the motivation and ability to elaborate the message, she had best come armed with facts and figures to support her case. A pleasant smile, an emotional appeal, or the loss of her daughter won't make any difference.

Since it's only by thoughtful consideration that her listeners may experience a lasting change in attitude, Rita probably hopes they can go the central route. But even if they do, it's still difficult to build a compelling persuasive case. If she fails to do her homework and presents weak arguments, the people who are ready to think will shift their attitude to a more antagonistic position.

If Rita determines that her hearers are unable or unwilling to think through the details of her plan, she'll be more successful choosing a delivery strategy that emphasizes the package rather than the contents. This could include a heartrending account of her daughter's death, a smooth presentation, and an ongoing effort to build friendships with the students. Perhaps bringing homemade cookies to class or offering rides to the mall would aid in making her an attractive source. But as we've already seen, the effects will probably be temporary.

It's not likely that Rita will get many people to elaborate her message in a way that ends up favorable for her cause. Most persuaders avoid appealing to the central route because the audience won't go with them or they find it too difficult to generate compelling arguments. But Rita really doesn't have a choice.

Driver's licenses (and perhaps beer) are so important to most of these students that they'll be ready to dissect every part of her plan. They won't be won over by a friendly smile. Rita will have to develop thoughtful and well-reasoned arguments if she is to change their minds. Given the depth of her conviction, she thinks it's worth a try.

ETHICAL REFLECTION: NILSEN'S SIGNIFICANT CHOICE

ELM describes persuasion that's effective. The late University of Washington professor emeritus Thomas Nilsen was concerned with what's ethical. Consistent with the democratic values of a free society, he proposed that persuasive speech is ethical to the extent that it maximizes people's ability to exercise free choice. Since many political, religious, and commercial messages are routinely designed to bypass rather than appeal to a listener's rational faculties, Nilsen upheld the value of significant choice in unequivocal terms:

> When we communicate to influence the attitudes, beliefs, and actions of others, the ethical touchstone is the degree of free, informed, rational and critical choice—significant choice—that is fostered by our speaking.[14]

For Nilsen, truly free choice was the test of ethical influence because "only a self-determining being can be a moral being; without significant choice, there is no morality."[15] To support his claim, he cited two classic essays on the freedom of speech. John Milton's *Areopagitica*[16] argues against prior restraint of any ideas, no matter how heretical. John Stuart Mill's *On Liberty*[17] advocates a free marketplace of ideas because the only way to test an argument is to hear it presented by a true believer who defends it in earnest.

Philosophers and rhetoricians have compared persuasion to a lover making fervent appeals to his beloved—wooing an audience, for example. Nilsen's ethic of significant choice is nicely captured in the courtship analogy because true love cannot be coerced; it must be freely given. Inspired by Danish philosopher Søren Kierkegaard's description of the ethical religious persuader as lover,[18] I have elsewhere presented a typology of false (unethical) lovers:[19]

> *Smother lovers* won't take no for an answer; their persistence is obnoxious.
> *Legalistic lovers* have a set image of what the other should be.
> *Flirts* are in love with love; they value response, not the other person.
> *Seducers* try deception and flattery to entice the other to submit.
> *Rapists* use force of threats, guilt, or conformity pressure to have their way.

In differing degrees, all five types of unethical persuader violate the human dignity of the people they pursue by taking away choice that is informed and free.

Nilsen obviously would have approved of persuasive appeals that encourage message elaboration through ELM's central route. But his standard of significant choice is not always easy to apply. Do emotional appeals seductively short-circuit our ability to make rational choices, or does heightened emotion actually free us to consider new options? Significant choice, like beauty and credibility, may be in the eye of the beholder.

CRITIQUE: ELABORATING THE MODEL

For the last 25 years, ELM has been a leading—if not *the* leading—theory of persuasion and attitude change. Petty, Cacioppo, and their students have published more than 100 articles on the model, and the dual-process conception has stimulated additional *quantitative research,* application, and critique that go beyond what I'm able to capture in a short chapter. On the other hand, since the time they introduced the theory, Petty and Cacioppo have made it more *complex,* less *predictive,* and less able to offer definitive *practical advice* to the influence practitioner. This is not the direction in which a scientific theory wants to go.

Arizona State University communication researcher Paul Mongeau and communication consultant James Stiff illustrate one of the specific problems with the theory when they charge that "descriptions of the ELM are sufficiently imprecise and ambiguous as to prevent an adequate test of the entire model."[20] For example, ELM views arguments as strong if people are persuaded, but weak if folks remain unmoved. There's no way apart from the persuasive outcome to know whether an argument is strong or weak. Like my childhood friend described in Chapter 3, ELM seems to have its own "never-miss shot." Petty and Cacioppo would say that they never intended to focus on defining factors like strong and weak arguments, high and low source credibility, and highly attractive or unattractive persuaders.[21] That may be true, but it doesn't help much in *testing* the theory. Objective theories that can't be clearly tested lose some of their luster.

Despite the criticisms, ELM is impressive because it pulls together and makes sense out of diverse research results that have puzzled communication theorists for years. For example, why do most people pay less attention to the communication than they do to the communicator? And if speaker credibility is so important, why does its effect dissipate so quickly? ELM's *explanation* is that few listeners are motivated and able to do the mental work required for a major shift in attitude. The two-path hypothesis also helps clarify why good evidence and reasoning can sometimes have a life-changing impact, but usually make no difference at all.

Attitude-change research often yields results that seem confusing or contradictory. Petty and Cacioppo's ELM takes many disjointed findings and pulls them together into a unified whole. This integrative function makes it a valuable theory of influence.

QUESTIONS TO SHARPEN YOUR FOCUS

1. Can you think of five different words or phrases that capture the idea of *message elaboration?*

2. What *peripheral cues* do you usually monitor when someone is trying to influence you?

3. Petty and Cacioppo want to persuade you that their elaboration likelihood model is a mirror of reality. Do you process their arguments for its accuracy closer to your *central route* or your *peripheral route?* Why not the other way?

4. Students of persuasion often wonder whether *high credibility* or *strong arguments* sway people more. How would ELM theorists respond to that question?

A SECOND LOOK

Recommended resource: Richard E. Petty, John T. Cacioppo, Alan J. Strathman, and Joseph R. Priester, "To Think or Not to Think: Exploring Two Routes to Persuasion," in *Persuasion: Psychological Insights and Perspectives,* 2nd ed., Timothy Brock and Melanie Green (eds.), Sage, Thousand Oaks, CA, 2005, pp. 81–116.

Full statement: Richard E. Petty and John T. Cacioppo, *Communication and Persuasion: Central and Peripheral Routes to Attitude Change,* Springer-Verlag, New York, 1986.

Selective exposure is a way to avoid dissonance in the first place. When that fails, the next two hypotheses try to explain how we reduce that anxious feeling.

Hypothesis 2: Postdecision Dissonance Creates a Need for Reassurance

According to Festinger, close-call decisions can generate huge amounts of internal tension after the decision has been made. Three conditions heighten *postdecision dissonance:* (1) the more important the issue, (2) the longer an individual delays in choosing between two equally attractive options, and (3) the greater the difficulty involved in reversing the decision once it has been made. To the extent that these conditions are present, the person will agonize over whether he or she made the right choice.[10] Sometimes referred to as "morning-after-the-night-before" regrets, the misgivings or second thoughts that plague us after a tough choice motivate us to seek reassuring information and social support for our decision.

Postdecision dissonance
Strong doubts experienced after making an important, close-call decision that is difficult to reverse.

A classic example of postdecision dissonance is the mental turmoil a person experiences after signing a contract to buy a new car. The cost is high, there are many competing models from which to choose, and the down payment commits the customer to go through with the purchase. It's not unusual to find a person examining online car reviews *after* they have the car. The buyer is seeking information that confirms the decision already made and quiets nagging doubts.

Many who recover from multiple addictions testify that quitting smoking is harder than giving up booze. Just as countless alcoholics turn to Alcoholics Anonymous for social support, people who try to give up tobacco often need at least one friend, family member, romantic partner, or co-worker who's also going through the pangs of withdrawal. They can remind each other that it's worth the effort. Of course, the decision to stop smoking doesn't fulfill Festinger's third condition of a once-and-for-all, no-going-back, final choice. One can always go back to smoking. In fact, those who swear off cigarettes typically have a few lapses, and total relapses are common. Encouragement and social support are necessary to tamp down the doubts and fears that follow such a tough decision.

Smokers who consciously decide *not* to quit face similar qualms and anxieties. They are bombarded with messages telling them they are putting their health at risk. People who care for them deeply urge them to stop, and nonsmokers look down on them because they don't. University of Kentucky communication professor Alan DeSantis describes the camaraderie he found among regular customers at a Kentucky cigar shop. Just as smoke from cigars drives some folks away, smokers keep postdecision dissonance at bay through collective rationalization with friends who smoke cigars together. DeSantis sees *Cigar Aficionado* as serving the same function. He writes that although the magazine professes to simply celebrate the good life, it actually serves "to relieve the cognitive dissonance associated with the consumption of a potentially dangerous product by adding cognitions, trivializing dissonant information, selectively exposing readers to pro-smoking information, and creating a social support network of fellow cigar smokers."[11]

Hypothesis 3: Minimal Justification for Action Induces Attitude Change

Suppose someone wanted to persuade an ex-smoker who is dying of lung cancer to stop publicly bashing the tobacco industry and to respect cigarette companies' right to market their product. That is one of the assignments given to Nick Naylor, chief spokesman for tobacco companies in the movie *Thank You for Smoking*. His job is to convince "Big Tobacco's" former advertising icon—the Marlboro Man—to switch from outspoken critic to silent partner. Before cognitive dissonance theory, conventional wisdom would have suggested that Naylor work first to change the bitter man's *attitude* toward the industry. If he could convince the cowboy that the cigarette companies are well-intentioned, then the man would change his communication *behavior*. It seemed natural to think of attitude and behavior as the beginning and end of a cause-and-effect sequence.

$$\text{Attitude} \rightarrow \text{Behavior}$$

But Festinger's *minimal justification hypothesis* reverses the sequence. This hypothesis suggests that the best way for Naylor to change the Marlboro Man's attitude toward his former employers is to get him to quit speaking out against them.

$$\text{Behavior} \rightarrow \text{Attitude}$$

Minimal justification hypothesis

A claim that the best way to stimulate an attitude change in others is to offer just enough incentive to elicit counterattitudinal behavior.

Festinger attached one important condition, however. Instead of giving the cowboy massive incentives to abandon his public critique ($100,000 in cash, lifetime health care for his wife, or a threat to harm his kids), Naylor should offer the minimum enticement necessary to induce him to quietly step off his soapbox. Festinger concluded:

> Thus if one wanted to obtain private change in addition to mere public compliance, the best way to do this would be to offer just enough reward or punishment to elicit overt compliance.[12]

Naylor doesn't follow Festinger's advice. Instead, he does it the old-fashioned way by throwing lots of money at the Marlboro Man. He goes to his rundown ranch with a briefcase filled with bundles of hundred-dollar bills, which he pours out on the floor. He labels the money a gift rather than a bribe, but makes it clear that the cowboy can't keep the money if he continues to denounce the tobacco companies. As it turns out, the offer is more than enough because the dying man is worried about how his family will manage after he's gone. So the Marlboro Man takes both the money and a vow of silence, but his antagonistic attitude toward his former employers hasn't changed. Outward *compliance* without inner conviction. For Naylor, that's enough.

Compliance

Public conformity to another's expectation without necessarily having a private conviction that matches the behavior.

There is, however, a brief moment in their discussion that suggests the potential of a minimal justification strategy. When the Marlboro Man looks longingly at the cash, he wonders out loud if he might keep half the money and still denounce the tobacco companies. His question reveals that somewhere between 50 percent and 100 percent of the cash on the floor there's a tipping point where the cowboy becomes willing to be bought off. Festinger predicted that if Naylor were to offer that "just-enough" amount, not only would the Marlboro Man alter his communication behavior, but the dissonance he would feel would also cause him to be less angry at the cigarette companies. Festinger's startling $1/$20 experiment shows how this might work.

A CLASSIC EXPERIMENT: "WOULD I LIE FOR A DOLLAR?"

There is nothing particularly radical about Festinger's first two hypotheses. His selective exposure prediction nicely explains why political rallies attract the party faithful and why the audience for religious radio and television tends to be made up of committed believers. As for postdecision dissonance, all of us have tried to convince ourselves that we've made the right choice after facing a close-call decision. But Festinger's minimal justification hypothesis is counterintuitive. Will a small incentive to act really induce a corresponding attitude change when heaping on the benefits won't? Festinger's famous $1/$20 experiment supported his claim that it will.

Festinger and social psychologist James Carlsmith recruited Stanford University men to participate in a psychological study supposedly investigating industrial relations.[13] As each man arrived at the lab, he was assigned the boring and repetitive task of sorting a large batch of spools into sets of 12 and turning square pegs a quarter turn to the right. The procedure was designed to be both monotonous and tiring. At the end of an hour the experimenter approached the subject and made a request. He claimed that a student assistant had failed to show up and that he needed someone to fill in. The experimenter wanted the subject to tell a potential female subject in the waiting room how much fun the experiment was. Dissonance researchers call this *counterattitudinal advocacy*. We'd call it lying.

Counterattitudinal advocacy
Publicly urging others to believe or do something that is opposed to what the advocate actually believes.

Some of the men were promised $20 to express enthusiasm about the task; others were offered only $1. After adjusting for inflation, that's about $170 or $8.50 today.[14] It's comforting to know that six of the men refused to take part in the deception, but most students tried to recruit the young woman. The gist of the typical conversation was similar for both payment conditions:

> SHE: "I heard it was boring."
> HE: "Oh no, it's really quite fun."

Publicly, that's what persuaders in both conditions said. What differed were the men's *privately* expressed attitudes after the study was over. Students who lied for $20 later confessed that they thought the task of sorting spools was dull. Those who lied for $1 maintained that it was quite enjoyable. (Festinger and Carlsmith practiced their own form of deception in the study—subjects never received the promised money.)

By now you should have a pretty good idea how Festinger interpreted the results. He noted that $20 was a huge sum of money at the time. If a student felt qualms about telling a "white lie," the cash was a ready justification. Thus, the student felt little or no tension between his action and his attitude. But the men who lied for a dollar had lots of cognitive work to do. Their internal dialogue tried to explain away the logical inconsistency of saying a boring task was actually interesting:

> I'm a Stanford man. Am I the kind of guy who would lie for a dollar? No way. Actually, what I told the girl was true. The experiment was a lot of fun.

Festinger said that $1 was just barely enough to induce compliance to the experimenter's request—enough to get them to lie, but not enough to justify it. So the students had to create another justification. They changed their attitude toward the task to bring it into line with their behavior—in other words, to eliminate dissonance.

THREE STATE-OF-THE-ART REVISIONS: THE CAUSE AND EFFECT OF DISSONANCE

The $1/$20 study has been replicated and modified many times in an effort to figure out what creates dissonance and how people reduce it. Based on hundreds of experimental studies, most persuasion researchers today subscribe to one of three revisions of Festinger's original theory.

To illustrate these revisions, we'll consider President Barack Obama, who has struggled with smoking during his adult life. Obama put away his cigarettes before

FIGURE 16–1   Festinger's Process Model of Cognitive Dissonance

Based on Festinger, *A Theory of Cognitive Dissonance*

his 2008 presidential bid, but relapsed during the campaign and his first two years in office. In 2011, however, Obama's doctors declared that he had broken his 30-year cigarette habit.[15] According to First Lady Michelle Obama, it seems that dissonance caused the president's decision to stop: "I think he didn't want to look his girls in the eye and tell them that they shouldn't do something that he was still doing."[16] That sounds like a straightforward explanation, but for cognitive dissonance theorists it isn't enough—they want to know what was going on in the mind of the president that generated and eliminated dissonance.

In order to understand each of the explanations described in the following sections, it will help you to picture the overall dissonance arousal and reduction process. Figure 16-1 shows that four-step sequence. So far we've discussed Festinger's belief that we experience dissonance when we face *logical inconsistency,* or beliefs and behaviors that don't quite add up. *(I value my health. My cigarette habit damages my health.)* That's a claim about the A → B link in the figure. Festinger further asserted that the way to reduce dissonance is to remove the logical inconsistency (point D). The three revisions question these assumptions, and each provides a somewhat different account for why Obama finally kicked his smoking habit.

1. Self-Consistency: The Rationalizing Animal

One of Festinger's early graduate students, University of California social psychologist Elliot Aronson, wasn't convinced that logical inconsistency produces dissonance. He noted that we sometimes find such inconsistencies curious or even amusing. For example, Andrew once received a university parking ticket in the mail dated several months after he'd graduated and moved out of the state. Two thoughts crossed his mind: *(1) I was not parked at the University of Kansas in October* and *(2) I have a parking ticket that says I was.* That's a logical inconsistency, and it made him feel mildly annoyed—but that's not the aversive discomfort Aronson claims is at the heart of dissonance.

Instead, Aronson thinks what produces dissonance is an inconsistency between a cognition and our *self-concept*—how we perceive ourselves. He interprets the $1/$20 experiment as a study of self-presentation.[17] The Stanford men were in a bind because they regarded themselves as decent, truthful human beings, in contrast to their deceptive behavior. In fact, the higher their opinion of their honesty, the more dissonance they would feel when they told the waiting woman that the study was fun. Conversely, if they had seen themselves as liars, cheats, or jerks, they would have felt no tension. As Aronson puts it, "If a person conceives of himself as a 'schnook,' he will be expected to behave like a 'schnook.'"[18]

Andrew's student Caitlin, a vegetarian, wrote about her feelings of guilt after eating meat. Clearly, she perceived that her choice was inconsistent with her self-concept:

When I ate meat for the first time in a year, I was at a hibachi grill where the chef gave each of us a sample of steak. At first I tried just one piece, but that provoked my decision to order fried rice and steak. This choice violated my vegetarian beliefs, but I justified it because it was only a small amount of meat. The day after, I experienced postdecision dissonance: I had strong doubts, a guilty conscience about my decision, and a very upset stomach.

If Aronson is right, what's the best way to persuade someone like President Obama to stop smoking? Showing him studies of tobacco's negative health effects might not be the route to go. Even if Obama acknowledges that his cigarette use is inconsistent with that information, Aronson doesn't think logical inconsistency is enough. The president will only feel dissonance if he sees smoking as inconsistent with his self-concept. Given the first lady's explanation ("I think he didn't want to look his girls in the eye . . ."), Aronson might suggest that the president perceived an inconsistency between his smoking and his fatherly image. Maybe Obama also thought that lighting up contradicted his appearance as a health-conscious person who regularly exercises through pickup basketball games. Throwing away his cigarettes reduced dissonance by removing those psychological inconsistencies.

2. Personal Responsibility for Bad Outcomes (the New Look)

For Princeton psychologist Joel Cooper, both Festinger and Aronson miss the true cause of dissonance. He doesn't think inconsistency—whether logical or psychological—is the main motivating factor. In his *new look* model of cognitive dissonance, Cooper argues that we experience dissonance when we believe our actions have unnecessarily hurt another person. For example, in the minimal justification condition of the $1/$20 experiment, the Stanford men willingly "duped a fellow student to look forward to an exciting experience" while knowing "full well that the waiting participant was in for an immense letdown."[19]

Cooper concludes that dissonance is "a state of arousal caused by behaving in such a way as to feel personally responsible for bringing about an aversive event."[20]

Note that the acceptance of personal *responsibility* requires that the person know ahead of time that his or her action will have negative consequences for someone else, and yet still choose to do the dirty deed. The reactions of participants in minimal justification experiments show that they often feel bad about the potential effects of their messages.

Purdue University social psychologists Richard Heslin and Michael Amo tested the new look by inducing college students to say something that might harm others. The researchers encouraged public speaking students to deliver impromptu speeches to persuade uninformed and uncommitted seventh grade kids that smoking pot wouldn't hurt them. The speakers saw their recorded speeches and were reminded that they'd be identified as actually having pro-marijuana sentiments. The speakers were quite aware that their message might harm kids. One speaker pleaded, "Please don't use my speech. I don't want the course credit; just don't use my speech!"[21] Clearly they felt dissonance, and new look theorists would argue that's because they perceived their actions as harmful (rather than inconsistent). Nevertheless, the speakers actually changed their attitude in the direction of their advocacy—they reduced dissonance by concluding that their actions weren't all that harmful.

New look theorists don't think inconsistency is enough to persuade someone like Obama to stop smoking. Sure, he may perceive that his actions are logically inconsistent with scientific research or psychologically inconsistent with his self-image. But if he only lights up in private—he never smoked publicly while president—he might believe his actions don't hurt anyone else. For Cooper, the first lady's explanation might suggest that the president thought his smoking could hurt their daughters. If Obama quit smoking because he was afraid Malia and Sasha would imitate him, or because he was concerned about their exposure to secondhand smoke, that's the new look in action.

3. Self-Affirmation to Dissipate Dissonance

While the revisions offered by Aronson (self-consistency) and Cooper (new look) address dissonance *creation* at the front end of Festinger's model (the link from A to B in Figure 16-1), Stanford psychologist Claude Steele's self-affirmation approach speaks to the question of dissonance *reduction* at the back end of the model—point D of the figure. Steele doesn't assume that dissonance always drives people to justify their actions by changing their attitudes. He thinks some fortunate people can call up a host of positive thoughts about themselves that will blot out a concern for restoring consistency. If he's right, high self-esteem is a resource for dissonance reduction.

According to Steele, most people are greatly motivated to maintain an overall self-image of moral adequacy. For a participant in the $1/$20 experiment, there's no question that lying to a fellow student makes it harder to preserve that favorable self-concept. But if the guy ignores the ethical slip and focuses instead on his good grades, athletic ability, social skills, and helpfulness to friends who are hurting, the dissonance will only be a blip on the radar screen of his mind and will quickly fade away. Thus, Steele believes that denial, forgetfulness, and trivialization of the incident are alternatives to attitude change, but only for the person who already has high self-esteem.

According to Steele's self-affirmation approach, Obama might have excused his smoking by reminding himself of his esteem-raising qualities, which include "gifted orator, award winning author, and proven intellect who was the first black president of the *Harvard Law Review*,"[22] not to mention president of the United States, winner of a Nobel Peace Prize, and the commander in chief who stopped Osama bin Laden for good. In light of these accomplishments, Obama might regard relapse as a minor inconsistency rather than a major contradiction. In Steele's view, the first lady's comment suggests that the president eventually couldn't rationalize that way anymore. As the son of a man who ignored his family obligations, perhaps Obama came to believe that smoking is a parenting flaw for which career success can't compensate.

Aronson, Cooper, and Steele offer their respective revisions as more accurate accounts of what goes on in people's heads than Festinger's original theory provided. But we don't have to pick one and trash the others. Self-consistency, personal responsibility for bad outcomes, and self-affirmation aren't mutually exclusive explanations. As Cooper suggests, "They each describe a distinct and important piece of the overall dissonance process and, in doing so, make a unique contribution to our understanding of how cognitions about the self [cause] cognitive dissonance and arousal and reduction."[23]

THEORY INTO PRACTICE: PERSUASION THROUGH DISSONANCE

We've placed this chapter in the section on interpersonal influence because Festinger and his followers focused on attitude change as an end product of dissonance. Suppose you know have a friend who holds an opinion that you're convinced is harmful or wrong. What practical advice does the theory offer that might help you alter your friend's conviction?

For openers, don't promise lavish benefits if your friend abandons that attitude or warn of dire consequences if she or he doesn't. A massive reward–punishment strategy may gain behavioral compliance, but the hard sell seldom wins the heart or mind of the person being bribed or pressured. Instead, cultivate your friendship. That way, your own position will tend to bypass the *selective exposure* screen that people put up to avoid threatening ideas. And if your friend eventually adopts your viewpoint, an ongoing bond means you'll be around to offer reassurance when *postdecision dissonance* kicks in.

To be an effective agent of change, you should offer just enough encouragement *(minimal justification)* for your friend to try out novel behavior that departs from old habits. Avoid making an offer that the friend can't refuse. As long as *counterattitudinal actions* are freely chosen and publicly taken, people are more likely to adopt beliefs that support what they've done. The greater the effort involved in acting this way, the greater the chance that their attitudes will change to match their actions.

Finally, as you seek to *induce compliance*, encourage your friend to count the cost of doing what you want and to grasp the potential downside of that behavior for others *(personal responsibility for negative outcomes)*. That kind of understanding will increase the probability that attitude will become consistent with actions. And if things turn sour, your friendship won't.

CRITIQUE: DISSONANCE OVER DISSONANCE

When Festinger died in 1989, his obituary in *American Psychologist* testified to the impact of his work:

> Like Dostoyevski and like Picasso, Festinger set in motion a *style* of research and theory in the social sciences that is now the common property of all creative

workers in the field. . . . Leon is to social psychology what Freud is to clinical psychology and Piaget to developmental psychology.[24]

For more than six decades, social scientists have invoked the theory to *predict future events* and *explain their data.* And as the *Dilbert* cartoon in this chapter suggests, cognitive dissonance is one of the few theories in this book that has achieved name recognition within popular culture. Like the cartoon dog, generations of persuaders have found the theory *practically useful.*

Where the theory falls short is *relative simplicity.* Cornell University psychologist Daryl Bem doesn't think we need the four-stage process diagrammed in Figure 16-1. He claims that *self-perception* is a much simpler explanation than cognitive dissonance. In other words, we simply judge our internal dispositions the same way others do—by observing our behavior.

Self-perception theory
The claim that we determine our attitudes the same way outside observers do—by observing our behavior; an alternative to cognitive dissonance theory.

Bem ran his own $1/$20 study to test his alternative explanation.[25] People heard a recording of a Stanford man's enthusiastic account of the spool-sorting, peg-turning task. Some listeners were told the man received $1 for recruiting the female subject. Since he had little obvious reason to lie, they assumed he really liked the task. Other listeners were told the man received $20 to recruit the woman. These folks assumed the man was bored with the task and was lying to get the money. Bem's subjects didn't speculate about what was going on inside the Stanford man's head. They simply judged his attitude by looking at what he did under the circumstances. If people don't need an understanding of cognitive dissonance to forecast how the men would react, Bem asks, why should social scientists? Bem is convinced that cognitive dissonance theory is like the mousetrap pictured on page 26—much too convoluted.

The theory has also received knocks for how difficult it is to actually observe dissonance. Look again at the four stages of the dissonance process diagram in Figure 16-1. Almost all the creative efforts of dissonance researchers have been aimed at inducing counterattitudinal advocacy at point A—getting people to say something in public that's inconsistent with what they believe in private. When researchers find an attitude shift at point C, they automatically assume that dissonance was built up at point B and is gone by point D. Festinger never specified a reliable way to detect the degree of dissonance a person experiences. If researchers can't observe dissonance, then the theory's core hypotheses aren't *testable*—a big problem for a scientific theory.

Dissonance thermometer
A hypothetical, reliable gauge of the dissonance a person feels as a result of inconsistency.

So scholars have searched for what University of Wisconsin psychologist Patricia Devine refers to as a *dissonance thermometer.*[26] Some researchers have tried to measure cognitive dissonance using self-report survey questions. For example, one survey designed to measure postdecision dissonance after a purchase asks participants to indicate their agreement with the statement, "After I bought this product, I felt furious with myself."[27] But will participants answer honestly? If the theory is right in claiming that humans desire to appear consistent, they very well might not. Other research has tried to gauge the *arousal* component of dissonance through physiological measures such as galvanic skin response.[28] However, sweaty palms are just one possible by-product of dissonance, not dissonance itself.

The most promising attempts to develop a dissonance thermometer have used neuroimaging. For example, Cameron Carter and his University of California, Davis, research team induced participants to engage in counterattitudinal advocacy while hooked up to a functional magnetic resonance imaging (fMRI) machine—basically, a brain scanner.[29] Marked differences in brain activity occurred for these participants compared to a separate group that was honest about their perceptions. Other brain research has found similar results, providing initial hard evidence that the experience of cognitive dissonance is indeed real. Even so, actually observing it is difficult and expensive. If the theory is testable, it certainly isn't simple.

Advocates of cognitive dissonance in the field of communication counter that nothing about mental processes is simple. When we deal with what goes on behind the eyes, we should expect and appreciate complexity. Festinger's theory has energized scientifically oriented communication scholars for more than 60 years. I feel no dissonance by including cognitive dissonance theory in this text.

QUESTIONS TO SHARPEN YOUR FOCUS

1. Cognitive dissonance is a *distressing mental state.* When did you last experience this *aversive drive?* Why might you have trouble answering that question?

2. The results of Festinger's famous *$1/$20 experiment* can be explained in a number of different ways. Which explanation do you find most satisfying?

3. Suppose you want your friends to change their sexist attitudes. What advice does the *minimal justification hypothesis* offer?

4. Cognitive dissonance theory says a lot about cognition—what goes on inside the mind. Why, then, is it in a *communication* theory textbook? What does communication have to do with *dissonance creation* and *reduction?*

A SECOND LOOK

Recommended resource: Joel Cooper, *Cognitive Dissonance: 50 Years of a Classic Theory,* Sage, Thousand Oaks, CA, 2007 (see especially Chapter 1, "Cognitive Dissonance: In the Beginning," pp. 1–27, and Chapter 3, "The Motivational Property of Dissonance," pp. 42–61).

Original statement: Leon Festinger, *A Theory of Cognitive Dissonance,* Stanford University, Stanford, CA, 1957.

Toward a dissonance thermometer: Patricia G. Devine, John M. Tauer et al., "Moving Beyond Attitude Change in the Study of Dissonance-Related Processes," in *Cognitive Dissonance: Progress on a Pivotal Theory in Social Psychology,* Eddie Harmon-Jones and Judson Mills (eds.), American Psychological Association, Washington, DC, 1999, pp. 297–323.

Engaging account of theory's development: Elliot Aronson, "The Evolution of Cognitive Dissonance Theory: A Personal Appraisal," in *The Science of Social Influence: Advances and Future Progress,* Anthon Prankanis (ed.), Psychology Press, New York, 2007, pp. 115–135.

Selective exposure: Silvia Knobloch-Westerwick and Jingbo Meng, "Looking the Other Way: Selective Exposure to Attitude-Consistent and Counterattitudinal Political Information," *Communication Research,* Vol. 36, 2009, pp. 426–448.

Postdecision dissonance: Dave D'Alessio and Mike Allen, "Selective Exposure and Dissonance after Decisions," *Psychological Reports,* Vol. 91, 2002, pp. 527–532.

$1/$20 experiment: Leon Festinger and James Carlsmith, "Cognitive Consequences of Forced Compliance," *Journal of Abnormal and Social Psychology,* Vol. 58, 1959, pp. 203–210.

Self-consistency revision: Ruth Thibodeau and Elliot Aronson, "Taking a Closer Look: Reasserting the Role of the Self-Concept in Dissonance Theory," *Personality and Social Psychology Bulletin,* Vol. 18, 1992, pp. 591–602.

New-look revision: Joel Cooper and Russell Fazio, "A New Look at Dissonance Theory," in *Advances in Experimental Social Psychology, Vol. 17,* Leonard Berkowitz (ed.), Academic Press, Orlando, FL, 1984, pp. 229–262.

Self-affirmation revision: Claude Steele, "The Psychology of Self-Affirmation: Sustaining the Integrity of the Self," in *Advances in Experimental Social Psychology, Vol. 21,* Leonard Berkowitz (ed.), Lawrence Erlbaum, Hillsdale, NJ, 1988, pp. 261–302.

Neuroimaging and cognitive dissonance: Vincent van Veen, Marie K. Krug, Jonathan W. Schooler, and Cameron S. Carter, "Neural Activity Predicts Attitude Change in Cognitive Dissonance," *Nature Neuroscience,* Vol. 12, 2009, pp. 1469–1474.

Critique: Daryl Bem, "Self-Perception: An Alternative Interpretation of Cognitive Dissonance Phenomena," *Psychological Review,* Vol. 74, 1967, pp. 183–200.

Experiencing cognitive dissonance may require a strong need for esteem.
To access a chapter on Abraham Maslow's theory of motivation,
click on Hierarchy of Needs in Archive under Theory Resources at
www.afirstlook.com.

DIVISION THREE

Group and Public Communication

On the morning of January 28, 1986, the space shuttle *Challenger* blasted off from the Kennedy Space Center in Florida. For the first time, the flight carried a civilian schoolteacher, Christa McAuliffe, as part of the crew. Seventy-three seconds after liftoff, millions of schoolchildren watched on television as the rocket disintegrated in a fiery explosion, and the capsule with its crew of seven plunged into the Atlantic Ocean. For many Americans, the *Challenger* disaster marked the end of a love affair with space. As they learned in the months that followed, the tragedy could have been—and should have been—avoided.

An independent presidential commission identified the primary cause of the accident as failure in an O-ring that was supposed to seal a joint, thus allowing volatile rocket fuel to spew out during the "burn." But the commission also concluded that a highly flawed decision process was an important contributing cause of the disaster. Communication, as well as combustion, was responsible for the tragedy. The day before the launch, rocket engineers had talked about the flight being risky. They worried that the O-ring seals had never been tested below 53 degrees Fahrenheit. As one of them later testified, with launch-time temperature in the 20s, getting the O-rings to seal gaps would be like "trying to shove a brick into a crack versus a sponge."[1] Yet during the final "go/no-go" conference, all agreed that the rocket was ready to fly.

Yale social psychologist Irving Janis was convinced that this grievous error wasn't an isolated incident. He had spotted the same group dynamic in other tragic government and corporate decisions. Janis didn't regard chief executives or their advisors as stupid, lazy, or evil. Rather he saw them as victims of "groupthink." He defined *groupthink* as "a mode of thinking that people engage in when they are deeply involved in a cohesive in-group, when the members' strivings for unanimity override their motivation to realistically appraise alternative courses of action."[2] This concurrence-seeking tendency emerges only when the group is characterized by "a warm clubby atmosphere" in which members desire to maintain relationships within the group at all costs. As a result, they automatically apply the "preserve group harmony" test to every decision they face.[3] Janis maintained that the superglue of solidarity that bonds people together can also cause their mental processes to get stuck.

Janis' concept of groupthink highlights the accepted wisdom in the field that there are two functions communication needs to address in any group—a *task function* and a *relationship function*. Task-focused communication moves the group along toward its goal; relational communication holds the group together. Some people concentrate on getting the job done, while others are much more concerned about relationships within the group. Task-oriented individuals are the pistons that drive the group machine. Relationship-oriented members are the lubricant that prevents excessive friction from destroying the group. Good groups require both kinds of people.

Harvard social psychologist Robert Bales was an early theorist who formally made the connection between specific types of communication and accomplishing these two functions.[4] Bales said group locomotion won't happen unless members *ask for* as well as *offer* information, opinions, and suggestions on how the group should proceed. Bales claimed that the most effective groups are those in which the verbal requests and responses are roughly equal in number. If everyone is asking and nobody's offering answers, the group won't make progress toward the goal. If, on the other hand, no one asks and everyone declares, the group will still be stuck.

As for *socio-emotional* communication (Bales' label for relational concern), he regarded showing agreement, showing solidarity, and dramatizing (reducing tension by storytelling) as positive forms of communication that make the group cohesive. He saw showing disagreement, antagonism, and tension as negative moves that tend to pull the group apart. Yet Bales found that groups make better decisions when there are a few negative voices. That squares with Janis' recommendation. He suggests that skepticism and blunt critiques are correctives to groupthink. That kind of communication might have saved the lives of the *Challenger* crew and Americans' support for the space shuttle program.[5]

Functional Perspective on Group Decision Making

of Randy Hirokawa & Dennis Gouran

A cynic once said that a camel is a horse put together by a committee. Others upset by their experience with group decision making give voice to their frustration with equally disparaging quips:[1]

"If you want something done, do it yourself."

"Too many cooks spoil the broth."

"A committee is a group that keeps minutes and wastes hours."

"Committees lure fresh ideas down a cul-de-sac and quietly strangle them."

Randy Hirokawa (professor of communication, University of Hawaii at Hilo) and Dennis Gouran (professor emeritus of communication, Pennsylvania State University) believe that these pessimistic views are unwarranted. Assuming that group members care about the issue, are reasonably intelligent, and face a challenging task that calls for more facts, new ideas, or clear thinking, Hirokawa and Gouran are convinced that group interaction has a positive effect on the final decision. Hirokawa seeks *quality* solutions.[2] Gouran desires decisions that are *appropriate*.[3] Both scholars regard talk as the social tool that helps groups reach better conclusions than they otherwise would. As the Hebrew proverb suggests, "Without counsel plans go wrong, but with many advisers they succeed."[4]

Functional perspective
A prescriptive approach that describes and predicts task-group performance when four communication functions are fulfilled.

The *functional perspective* specifies what communication must accomplish for jointly made decisions to be wise. Gouran laid the groundwork for the theory with his early writing on group decision making. Hirokawa developed the core principles of the theory during his graduate studies, and for 20 years his research tested and refined the theory. On the chance that you would be intrigued by a behind-the-scenes look at real-life group decisions made by college students living together, I'll illustrate the functional perspective by drawing on my experience conducting a two-week off-campus class that students called the "Island Course."

For 20 years I taught a group dynamics seminar limited to eight students on a remote island in northern Lake Michigan. Travel to and from the island was by a single-engine airplane, and we lived together in a cabin—the only structure on the island. Except when a few of us flew off the island to the mainland to get food, our sole communication was with each other. There's no cell phone service or Internet access on the island. Course alumni look back and consider our isolation similar to the reality TV show *Survivor,* yet with a cooperative rather than competitive agenda. No one was ever voted off the island.

The island course was primarily a venture in experiential education. We learned about group dynamics by studying our own interaction. I asked students to adopt the role of participant-observer. Whatever happened among us became a subject for group discussion. Still, the course maintained traditional academic features—four hours of class per day, assigned readings, and final grades. Within that hybrid framework, class members had to decide on a daily schedule, who would do each job necessary for group living, how limited funds for food and fuel would be spent, and on what basis I would assign grades. They understood that they had to live with their decisions for the first half of the course, but could change things for the second week.

As for my role, I let them know that I wouldn't be an active participant in the choices they made—they were free to decide as they saw fit. I'd provide any information they asked for, with the exception of revealing how other island-course groups had handled these issues or disclosing my own personal preferences. In the survey that alums filled out up to two decades after the course, Kelly's response reflected the general consensus:

> I remember Em's role best for what he didn't do. It was my first real experience with a leader who laid back intentionally so that we had to come to our own conclusion—a real democracy. It was refreshing to deal with someone in charge who didn't give all the answers. We were responsible for how things turned out.

As Hirokawa and Gouran predict, how things turned out hinged on the absence or presence of four types of communication.

FOUR FUNCTIONS OF EFFECTIVE DECISION MAKING

Consistent with the approach of Harvard social psychologist Robert Bales and other pioneer researchers, Hirokawa and Gouran draw an analogy between small groups and biological systems. Complex living organisms must satisfy a number of functions, such as respiration, circulation, digestion, and elimination of bodily waste, if they are to survive and thrive in an ever-changing environment. In like manner, Hirokawa and Gouran see the group decision-making process as needing to fulfill four task requirements if members are to reach a high-quality solution. They refer to these conditions as *requisite functions* of effective decision making—thus the "functional perspective" label.[5] The four functions are (1) problem analysis, (2) goal setting, (3) identification of alternatives, and (4) evaluation of positive and negative characteristics of each alternative.

Requisite functions
Requirements for positive group outcome; problem analysis, goal setting, identification of alternatives, and evaluation of pluses and minuses for each.

1. Analysis of the Problem

Is something going on that requires improvement or change? To answer that question, group members must take a realistic look at current conditions. Defenders of the status quo are fond of saying, "If it ain't broke, don't fix it." But, as Hirokawa warns, any misunderstanding of the situation tends to be compounded when the members make their final decision. He also notes that the clearest example of faulty analysis is the failure to recognize a potential threat when one really exists.[6] After people acknowledge a need to be addressed, they still must figure out the nature, extent, and probable cause(s) of the problem that confronts the group.

The first night on the island, students faced the task of drawing up a daily schedule. Because that decision affected other choices, I'll describe how two groups in different summers handled *problem analysis* and how they fulfilled the other three requisite functions that Hirokawa and Gouran identify. I'll refer to them as the *blue group* and the *green group.*

The blue group never did any overt problem analysis. To them, scheduling seemed a simple matter. They jumped to pooling suggestions for what would make the two weeks ideal without ever considering the unique problems that island living posed. Their conversation centered on building in as much time as possible to go outside to enjoy the island during the day and each other at night. Most class members noted that sleeping in late was also an idea with great appeal.

Conversely, the green group started out by exploring what situational limitations they had to factor into their decision. The close quarters of the small cabin proved to be a problem because it provided no aural—and very little visual—privacy. A few light sleepers admitted that it would be impossible for them to get to sleep at night, or to stay asleep in the morning, if someone was talking or walking around. Before budgeting their limited funds for food and fuel, they also figured out the cost for each member to ride the all-terrain cycle (ATC) around the island for 30 minutes a day—something all were eager to do. Their figures showed that they'd run out of money before the end of the course unless they could limit the use of the diesel generator to no more than 10 hours a day. This problem analysis strongly informed the schedule they finally worked out.

2. Goal Setting

Goal setting
Establishing criteria by which to judge proposed solutions.

Because group members need to be clear on what they are trying to accomplish, Hirokawa and Gouran regard discussion of goals and objectives as the second requisite function of decision making. A group needs to establish criteria by which to judge proposed solutions. These criteria must set forth the minimal qualities that an acceptable solution must possess. If the group fails to satisfy this task requirement, it's likely that the decision will be driven by power or passion rather than reason.[7]

Even before they began discussing alternatives, the green group reached a consensus on the specific criteria their schedule had to meet. They agreed that the schedule should include four hours of class as well as enough time for students to prepare and enjoy decent meals and clean up afterward. Members insisted there be a minimum of six hours of free time to play, study, or chill out. They also specified a nighttime block of at least seven hours for sleeping, where both the generator and conversation in the cabin would be turned off. And based on their problem analysis, they wanted to craft an energy-sensitive schedule that wouldn't require the generator to be used for more than 10 hours a day. With the possible exceptions of *decent meals* and *energy sensitive,* these were measurable goals that could be used to gauge the quality of their final decision.

Unlike the green group, the blue group never spoke of goals, objectives, standards, targets, or criteria. Their discussion made it clear that fun in the sun and lots of casual time together were high priorities. But these overlapping desires are quite subjective and open to multiple interpretations. With no definitive goals to focus their discussion, it's difficult for group members to know whether they're

Problem analysis
Determining the nature, extent, and cause(s) of the problem facing the group.

making an appropriate decision. Or, as sports enthusiasts put it, *You don't know you're winning if you don't keep score.*

3. Identification of Alternatives

Hirokawa and Gouran stress the importance of marshaling a number of alternative solutions from which group members can choose:

> If no one calls attention to the need for generating as many alternatives as is realistically possible, then relatively few may be introduced, and the corresponding possibility of finding the acceptable answer will be low.[8]

Identification of alternatives
Generation of options to sufficiently solve the problem.

Both island-course groups wanted to schedule time when they could enjoy the island. Swimming, sunbathing, stone skipping, playing volleyball or soccer, trailblazing, riding the ATC, treasure hunting, bird watching, picking wild raspberries, building tree forts in the woods, and just lolling in the hammock were a few of the daylight activities suggested by blue and green course members alike. But the groups varied greatly on the number of options they generated for scheduling class and meals. The blue group seemed to have tunnel vision and could only picture

"Gentlemen, the fact that all my horses and all my men couldn't put Humpty together again simply proves to me that I must have more horses and more men."

©Dana Fradon/The New Yorker Collection/The Cartoon Bank

a schedule with two hours of class in the morning and two hours at night. No other options were seriously considered. They were equally locked into the traditional practice of lunch at noon and dinner at six. One tentatively suggested alternative was shot down before it could be explained.

A girl in the green group had read an article on brainstorming before the course and urged classmates, "Let's see how many different ideas we can think of for when we'll eat." They took her up on it and suggested a dozen meal plans: late breakfast; no breakfast; brunch instead of breakfast and lunch; one big meal a day at noon; dinner at noon and light supper in the evening; a picnic snack to eat in the afternoon; four light meals a day; and a mix of these options.

The green group wasn't quite as creative with alternatives for class, yet they went beyond the two-hours-in-the-morning-and-two-at-night plan that seemed written in stone for the blue group. Different class members suggested three hours in the morning and one at night; four hours in the morning with two breaks; three class sessions of 80 minutes in the morning, afternoon, and night; three hours of class at night when the generator would be on anyway; all classes during daylight hours so the generator wouldn't have to be on. Their final decision turned out to be a combination of these ideas.

4. Evaluation of Positive and Negative Characteristics

After a group has identified alternative solutions, the participants must take care to test the relative merits of each option against the criteria they believe are important. This point-by-point comparison doesn't take place automatically. Hirokawa and Gouran warn that groups get sloppy and often need one member to remind the others to consider both the positive and negative features of each alternative.

Evaluation of positive and negative characteristics
Testing the relative merits of each option against the criteria selected; weighing the benefits and costs.

Because blue group members concentrated on only one schedule option, their evaluation of its characteristics was rather brief. They did a nice job of articulating the benefits they saw in their plan—a similarity to campus schedule, afternoons free for outdoor recreation, late-night opportunity to strengthen relationships, and a chance to sleep in before a late morning class. What's not to like? But the blue group never addressed that issue. Hirokawa notes that some group tasks have a negative *bias* in that spotting the downside of each alternative is more important than identifying its positive qualities.[9] Since students were new to island living, it turned out that focusing on the disadvantages inherent in any plan would have been time well spent.

The green group discussed the pluses and minuses of every alternative. They concluded that late-night activity came at the cost of money they'd rather spend on food. They also saw that long class sessions in this idyllic setting could result in boredom and resentment. And for many of the meal plans they were considering, the amount of time spent in preparation, eating, and cleanup struck them as excessive. These realizations led them to adopt the novel schedule displayed on the bottom of Figure 17-1. Note that the three shorter classes meet in daylight hours. Since there are only two sit-down meals with prep and cleanup, there's more free time for whatever people want to do. And there are more than eight hours of darkness for course members and the generator to be at rest.

When the green group members first looked at their schedule shown in Figure 17-1, some had second thoughts. For them, it seemed bizarre to be going to bed at 10 P.M., with some folks rising at 6:30 in the morning. But one girl suggested advancing all clocks, watches, and times on the schedule ahead by one hour. "We'll

BLUE GROUP	Sleep in Generator on when needed	Breakfast	Class (2 hours)	Lunch	Free time	Class (2 hours)	Dinner	Free time	Lights out

	7	8	9	10	11	12	1	2	3	4	5	6	7	8	9	10	11	12

GREEN GROUP	Coffee Tea Cocoa	Class (90 min)	Complete brunch	Class (90 min)	Free time Picnic at leisure	Class (1 hour)	Dinner	Free time	Lights out

[The Green Group time line depicts their proposal before advancing it an hour to "Island Daylight Saving Time."]

FIGURE 17-1   Blue and Green Group Schedules for the Island Course

feel better about going to bed at 11, and our schedule will still be in sync with the sun," she explained. The others were intrigued by the elegant simplicity of her idea, so before turning in that night, we switched to Island Daylight Saving Time. Our body clocks were quick to adjust as well.

Predictable Outcomes

So what difference did Hirokawa and Gouran's four requisite functions make for these two island groups? Over the course of two weeks, how did these contrasting schedules turn out in practice? Both groups stuck to their plan for the first week, but by the fifth day, the class that didn't address the four functions was struggling. No one in the blue group went to sleep before midnight, and once someone got up early in the morning, no one else could sleep. Students slept only six or seven hours, and those who planned to sleep in were irritated at others who woke them up. The two-hour class at night became a real drag; no one looked forward to that time together.

Perhaps the biggest problem triggered by the blue group's decision was prolonged use of the generator. Extended activity in the cabin resulted in the generator running more than 12 hours a day, at a cost that took a big bite out of the food budget. The blue group made some adjustments the second week, but the menu for our last few meals seemed to consist of grubs and yucca roots. And there was no gas for the ATC.

On the other hand, the eight students in the green group were quite satisfied with the schedule they crafted. They saved time and energy by eating only two meals in the cabin, holding all classes during daylight hours, and preparing the afternoon picnic snack and the brunch at the same time. They had more time for fun in the sun than the blue group did, and looked forward to the abbreviated evening class as a lead-in to a relaxed dinner.

The well-rested green group took great pride in limiting generator use to eight hours per day and celebrated with a T-bone steak dinner the last night with the money they'd saved. In addition, there was enough room in the budget to guarantee unlimited rides on the ATC. As Hirokawa and Gouran suggest, it took discussion of all four requisite functions to hammer out a quality solution that was appropriate for the island course.

PRIORITIZING THE FOUR FUNCTIONS

The word *prioritizing* refers to addressing the four requisite functions in a logical progression. Hirokawa originally thought that no one sequence or group agenda does the job better than another. As long as the group ends up dealing with all four

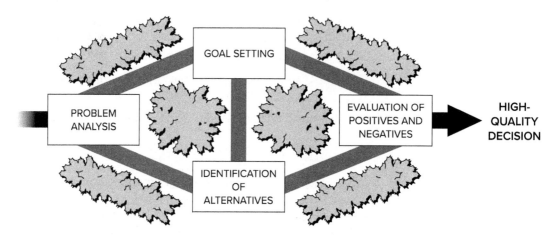

FIGURE 17–2   An Effective Decision-Making Path from the Functional Perspective

functions, the route its members take won't make much difference. Yet he's discovered the groups that successfully resolve especially difficult problems usually take a common decision-making path.[10]

The term *prioritizing* in the heading also refers to the question of which function is most important in order for a group to maximize the probability of a high-quality decision. Hirokawa and Gouran originally thought that no single function is inherently more important than any of the others.[11] But as Hirokawa admits in a paper entitled, "To Err Is Human, To Correct for It Divine," they were wrong. The paper reports on a meta-analysis of 60 empirical research studies on the functional perspective. The study concludes that of the four functions, *evaluation of negative consequences of alternative solutions* is by far the most crucial to ensure a quality decision.[12] Perhaps to stress its importance, Hirokawa now splits up the evaluation of alternatives function into positive outcomes and negative outcomes for each option, and speaks of five requisite functions rather than four.

Figure 17–2 portrays the path that seems to offer the best problem-solving progression. Groups start with problem analysis, then deal with goal setting and identifying alternatives, and end by evaluating the positive and negative characteristics of each alternative before making a final choice. This decision-making flow parallels the advice I once heard on National Public Radio's *Car Talk*. Asked how car owners should handle close-call decisions on auto repair, mechanics Tom and Ray Magliozzi ("Click and Clack, the Tappet Brothers") gave a street-smart answer that ran something like this:

> First, figure out what's broke. Then, make up your mind how good you want to fix it. Or before that ask your mechanic to list the choices you've got. Either way, you gotta do both. Finally, weigh the bang-for-the-buck that each job gives. Then decide.

THE ROLE OF COMMUNICATION IN FULFILLING THE FUNCTIONS

Most communication scholars believe that discussion among members has a significant effect on the quality of group decisions. Traditional wisdom suggests that talk is the medium, channel, or conduit through which information travels between participants.[13] Verbal interaction makes it possible for members to (1) distribute and pool information, (2) catch and remedy errors, and (3) influence each other. But distractions and nonproductive conversation create channel noise, causing a loss of information. Group researcher Ivan Steiner claimed that[14]

$$\begin{matrix} \text{Actual Group} \\ \text{Productivity} \end{matrix} = \begin{matrix} \text{Potential} \\ \text{Productivity} \end{matrix} - \begin{matrix} \text{Losses Due} \\ \text{to Processes} \end{matrix}$$

It follows that communication is best when it doesn't obstruct or distort the free flow of ideas.

While not rejecting this traditional view, Hirokawa believes that communication plays a more active role in crafting quality decisions. Like social constructionists (see Chapters 5, 6, and 11), he regards group discussion as a tool or instrument that group members use to create the social reality in which decisions are made.[15] Discussion exerts its own impact on the end product of the group.

How does this work in practice? Think of the dark, wide lines in Figure 17–2 as safe trails through a dense thicket—paths that connect the four key task functions and lead ultimately to the goal of a high-quality group decision. Members can easily wander off that goal path and get caught up in a tangle of prickerbushes that thwart the group's progress. The bushes in this analogy represent distractions or barriers that hinder movement toward the goal. Hirokawa and Gouran list a number of thorny obstacles—ignorance of the issue, faulty facts, misguided assumptions, sloppy evaluation of options, illogical inferences, disregard of procedural norms, and undue influence by powerful members. They believe that people go astray through talk, but they also believe that communication has the power to pull them back onto the goal-directed path.

Consistent with these convictions, Hirokawa and Gouran outline three types of communication in decision-making groups:

1. **Promotive**—interaction that moves the group along the goal path by calling attention to one of the four requisite decision-making functions.

2. **Disruptive**—interaction that diverts, hinders, or frustrates group members' ability to achieve the four task functions.

3. **Counteractive**—interaction that members use to get the group back on track.

Hirokawa and Gouran suggest that most comments from group members disrupt rather than promote progress toward the goal. They conclude, therefore, that "effective group decision-making is perhaps best understood as a consequence of the exercise of counteractive influence."[16] In other words, someone has to say something that will get the group back on track. After reading about these three types of communication in her comm theory course, Lydia recognized that her comments during a critical discussion had been disruptive rather than counteractive:

> I think group decision making is important, even vital, yet I am the worst at it. When I was in high school, I applied to be a foreign exchange student to Germany. For our final selection task the six finalists had to come up with a solution to a problem, then present it to the directors. Based on the group process, the directors would select the four of us who would go. Judging by Hirokawa and Gouran's theory, I see why I never went to Germany. I'd like to say it's because I tend to promote different alternatives, however, I can see how my smart/sarcastic comments tend to disrupt and take away from the task of problem analysis and goal setting. I wish I had a chance to do it over—after my big personality change, of course.

THOUGHTFUL ADVICE FOR THOSE WHO KNOW THEY ARE RIGHT

How can you and I use the functional perspective to facilitate better group decisions? We can start with a healthy dose of humility concerning the wisdom of our own opinions. Hirokawa and Gouran report that groups often abandon the rational path due to the persuasive efforts of members who are convinced that they alone have the right answer. Their discussion style proclaims, "Don't confuse me with the facts; my mind's made up," and they wear down the opposition. We can make sure we don't come to the table with the sort of closed-minded attitude that torpedoes honest discussion. Additionally, we should be wary of pushing any "intuitive hunch" or "gut feeling" that we can't back up with reasonable evidence. These are errors to avoid.

We can also take proactive measures to promote clear thinking within the group. In almost every article they write, Hirokawa and Gouran acknowledge their intellectual debt to early-twentieth-century American pragmatist philosopher John Dewey.[17] Dewey's pragmatism was based on the hopeful assumption that practical decisions can be brought under more intelligent control through the process of rational inquiry.[18] He advocated a six-step process of *reflective thinking* that parallels a doctor's approach to treating a patient:[19]

1. Recognize symptoms of illness.
2. Diagnose the cause of the ailment.
3. Establish criteria for wellness.
4. Consider possible remedies.
5. Test to determine which solutions will work.
6. Implement or prescribe the best solution.

Reflective thinking
Thinking that favors rational consideration over intuitive hunches or pressure from those with clout.

Note that Hirokawa and Gouran's four requisite functions are almost exact replicas of steps 2, 3, 4, and 5 in Dewey's reflective-thinking process. Both lists recommend that group members discuss issues in a way that promotes problem analysis, goal setting, discovery of alternatives, and evaluation of these options. When we're tempted to make remarks that will detract from the process, Hirokawa and Gouran suggest we bite our tongues. And when others say things that sidetrack the group from fulfilling the four functional requisites, the theorists urge us to counter with a comment aimed at getting the group back on a rational path.

You may be hesitant to counteract the dubious logic of a powerful leader or a high-status member of the group, but Hirokawa and Gouran don't advocate direct criticism. Instead, they recommend a strategy of insisting on a careful process. By raising questions, calling for more alternatives, and urging a thorough evaluation of evidence, a low-status member can have a high-power impact on the quality of the final decision.

ETHICAL REFLECTION: HABERMAS' DISCOURSE ETHICS

German philosopher Jürgen Habermas suggests a rational group process through which people can determine right from wrong—a different kind of decision than Hirokawa and Gouran usually study. In order to develop guidelines for ethical action, the Frankfurt School critical theorist pictures a diverse group of people engaged in public discourse. Habermas' ethical approach seeks an after-the-fact discussion about what we did in a particular situation and why we decided to do it. Being ethical means being accountable.[20]

Habermas assumes that people within a given culture or community can pretty much agree on the good they want to accomplish, and that over time they've built up practical wisdom on how to achieve it. For example, your campus newspaper reporters assume that it's good for students to know more about what's going on within the school's administration ("the people's right to know") and that guaranteeing confidentiality to insiders is the best way to find out ("protecting their sources"). This newsroom common sense is a good place to start doing journalistic ethics, but reporters' justification of the practice typically lacks reflective rigor. It often doesn't take into account the interests of everyone affected by their stories.

Discourse ethics

Jürgen Habermas' vision of the ideal speech situation in which diverse participants could rationally reach a consensus on universal ethical standards.

Habermas' *discourse ethics* sets up a discursive test for the validity of any moral claim. The person who performed an act must be prepared to discuss what he or she did and why he or she did it—in an open forum. This deliberative process is a two-stage process of justification and application. The actor must reveal the general ethical principle that he or she used to justify the action and then show why it was the appropriate thing to do in those particular circumstances. Habermas imagines an *ideal speech situation* where participants are free to listen to reason and speak their minds without fear of constraint or control.[21] He's convinced that the validity of any ethical consensus can be reached only to the extent that three requirements are met:[22]

1. *Requirement for access.* All people affected by the ethical norm being debated can attend and be heard, regardless of their status. That means donors, administrators, professors, students, and minimum-wage staff at the school are welcome at the table without prejudice.

2. *Requirement for argument.* All participants are expected to exchange their points of view in the spirit of genuine reciprocity and mutual understanding. They aren't merely trying to advance their own interests, but are trying to figure out whether an action serves the common good.

Ideal speech situation

A discourse on ethical accountability in which discussants represent all who will be affected by the decision, pursue discourse in a spirit of seeking the common good, and are committed to finding universal standards.

3. *Requirement for justification.* Everyone is committed to a standard of universalization. What makes ethical claims legitimate is their "acceptance not only among those who agree to live with and by them but by anyone *affected* by them."[23]

Habermas understands that thoroughly noncoercive dialogue is a utopian dream, yet he finds his conception of the ideal speech situation helpful in gauging the degree to which a discussion is rational. This, of course, is a major goal of Hirokawa's, Gouran's, and Dewey's. The trick is getting group members to do it.

CRITIQUE: VALID ONLY IF NEW FUNCTIONS ARE ADDED OR SCOPE IS NARROWED

In their premillennial review of small-group communication literature, John Cragan and David Wright conclude that there are three leading theories.[24] One is Bormann's *symbolic convergence theory,* discussed in the next chapter. The second is Scott Poole's *adaptive structuration theory,* which you can read about in the theory archive at *www.afirstlook.com.* The third is Hirokawa and Gouran's functional perspective. In their critique of the functional perspective, communication professor Cynthia Stohl (University of California, Santa Barbara) and research consultant Michael Holmes explain why it is so highly regarded:

The basic premise of the perspective, that communication serves task functions and the accomplishment of those functions should be associated with effective group decisions, is intuitively appealing and sensible. It also meets the standards of an objective theory in that it explains, is testable, simple, and practical.[25]

As a result, many communication scholars endorse the theory as a model for group discussion and decision making. One of my students is so convinced that he wrote, "A list of the four functions should be woven into the carpet of every committee room."

Yet Stohl and Holmes note that researchers get mixed results when they test the theory's prediction. They claim it's because the functional perspective "treats all groups as if they were self-contained, zero-history systems."[26] They're referring to the research and development of the theory that was based on forming small groups of strangers in a laboratory and asking them to reach agreement on the best way to solve a hypothetical problem. For example, the groups were asked to decide the consequences for students caught cheating on an exam, or to rank-order the importance of supplies for survival if lost at sea in a lifeboat. Their decisions had no effect on them or anyone else actually facing the problem.

Stohl and Holmes suggest that unless the theorists adopt a *bona fide group* approach, the theory is irrelevant for most real-life group decisions. Stohl and her colleague at UC Santa Barbara, Linda Putnam, introduced the term *bona fide group* to refer to "intact groups with stable, yet permeable boundaries and interdependent with their immediate context."[27] In *bona fide groups,* most participants already know each other and often have relationships with each other outside the group. Membership is established, but fluid in that a new person might join the group, or another member may drop out or be absent when the decision is made. In these authentic situations, many members have roles in overlapping groups that have a stake in the decision they make, and are typically responsible to a leader or manager outside the group.

Bona fide groups
Intact groups with stable, yet permeable boundaries and interdependent with their immediate context; real-life groups.

Since most real-life groups have a prior decision-making history and are embedded within a larger organization, Stohl and Holmes advocate a *historical function* that requires the group to talk about how past decisions were made. They also recommend an *institutional function* that is satisfied when members discuss the reality of power brokers and stakeholders who aren't at the table, but whose views clearly affect and are affected by the group decision.

Two decades after introducing the theory, Gouran also raised doubts about how useful the functional perspective is for many small-group discussions.[28] He notes that almost all group dynamics research has dealt with decision making and problem solving. Although he and Hirokawa attempted to craft a one-size-fits-all model for group communication, he now believes it's beneficial for members to fulfill the four requisite functions only when they are addressing *questions of policy.* That's not always the case.

Investigative panels and juries deal with *questions of fact* such as "What happened?" or "Who's responsible?" College admission boards and product design teams face *questions of conjecture,* trying to figure out what's likely to happen in an uncertain future without any current way of knowing if their predictions are right. Religious groups and addiction recovery support groups face emotionally loaded *questions of value,* with members sharing or debating what they believe is acceptable, appropriate, ethical, or morally right. None of these questions has a discernable "right" or "high-quality" answer. Gouran doesn't believe that these alternative group goals invalidate the functional perspective, but he does suggest their existence shows that the theory isn't relevant in every situation. The scope of the functional perspective is more limited than first believed.

QUESTIONS TO SHARPEN YOUR FOCUS

1. Hirokawa and Gouran claim that small groups are like living *systems.* Do you see parallels between the four *functional requisites* of task groups and the body's need for respiration, circulation, digestion, and elimination?

2. Given that the functional theory focuses on *decision-making* and *problem-solving* groups, why is its silence on *relationship* issues a problem?

3. Think of a time when you've been part of a task group that strayed from the *goal path.* What *counteractive statement* could you have made that might have brought it back on track?

4. Are you part of a *bona fide* small group? What *institutional* and *historical* issues would need to be discussed in order to reach a quality decision you could embrace and implement?

CONVERSATIONS

View this segment online at www.afirstlook.com.

As you might expect from an objective theorist discussing a rational theory, Randy Hirokawa gives clear, concise responses to my opening questions about group decision making. Is it possible he will find a yet undiscovered requisite function? Are jokes a form of disruptive communication? But as the conversation continues, Hirokawa voices ideas not usually heard from thoroughgoing empiricists. He refers to the irony of questionable motives producing beneficial actions, a subjective standard to determine whether a decision is good, and his belief that there are no guarantees in life. Many students consider this conversation the best of the bunch.

A SECOND LOOK

Recommended resource: Dennis Gouran, Randy Hirokawa, Kelly Julian, and Geoff Leatham, "The Evolution and Current Status of the Functional Perspective on Communication in Decision-Making and Problem-Solving Groups," in *Communication Yearbook 16,* Stanley Deetz (ed.), Sage, Newbury Park, CA, 1993, pp. 573–600.

Original statement: Dennis Gouran and Randy Hirokawa, "The Role of Communication in Decision-Making Groups: A Functional Perspective," in *Communications in Transition,* Mary Mander (ed.), Praeger, New York, 1983, pp. 168–185.

Research review: Randy Hirokawa, "From the Tiny Pond to the Big Ocean: Studying Communication and Group Decision-Making Effectiveness from a Functional Perspective," 1999 B. Aubrey Fisher Memorial Lecture, Department of Communication, University of Utah, Salt Lake City, UT.

Role of communication: Randy Hirokawa and Dirk Scheerhorn, "Communication in Faulty Group Decision-Making," in *Communication and Group Decision-Making,* Randy Hirokawa and M. Scott Poole (eds.), Sage, Beverly Hills, CA, 1986, pp. 63–80.

Additional propositions: Dennis Gouran and Randy Hirokawa, "Effective Decision Making and Problem Solving in Groups: A Functional Perspective," in *Small Group Communication: Theory and Practice,* 8th ed., Randy Hirokawa, Robert Cathcart et al. (eds.), Roxbury, Los Angeles, CA, 2003, pp. 27–38.

Survey of group theories taking a functional perspective: Andrea B. Hollingshead, Gwen Wittenbaum et al., "A Look at Groups from the Functional Perspective," in *Theories of Small Groups: Interdisciplinary Perspectives,* M. Scott Poole and Andrea B. Hollingshead (eds.), Sage, London, 2005, pp. 21–62.

Requisite functions accomplished face-to-face vs. online: Shu-Chu Sarrina Li, "Computer-Mediated Communication and Group Decision Making: A Functional Perspective," *Small Group Research,* Vol. 38, 2007, pp. 593–614.

Equivocal evidence that communication changes group decisions: Dean E. Hewes, "The Influence of Communication Processes on Group Outcomes: Antithesis and Thesis," *Human Communication Research,* Vol. 35, 2009, pp. 249–271.

Critique: Cynthia Stohl and Michael Holmes, "A Functional Perspective for Bona Fide Groups," *Communication Yearbook 16,* 1993, pp. 601–614.

Theorist's assessment of limited scope: Dennis Gouran, "Reflections on the Type of Question as a Determinant of the Form of Interaction in Decision-Making and Problem-Solving Discussions," *Communication Quarterly,* Vol. 53, 2003, pp. 111–125.

To access a chapter on Irving Janis' Groupthink,
click on Archive under Theory Resources at
www.afirstlook.com.

Symbolic Convergence Theory

of Ernest Bormann

In the introduction to this section on group communication, I refer to Harvard social psychologist Robert Bales' work to categorize comments made in small-group discussions. On the basis of his research with zero-history problem-solving groups in his lab, Bales discovered that *dramatizing* was a significant type of communication that often fostered group cohesiveness.[1] The late University of Minnesota communication professor Ernest Bormann picked up on Bales' finding and undertook a more extensive study of newly formed groups to examine leadership emergence, decision making, norms, cohesiveness, and a number of other features of group life.[2]

Similar to Bales, Bormann and his team of colleagues observed that group members often dramatized events happening outside the group, things that took place at previous meetings, or what might possibly occur among them in the future. Sometimes these stories fell flat and the discussion moved in a different direction. But at other times group members responded enthusiastically by adding on to the story or chiming in with their own matching narratives. When the drama was enhanced in this way, members developed a common group consciousness and drew closer together. On the basis of extensive case studies, Bormann set forth the central explanatory principle of symbolic convergence theory (SCT):

Sharing group fantasies creates symbolic convergence.[3]

When she read about Bormann's theory, communication theory student Maggie had no difficulty illustrating this core claim. Two weeks before her class began, she served as a student leader in the Wheaton Passage program for new freshmen that's held at a camp in Wisconsin's Northwoods. One of the stated goals of this optional offering is to build intentional community. In her application log, Maggie wrote of unplanned communication that achieved this end.

> Cabin 8 was the rustic, run-down cabin that my group of Passage students was assigned to live in for the week. My co-leader and I decked the cabin out with decorations by hanging Christmas lights and origami doves, yet there was no escaping the massive holes in the screens, sticky messes in the drawers, and the spiders

residing in the rafters. The night students arrived, we walked our group of girls past the brand new cabins, arrived at our old cabin, and presented Cabin 8—their home for a week. Needless to say, they were less than pleased.

The next day as our group was trekking to our morning activity, one of the girls brought up what she thought the perfect cabin would look like. Others jumped in with their ideas. For 10 minutes, each girl contributed something to the discussion of the fantasy cabin. Hot tubs, screened-in porches, soft carpet, lounge chairs, and a glass roof for stargazing were all mentioned as features in their ideal cabin. Looking back on this experience, I see how this shared fantasy played a role in our cabin bonding. As the week went on, our dream cabin became a running joke within our group that helped students develop a sense of closeness—what they deemed "hardcoreness." While living in the crummy cabin, they frequently revisited the image of the ideal cabin they created in their conversation.

DRAMATIZING MESSAGES: CREATIVE INTERPRETATIONS OF THERE-AND-THEN

Many comments in task-oriented discussion groups offer lines of argument, factual information, members' opinions, and suggestions for how the group should proceed. That's the kind of member contribution Hirokawa and Gouran's functional perspective values (see Chapter 17). Advocates of rational discussion believe it's usually disruptive and counterproductive when someone cracks a joke, describes a movie, or starts talking about plans for the upcoming weekend. Not so for Bormann. SCT classifies these examples and many other forms of speaking as *dramatizing messages* and believes that conversations about things outside of what's going on right now can often serve the group well.

A dramatizing message is one that contains imaginative language such as a pun or other wordplay, figure of speech (e.g., metaphor, simile, personification), analogy, anecdote, allegory, fable, narrative, story, or other creative expression of ideas. Whatever the form, the dramatizing message describes events occurring somewhere else and/or at some time other than the here-and-now.[4]

Dramatizing message
Imaginative language by a group member describing past, future, or outside events; creative interpretations of there-and-then.

Notice first that a group member's words must paint a picture or call to mind an image in order to be labeled a dramatizing message. A comment that groups need conflict in order to make good decisions might stimulate discussion among members, but that's not dramatizing in the way Bormann used the term. Second, a vivid message qualifies as dramatizing if it either describes something outside the group or portrays an event that has happened within the group in the past or might happen to the group in the future. Comments that have no imagery or those that refer to what's currently going on in the group make up the bulk of most group discussions. They aren't dramatizing messages.

When Maggie's girls started to verbally construct their ideal cabin, they were using imaginative language to talk about what they'd like to see in the future, probably wishing it would magically appear that night. If in a darker tone one of the girls expressed her hope that someone would set fire to the cabin before they returned, that message would also be dramatizing. But if the group of girls sat around in the cabin grousing about the spiders, mosquitoes, and sticky goo in the drawers, those comments would be about the here-and-now and wouldn't be defined as dramatizing messages.

Why is this distinction so important to Bormann and SCT advocates? Because dramatizing messages are interpretive. They aren't knee-jerk responses to experiences of the moment. "Dramatizing accounts of past occurrences artistically organize what are usually more complex, ambiguous, and chaotic experiences."[5] They help the speaker, and sometimes the listeners, make sense out of a confusing situation or bring some clarity to an uncertain future. Whether or not other group members connect with their imagery, dramatizing messages are creative interpretations of the there-and-then.

FANTASY CHAIN REACTIONS: UNPREDICTABLE SYMBOLIC EXPLOSIONS

Some people use the term *fantasy* to refer to children's literature, sexual desire, or things "not true." Bormann, however, reserved the term *fantasy* for dramatizing messages that are enthusiastically embraced by the whole group. Most dramatizing messages don't get that kind of reaction. They often fall on deaf ears, or group members listen but take a ho-hum attitude toward what was said. Of course, an embarrassing silence or a quick change of subject makes it obvious that the dramatizing message has fallen flat. As the cartoon below illustrates, there may even be group members who openly oppose what was said. Yet as Bormann noted, "Some dramatizing messages cause a symbolic explosion in the form of a chain reaction in which members join in until the entire group comes alive."[6] He described what he had seen when a fantasy chains out in this way:

> The tempo of the conversation would pick up. People would grow excited, interrupt one another, blush, laugh, forget their self-consciousness. The tone of the meeting, often quiet and tense immediately prior to the dramatizing, would become lively, animated, and boisterous, the chaining process, involving both the verbal and nonverbal communication, indicating participation in the drama.[7]

"Pardon us, Harrison, if the board fails to share your enthusiasm for the foliage up in Darien."
©Jack Ziegler/The New Yorker Collection/The Cartoon Bank

A concrete example of a fantasy chain and its results may be helpful. University of Kentucky communication professor Alan DeSantis asks us to picture a group of Kentucky-born, middle-aged white guys sitting around a cigar store smoking hand-rolled imported cigars. As the topic shifts from college basketball to the risk of smoking, the owner tells the story of a heart surgeon who came into the shop after having been on duty for 36 hours. After lighting up, the doctor blew out a big mouthful of smoke and said, "This is the most relaxed I have felt in days. Now how can that be bad for you?"[8]

Whether or not the doctor really said this isn't the issue. Symbolic convergence theory is concerned with the group's response to the tale. In this case the patrons chuckle in appreciation, nod in agreement, or say "You've got it!" to punctuate the narrative. Some vie to tell their own stories that dismiss the harm of cigar smoking, a pastime they consider a benign practice. Bormann said that we can spot a *fantasy chain* through a common response to the imagery. DeSantis, who was a cigar-smoking participant-observer among the shop's regular customers, affirms that the group's response to the owner's story paralleled Bormann's description above.

Symbolic convergence researchers have had little success predicting when a fantasy will ignite and trigger a chain reaction. They've found there's a better chance of a fantasy chaining out when the group is frustrated (as with Maggie's girls) or when they are bogged down in an effort to solve a thorny problem. Also, members with rhetorical skill seem to have a better chance of providing the spark, but there's no guarantee that their words will ignite others. And even when a skillful image-maker does spark a fantasy chain, he or she has little control over where the conversation will go. Fantasy chains seem to have a life of their own. But once a fantasy chain catches fire, symbolic convergence theory predicts that the group will converge around a fantasy theme.

Fantasy chain
A symbolic explosion of lively agreement within a group in response to a member's dramatizing message.

FANTASY THEMES—CONTENT, MOTIVES, CUES, TYPES

Bormann's technical definition of *fantasy* is "the creative and imaginative shared interpretation of events that fulfills a group's psychological or rhetorical needs."[9]

Fantasy
The creative and imaginative shared interpretation of events that fulfills a group's psychological or rhetorical needs.

Think of a *fantasy theme* as the *content* of the dramatizing message that successfully sparks a fantasy chain. As such, it's the theory's basic unit of analysis. Because fantasy themes reflect and create a group's culture, all SCT researchers seek to identify the fantasy theme or themes that group members share. When spotted, fantasy themes are consistently ordered, always interpretive, and they inevitably put the group's slant on things. Fantasy themes act as a rhetorical means to sway doubters or naysayers.

Fantasy theme
Content of the fantasy that has chained out within a group; SCT's basic unit of analysis.

When a fantasy chains out among core patrons in the cigar store, we would expect to see that same theme run throughout multiple narratives. Perhaps the hero of every man's account is a famous cigar smoker who lived into old age without ill effects—think George Burns, Winston Churchill, or Fidel Castro. Or maybe each image reflects a meddling government bureaucrat who wants to limit their right to enjoy a cigar in a public place. Along with examples of long-lived smokers, group fantasies might focus on the difference between cigars and cigarettes, safety in moderation, inconsistent scientific findings concerning cancer, the greater risks of everyday living, and the health benefits of relaxation that come from smoking a good cigar. All of these fantasies have the same basic theme—*cigar smoking is safe.*

Bormann suggested that group members' *meanings, emotions, motives,* and *actions* are apparent in their fantasy themes. We can see all four of these in DeSantis' description of the angst that the core group of patrons experienced at the premature death of their friend Greg. Like the rest of the store's regulars who sat around smoking, Greg had scoffed at the health risks of their practice. Now they were confronted with the sobering fact of his fatal heart attack. Within a week of the funeral, however, his smoking buddies had constructed a verbal collage of images depicting Greg's stressful lifestyle. The store owner voiced their consensus: "Smoking had nothing to do with his death. He lived, drank and played hard and it took a toll on him at the end."[10] *Meaning:* Hard living killed Greg. *Emotion:* Reduction of fear; relief. *Motive:* Desire to smoke with buddies. *Action:* Not going to quit. Fantasy themes create a group's social reality.

Bormann and symbolic convergence theory advocates have found that many fantasy themes are indexed by a *symbolic cue.* A symbolic cue is "an agreed-upon trigger that sets off the group members to respond as they did when they first shared the fantasy."[11] It could be a code word, nonverbal gesture, phrase, slogan, inside joke, bumper sticker, or any shorthand way of re-establishing the full force of shared fantasy. In the Kentucky smoke shop where these fantasy themes were voiced, any mention of criticism of cigar smoking from family or friends was the cue that set off a new round of protest among store regulars. Their emotional reaction was captured on a T-shirt sold at the store that satirized the surgeon general's cautionary statement: "Warning—Harassing me about my smoking can be hazardous to your health."[12]

The meaning of a given fantasy theme is quite specific. Since clusters of related fantasy themes sometimes surface again and again in different groups, Bormann found it helpful to have a label to classify this phenomenon when it occurs. He used the term *fantasy type* to describe these well-worn symbolic paths. Fantasy types are "greater abstractions incorporating several concrete fantasy themes" and they exist "when shared meaning is taken for granted."[13] The cigar store group's fantasy theme of family and friends criticizing their smoking could be considered part of a larger "get-off-my-case" fantasy type. Perhaps that's a fantasy type that you and your friends have drawn upon when talking about your lifestyle, even if you've never smoked a cigar. Or students at your school may share stock fantasy types about Saturday night parties, the food on campus, professors who never seem to be in their offices, or the guy who always bails on a group project at the last minute.

Symbolic cue
An agreed-upon trigger that sets off group members to respond as they did when they first shared the fantasy.

Fantasy type
A cluster of related fantasy themes; greater abstractions incorporating several concrete fantasy themes that exist when shared meaning is taken for granted.

SYMBOLIC CONVERGENCE: GROUP CONSCIOUSNESS AND OFTEN COHESIVENESS

The discussion of dramatizing messages, fantasy chains, and fantasy themes has dealt with the first part of SCT's core principle: *Sharing group fantasies creates symbolic convergence.* We're now ready to look at the second part—symbolic convergence. For Bormann, *symbolic convergence* meant the way in which "two or more private symbol worlds incline toward each other, come more closely together, or even overlap."[14] As those worlds intersect, group members develop a unique group consciousness. No longer do members think in terms of *I, me,* and *mine.* As symbolic overlap takes place, they begin to think and speak about *we, us,* and *ours.*

Do shared fantasies really cause this group transformation? Bormann insisted they do. Some limited commonality of words and images may naturally occur when group members interact often enough over a long period of time. But the process is accelerated and extended way beyond what otherwise might happen when

Symbolic convergence
Two or more private symbol worlds incline toward each other, come more closely together, or even overlap; group consciousness, cohesiveness.

members participate in one or more fantasy chains that create joint fantasy themes. Bormann used a variety of terms to portray the effect of group consciousness—*common ground, meeting of the minds, mutual understanding, groupiness, common social reality,* and *empathic communion.*

Once a group experiences symbolic convergence, Bormann suggested it's important for members to memorialize their group consciousness with a name and recorded history (*saga*) that recalls moments when fantasies chained out. He did that with his University of Minnesota colleagues who met in the Bormann home every Wednesday night to discuss the ideas that make up symbolic convergence theory. They called themselves the *Turtle Racers*—presumably based on an illustrated poster with the caption "Behold the turtle who makes progress only when he sticks his neck out." The image of a turtle race seemed doubly appropriate to their history of theory building when Bormann described the work going forward in fits and starts.

Symbolic convergence usually results in heightened group *cohesiveness*—members attracted to each other and sticking together through thick and thin. But not always. Bormann regarded symbolic convergence as usually a necessary but not sufficient cause of cohesiveness.

> Groups that do little fantasizing are seldom highly attractive and cohesive. Such groups tend to be boring and ordinary. The cohesive groups have usually done considerable fantasizing, but not all groups that fantasize a lot are rewarding and cohesive. The fantasies that chain may contribute to creating a social reality that is warm, friendly and hard working, that provides the group with a strong identity and self image, and that gives members a sense of purpose and meaning for their group's work. On the other hand, the fantasies may develop a group climate that is fascinating, frustrating, and punishing.[15]

Bormann went on to say that fantasy themes in those negative groups are riddled with conflict and that the humor expressed tends to be satire, ridicule, or sarcasm. I was in such a group my sophomore year of college, and he was right—it was fascinating. Fortunately I had enough sense to bail out.

RHETORICAL VISION: A COMPOSITE DRAMA SHARED BY A RHETORICAL COMMUNITY

Up to this point in the chapter, my description and illustration of symbolic convergence theory has focused on shared fantasies in small-group settings. That's where SCT was spawned. But early in the theory's development, the Turtle Racers discovered that shared fantasies weren't confined to a small-group context. As Bormann explained, "Fantasies that begin in small groups often are worked into public speeches, become picked up by mass media and 'spread out across larger publics.'"[16] Once attuned to the basic concepts of SCT, these scholars spotted swirling batches of related fantasy themes and types in all sorts of communication texts. Bormann coined the term *rhetorical vision* to designate "a composite drama that catches up large groups of people into a common symbolic reality."[17] He called the wide-ranging body of people who share that reality a *rhetorical community.*

Rhetorical vision
A composite drama that catches up large groups of people into a common symbolic reality.

The majority of research conducted using SCT has been aimed at capturing the rhetorical visions of dispersed rhetorical communities and figuring out how their communication created their unified fantasies. Researchers don't have the benefit of sitting in a room with the whole community while waiting for a fantasy to chain out as evidence of a fantasy theme. So Bormann and his colleagues developed a procedure called *fantasy theme analysis* to discover fantasy themes and rhetorical visions that have already been created.

Fantasy Theme Analysis

Fantasy theme analysis is a specific type of rhetorical criticism that's built on two basic assumptions. First, people create their social reality—a premise shared by many interpretive theorists (see Chapters 5, 6, and 11). Second, people's meanings, motives, and emotions can be seen in their rhetoric. So when a dispersed community embraces the same rhetorical vision, that's reality for them. They aren't pretending.

A rhetorical critic using fantasy theme analysis looks for recurring fantasy themes in the text. If found, the critic should then figure out if these shared fantasies are woven together into a rhetorical vision. In addition to using the basic SCT concepts already discussed, Bormann suggested the critic look for at least four features that are present in all rhetorical visions.[18]

Fantasy theme analysis
A type of rhetorical criticism used to detect fantasy themes and rhetorical visions; the interpretive methodology of SCT.

1. **Characters:** Are there heroes to root for and villains to despise?
2. **Plotlines:** Do characters act in a way consistent with the rhetorical vision?
3. **Scene:** How do descriptions of time and place increase the drama's impact?
4. **Sanctioning agent:** Who or what legitimates the rhetorical vision?

I'll describe a fantasy theme analysis of Internet websites to demonstrate how these tools can reveal a rhetorical vision and show how that vision is created and sustained within a dispersed rhetorical community.

The Symbolic Creation of a Pro-Eating Disorder Rhetorical Vision

For those who are anorexic and/or bulimic, the world of face-to-face communication can be a lonely place. Afraid of condemnation if they reveal their eating disorder, they often live a life of secrecy, deception, and guilt. Although 12-step programs extend social support to those who want to overcome their disease, not all people with food disorders want to change. The Internet offers hundreds of pro-eating disorder websites where those who resist recovery can anonymously interact with like-minded others. Wayne State University communication professor Jessi McCabe conducted a fantasy theme analysis to "explore how group exchanges on these websites redefine a reality largely rejected by the cultural norm and what elements contribute to creating this worldview."[19] She chose the 12 most active pro-food disorder sites for her analysis. The message boards on the three most popular sites—Blue Dragon Fly, Pro-Ana Suicide Society, and Fragile Innocence—had a combined membership of more than 25,000 users.

Fantasy types are an SCT category midway between specific fantasy themes and an overall rhetorical vision. McCabe found that two contrasting fantasy types emerged in her analysis—a positive one and a negative one. She labeled the positive fantasy type "The humorous world of Ana and Mia." Within this world, fantasy chains reinforce site users' eating habits and shared reality. Across the message boards, members personify their disorders as characters in an ongoing drama.

Members depict their own goals, struggles, and emotions through the personification of Ana and Mia. Anorexia and bulimia are given life and attributed human-like emotions and qualities, which are justified by the sanctioning agent, humor. The most favorable depiction is a girl named Ana (anorexia), who represents the goal of the group, the idolization of perfection in this reality. Perfection is about having self-control and being thin. Personified through Ana is a yearning for being untouchable and perfect.[20]

Message-board users write about Ana as their hero. ("Ana knows what to say to make me feel better."[21]) They also confess lapses and seek her forgiveness. ("Dear Ana, I am sorry that I failed you. . . . Not only did I fail you but I binged."[22])

Unlike Ana, Mia (bulimia) isn't seen as perfect. Her role in the drama is to stir up the emotions users feel as they struggle to get down to the elusive perfect weight. Site users rarely describe Mia in positive terms. One post complains, "Mia is SO loud and annoying . . . my Mom heard Mia because she can't keep her [stinking] mouth shut!"[23] Yet other messages reluctantly suggest Mia is needed. "Sometimes she is all right . . . she lets me eat . . . keeps my body pure."[24] The third character in this ongoing drama is the villainous ED (eating disorder). He represents the social norm of moderation and recovery from addiction. McCabe explains why he's so feared: "Members not only try to avoid ED for fear of recovery but the group knows that accepting ED means a loss of community and a reentry into a reality in which eating disorders are a negative attribute."[25]

The discussion of these three characters constructs an alternative world where high-risk dieters aren't hassled. Despite the lurking presence of ED, who reminds everyone of another reality "out there," this positive fantasy type is a closed world where anorexics and bulimics feel safe. McCabe sees humor as the *sanctioning agent* that makes this constructed reality legitimate for site users. The satirical exchange of experiences turns discussion of a deadly disease into a game that validates what these users are doing, saying, and living.

Conversely, the negative fantasy type portrayed on these message boards is "Surviving encounters with The Real World," a distressing place for those who visit these websites. McCabe notes that almost all users log on to get tips on "safe" foods and how to hide their eating habits and symptoms from friends and family. The *scene* of the struggle in "the real world" is almost always part of this fantasy type. Many posts include references to time and space.

> I hate coming home at night. . . . I am with Ana all day and I cannot eat . . . but when I get home Ana stays at the door and I just binge.[26]

> How can I live with Mia if we are sharing community bathrooms in our dorm?[27]

McCabe doesn't explicitly address *plotlines* in her fantasy theme analysis, but from her rich description two plots seem paramount. The first is acting in multiple ways to reduce weight—dieting, exercising, and purging. The second plot is doing whatever one has to do to keep the extent of this obsession with food a secret from those who don't share it.

McCabe concludes that the rhetorical vision of the pro-eating disorder community is the uneasy coexistence of these two contrasting fantasy types—*The humorous world of Ana and Mia* and *Surviving encounters with The Real World*. She writes, "The rhetorical vision shared by this group is the effort to maintain a disease within settings where their belief is challenged and get back to the state where the personification of the disease can proliferate."[28]

An Alternative Rhetorical Vision—Make America Great Again

If the rhetorical vision that includes Ana and Mia is foreign to your experience, consider the impact of the "Make America Great Again" movement during the run-up to the 2016 US presidential election. This rhetorical vision was shared mainly among white, small-town, rural Americans who dreamed of a return to the lives they had a few decades prior—full employment, cheap energy, less ethnic diversity, and noninterference from Washington bureaucrats. This widespread rhetorical vision could be triggered and spread by a number of pithy slogans:

Drill, baby, drill. Build the wall. Drain the swamp. Lock her up. Repeal Obamacare.

The main *characters* in the drama were the hero, Donald Trump, and the villain, Hillary Clinton. The *plotline* involved rallying together, voting for Trump, and cheering him on as he turned things around his first days in office. The *scene* was sketched as a nation in crisis and getting worse, as opposed to what they remembered as an idyllic America—one that could be brought back. The *sanctioning agents* were Trump's business know-how, immense wealth, success in the primaries, and candor to say whatever he thought. Hillary had a larger base, and even garnered more votes, but this vivid rhetorical vision motivated its believers to turn the tide in states where it mattered. Rhetorical visions have power.

THEORY INTO PRACTICE: ADVICE TO IMPROVE YOUR COLLEGE EXPERIENCE

As you've gained an understanding of symbolic convergence theory, hopefully you've thought about its implications for a group in which you take part. No matter what your role in the group, Bormann has offered the following advice:[29]

- When the group begins to share a drama that in your opinion would contribute to a healthy culture, you should pick up the drama and feed the chain. You don't have to be an artist or wordsmith to tell a story that promotes an emerging fantasy theme.
- If the fantasies are destructive, creating group paranoia or depression, cut the chain off whenever possible. Change the subject.
- To build cohesiveness, use personification to identify your group.
- Early on, be sure to encourage the sharing of dramas depicting your group history.
- Even though a conscious rhetorical effort on your part can succeed in igniting a chain reaction, remember that the fantasy may take an unexpected turn.

Bormann and his followers have also used fantasy theme analysis to improve organizational communication, conduct market research, and assess public opinion. To illustrate the pragmatic value of the methodology, John Cragan (University of St. Thomas) and Donald Shields (University of Missouri) require students in their applied research classes to analyze the way high school seniors talk about college. They find that most rhetorical visions employ one of three competing master analogues—a righteous vision, a social vision, or a pragmatic vision.[30]

Potential applicants who embrace a *righteous* vision are interested in a school's academic excellence, the reputation of its faculty, and special programs it offers. Those who adopt a *social* vision view college as a means of getting away from home, meeting new friends, and joining others in a variety of social activities. High school seniors who buy into a *pragmatic* vision are looking for a marketable degree that will help them get a good job. (What was your vision when you entered college?) Knowledge of these distinct visions could help admissions officers at your school develop a strategy to appeal to prospective students who would most appreciate the character of your campus. That knowledge could also help you figure out if you're at a school that can best meet your needs.

CRITIQUE: JUDGING SCT AS BOTH A SCIENTIFIC AND INTERPRETIVE THEORY

Ernest Bormann claimed that symbolic convergence theory is both objective and interpretive. The theory's basic explanatory hypothesis—*sharing group fantasies creates symbolic convergence*—is framed as a universal principle that holds for all people, in any culture, at any time, in any communication context.[31] Definitely objective. But the methodology of determining fantasy themes, fantasy types, and rhetorical visions is rhetorical criticism—a humanistic approach that's undeniably interpretive. This unusual mix has stimulated many of the 1,000 original research studies that have examined and applied the theory over the last 45 years.[32] When the six standards for judging a social science theory and the six criteria for evaluating an interpretive theory are applied to SCT, the theory stacks up remarkably well (see Chapter 3). Despite this success, SCT fails to meet two benchmarks of a good theory—one objective and one interpretive.

A good objective theory predicts what's going to happen. SCT clearly predicts symbolic convergence will occur when a fantasy chain erupts among members. The theory even suggests that without shared fantasies, there will be little or no cohesiveness. But as discussed earlier in the chapter, SCT researchers have had minimal success predicting when a dramatizing message will trigger a chain reaction. To that point, Bormann responded that uncertainty about the future isn't bothersome in other scientific theories. He saw symbolic convergence theory as similar to Darwin's biological theory of evolution in that respect.

> An evolutionary theory can explain the way modern humans evolved from earlier humanoid individuals. But, such theories cannot predict the future path of evolution. . . . SCT involves a careful cataloguing of group consciousness through time. The theory also includes a description of the dynamic forces that provide a necessary and sufficient set of causes to explain the discovered communication patterns. For an evolution theory the dynamic may be the survival of the fittest. For SCT the dynamic is the process of group sharing.[33]

But without the ability to forecast when a fantasy chain reaction will occur, SCT is difficult to test and not as useful as group practitioners desire. Perhaps that's why the vast majority of research on SCT this century has focused on rhetorical visions rather than symbolic convergence in small groups.

A good interpretive theory clarifies people's values. There's no doubt that fantasy theme analysis uncovers the values of a rhetorical community. It does this well. But University of Oklahoma communication professor James Olufowote is concerned about the unexamined values that undergird SCT.[34] One concern is an ideology of convergence. The terms that describe its effects—*common ground, meeting of the minds, empathic communion,* etc.—make it clear that the theory has a pro-social bias. Shall we look at the convergence of hate groups or pro-eating disorder websites as a positive outcome?

A second value concern Olufowote expresses is an egalitarian assumption that ignores issues of power within groups. For example, do all members of a group benefit equally when a fantasy chains out? Does an *inside joke* become a symbolic cue at the expense of one of the members? A final concern is about the way members of a rhetorical community are characterized. The communities described come across as conflict-free. Differences among members are ignored, and there's little discussion of the inner tension a member feels when the multiple rhetorical visions he or she embraces don't mesh. Olufowote is an advocate of social convergence theory, but its silence on these questions of value provide some cause for pause.

QUESTIONS TO SHARPEN YOUR FOCUS

1. As a rhetorically sensitive scholar, Bormann defined SCT terms carefully. Can you distinguish between *dramatizing messages* and *fantasies?* Do you understand why it's a difference that makes a difference?

2. Some critics dismiss SCT as a cookie-cutter approach to group analysis. Could this be said of most social science theories? Bormann regarded the charge as a compliment.[35] Can you figure out why he was pleased rather than offended?

3. Bormann insisted that SCT is an objective theory that's valid *any time* and in *any culture,* but that its methodology, *fantasy theme analysis,* is interpretive. Do you regard SCT as a better *objective* or *interpretive* theory? Why?

4. Bormann was intrigued with a T-shirt that proclaims, "I have given up my search for truth. Now I want to find a good fantasy."[36] Based on what you've read, does this slogan reflect the *symbolic world* of SCT advocates? Does it reflect yours?

A SECOND LOOK

Recommended resource: Ernest G. Bormann, John Cragan, and Donald Shields, "Three Decades of Developing, Grounding, and Using Symbolic Convergence Theory (SCT)," in *Communication Yearbook 25,* William Gudykunst (ed.), Lawrence Erlbaum, Mahwah, NJ, 2001, pp. 271-313.

Brief summary: Ernest Bormann, "Symbolic Convergence Theory," in *Small Group Communication Theory & Practice: An Anthology,* 8th ed., Randy Hirokawa, Robert Cathcart, Larry Samovar, and Linda Henman (eds.), Roxbury, Los Angeles, CA, 2003, pp. 39-47.

Early statement of the theory: Ernest G. Bormann, "Fantasy and Rhetorical Vision: The Rhetorical Criticism of Social Reality," *Quarterly Journal of Speech,* Vol. 58, 1972, pp. 396-407.

Small-group context: Ernest G. Bormann and Nancy C. Bormann, *Effective Small Group Communication,* 5th ed., Burgess, Edina, MN, 1992, pp. 105-126.

Fantasy theme analysis: Sonja K. Foss, *Rhetorical Criticism: Exploration and Practice,* 4th ed., Waveland, Prospect Heights, IL, 2009, pp. 97-136.

Practical applications of assessing rhetorical visions: John F. Cragan and Donald C. Shields, *Symbolic Theories in Applied Communication Research: Bormann, Burke, and Fisher,* Hampton, Cresskill, NJ, 1995, pp. 161-198.

Cigar store ethnography: Alan D. DeSantis, "Smoke Screen: An Ethnographic Study of a Cigar Shop's Collective Rationalization," *Health Communication,* Vol. 14, 2002, pp. 167-198.

Symbolic convergence in a neighborhood watch group: Cheryl Broom and Susan Avanzino, "The Communication of Community Collaboration: When Rhetorical Visions Collide," *Communication Quarterly,* Vol. 58, 2010, pp. 480-501.

Pro-eating disorder website analysis: Jessi McCabe, "Resisting Alienation: The Social Construction of Internet Communities Supporting Eating Disorders," *Communication Studies,* Vol. 60, 2009, pp. 1-15.

Small-group fantasies becoming rhetorical visions: Ernest Bormann, "The Critical Analysis of Seminal American Fantasies," in *The Force of Fantasy: Restoring the American Dream,* Southern Illinois University, Carbondale, IL, 2001, pp. 1-25.

Symbolic convergence in families: Dawn O Braithwaite, Paul Schrodt, Jody Koenig Kellas, "Symbolic Convergence Theory: Communication, Dramatizing Messages, and Rhetorical Visions in Families," in *Engaging Theories in Family Communication: Multiple Perspectives,* Dawn O. Braithwaite and Leslie A. Baxter (eds.), Sage, Thousand Oaks, CA, 2006, pp. 146-161.

Response to early critics: Ernest G. Bormann, John Cragan, and Donald Shields, "In Defense of Symbolic Convergence Theory: A Look at the Theory and Its Criticisms After Two Decades," *Communication Theory,* Vol. 4, 1994, pp. 259-294.

Contemporary critique: James O. Olufowote, "Rousing and Redirecting a Sleeping Giant: Symbolic Convergence Theory and Complexities in the Communicative Constitution of Collective Action," *Management Communication Quarterly,* Vol. 19, 2006, pp. 451-492.

Will our group stay like this or will it change?
Poole's Adaptive Structuration Theory answers this question.
Click on Archive under Theory Resources at
www.afirstlook.com.

What do the following organizations have in common—the *United States Navy, McDonald's, General Motors,* and the *Green Bay Packers?* The first three are gigantic organizations, the middle two sell a tangible product, and the last three are publicly owned corporations that try to make a profit. But in terms of organizational communication, their most important common feature is that each is a prime example of *classical management theory, which embraces the following principles of organizational leadership.*

- Command is from the top. The CEO, president, or executive director calls the shots. That leader delegates some of his or her authority to subordinates, but is ultimately responsible for the organization's performance. Tight control is necessary.

- All employees should have well-defined tasks and report to only one boss. Their authority and resources should match the responsibility they've been given.

- The organization will be most effective if work is divided into specialized roles. The way to perform each job should be standardized and outlined in an operations manual.

- Patterns of communication should be clearly defined, usually running parallel to the lines on the hierarchical organizational chart. Those expected and allowed to talk to or text each other should be specified.

- The organization is engineered for maximum efficiency. Workers or staff should be hired on the basis of their ability and willingness to fit in and make the organization run smoothly.

- Those who break the rules or cause conflict jeopardize the organization's mission. Through constant supervision, firmness, and leading by example, managers should maintain discipline.

- Everyone in the organization is expected to subordinate their own interests for the good of the whole.

Classical management theory places a premium on productivity, precision, and efficiency. As York University professor Gareth Morgan notes, these are the very qualities you expect from a well-designed, smoothly running machine. Morgan uses the mechanistic metaphor because he finds significant parallels between mechanical devices and the way managers traditionally think about their organizations.[1] In classical management theory, workers are seen as cogs in vast machines that function smoothly as long as their range of motion is clearly defined and their actions are lubricated with an adequate hourly wage.

Machines repeat straightforward, repetitive tasks, just as McDonald's workers have cooked billions of hamburgers, each one in exactly the same way. Machines have interchangeable parts that can be replaced when broken or worn out, just as a National Football League coach can insert a new player into the tight-end slot when the current starter is injured or begins to slow down. A new Chevy Tahoe comes with a thick operator's manual that specifies how the SUV should be driven, but the GM employee handbook is thicker and contains even more detailed instructions on how things are done within the company. As for the US Navy, the fleet is an integral part of the country's war machine, and officers at every level are most comfortable when it runs like one.

The three theories in this section view classical management theory as outmoded and reject the idea that organization members are like replaceable parts. Each approach searches for ways of thinking about organizations other than as machines. The *cultural approach* looks for stories and shared meanings that are unique to a given organization. The *constitutive approach* believes the essence of any organization is communication itself. And the *critical approach* looks at organizations as political systems where conflict and power should be negotiated openly. Above all, the theorists who employ these approaches are committed to developing humane ways of talking about people and the organizational tasks they do.

Cultural Approach to Organizations

of Clifford Geertz & Michael Pacanowsky

The late Princeton anthropologist Clifford Geertz wrote that "man is an animal suspended in webs of significance that he himself has spun."[1] He pictured culture as those webs. In order to travel across the strands toward the center of the web, an outsider must discover the common interpretations that hold the web together. Culture is shared meaning, shared understanding, shared sensemaking.

Geertz conducted field research in the islands of Indonesia and on the Moroccan highlands, rural settings remote from industrial activity. His best-known monograph is an in-depth symbolic analysis of the Balinese cockfight. Geertz never wrote a treatise on the bottom line, never tried to decipher the significance of the office Christmas party, and never met a payroll—a disqualifying sin in the eyes of many business professionals. Despite his silence on the topic of big business, Geertz' interpretive approach has proved useful in making sense of organizational activity.

In the field of communication, former University of Colorado professor Michael Pacanowsky has applied Geertz' cultural insights to organizational life. He says that if culture consists of webs of meaning that people have spun, and if spun webs imply the act of spinning, "then we need to concern ourselves not only with the structures of cultural webs, but with the process of their spinning as well."[2] That process is communication. It is communication that "creates and constitutes the taken-for-granted reality of the world."[3]

CULTURE AS A METAPHOR OF ORGANIZATIONAL LIFE

The use of culture as a root metaphor was undoubtedly stimulated by Western fascination with the economic success of Japanese corporations in the 1970s and 1980s. Back then, when American business leaders traveled to the Far East to study methods of production, they discovered that the superior quantity and quality of Japan's industrial output had less to do with technology than with workers' shared cultural value of loyalty to each other and to their corporation. Organizations look radically different depending on how people in the host culture structure meaning. Communal face-saving in Japan is foreign to the class antagonism of Great Britain or the we're-number-one competitive mindset of the United States.

Today the term *corporate culture* means different things to different people. Some observers use the phrase to describe the surrounding environment that constrains a company's freedom of action. (US workers would scoff at singing a corporate anthem at the start of their working day.) Others use the term to refer to a quality or property of the organization. (Acme Gizmo is a friendly place to work.) They speak of *culture* as synonymous with *image, character,* or *climate.* But Pacanowsky is committed to Geertz' symbolic approach and thus considers culture as more than a single variable in organizational research:

> Organizational culture is not just another piece of the puzzle; it is the puzzle. From our point of view, culture is not something an organization has; a culture is something an organization is.[4]

WHAT CULTURE IS; WHAT CULTURE IS NOT

Geertz admitted that the concept of culture as *systems of shared meaning* is somewhat vague and difficult to grasp. Though popular usage equates culture with concerts and art museums, he refused to use the word to signify *less primitive.* No modern anthropologist would fall into the trap of classifying people as high- or low-culture.

Culture
Webs of significance; systems of shared meaning.

Culture is not whole or undivided. Geertz pointed out that even close-knit societies have subcultures and countercultures within their boundaries. For example, employees in the sales and accounting departments of the same company may eye each other warily—the first group calling the accountants *number crunchers* and *bean counters,* the accountants in turn labeling members of the sales force *fast talkers* and *glad-handers.* Despite their differences, both groups may regard the blue-collar bowling night of the production workers as a strange ritual compared with their own weekend ritual of a round of golf.

For Pacanowsky, the web of organizational culture is the residue of employees' performance—"those very actions by which members constitute and reveal their culture to themselves and to others."[5] He notes that job performance may play only a minor role in the enactment of corporate culture.

> People do get the job done, true (though probably not with the singleminded task-orientation communication texts would have us believe); but people in organizations also gossip, joke, knife one another, initiate romantic involvements, cue new employees to ways of doing the least amount of work that still avoids hassles from a supervisor, talk sports, arrange picnics.[6]

Cultural performance
Actions by which members constitute and reveal their culture to themselves and others; an ensemble of texts.

Geertz called these *cultural performances* "an ensemble of texts . . . which the anthropologist strains to read over the shoulder of those to whom they properly belong."[7] The elusive nature of culture prompted Geertz to label its study a *soft science.* It is "not an experimental science in search of law, but an interpretive one in search of meaning."[8] The corporate observer is one part scientist, one part drama critic.

The fact that symbolic expression requires interpretation is nicely captured in a story about Pablo Picasso recorded by York University professor Gareth Morgan.[9]

A man commissioned Picasso to paint a portrait of his wife. Startled by the non-representational image on the canvas, the woman's husband complained, "It isn't how she really looks." When asked by the painter how she really looked, the man produced a photograph from his wallet. Picasso's comment: "Small, isn't she?"

THICK DESCRIPTION: WHAT ETHNOGRAPHERS DO

Ethnography
Mapping out social discourse; discovering who people within a culture think they are, what they think they are doing, and to what end they think they are doing it.

Geertz referred to himself as an *ethnographer,* one whose job is to sort out the symbolic meanings of people's actions within their culture. Just as geographers chart the physical territory, ethnographers map out social discourse. They do this "to discover who people think they are, what they think they are doing, and to what end they think they are doing it."[10] There's no shortcut for the months of participant observation required to collect an exhaustive account of interaction. Without that raw material, there would be nothing to interpret.

Geertz spent years in Indonesia and Morocco, developing his deep description of separate cultures. Pacanowsky initially invested nine months with W. L. Gore & Associates, best known for its Gore-Tex line of sports clothing and equipment. Like Geertz, he was completely open about his research goals, and during the last five months of his research he participated fully in problem-solving conferences at the company. Later, Pacanowsky spent additional time at the W. L. Gore plants in Delaware as a consultant. In order to become intimately familiar with an organization *as members experience it,* ethnographers must commit to the long haul. Pacanowsky did commit to the long haul of working full time at Gore, this despite his earlier caution against "going native." He had previously advised ethnographers to assume an attitude of "radical naivete" that would make it possible for them to "experience organizational life as 'strange.'" This stance of wonder would help them get past taken-for-granted interpretations of what's going on and what it means to insiders. When Pacanowsky went to work for Gore, he no longer had that opportunity.[11]

The daily written accounts of intensive observation invariably fill the pages of many ethnographic notebooks. The visual image of these journals stacked on top of each other would be sufficient justification for Geertz to refer to ethnography as *thick description.* The term, however, describes the intertwined layers of common meaning that underlie what a particular people say and do. Thick descriptions are powerful reconstructions, not just detailed observations.[12] After Geertz popularized the concept, most ethnographers realized their task is to:

Thick description
A record of the intertwined layers of common meaning that underlie what a particular people say and do.

1. Accurately describe talk and actions and the context in which they occur.
2. Capture the thoughts, emotions, and web of social interactions.
3. Assign motivation, intention, or purpose to what people say and do.
4. Artfully write this up so readers feel they've experienced the events.
5. Interpret what happened; explain what it means within this culture.[13]

Thick description is tracing the many strands of a cultural web and tracking evolving meaning. No matter how high the stack of an ethnographer's notes, without interpretation, they would still be *thin* description.

Thick description starts with a state of bewilderment. *What the devil's going on?* Geertz asked himself as he waded into a new culture. The only way to reduce the puzzlement is to observe as if one were a stranger in a foreign land. This can be difficult for a manager who is already enmeshed in a specific corporate culture. He or she might overlook many of the signs that point to common interpretation.

Worse, the manager might assume that office humor or the company grapevine has the same significance for people in this culture as it does for those in a previous place of employment. Geertz said it will always be different.

Behaviorists would probably consider employee trips to the office watercooler or coffee machine of little interest. If they did regard these breaks worth studying, they would tend to note the number of trips and length of stay for each worker. Ethnographers would be more interested in the significance this seemingly mundane activity had for these particular employees. Instead of a neat statistical summary, they'd record pages of dialogue while workers were standing around with a cup in their hands. Pacanowsky fears that a frequency count would only bleach human behavior of the very properties that interest him. Classifying performances across organizations would yield superficial generalizations at the cost of localized insight. He'd rather find out what makes a particular tribal culture unique.

Although Pacanowsky would pay attention to all cultural performances, he would be particularly sensitive to the imaginative language members used, the stories they told, and the nonverbal rites and rituals they practiced. Taken together, these three forms of communication provide helpful access to the unique shared meanings within an organization.

METAPHORS: TAKING LANGUAGE SERIOUSLY

Metaphor
Clarifies what is unknown or confusing by equating it with an image that's more familiar or vivid.

When used by members throughout an organization (and not just management), *metaphors* can offer the ethnographer a starting place for accessing the shared meaning of a corporate culture. Pacanowsky records a number of prominent metaphors used at W. L. Gore & Associates, none more significant than the oft-heard reference within the company to Gore as a *lattice organization.*[14] If one tried to graph the lines of communication at Gore, the map would look like a lattice rather than the traditional pyramid-shaped organizational chart. The crosshatched lines would show the importance of one-on-one communication and reflect the fact that no person within the company needs permission to talk to anyone else. Easy access to others is facilitated by an average plant size of 150 employees and a variety of electronic media that encourage quick responses.

This lack of hierarchical authority within the lattice organization is captured in the egalitarian title of *associate* given to every worker. People do have differential status at Gore, but it comes from technical expertise, a track record of good judgment, and evidence of follow-through that leads to accomplishment.

The company's stated objective (singular) is "to make money and have fun."[15] The founder, Bill Gore, was famous for popping into associates' offices and asking, "Did you make any money today? Did you have any fun today?" But work at Gore is not frivolous. The *waterline* operating principle makes it clear that associates should check with others before making significant decisions:

> Each of us will consult with appropriate Associates who will share the responsibility of taking any action that has the potential of serious harm to the reputation, success, or survival of the Enterprise. The analogy is that our Enterprise is like a ship that we are all in together. Boring holes above the waterline is not serious, but below the waterline, holes could sink us.[16]

When Brandy read about the emphasis Pacanowsky placed on metaphors, she analyzed their use among the tech crew in her high school theater department.

My role in the crew was managing the stagehands and taking care of all the props in the show. We were a distinct subculture best described through religious metaphors. For instance, the faculty Tech Director was viewed as "God." He was our superior, always vigilant and often appearing out of nowhere to correct our behavior. We also called him Apollo—the Greek god of light—since he designed the lighting plan for every production. His technical production book for the play was considered our "bible." One of the photos I have of the crew shows us bowing before that holy text.

Despite our tech director's sarcasm and skepticism toward organized religion, he introduced and reinforced many of these metaphors. They suggested that theater was as serious to us as religion was to other people. They also gave his insights and directives a divine stamp of approval. No one opposes what a god says. We willingly worked countless hours and skipped sleep in order to produce a great production. Amen.

Pacanowsky suggests that "fictional descriptions, by the very nature of their implicitness and impressionism can fully capture . . . both the bold outlines and the crucial nuances of cultural ethos."[17] Many TV critics believed the show *Mad Men* reliably reflects the culture of a 1960s New York advertising agency—not just in the retro style of clothing and cars, but in the dialogue. If so, the metaphors these men employ should reveal the shared meaning within their organizational culture.

In the very first episode of the series, Pete Campbell, a junior account executive, sucks up to Don Draper, creative director at the Sterling Cooper ad agency: "A man like you, I'd follow you into combat blindfolded and I wouldn't be the first. Am I right, buddy?" Don responds, "Let's take it a little slower. I don't want to wake up pregnant."[18] The obvious meaning is for Pete to back off, and Pete's muttered curse as Don walks away shows he gets the message. But there are overlapping layers of meaning within the *wake-up-pregnant* imagery that reflect the underlying culture that's Sterling Cooper.

Sexual allusions are present in almost every conversation among men at the agency, regardless of whether women are present. So is power. The self-described *mad men* are all highly competitive. Despite a surface backslapping camaraderie, in this ad game it's every man for himself. Men at Sterling Cooper score by winning the multimillion dollar account or sleeping with a pretty associate. Losing is getting pregnant, which doesn't happen to men. And if it happens to you physically or metaphorically, you're on your own. So a guy has to be on guard lest he come to the office one morning and discover he's been screwed.

Can these multiple meanings really be teased out of a single metaphor heard only once? Probably not without other symbolic clues to collaborate the interpretation. Yet regular viewers of *Mad Men* who listened and watched with an ethnographer's mindset could look back on this first episode and realize that Draper's *wake-up-pregnant* metaphor was both a lens into the culture they came to know and an artifact of it.

THE SYMBOLIC INTERPRETATION OF STORY

Stories that are told over and over provide a convenient window through which to view corporate webs of significance. Pacanowsky asks, "Has a good story been told that takes you to the heart of the matter?"[19] He focuses on the scriptlike qualities of narratives that portray an employee's part in the company play. Although workers have room to improvise, the anecdotes provide clues to what it means to perform a task in this particular theater. Stories capture memorable performances and convey the passion the actor felt at the time.

Pacanowsky suggests three types of narrative that dramatize organizational life. *Corporate stories* carry the ideology of management and reinforce company policy. Every McDonald's franchisee hears about the late Ray Kroc, who, when he was chairman of the board, picked up trash from the parking lot when he'd visit a store.

Personal stories are those that employees tell about themselves, often defining how they would like to be seen within the organization. If you've seen reruns of NBC's *The Office*, you've witnessed Dwight Schrute's interviews with the camera crew. During these interviews, he talks about his excellence as an employee and how he deserves the respect of others in the Dunder Mifflin paper company. These are Dwight's personal accounts.

Collegial stories are positive or negative anecdotes told about others in the organization. When the camera crew interviews Dwight's colleagues Jim and Pam, we hear stories of Dwight's eccentricity and lack of basic social awareness. These collegial stories describe Dwight as someone who is not to be taken seriously. Since these tales aren't usually sanctioned by management, collegial accounts convey how the organization "really works."

Corporate stories
Tales that carry management ideology and reinforce company policy.

Personal stories
Tales told by employees that put them in a favorable light.

Collegial stories
Positive or negative anecdotes about others in the organization; descriptions of how things "really work."

Stories at Dixie

Throughout most of my life, I've had access to some of the cultural lore of Dixie Communications, a medium-sized corporation that operates a newspaper and a television station in a Southern city. Like so many other regional companies, Dixie has been taken over by an out-of-state corporation that has no local ties. The following three narratives are shorthand versions of stories heard again and again throughout the company.

> Although the original publisher has been dead for many years, old-timers fondly recall how he would spend Christmas Eve with the workers in the pressroom. Their account is invariably linked with reminders that he initiated health benefits and profit sharing prior to any union demand. (Corporate story)

> The current comptroller is the highest ranking "local boy" in the corporation. He often tells the story about the first annual audit he performed long before computers were installed. Puzzled when he ran across a bill for 50 pounds of pigeon feed, he discovered that the company used homing pigeons to send in news copy and circulation orders from a town across the bay. The story usually concludes with an editorial comment about pigeons being more reliable than the new machines. His self-presentation reminds listeners that he has always been cost-conscious, yet it also aligns him with the human side of the "warm people versus cold machines" issue. (Personal story)

> Shortly after the takeover, a department head encouraged the new publisher to meet with his people for a few minutes at the end of the day. The new boss declined the invitation on the grounds of efficiency: "To be quite candid, I don't want to know about a woman's sick child or a man's vacation plans. That kind of information makes it harder to fire a person." Spoken in a cold, superior tone, the words *quite candid* are always part of the story. (Collegial story)

Both Geertz and Pacanowsky caution against any analysis that says, "This story means. . . ." Narratives contain a mosaic of significance and defy a simplistic, one-on-one translation of symbols. Yet taken as a whole, the three stories reveal an uneasiness with the new management. This interpretation is consistent with repeated metaphorical references to the old Dixie as *family* and the new Dixie as *a faceless computer.*

RITUAL: THIS IS THE WAY IT'S ALWAYS BEEN AND ALWAYS WILL BE

Geertz wrote about the Balinese rite of cockfighting because the contest represented more than a game. "It is only apparently cocks that are fighting there. Actually it is men." The cockfight is a dramatization of status. "Its function is interpretive: It is a Balinese reading of Balinese experience, a story they tell themselves about themselves."[20]

Pacanowsky agrees with Geertz that some rituals (like the Balinese cockfight) are "texts" that articulate *multiple* aspects of cultural life.[21] These rituals are nearly sacred, and any attempt to change them meets with strong resistance. Although the emphasis on improvisation and novelty reduces the importance of ritual at Gore, organizational rites at more traditional companies weave together many threads of corporate culture.

Ritual
Texts that articulate multiple aspects of cultural life, often marking rites of passage or life transitions.

Before eBay became the preferred way to connect buyers and sellers, workers in the classified advertising department at Dixie created an *integrative rite* consistent with its low employee turnover and premerger family atmosphere. The department was staffed by 50 telephone sales representatives who worked out of a large common room. These sales reps not only took "two lines/two days/two dollars" personal ads over the phone, they called back after the ad ran to find out if customers were successful and might want to sell other items.

Most of the phone reps were women under the age of 40. They regarded Max, the manager for three decades, as a *father confessor. He was a* warm, nonjudgmental person who had genuine concern for their lives. Whenever a female employee had a baby, Max visited her in the hospital and offered help to those at home preparing for her return. A woman announced her pregnancy by taping a dime within a large picture frame on the outer wall of Max' office, inscribing her name and anticipated day of delivery.

This *rite of integration* served multiple functions for the women. At a time of potential anxiety, it was an occasion for public affirmation from the larger community. The rite was a point of contact between work and those outside Dixie. Employees took pride in describing the ritual to customers and friends.

Although the dime-on-the-wall practice originated with the workers, this authorized chronicle of decades of expected births proclaimed a sense of permanence. It said, in effect: "The company doesn't consider motherhood a liability; your job will be here when you get back."

From the management's standpoint, the rite ensured there would be no surprises. Max had plenty of time to schedule the employee's maternity leave, arrange for another salesperson to cover her accounts, and anticipate stresses she might be encountering. It's tempting to read economic significance into the fact that employees used dimes to symbolize this major change in their lives. But the women involved referred to the small size of the token rather than its monetary value. Geertz and Pacanowsky would caution that this is *their* ritual. We should listen to *their* interpretation.

CAN THE MANAGER BE AN AGENT OF CULTURAL CHANGE?

The popularity of the cultural metaphor when it was first introduced to the corporate world in the 1980s was undoubtedly due to business leaders' desire to shape interpretation within the organization. Symbols are the tools of management. Executives don't operate forklifts or produce widgets; they cast vision, state goals, process information, send memos, and engage in other symbolic behavior. If they believe culture is the key to worker commitment, productivity, and sales, the possibility of changing culture becomes a seductive idea. Creating favorable metaphors, planting organizational stories, and establishing rites would seem an ideal way to create a corporate myth that would serve managerial interests.

Linguist Chengxiu Suo (Southern Illinois University) relates the corporate turn-around story of Haier, a consumer appliance manufacturer and Fortune Global 500 company now known as the "GE of China." It started as a small company that made only one product—refrigerators, and those not very well. When Zhang Ruimin was appointed chief executive officer, he discovered that 76 of 400 units about to be shipped were defective. Ruimin lined up the workers who made the flawed products and announced, "At Haier, a defective item is nothing but a reject." He then handed them sledgehammers and demanded they smash the refrigerators into small pieces. Sou reports that this dramatic move was strategically planned by the CEO to create a new culture of quality control.[22] Haier's literature, films, and website retell this corporate story, and a sledgehammer is prominently displayed at corporate headquarters. But once a corporate culture exists, can it be altered by a manager?

Geertz regarded shared interpretations as naturally emerging from all members of a group rather than consciously engineered by leaders. Leaders may articulate a new vision in a fresh vocabulary, but it is the workers who smile, sigh, snicker, or scoff. Organizational consultants who share Geertz' approach are fond of citing management guru Peter Drucker's pithy conclusion: *Culture eats strategy for lunch.*[23]

Shared meanings are hard to dispel. Symbol watchers within a company quickly discount the words of management if they don't square with performance. But even if culture *could* be changed, there still remains the question of whether it *should* be. Symbolic anthropologists have traditionally adopted a non-intrusive style appropriate to examining fine crystal—look, admire, but don't touch. So managers who regard themselves as agents of cultural change create bull-in-a-china-shop fears for ethnographers who have ethical concerns about how

DILBERT © 1996 Scott Adams. Used By permission of ANDREWS MCMEEL SYNDICATION. All rights reserved.

those corporate analyses might be used. University of Massachusetts management professor Linda Smircich notes that ethnographers would draw back in horror at the idea of using their data to extend a tribal priest's control over the population, yet most communication consultants are hired by top management to do just that.[24]

CRITIQUE: IS THE CULTURAL APPROACH USEFUL?

The cultural approach adopts and refines the *qualitative research methodology* of ethnography to gain a *new understanding of a specific group of people.* A crucial part of that understanding is a *clarification of values* within the culture under study. Today, however, there isn't the excitement about the cultural approach to organizations that there was when interpretive scholars introduced it in the 1980s. Perhaps that's because many researchers trained in organizational communication are hired as consultants by corporate managers looking for change. By now you understand that Geertz would regard the quest to alter culture as both inappropriate and virtually impossible. This purist position exposes him and his admirers within our discipline to criticism from corporate consultants who not only desire to understand organizational communication, but also want to influence it.

If a thick description of the web of meanings within an organization can't be used to change the culture, how can the cost in time and money of an ethnographic study be justified? Better employee recruitment is one answer. Traditionally, companies stress their attractive features and downplay characteristics that potential hires would find disturbing. So it's only after the firm has spent about $15,000 to recruit, assess, orient, and train a new employee that the newcomer finds out if he or she is suited for the job. Early resignations are costly and leave everyone disgruntled.

Managers are learning that they can cut costs and avoid hassles by providing a realistic job preview right from the start.[25] Offering recruits a sensitive analysis of the culture they'd be entering gives potential hires the chance to make an informed decision as to whether they will fit within it or not. And for those who take the plunge, the shared knowledge of what means what within the organization will reduce mistakes and misunderstandings. W. C. Gore's subsequent hiring of Pacanowsky shows the high regard the founder placed on the theorist's thick description.

A different kind of objection comes from critical theorists who fault the cultural approach because interpretive scholars like Geertz and Pacanowsky refuse to evaluate the customs they portray. For example, if Pacanowsky were to discover that female associates at Gore hit a glass ceiling when they try to advance, these advocates insist he should *expose* and *deplore* this injustice rather than merely *describe* and *interpret* it for readers.[26] For researchers who take a cultural approach to organizational life, this criticism misses the point of their work. The purpose of ethnography is not to pass moral judgment or *reform society.* The goal of symbolic analysis is to create a better understanding of what it takes to function effectively within a culture.

Anthropologist Adam Kuper is critical of Geertz for his emphasis on interpretation rather than behavioral observation. Because if, as Geertz claimed, "we begin with our own interpretations of what our informants are up to or think they are up to and then systematize those,"[27] who's to say the meaning assigned by the ethnographer is right?[28] Kuper is afraid that the past experiences and biases of interpretive researchers will shape the conclusions they reach. But for Geertz, members within the culture are the ones who verify a thick description. Participant-observers need to check out their interpretation with the "natives" in their study. It's their culture—they should recognize the "truth" of the story told about them.[29] In organizational research, that means members affirming the ethnographer's construction of what's going on. *(Right. You've got it. That's what this means.)*

There might be another reason why interest in the cultural approach has waned in recent years. In Chapter 3, we cited *aesthetic appeal* as one of the criteria for a good interpretive theory. The force of an ethnographic analysis depends in large measure on the prose in which it's couched. In the *Times Literary Supplement* (UK), T. M. Luhrmann gives testimony to the compelling power of Geertz' writing: "Rarely has there been a social scientist who has also been so acute a writer; perhaps there has never been one so quotable."[30] Indeed, Geertz' interpretation of a Balinese cockfight reads like an engrossing novel that the reader can't put down. Though Pacanowsky writes well, it may not be until a perceptive ethnographer with Geertz' compelling way with words focuses on organizational life that the cultural approach to organizations will spark renewed interest.

QUESTIONS TO SHARPEN YOUR FOCUS

1. Based on the concept of organizational culture as a system of *shared meaning,* how would you describe the culture at your school to a prospective student?

2. Anthropologists say, "We don't know who discovered water, but we know it wasn't the fish." Does this adage suggest that it's foolish to ask members of a culture to verify or challenge an *ethnographer's interpretation?*

3. Think of your extended family as an *organizational culture.* What family *ritual* might you analyze to *interpret* the webs of significance you share for someone visiting your home?

4. What favorite *story* do you tell others about your most recent place of employment? Is it a *corporate, personal,* or *collegial* narrative?

A SECOND LOOK

Recommended resource: Clifford Geertz, *The Interpretation of Cultures,* Basic Books, New York, 1973. (See especially "Thick Description: Toward an Interpretive Theory of Culture," pp. 3–30; and "Deep Play: Notes on the Balinese Cockfight," pp. 412–453.)

Culture as performance: Michael Pacanowsky and Nick O'Donnell-Trujillo, "Organizational Communication as Cultural Performance," *Communication Monographs,* Vol. 50, 1983, pp. 127–147.

Nonmanagerial orientation: Michael Pacanowsky and Nick O'Donnell-Trujillo, "Communication and Organizational Cultures," *Western Journal of Speech Communication,* Vol. 46, 1982, pp. 115–130.

Thick description: Joseph G. Ponterotto, "Brief Note on the Origins, Evolution, and Meaning of the Qualitative Research Concept 'Thick Description,'" *The Qualitative Report,* Vol. 11, 2006, pp. 538–549.

Cultural metaphor: Gareth Morgan, "Creating Social Reality: Organizations as Cultures," in *Images of Organization,* Sage, Newbury Park, CA, 1986, pp. 111–140.

Corporate ethnography: Michael Pacanowsky, "Communication in the Empowering Organization," in *Communication Yearbook 11,* James Anderson (ed.), Sage, Newbury Park, CA, 1988, pp. 356–379.

Corporate stories: Joanne Martin, Martha Feldman, Mary Jo Hatch, and Sim Sitkin, "The Uniqueness Paradox in Organizational Stories," *Administrative Science Quarterly,* Vol. 28, 1983, pp. 438–453.

Rites: Harrison Trice and Janice Beyer, "Studying Organizational Cultures Through Rites and Ceremonials," *Academy of Management Review,* Vol. 9, 1984, pp. 653–669.

Interpretive vs. objective approach: Linda L. Putnam, "The Interpretive Perspective: An Alternative to Functionalism," in *Communication and Organizations: An Interpretive Approach,* Linda L. Putnam and Michael Pacanowsky (eds.), Sage, Newbury Park, CA, 1982, pp. 31–54.

Webs of shared meaning in sports: Nick Trujillo, "Reflections on Communication and Sport: On Ethnography and Organizations," *Communication and Sport,* Vol. 1, 2013, pp. 68–75.

Examples of corporate culture handbooks: Jim Robinson, "6 Inspiring Employee Handbook Examples," *Nasdaq,* March 26, 2015, http://www.nasdaq.com/article/6-inspiring-employee-handbook-examples-cm459464, accessed April 16, 2017.

Interpretive research: Bryan Taylor and Nick Trujillo, "Qualitative Research Methods," in *The New Handbook of Organizational Communication,* Fredric Jablin and Linda L. Putnam (eds.), Sage, Thousand Oaks, CA, 2001, pp. 161–194.

History and critique of Geertz: Adam Kuper, *Culture: The Anthropologists' Account,* Harvard University, Cambridge, MA, 1999, pp. 75–121.

Communicative Constitution of Organizations

of Robert McPhee

Valve Corporation has achieved a reputation as one of the most innovative publishers in the video game industry. If you're a video gamer like me (Andrew), you've probably heard of Valve. It has produced *Portal,* a physics-based puzzle game so artistic that the Smithsonian American Art Museum showcased it for several months. Millions of players have battled online opponents in hit games like *Counter-Strike* and *Half-Life,* or purchased classic games from Valve's popular Steam app store. Valve's success has earned more than a reputation. Although Valve keeps its financial information private, in 2012 one industry analyst estimated Valve's worth at $2.5 billion.[1] By comparison, that's about a half billion higher than the value of Wendy's fast-food restaurants at the time.[2]

Although Valve leads in the video game industry, it isn't clear who leads Valve. Among its approximately 300 employees, the company insists that no one holds the title of manager, supervisor, boss, or head honcho. In fact, the company handbook even describes founder Gabe Newell this way: "Of all the people at this company who aren't your boss, Gabe is the MOST not your boss, if you get what we're saying."[3] Instead of a manager dictating priorities, all employees possess the freedom to initiate projects they believe will benefit the company. Although Valve believes such an environment unleashes employees' creative potential, it's unsettling to those who've spent a career working in traditional organizations. For this reason, the new employee handbook bluntly describes its purpose: "Mainly, it's about how not to freak out now that you're here."[4]

Robert McPhee and other *communicative constitution of organizations (CCO)* theorists believe that Valve's business practices arise from the daily interactions of the organization's members. Their conclusion isn't based on the unusual structure of the company. They insist *all* companies are what they are because communication brings organization into existence. In other words, like CMM theorists, they believe that persons-in-conversation co-construct their social worlds (see Chapter 6)—and forms are continually produced and reproduced through language, we'll understand that corporations produce not only goods and services, but also meaning.

People who adopt the lingo of big business may not be aware that they are putting corporate values into play. For example, the bottom line on a profit-and-loss statement is only that—the last line on the financial report. But a CEO's continual use of the term *bottom line* to justify all managerial decisions produces a perceived reality that shuts out nonfinancial considerations. When ordinary citizens use this economic idiom to characterize the deciding or crucial factor in their own family decisions, they reinforce and expand the influence of corporate thinking in life without even realizing they are doing so.

Figure 21-1 contrasts Deetz' communication approach to organizational practices with an information approach that regards language as neutral and neutered. Like Pearce and Cronen (see Chapter 6), Deetz considers communication the ongoing social construction of meaning. But his critical theory differs from CMM in that he thinks the issue of power runs through all language and communication. He believes managerial control often takes precedence over representation of conflicting interests and long-term company and community health.

> The fundamental issue in my analysis is control and how different groups are represented in decision making. . . . Since industrialization, managers in American corporations have primarily operated from a philosophy of control.[8]

The upper level of Figure 21-1 represents corporate decision processes that systematically exclude the voices of people who are directly affected by the decisions. Deetz labels this practice *managerial control*. The bottom half of the figure pictures decision processes that invite open dialogue among all stakeholders. Deetz calls this practice *codetermination*. When coupled with the constitutive view of communication, codetermination represents the "collaborative collective constructions

Codetermination
Collaborative decision making; participatory democracy in the workplace.

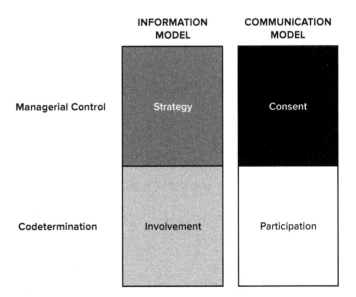

FIGURE 21-1 Two Approaches to Organizational Practice
Source: Based on Deetz, *Transforming Communication, Transforming Business*, Chapter 7

of self, other, and the world"[9] that Deetz believes are the product of participatory democracy.

The 2 × 2 nature of Figure 21-1 yields four different ways in which public decisions—including corporate ones—can be made: *strategy, consent, involvement,* and *participation.* Deetz' analysis of these four corporate practices provides the core of his critique of managerialism.

STRATEGY: OVERT MANAGERIAL MOVES TO EXTEND CONTROL

Managerialism
A systematic logic, set of routine practices, and ideology that values control over all other concerns.

Deetz doesn't portray individual managers as scoundrels in his saga of corporate control. He makes it clear that managers are not the problem—the real culprit is *managerialism.* Deetz describes managerialism as discourse based on "a kind of systematic logic, a set of routine practices, and ideology" that values control above all else.[10] Stockholders want profits and workers desire freedom, but management craves control.

Whenever there's a corporate disaster or scandal, the public and media look for a scapegoat or "bad apple" who's responsible. Deetz thinks that's shortsighted because it diverts attention from a failed managerial system based on control. He cites social psychologist Philip Zimbardo's book *The Lucifer Effect,* which suggests we'd do well to stop talking about a few bad apples and look at the consequences of what happens when you put good people in bad barrels.[11]

No matter what their job, workers around the world often experience the same dictatorial style in the expressed and implied messages that come from the top:

"Because I'm the boss."
"Because I say so."
"If you don't like it, quit."
"It's my way or the highway."

Some employees do object by saying, in effect, "Take this job and shove it," but that doesn't increase collaboration. Their choice is often limited to loyalty or exit—"love it or leave it." Without a voice, workers have no say in the decisions that affect them during the majority of their waking hours. Deetz argues that while control of this sort is disappearing in most enlightened corporations, new forms of control based in communication systems impede any real worker voice in structuring their work.

Stockholders face the same either/or dilemma. They can choose to hold their shares or sell them, but neither option offers a way to influence corporate policy. Although management presents itself as making decisions on behalf of stockholders (the owners), Deetz says that the interests of the two groups are often at odds. Because of stock options and "golden parachutes," top management has benefited more than any other group from the merger mania and cost-cutting strategies of the last two decades. Whereas long-term growth would help the average investor, quick profits and tight control of costs are the manager's ticket up the corporate ladder. Regardless of a company's product line or service, "control is the management product and is most clearly the one on which individual advancement rests."[12]

Initially, managers may regard efficiency as a means to the end goal of higher profits. Deetz is convinced, however, that the desire for control soon becomes a valued end in itself. That desire can even exceed the desire for corporate performance. Talking in terms of money is often more for control than for efficiency or profits.

The control drive of managerialism seeks the medium of its extension, and money is it. . . . Everything that cannot be adequately translated into money is implicitly suppressed, and all competing rights of decisions regarding one's life are made marginal.[13]

Nowhere is this quest for control more apparent than in corporate aversion to public conflict. The managerial rule of thumb seems to be that conflict is to be "dealt with" rather than openly discussed. Managers are rewarded for "putting out fires," "running a tight ship," or "making things run smoothly." The impersonal nature of these metaphors suggests that executives should place responsibility to the company ahead of personal feelings or ethical concerns. In the corporate context, claims of "company policy" and "just doing my job" provide sufficient moral justification for suppressing almost any act of employee resistance or dissent.

Deetz argues there is little evidence that strategic control has beneficial effects beyond accelerating advancement on the managerial career path. He claims that most corporate successes (or failures) are the result of factors beyond managerial control.[14] Control does have distinct disadvantages, however. The cost is high, and workers resent the constant surveillance. Frequent references to "clearing out the deadwood" or "trimming the fat" create an understandable jumpiness among employees, and sometimes their fear is acted out in covert rebellion. Since dominance creates this kind of resistance, most modern managers prefer to maintain control through the voluntary consent of the worker rather than the strategic use of raw power.

CONSENT: UNWITTING ALLEGIANCE TO COVERT CONTROL

Deetz believes in capitalism, but he's convinced that corporations are unreasonable. "They expect more than a fair day's work for a fair day's pay; they want love, respect, and above all loyalty."[15] Even though the company gets the workers' most rested, alert, and chemical-free portion of the day, apparently that's not enough. Management insists that allegiance to the company should come before family, friends, church, and community. Through the process that Deetz calls *consent,* most employees willingly give that loyalty without getting much in return. "Consent is the term I use to designate the variety of situations and processes in which someone actively, though unknowingly, accomplishes the interests of others in the faulty attempt to fulfill his or her own interests. The person is complicit in her or his own victimization."[16]

Lynn, a former student of mine, wrote an application log entry for Deetz' critical theory that poignantly captures the human cost of consent:

Consent
The process by which employees actively, though unknowingly, accomplish managerial interests in a faulty attempt to fulfill their own.

My father was very loyal to his company in the interest of moving up the ladder for pay increases. When my brother and I were babies and toddlers, my family lived in four different places in three years because the company required that we move. Later on, my father spent much of his time traveling and lived in New York for over six months while the rest of us lived in Baltimore. During my high school years, he worked until about eight or nine o'clock in the evening even though it wasn't demanded of him. His entire department was often there because it was common practice to spend that much time getting the job done.

I would love to see the ideal world where employees have a lot more power in their communication within a large company. I think that it would possibly save families like mine from growing up without a full-time father.

I can see further implications. If employees, especially men, feel like they have more power in the workplace, they will be less likely to come home and feel the need to prove their power at home by demeaning their wives in many different ways. I think that if Deetz' proposals ever worked on a wide scale, our country would see a decrease in domestic violence.

How do companies manage to strike such an unfair bargain with their employees? It's tempting to point to the workaholism of Lynn's father as the core of the problem, but Deetz lays more of the blame on managerial control of workplace language, information, forms, symbols, rituals, and stories. Although these are the practices that Pacanowsky and other interpretive scholars treat as indicators of a given organizational culture (see Chapter 19), Deetz views them as attempts to produce and reproduce a culture that is sympathetic to managerial interests. As McPhee's CCO states, all corporations have their own sets of constitutive practices. The question Deetz asks is not *What do these mean?* Rather, it is *Whose meanings are these?*

Systematically distorted communication
Operating outside of employees' awareness, a form of discourse that restricts what can be said or even considered.

Managerialism promotes workers' unwitting consent through a process of *systematically distorted communication.* Unlike strategic control, which is open and deliberate, systematically distorted communication operates under the radar. When this happens, expectations and norms within a group setting restrict what can be openly expressed or even thought. Deetz emphasizes that the workers deceive themselves because they believe they are interacting freely, while in reality only certain options are available. As an example, Deetz notes that arbitrary authority relations within an organization may be disguised as legitimate divisions of labor. That way any talk about power relations must assume the validity of the status quo, thus reproducing the organizational hierarchy rather than challenging it. Real interactive decisions can't be made in such a context.

Discursive closure
Suppression of conflict without employees realizing that they are complicit in their own censorship.

Systematically distorted communication requires suppression of potential conflict. This process, which Deetz calls *discursive closure,* occurs in a variety of ways. For example, certain groups of people within an organization may be classified as "disqualified" to speak on important issues. Arbitrary definitions can be labeled "natural" to avoid further discussion. The values that guided a manager's judgment call may be kept hidden so that it appears to be an objective decision (see Chapter 20). A group may discourage members from talking about certain subjects. Or the organization may allow the discussion of a topic such as gender-linked job classification or pay differences but discount its importance or quickly divert attention to other issues.

Deetz suggests that the force of an organizational practice is strongest when no one even thinks about it. If someone were to question such a routine, employees would be hard-pressed to explain why it is standard operating procedure. The best response they could muster would be a nonanswer: "That's the way it's done around here." Practices that have this taken-for-granted quality are often equated with common sense. Without a clear understanding that communication produces rather than reflects reality (the right side of Figure 21-1), employees will unknowingly consent to the managerial mentality that wants to expand corporate control—even though it doesn't benefit them or other stakeholders.

INVOLVEMENT: FREE EXPRESSION OF IDEAS, BUT NO VOICE

For anyone who has a stake in corporate decisions (all of us), shifting from managerial control at the top of Figure 21-1 to involvement at the bottom is a crucial move. In political terms, it represents a switch from autocracy to liberal democracy—from managerial decisions made behind closed doors to open discussions where all have the opportunity to express their opinions.

Employee *involvement* in corporate choices began with a suggestion box mounted on a wall. In some companies, this invitation for expression evolved over decades into open forums that look like early-American town meetings. At their best, these attempts at corporate democracy are based on a commitment to free speech and the value of an open marketplace of ideas (see Nilsen's ethic of significant choice, p. 191).

Deetz claims that liberal eighteenth-century Jeffersonian democracy was based on three notions about communication: (1) freedom of speech guaranteed equitable participation in decision making; (2) persuasion and advocacy were the best ways to reach a good decision; and (3) autonomous individuals could then make up their own minds. Taken together, this meant truth would emerge from the free flow of information in an open marketplace of ideas. As long as people shared the same values, an information-transfer model of communication worked well.[17] But not in today's society. Freedom of speech doesn't mean the right to be in on the decision. Adversarial posturing doesn't lend itself to creative consensus. And consent conditions make autonomy rare.

Involvement
Stakeholders' free expression of ideas that may, or may not, affect managerial decisions.

Organizations in the twenty-first century must operate in a pluralistic and interdependent world. People have always been different, but it used to be that mountains and oceans made it possible to stick with your own kind. In business and government today, that's almost impossible. You can't expect much empathy from a person raised in a different culture, who has had radically different experiences, and who holds a worldview that you might find disturbing. And isolation is no longer an option. As the worldwide economic meltdown in 2008, the 2010 BP Gulf oil spill, and bankrupt European economies in 2012 illustrate, whatever happens up the road or overseas will surely affect us all. Deetz is convinced that if Thomas Jefferson lived downwind or downstream from a factory hog farm, the Declaration of Independence he wrote would be a different document.[18] It might well have been a Declaraton of Interdependence.

As Deetz surveys present-day corporate communication practices, he concludes that "the right of expression appears more central than the right to be informed or to have an effect."[19] Through involvement in discussions of company policy, employees have a chance to air their grievances, state their desires, and recommend alternative ways of working. Many managers use these sessions as a way to give employees a chance to let off steam. But advocacy is not negotiation. If workers find out their ideas aren't represented in the final decision, they quickly become cynical about the process. And when consent is present, the right to freely express ideas is only the right to express the meanings belonging to someone else.

In national politics as well as corporate governance, meaningful democracy requires that people not only have a chance to discuss the issues, but also have a voice in the final outcome. Forums provide the opportunity for involvement, yet *voice* is not just having a say. It means expressing interests that are freely and openly formed, and then having those interests reflected in joint decisions. That's real participation. Deetz says it's only possible when all stakeholders realize that their communication creates reality rather than merely describing it.

PARTICIPATION: STAKEHOLDER DEMOCRACY IN ACTION

Deetz' theory of communication is critical, but not just negative. While he strongly criticizes the managerial strategy of increasing control over workers, engineering their consent, and granting them free expression without giving them a voice in decisions, he also believes that joint, open decisions in the workplace are possible. Deetz is convinced that "meaningful democratic participation creates better citizens and better social choices, and provides important economic benefits."[20] One of the goals of his theory is to reclaim the possibility of open negotiations of power. He calls it *stakeholder democracy* or generative democracy—this alternative term emphasizing that participants are creating something new.

The first move Deetz makes is to expand the list of people who should have a say in how a corporation is run. Besides managers, he sees at least six groups of stakeholders with multiple needs and desires.[21]

Participation
Stakeholder democracy; the process by which all stakeholders in an organization negotiate power and openly reach collaborative decisions.

Investors seek security of principal and a decent return on their investment.

Workers seek a reasonable wage, safe working conditions, a chance to take pride in their labor, security of employment, and time for their families.

Consumers seek quality goods and services at a fair price.

Suppliers seek a stable demand for their resource with timely payment upon delivery.

Host communities seek payment for services provided, stable employment, environmental care, and the quality of family and public life enhanced rather than diminished.

Greater society and the world community seek environmental care, economic stability, overall civility, and fair treatment of all constituent groups (racial, ethnic, gender).

Deetz notes that some stakeholders have taken greater risks and made longer-term investments in a company than typical owners of stock or top-level managers.[22]

He believes it's imperative that those who are affected by corporate decisions have a say in how such decisions are made. Of course, this stance runs counter to traditional notions of exclusive stockholder rights or managerial prerogatives, but Deetz says there's no legitimate basis for privileging one group of stakeholders over another. He reminds us that nature did not make corporations—we did. "The rights and responsibilities of people are not given in advance by nature or by a privileged, universal value structure, but are negotiated through interaction."[23]

As you scan the list of stakeholders and their interests, it's obvious that current corporate governance is not set up to address their social, financial, and ecological goals. In light of the widespread corporate greed and corruption that led to the financial meltdown and Great Recession of the last decade, relying on managerial goodwill would seem a joke. Some would expect government to insert social values into the marketplace, but, except for brief periods of time following a crisis, government policy is largely influenced by business leaders and lobbyists. Free-enterprise advocates suggest that the unseen hand of the market will sort things out, but that reduces all values to a matter of dollars and cents—and those not equitably.

Deetz offers his appraisal and previews his solution: Taken together, corporate "stewardship, government regulation, and markets offer weak mechanisms for value inclusion and virtually no support for communication processes that create win/win situations where multiple stakeholders can successfully pursue their mutual interests."[24] Rather than trying to leverage participatory governance from the outside, Deetz believes building stakeholder values into corporate decision-making practices is the route to go. In addition to his academic work, he acts as a consultant to companies' top management and their boards of directors, showing why it's in their long-term interest to initiate collaborative practices themselves. He stresses that the diversity among stakeholders generates productive interaction and creativity instead of merely reproducing what's always been.

POLITICALLY ATTENTIVE RELATIONAL CONSTRUCTIONISM (PARC)

Deetz proposes an extension of his critical theory that describes six types of conflict that must be addressed in organizations. He calls it *politically attentive relational constructionism (PARC).*[25] He suggests it can also serve as a framework or metatheory within which to compare his theory with other organizational and/or critical theories. Although the four-word label to which PARC refers may strike you as daunting, when split into two-word pairs you can see that the phrase reflects the *communication model* and *codetermination* features of stakeholder participation shown in Figure 21–1.

PARC model

Politically attentive relational constructionism; a collaborative view of communication based in stakeholder conflict.

Relational Constructionism

Deetz maintains that most organizational theories are based on some form of social construction. That's certainly the case with Pacanowsky's cultural approach, which looks at cultural artifacts and seeks to interpret what they mean (see Chapter 19). It's also true with McPhee's version of CCO, which describes the four flows constituted by communication within an organization (see Chapter 20). Both theories focus on *what* has been created, not *how* it was done. Since Deetz is just as concerned with the process of construction as he is with its end product, he uses the designation *relational* rather than the more common term *social.* He makes this switch to signal that he differs from those who think they're looking at an already etched-in-stone culture or, conversely, those who think they're writing on a blank slate. "Relational constructionism asks us to return to explore the moments of co-constructions and the conditions making particular constructions possible rather than accept the productions as given."[26]

Deetz outlines nine conditions that must be met in order for diverse stakeholders to successfully negotiate their needs and interests:[27]

1. Stakeholders have divergent interests, not set positions.
2. Stakeholders possess roughly the same level of communication skill.
3. Authority relationships and power positions are set aside.
4. All stakeholders have an equal opportunity to express themselves.
5. Stakeholders' wants are openly investigated to determine their interests.
6. Participants transparently share information and how decisions are made.
7. Facts and knowledge claims are revisited to see how they were created.
8. Focus on outcomes and interests rather than bargaining on rival solutions.
9. Stakeholders jointly make decisions rather than just having "their say."

This batch of preconditions might seem impossible to meet, but those trained in the art of negotiation and conflict mediation are quite familiar with most of the requirements and are committed to using them for the benefit of all parties. It's not surprising that Deetz, former director of peace and conflict studies at his university, finds them useful in his PARC model.

Politically Attentive

Deetz uses the term "political" to refer to the presence of power dynamics in relationships. He's convinced that the world is "fundamentally based on conflict and tension rather than consensus and order,"[28] so all communication is political and we should be frequently aware of that fact. Deetz sees power as an ever-present part of our relationships—certainly so in our organizational lives. To be *politically attentive* means to honestly explore the power in play behind so-called neutral facts and taken-for-granted positions.

In corporations, for example, political awareness might lead us to examine specific "standard accounting practices" to uncover how they came to be—who benefited and who suffered loss by their adoption. Deetz isn't bothered that the world is political, and he thinks it's disingenuous and deceptive when managers pretend it isn't. An organization's stakeholders need to recover the conflict that was repressed so that all interests are on the table and openly discussed. Only in this way can fair and beneficial negotiations take place.

Deetz would have managers take the role of mediator rather than persuader, manipulator, or dictator. They would coordinate the conflicting interests of all parties affected by corporate decisions. He understands that even those who are committed to open dialogue will feel insecure as they relinquish control. He suggests that a good way for them to start is to "complicate" their perceptions of subordinates and other stakeholders by being around them, talking with them, and learning their hopes, dreams, fears, values, and needs. And when stakeholders come together to discuss corporate policy, managers should make sure all areas of conflict are considered. PARC suggests six that are almost always an issue.[29]

Inner life: What feelings are present and possible? What organizational practices are necessary for those feelings to surface?

Identity and recognition: Who are the people involved? Given their identities, what rights and responsibilities do they have?

Social order: What behaviors, actions, and ways of talking are considered appropriate? What norms and rules support these?

Truth: What do members think is true? How do they back up these claims? What are the processes for resolving different views?

Life narratives: How does the world work for them? What would a good and beautiful future look like?

Justice: What is fair? How should limited goods and services be distributed?

AVOIDING MELTDOWN—PUTTING THEORY INTO PRACTICE

Given entrenched managerial power and privilege in corporations, most economic observers are skeptical that the workplace participation Deetz advocates will become reality. But Deetz' work with the International Atomic Energy Agency (IAEA) might give naysayers cause for pause. The agency invited Deetz to join a working group of international experts, nuclear plant supervisors, and government regulators concerned with creating "cultures of safety" around the construction and operation of atomic generating sites. Although anything involving radiation is always a concern, fears of power-plant disasters skyrocketed after the 2011 Fukushima meltdown following an earthquake and subsequent tsunami. The chairman of the independent commission that investigated the accident made it clear this wasn't a natural disaster:

> What must be admitted—very painfully—is that this was a disaster "Made in Japan." Its fundamental causes are to be found in the ingrained conventions of Japanese culture: our reflexive obedience; our reluctance to question authority; our devotion to 'sticking with the program'; our groupism; and our insularity.[30]

Deetz would call this consent actively reproduced at work. The nuclear community was shocked the meltdown took place in a technologically sophisticated nation known for quality control and a highly skilled workforce. If this could happen in Japan, how much more risk will atomic energy pose in less developed countries such as Mexico, Poland, or Vietnam, where plans are quickly moving ahead?

Most members of IAEA admit that a checklist approach to safety isn't working and that nuclear engineers know little about the human side of organizational dynamics. This is why communication experts looking at the consent production and change process need to be involved. Deetz, of course, advocates bringing the workers into the process, with places for active participatory dialogue. (See a link to his presentation at the IAEA 2012 annual meeting in the Second Look bibliography.) Members of his working group realize that people welding pipe know things that people who aren't welding pipe don't know. So if welders are part of the decision-making process, the decision will be based on better information.

Imagine Deetz on a video conference call with nuclear plant managers around the world.

SUPERVISOR #1: At our safety meetings, I have a lot of trouble getting people to pay attention, listen, or even care.

SUPERVISOR #2: You know, I just don't let that happen. I get in their face and tell them to pay attention and listen.

DEETZ: Have you ever asked them why they're not paying attention—what there is about this that makes it seem unworthy of them? You might ask them what conversations about safety they'd want to turn off their cell phones to be part of.[31]

Deetz says you'll never know unless you ask and then treat their answers as valuable. You may find out that workers believe safety is just managerial lip service because what their boss really wants is the job done fast. Perhaps a lot of the crew thinks everything in the building of these plants is overengineered. They're pouring twice as much concrete as needed, so cutting a few corners doesn't seem dangerous. Or you might pick up a machismo swagger that sees caution as unmanly. Only when the discussion turns to the safety of one's family or the chance of radiation rendering a guy sterile does there seem to be a reason to turn off the cell phone.

Stan Deetz is not naive. He knows atomic energy is not just an alternative way to boil water. Moving toward an industry culture of safety through stakeholder participation is a complex and difficult process, and there aren't enough regulators to look over the shoulder of every worker eight hours a day. So the goal is to reach a point where all stakeholders voluntarily do the right thing because they see it's in their own interest or the interests of those they love. But if Deetz is wrong—or managers ignore his advice—you might learn about it first on the evening news.

CRITIQUE: A QUALITY CRITICAL THEORY, BUT IS WORKPLACE DEMOCRACY JUST A DREAM?

Applied to organizational life, Deetz' critical approach is an exemplar of what this type of interpretive theory should be. He *clarifies the harmful values* of managerialism and affirms the importance of participation, fairness, equality, diversity, and cooperation—values that many of us in the field of communication share. He also provides a *new understanding* of why and how corporate managers exert control, even when it ultimately benefits no one—not even themselves.

Deetz' *reform agenda* is to expose unequal and destructive power relationships in a quest to make society more democratic. His extensive experience with organizations like IAEA provides rich *qualitative data* that supports his theory. His work has created a *community of agreement* among other critical theorists and social constructionists, and it's also a must-read among organizational communication scholars who don't share those commitments.

Like prophets, critical theorists have the reputation of being a rather grim bunch. But Deetz insists that critical scholars be "filled with care, thought, and good humor.[32] That third quality may surprise you, but he suggests that with good humor we can smile at our inconsistencies, contradictions, and bruised pride. We are to take the plight of the oppressed—but not ourselves—seriously. "The righteousness and pretense is gone, we must act without knowing for sure. The grand narratives are dead, but there is meaning and pleasure in the little ones. The pleasure embarrasses us but also gives us energy and a smile at ourselves."[33] For me, that makes this theory *aesthetically pleasing.* You can catch some of Deetz' earnestness and humor in the conversation referenced at the end of this chapter.

Robert McPhee employs a different kind of humor in his ironic summary of Deetz' vision of democracy in the workplace: "If we just didn't find it natural and right and unavoidable to hand power over to managers, everything would be different and all our problems would be solved."[34] Deetz understands the difficulty in altering entrenched power, but the number of problems like those faced in nuclear power plants may put the forces of a changing world on the side of collaboration between management and workers. He cites the example of Five-Stars, a customer loyalty technology company that has 80 managers (referred to as "coaches").

At FiveStars, coaches are selected for their ability and desire to build authentic relationships with employees. FiveStars announces to all in the company and community that "our goal is to make sure our managers have an honest, genuine, and trusting relationship with their direct reports that lasts a lifetime, not just the duration of an employee's tenure here. This means that we are responsible for coaching our managers to lead from a place of humility, rather than authority. . . . Leaders succeed by getting to know their employees and connecting with them personally."[35] Not every manager wants or is able to coach this way, but that's what's expected and rewarded at FiveStars. Of course, that kind of commitment has to start with and be modeled by the top leaders at the company—which it is.

Deetz is convinced that other organizations can and will catch the same vision. In summarizing his life work, he writes, "My job and joy is to remove structural and systemic features of life that are designed to advantage some and reduce the capacity of democracy to work, to get rid of systematically distorted communication and various discursive closures to enable creative mutually beneficial choices."[36]

QUESTIONS TO SHARPEN YOUR FOCUS

1. Deetz contrasts *information models* that assume language *reflects* reality with *communication models* that assume reality emerges out of a *relationship* among self, others, language, and the world. Which theories that we've already covered fit the communication model?

2. Managers use *strategy* and *consent* to maintain *control* over subordinates. According to Deetz, which practice is more effective? Why?

3. The *stakeholder model* requires *participation*, not just *involvement*. What is the difference between the two practices?

4. To what extent do you agree with the following statement: "Autocracy at work is the price we pay for *democracy* after hours"? Does it apply equally to work in the classroom?

CONVERSATIONS

View this segment online at www.afirstlook.com.

In this eight-minute segment, critical theorist Stan Deetz offers a host of pithy opinions. Here's a sample. *On communication:* "The field for a long time argued that meanings were in people. I raise the opposite kind of question: Whose meanings are in people?" *On management:* "A lot of managers talk about thinking out of the box, but they don't understand . . . that you do not think out of the box by commanding the box." *On corporate assets:* "Their primary assets are not what investors gave them, but what employees gave them. . . . Their primary assets go down the elevator every night." And there are lots more. Watch and discover your favorites.

A SECOND LOOK

Recommended resource: Stanley Deetz, *Transforming Communication, Transforming Business: Building Responsive and Responsible Workplaces,* Hampton, Cresskill, NJ, 1995.

Critical foundation: Stanley Deetz, *Democracy in an Age of Corporate Colonization: Developments in Communication and the Politics of Everyday Life,* State University of New York, Albany, NY, 1992.

Critique of communication theory and practice: Stanley Deetz, "Critical Theory," in *Engaging Organizational Communication Theory: Multiple Perspectives,* S. May and Dennis Mumby (eds.), Sage, Thousand Oaks, CA, 2004, pp. 85–111.

Organizational politics: "Interests, Conflict, and Power: Organizations as Political Systems," in Gareth Morgan, *Images of Organization,* 2nd ed., Sage, Thousand Oaks, CA, 1997, pp. 153–213.

PARC model compared to McPhee's CCO: Stanley Deetz and Elizabeth K. Eger, "Developing a Metatheoretical Perspective for Organizational Communication Studies," in *The New Handbook of Organizational Communication: Advances in Theory, Research, and Methods,* 2nd ed., Fredrick Jablin and Linda L. Putnam (eds.), Sage, Thousand Oaks, CA, 2013.

PARC model compared to CMM: Stanley Deetz, "Power and the Possibility of Generative Community Dialogue," in *The Coordinated Management of Meaning: A Festschrift in Honor of W. Barnett Pearce,* Stephen Littlejohn (ed.), Rowman & Littlefield, Lanham, MD, 2014, pp. 217–234.

Deetz' end goal: Stanley Deetz, "Generative Democracy," in *Interorganizational Collaboration: Complexity, Ethics, and Communication,* Renee Guarriello Heath and Matthew G. Isbell (eds.), Waveland, Long Grove, IL, 2017, pp. 129–131.

Deetz' IAEA paper on creating a safe nuclear culture: http://gnssn.iaea.org/NSNI/SC/SCPoP/Papers prepared for meeting/Stanley Deetz_Being Transformative - How Hearts, Minds and Souls All Matter_Paper.pdf

Review and critique: Branislav Kovačić, "The Democracy and Organizational Communication Theories of Deetz, Mumby, and Associates," in *Watershed Research Traditions in Communication Theory,* Donald Cushman and Branislav Kovačić (eds.), State University of New York, Albany, NY, 1995, pp. 211–238.

To access scenes from feature films that illustrate the
Critical Theory of Communication in Organizations, click on
Suggested Movie Clips under Theory Resources at
www.afirstlook.com.

Public Rhetoric

Aristotle wrote that rhetoric is "an ability, in each particular case, to see the available means of persuasion."[1] That definition centers attention on the intentional act of using words to have an effect. We use the term *public rhetoric* in this section to refer to a speaking context in which the orator has an opportunity to monitor and adjust to the response of his or her immediate audience.

For citizens of ancient Greece, knowing how to speak in public was part of their democratic responsibility. Later on, when Rome ruled the world, rhetorical ability was a survival skill in the rough-and-tumble politics of the forum. Rhetoricians have always had a special interest in judicial argument, legislative debate, political rallies, religious sermons, and speeches given at celebrations. In each setting, teachers and practitioners champion the art of rhetoric as a means of ensuring that speakers of truth are not at a disadvantage when trying to win the hearts and minds of an audience.

The Greeks and Romans distinguished five parts, or divisions, of the study of rhetoric:

1. *Invention*—discovery of convincing arguments
2. *Arrangement*—organization of material for best impact
3. *Style*—selection of compelling and appropriate language
4. *Delivery*—coordination of voice and gestures
5. *Memory*—mastery and rehearsal of content

With the possible exception of memory, these concerns of rhetoric require that a speaker first analyze and then adapt to a specific group of listeners. We can, of course, react to the idea of audience adaptation in two different ways. If we view speakers who adjust their message to fit a specific audience in a positive light, we'll praise their rhetorical sensitivity and flexibility. If we view them negatively, we'll condemn them for their pandering and lack of commitment to the truth. Rhetorical thought across history swings back and forth between these two conflicting poles. The words of most rhetoricians reflect the tension they feel between "telling it like it is" and telling it in such a way that the audience will listen.

Greek philosopher Plato regarded rhetoric as mostly flattery. Far from seeing it as an art, he described rhetoric as a "knack," similar to the clever use of cosmetics. Both are attempts to make things look better than they really are.[2] In spite of his scorn, Plato imagined an ideal rhetoric based on a speaker's understanding of listeners with different natures and dispositions.

Plato's ideal discourse was an elite form of dialogue meant for private, rather than public, consumption. This philosophic, one-on-one mode of communication is known as *dialectic* (a different meaning for the term than its use in Baxter and Bakhtin's relational dialectics theory). Unlike typical oratory in Athens, where speakers addressed large audiences on civic issues, Plato's dialectic focused on exploring eternal Truths in an intimate setting.

Although Plato hoped that philosophic dialectic would supplant public rhetoric, his best student, Aristotle, rejuvenated public rhetoric as a serious academic subject.

More than 2,000 years ago, Aristotle's *Rhetoric* systematically explored the topics of speaker, message, and audience. His ideas have stood the test of time and form a large portion of the advice presented in contemporary public speaking texts. But even though Aristotle defined rhetoric as the art of discovering all available means of persuasion, this conception doesn't solve the problem of how to get audiences to listen to hard truths.

Religious rhetors face the same paradox. In many ways, the apostle Paul seemed to personify the lover of diverse souls that Plato had earlier described. In his first letter to the Corinthians, Paul reminds the people of Corinth that he made a conscious decision to let his message speak for itself: "My speech and my proclamation were not with plausible words of wisdom."[3] Yet further on in the same letter he outlines a conscious rhetorical strategy: "I have become all things to all people, that I might by all means save some."[4] Four centuries later, Augustine continued to justify the conscious use of rhetoric by the church. Why, he asked, should defenders of truth be long-winded, confusing, and boring, when the speech of liars was brief, clear, and persuasive?

The tension between the logic of a message and the appeal it has for an audience isn't easily resolved. British philosopher Francis Bacon sought to integrate the two concerns when he wrote that "the duty of rhetoric is to apply Reason to Imagination for the better moving of the will."[5]

The three rhetoricians we introduce in this section face the dilemma that rhetoricians have struggled with since Plato: "How do you move an audience without changing your message or losing your integrity?" As you read, see which theorist comes up with an answer that is most satisfying for you.

The Rhetoric

of Aristotle

Aristotle was a student of Plato's in the golden age of Greek civilization, four centuries before the birth of Christ. He became a respected instructor at Plato's Academy but disagreed with his mentor over the place of public speaking in Athenian life.

Ancient Greece was known for its traveling speech teachers, called Sophists. Particularly in Athens, those teachers trained aspiring lawyers and politicians to participate effectively in the courts and deliberative councils. In hindsight, they appear to have been innovative educators who offered a needed and wanted service.[1] But since their advice was underdeveloped theoretically, Plato scoffed at the Sophists' oratorical devices. His skepticism is mirrored today in the negative way people use the term *mere rhetoric* to label the speech of *tricky* lawyers, *mealy-mouthed* politicians, *spellbinding* preachers, and *fast-talking* salespeople.

Aristotle, like Plato, deplored the demagoguery of speakers using their skill to move an audience while showing a casual indifference to the truth. But unlike Plato, he saw the tools of rhetoric as a neutral means by which the orator could either accomplish noble ends or further fraud: ". . . by using these justly one would do the greatest good, and unjustly, the greatest harm."[2] Aristotle believed truth has a moral superiority that makes it more acceptable than falsehood. But unscrupulous opponents of the truth may fool a dull audience unless an ethical speaker uses all possible means of persuasion to counter the error. Speakers who neglect the art of rhetoric have only themselves to blame when their hearers choose falsehood. Success requires wisdom *and* eloquence.

Both the *Politics* and the *Ethics* of Aristotle are polished and well-organized books compared with the rough prose and arrangement of his text on rhetoric. The *Rhetoric* apparently consists of Aristotle's reworked lecture notes for his course at the academy. Despite the uneven nature of the writing, the *Rhetoric* is a searching study of audience psychology. Aristotle raised rhetoric to a science by systematically exploring the effects of the speaker, the speech, and the audience. He regarded the speaker's use of this knowledge as an art. Quite likely, the text your communication department uses for its public speaking classes is basically a contemporary recasting of the audience analysis provided by Aristotle more than 2,000 years ago.

RHETORIC: MAKING PERSUASION PROBABLE

Rhetoric
Discovering in each case all possible means of persuasion.

Aristotle saw the function of *rhetoric* as the discovery in each case of "the available means of persuasion." He never spelled out what he meant by persuasion, but his concern with noncoercive methods makes it clear that he ruled out force of law, torture, and war. His threefold classification of speech situations according to the nature of the audience shows that he had affairs of state in mind.

The first in Aristotle's classification is courtroom (forensic) speaking, which addresses judges who are trying to render a just decision about actions alleged to have taken place in the *past*. The closing arguments presented by the prosecution and defense in the trial of George Zimmerman for killing an unarmed Trayvon Martin are examples of judicial rhetoric centered on guilt or innocence. The second, ceremonial (epideictic) speaking, heaps praise or blame on another for the benefit of *present-day* audiences. For example, President Obama's remarks in the aftermath of the shooting deaths of five Dallas police officers gave the nation a chance to celebrate those who seek to protect us. It also expressed regret and disapproval for those who choose violence as a political solution to their problems. The third, political (deliberative) speaking, attempts to influence legislators or voters who decide *future* policy. The 2016 presidential debates gave candidates Donald Trump and Secretary Hillary Clinton the chance to sway undecided voters. These different temporal orientations could call for diverse rhetorical appeals.

Because his students were familiar with the question-and-answer style of Socratic dialogue, Aristotle classified rhetoric as a counterpart or an offshoot of dialectic. Dialectic is one-on-one discussion; rhetoric is one person addressing many. Dialectic is a search for truth; rhetoric tries to demonstrate truth that's already been found. Dialectic answers general philosophical questions; rhetoric addresses specific, practical ones. Dialectic claims certainty; rhetoric deals with probability. Aristotle saw this last distinction as particularly important: Rhetoric is the art of discovering ways to make truth seem more probable to an audience that isn't completely convinced.

RHETORICAL PROOF: *LOGOS, PATHOS, ETHOS*

Inartistic proofs
External evidence the speaker doesn't create.

Artistic proofs
Internal proofs that rely on *logos, pathos,* and *ethos* appeals.

According to Aristotle, the available means of persuasion can be artistic or inartistic. *Inartistic* or external proofs are those the speaker doesn't create. They would include testimonies of witnesses or documents such as letters and contracts. *Artistic* or internal proofs are those the speaker creates. There are three kinds of artistic proofs: *logos, pathos,* and *ethos.* In English, these Greek words are often rendered as *logical, emotional,* and *ethical* proofs, but for the first and last terms, some of their meaning gets lost in translation. *Logos* is an appeal to listeners' rationality—what seems reasonable to the audience, not ironclad logic. Its appeal comes from lines of argument in the speech. *Pathos* is the feeling the speech draws out of the hearers. It's the root of the English word *pathetic,* so you might assume pathos had a negative connotation for Aristotle and his Greek readers. Not so. Pathos refers to both positive and distressing emotional responses that a speaker tries to stimulate. *Ethos* refers to credibility—how a member of the audience perceives a speaker's entire character based on the message and the way it's delivered. Ethical integrity is only part of that overall judgment that's in the eye of the beholder. Some form of *logos, pathos,* and *ethos* is present in every public presentation, but one speech delivered during your lifetime that has done this exceedingly well is President Barack

Obama's commencement address to graduating seniors at the University of Notre Dame in 2009.

Case Study: Barack Obama's Commencement Address at Notre Dame

A few months into his first term of office, President Obama accepted an invitation to address the 2009 graduating class at their University of Notre Dame commencement service and receive an honorary Doctor of Laws degree. The announcement by the school's President, Rev. John I. Jenkins, triggered angry protests from many alumni, some students, and Roman Catholic church leaders. John D'Arcy, Bishop of the Catholic Diocese of Fort Wayne-South Bend, issued a statement that he would boycott the ceremony because of Obama's approval of abortion and stem cell research—practices that longstanding Catholic doctrine holds to be morally wrong. He cited a 2004 pronouncement of the US Catholic Bishops:

> The Catholic community and Catholic institutions should not honor those who act in defiance of our fundamental moral principles. They should not be given awards, honors or platforms which would suggest support for their actions. Indeed, the measure of any Catholic institution is not only what it stands for, but also what it will not stand for.[3]

Despite the pro-and-con arguments about abortion that created a highly charged atmosphere surrounding the event, Obama's speech was not *judicial*. He neither defended his pro-choice stance nor criticized the pro-life commitment of those who opposed his presence. And although congratulations are a standard feature of graduation ceremonies, praise for a specific individual was not the thrust of the president's address. This was a *deliberative* speech—not about any specific government policy, but one in which he urged listeners to be mindful of the way they interact with those who hold opposing views. At root, the speech wasn't about abortion; it was about communicating deep-seated commitments in a way that builds community rather than tearing it apart.[4]

Following introductory remarks that established a warm connection with his Notre Dame audience, Obama briefly listed challenges graduates would face and summed up: "In short, we must find a way to live together as one human family. And it's this last challenge that I'd like to talk about today." This was the goal that was paraphrased in multiple ways throughout the speech.

> Making our case in public without reducing those with different views to caricature.
> Finding common ground. Bringing people together. A more perfect union.
> Promoting greater understanding and cooperation among people.
> Open heart. Open mind. Fair-minded words.

The three types of proof Aristotle discussed demonstrate how President Obama might speak in a way that makes reaching his goal possible, maybe even probable, but never with absolute certainty. He started with logos.

Logos
Proofs that appeal to listeners' rationality; lines of argument that seem reasonable; enthymemes and examples.

Logos: Quasi-Logical Arguments That Make Sense

Aristotle focused on two forms of *logos*—the *enthymeme* and the *example*. He regarded the enthymeme as "the strongest of the proofs."[5]

Enthymeme. An enthymeme is an incomplete version of a formal deductive syllogism. To illustrate, logicians might create the following syllogism from one of Obama's lines of reasoning:

Major or general premise: *Catholics have promoted the use of fair-minded words.*
Minor or specific premise: *Notre Dame is a Catholic university.*
Conclusion: *We should use fair-minded words.*

Typical enthymemes, however, leave out a premise that is already accepted by the audience. So the line of argument becomes: *Catholics have promoted the use of fair-minded words. . . . We should use fair-minded words.* In terms of style, the enthymeme is more artistic than a stilted syllogistic argument. But as University of Wisconsin rhetorician Lloyd Bitzer noted, Aristotle had a greater reason for advising the speaker to suppress the statement of a premise the listeners already believe. "Because they are jointly produced by the audience, enthymemes intuitively unite speaker and audience and provide the strongest possible proof. . . . The audience itself helps construct the proof by which it is persuaded."[6]

Enthymeme
An incomplete version of a formal deductive syllogism that is created by leaving out a premise already accepted by the audience or not drawing the obvious conclusion; a reasonable argument.

President Obama constructed a more pointed enthymeme when he addressed the practice of demonizing those who express deeply held convictions opposed to our own—specifically on the issue of abortion.

Major premise: *It is wrong to reduce those who disagree with us to a caricature.*
Minor premise: *We have reduced our opponents to a caricature.*
Conclusion: *We can right those wrongs by ceasing to caricature those we oppose.*

To state the minor premise might have produced a defensive reaction—"No, not me!" Leaving it unsaid gave listeners the space to admit to themselves, "I've done that," and accept the conclusion.

Example. Enthymemes are deductive. If listeners accept the premises, the claim of truth logically follows. Examples, on the other hand, are inductive. If an illustration strikes a responsive chord in the listener, the truth it suggests seems evident. Aristotle said that both forms of *logos* are persuasive, but examples are especially so when they illustrate a premise or the conclusion of an enthymeme that's already been stated.[7]

President Obama offered Cardinal Joseph Bernardin as an example to support the major premise of the first enthymeme I mentioned above. That enthymeme claimed that Catholics have promoted the use of fair-minded words. Obama regarded Bernardin as a kind, wise, and good man when they labored together to help unemployed people in impoverished South Side Chicago neighborhoods. The President recalled Bernardin speaking at one of the first meetings Obama attended as a community organizer. He said the Cardinal was "unafraid to speak his mind on moral issues ranging from poverty and AIDS and abortion to the death penalty and nuclear war. And yet, he was congenial and gentle in his persuasion, always trying to bring people together, always trying to find common ground."

As an example that it's wrong to reduce those who express differing views to a caricature—the major premise of the second enthymeme charted above—the president offered a personal illustration. During the run-up to his election as Senator, he received a letter from a doctor who was strongly pro-life, but who voted for him in the Illinois primary because he assumed that Obama was "a reasonable person." But now his campaign website declared that Obama would fight "right-wing ideologues who want to take away a woman's right to choose." If Obama truly believed that every pro-life individual was simply an ideologue who wanted to inflict suffering on women, he wasn't very reasonable. The doctor concluded, "I do not ask at this point that you oppose abortion, only that you speak about this issue in fair-minded words." So Obama told his staff to change his website.

Aristotle noted that examples drawn from the past, such as these, are more compelling than made-up illustrations. That's because most audiences realize the past is a better predictor of the future than are speculative descriptions. But he admitted that it's easier to create stories or paint future scenarios than it is to find apt historical events, and that hypothetical examples or fictional tales can be quite persuasive as well.[8]

Pathos: Emotional Appeals That Strike a Responsive Chord

Pathos
Proofs consisting of feelings and emotions elicited by the speech.

Aristotle was skeptical of the emotion-laden public oratory typical of his era.[9] He preferred the reason-based discussion characteristic of relatively small councils and executive deliberative bodies. Yet he understood that public rhetoric, if practiced ethically, benefits society. Thus, Aristotle set forth a theory of *pathos.* He offered it not to take advantage of an audience's destructive emotions, but as a corrective measure that could help a speaker craft emotional appeals that inspire reasoned civic decision-making. To this end, he cataloged a series of opposite feelings, explained the conditions under which each mood is experienced, and described how the speaker can get an audience to feel that way.[10] Aristotle scholar and translator George Kennedy claims that this analysis of *pathos* is "the earliest systematic discussion of human psychology."[11] If Aristotle's advice sounds familiar, it may be a sign that human nature hasn't changed much in the last 2,300 years.

Anger vs. Calmness. Aristotle's discussion of anger was an early version of Freud's frustration–aggression hypothesis. People feel angry when they are thwarted in their attempt to fulfill a need. Remind them of interpersonal slights and they'll become irate. Show them that the offender is sorry, deserves praise, or has great power, and they will calm down.

Friendliness vs. Enmity. Consistent with present-day research on attraction, Aristotle considered similarity the key to mutual warmth. The speaker should point out common goals, experiences, attitudes, and desires. In the absence of these positive forces, hatred of a common enemy can be used to create solidarity.

Fear vs. Confidence. Fear comes from a mental image of potential disaster. The speaker should paint a vivid word picture of the tragedy, showing that its occurrence is probable. Confidence can be built by describing the danger as remote.

Indignation vs. Pity. We all have a built-in sense of fairness. As the producers of *60 Minutes* prove weekly, it's easy to arouse a sense of injustice by describing an arbitrary use of power upon those who are helpless.

Admiration vs. Envy. People admire moral virtue, power, wealth, and beauty. By demonstrating that an individual has acquired life's goods through hard work rather than mere luck, admiration will increase.

In his address, President Obama sought to shift any sentiment of *enmity* in the audience to a feeling of *friendliness.* He did this with warm words for former Notre Dame President Father Theodore Hesburgh and praise for the volunteer service performed by 80 percent of the students in the graduating class. ("That's incredibly impressive, a powerful testimony to this institution.")

He also used self-deprecating humor. After thanking the University for the honorary Doctor of Laws degree, he acknowledged that the grant hadn't been without controversy, and ruefully quipped:

> I don't know if you're aware of this, but these honorary degrees are apparently pretty hard to come by. So far I'm only 1 for 2 as president. [Arizona State University did not bestow this traditional honor when he spoke at its commencement in 2009.] Father Hesburgh is 150 for 150. So Father Ted, after the ceremony, maybe you can give me some pointers to boost my average.

Obama's nonbiting humor evoked laughter 8 times in the first 10 minutes of the speech—the kind of interaction you'd have with a friend.

As for tamping down *fear* and anxiety that graduates might feel if they try to find common ground with those who oppose their deepest convictions, Obama acknowledged it wouldn't be easy. To connect with the audience in a *confident* and upbeat way, he told a story about Father Hesburgh, who was one of six men appointed to a presidential Civil Rights Commission tasked with implementing the Supreme Court's mandate for racial integration in education. The commission was made up of five Caucasians and one African American, encompassing both Democrats and Republicans. Members included two Southern governors, the dean of a Southern law school, Father Hesburgh, and another Northern university president.

After two of years of heated debate, the six men were at an impasse. Father Hesburgh invited them to Notre Dame's retreat center in Land O'Lakes, Wisconsin. At their first dinner they discovered they were all fishermen. So Hesburgh quickly readied a boat for a twilight trip out on the lake. While at the center they "overcame their differences and hammered out a final deal." The 12 resolutions they drafted became the backbone of the US Civil Rights Act passed by Congress. President Obama asked graduates to never forget "that each of us, endowed with the dignity possessed by all children of God, has the grace to recognize ourselves in one another; to understand that we all seek the same love of family, the same fulfillment of a life well lived. Remember that in the end, in some way we are all fishermen." The story functioned as an emotional appeal to forgo *anger* and instead *calmly* work across lines of ideological difference.

Ethos: Perceived Source Credibility

According to Aristotle, it's not enough for a speech to contain plausible arguments. The speaker must *seem* credible as well. Many audience impressions are formed before the speaker even begins. As poet Ralph Waldo Emerson cautioned more than a century ago, "Use what language you will, you can never say anything but what you are."[12] Quite likely, some in the audience rejected what Obama said due to his pro-choice stance or because he was a Democrat. But surprisingly, Aristotle said little about a speaker's background or reputation. He was more interested in audience perceptions that are shaped by what the speaker says or doesn't say. In the *Rhetoric* he identified three qualities that build high source credibility—*intelligence, character,* and *goodwill.*

1. Perceived intelligence. Aristotle believed that audiences judge intelligence by the overlap between their beliefs and the speaker's ideas. Their perception has more

Ethos
Perceived credibility consisting of auditors' judgment of the speaker's intelligence, character, and goodwill toward the audience, as these personal characteristics are revealed throughout the speech.

to do with practical wisdom (*phronesis*) and shared values than it does with training at Plato's Academy or an Ivy League school. Obama proposed four places where pro-life and pro-choice advocates might find common ground. (See the Ethical Reflection section ahead.) The applause each suggestion received indicated that many of his thoughts on this crucial matter coincided with theirs. And perhaps for some, his references to the Supreme Court case of Brown v. Board of Education and living at "a rare inflection point of history" bespoke a person with an active and sophisticated mind.

2. Virtuous character. Character has to do with the speaker's image as a good and honest person. Obama described "our selfishness, our pride, our stubbornness, our insecurities, our egos" as character flaws that make finding common ground so difficult. His use of the pronoun *our* rather than an accusatory *your* or *their* subtly communicates honesty and humility—the president knows he isn't perfect and is willing to own his weaknesses. For this audience of students who performed voluntary service while studying at Notre Dame, Obama's reference to working with Cardinal Bernardin to help the poor would enhance their opinion of his character rather than tarnish it.

Of course, not everyone in the audience was convinced that Obama was a good man—especially not the protesters who interrupted with shouts of "Abortion is murder!" and "Stop the baby killers!" early in the speech. But Obama's calm, impromptu response of "That's all right" seemed to align him with the student audience who then chanted, "We're Notre Dame. We're Notre Dame," implying that "We don't

"Trust me, at this point it's the only way we can boost your numbers on likability."

do things like that around here." Obama's charitable approach to his adversaries demonstrated virtuous character. It also emphasized the main point of his speech.

3. Goodwill. Goodwill is a positive judgment of the speaker's intention toward the audience. Aristotle thought it possible for an orator to possess extraordinary intelligence and sterling character yet still not have the listeners' best interests at heart. Obama's basketball humor at the start of the speech showed a genuine care for students' lives that would be hard for other US presidents to successfully project. He noted that they had the largest student five-on-five outdoor basketball tournament in the country and congratulated the winning team—the "Hallelujah Holla Backs." But much to the delight of the crowd, he expressed disappointment that the "Barack O'Ballers" had come up short and quipped, "So next year, if you need a six-foot, two-inch forward with a decent jump shot, you know where I live." He had the crowd. He was on their side.

Although Aristotle's comments on *ethos* were stated in a few brief sentences, no other portion of his *Rhetoric* has received such close scientific scrutiny. The results of sophisticated testing of audience attitudes show that his three-factor theory of source credibility stands up remarkably well.[13] Listeners definitely think in terms of competence (intelligence), trustworthiness (character), and care (goodwill). As Barack Obama spoke at Notre Dame, it seems likely that most listeners perceived him as strong in all three.

THE FIVE CANONS OF RHETORIC

Canons of rhetoric
The principle divisions of the art of persuasion established by ancient rhetoricians—invention, arrangement, style, delivery, and memory.

Although the organization of Aristotle's *Rhetoric* is somewhat puzzling, scholars and practitioners synthesize his words into four distinct standards for measuring the quality of a speaker's ability and performance: the construction of an argument (invention), ordering of material (arrangement), selection of language (style), and technique of presentation (delivery). Later writers add memory to the list of skills the accomplished speaker must master. As previewed in the introduction to this section on public rhetoric, the five *canons of rhetoric* have set the agenda of public address instruction for more than 2,000 years. Aristotle's advice strikes most students of public speaking as surprisingly up-to-date.

Invention
A speaker's "hunt" for arguments that will be effective in a particular speech.

Invention. To generate effective enthymemes and examples, the speaker draws on both specialized knowledge about the subject and general lines of reasoning common to all kinds of speeches. Imagining the mind as a storehouse of wisdom or an informational landscape, Aristotle called these stock arguments *topoi,* a Greek term that can be translated as "topics" or "places." As Cornell University literature professor Lane Cooper explained, "In these special regions the orator hunts for arguments as a hunter hunts for game."[14] Obama didn't have to go far afield to discover arguments and examples to support his appeal for open hearts, open minds, and fair-minded words. Most graduates and their family members were Catholics who held Notre Dame and its iconic former president Father Hesburgh in high esteem. Six times Obama mentioned him by name, and the words and deeds the President cited were powerful proof for the wisdom of seeking common ground.

Arrangement. According to Aristotle, we should avoid complicated schemes of organization. He wrote that "there are two parts to a speech; for it is necessary first to state the subject and then to demonstrate it."[15] First the thesis, then the proof. That's what Obama did at Notre Dame. Like public address teachers today,

Aristotle decried starting with jokes that have nothing to do with the topic or situation, insisting on three-point outlines, or waiting until the end of the speech to reveal the main point. The introduction should capture attention, establish our credibility, and make clear the purpose of the speech. The conclusion should remind listeners what we've said and leave them feeling good about us and our ideas.

Style. Aristotle's treatment of style in the *Rhetoric* focuses on metaphor. He believed that "to learn easily is naturally pleasant to all people" and that "metaphor most brings about learning."[16] Furthermore, he taught that "metaphor especially has clarity and sweetness and strangeness."[17] But for Aristotle, metaphors were more than aids for comprehension or aesthetic appreciation. Metaphors help an audience visualize—a "bringing-before-the-eyes" process that energizes listeners and moves them to action.[18] In this rhetorical situation, Obama couldn't have done better than to borrow a metaphor from Father Hesburgh, who pictured Notre Dame as both a lighthouse and a crossroads: "A lighthouse that stands apart, shining with the wisdom of the Catholic tradition, while the crossroads is where difference of culture and religion and conviction can coexist with friendship, civility, hospitality, and especially love." Students who had chanted, "We are Notre Dame" minutes before were reminded that this identification meant interacting and even intertwining with fellow human beings of all persuasions at the crossroads after graduation.

Delivery. Audiences reject delivery that seems planned or staged. Naturalness is persuasive, artifice just the opposite. Any form of presentation that calls attention to itself takes away from the speaker's proofs. In his 40-page analysis of the president's commencement address, Duquesne University rhetorician Ron Arnett never once mentions Obama's delivery.[19] That's high praise.

Memory. Aristotle's students needed no reminder that good speakers are able to draw upon a collection of ideas and phrases stored in the mind, yet Greek and Roman teachers of rhetoric found it necessary to stress the importance of memory. In our present age of instant information on the Internet and teleprompters that guarantee a speaker will never be at a loss for words, memory seems to be a lost art. Unlike presidents and Athenian orators, most of us aren't speaking in public every day. Perhaps for us, the modern equivalent of memory is rehearsal.

ETHICAL REFLECTION: ARISTOTLE'S GOLDEN MEAN

Aristotle's *Rhetoric* is the first known systematic treatise on audience analysis and adaptation. His work therefore begs the same kind of question discussed in the introduction to this section on public rhetoric: Was it ethical for President Obama to cloak himself in Father Hesburgh's clerical cloth in order to make his message more acceptable for this particular audience? The way I've phrased the question reflects a Western bias for linking morality with behavior. Does an act produce benefit or harm? Is it right or wrong to do a certain deed? Aristotle, however, spoke of ethics in terms of character rather than conduct, inward disposition instead of outward behavior. He took the Greek admiration for moderation and elevated it to a theory of virtue.

Golden mean
The virtue of moderation; the virtuous person develops habits that avoid extremes.

Aristotle assumed virtue stands between two vices.[20] He saw wisdom in the person who avoids excess on either side. Moderation is best; virtue develops habits that seek to walk an intermediate path. This middle way is known as the *golden mean*. That's because out of the four cardinal Hellenistic virtues—courage, justice, temperance, and practical wisdom—temperance is the one that explains the three others.

Whether the issue is truth-telling, self-disclosure, risk-taking when making decisions, or other communication choices, Aristotle's golden mean suggests a middle way.

Extreme	Golden Mean	Extreme
Lies	Truthful statements	Brutal honesty
Secrecy	Transparency	Soul-baring
Cowardice	Courage	Recklessness

As for audience adaptation at Notre Dame, Aristotle would have counseled Obama against the practice of telling people only what they want to hear, pandering to the crowd, or "wimping out" by not stating what he really thought. Aristotle would be equally against a disregard of audience sensitivities, riding roughshod over listeners' beliefs, or adopting a take-no-prisoners, lay-waste-the-town rhetorical belligerence. Obama's strategic identification with Father Hesburgh doesn't seem to fit either extreme. Using his golden mean standard, I believe Aristotle would condemn the mindset of protesters shouting "Stop the baby killers," just as he would denounce the prejudiced words on Obama's website that implied all people opposed to abortion are right-wing ideologues. The golden mean is the path that embraces winsome straight talk, gentle assertiveness, and adaptation.

After acknowledging that good-hearted people will never completely agree on abortion, Obama sketched out potential common ground.

> So let us work together to reduce the number of women seeking abortions; let's reduce unintended pregnancies. Let's make adoption more available. Let's provide care and support for women who do carry their children to term. Let's honor the conscience of those who disagree with abortion, and draft a sensible conscience clause, and make sure that all of our health care policies are grounded not only in sound science, but also in clear ethics, as well as respect for the equality of women.

This type of golden mean communication will often prove to be the best way to persuade others. But for Aristotle, that wasn't the ethical issue. Aristotle advocated the middle way because it is the well-worn path taken by virtuous people.

CRITIQUE: A THEORY THAT STANDS THE TEST OF TIME

You'll note that at the start of the chapter I classified Aristotle's *Rhetoric* as both an objective and interpretive theory—a surprise for many rhetoricians who consider it highly interpretive. I've made this assignment based on three distinct criteria for both types of theory that the *Rhetoric* fulfills. Operating within a cause-and-effect logic, Aristotle *predicted future* audience response based on the rhetorical choices the speaker makes. He not only forecasted how listeners will react, he *explained* why they will respond this way, often drawing upon historical cases known to his students. Equally impressive is the *practical utility* of his advice, which is taught in almost all public speaking classes and professional seminars on effective oral presentations.

As for fulfilling the requirements for a good interpretive theory, the thrust of Aristotle's *Rhetoric* is offering a *new understanding of people* in a speaker's audience. He *clarified the values* they are likely to hold as well as his own personal ideals. Although he believed that discovering all possible means of persuasion is a morally neutral quest, he considered how one used that knowledge as the ethical issue. For example, he regarded promoting rational deliberation as a morally superior strategy to stirring up negative emotions that trigger unthinking responses. And the *community of agreement* over the quality of his audience analysis and advice for speakers has spanned 24 centuries. Referring to Aristotle's manuscript in a rare moment of sincere appreciation, French skeptic Voltaire declared what many communication teachers would echo today: "I do not believe there is a single refinement of the art that escapes him."[21]

For some teachers of public speaking and rhetoric, criticizing Aristotle's *Rhetoric* is like doubting Einstein's theory of relativity or belittling Shakespeare's *King Lear.* Yet most interpretive and objective scholars agree that the *Rhetoric* falls short of meeting the dual standards of *relative simplicity* and *aesthetic appeal*—which include clarity. The organization of the book seems less simple and clear than he urged his students to be. For example, at the beginning of his *Rhetoric,* Aristotle promised a systematic study of *logos, ethos,* and *pathos,* but failed to follow that three-part plan. Instead, it appears that he grouped the material in a speech-audience-speaker order. Even those who claim there's a conceptual unity to Aristotle's theory admit the book is "an editorial jumble."[22] We must remember, however, that just like Mead's theory of symbolic interactionism (see Chapter 5), Aristotle's *Rhetoric* consists of lecture notes rather than a treatise prepared for the public.

Despite the shortcomings and perplexities of the *Rhetoric,* it remains a foundational text of our discipline—a starting point for objective and interpretive scholars alike. I was trained as a social scientist and have never taught a course in rhetoric. But I regard Aristotle—more than any other figure in the past—as the founding father of the communication discipline.

QUESTIONS TO SHARPEN YOUR FOCUS

1. For most people today, the term *rhetoric* has unfavorable associations. What synonym or phrase captures what Aristotle meant yet doesn't carry a negative connotation?

2. What *enthymemes* have advocates on each side of the abortion issue employed in their public *deliberative rhetoric?*

3. Aristotle divided *ethos* into issues of *intelligence, character,* and *goodwill.* Which quality is most important to you when you hear a campaign address, sermon, TED Talk, or other public speech?

4. Most scholars who define themselves as rhetoricians identify with the humanities rather than the sciences. Can you support the claim that Aristotle took a *scientific approach to rhetoric?*

A SECOND LOOK

Recommended resource: Aristotle, *On Rhetoric: A Theory of Civil Discourse,* 2ⁿᵈ ed., George A. Kennedy (ed. and trans.), Oxford University, New York, 1991.

Key scholarship: Richard Leo Enos and Lois Peters Agnew (eds.), *Landmark Essays on Aristotelian Rhetoric,* Lawrence Erlbaum, Mahwah, NJ, 1998.

Rhetoric as art: George A. Kennedy, "Philosophical Rhetoric," in *Classical Rhetoric,* University of North Carolina, Chapel Hill, 1980, pp. 41–85.

Rhetoric as science: James L. Golden, Goodwin F. Berquist, and William E. Coleman, *The Rhetoric of Western Thought,* Kendall/Hunt, Dubuque, IA, 1976, pp. 25–39.

Twenty-first-century interpretation: Alan Gross and Arthur Walzer (eds.), *Rereading Aristotle's Rhetoric,* Southern Illinois University, Carbondale, 2000.

Enthymeme: Lloyd F. Bitzer, "Aristotle's Enthymeme Revisited," *Quarterly Journal of Speech,* Vol. 45, 1959, pp. 399–409; also in Enos and Agnew, pp. 179–191.

Metaphor: Sara Newman, "Aristotle's Notion of 'Bringing-Before-the-Eyes': Its Contributions to Aristotelian and Contemporary Conceptualizations of Metaphor, Style, and Audience," *Rhetorica,* Vol. 20, 2002, pp. 1–23.

Measuring ethos: James McCroskey and Jason Teven, "Goodwill: A Reexamination of the Construct and Its Measurement," *Communication Monographs,* Vol. 66, 1999, pp. 90–103.

Ethos and oral morality: Charles Marsh, "Aristotelian Ethos and the New Orality: Implications for Media Literacy and Media Ethics," *Journal of Mass Media Ethics,* Vol. 21, 2006, pp. 338–352.

Rhetoric and ethics: Eugene Garver, *Aristotle's Rhetoric: An Art of Character,* University of Chicago, IL, 1994.

Rhetorical criticism of Obama's Notre Dame speech: Ronald C. Arnett, "Civic Rhetoric—Meeting the Communal Interplay of the Provincial and the Cosmopolitan: Barack Obama's Notre Dame Speech, May 17, 2009," *Rhetoric & Public Affairs,* Vol. 14, 2011, pp. 631–672.

For a twentieth-century theory of rhetoric, click on
I. A. Richards' Meaning of Meaning in
Archive under Theory Resources at
www.afirstlook.com.

Dramatism

of Kenneth Burke

For Kenneth Burke, words are first and foremost action—*symbolic action.* And where there's action, there's drama.

So when a political candidate says her opponent lacks character or competence, what is she doing? To Burke, her words don't just advance a claim of fact or opinion. Instead, the words are an *attack.* The target might craft words to *defend,* or engage in a *counterattack* of his own. Like an engrossing reality show, each may play the role of hero, victim, or villain. As a rhetorical critic, Burke believed close analysis of each candidate's words could reveal their hidden motives in the drama of the campaign. Such analysis can also unmask the drama inherent in religious sermons, stand-up comedy, corporate training events, sports commentary, or any situation where someone engages in public symbolic action.

When you see the word *critic,* you might think of movie reviewers or people who nag and complain. That's not what Burke and other rhetoricians mean. In their world, critics carefully analyze the language that speakers and authors use. They try to discern the motivations behind their messages—and often these motivations aren't obvious. Burke devoted his career to developing vocabulary and methods that help theorists understand the connection between the symbols speakers use and their motives for speaking in the first place.

Critic
Rhetorical scholar who carefully analyzes the language of speakers and authors.

Until his death in 1993 at the age of 96, Burke picked his way through the human "motivational jungle" by using the tools of philosophy, literature, psychology, economics, linguistics, sociology, and communication. He spent his young adult years in Greenwich Village, a New York bohemian community that included poets E. E. Cummings and Edna St. Vincent Millay. Like many intellectuals during the Depression of the 1930s, Burke flirted with communism but was disillusioned by Stalin's intolerance and brutality. Although he never earned a college degree, he taught for 15 years at Bennington College in Vermont and filled visiting lectureships at Harvard, Princeton, Northwestern, and the University of Chicago. Burke's writing shows an intellectual breadth and depth that leads admirers to refer to him as a Renaissance man. He called himself a "gypsy scholar" and responded to questions about his field of interest by asking, "What am I but a word man?"[1]

Like Barnett Pearce in CMM and Stan Deetz in his critical theory of communication (see Chapters 6 and 21), Burke rejected the commonly held notion that

Realm of motion
Things moving according to cause/effect laws without purpose.

Symbolic action
Words as intentional action, giving life to particular motives and goals.

Dramatism
A technique of analysis of language and thought as modes of action rather than as means of conveying information.

communication is primarily a process of message transmission. The transmission approach treats communication as just one part of the *realm of motion,* where things move according to cause-and-effect laws without meaning or purpose. Although clouds, rocks, planets, and even animals exist only in that realm of motion, Burke believed humans are different. Yes, like animals, humans have material bodies that occupy the realm of motion and obey its laws. But unlike animals, we also possess the capacity to engage in intentional *action.*[2] This ability to plan and act arises from our ability to use symbols. Thus, when we speak, we're engaging in *symbolic action—*using words to give life to particular motives and pursue particular goals.[3] Drama inevitably follows this dance between symbols and the motives underlying them. For Burke, life is not *like* a drama; human life *is* drama.

So Burke coined the umbrella term *dramatism* to describe "a technique of analysis of language and thought as basically modes of action rather than as means of conveying information."[4] Almost every public utterance speaks to a moral conflict where something has gone wrong or might soon go awry. Presidential candidates try to craft memorable campaign slogans that capture this sense in just a few words. In the 1920s, Warren Harding promised a "return to normalcy." In the 1960s, Lyndon Johnson told voters that "the stakes are too high for you to stay at home." In 2008 Barack Obama called for "change we need," and in 2016 Donald Trump pledged to "make America great again."[5] But why do the words of presidential candidates so frequently drip with doom-and-gloom negativity? For Burke, that isn't just a rhetorical question. He had an answer: The nature of language itself leads us to believe that something is wrong with the world. And if something is wrong, somebody or something needs to pay the price to make things right.

LANGUAGE AS THE GENESIS OF GUILT

Burke regarded human beings as symbol-using animals, and he obviously enjoyed exploring how symbol use separates us from other creatures. He examined words, defined words, played with words, and made up his own words. But Burke also regarded our capacity for language as the source of our downfall. That's because language introduced the negative. The animalistic world of motion just *is*; it contains no negative commands. But our language is filled with words like *no, not, nothing, never,* and prefixes such as *un-, dis-,* and *non-* that negate the meaning of other words.[6] Even our definitions of words are dependent on the negative. As Burke said, "You can go on forever saying what a thing is not."[7]

Likewise, most laws tell us what we *shouldn't* do: we shouldn't steal, shouldn't drive over the speed limit, shouldn't smoke in a public building. We couldn't have laws without the negative. It's necessary for humans to create the rules and standards for behavior that Burke called the "thou shalt nots" of life.[8] These *shoulds* and *oughts* inevitably produce guilt when we fail to live up to their moral imperatives.

Guilt
Burke's catchall term to cover every form of tension, anxiety, embarrassment, shame, disgust, and other noxious feelings inherent in human symbol-using activity.

For Burke, guilt wasn't only a specific emotional response to a specific rule violation, like the remorse a student might feel when caught cheating on a test. Rather, Burke uses *guilt* as his catchall term to cover every form of tension, anxiety, embarrassment, shame, disgust, and other noxious feelings inherent in human symbol-using activity. When we feel like the world isn't as it should be, we're experiencing Burke's style of guilt.

Burke's *Definition of Man* oozes with this sense of guilt. Like most writers of an earlier generation, Burke used the word *man* to designate both men and women. Given his record of using words to startle his readers, I wonder if he might recast his definition with feminine vocabulary if he were writing today. But in order to remain faithful to what he wrote, I won't alter his gender-loaded references.

> Man is
> the symbol-using inventor of the negative
> separated from his natural condition by instruments
> of his own making
> goaded by the spirit of hierarchy
> and rotten with perfection.[9]

Like Mead (see Chapter 5), Burke starts with the uniquely human ability to create, use, and abuse language. The rest of his definition makes it clear that the capacity to manipulate symbols is a mixed blessing. The remaining lines suggest three linguistic causes for the sense of inner pollution.

By writing "inventor of the negative," Burke reiterates that it's only through human-made language that the possibility of choice comes into being. In a world without human beings, there are no negative commands, no prohibitions. It's only when humans act symbolically that the possibility of *No! Don't do it!* arrives.

The phrase "separated from his natural condition by instruments of his own making" bounces off the traditional description of humans as *tool-using animals.* Here again, Burke suggests that our inventions—language and all the tools developed with language—cause us grief. Murphy's Law states that anything that can go wrong will.[10] When it comes to relations among people, Burke would say Murphy was an optimist. That's because language is morally loaded.

Burke wrote extensively about hierarchies, bureaucracies, and other ordered systems that rank how well people observe society's negative rules. He was convinced that no matter how high you climb on the performance ladder, you'll always feel a strong sense of embarrassment for not having achieved perfection. A perfect 10 on the ladder of esteem, privilege, or power is exceedingly rare, and if ever achieved, fleeting. The guilt-inducing high priests of the hierarchy are the professional symbol users of society—lawyers, journalists, artists, advertisers, and even your professors when they assign grades at the end of the term.

In the final phrase, Burke suggests that our seemingly admirable drive to do things perfectly can hurt us and others in the process. This is an example of *perspective by incongruity,* or the linking of two dissonant ideas in order to provide shocking new insight.[11] *Rolling Stone* magazine used perspective by incongruity when they featured Boston marathon bomber Dzhokhar Tsarnaev on the cover. He appeared relaxed and stylish in the photo, like a hot new rock star might. Some people criticized the seeming glorification of a murderer, but an editor defended the choice: "The jarringly non-threatening image of Tsarnaev is exactly the point. . . . it's Tsarnaev's very normalcy and niceness that is the most monstrous and terrifying thing about him."[12] Perspective by incongruity shocks our sensibilities but helps us see things from a different angle.

Perspective by incongruity
Providing shocking new insight by linking two dissonant words.

THE GUILT-REDEMPTION CYCLE: A UNIVERSAL MOTIVE FOR RHETORIC

Scapegoat
Someone or something blamed for guilt.

Whatever private purpose a speaker, singer, or writer has, Burke believed that purging guilt is the ultimate motive for public rhetoric. He saw the quest for redemption as the basic plot of the human drama, even if the speaker is unaware of its force. Rhetoric is the public search for someone or something to blame, a quest for a perfect *scapegoat.*

Devil-term
A term that sums up all that a speaker regards as bad, wrong, or evil.

God-term
A term that sums up all that a speaker regards as righteous and good.

Mortification
Confession of guilt and request for forgiveness.

Victimage
Naming an external enemy as the source of our ills.

To identify a speaker's chosen scapegoat, Burke instructed critics to look for *devil-terms,* or words used by the speaker that sum up all that a speaker regards as bad, wrong, or evil. For example, in his nationally broadcast address to Congress following the 9/11 attacks, President Bush used the word *terror* or *terrorist* 34 times.[13] In that speech he declared a "War on Terror," a devil-term that shaped the country's foreign policy for more than a decade. More recently, in the 2016 campaign Donald Trump frequently blamed *immigrants* and *illegal immigration* for the nation's economic, crime, and security problems.

Devil-terms call for *god-terms* to oppose them—words summing up what the speaker regards as righteous and good. Against the devil-term of *illegal immigration,* Trump often mentioned a *wall* he hoped to build along the southern border of the United States. Burke said a speaker's god-term is best understood by other words that cluster around it—it can be known by the company it keeps. When he announced his candidacy, Trump said it would be a "great, great wall," that "nobody builds walls better than me," and "I will have Mexico pay for that wall."[14] These words clarify Trump's meaning by drawing attention to how the wall would demonstrate his own negotiating skill and grandeur.

Devil- and god-terms reveal another aspect of Burke's theory: his frequent use of spiritual language. Those who have rejected or never had a religious commitment may be impatient with Burke's use of theological terms. He made no claim to be a man of faith, nor did he ask his readers to believe in God. Regardless of whether you accept the Christian doctrine of human sin, purification through the death of Jesus, and divine redemption, Burke claimed that the "purely social terminology of human relations cannot do better than to hover about that accurate and succinct theological formula."[15] He regarded theology as a field that has fine-tuned its use of language, and he urged the social critic to look for secular equivalents of the major religious themes of guilt, purification, and redemption.

Burke said that the speaker or author has two possible ways of off-loading guilt. The first option is to purge guilt through self-blame. Described theologically as *mortification,* this route requires confession of sin and a request for forgiveness.[16] In the 2016 presidential campaign, Hillary Clinton seemed equivocal when acknowledging she'd made a mistake by maintaining an email server in her home while secretary of state. Donald Trump's grudging apology for lewd comments caught on video seemed half-hearted at best. They aren't alone. For example, several years after allegations first surfaced, cycling superstar Lance Armstrong finally confessed to illegal performance-enhancing drug use.[17] Obvious candidates for mortification often find it excruciatingly difficult to admit publicly that they are the cause of their own grief. Since it's much easier for people to blame their problems on someone else—the second option—Burke suggested we look for signs of *victimage* in every rhetorical act.[18] He was sure we would find them.

Victimage is the process of designating an external enemy as the source of our ills. Presidential candidates do that all the time in American rhetoric. Reagan blamed Soviet communists; Bush blamed al-Qaeda and Islamic terrorism; Obama blamed the economic policies of the Bush administration. In 2016, Bernie Sanders criticized wealthy Wall Street bankers, Hillary Clinton branded some Trump supporters as "deplorables" and "irredeemable,"[19] and Donald Trump characterized some Mexican immigrants as "criminals, drug dealers, rapists."[20] He also gave his opponents condescending nicknames like "Lyin' Ted" and "Crooked Hillary." Presidential candidates aren't shy about naming people and groups they oppose, and they hope you'll identify with their victimage in one key way: supporting their candidacy. Beyond

"My fellow victims . . ."
©Peter Steiner/The New Yorker Collection/The Cartoon Bank

politics, other types of speakers hope you'll identify with them so much that you'll buy their product, donate to their cause, or convert to their religious faith.

IDENTIFICATION: WITHOUT IT, THERE IS NO PERSUASION

The late Harry Chapin (who happened to be Burke's grandson) captured some of the tragedy and comedy of everyday life by putting words to music in *story songs* people could identify with. His classic "Cat's in the Cradle" is the timeless tale of a father too busy to spend time with his son. Parents who listen to the lyrics realize they have a part in the drama rather than the role of passive listener. They can't help but identify with the drama portrayed in the song.

For Burke, identification with the speaker isn't just a fleeting sense of connection. *Instead, without identification, there is no persuasion.*[21] Unless we identify with the drama portrayed by the speaker, persuasion won't occur. Although he was a great admirer of Aristotle's *Rhetoric* (see Chapter 22), Burke was less concerned with enthymeme and example than he was with a speaker's overall ability to identify with the audience and vice versa.

Identification
The common ground between speaker and audience; consubstantiality.

Identification is the common ground that exists between speaker and audience. Burke used the word *substance* to describe a person's physical characteristics, talents, occupation, friends, experiences, personality, beliefs, and attitudes. The more overlap between the substance of the speaker and the substance of the listener, the greater the identification. Behavioral scientists have used the term *homophily* to describe perceived similarity between speaker and listener,[22] but again, Burke preferred religious language rather than scientific jargon. Borrowing from Martin Luther's description of what takes place at the communion table, Burke said identification is *consubstantiality.*[23] This religious term calls to mind the oft-quoted Old Testament passage where Ruth pledges solidarity with her mother-in-law, Naomi: "For where you go I will go, and where you lodge I will lodge; your people shall be my people, and your God my

God."[24] Although Ruth and Naomi came from different generations, cultures, and religious upbringings, they found common ground. That's identification.

One of the most common ways for speakers to identify with audiences is to lash out at whatever or whomever people fear. ("My friend is one who hates what I hate.") Burke was not an advocate of such identification through devil-terms and victimage, but he said he couldn't ignore the historical pattern of people uniting against a common enemy ("congregation through segregation"[25]). His most famous rhetorical analysis was of Hitler's *Mein Kampf,* a book that blamed Jewish people for all of Germany's problems.[26] This symbolic victimage was followed by extermination in death camps.

Audiences sense a joining of interests through style as much as through content. Burke said the effective communicator can show consubstantiality by giving signs in language and delivery that his or her properties are the same as theirs. During World War II, President Roosevelt achieved identification with the American public through his "fireside chats" on the radio, a popular medium at the time. Although Donald Trump is a wealthy New York businessman, during his campaign he spoke in plain, simple sentences that connected with the rural poor. For both presidents, their form led some members of their audience to think they were "talking sense." On the other hand, Trump's simple style alienated some affluent and educated voters.

For Burke, identification is the key to persuasion—without identification, there is no persuasion. For an aspiring presidential candidate, that means crafting messages designed to build that sense of identification. But that wasn't Burke's main concern. He was more interested in examining rhetoric after the fact to discover what motivates the speaker. His dramatistic pentad is a tool for doing just that.

THE DRAMATISTIC PENTAD: A LENS FOR INTERPRETING SYMBOLIC ACTION

Dramatistic pentad
A tool critics can use to discern the motives of a speaker by labeling five key elements of the drama: act, scene, agent, agency, and purpose.

Burke's *dramatistic pentad* enables the critic to dig beneath surface impressions in order to identify the complex motives of a speaker or writer. As Burke said, it's a shorthand way the rhetorical critic can "talk about their talk about" in a meaningful way.

> In a well-rounded statement about motives, you must have some word that names the act (names what took place in thought or deed), and another that names the scene (the background of the act, the situation in which it occurred); also you must indicate what person or kind of person (agent) performed the act, what means or instruments he used (agency), and the purpose.[27]

To demonstrate the dramatistic pentad, I'll focus on a speech President Obama gave at a campaign rally on July 13, 2012. After calling for wealthy Americans to pay higher taxes to develop infrastructure, he said:

> If you've been successful, you didn't get there on your own. You didn't get there on your own. I'm always struck by people who think, well, it must be because I was just so smart. There are a lot of smart people out there. It must be because I worked harder than everybody else. Let me tell you something—there are a whole bunch of hardworking people out there. If you were successful, somebody along the line gave you some help. There was a great teacher somewhere in your life. Somebody helped to create this unbelievable American system that we have that allowed you to thrive. Somebody invested in roads and bridges. If you've got a business—you didn't build that. Somebody else made that happen. The Internet didn't get invented

on its own. Government research created the Internet so that all the companies could make money off the Internet.[28]

Some people identified strongly with Obama's words. Others opposed the drama he described. The pentad helps us understand why. We'll start by identifying the five elements present in the speech.

Act. To Burke, the act is the most important element of the pentad, "foremost among the equals."[29] The act is what was done. Without action, there is no drama, and multiple acts form the plot of the drama. In Obama's speech, the central act is *achieving success,* particularly in business.

Agent. An act implies an agent—the person who committed the act. In Obama's speech, the agents are the people (particularly business owners) who have achieved success.

Agency. An act also implies a procedure for how the act was done. In this speech, Obama doesn't give a tutorial on how he thinks business owners achieve success. Instead, he argues what agency is *not.* Intelligence and hard work aren't it, because some smart people who work hard don't succeed.

Scene. Agent, act, and agency imply a scene where they take place. Obama describes the environment of business owners (agents) who have achieved success (acts)—the infrastructural, technological, and educational features around them.

Purpose. The purpose behind the act addresses the motive of the agent. The final sentence quoted above suggests why Obama thinks business owners seek success: to earn money.

Now, before we go further, I need to warn you against a misunderstanding that trips up some students. Observe that the elements of the pentad describe *the drama described in the speech.* They do not describe *the speech itself.* In other words, the agent isn't President Obama, the scene isn't the campaign rally, the act isn't giving a speech, the agency isn't the rhetorical devices he used, and the purpose isn't to persuade voters. That basic description isn't rhetorical criticism. Remember that Burke was interested in how speakers engage in symbolic action. He thinks Obama is portraying a drama for his audience. If we identify with the drama, then we're persuaded, and Obama's symbolic action worked. The pentad helps us map how Obama tries to build that identification by examining relationships, or *ratios,* among the pentad's parts.

RATIO: THE RELATIVE IMPORTANCE OF EACH PART OF THE PENTAD

Burke associated each part of the pentad with a corresponding philosophy.[30] Speakers who emphasize the act demonstrate a commitment to philosophical *realism* ("actions speak louder than words"). A focus on the agent as instigator of the act is consistent with philosophical *idealism* ("the mind and heart of the person is what matters"). A long description of agency resonates with *pragmatism* ("let's just get the job done"). Emphasis on scene downplays free will and exhibits an attitude of situational *determinism* ("I couldn't help it"). And an extended discussion of the agent's purpose reflects a quest for ultimate meaning that resonates with *mysticism* ("what is the real meaning of life?").

After the critic has labeled the act, scene, agent, agency, and purpose, the next step is to discern the relative importance that the speaker gives to each of these

Ratio
The relative importance of any two terms of the pentad as determined by their relationship.

five elements (and, therefore, each of these philosophies). The critic can start by identifying the two elements of the pentad most heavily emphasized in the speech. These two elements create the dominant *ratio* that provides the most insight into the speaker's motivations.[31] Obama's speech emphasizes *scene* first, and then *act*. In the second half of the passage, he devotes five full sentences to describing aspects of the scene around successful businesspeople: teachers, roads, bridges, the Internet, the American system. In the drama he describes, the scene drives the successful acts within it. In this *scene-act ratio,* business success and failure occur as a by-product of elements of the scene, not the purpose or agency of business owners.

Obama's immediate audience seemed to identify with this deterministic drama. They applauded, laughed, and cheered "yeah!" and "right!" throughout.[32] Business owners had a very different reaction and countered with a drama of their own. Obama's challenger Mitt Romney voiced their version of the story: "To say that Steve Jobs didn't build Apple, that Henry Ford didn't build Ford Motors . . . to say something like that . . . [is] insulting to every entrepreneur, every innovator in America."[33] Many of Obama's opponents adopted the refrain featured at the 2012 Republican convention: "We built it." Those three words establish an *agent-act ratio.* In that story, good deeds (like success) come from good people. That also implies bad deeds (failure) come from bad people—an unsettling thought for those who fall on hard times through no fault of their own.

CRITIQUE: EVALUATING THE CRITIC'S ANALYSIS

Kenneth Burke was perhaps the foremost rhetorician of the twentieth century. Today, rhetorical critics continue to draw on the pentad to analyze a speaker's words and motivations. Universities offer entire courses on Burkean analysis. The Kenneth Burke Society holds conferences and competitions that give his followers the opportunity to discuss and delight over his wide-ranging thoughts. *KB Journal* exists solely to explain, clarify, and critique Burke's ideas through debate and *qualitative research.* He obviously had something to say, and a *community of agreement* continues to have something to say about him.

Burke's concept of rhetoric as identification was a major advance in a field of knowledge that many scholars had thought complete. Rather than opposing Aristotle's definition, he gave it a contemporary luster by showing that common ground is the foundation of persuasive appeals. Nevertheless, his thoughts about redemption remain controversial. Perhaps that's because his "secular religion" takes God too seriously for those who don't believe, yet not seriously enough for those who do. Both camps have trouble with Burke's unsubstantiated assumption that guilt is the primary human emotion that underlies all symbolic action. Whatever you think about these issues, it's clear Burke provided *creative and new understanding* of what people are *really* doing when they talk.

I appreciate Burke's commitment to an ethical stance that refuses to let desirable ends justify unfair means. He urged speakers not to make a victim out of someone else in order to become unified with the audience. But some scholars don't think he did enough to *clarify values* or *reform society.* The late Phyllis Japp (University of Nebraska-Lincoln) wrote that, as a feminist reader of Burke, she found in his writings "an indispensable array of guerrilla tactics for survival in a field of masculinist symbols." But at other times, she met "passages that seem alien to my [female] experience of the world and engage concepts that fail to include my perspectives."[34] Her mixed assessment seems to agree with that of Kevin McClure and Julia Skwar (University of Rhode Island), who applaud Burke for building moral concerns into dramatism but contend that more needs to be done to flesh out the theory's ethical implications.[35]

Perhaps the greatest weakness of dramatism is this: Burke isn't an easy read. Most of the time, he said what he said in a roundabout way. His frequent use of literary allusions overwhelms the new reader. Unless a student is prepared to grapple with Coleridge's *The Rime of the Ancient Mariner,* Augustine's *Confessions,* and Freud's *The Psychopathology of Everyday Life*—all on the same page—Burke's mental leaps and breadth of scholarship will prove more frustrating than informative. Even advocates like Marie Hochmuth Nichols, who introduced Burke to the communication discipline in 1952, have defended why Burke was frequently confusing and sometimes obscure: "In part the difficulty arises from the numerous vocabularies he employs. His words in isolation are usually simple enough, but he often uses them in new contexts."[36] Although Burke's followers think he was brilliant, it's hard to argue that his writings have *aesthetic appeal.*

Yet Burke enthusiasts insist that the process of discovery is half the fun. Like a choice enthymeme, Burke's writing invites active reader participation as he surrounds an idea. And here, I've only given you a taste of what Burke has to offer. No matter what aspect of rhetoric his ideas address, the reader will never again be able to dismiss words as "mere rhetoric." Burke has done us all a favor by celebrating the life-giving quality of language.

QUESTIONS TO SHARPEN YOUR FOCUS

1. Despite the fact that Burke was a *rhetorical critic* who described himself as a "word man," he was convinced that the creation of *language* began the downfall of the human race. Why?

2. Find a popular song and examine its lyrics using the *pentad.* What elements do the lyrics emphasize? What is the dominant *ratio?* What does that say about the songwriter's motivation?

3. Burke claims that all rhetoric ultimately *expiates guilt through victimage.* Pick one of the ethical reflections from another chapter. How would that ethical stance evaluate victimage? When is victimage right (if ever), and when is it wrong (if ever)?

4. Based on what you know of Burke, how would you apply Burke's ideas to his own theory? What does he *scapegoat?* What are his *god-terms* and *devil-terms?* What elements of the *pentad* does he emphasize as he portrays the drama of human life?

A SECOND LOOK

Recommended resource: Sonja Foss and Karen Foss, *Contemporary Perspectives on Rhetoric: 30ᵗʰ Anniversary Edition,* Waveland, Long Grove, IL, 2014, pp. 185–231.

Dramatism: Kenneth Burke, "Dramatism," in *The International Encyclopedia of the Social Sciences,* Vol. 7, David L. Sills (ed.), Macmillan, New York, 1968, pp. 445–451.

Summary of key concepts: Edward Appel, *Language, Life, Literature, Rhetoric and Composition as Dramatic Action: A Burkean Primer,* Oar Press, Leola, PA, 2012, pp. 265–271.

Identification: Kenneth Burke, *A Rhetoric of Motives,* University of California, Berkeley, 1969, pp. 20–46.

Dramatistic pentad: Kenneth Burke, *A Grammar of Motives,* University of California, Berkeley, 1969, pp. xv–xxiii.

Guilt–redemption cycle: Kenneth Burke, "On Human Behavior Considered 'Dramatistically,'" in *Permanence and Change,* Bobbs-Merrill, Indianapolis, IN, 1965, pp. 274–294.

Human nature: Kenneth Burke, "Definition of Man," in *Language as Symbolic Action,* University of California, Berkeley, 1966, pp. 3–24.

Burkean analysis of King's "I Have a Dream": David Bobbitt, *The Rhetoric of Redemption: Kenneth Burke's Redemption Drama and Martin Luther King Jr.'s "I Have a Dream" Speech,* Rowman & Littlefield, Lanham, MD, 2004.

Burkean analysis of obesity and sexual assault: Sandra L. French and Sonya C. Brown, "It's All Your Fault: Kenneth Burke, Symbolic Action, and the Assigning of Guilt and Blame to Women," *Southern Communication Journal,* Vol. 76, 2011, pp. 1–16.

Explication and critique of guilt–redemption cycle: Kristy Maddux, "Finding Comedy in Theology: A Hopeful Supplement to Kenneth Burke's Logology," *Philosophy and Rhetoric,* Vol. 39, 2006, pp. 208–232.

Feminist critique: Celeste Michelle Condit, "Post-Burke: Transcending the Substance of Dramatism," *Quarterly Journal of Speech,* Vol. 78, 1992, pp. 349–355; also in Barry Brummet (ed.), *Landmark Essays on Kenneth Burke,* Hermagoras, Davis, CA, 1993, pp. 3–18.

Narrative Paradigm

of Walter Fisher

People are storytelling animals. This simple assertion is Walter Fisher's answer to the philosophical question *What is the essence of human nature?*

Many of the theorists discussed in preceding chapters offer different answers to this key question of human existence. For example, Thibaut and Kelley's social exchange theory operates on the premise that humans are rational creatures. Berger's uncertainty reduction theory assumes that people are basically curious. More relevant to all students of communication, Mead's symbolic interactionism insists that our ability to use symbols is what makes us uniquely human. (See Chapters 8, 9, and 5.)

Fisher doesn't argue against any of these ideas, but he thinks that human communication reveals something more basic than rationality, curiosity, or even symbol-using capacity. He is convinced that we are narrative beings who "experience and comprehend life as a series of ongoing narratives, as conflicts, characters, beginnings, middles, and ends."[1] If this is true, then all forms of human communication that seek to affect belief, attitude, or action need to be seen fundamentally as stories.[2]

Walter Fisher is an emeritus professor at the University of Southern California's Annenberg School of Communication. Throughout his professional life, he has been uncomfortable with the prevailing view that rhetoric is only a matter of evidence, facts, arguments, reason, and logic that has its highest expression in courts of law, legislatures, and other deliberative bodies. In 1978, he introduced the concept of *good reasons,* which led to his proposal of the narrative paradigm in 1984.[3] He claimed that offering good reasons has more to do with telling a compelling story than it does with piling up evidence or constructing a tight argument.

Fisher soon became convinced that all forms of communication that appeal to our reason are best viewed as stories shaped by history, culture, and character. When we hear the word *story,* most of us tend to think of novels, plays, movies, TV sitcoms, and yarns told around a campfire. Some of us also call to mind accounts of our past—tales we tell to others in which we are the central character. But with the exception of jokes, *Hi, How are you?* greetings, and other forms of *phatic communication,* Fisher regards almost *all* types of communication as story.

Phatic communication
Communication aimed at maintaining relationships rather than passing along information or saying something new.

Obviously, he sees differences in form between a Robert Frost poem, a *Harry Potter* book, or a performance of *As You Like It* on the one hand, and a philosophical essay, historical report, political debate, theological discussion, or scientific treatise on the other. But if we want to know whether we should believe the "truth" each of these genres proclaims, Fisher maintains that all of them can and should be viewed as narrative. He uses the term *narrative paradigm* to highlight his belief that there is no communication of ideas that is purely descriptive or didactic.

TELLING A COMPELLING STORY

Most religious traditions are passed on from generation to generation through the retelling of stories. The faithful are urged to "tell the old, old story" to encourage believers and convince those in doubt. American writer Frederick Buechner takes a fresh approach to passing on religious story. For example, he retells the eighth-century BC biblical story of the rocky marriage between Hosea and Gomer in twenty-first-century style.[4] Buechner's account of love, unfaithfulness, and forgiveness provides a vehicle for examining Fisher's narrative paradigm in the rest of the chapter.

The story begins when the startling word-of-the-Lord came to the Israeli prophet Hosea that he was to marry a prostitute. He chose Gomer. "She was always good company—a little heavy with the lipstick maybe, a little less than choosy about men and booze, a little loud, but great at a party." Then along came Hosea, wearing a black T-shirt that warned, "The End is at Hand" on the front and "Watch Out" on back. When he told Gomer he wanted to marry her, she thought it was a joke. When he proposed a second time she knew he meant it, but thought he was nuts. But she finally gave in. "He wasn't exactly a swinger, but he had a kind face, and he was generous, and he wasn't all that crazier than everybody else. Besides, any fool could see he loved her."

Hosea named one of their children *Not my people* and another *Not loved*, "so that every time the roll was called at school, Hosea would be scoring a prophetic bullseye in absentia." But while Hosea was proclaiming God's judgment on a nation whoring after false gods, Gomer was partying and sleeping around. "Any resemblance between her next batch of children and Hosea was purely coincidental. It almost killed him, of course." He tried kicking her out of the house, but every time she came back it was Hosea who ended up apologizing. "Then one day she didn't show up at all." He vowed their marriage was over for good, yet searched for her day and night.

> When he finally found her, she was lying passed out in a highly specialized establishment located above an adult bookstore, and he had to pay the management plenty to let her out of her contract. She'd lost her front teeth and picked up some scars you had to see to believe, but Hosea had her back again and that seemed to be all that mattered.

He put on a new T-shirt that proclaimed "God is love" on the front and "There's no end to it" on the back. We don't know how many people returned to the faith, "but one thing that's for sure is that, including Gomer's, there was seldom a dry eye in the house."[5]

NARRATION AND PARADIGM: DEFINING THE TERMS

Fisher defines *narration* as "symbolic actions—words and/or deeds—that have sequence and meaning for those who live, create, or interpret them."[6] Hosea's experience and Buechner's account of it clearly qualify as narrative. But Fisher's definition is broad and is especially notable for what it doesn't exclude. On the basis of his further elaboration,[7] I offer this expanded paraphrase of his definition:

Narration
Symbolic actions—words and/or deeds—that have sequence and meaning for those who live, create, or interpret them.

> Narration is communication rooted in time and space. It covers every aspect of our lives and the lives of others in regard to character, motive, and action. The term also refers to every verbal or nonverbal bid for a person to believe or act in a certain way. Even when a message seems abstract—devoid of imagery—it is narration because it is embedded in the speaker's ongoing story that has a beginning, middle, and end, and it invites listeners to interpret its meaning and assess its value for their own lives.

Under this expanded definition, the didactic God-is-love statement on Hosea's T-shirt is the premise for much of religious rhetoric. Those who dwell in the story cannot help but identify with the commitment, love, and forgiveness that Hosea gives to Gomer.

Fisher uses the term *paradigm* to refer to a *conceptual framework*—a widely shared perceptual filter. Perception is not so much a matter of the physics of sight and sound as it is one of interpretation. Meaning isn't inherent in events; it's attached to the raw physical stimuli at the workbench of the mind. A paradigm is a universal model that calls for people to view events through a common interpretive lens.

Paradigm
A conceptual framework; a universal model that calls for people to view events through a common interpretive lens.

In *The Structure of Scientific Revolutions,* Thomas Kuhn argues that an accepted paradigm is the mark of a mature science.[8] Responding to this challenge, communication scientists in the 1970s sought to discover a universal model that would explain communication behavior. Fisher's narrative paradigm is an interpretive counterpart to their efforts. Fisher offers a way to understand all communication and to direct rhetorical inquiry. He doesn't regard the narrative paradigm as a specific rhetoric. Rather, he sees it as "the foundation on which a complete rhetoric needs to be built. This structure would provide a comprehensive explanation of the creation, composition, adaptation, presentation, and reception of symbolic messages."[9]

PARADIGM SHIFT: FROM A RATIONAL-WORLD PARADIGM TO A NARRATIVE ONE

Fisher begins his book *Human Communication as Narration* with a reference to the opening line of the Gospel of John: "In the beginning was the word (*logos*)." He notes that the Greek word *logos* originally included story, reason, rationale, conception, discourse, thought—all forms of human communication. Imagination and thought were not yet distinct. So the story of Hosea and Gomer was *logos*.

According to Fisher, the writings of Plato and Aristotle reflect the early evolution from a generic to a specific use of *logos*—from story to statement. *Logos* had already begun to refer only to philosophical discourse, a lofty enterprise that relegated imagination, poetry, and other aesthetic concerns to second-class status. Rhetoric fell somewhere between *logos* and *mythos*. As opposed to the abstract discourse of philosophy, it was practical speech—the secular combination of pure logic on the one hand and emotional stories that stir up passions on the other. The Greek citizen concerned with truth alone should steer clear of rhetoric and consult an expert on wisdom—the philosopher.

Fisher says that 2,000 years later, the scientific revolution dethroned the philosopher-king. In the last few centuries, the only knowledge that seems to be worth knowing in academia is that which can be spotted in the physical world. The person who wants to understand the way things are needs to check with a doctor, a scientist, an engineer, or another technical expert. Despite the elevation of technology and the demotion of philosophy, both modes of decision making are similar in their elitist tendencies to "place that which is not *formally* logical or which is not characterized by *expertise* within a somehow subhuman framework of behavior."[10] Fisher sees philosophical and technical discussion as scholars' standard approach to knowledge. He calls this mindset the *rational-world paradigm*. Hirokawa and Gouran's functional perspective on group decision making is a perfect example (see Chapter 17).

Fisher lists five assumptions of the prevailing rational-world paradigm. See if they match what you've been taught in school.[11]

1. People are essentially rational.
2. We make decisions on the basis of arguments.
3. The type of speaking situation (legal, scientific, legislative) determines the course of our argument.

Rational-world paradigm
A scientific or philosophical approach to knowledge that assumes people are logical, making decisions on the basis of evidence and lines of argument.

4. Rationality is determined by how much we know and how well we argue.
5. The world is a set of logical puzzles that we can solve through rational analysis.

Viewed through the rational-world paradigm, the story of Hosea seems ridiculous. Hosea's marriage to Gomer is irrational. The only logical conclusion is that the man had an unhealthy sexual obsession with a destructive woman. Buechner's words offer no plausible argument why Hosea's willingness to let Gomer walk all over him is a superior strategy to separation or divorce. The author presents no evidence that Hosea and Gomer are historical characters, that any kind of god exists, or how this supreme being communicated to Hosea that he should marry a prostitute. And the implication that Hosea and Gomer's dysfunctional marriage illustrates the divine–human relationship has no basis in fact. So from a rational-world perspective, the story makes no sense.

Fisher is convinced that the assumptions of the rational-world paradigm are too limited. He calls for a new conceptual framework (a paradigm shift) in order to better understand human communication. His *narrative paradigm* is built on five assumptions similar in form to the rational-world paradigm, but quite different in content.[12]

1. People are essentially storytellers.
2. We make decisions on the basis of good reasons, which vary depending on the communication situation, media, and genre (philosophical, technical, rhetorical, or artistic).
3. History, biography, culture, and character determine what we consider good reasons.

Narrative paradigm
A theoretical framework that views narrative as the basis of all human communication.

4. Narrative rationality is determined by the coherence and fidelity of our stories.
5. The world is a set of stories from which we choose, and thus constantly re-create, our lives.

Viewing human beings as storytellers who reason in various ways is a major conceptual shift. For example, in a logical system, values are emotional nonsense. From the narrative perspective, however, values are the stuff of stories and provide the reason for actions. Working from a strictly logical standpoint, aesthetic proof is irrelevant, but within a narrative framework, style and beauty play a pivotal role in determining whether we get into a story.

Perhaps the biggest shift in thinking has to do with who is qualified to assess the quality of communication. Whereas the rational-world model holds that only experts are capable of presenting or discerning sound arguments, the narrative paradigm maintains that, armed with a bit of common sense, almost any of us can see the point of a good story and judge its merits as the basis for belief and action. No one taught us how to do this. It's an inherent awareness that's honed by life experience. Fisher would say that each of us will make a judgment about Buechner's account of Hosea's actions (or any story) based upon *narrative rationality.*

NARRATIVE RATIONALITY: COHERENCE AND FIDELITY

Narrative rationality
A way to evaluate the worth of stories based on the twin standards of narrative coherence and narrative fidelity.

According to Fisher, not all stories are equally good. Even though there's no guarantee that people won't adopt a bad story, he thinks everybody applies the same standards of *narrative rationality* to whatever stories they hear: "The operative principle of narrative rationality is identification rather than deliberation."[13] Have we screwed up our lives to the extent that we can see a bit of ourselves in Gomer? Do we hope that someone out there will be as loving and forgiving of us as Hosea is of Gomer? Fisher believes that our answer will depend on whether Buechner's account meets the twin tests of *narrative coherence* and *narrative fidelity.* Together they are measures of a story's truthfulness and humanity.

Narrative Coherence: Does the Story Hang Together?

Narrative coherence
Internal consistency with characters acting in a reliable fashion; the story hangs together.

Narrative coherence has to do with how probable the story sounds to the hearer.[14] Does the narrative *hang together?* Do the people and events it portrays seem of one piece? Are they part of an organic whole? Fisher suggests a number of ways we judge whether a story hangs together.

First, we find out if there are contradictions in the story. Fisher regards the internal consistency of a narrative as similar to lines of argument in a rational-world paradigm. In that sense, his narrative paradigm doesn't discount or replace logic. Instead, he lists the test of reason as only one of the factors that affect narrative coherence.

A sense of coherence is strengthened when the storyteller adapts to the intended audience. Note that Buechner makes that accommodation by referring to a swinger, roll call in school, and an adult bookstore—words that bring the story into the present.

Second, stories hang together when we're convinced that the narrator hasn't left out important details, fudged the facts, or ignored other plausible interpretations. Although the TV series *How I Met Your Mother* and the re-imagined *Battlestar Galactica* garnered critical acclaim throughout their runs, their final episodes were roundly panned by fans and critics because they didn't meet those criteria. At the end, both shows lacked narrative coherence.

We often judge the coherence of a narrative by comparing it with other stories we've heard that deal with the same theme. A generation ago, many Hollywood stars—Jane Fonda, Julie Christie, Brooke Shields, Lynn Redgrave, Nicole Kidman,

"I know what you're thinking, but let me offer a competing narrative."
©Harry Bliss/The New Yorker Collection/The Cartoon Bank

Jodie Foster—portrayed the role of prostitutes in movies that put a positive spin on the practice. The most popular was Julia Roberts in *Pretty Woman,* a film where the beautiful hooker with a heart of gold is swept away by a steely-eyed business tycoon, who, inspired by her, develops a social conscience. Communication scholars maintain that *Pretty Woman* plays more like a fairy tale than reality, and thus lacks narrative coherence.[15] Buechner, on the other hand, doesn't glamorize Gomer's selfish and destructive behavior, which makes his prostitution narrative more probable.

But for Fisher, the ultimate test of narrative coherence is whether we can count on the characters to act in a reliable manner. We are suspicious of accounts where characters behave uncharacteristically. We tend to trust stories of people who show continuity of thought, motive, and action. Whether you regard Hosea as an admirable husband or a spineless wimp, the constancy of his love for Gomer in spite of her unfaithfulness is a thread that gives the fabric of the story a tight weave.

Narrative Fidelity: Does the Story Ring True and Humane?

Narrative fidelity
Congruence between values embedded in a message and what listeners regard as truthful and humane; the story strikes a responsive chord.

Narrative fidelity is the quality of a story that causes the words to strike a responsive chord in the life of the listener. A story has fidelity when it rings true with the hearers' experiences—it squares with the stories they might tell about themselves.[16] Have we, like Gomer, ever been caught up in the party scene, cheated on a faithful lover, been forgiven when we didn't deserve it, or shed tears over the hurt we've caused others and ourselves? Or, like Hosea, have we forgiven another who did us great harm, rather than seeking revenge? To the extent that the details of this 3,000-year-old story portray our experiences and aspirations, the narrative has fidelity.

Fisher's book *Human Communication as Narration* has the subtitle *Toward a Philosophy of Reason, Value, and Action.* He believes a story has fidelity when it provides good reasons to guide our future actions. When we buy into a story, we buy into the type of character we should be. Thus, values are what set the narrative paradigm's logic of good reasons apart from the rational-world paradigm's mere logic of reasons.

The *logic of good reasons* centers on five value-related issues. Fisher says we are concerned with (1) the values embedded in the message, (2) the relevance of those values to decisions made, (3) the consequence of adhering to those values, (4) the overlap with the worldview of the audience, and (5) conformity with what the audience members believe is "an ideal basis for conduct."[17] The last two concerns—congruity with the listeners' values and the actions they think best—form the basis of Fisher's contention that people tend to prefer accounts that fit with what they view as truthful and humane. But what specific values guide audiences as they gauge a story's truth or fidelity? Fisher suggests there is an *ideal audience* or permanent public that identifies the humane values a good story embodies:

> It appears that there is a permanent public, an actual community existing over time, that believes in the values of truth, the good, beauty, health, wisdom, courage, temperance, justice, harmony, order, communion, friendship, and oneness with the Cosmos—as variously as those values may be defined or practiced in "real" life.[18]

Ideal audience
An actual community existing over time that believes in the values of truth, the good, beauty, health, wisdom, courage, temperance, justice, harmony, order, communion, friendship, and oneness with the cosmos.

Fisher admits that other communities are possible—ones based on greed or power, for example. But he maintains that when people are confronted by "the better part of themselves," these less-idealistic value systems won't be "entirely coherent or true to their whole lives, or to the life that they would most like to live."[19] Fisher believes, then, that the humane virtues of the ideal audience shape our logic of good reasons. They help us pick which stories are reliable and trustworthy.

If we think Hosea's response to Gomer's unfaithfulness merely enables her destructive behavior, or scoff at the idea that her tears mean she's home to stay, Buechner's version of the biblical narrative will lack fidelity. But inasmuch as we think these ideal auditors would applaud Hosea's love and forgiveness of Gomer—and believe they might even illustrate the revised message on his T-shirt—Buechner's words will have the ring of humanity and truth. If so, Fisher says we aren't merely affirming shared values. We are opening ourselves to the possibility that they will influence our beliefs and actions.

I have employed the story of Hosea to illustrate features of the narrative paradigm. In like manner, most of my students—like Chris below—pick a book or a film to demonstrate their application of Fisher's theory.

> Beginning with *The Lion, the Witch, and the Wardrobe* in *The Chronicles of Narnia*, C. S. Lewis presents a coherent set of stories. While the characters, places, and events may not be "of this world"—the rational world we live in—Lewis has constructed a set of relationships and rules so consistent that it makes the fictional world seem plausible. The stories also have fidelity because Lewis skillfully creates parallels to our common human reality. The characters relate directly to people in my life (including me). For instance, I can identify with "doubting" Susan as she grows out of her childlike faith. Yet I long for the innocent passion of Lucy and the nobleness of Peter.

A good story is a powerful means of persuasion. Fisher would remind us, however, that almost *all* communication is narrative, and we evaluate it on that basis. This chapter and all the others in this book are story. According to his narrative paradigm, you can (and will) judge whether they hang together and ring true to the values held by the people who make up your ideal audience.

CRITIQUE: DOES FISHER'S STORY HAVE COHERENCE AND FIDELITY?

Fisher's theory excels in fulfilling most of the requirements of a good interpretive theory. He expands our *understanding of human nature,* is specific about the *values we prefer,* and supports his new paradigm with intriguing rhetorical criticism of significant texts—a classic method of *qualitative research.* Since most of us like stories and Fisher's twin criteria for judging them is easy to grasp, his narrative paradigm has *aesthetic appeal.*

Many readers appreciate his fresh reworking of Aristotelian analysis, which has dominated rhetorical thinking in the field of communication. His approach is strongly democratic—people usually don't need specialized training or expertise to figure out if a story holds together or offers good reasons for believing it to be true. There's still a place for experts to provide information and explanation in specialized fields, but when it comes to evaluating coherence and fidelity, people with ordinary common sense are competent rhetorical critics.

Of course, Fisher's theory is itself a story, and as you might expect, not everyone accepts his tale. The *community of agreement* among scholars is by no means unanimous. For example, many critics charge that he is overly optimistic when, similar to Aristotle, he argues that people have a natural tendency to prefer the true and the just. Challenging Fisher's upbeat view of human nature, rhetorical critic Barbara Warnick at the University of Pittsburgh calls attention to the great communicative power of evil or wrongheaded stories such as Hitler's *Mein Kampf,* which "struck a chord in an alienated, disunited, and despairing people."[20] Fisher grants that evil can overwhelm our tendency to adopt good stories, but argues that's all the more reason to identify and promote the humane values described by the narrative paradigm.

William Kirkwood at East Tennessee State University claims there is another problem with the logic of good reasons. Kirkwood says a standard of narrative rationality implies that good stories cannot and perhaps should not go beyond what people already believe and value. He charges that the logic of good reasons encourages writers and speakers to adjust their ideas to people rather than people to their ideas, and thus denies the "rhetoric of possibility"—the chance to be swayed by that which is unfamiliar or radically different.[21] (If true, *reform of society* is certainly off the table.) But Fisher thinks Kirkwood's charge is ridiculous. He explicitly states that people have the capacity "to formulate and adopt new stories that better account for their lives or the mystery of life itself."[22] Certainly, the forgiveness that Hosea extends to Gomer goes beyond anything most of us have experienced on a human level, yet the story still strikes a responsive chord in many who hear it.

Is most communication story, and do we judge every message we hear on the basis of whether it hangs together and rings true with our values? If you take Fisher's ideas seriously, you won't need me or a trained rhetorician to give you the final word. Like everyone else, you can spot the difference between a good story and a bad one.

QUESTIONS TO SHARPEN YOUR FOCUS

1. Using Fisher's definition of *narration,* can you think of any types of communication—other than jokes or phatic communication—that don't fit within the *narrative paradigm?*

2. Fisher claims that the *rational-world paradigm* dominates Western education. Can you list college courses you've taken that adopt the assumptions of this conceptual framework?

3. What is the difference between *narrative coherence* and *narrative fidelity?*

4. You apply a *logic of good reasons* to the stories you hear. What are the *values* undergirding Buechner's story of Hosea and Gomer? Which one do you most admire? What *values* do you hold that cause you to ultimately accept or reject his narrative?

A SECOND LOOK

Recommended resource: Walter R. Fisher, *Human Communication as Narration: Toward a Philosophy of Reason, Value, and Action,* University of South Carolina, Columbia, 1987.

Original statement: Walter R. Fisher, "Narration as a Human Communication Paradigm: The Case of Public Moral Argument," *Communication Monographs,* Vol. 51, 1984, pp. 1–22.

Storytelling and narrativity in communication research: Journal of Communication, Vol. 35, No. 4, 1985, entire issue.

Scientific communication as story: Walter R. Fisher, "Narration, Knowledge, and the Possibility of Wisdom," in *Rethinking Knowledge: Reflections Across the Disciplines,* Robert F. Goodman and Walter R. Fisher (eds.), State University of New York, Albany, 1995, pp. 169–197.

Narrative ethics: Walter R. Fisher, "The Ethic(s) of Argument and Practical Wisdom," in *Argument at Century's End,* Thomas Hollihan (ed.), National Communication Association, Annandale, VA, 1999, pp. 1–15.

Telling the old story in a new way: Frederick Buechner, *Peculiar Treasures,* Harper & Row, New York, 1979.

History of narrative theory in the field of communication: Robin P. Clair, Stephanie Carlo et al., "Narrative Theory and Criticism: An Overview Toward Clusters and Empathy," *Review of Communication,* Vol.14, 2014, pp. 1–18.

Ethics as story: Richard Johannesen, "A Rational World Ethic Versus a Narrative Ethic for Political Communication," in *Ethics in Human Communication,* 6th ed., Waveland, Prospect Heights, IL, 2008, pp. 254–262.

Empirical measure of believability: Robert Yale, "Measuring Narrative Believability: Development and Validation of the Narrative Believability Scale (NBS-12)," *Journal of Communication,* Vol. 63, 2013, pp. 578–599.

Critique: Barbara Warnick, "The Narrative Paradigm: Another Story," *Quarterly Journal of Speech,* Vol. 73, 1987, pp. 172–182.

Critique: William G. Kirkwood, "Narration and the Rhetoric of Possibility," *Communication Monographs,* Vol. 59, 1992, pp. 30–47.

Critique: Robert Rowland, "On Limiting the Narrative Paradigm: Three Case Studies," *Communication Monographs,* Vol. 56, 1989, pp. 39–54.

Response to critics: Walter R. Fisher, "Clarifying the Narrative Paradigm," *Communication Monographs,* Vol. 56, 1989, pp. 55–58.

Are you convinced you can detect when a story is false?
Click on Interpersonal Deception Theory in
Archive under Theory Resources at
www.afirstlook.com.

DIVISION FOUR

Mass Communication

Students who begin to learn about the relationship between media and culture quickly run across multiple references to *postmodernism*. While most of us understand that this term refers to many elements of contemporary Western society, we may be hard-pressed to explain the specific values or practices that distinguish a postmodern culture from others. Since media expression is at the heart of postmodernism, we'll illustrate six of its defining features.[1]

1. Postmodern *describes a period of time when the promise of modernism no longer seems justified.* The modernistic ideologies that postmodernism rejects include the Industrial Revolution, nationalistic imperialism, the rationality of the Enlightenment, faith in science, and any sense that the world is on an upward trajectory. In his essay "On Nihilism," Jean Baudrillard, a leading French postmodernist, claims that he and his colleagues are neither optimistic nor pessimistic. Yet the absence of meaning he describes strikes most readers as devoid of hope.

> I have the impression with postmodernism that there is an attempt to rediscover a certain pleasure in the irony of things. Right now one can tumble into total hopelessness—all the definitions, everything, it's all been done. What can one do? What can one become? And postmodernity is the attempt . . . to reach a point where one can live with what is left. It is more a survival amongst the remnants than anything else.[2]

2. *We have become tools of our tools.* Canadian Marshall McLuhan surveyed the history of media technology and observed that *we shape our tools and they in turn shape us.* According to McLuhan, when we continually use a communication technology, it alters our symbolic environment—the socially constructed, sensory world of meanings that shapes our perceptions, experiences, attitudes, and behavior. If we concentrate on analyzing the content of media messages or strive to resist their impact, we miss the fact that the medium itself is the "message" that shapes us.

3. *In a postmodern world, any claim of truth or moral certainty is suspect.* In his book *The Postmodern Condition,* Baudrillard's compatriot Jean-François Lyotard was the first to popularize the use of the term *postmodern* to describe our culture. "Simplifying to the extreme," wrote Lyotard, "I define *postmodern* as incredulity towards metanarratives."[3] He was referring specifically to any systems of thought that claimed to be true for all people, such as Marxism, Freudianism, or Christianity. But the relativity of knowledge applies to any assertion of truth. In postmodern thinking, there are no facts, only interpretations. We can't know anything for certain. (As you ponder this idea, you might wonder how certain we can be that we can't know anything for certain.) In the world of art, postmodernism ignores universal principles of aesthetic beauty. There are no standard rules for creating a painting, sculpture, movie, or concerto.

4. *Images become more important than what they represent.* Postmodernists are convinced that recurrent media images take on a *hyperreality*—they are more real than reality. Our mental pictures of the perfect body, house, meal, vacation, and sexual relationship have been created through exposure to constantly recycled media depictions that have no basis in fact—but it is these images that shape our expectations. As Baudrillard suggested, "It's not TV as a mirror of society but just the reverse: *it's society as the mirror of television.*"[4] For postmodernists, the issue is not whether media distort reality. In today's world, media have become reality—the only one we have.

5. ***With a media assist, we can mix and match diverse styles and tastes to create a unique identity.*** Lyotard regarded this kind of eclecticism as the norm for postmodern culture. "One listens to reggae, watches a Western, eats McDonald's food for lunch and local cuisine for dinner, wears Paris perfume in Tokyo and 'retro' clothes in Hong Kong; knowledge is a matter for TV games."[5] The possibilities of identity construction are endless in an urban setting with thousands of cable channels, Netflix, Amazon Prime, and high-speed Internet to provide infinite variety. Postmodernism is an age of individualism rather than one of community.

6. ***Postmodernism can also be seen as a new kind of economic order—a consumer society based on multinational capitalism.*** In a postmodern society, information rather than production is the key to profits. Money is especially important in a consumer society because *people are what they consume.*

Operating from a neo-Marxist perspective, Duke University literature professor Fredric Jameson is a high-profile postmodernist who takes this economic view. He sees in our current era "the emergence of a new type of social life and a new economic order,"[6] specifically a late stage of capitalism. He is not surprised to see the erosion of the old distinction between high culture and so-called popular culture. In the absence of aesthetic standards, profits become the measure of whether art is good or bad. Thus, media conglomerates such as Disney and Time Warner cannot help but work in the interest of those who already have financial control.

The theorists featured in this section don't identify themselves as postmodernists, but their analysis of media and culture certainly places them in that camp. Their highly interpretive methodological approach is in sharp contrast with the empirical approach that marks the social science-based media theorists featured in the section following this one.

Media Ecology

of Marshall McLuhan

Award-winning filmmaker Rachel Dretzin began her 2010 PBS documentary, *Digital Nation,*[1] with a personal observation:

> So it really hit me one night not that long ago. I was in the kitchen and I was cooking dinner, chopping vegetables—and my husband was in the next room on his laptop and across the table from my husband was my oldest son—who was also on a laptop doing his homework—and my younger kids had picked up my iPhone and were playing a game on it or something and it just hit me. We're all in the same house but we're also in *other* worlds—and it just kind of snuck up on us. I didn't see it coming.

The heart of Dretzin's insight is the fact that her entire home *environment* had changed dramatically due to electronic media—a change she'd never noticed until that one evening chopping vegetables.

Dretzin's realization highlights what media ecologists study. You're probably familiar with the word *ecology* because it comes up in discussions about global warming, recycling garbage, and saving rain forests. Ecologists study the environment, how people interact with it, and the way these interactions result in change. *Media* ecologists study *media* environments. They seek to understand how people interact with media and how those interactions shape our culture and our daily experiences. If Marshall McLuhan could have heard Dretzin's comment, he would have probably smiled knowingly. At the same time that McLuhan claimed to understand the changes media bring, he also confidently theorized about why most of us are oblivious to those changes.

In the 1960s, Marshall McLuhan was an English professor at the University of Toronto. He burst onto the public scene by asking questions about the relationship between media and culture. His book *Understanding Media* was a surprise hit that generated both admiration and dissension. His theory suggests that media should be understood ecologically. Changes in technology alter the *symbolic environment*—the socially constructed, sensory world of meanings that in turn shapes our perceptions, experiences, attitudes, and behavior.

Symbolic environment
The socially constructed, sensory world of meanings.

THE MEDIUM IS THE MESSAGE

McLuhan's theory of media ecology is best captured in his famous aphorism "The medium is the message." This pithy statement is meant to upset our expectations. We're accustomed to thinking that people change because of the messages they consume. The whole field of persuasion revolves around message content (see Chapter 15). We think of media as mere channels of message delivery that play a minor role in effecting change.

When McLuhan said, "the medium is the message," he wanted us to see that media—regardless of content—reshape human experience and exert far more change in our world than the sum total of the messages they contain. He made this point forcefully in a famous interview with *Playboy* magazine in 1969: "The content or message of any particular medium has about as much importance as the stenciling on the casing of an atomic bomb."[2]

Media
Generic term for all human-invented technology that extends the range, speed, or channels of communication.

McLuhan loved using metaphors to explain theoretical concepts. He was convinced that when we consider the cultural influence of *media,* we are usually misled by the illusion of *content.* One metaphor that he used to make this point was particularly colorful. He wrote, "For the 'content' of a medium is like the juicy piece of meat carried by the burglar to distract the watchdog of the mind."[3] We focus on the content and overlook the *medium*—even though content doesn't exist outside of the way it's mediated. *Moby Dick* is a book. *Moby Dick* is a movie. *Moby Dick* is an oral tale. These are different stories. For this reason, we shouldn't complain that a movie is not like the book, because a movie can never be like a book. A movie can only be a movie.

Medium
A specific type of media; for example, a book, newspaper, radio, television, telephone, film, website, or email.

Whether a TV show is about killer whales, current events, crime scene investigations, the next American pop star, or *The Real Housewives of New Jersey,* the message is always television. It is the distinct experience of TV that alters the symbolic environment. From the perspective of media ecology, the Clydesdale ad discussed in Chapter 2 is important not because of its content, but because it offered a shared media experience that captured the time and attention of millions of people. It also triggered nearly 3 million visits to YouTube to watch the ad again.[4] Media ecologists might point out that neither Glenn nor Marty even mentioned these features in their analysis.

After reading about McLuhan's theory, John had no problem recognizing the message of a medium. In his application log, he wrote:

> Text messages are a recent fad as society moves deeper into the digital age. I don't regard texting as necessary for exchanging information. Emails and phone calls can take care of that. For me, texts are a sign of affection; they are "flirtatious." I've got a crush on Ashley, and when I see that I have text from her, I can't help but smile— this even before I read the message. Overshadowed by a media form that signifies intimacy and fondness, the content seems irrelevant. The medium is the message.

THE CHALLENGE OF MEDIA ECOLOGY

Media ecology
The study of different personal and social environments created by the use of different communication technologies.

Any understanding of social and cultural change is impossible without a knowledge of the way media work as environments.[5] But evaluating the *ecology of media* is a difficult enterprise because all environments are inherently intangible and interrelated. An environment is not a thing to identify; rather, it is the intricate association of many things. By definition, these things are part of the background. They are everything and no thing. McLuhan noted that "their ground rules, pervasive structure, and overall patterns elude easy perception."[6]

"We have a calendar based on the book, stationery based on the book, an audiotape of the book, and a videotape of the movie based on the book, but we don't have the book."

©Michael Maslin/The New Yorker Collection/The Cartoon Bank

Invisibility of Environments

McLuhan was fond of quoting the mantra of anthropologists: "We don't know who discovered water, but we're pretty sure it wasn't the fish." In the same way, we have trouble recognizing "the way media work as environments" because we are so immersed in them.

McLuhan's theory of media differs from the traditional warnings against technological advances. The tales of *Ex Machina, Blade Runner, Jurassic Park, Inception, The Matrix,* and *The Terminator* tell of technology gone awry and turning on its maker. These fantastical threats prove terribly obvious. As long as our technologies are not chasing after us, we are supposedly safe from the consequences of our creations.

According to McLuhan, it's not technological abnormality that demands our attention. It's hard *not* to notice what's new and different. Instead, we need to focus on our everyday experience of *technology*. A medium shapes us because we partake of it over and over until it becomes an extension of ourselves. Because every medium emphasizes different senses and encourages different habits, engaging a medium day after day conditions the senses to take in some stimuli and not register others. A medium that emphasizes the ear over the eye alters the ratios of sense perception.

Technology
According to McLuhan, human inventions that enhance communication.

Like a blind man who begins to develop a heightened sense of hearing, society is shaped in accordance with the dominant medium of the day.

The ordinariness of media is what makes them invisible. When a new medium enters society, there's a period of time in which we're aware of its novelty. But when it fades into the background of our lives we become vulnerable to its patterns—its environmental influence. In the same way that a girl growing up in California may unconsciously absorb a West Coast attitude, a boy growing up in our electronic age may unconsciously absorb a digital attitude. Rachel Dretzin noted that the media changes that transformed her family's home environment had "snuck up" on them.

Complexity of Environments

If you surveyed the landscape of media research, you'd discover plenty of material devoted to the effects of content. You'd also discover numerous studies focusing instead on specific media such as television, computers, and iPhones, as well as applications like Facebook, Twitter, and LinkedIn. In contrast, research on media ecology is rather sparse because it takes up the challenge of trying to understand the interplay between all of these things in a culture that changes at blazing speed.

McLuhan believed it took a special ability to stand back from the action and take in the big picture. Dretzin realized what was going on inside her home only when she was able to assume the role of a sideline observer preparing dinner. One way McLuhan tried to gain a broader perspective was by stepping outside the moment and considering all of human history. He found it helpful to trace the major ecological shifts in media over thousands of years. That grand historical perspective is the foundation of McLuhan's theory. It also illustrates his conviction that "We shape our tools, and thereafter they shape us."[7]

A MEDIA ANALYSIS OF HUMAN HISTORY

McLuhan was critical of social observers who analyzed the Western world but bypassed the effects of symbolic environments, be they oral, print, or electronic. He specifically accused modern scholars of being "ostrichlike" in refusing to acknowledge the revolutionary impact of electronic media on the sensory experience of contemporary society.

As Figure 25-1 shows, McLuhan divided all human history into four periods, or epochs—a tribal age, a literate age, a print age, and an electronic age. According to McLuhan, the crucial inventions that changed life on this planet were the phonetic alphabet, the printing press, and the telegraph. In each case the world was wrenched from one era into the next because of new developments in media technology. Those who were born in the twentieth century are living through one of those turbulent transitions—from the tail end of the *print* age to the very beginning of the *electronic* age. McLuhan believed the transitions (shaded in gray in Figure 25-1) take 300 to 400 years to complete. While you might think you're living in the electronic age right now, you're not there yet. The full transition will take another two centuries.

1. The Tribal Age: An Acoustic Place in History

According to McLuhan, the tribal village was an acoustic place where the senses of hearing, touch, taste, and smell were developed far beyond the ability to visualize. In untamed settings, hearing is more valuable than seeing because it allows you to

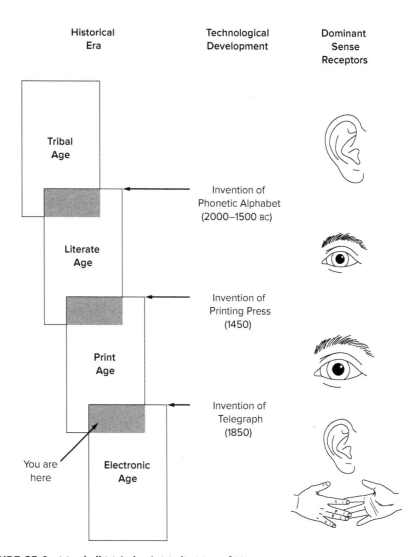

FIGURE 25-1 Marshall McLuhan's Media Map of History

be more immediately aware of your surroundings. With sight, we are limited to direction and distance. We can only sense what is clearly in front of us. If a preying animal is behind us or hidden by a tree, we are hopelessly unaware without a sensitivity to sound or smell. Hearing and smelling provide a sense of that which we cannot see—a crucial ability in the tribal age.

The omnidirectional quality of sound also enhances community. The spoken word is primarily a communal experience. To tell a secret, we must whisper or speak directly into someone's ear or make sure no one else is listening. The sense of sound works against privatization. Listening to someone speak in a group is a unifying act. Everyone hears at the same time.

The spoken word is also immediate and alive. It exists only at the moment it is heard. There is no sense of the word as something that is fixed or objectified. Spoken words lack materiality. In order to keep an idea or an event alive, it must

Tribal age

An acoustic era; a time of community because the ear is the dominant sense organ.

constantly be shared and reiterated and passed down. The ethereal quality of speech doesn't allow for detached analysis. In a tribal age, hearing is believing.

McLuhan claimed that "primitive" people led richer and more complex lives than their literate descendants because the ear, unlike the eye, encourages a more holistic sense of the world. There is a deeper feeling of community and greater awareness of the surrounding existence. The acoustic environment also fosters more passion and spontaneity. In that world of surround sound, everything is more immediate, more present, and more actual.

Then someone invented the alphabet.

2. The Age of Literacy: A Visual Point of View

Turning sounds into visible objects radically altered the symbolic environment. Suddenly, the eye became the heir apparent. Hearing diminished in value and quality. To disagree with this assessment merely illustrates McLuhan's belief that a private, left-brain "point of view" becomes possible in a world that encourages the visual practice of reading texts.

Words fixed on a page detach meaning from the immediacy of context. In an acoustic environment, taking something out of context is nearly impossible. In the age of literacy, it's a reality. Both writer and reader are always separate from the text. Words are no longer alive and immediate. They can be read and reread. They can be thoroughly analyzed. Hearing no longer becomes trustworthy. "Seeing it in writing" becomes proof that it's true.

Literary age
A visual era; a time of private detachment because the eye is the dominant sense organ.

Literacy also jarred people out of collective tribal involvement into "civilized" private detachment. Reading words, instead of hearing them, transforms group members into individuals. Even though the words may be the same, the act of reading a text is an individual one. It requires singular focus. A tribe no longer needs to come together to get information. Proximity becomes less important.

McLuhan also claimed that the phonetic alphabet established the line as the organizing principle in life. In writing, letter follows letter in a connected, orderly line. Logic is modeled on that step-by-step, linear progression. According to McLuhan, when literate people say, "I don't follow you," they mean, "I don't think you are logical." He alleged that the invention of the alphabet fostered the sudden emergence of mathematics, science, and philosophy in ancient Greece. He cited the political upheaval in colonial Africa as twentieth-century evidence that literacy triggers an ear-to-eye switch that isolates the reader. When oppressed people learned to read, they became independent thinkers.

3. The Print Age: Prototype of the Industrial Revolution

If the phonetic alphabet made visual dependence possible, the printing press made it widespread. In *The Gutenberg Galaxy,* McLuhan argued that the most important aspect of movable type was its ability to reproduce the same text over and over again, and a press run of 100,000 copies of *Understanding Media* suggests he was right. Because the print revolution demonstrated mass production of identical products, McLuhan called it the forerunner of the industrial revolution.

Print age
A visual era; mass-produced books usher in the industrial revolution and nationalism, yet individuals are isolated.

He saw other unintended side effects of Gutenberg's invention. The homogenization of fluid regional tongues into a fixed national language was followed closely by the rise of nationalism. Concurring with this new sense of unification was a countering sense of separation and aloneness.

Printing, a ditto device, confirmed and extended the new visual stress. It created the portable book, which men could read in privacy and in isolation from others.[8]

Many libraries have the words "The truth will set you free" carved in stone above the main entrance.[9] From McLuhan's perspective, libraries provide readers with the freedom to be alienated from others and from the immediacy of their surroundings.

4. The Electronic Age: The Rise of the Global Village

With the tap-tap-tap of the telegraph, the power of the printed word lost its bearings. Of course, Samuel Morse's invention was only the first of the new electronic media devices that would make the local Best Buy seem, to previous generations, like a magic shop.

Telegraph   Radio   Telephone   Film projector   Phonograph   TV
Photocopier   Tape recorder   Answering machine   VCR   Computer
Fax   CD   DVD   Cell phone   GPS   Video game   MP3
Internet   Laptop   Smartphone   Tablet   Touchscreen

Electronic age
An era of instant communication; a return to the global village with all-at-once sound and touch.

McLuhan insisted that electronic media are retribalizing the human race. Instant communication has returned us to a pre-alphabetic oral tradition where sound and touch are more important than sight. We've gone "back to the future" to become a village unlike any other previous village. We're now a *global village.*

Electronic media bring us in contact with everyone, everywhere, instantaneously. Whereas the book extended the eye, electronic circuitry extends the central nervous system.[10] Constant contact with the world becomes a daily reality. All-at-once-ness is our state of being. Closed human systems no longer exist. The rumble of empty stomachs in Bangladesh and of roadside bombs in Baghdad vibrate in the living rooms of Boston. For us, the first postliterate generation, privacy is either a luxury or a curse of the past. The planet is like a general store where nosy people keep track of everyone else's business—a 12-way party line or an "Ask Amy" column writ large. "The new tribalism is one where everyone's business is everyone else's and where we all are somewhat testy."[11] Citizens of the world are back in acoustic space.

Global village
A worldwide electronic community where everyone knows everyone's business and all are somewhat testy.

Linear logic is useless in the electronic society McLuhan described. Acoustic people no longer inquire, "Do you see my point?" Instead we ask, "How does that grab you?" What we feel is more important than what we think.

5. The Digital Age? A Wireless Global Village

When *Wired,* a magazine on digital culture, was launched in 1992, the editors declared Marshall McLuhan the magazine's "patron saint." There was a sense that another revolution was looming, even though digital technology is wholly electronic.

There's no doubt that the introduction of digital technology is altering the electronic environment. The mass age of electronic media is becoming increasingly personalized. Instead of one unified electronic tribe, we have a growing number of digital tribes forming around the most specialized ideas, beliefs, values, interests, and fetishes. Instead of mass consciousness, which McLuhan viewed rather favorably, we have the emergence of a tribal warfare mentality.

Digital age
A possible fifth era of specialized electronic tribes contentious over diverse beliefs and values.

Twitter is a recent example of a digital creation that now shapes our communication environment. Texas Tech University media scholar Brian Ott claims there are three inherent features of the app that have altered the nature of public discourse.[12] First, the 140-character limit demands *simplicity*. There's no room for complex ideas, subtle nuances, or evidence to support a claim. Second, Twitter promotes *impulsivity*. The ease of sending a quick tweet from any place whenever a thought crosses the brain pan almost guarantees a lack of reflection or consideration of consequences. Finally, Twitter fosters *incivility*. The lack of formality and intimacy encourages negative zingers that demean others. If Ott is right, President Trump's famous reliance on this form of social media may be changing the world's social ecology just as much as scientists attribute climate change to global warming.

A SOURCE OF INSPIRATION FOR MCLUHAN'S IDEAS: HIS CATHOLIC FAITH

McLuhan grew up in a Presbyterian family but converted to Catholicism when he was 25 years old. He held a deep faith in God, was well read in theology, and attended Mass almost every day. It's widely known that McLuhan's ideas were informed by the work of Canadian professor of economic history Harold Innis.[13] But many McLuhan scholars are also quick to note the impact of two Jesuit priests on his thinking: Walter Ong[14] and Pierre Teilhard de Chardin.[15] That's why it's surprising that McLuhan rarely discussed his faith in the context of his theory or voiced ethical judgments on the cultural effects of media technology.

In his essay, "The Medium is the Messiah," Read Schuchardt, a communication professor at my alma mater wrote: "To say that Marshall McLuhan was incidentally a Christian, or that his Catholicism was just part of his private life, is a little like saying that Karl Marx was only incidentally a Marxist." Schuchardt endorses media technology critic Nicolas Carr's analysis of McLuhan's approach to scholarship. "Though he never discussed it, his faith forms the intellectual backdrop to all his mature work. . . . His role as a thinker was not to celebrate or denigrate the world, but simply to understand it." Similar to most artists, he thought it was his responsibility to offer a perspective rather than a prescription.[16]

As a professor, McLuhan believed he should keep his personal beliefs private, and rarely referred directly to his faith when discussing his theory.[17] In a letter to anthropologist Edward Hall, he made one of his few direct references to his faith's connection to the theory. "I deliberately keep Christianity out of these discussions lest perception be diverted from structural processes by doctrinal sectarian passions."[18] But as a comment he made during a radio interview reveals, his scholarship informed his faith and his faith informed his scholarship. "In Jesus Christ, there is no distance or separation between the medium and the message: it is the one case where we can say that the medium and the message are fully one and the same."[19]

ETHICAL REFLECTION: POSTMAN'S FAUSTIAN BARGAIN

McLuhan's probes stimulated others to ponder whether specific media environments were beneficial or destructive for those immersed in them. Neil Postman founded the media ecology program at New York University and was regarded by many as McLuhan's heir apparent. Like McLuhan, Postman believed that the forms of media regulate and even dictate what kind of content the form of a given medium can carry.[20] For example:

> Puffs of smoke are insufficiently complex to express ideas on the nature of existence and even if they were not, a Cherokee philosopher would run short of either

wood or blankets long before he reached his second axiom. You cannot use smoke to do philosophy. Its form excludes the content.[21]

But unlike McLuhan, Postman believed that the primary task of media ecology is to make moral judgments. "To be quite honest about it," he once proclaimed, "I don't see any point in studying media unless one does so within a moral or ethical context."[22]

According to Postman, a new technology always presents us with a *Faustian bargain*—a potential deal with the devil. As Postman was fond of saying, "Technology giveth and technology taketh away. . . . A new technology sometimes creates more than it destroys. Sometimes, it destroys more than it creates. But it is never one-sided."[23] His media ecology approach asks, *What are the moral implications of this bargain? Are the consequences more humanistic or antihumanistic? Do we, as a society, gain more than we lose, or do we lose more than we gain?*

As for television, Postman argued that society lost more than it gained. He believed whatever advantages TV offers are more than offset by the fact that it has led to the loss of serious public discourse. Television changes the form of information "from discursive to nondiscursive, from propositional to presentational, from rationalistic to emotive."[24] He set forth this argument in his popular book *Amusing Ourselves to Death,* which argues that TV has transformed our culture into one that is focused too heavily on entertainment. In 2016, cable news shows couldn't get enough of presidential candidate Donald Trump's surprising rhetoric. Postman would likely have seen this as direct evidence that TV transforms serious political news into a grand spectacle of entertainment.

Postman died in 2003, just before social media exploded in American culture. Had he been here to witness this change, he could have easily cast his analysis in terms of the *Faustian bargain.* Social media offers unprecedented opportunities to maintain electronic connections with family and friends. But, similar to Sherry Turkle (see Chapter 10), Postman feared that virtual interaction may sabotage the kind of intimacy that only comes by being in the physical presence of others. Have we gained more than we've lost?

Faustian bargain
A deal with the devil; selling your soul for temporary earthly gain.

CRITIQUE: HOW COULD MCLUHAN BE RIGHT? BUT WHAT IF HE IS?

McLuhan likened himself to "Louis Pasteur telling doctors that their greatest enemy is quite invisible, and quite unrecognized by them."[25] Of course, the major difference is that Pasteur was a scientist who ultimately gave tangible evidence that invisible germs cause infection. McLuhan's theory suggests objectivity without scientific evidence. In other words, he used an interpretive approach to make objective claims, but his theory fails to meet most of the standard criteria used to assess either type of theory.

For readers who desire a scientific theory, McLuhan does offer an *explanation* of the way different media engage our different senses of sound, sight, and touch. But this is after-the-fact analysis rather than specific *predictions* of future cultural change. As George Gordon, former chairman of the department of communication at Fordham University, observed, "Not one bit of sustained and replicated scientific evidence, inductive or deductive, has to date justified any one of McLuhan's most famous slogans, metaphors, or dicta."[26] Indeed, it's hard to know how *empirical research* could prove the phonetic alphabet created Greek philosophy, the printing press fostered nationalism, or television is a tactile medium. The theory can't be *tested.* Even if these claims were found valid, the *practical utility* of that knowledge is questionable.

Regarded as an interpretive theory, media ecology fares somewhat better. McLuhan connected the essence of key communication media with the rapid changes in culture people knew were occurring, but didn't know why. Media ecology offers a *new understanding* of the rise in drug abuse, shortened attention spans, decline in standardized test scores, popularity of rock music and tattoos, and the success and failure of specific political candidates.

As for *aesthetic appeal,* McLuhan was superb at crafting memorable phrases, catchy statements, and 10-second sound bites that appealed to media practitioners and a popular audience, which formed a loose *community of agreement.* But his often enigmatic statements that weren't woven into a comprehensive system have drawn disdain and resistance among a counter-community of media scholars. Certainly he made no effort to *reform society,* and unlike many critical and interpretive theorists, he didn't *clarify the values* that undergirded his work. McLuhan obviously had a facile mind, but the *qualitative research* that informed his theory wasn't discussed.

Given that Marshall McLuhan's media ecology fails to meet many of the standards of a good theory—scientific or interpretive—why have we included a chapter on his work in this text? The answer is that McLuhan's historical analysis has heightened awareness of the possible cultural effects of new media technologies. Other scholars have been more tempered in their statements and more rigorous in their documentation, but none has raised media consciousness to the level achieved by McLuhan. We believe that all students of media should be conversant with his ideas and have some awareness of his impact, which continues to be fanned by the passionate members of the Media Ecology Association.

History is littered with theories that were ahead of their time and couldn't immediately be tested. When McLuhan was alive, journalist Tom Wolfe asked, "What if he's right? Suppose he is what he sounds like, the most important thinker since Newton, Darwin, Freud, Einstein, and Pavlov?"[27] The late economist Kenneth Boulding, who headed the Institute of Behavioral Science at the University of Colorado, captured both the pro and con reactions to McLuhan with a metaphor of his own: "It is perhaps typical of very creative minds that they hit very large nails not quite on the head."[28]

QUESTIONS TO SHARPEN YOUR FOCUS

1. What would McLuhan say about the impact of the Internet on the *global village?* Consider the fact that civic, political, and religious participation are declining in America.[29] Has *electronic technology* increased social connectedness?

2. How are portable media devices such as smartphones, iPads, and handheld video games altering the *media environment?* How are these devices shaping sensibilities?

3. Beyond changes in content, what are the differences in experiencing a book and its translations into film or television?

4. Can you conceive of any way that McLuhan's idea of *media ecology* could be proved false?

A SECOND LOOK

Recommended resource: Marshall McLuhan, "*Playboy* Interview: A Candid Conversation with the High Priest of Popcult and Metaphysician of Media," March 1969, p. 53ff. Reprinted in *Essential McLuhan,* Eric McLuhan and Frank Zingrone (eds.), BasicBooks, New York, 1995, pp. 233–269.

McLuhan primer: Marshall McLuhan and Quentin Fiore, *The Medium Is the Massage,* Gingko, Corte Madera, CA, 2005.

Impact of print media: Marshall McLuhan, *The Gutenberg Galaxy,* University of Toronto, 1962.

Impact of electronic media: Marshall McLuhan, *Understanding Media,* McGraw-Hill, New York, 1964.

Impact of digital media à la McLuhan: Paul Levinson, *Digital McLuhan: A Guide to the Information Millennium,* Routledge, London, 1999.

Early vs. late McLuhan: Bruce E. Gronbeck, "McLuhan as Rhetorical Theorist," *Journal of Communication,* Vol. 31, 1981, pp. 117–128.

Intellectual roots: Harold Innis, *The Bias of Communication,* University of Toronto, 1964.

Methodology: Paul Levinson, "McLuhan and Rationality," *Journal of Communication,* Vol. 31, 1981, pp. 179–188.

Scientific claims: Marshall McLuhan and Eric McLuhan, *Laws of Media: The New Science,* University of Toronto, 1988.

Recent scholarship: Eric McLuhan and Marshall McLuhan, *Theories of Communication,* Peter Lang, New York, 2010.

Rethinking McLuhan through critical theory: Paul Grosswiler, *Method Is the Message,* Black Rose, Montreal, 1998.

Postmodern connections: Gary Genosko, "McLuhan's Legacy of Indiscipline," in *Undisciplined Theory,* Sage, London, 1998, pp. 154–182.

Brief interpretive biography: Douglas Coupland, *Extraordinary Canadians: Marshall McLuhan,* Penguin, Viking Canada, 2010.

Legacy of McLuhan: Lance Strate and Edward Wachtel (eds.), *The Legacy of McLuhan,* Hampton, Cresskill, NJ, 2005, Chapters 1–4.

Neil Postman's ethical view of new media: Neil Postman, *Amusing Ourselves to Death: Public Discourse in the Age of Show Business,* Viking, NY, 1985; Neil Postman, *Technopoly: The Surrender of Culture to Technology,* Knopf, New York, 1992.

Critique: Gerald Stearn (ed.), *McLuhan: Hot & Cool,* Dial, New York, 1967.

Do we respond to people and digital media in the same way?
Click on The Media Equation in Archive
under Theory Resources at
www.afirstlook.com.

Semiotics

of Roland Barthes

French literary critic and semiologist Roland Barthes (rhymes with "smart") wrote that for him, semiotics was not a cause, a science, a discipline, a school, a movement, nor presumably even a theory. "It is," he claimed, "an adventure."[1] The goal of semiotics is interpreting both verbal and nonverbal *signs*. The verbal side of the field is called *linguistics*. Barthes, however, was mainly interested in the nonverbal side—multifaceted visual signs just waiting to be read. Barthes held the chair of literary semiology at the College of France when he was struck and killed by a laundry truck in 1980. In his highly regarded book *Mythologies,* Barthes sought to decipher the cultural meaning of a wide variety of visual signs—from sweat on the faces of actors in the film *Julius Caesar* to a magazine photograph of a young African soldier saluting the French flag.

Semiotics (semiology)
The study of the social production of meaning from sign systems; the analysis of anything that can stand for something else.

Semiology (or semiotics, as it is better known in America) is concerned with *anything that can stand for something else.* Italian semiologist and novelist Umberto Eco had a clever way of expressing that focus. Semiotics, he said, is "the discipline studying everything which can be used in order to lie, because if something cannot be used to tell a lie, conversely it cannot be used to tell the truth; it cannot, in fact, be used to tell at all."[2] Barthes was interested in signs that are seemingly straightforward but that subtly communicate ideological or connotative meaning and perpetuate the dominant values of society. As such, they are deceptive.

Barthes was a mercurial thinker who changed his mind about the way signs work more than once over the course of his career. Yet most current practitioners of semiotics follow the basic analytical concepts of his original theory. His approach provides great insight into the use of signs, particularly those channeled through the mass media.

WRESTLING WITH SIGNS

Barthes initially described his semiotic theory as an explanation of *myth.* He later substituted the term *connotation* to label the ideological baggage that signs carry wherever they go, and most students of Barthes' work regard connotation as a better word choice to convey his true concern.

Myth
The connotative meaning that signs carry wherever they go; myth makes what is cultural seem natural.

Barthes' theory of connotative meaning won't make sense to us, however, unless we first understand the way he viewed the structure of signs. His thinking was strongly influenced by the work of Swiss linguist Ferdinand de Saussure, who coined the term *semiology* and advocated its study.[3] To illustrate Barthes' core principles, I'll feature portions of his essay on professional wrestling as entertainment.

1. A Sign Is the Combination of Its Signifier and Signified

The distinction between signifier and signified can be seen in Barthes' graphic description of the body of a French wrestler who was selected by the promoter because he typified the repulsive slob:

> As soon as the adversaries are in the ring, the public is overwhelmed with the obviousness of the roles. As in the theatre, each physical type expresses to excess the part which has been assigned to the contestant. Thauvin, a fifty-year-old with an obese and sagging body . . . displays in his flesh the characters of baseness. . . . The physique of the wrestlers therefore constitutes a basic sign, which like a seed contains the whole fight.[4]

According to Barthes, the image of the wrestler's physique is the *signifier*. The concept of baseness is the *signified*. The combination of the two—the villainous body—is the *sign*.

This way of defining a sign differs from our customary use of the word. We would probably say the wrestler's body *is a sign* of his baseness—or whatever else comes to mind. But Barthes considered the wrestler's body just *part* of the overall sign; it's the signifier. The other part is the concept of hideous baseness. The signifier isn't a sign of the signified. Rather, they work together in an inseparable bond to form a unified sign.

Sign
The inseparable combination of the signifier and the signified.

Signifier
The physical form of the sign as we perceive it through our senses; an image.

Barthes' description of a sign as the correlation between the signifier and the signified came directly from Saussure. The Swiss linguist visualized a sign as a piece of paper with writing on both sides—the signifier on one side, the signified on the other. If you cut off part of one side, an equal amount of the other side automatically goes with it.

Using a similar metaphor, I see signs as coins. For example, the image of a country's president is stamped on the "heads" side of a gold coin—the signifier. It's only on the flip side of the coin that we see its value in the United States of America is $1—the signified. The signifier and the signified can't be separated. They are combined in our reference to that monetary sign as a US gold dollar.

Signified
The meaning we associate with the sign.

Is there any logical connection between the image of the signifier and the content of the signified? Saussure insisted the relationship is arbitrary—one of correlation rather than cause and effect. Barthes wasn't so sure. He was willing to grant the claim of Saussure that words have no inherent meaning. For example, there is nothing about the word *referee* that makes it stand for the third party in the ring who is inept at making Thauvin follow the rules. But nonverbal signifiers seem to have a natural affinity with their signifieds. Barthes noted that Thauvin's body was so repugnant that it provoked nausea. He classified the relationship between signifiers and signifieds as "quasi-arbitrary." After all, Thauvin really did strike the crowd as vileness personified.

2. A Sign Does Not Stand on Its Own: It Is Part of a System

Barthes entitled his essay "The World of Wrestling" because, like all other semiotic systems, wrestling creates its own separate world of interrelated signs:

> Each moment in wrestling is therefore like an algebra which instantaneously unveils the relationship between a cause and its represented effect. Wrestling fans certainly experience a kind of intellectual pleasure in *seeing* the moral mechanism function so perfectly. . . . A wrestler can irritate or disgust, he never disappoints, for he always accomplishes completely, by a progressive solidification of signs, what the public expects of him.[5]

Barthes noted that the grapplers' roles are tightly drawn. There is little room for innovation; the men in the ring work within a closed system of signs. By responding to the unwavering expectation of the crowd, the wrestlers are as much spectators as the fans who cheer or jeer on cue.

Wrestling is just one of many semiotic systems. Barthes also explored the cultural meaning of designer clothes, French cooking, automobiles, Japanese gift giving, household furniture, urban layout, and public displays of sexuality. He attempted to define and classify the features common to all semiotic systems. This kind of structural analysis is called *taxonomy,* and Barthes' book *Elements of Semiology* is a "veritable frenzy of classifications."[6] Barthes later admitted that his taxonomy "risked being tedious," but the project strengthened his conviction that all semiotic systems function the same way, despite their apparent diversity.

Barthes believed that the significant semiotic systems of a culture lock in the status quo. The mythology that surrounds a society's crucial signs displays the world as it is today—however chaotic and unjust—as *natural, inevitable,* and *eternal.* The function of myth is to bless the mess. We now turn to Barthes' theory of connotation, or myth, which suggests how a seemingly neutral or inanimate sign can accomplish so much.

THE YELLOW RIBBON TRANSFORMATION: FROM FORGIVENESS TO PRIDE

According to Barthes, not all semiological systems are mythic. Not every sign carries ideological baggage. How is it that one sign can remain emotionally neutral while other signs acquire powerful inflections or connotations that suck people into a specific worldview? Barthes contended that a mythic or connotative system is a *second-order semiological system*—built off a pre-existing sign system. The sign of the first system becomes the signifier of the second. A concrete example will help us understand Barthes' explanation.

In an *American Journal of Semiotics* article, Donald and Virginia Fry of Emerson College examined the widespread American practice of displaying yellow ribbons during the 1980 Iranian hostage crisis,[7] which began with the storming of the US embassy vividly portrayed in the Academy Award-winning film *Argo.* They traced the transformation of this straightforward yellow symbol into an ideological sign. Americans' lavish display of yellow ribbons during Operation Desert Storm in 1991 and the occupation of Iraq that began in 2003 adds a new twist to the Frys' analysis. I'll update their yellow ribbon example to illustrate Barthes' semiotic theory.

"Tie a Yellow Ribbon Round the Ole Oak Tree" was the best-selling pop song of 1972 in the United States.[8] Sung by Tony Orlando and Dawn, the lyrics express the thoughts of a convict in prison who is writing to the woman he loves.

After three years in jail, the man is about to be released and will travel home by bus. Fearing her possible rejection, he devises a plan that will give her a way to signal her intentions without the potential embarrassment of a face-to-face confrontation.

Since he'll be able to see the huge oak planted in front of her house when the bus passes through town, he asks her to use the tree as a message board. If she still loves him, wants him back, and can overlook the past, she should tie a yellow ribbon around the trunk of the tree. He will know that all is forgiven and join her in rebuilding a life together. But if this bright sign of reconciliation isn't there, he'll stay on the bus, accept the blame for a failed relationship, and try to get on with his life without her.

The yellow ribbon is obviously a sign of acceptance, but one not casually offered. There's a taint on the relationship, hurts to be healed. Donald and Virginia Fry labeled the original meaning of the yellow ribbon in the song as "forgiveness of a stigma."

Yellow ribbons continued to carry a "We want you back" message in 1991 when US armed forces fought in Operation Desert Storm. Whether tied to trees, worn in hair, or pinned to lapels, yellow ribbons still proclaimed, "Welcome home." But there was no longer any sense of shameful acts to be forgiven or disgrace to be overcome. Vietnam was ancient history and America was the leader of the "new world order." Hail the conquering heroes.

The mood surrounding the yellow ribbon had become one of triumph, pride, and even arrogance. After all, hadn't we intercepted Scud missiles in the air, guided "smart bombs" into air-conditioning shafts, and "kicked Saddam Hussein's butt across the desert"? People were swept up in a tide of "yellow fever." More than 90 percent of US citizens approved of America's actions in the Persian Gulf. The simple yellow ribbon of personal reconciliation now served as a blatant sign of nationalism.

The yellow-ribbon sign functioned the same way for about three years after the 2003 US invasion of Iraq, which was the centerpiece of America's "War on Terror." Millions of citizens displayed yellow-ribbon decals and magnets on their cars and trucks that urged all to "Support Our Troops." The ribbon called up feelings of national pride and memories of the shock-and-awe attack on Baghdad that had squashed immediate resistance. Saddam Hussein had been driven from office, his statue toppled; democracy was being established; and President George W. Bush had dramatically landed a fighter jet on an aircraft carrier proclaiming "Mission Accomplished." The yellow ribbon continued to signify that the soldiers' return would be joyous, but its message held no sense of shame. What had originally signified forgiveness of a stigma now symbolized pride in victory.

THE MAKING OF MYTH: STRIPPING THE SIGN OF ITS HISTORY

According to Barthes' theory, the shift from "forgiveness of stigma" to "pride in victory" followed a typical semiotic pattern. Figure 26–1 shows how it's done.

Barthes claimed that every ideological sign is the result of two interconnected sign systems. The first system represented by the smaller coins is strictly descriptive—the signifier image and the signified concept combining to produce a denotative sign.

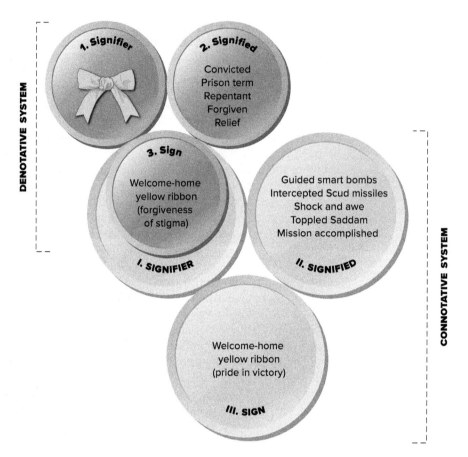

FIGURE 26-1   Connotation as a Second-Order Semiotic System
Source: Based on Barthes, "Myth Today"

The three elements of the sign system based on the "Tie a Yellow Ribbon . . ." lyrics are marked with Arabic numerals on the three images of the smaller coins. The three segments of the connotative system are marked with Roman numerals on the images of the larger coins. Note that the sign of the first system does double duty as the signifier of the Iraqi war connotative system. According to Barthes, this lateral shift, or connotative sidestep, is the key to transforming a neutral sign into an ideological tool. Follow his thinking step-by-step through the diagram.

The signifier (1) of the *denotative sign system* is the image of a yellow ribbon that forms in the mind of the person who hears the 1972 song. The content of the signified (2) includes the stigma that comes from the conviction of a crime, a term in jail, the prisoner's willingness to take responsibility for the three-year separation, and the explosive release of tension when the Greyhound passengers cheer at the sight of the oak tree awash in yellow ribbons. The corresponding denotative sign (3) is "forgiveness of a stigma." For those who heard the song on the radio, the yellow-ribbon sign spoke for itself. It was a meaningful sign, rich in regret and relief.

Current usage takes over the sign of the denotative system and makes it the signifier (I) of a secondary (connotative) system. The "welcome-home" yellow ribbon is paired with the mythic content of a signified (II) that shouts to the world, "Our technology can beat up your technology." But as the symbol of the yellow

Denotative sign system
A descriptive sign without ideological content.

©Mark Parisi/offthemark.com. Used by permission.

ribbon is expropriated to support the myth of American nationalism, the sign loses its historical grounding.

As a mere signifier of the *connotative sign system,* the yellow ribbon is no longer rooted in the details of the song. It ceases to stand for three years of hard time in prison, repentance, wrongdoing, or forgiveness that gains meaning because there is so much to be forgiven. Now in the service of the mythic semiotic system, the yellow ribbon becomes empty and timeless, a form without substance. But according to Barthes, the meaning of the original denotative sign is not completely lost:

> The essential point in all this is that the form does not suppress the meaning, it only impoverishes it, it puts it at a distance. . . . One believes that the meaning is going to die, but it is a death with reprieve; the meaning loses its value, but keeps its life, from which . . . the myth will draw its nourishment.[9]

In the connotative system, the generalized image of a yellow ribbon is now paired with the signified content of victory in the Iraqi wars as seen on television. But since the signifier can't call up a historical or cultural past, the mythic sign (III) of which it is a part carries the "crust of falsity."[10] For example, there was no sense of American culpability in supplying arms to Saddam Hussein until he invaded Kuwait, no confession that a postwar plan for peace hadn't been prepared, and no shame for allowing the abuse of prisoners at Abu Ghraib. And since mythic

Connotative sign system
A mythic sign that has lost its historical referent; form without substance.

communication is unable to imagine anything alien, novel, or other, the sign sweeps away second thoughts about civilian deaths in Baghdad. The transformed yellow ribbon is now a lofty sign that allows no room for nagging doubts that love of oil may have been our country's prime motivation for championing the United Nations' "humanitarian" intervention.

As a semiologist who relished uncovering the ideological subtext in apparently straightforward signs, Barthes might also note that the support-our-troops yellow ribbon is not merely an appeal to write encouraging letters, pray for their safety, and praise them for their service when they come home. In effect, the exhortation makes it unpatriotic to openly criticize George W. Bush's decision to invade Iraq. The juxtaposition of yellow ribbons with Bush-Cheney bumper stickers prior to the 2004 election, as well as the conservative stance of websites selling the magnets, makes it clear that these are not neutral denotative signs.

UNMASKING THE MYTH OF A HOMOGENEOUS SOCIETY

Barthes was convinced that only those with semiotic savvy can spot the hollowness of connotative signs. For most Americans, the yellow ribbon will continue to elicit an unreflective "we're number one" feeling of national pride. Of course, it goes without saying that people will love their country. But that's precisely the problem with mythic signs. They *go without saying*. They don't explain, they don't defend, and they certainly don't raise questions. So it's up to the semiologist to expose or deconstruct the mythic system.

Deconstruction
The process of unmasking contradictions within a text; debunking.

Throughout his life, Roland Barthes deciphered and labeled the *ideologies* foisted upon naïve consumers of images. Although the starting-point signifiers varied, Barthes concluded that society's connotative spin always ends up the same. *Mythic signs reinforce the dominant values of their culture.* For example, the wrestling match we examined earlier seems at first glance to be no more than a harmless Saturday night diversion. Under Barthes' watchful eye, however, it was the site of dangerous mythmaking. He explained that the honorable wrestler's eventual triumph over the rule-breaking villain signifies a make-believe ideology of pure "justice." The "good guys win" simplicity of the spectacle provides false comfort for an audience that lives in a world of dubious morality and inherent inequality.

Ideology
Knowledge presented as common sense or natural, especially when its social construction is ignored or suppressed.

According to Barthes, ideological signs enlist support for the status quo by transforming history into nature—pretending that current conditions are the natural order of things. Without any basis in fact, life has become simple, the complexity of human activity invisible. As with the ribbons and the wrestling match, everything that is personal, conditional, cultural, and temporal disappears. We are left with a sign that makes the world seem inevitable and eternal. Barthes' analysis calls to mind the final words of the "Gloria Patri," a choral response that many Christians sing in worship:

As it was in the beginning,
Is now and ever shall be,
World without end. Amen. Amen.

For believers, singing these words about anything or anyone but God would be unthinkable. Barthes wouldn't grant even that exception. All his semiotic efforts were directed at unmasking what he considered the heresy of those who controlled the images of society—the naturalizing of history.

THE SEMIOTICS OF MASS COMMUNICATION: "I'D LIKE TO BE LIKE MIKE"

Like wrestlers and ribbons, most semiotic signs gain cultural prominence when broadcast through the electronic and print media. Because signs—as well as issues of power and dominance—are integral to mass communication, Barthes' semiotic analysis has become a seminal media theory. As Kyong Kim, author of a book on semiotics, concludes:

> Information delivered by mass media is no longer information. It is a commodity saturated by fantasized themes. Mass audiences are nothing more than consumers of such commodities. One should not forget that, unlike nature, the media's reality is always political. The mass signification arising in response to signs pouring from the mass media is not a natural process. Rather it is an artificial effect calculated and induced by the mass media to achieve something else.[11]

The advertisements that make commercial television so profitable also create layers of connotation that reaffirm the status quo. During the 1998 NBA playoffs, one of the most frequently aired spots featured Chicago Bulls' superstar Michael Jordan slam-dunking the basketball over a variety of helpless defenders.[12] He then gulps down Gatorade while a host of celebrity and everyday admirers croon his praises. The most memorable of these adoring fans is a preschool African American boy, who stares up in awe at the towering Jordan. "Sometimes I dream," we hear him sing, "that he is me." He *really* wants to be like Mike.

Obviously, the commercial is designed to sell Gatorade by linking it to the virtually unlimited achievement of one of basketball's greatest players. To partake of this liquid is to reach for the stars. In that sense, the little boy, rather than MJ himself, becomes the ad's crucial sign. Within this denotative system, the youngster's rapt gaze is the signifier, and his dream of becoming a famous athlete is the signified. The resultant denotative sign—a look of yearning—has the potential to move cartons of Gatorade off the shelf. But as the signifier of a secondary connotative system, it has greater cultural impact.

At the connotative level, the original "look of yearning" suggests a new second-order signified—a more general kind of dreaming about one's future in which the ad's audience is invited to participate. Viewers are encouraged to wish for careers and goals that are virtually unattainable, even in the best of circumstances. The CEO of Microsoft, the conductor of the New York Philharmonic, Hollywood's greatest star, the president of the United States, and the scientist who discovers a vaccine for Alzheimer's constitute the lofty heights surveyed by the gaze that the connotative shift implies.

With its attractive visuals, uplifting soundtrack, and good-natured humor, the commercial functions as a glorification of *unfulfilled desire,* the very essence of its second-order sign. This is America, after all, so think big, aim high, and don't be satisfied with anything but the top. Do what it takes—and purchase what is required—to be the very best. Ideologically speaking, it is this kind of naturalized longing that enslaves the average citizen and fuels the capitalist system. Although the commercial evokes a warm, fuzzy reaction from the viewer, it surreptitiously enforces our fundamental cultural myths about unlimited possibilities for success, myths that—according to Barthes—maintain the dominance of those who hold the reins of commerce and power.

Furthermore, Barthes would no doubt seek to expose the semiotic sleight of hand that subtly drains the second-order connotative system of the historical reality implicit in the original sign. At this denotative level, the African American boy's fixation with MJ is necessarily embedded in a long history of racial injustice and economic hardship. Michael Jordan's accomplishments, as well as the dream of his pint-sized fan, exist in a world in which African Americans must strive particularly hard to succeed. As the documentary *Hoop Dreams* brilliantly portrays, the desire-filled faces of the kids who populate the rough basketball courts of urban America also reflect the poverty; substance abuse; shattered families; and harsh, big-city surroundings that constantly threaten to engulf them. Nonetheless, the yearning connoted by the second-order system generated by the commercial is utterly stripped of this rather grim social reality. The boy, his life, and his dream are deftly co-opted by the system. Or so Barthes would argue.

Katherine, a student who read the semiotic analysis above, was inspired to look for another connotative sign system involving Michael Jordan and his admirers.

> Michael Jordan played most of his games (especially his slam dunks) with his mouth hanging wide and his tongue wagging. This came to signify talent, expectation of greatness, and pride. Jordan wannabes across the country picked up this little quirk. For them, keeping their mouth open signifies Michael Jordan and, therefore, being cool, talented, and better than everyone else. The image of superiority, however, is not derived from any comparable history of success or talent of their own; it's based on myth.

She could have added that after his retirement, some less talented NBA players adopted the Jordanesque tongue wag to signal great skill when sinking even a routine shot.

SEMIOTICS GOES TO THE MOVIES

More than 100 years ago, when Ferdinand de Saussure was describing a *sign* as the combination of the *signifier* and *signified,* American philosopher Charles Sanders Peirce (pronounced "purse") was independently developing his own model of how signs work. Similar to Barthes, but unlike Saussure whose concern was with spoken and written words, Peirce included nonverbal signs in his semiotic theorizing right from the start. He classified signs by type based on their relationship to what they represent.

Symbolic signs bear no resemblance to the objects to which they refer. The association is arbitrary and must be learned within the culture as a matter of convention. Examples: almost all words; mathematical symbols; the meaning of a red light on a traffic signal; a yellow ribbon.

Iconic signs have a perceived resemblance with the objects they portray. They look, sound, taste, smell, or feel similar to their referents. Examples: cartoon art; metaphors; onomatopoeic words like *slush* or *ring;* shadows; a wrestler's ignoble body.

Indexical signs are directly connected with their referents spatially, temporally, or by cause and effect. Like an index finger, they point to the object, action, or idea to which they refer. Examples: smoke as a sign of fire; fever as a sign of illness; a wind sock as a sign of the direction and speed of the wind; a wrinkled brow as a sign of confusion.

Cinesemiotics, a branch of semiotics that informs filmmaking, draws upon Peirce's distinctions among signs.[13] Symbolic signs are usually quite obvious—religious films that use the sign of the cross; courtroom dramas that show the scales of justice; adventure thrillers that quickly train audiences to associate a particular musical score with impending disaster. (Zombie movies, anyone?)

Directors known for realism draw upon signs that index, but film them sparingly. They foreground natural scenes and actions rather than scripted images. Their aim is for the film to reveal the world as it is rather than for what it signifies. They believe that indexical connections should be captured rather than created or contrived. That way, the movie evokes reality instead of an imaginary world. The classic film *Bicycle Thieves* exemplifies the use of indexical signs.

Expressionistic directors use iconic signs to create a fantasy world of their own choosing. When artfully done, the choices they make present an interpretation of life that's difficult for viewers to resist. The film *Avatar* did this well. Not many viewers left the theater convinced that the need for minerals justified displacing or dispatching human beings.

CRITIQUE: DO MYTHIC SIGNS ALWAYS REAFFIRM THE STATUS QUO?

Roland Barthes' semiotics fulfills five of the criteria of a good interpretive theory (see Chapter 3) exceedingly well. His *qualitative analyses* of middle-class *values* and practices are *fascinating and well-written*. As readers of his essays, we chuckle with *new understanding* at how consumers of mediated images are taken in, and only belatedly realize that Barthes was describing us. More than most interpretive scholars, Barthes intended that this new realization would inoculate us against being sucked into thinking that life should not, and could not, be altered. He wanted to *change the world.*

When it comes to the good-theory standard of a *community of agreement,* however, Barthes' theory draws mixed reviews. With the exception of Aristotle, the four-volume *International Encyclopedia of Communication* refers to Barthes more than any other theorist in this book.[14] Barthes spoke and wrote for wide audiences, so he can't be accused of presenting his ideas only to true believers. Yet the majority of communication scholars in the United States ignore the field of semiotics and the work of its central theorists, including Barthes, Peirce, and Eco.[15]

For those who do interact with Barthes' theory, the crucial question is whether connotative systems are always ideological, and if they inevitably uphold the values of the dominant class. Many who study the theory are dubious. For them, Barthes' monolithic Marxist approach to mythmaking borders on being a conspiracy theory. These critics are unwilling to accept the idea that all representation is a capitalistic plot, or that familiar visual signs can't be used to promote resistance to dominant cultural values.

Perhaps there are significant semiotic systems that suggest divergent perspectives or support alternative voices. University of Pennsylvania political scientist Anne Norton expands Barthes' semiotic approach to account for other possibilities. For example, she has argued that Madonna's MTV persona signifies an autonomous, independent sexuality that inspires young girls to control—rather than be controlled by—their environment.[16] In the same vein, UCLA media scholar Douglas Kellner suggests that Madonna's provocative outfits and unabashed eroticism may seem at first glance to reinforce traditionally patriarchal views of women, but her onstage character refigures her body as "the means to her wealth" and recasts her sexuality as "a form of feminine power."[17]

Consider Lauren's faithful application of Barthes' theory to her own self-presentation. Does the semiotic shift she describes below reinforce the dominant values of our society?

My senior year in high school, I thought classmates with a lanyard hanging out of their pocket were very cool. In this denotative sign system, the signifier was the lanyard itself. To me, it signified that the guy or gal had a set of car keys and rich parents. Or perhaps the lanyard advertised acceptance at a great college or deep attachment to a successful sports team. Any of these things meant the person was popular.

Here at Wheaton I've decided to sport a lanyard from Honey Rock, where I counseled last summer. For me the signifier of the secondary connotative sign system is the cool lanyard of status, which was the sign of the denotative system. The signified is higher self-esteem and popularity. I realize that in this connotative system the sign has lost its history. I don't have a car or a record of great achievement, so I just attach the lanyard to my wallet. But I feel the epitome of cool when I see my shadow with the prestigious loop swinging as I walk from my apartment to campus.

Whether or not we accept Barthes' claim that all connotative signs reinforce dominant values, his semiotic approach to imagery remains a core theoretical perspective for a wide variety of communication scholars, particularly those who emphasize media and culture. For example, cultural studies guru Stuart Hall built directly on Barthes' analysis of myth to establish his critique of the "hegemonic" effects of mass communication.[18] Hall's innovative analysis, though, deserves a chapter all its own.

QUESTIONS TO SHARPEN YOUR FOCUS

1. What are the *signifier* and *signified* of an engagement ring? Can you think of a way that this sign has already been *stripped of history?*

2. Why did Barthes think it was crucial to *unmask* or *deconstruct* the original *denotation* of a sign?

3. Identify two or more distinct *nonverbal signifiers* from different reality TV shows that have basically the same *signified*—"You're out of here."

4. "It's not over 'til the fat lady sings": what are the *denotative signifier, signified,* and *sign* to which this statement originally referred? When spoken about a baseball game, what *connotative shift* has altered the meaning of the original sign?

A SECOND LOOK

Recommended resource: Roland Barthes, *Mythologies,* Annette Lavers (trans.), Hill and Wang, New York, 1972, especially "The World of Wrestling" and "Myth Today," pp. 15–25, 109–159.

Barthes' structuralism: Annette Lavers, *Roland Barthes: Structuralism and After,* Harvard University, Cambridge, MA, 1982.

Essays on semiotics: Roland Barthes, *The Semiotic Challenge,* Richard Howard (trans.), Hill and Wang, New York, 1988.

Saussure on signs: Ferdinand de Saussure, *A Course in General Linguistics,* McGraw-Hill, New York, 1966.

Introduction to semiotics: Daniel Chandler, *Semiotics: The Basics,* 3rd ed., Routledge, London, 2007.

Intermediate semiotics: Kyong Kim, *Caged in Our Own Signs: A Book About Semiotics,* Ablex, Norwood, NJ, 1996.

Applied semiotics: Wendy Leeds-Hurwitz, *Semiotics and Communication: Signs, Codes, Cultures,* Lawrence Erlbaum, Hillsdale, NJ, 1993.

Yellow ribbon in a connotative semiotic system: Donald Fry and Virginia Fry, "Continuing the Conversation Regarding Myth and Culture: An Alternative Reading of Barthes," *American Journal of Semiotics,* Vol. 6, No. 2/3, 1989, pp. 183–197.

Barthes' critique of his own theory: Roland Barthes, "Inaugural Lecture, College de France," in *A Barthes Reader,* Susan Sontag (ed.), Hill and Wang, New York, 1982, pp. 457–478.

Barthes' semiotics is a theory about connotation. To access
a theory on linguistic denotation, click on General Semantics in
Archive under Theory Resources at
www.afirstlook.com.

Cultural Studies

of Stuart Hall

Stuart Hall was a Jamaican-born emeritus professor of sociology at the Open University in the UK who died in 2014. In previous pages you read about the ideas of the Frankfurt School sociologists, Stanley Deetz, and Roland Barthes (see Chapters 4, 21, and 26). Hall joins this group of critical scholars who attack "mainstream" communication research that is empirical, quantitative, and narrowly focused on discovering cause-and-effect relationships. In particular, Hall doubted social scientists' ability to find useful answers to important questions about media influence. He rejected the "body counts" of survey research, which are "consistently translating matters that have to do with signification, meaning, language, and symbolization into crude behavioral indicators."[1] He was not a fan of the three theories in the Media Effects section ahead.

CULTURAL STUDIES VERSUS MEDIA STUDIES: AN IDEOLOGICAL DIFFERENCE

Hall believed the mass media maintain the dominance of those already in positions of power. Broadcast and print outlets serve the Warren Buffetts, Michael Bloombergs, and Bill Gateses of this world. Conversely, the media exploit the poor and powerless. Hall charged that the field of communication continues to be "stubbornly sociologically innocent." He was "deeply suspicious of and hostile to empirical work that has no ideas because that simply means that it does not know the ideas it has."[2] Noncritical researchers represent their work as pure science with no presuppositions, but every media theory by its very nature has ideological content. Hall defined *ideologies* as "the mental frameworks—the languages, the concepts, categories, imagery of thought, and the representation—which different classes and social groups deploy in order to make sense of, define, figure out and render intelligible the way society works."[3] Most of us are unaware of our ideologies and the tremendous impact they can have on our lives.

As for mainstream mass communication research in the United States, Hall believed that it serves the myth of *democratic pluralism*—the pretense that society is held together by common norms, including equal opportunity, respect for diversity, one person–one vote, individual rights, and rule of law. The usual finding that media messages have little effect celebrates the political claim that democracy works. Such research claims that the American Dream has been empirically verified, and science beckons developing countries to become "fully paid-up members of the consensus club."

Ideologies
The mental frameworks different classes and social groups deploy in order to make sense of the way society works.

Democratic pluralism
The myth that society is held together by common norms such as equal opportunity, respect for diversity, one person-one vote, individual rights, and rule of law.

Hall believed that typical research on individual voting behavior, brand loyalty, or response to dramatic violence fails to uncover the struggle for power that the media mask. He thought it was a mistake to treat communication as a separate academic discipline (a view that may or may not endear him to your instructor). Academic isolation tends to separate messages from the culture they inhabit:

> All the repetition and incantation of the sanitized term *information,* with its cleansing cybernetic properties, cannot wash away or obliterate the fundamentally dirty, semiotic, semantic, discursive character of the media in their cultural dimensions.[4]

Therefore, Hall referred to his work as *cultural studies* rather than *media studies,* and in the 1970s he directed the Center for Contemporary Cultural Studies (CCCS) at the University of Birmingham in the UK. Under Hall, the staff and graduate students at CCCS sought to articulate their perceptions of the cultural struggle between the haves and the have-nots. Hall used the term *articulate* in the dual sense of *speaking out* on oppression and *linking* that subjugation with the communication media because they provide the terrain where meaning is shaped. He said he didn't seek to be a "ventriloquist" for the masses, but he did desire to "win some space" where their voices can be heard.[5] The effort to jar people loose from their entrenched power positions often requires harsh words, because a "cozy chat among consenting scholars" won't dissolve the ideology that is the glue binding together most communication study.

Since one of Hall's stated aims was to unmask the power imbalances within society, he said the cultural studies approach is valid if it "deconstructs" the current structure of a media research establishment that fails to deal with ideology. Just as Deetz wants to give a meaningful voice to stakeholders affected by corporate decisions (see Chapter 21), Hall wanted to liberate people from an unknowing acquiescence to the dominant ideology of the culture. Obviously, *critical theory* and *cultural studies* are close relatives. However, Hall placed less emphasis on rationality and more emphasis on resistance. As far as he was concerned, the truth of cultural studies is established by its ability to raise our consciousness of the media's role in preserving the status quo.

Hall was suspicious of any cultural analysis that ignores power relationships. That's because he believed the purpose of theory and research is to empower people who live on the margins of society, people who have little say in the direction of their lives and who are scrambling to survive. He took the epitaph on Karl Marx' tombstone as a mission statement for cultural studies: "The philosophers have only *interpreted* the world in various ways; the point, however, is to *change* it."

Articulate
The process of speaking out on oppression and linking that subjugation with media representations; the work of cultural studies.

Cultural studies
A neo-Marxist critique that sets forth the position that mass media manufacture consent for dominant ideologies.

HEGEMONY: MARXISM WITHOUT GUARANTEES

Stuart Hall owed an intellectual debt to Karl Marx. Of course, for many students in the West, the word *Marxist* conjures up images of failed Communist states, repressive dictators, or North Korean intercontinental ballistic missiles (ICBMs) that can reach the United States. Marxism, however, is at root a theory of economics and power. At the risk of oversimplifying, the Marxist golden rule suggests that *he who has the gold, rules.* Because workers lack capital or the means of production, they must sell their labor to live. Therefore, in a capitalistic society, people who own the means of production gain more wealth by extracting labor from workers, who get no extra benefit from the wealth created by their work. So the rich get richer and the poor get poorer. Great wealth comes to the privileged few who did little to create it. According to Marx, as the gap between the managerial class and the working class grows ever larger, desperate workers will overthrow the owners and create a classless society.

Although Hall was strongly influenced by Marxist thought, he didn't subscribe to the hard-line brand of *economic determinism* that sees all economic, political, and social relationships as ultimately based on money. He thought that would be an oversimplification. As a Jamaican person of color who immigrated to England as a young adult, Hall found that his physical appearance was often as important as his economic class in the way people reacted to him. Nor was he convinced that the masses will inevitably revolt against those who control the means of production in a capitalistic society. Instead, he adopted a Marxism without guarantees. He realized that his theory was not pure, but he preferred to be "right but not rigorous" rather than "rigorous but wrong."[6]

Hall drew upon Italian political theorist Antonio Gramsci's concept of *hegemony* to explain why the revolution Marx predicted hasn't occurred in any industrial society.[7] On the international scene, *hegemony* usually refers to the preponderant influence or domination of one nation over another. The word is little used by Americans, perhaps because it describes how many countries see the United States. In a specific cultural context, Hall employed the term to describe the subtle sway of society's *haves* over its *have-nots*. He emphasized that media hegemony is not a conscious plot, it's not overtly coercive, and its effects are not total. The broadcast and print media present a variety of ideas, but then they tend to prop up the status quo by privileging the already-accepted interpretation of reality. The result is that the role of mass media turns out to be *production of consent* rather than a *reflection of consensus* that already exists.

Recall that Stan Deetz uses the term *consent* to describe how workers unwittingly accomplish the desires of management in the faulty attempt to fulfill their own interests. They are complicit in their own victimization (see Chapter 21). In the same way, Hall believed that the consent-making function of the mass media is to convince readers and viewers that they share the same interests as those who hold the reins of power. Because the media's hegemonic influence has been relatively successful, it has played an important role in maintaining worker unrest at the level of moaning and groaning rather than escalating into revolutionary fervor.

MAKING MEANING THROUGH DISCOURSE

In his book *Representation*, Hall stated that the primary function of discourse is to *make meaning*. Many students of communication would agree that words and other signs contain no intrinsic meaning. A catchy way of stating this reality is "Words don't mean; people mean." But Hall wanted us to push further and ask, *Where do people get their meanings?* After all, humans don't come equipped with ready-made meanings, either. Hall's answer was that we learn what signs mean through *discourse*—communication that establishes frameworks of interpretation.

To illustrate this, Hall asked his readers how they know that a red light means *stop* and a green light means *go*. The answer is that someone, many years ago, told them so. The process is the same when we consider signs such as a picture of a cigarette covered by a circle slash, the golden arches, or the word *terrorist*. But it is not enough to simply recognize that meaning is created in discourse. We must also examine the *sources* of that discourse, especially the originators or "speakers" of it.[8]

Economic determinism
The belief that human behavior and relationships are ultimately caused by differences in financial resources and the disparity in power that those gaps create.

Hegemony
The subtle sway of society's haves over its have-nots.

Discourse
Communication that establishes frameworks of interpretation.

Hall was struck by French philosopher Michel Foucault's extensive study of mental illness, sexuality, and criminality in different historical eras. Foucault concentrated on what people were saying, what people were *not* saying, and *who* got to say it. As you might suspect, he discovered that throughout history, not everyone in society had an equal voice or power. That's certainly true in America today. Undoubtedly, CNN founder Ted Turner has more discursive power than I have. But, due to the fact that I'm an author of a college textbook, I'm aware that I have more power to frame meaning than do many of the students who read it.

Discursive formation
The process by which unquestioned and seemingly natural ways of interpreting the world become ideologies.

In terms of mental illness, Foucault found that the definition of what constitutes insanity and what to do about it have changed dramatically over time.[9] People with power drew arbitrary lines between the normal and the abnormal, and these distinctions became *discursive formations* that had real, physical effects on those deemed to belong to each group.[10] Over time, these unquestioned and seemingly natural ways of interpreting the world became ideologies, which then perpetuated themselves through further discourse. The right to make meaning can literally be the power to make others crazy.

CORPORATE CONTROL OF MASS COMMUNICATION

Hall worked to move the study of communication away from the compartmentalized areas reflected in the organization of this text: relationship development, influence, media effects, and so on. He believed we should be studying the unifying *atmosphere* in which they all occur and from which they emanate—human culture. Consistent with Marxist theory, he also insisted that communication scholarship should examine power relations and social structures. For Hall, stripping the study of communication away from the cultural context in which it is found and ignoring the realities of unequal power distribution in society have weakened our field and made it less theoretically relevant.

Scholars who follow Hall's lead wish to place the academic spotlight directly on the ways media representations of culture reproduce social inequalities and keep the average person more or less powerless to do anything but operate within a corporatized, commodified world. At least within the United States, the vast majority of information we receive is produced and distributed by corporations. If your family-room television is tuned to CNN, your home is a virtual advertisement for a media conglomerate. Time Warner owns CNN, and most likely the cable company that brings the signal to your house. And if you switch channels to HBO to watch a flick produced by the largest Hollywood studio, you'll get a double dose of meanings produced and sponsored by Time Warner.

Why is that such a big deal? Hall would answer that corporate control of such influential information sources prevents many stories from being told. Consider the plight of the vast majority of the people in Africa. Except for a vague knowledge of terrorism across the continent and waves of refugees fleeing to Europe, that may be hard for you to do. For example, there's almost no reporting of decades of genocide in Sudan. It's not the subject of a television drama and it rarely makes the evening news. On the few occasions when the atrocities are mentioned, they are paired with the issue of who will control the country's oil reserves. That linkage squares with Hall's belief that news comes with a spin reflecting the interests of Western multinational corporations. A growing economy and rising stock prices are good news. A labor strike for higher wages is bad news. The ultimate issue for cultural studies is not *what* information is presented, but *whose* information it is.

"What about business—which branch is that?"
©David Sipress/The New Yorker Collection/The Cartoon Bank

CULTURAL FACTORS THAT AFFECT THE SELECTION OF NEWS

Hall saw corporate clout as only one reason broadcast and print journalism support the *status quo.* Consistent with his brand of Marxism without guarantees, he believed a number of cultural factors also influence the selection of news that furthers the interests of those who already have money and power. While Hall was articulating his theory at CCCS in Great Britain, an extensive study of national news organizations in the United States gave credence to his cultural studies approach.

Over an eight-year period, Herbert Gans of Columbia University conducted a content analysis of newscasts at CBS and NBC along with the coverage of two news magazines—*Newsweek* and *Time.* He spent additional months observing and talking with reporters and editors in the newsrooms of these organizations.[11] Gans discovered multiple values, procedures, and publishing realities that ensure their stories favor people who already have power, fame, and fortune.

Source of news.   The bulk of broadcast and print news comes from those who already have power. Government officials, corporate CEOs, trade associations, Washington think tanks, and large foundations issue frequent press releases and hold news conferences. Given the time pressure of deadlines and media management's insistence on cutting costs, a reporter is more likely to draw upon these readily available sources than go into the field to discover the plight or opinion of a "nobody." So readers and viewers are much more likely to hear about failing public schools according to the Bill & Melinda Gates Foundation than they are to hear about classroom success from an inner-city schoolteacher.[12]

Individualism.   Americans value individual effort. Part of the American myth is the "rugged individual" who is a "self-made" man or woman. News stories are usually framed around a single person. *Time* magazine regularly features a single face on its weekly cover. With the exception of major criminals and their victims, almost all those covered are powerful and wealthy people who have a vested interest in the status quo. (How many people living in poverty can you name?)

Ethnocentrism.   Like reporters in other nations, US journalists value their own country over others. They don't want the United States to look bad. So despite the fact that the rate of infant mortality in America is worse than in 50 other countries, claims that Americans receive the best medical care in the world are seldom challenged.[13] The exorbitant cost of health care in the United States isn't ignored, but it's often framed as the price of getting the best care possible.

Democratic process.   Gans found that reporters are committed to democracy. They believe Americans will elect better representatives more often if reporters honor the "public's right to know" about what's happening. But journalists tend to frame every election in terms of who won and who lost rather than dwell on the complexity of the issues. So the immigration debate is reduced to bumper stickers—*Build the wall* vs. *We are not afraid*—and nothing is resolved.

Objectivity.   Most journalists have a strong commitment to report the news without bias—objective reporting of facts without taking sides. The desire to be fair is reinforced by editors and lawyers who fear the flak that comes from groups who perceive media bias. This effort to be impartial often leads to "on the one hand . . . on the other" type of reporting. So journalists' attempt to be fair creates the public impression that climate scientists are split as to global warming's reality and cause. They aren't.

In 2011, Hall wrote that the way the working poor, people of color, and immigrants had been represented (or not represented) by the media in Great Britain contributed to a sharp decline in their quality of life. These negative outcomes included massive layoffs; wage freezes; pension cuts; support for the vulnerable whittled away; college students building lifelong debt; and the closing of libraries, parks, and museums. The list looks quite familiar on this side of the Atlantic as well.[14]

EXTREME MAKEOVER: THE IDEOLOGICAL WORK OF REALITY TV

Not all of the media's ideological work is accomplished through the presentation of news. Luke Winslow, a professor of communication at San Diego State University, claims that the representation of ordinary people on reality TV "offers its viewer more explicit 'guidelines for living' than other television genres."[15] Specifically, he analyzed *Extreme Makeover: Home Edition* to show how it reinforces the myth of the American Dream.

For a decade, the show featured the fairy-tale story of a down-and-out family living in a decrepit house and then having it transformed into a dream home in seven days, at no cost to them.[16] But as Winslow notes, the weekly feel-good program didn't "become ABC's top-rated series and the winner of back-to-back Emmy awards because it is concerned with concrete and drywall."[17] The real focus is on a deserving family that has suffered misfortune and on their restoration to a perfect life.

Although the show spotlights a different family each week, they have much in common. The producers intentionally sought out all-American families whose moral character, love for each other, and demonstrated care for others make it clear that they are worthy recipients. In the first segment of the show we meet the family and hear their story. Through his questions and comments, host Ty Pennington assures his team that these are good folks who play by the rules. In the second segment we learn that, through no fault of their own, the family has fallen on hard times made much worse by the dump they live in. Whether victims of heinous crime, survivors of a natural disaster, or those who suffer from medical problems that insurance companies refuse to cover, they've all hit rock bottom. The combination of their moral goodness and tragic circumstances convinces Ty and his viewers that these are *deserving people*—truly worthy of being chosen to get an extreme makeover or a brand new home.

The rest of the show chronicles the ingenuity and commitment of the designers, contractors, and volunteers as they frantically race against time. We learn to appreciate ABC and other major corporations that donate materials and services to make this extreme makeover possible. Meanwhile, the family has been sent away for an all-expenses-paid week of vacation. At the end of the show they are brought back in a stretch limousine to see their new home, but their view is intentionally blocked by a bus. Then Ty and the whole crew yell to the driver, "Move that bus!" When they can see their new home, family members are blown away by the total transformation. Amid tears of joy they tell Ty that it's unbelievable, miraculous, an answer to prayer. As for television viewers, their belief that good things happen to good people is reinforced and reaffirmed. All's right with the world.[18]

Perhaps you've already anticipated Winslow's cultural critique of the show. He believes the real work done in *Extreme Makeover* is on the audience rather than the house. Each episode is a mini morality play that suggests wealth goes only to those who deserve it. These good people deserved a decent house and they got it. The system works. Winslow cites Stuart Hall when he summarizes the message that's enacted every week:

> The result is a reduced and simplified ideology regarding the connection between morality and economics: who should be poor and who should not, and, more importantly, frameworks of thinking about how the social world works, what the viewers' place is in it, and what they ought to do. We not only learn who deserves to be rich, and who deserves to be poor, but also how each should be treated.[19]

Winslow's critique is typical of scholarship done under the banner of Hall's cultural studies. As he explains, "Ultimately, a primary goal of ideological scholarship is to bring comfort to the afflicted and [to] afflict the comfortable by questioning taken-for-granted assumptions, giving voice to the voiceless, and bringing in those on the margins of society."[20]

Although many intellectuals dismiss the study of popular culture as frivolous, Hall sees it as a key site where the struggle for power between the haves and the have-nots takes place. "That's why 'popular culture' matters," he writes. "Otherwise, to tell you the truth, I don't give a damn about it."[21]

I'm sure Hall would have appreciated the resistance of an Australian street artist who ironically calls himself "Meek." Using the little-known medium of stencil art, he painted the typical image of a homeless beggar on the wall of the Melbourne train station where thousands of commuters would see it. The man holds a large sign that proclaims: **Keep your coins, I WANT CHANGE.** People who passed by smiled at the unexpected wordplay on the beggar's sign, but many also thought about his disdain for a handout and call for profound change in society. An inscribed imprint of Meek's "Begging for Change" now hangs in the National Gallery of Australia.[22]

AN OBSTINATE AUDIENCE

The fact that the media present a preferred interpretation of human events is no reason to assume that the audience will correctly "take in" the offered ideology. Hall held out the possibility that the powerless may be obstinate, resist the dominant ideology, and translate the message in a way that's more congenial to their own interests. He outlined three decoding options:

1. *Operating inside the dominant code.* The media produce the message; the masses consume it. The *audience reading* coincides with the *preferred reading.*

2. *Applying a negotiable code.* The audience assimilates the leading ideology in general but opposes its application in specific cases.

3. *Substituting an oppositional code.* The audience sees through the establishment bias in the media presentation and mounts an organized effort to demythologize the news.

With all the channels of mass communication in the unwitting service of the dominant ideology, Hall had trouble believing that the powerless can change the system. He called this his "pessimism of the intellect."[23] Yet he was determined to do everything he could to expose and alter the media's structuring of reality. He referred to this as his "optimism of the will." Hall had genuine respect for the ability of people to resist the dominant code. He didn't regard the masses as cultural dupes who are easily manipulated by those who control the media, but he was unable to predict when and where resistance will spring up.

Of all the programs on American television, the satires of Jon Stewart on *The Daily Show* and Stephen Colbert on *The Late Show* seem to offer the most effective challenge to the dominant political ideology. Each program mocks the pretentious statements of people in power and ridicules the positions of television commentators. Stewart's and Colbert's humor are highly popular, so network heads and advertisers haven't had the option of censoring their shows. And surprisingly, not only was *The Daily Show* rated "the most trusted source for political news on television," but viewers who only watched Stewart proved to be better informed on domestic and international affairs than viewers who only got their news from Fox News, CNN, or MSNBC.[24]

Despite Stewart's and Colbert's withering parodies of those in power, two University of Illinois professors suggest that these shows may actually support the hegemony their stars skewer with their wit. James Anderson and Amie Kincaid (University of Illinois) point out the paradox of satire used by Stewart and Colbert.[25] In order to lampoon an idea or practice, the satirists have to make sure the audience knows what they're knocking. Their very exposure and reiteration of the dominant ideology may make it more acceptable. And some in the audience may miss the satire and think Stewart and Colbert are advocating the position they voice. At the very least, talking about an idea or practice increases the chance that viewers will recall it in the future.

Anderson and Kincaid also point out that after getting their laughs, both comedians fail to offer a better way of thinking or acting. Without naming a viable alternative, the dominant ideology will have no rival and seem natural. All of this suggests that while hegemony is never total, effective resistance is never easy.

Hall cited one small victory by activists in the organized struggle to establish that black is beautiful. By insisting on the term *black* rather than *Negro* or *colored,* people of African heritage began to give dignity in the 1970s to what was once a racial slur. Jesse Jackson's call for an African American identity is a continuing effort to control the use of symbols. This is not a matter of "mere" semantics, as some would charge. Although there is nothing inherently positive or negative in any of these racial designations, the connotative difference is important because the effects are real. The ideological fight is a struggle to capture language. Hall saw those on the margins of society doing semantic battle on a media playing field that will never be quite level. In her cultural studies application log written a decade ago, Sharon perceived a clear winner in the linguistic struggle within the abortion debate:

> The media seems to favor those with "pro-choice" beliefs. I wish copywriters would even the debate by referring to the other side as "pro-life" rather than "anti-abortion." This would be a sign that pro-life groups are seen as reasonable, positive people. Up to this point, they haven't been able to make that label stick in the public arena. The media gives an ideological spin by the use of connotative language.

ETHICAL REFLECTION: LARRY FREY'S COMMUNICATION ACTIVISM FOR SOCIAL JUSTICE

Social justice activism is based on identification and solidarity with oppressed, marginalized, and under-resourced communities.[26] These groups include those who are treated as outsiders because of their poverty, race, creed, lifestyle, or medical condition, or simply because they are in the way of someone else's project.

Larry Frey, professor of communication at the University of Colorado, says action to address these wrongs starts with a social justice sensibility—the ethical conviction that "none of us is truly free while others of us are oppressed."[27] He notes that Stuart Hall sought to raise consciousness about how communication is often used to preserve a status quo that perpetuates social injustice. But, according to Frey, most current cultural studies scholars have turned to merely gazing with interest at cultural phenomena. They ignore any attempt to meaningfully intervene to aid those trapped in the cultural systems Hall described.[28]

In contrast, the ethical mandate of *communication activism for social justice* insists we act to change structural conditions and attempt to make the world more just. Frey notes that as communication students and scholars, we are trained and well placed to do this. Our activism might involve speaking out against corruption, human trafficking, war, or genocide. It may include organizing groups to protest racial or sexual discrimination, destruction of the environment, or inhumane treatment of prisoners. Or it could be working to persuade those in power to offer quality public education, a living wage, or opportunities for the poor.

In the 1990s, when a diagnosis of AIDS seemed like an automatic death certificate, social justice activism for Frey and Seattle University communication professor Mara Adelman meant using their communication skills at Bonaventure House, a residential home in Chicago for people with AIDS. They trained staff and residents how to understand and massage the tensions of living in a communal setting. They also offered suggestions for changes in policies and practices, and helped implement these when requested.

Adelman filmed a documentary of life at Bonaventure House, which Frey then promoted. It was shown on PBS in Chicago and is available on YouTube in three parts, under "The Pilgrim Must Embark: Living in Community." The video and subsequent book not only raised funds from around the country for Bonaventure House,[29] but it also changed perceptions of people living with AIDS and the nature of the disease—a great example of communication activism for social justice.

CRITIQUE: YOUR JUDGMENT MAY DEPEND ON YOUR IDEOLOGY

Although the label *cultural studies* describes the work of a wide range of communication and sociology scholars, Stuart Hall comes the closest to being the founder or godfather of this critical interpretive approach. The six standards presented in Chapter 3 offer a helpful framework to evaluate the theory.

Reform of society. In his early work, Marshall McLuhan was highly critical of television. But Hall accused McLuhan of being co-opted by the media establishment in his later years, characterizing McLuhan's final position as one of "lying back and letting the media roll over him; he celebrated the very things he had most bitterly attacked."[30] No one ever accused Stuart Hall of selling out to the dominant ideology of Western society. Throughout his life, he exposed what he saw as the unjust use of power by those who controlled the media in order to maintain their privileged position. Perhaps more than any other theorist covered in this book, he sought to change the world.

New understanding of people. Cultural studies involve learning what the "other" is like. As a Jamaican man of color living in a white British culture, Hall experienced and shared what the slights, put-downs, discrimination, and lack of opportunity do to a person. That knowledge informed his theory and can help us be aware of what others face.

Clarification of values. Hall was critical of scholars who didn't realize—or didn't reveal—their value commitments. He was quite open about the quasi-Marxist ideas that motivated his work. Many communication scholars, however, question the wisdom of performing scholarship under an ideological banner. Do explicit value commitments inevitably compromise the integrity of research or theorizing? Former Surgeon General C. Everett Koop lamented that pro-choice researchers always conclude that abortion does no psychological harm to the mother, whereas pro-life researchers always find that abortion leaves long-term emotional scars. Ever since Copernicus thought the unthinkable—that the earth is not the center of the universe—truth has prospered by investigating what *is*, separately from what we think it *ought* to be. Hall seemed to blur that distinction.

Qualitative research. The book *Policing the Crisis: Mugging, the State, and Law and Order* is Hall's best known qualitative research.[31] He analyzes how street mugging by black teenagers in London become police statistics of increasing crime, which in turn are the rationale for stiffer sentences in court, which are reported by the media as a crime wave, causing panic among the public who vote for "law and order" candidates. The escalating progression is strikingly similar to the intertwined events depicted 40 years later in the HBO show "The Wire."[32]

Aesthetic appeal. Students first reading a typical Stuart Hall monograph may find it daunting, both in clarity and in style. Hall uses terminology that's not in most newcomers' working vocabulary—conjuncture, overdetermination, dearticulation, etc. It's also necessary to think through what Hall is saying almost line by line. However, he's quite clear in his essay critiquing the empirical research of communication scholars, which is cited in the Second Look feature of this chapter. As for style, Cliff Christians, former director of the Institute of Communications Research at the University of Illinois, is lavish in his praise. "His essay, like the Taj Mahal, is an artistic masterpiece inviting a pilgrimage."[33]

Community of agreement.   Claire Alexander is the editor of a special edition of *Cultural Studies* exploring Stuart Hall and race. She describes a "Race Matters" conference held in honor of pragmatist philosopher Cornel West, which was attended by a who's who of black intellectuals. Following the first panel discussion, the chair invited questions and comments. The first person who came to the microphone simply introduced himself, "Stuart Hall, the Open University." The packed room exploded in applause. When Alexander later mentioned to West that she'd never seen a person get this kind of response just by saying his or her name, he explained: "The thing you have to understand, Claire, is that we all grew up reading Stuart. We wouldn't be here without him. We all stand on his shoulders."[34] That's a community of agreement.

QUESTIONS TO SHARPEN YOUR FOCUS

1. *Hegemony* is not a household word in the United States. How would you explain what the term means to your roommate? Can you think of a metaphor or an analogy that would clarify this critical concept?

2. What is the nature of Hall's complaint about *American media scholarship?*

3. Hall said that the *media encode the dominant ideology of our culture.* If you don't agree with his thesis, what *evidence* could he have mustered that would convince you he's right? What evidence would you provide to counter his argument?

4. In what way is Roland Barthes' *semiotic* perspective (see Chapter 26) similar to Hall's cultural studies? How do they differ?

A SECOND LOOK

Recommended resource: Stuart Hall, "Introduction" and "The Work of Representation," in *Representation: Cultural Representations and Signifying Practices,* Stuart Hall (ed.), Sage, London, 1997, pp. 1–64.

Intellectual biography: Helen Davis, *Understanding Stuart Hall,* Sage, Thousand Oaks, CA, 2004.

Anthology of theory and practice: Rhonda Hammer and Douglas Kellner (eds.), *Media/Cultural Studies,* Peter Lang, New York, 2009.

Hall's critique of the dominant communication paradigm: Stuart Hall, "Ideology and Communication Theory," in *Rethinking Communication Theory: Vol. 1,* Brenda Dervin, Lawrence Grossberg, Barbara O'Keefe, and Ellen Wartella (eds.), Sage, Newbury Park, CA, 1989, pp. 40–52. (See also multiple reactions following.)

Hegemony, ideology, Marxism, and postmodernism: Journal of Communication Inquiry, Vol. 10, No. 2, 1986. The entire issue addresses Stuart Hall's cultural studies.

Marxist interpretations: Samuel Becker, "Marxist Approaches to Media Studies: The British Experience," *Critical Studies in Mass Communication,* Vol. 1, 1984, pp. 66–80.

Race and ethnicity: Cultural Studies, Vol. 23, No. 4, 2009. The entire issue addresses Stuart Hall and race.

Historical perspective: Stuart Hall, "Cultural Studies and Its Theoretical Legacies," in *Cultural Studies,* Lawrence Grossberg, Cary Nelson, and Paula Treichler (eds.), Routledge, New York, 1992, pp. 277–294.

Autobiographical account of work at CCCS: Stuart Hall, "Stuart Hall Interview—2 June 2011," *Cultural Studies,* Vol. 27, 2013, pp. 757–777.

Ideology in reality TV: Luke Winslow, "Comforting the Comfortable: *Extreme Makeover Home Edition's* Ideological Conquest," *Critical Studies in Mass Communication,* Vol. 27, 2010, pp. 267–290.

Appreciative retrospective: Paul Gilroy, Lawrence Grossberg, and Angela McRobbie (eds.), *Without Guarantees: In Honour of Stuart Hall,* Verso, London, 2000.

Critique from quantitative perspective: Justin Lewis, "What Counts in Cultural Studies?" *Media, Culture & Society,* Vol. 19, 1997, pp. 83–97.

Critique from qualitative perspective: Patrick Murphy, "Media Cultural Studies' Uncomfortable Embrace of Ethnography," *Journal of Communication Inquiry,* Vol. 23, 1999, pp. 205–221.

Media Effects

In 1940, before the era of television, a team of researchers from Columbia University, headed by Paul Lazarsfeld, descended on Erie County, Ohio—an area that had reflected national voting patterns in every twentieth-century presidential election. By surveying people once a month from June to November, the interviewers sought to determine how the press and radio affected the people's choice for the upcoming presidential election.[1]

Contrary to the then-accepted *magic-bullet* model of direct media influence, the researchers found little evidence that voters were swayed by what they read or heard. Political conversions were rare. The media seemed merely to reinforce the decisions of those who had already made up their minds.

Lazarsfeld attributed the lack of media effect to *selective exposure* (see Chapter 16). Republicans avoided articles and programs that were favorable to President Franklin Roosevelt; Democrats bypassed news stories and features sympathetic to Republican Wendell Willkie. The principle of selective exposure didn't always test out in the laboratory, where people's attention was virtually guaranteed, but in a free marketplace of ideas it accounted for the limited, short-term effects of mass communication.

The Erie County results forced media analysts to recognize that friends and family affect the impact of media messages. They concluded that print and electronic media influence masses of people only through an indirect *two-step flow of communication.* The first stage is the direct transmission of information to a small group of people who stay well informed. In the second stage, those opinion leaders pass on and interpret the messages to others in face-to-face discussion.

The two-step flow theory surfaced at a time of rapid scientific advancement in the fields of medicine and agriculture. The model accurately described the diffusion of innovation among American doctors and farmers in the 1950s, but the present era of saturation television and Internet news has made alterations necessary. The first step of the *revised two-step theory* of media influence is the transmission of information to a mass audience. The second step is validation of the message by people the viewer respects.[2]

By the 1970s, empirical studies on viewer response to television had resurrected belief in a *powerful-effects* model of media influence, and the explanatory links between the two were becoming clear. The possible connection between violence on the screen and subsequent viewer aggression was of particular interest to media theorists, and remains an important research focus today.

In the 1980s and 1990s, theorists continued to study how media content affects behavior, but expanded their focus to include thoughts and feelings. Dolf Zillmann, professor emeritus at the University of Alabama, used his *excitation transfer theory* to highlight the role of physiological arousal when we react to media.[3] According to the theory, emotional reactions like fear, anger, joy, and lust all generate heightened arousal that takes a while to dissipate after media exposure. The leftover excitation can amplify any mood we feel afterward. If a man becomes angry at his wife, the arousal he experiences from watching televised aggression can fuel his anger and lead to domestic violence. But Zillmann says that arousal from an erotic bedroom scene or a protagonist's joyful triumph can cause the same effect.

Excitation transfer can account for violent acts performed immediately after TV viewing. But Stanford psychologist Albert Bandura's *social learning theory* takes the findings a step further and predicts that the use of force modeled on television today may erupt in antisocial behavior years later.[4] Although Bandura's theory can explain imitation in many contexts, most students of his work apply it specifically to the vicarious learning of aggression through television.

Social learning theory postulates three necessary stages in the causal link between television and the actual physical harm we might inflict on another some time in the future. The three-step process is attention, retention, and motivation. Video violence grabs our *attention* because it's simple, distinctive, prevalent, useful, and depicted positively. If you doubt that last quality, remember that television draws in viewers by placing attractive people in front of the camera. There are very few overweight bodies or pimply faces on TV. When the winsome star roughs up a few hoods to rescue the lovely young woman, aggression is given a positive cast.

Without any risk to ourselves, watching media violence can expand our repertoire of behavioral options far beyond what we'd discover on our own through trial-and-error learning. For example, we see a knife fighter holding a switchblade at an inclined angle of 45 degrees and that he jabs up rather than lunging down. This kind of street smarts is mentally filed away as a visual image. But Bandura says *retention* is strongest when we also encode vicarious learning into words: *Hold the pistol with both hands. Don't jerk the trigger; squeeze it. Aim six inches low to compensate for recoil.*

Without sufficient *motivation*, we may never imitate the violence we saw and remember. But years later we may be convinced that we won't go to jail for shooting a prowler lurking in our backyard, or that we might gain status by punching out a jerk who's hassling a friend. If so, what we learned earlier and stored in our memory bank is now at our disposal.

Communication scholars are playing catch-up to document the effects of the rapid changes brought by new media technology. We need to be patient before a strong consensus forms about some of the effects. A few researchers blame Facebook content for increasing feelings of depression,[5] while others find no such relationship.[6] Still others tout the social network's benefits for keeping us closely connected to friends.[7] Theorists are busy scoping out the conditions that might explain these divergent findings.

Uses and Gratifications

of Elihu Katz

Paul and Alex are college sophomores who have roomed together since freshman year. At the end of their first year, Paul notices that Alex is spending more and more time playing the latest *Call of Duty game,* one of a series of online games in which many players join together in a common mission. During their second year, the gaming gets even more intense. Paul becomes concerned that his roommate's game playing is draining time from his studies and ruining his social life.

Thinking about Alex, Paul remembers what he heard in his media class about Hsieh, the 32-year-old Taiwanese man who died of exhaustion in 2015 after playing a video game for three days straight.[1] It wasn't the first time a person expired during an extraordinary video game session. In 2005, a South Korean man died after playing a game for 50 consecutive hours. Authorities said the man had hardly eaten during his game playing and hadn't slept.[2] While Paul knows that these deaths happened in Asian countries where addiction to video games has been a greater problem than in the United States,[3] he wonders if he should try to have a serious talk with Alex about his game playing. He feels especially motivated to talk with Alex after reading about Chris Staniforth, the 20-year-old British man who died in 2011 after playing *Halo* on his Xbox. Staniforth sat for 12 hours straight while playing the game and developed a blood clot in his leg that eventually hit his heart and killed him.[4] Thinking about these examples, Paul is convinced that talking to Alex would be a good idea.

Whether or not we spend time playing video games like Alex does, we do make daily choices to consume different types of media. In the late 1950s, when communication scholar Elihu Katz began his work on uses and gratifications theory (commonly referred to as *uses & grats*), no one was playing video games on campus. But newspapers, magazines, radio, and movies were well established, and 80 percent of American households had a TV. There were plenty of media to choose from.

Katz thought studying all of those media choices was so important that it could save the entire field of communication.[5] He made his argument about saving the field in response to another communication scholar, Bernard Berelson, who had just published an influential essay arguing that the future of communication research was bleak.[6] Berelson based his case on the study of the persuasive power of radio during the 1940 presidential campaign[7]—research described in the introduction to this section. The study showed that media didn't do anything to change people's attitudes. Berelson reasoned that if media weren't persuasive, the field of communication research would simply wither away.

Katz, who is now a professor emeritus of both sociology and communication at the Hebrew University of Jerusalem, introduced a different logic. In order to prevent the disintegration of the field, he suggested that scholars change the question used to generate their research. Instead of asking, "What do media do to people?" Katz flipped the question around to ask, "What do people do with media?"[8] In retrospect, the field of communication was hardly on its deathbed. Berelson's perspective was overly pessimistic and, by focusing only on media effects, it was overly narrow as well. Though Katz' theory didn't "save" the discipline, it is valuable because it encourages scholars to think about mass communication in a different way. As it turns out, uses & grats has endured for more than 50 years and still inspires cutting-edge research.

The theory attempts to make sense of the fact that people consume a dizzying array of media messages for all sorts of reasons, and that the effect of a given message is unlikely to be the same for everyone. The driving mechanism of the theory is need gratification. By understanding the particular needs of media consumers, the reasons for media consumption become clear. Particular media effects, or lack of effects, can also be clarified. For example, radio listeners in 1940 may have been so loyal to their political party that they had little need to listen to the opposing party's campaign ads. If they didn't attend to the ads, the ads couldn't have any effect. Let's look more closely at the five key assumptions that underlie uses & grats.[9]

ASSUMPTION 1: PEOPLE USE MEDIA FOR THEIR OWN PARTICULAR PURPOSES

The theory's fundamental assumption was revolutionary at the time Katz proposed it: *The study of how media affect people must take account of the fact that people deliberately use media for particular purposes.* Prior to this proposal, scholars thought audiences were passive targets waiting to be hit by a magic bullet (the media message) that would affect everyone in the same way. In uses & grats, audiences are seen as anything but passive. They decide which media they want to use and what effects they want the media to have.

For example, when Game 6 of the 2010 NHL Stanley Cup Finals was on TV, I (Glenn) wanted to watch in hopes of seeing the Chicago Blackhawks become hockey champions. I wasn't a big fan of the sport, but after talking with Em, a hockey aficionado, I got sucked into the series. When I sat down to watch I was already prepared to celebrate. My wife, Cheri, would ordinarily choose to watch *anything* but hockey. Yet she decided that the clacking of hockey sticks was exactly what she needed to prevent her from stumbling upon the depressing CNN videos of oil gushing into the Gulf of Mexico from BP's uncapped well. So we decided to watch the game together—each for very different reasons and with very different effects. For me, watching the game resulted in happiness as I basked in the Blackhawks' victory. For her, the game provided a boring, but safe, distraction from unpleasant news she wanted to avoid. According to uses & grats, audiences play a pivotal role in determining the influence of media. So when Cheri and I decided to watch that hockey game for different reasons, we each behaved in a way consistent with the theory.

Fast-forward to 2013 with the Blackhawks again trying to win the Stanley Cup in Game 6, but trailing the Boston Bruins 2 to 1 with just 76 seconds left in the game. When the Hawks scored two goals in 17 seconds to win the championship, I was once again basking in their success. But this time around, Cheri wasn't watching just to hear the clack of hockey sticks. She'd become a fan, and her excitement for the Blackhawks matched mine. This illustrates an underlying premise of uses and gratifications theory. The reasons to consume media—even the same type of media—can change over time.

In the history of media theory, uses & grats is known for its deliberate shift away from the notion that powerful media messages have the same effect on everyone in the audience. This *uniform-effects model* of media evokes the image of a parent who force-feeds the kids with a prepared formula that's guaranteed to have the same effect on each child. It doesn't easily account for Paul's and Alex' different response to video games. Uses & grats rejects that image and replaces it with one of adults in a cafeteria freely choosing what to eat based on individual yearnings at particular times. You might compare Alex' obsession with playing video games to someone craving the same food for every meal.

Some of the latest research indicates that comparing a biological urge like hunger to a drive to use certain types of media isn't so far-fetched. Geneticist Robert Plomin and his research team at King's College London studied several thousand pairs of twins brought up in different homes and examined their self-reported use of video games, entertainment and educational websites, and Facebook. They discovered that genetics accounted for as much as 25 percent of the variance in media use.[10] Rarely can scientists predict human behavior with that amount of accuracy. But 75 percent of the twins' media-choice behavior was *not* due to their biological makeup. This suggests that while we may have a genetic predisposition to be attracted to a given type of media, the active media choices we make can't be completely explained by DNA. Those choices are undoubtedly influenced by a host of other factors, including the environment in which we were raised, our friends, and our past media exposure.

Uniform-effects model
The view that exposure to a media message affects everyone in the audience in the same way; often referred to as the "magic-bullet" or "hypodermic-needle" model of mass communication.

ASSUMPTION 2: PEOPLE SEEK TO GRATIFY NEEDS

Just as people eat in order to satisfy certain cravings, uses & grats assumes people have needs that they seek to gratify through media use. Note the close connection between the concepts of *media use* and *gratification from media*. The deliberate choices people make in using media are presumably based on the gratifications they seek from those media. Thus, *uses* and *gratifications* are inextricably linked. By taking this position, Katz was swimming against the tide of media theory at the time. In 1974, he wrote an essay with Jay Blumler and Michael Gurevitch, two scholars often considered co-creators of the theory. The essay states:

> In the mass communication process much initiative in linking need gratification and media choice lies with the audience member. This places a strong limitation on theorizing about any form of straight-line effect of media content on attitudes and behavior.[11]

Straight-line effect of media
A specific effect on behavior that is predicted from media content alone, with little consideration of the differences in people who consume that content.

A *straight-line effect of media* is a specific effect on behavior that is predicted from media content alone, with little consideration of the differences in people who consume that content. A theory predicting this sort of effect might forecast that *both* Cheri and I would have become excited watching the Blackhawks win the Stanley Cup in 2010. But Katz thinks the key to understanding media depends upon which need(s) a person is trying to satisfy when selecting a media message. One reason that hockey game affected Cheri and I differently is that we were watching it to satisfy different needs.

ASSUMPTION 3: MEDIA COMPETE FOR OUR ATTENTION AND TIME

One of Paul's concerns as he watches Alex spend so much time playing video games is that gaming is ruining Alex' social life. From Paul's perspective, the technology that permits Alex to interact with other gamers online is competing with opportunities to interact with peers on campus. The uses & grats approach directly acknowledges the competition. Not only do media compete with each other for your time, they compete with other activities that don't involve media exposure.

While Paul evaluates Alex' situation as unhealthy, Katz would suggest he try to understand what specific needs motivate Alex' use of video games. Why does Alex choose to spend his time gaming instead of socializing with Paul and the other guys who live in the dorm? Some of the more recent attempts to understand these sorts of choices might provide an answer. Uses & grats researchers have discovered that some people experience high levels of anxiety when they think about talking face-to-face; they don't enjoy these sorts of interactions or find them rewarding.[12] Meeting in person just doesn't gratify their needs. In contrast, extroverts express a clear preference for one-on-one conversations over spending time with media.[13]

The notion that media compete for attention and time is only an initial step in understanding the choices people eventually make. The more interesting question is *why* some people choose to watch TV while others decide to play a video game or read a book, and still others decide to have coffee with a friend. On any given day, the number of ways we can choose to spend our time is almost limitless. According to uses & grats, we won't understand the media choices we make until we first recognize the underlying needs that motivate our behavior. Paul's well-intentioned concern might cause him to overlook the needs Alex has that are gratified by playing video games. Helping Alex get a good grasp of the reasons he plays may be the key to helping him alter his behavior.

ASSUMPTION 4: MEDIA AFFECT DIFFERENT PEOPLE DIFFERENTLY

My own studies on the effects of frightening media confirm that the same media message doesn't affect everyone in the same way.[14] Assuming that Hollywood makes so many scary movies because of the popularity of the genre, journalists often ask me, "Why do people enjoy watching scary movies?" My first response to this question is always the same and echoes the fundamental point of uses & grats: Not everyone *does* enjoy scary movies. Some people systematically avoid them and can suffer for days if they become emotionally upset from what they see in a film.

As it turns out, few people voluntarily expose themselves to scary movies in order to experience fear. Fear is a negative emotion and, in general, people want to avoid it. However, some people are willing to tolerate fear in order to ooh and aah at high-tech special effects they can't see anywhere else. Others are willing to endure fear to experience a sense of mastery over something threatening—much like the effect of riding a roller coaster. Still others might actually enjoy the adrenaline rush that accompanies a scary movie and the intense relief that comes when the film is over. Current research seeks to understand the factors that lead some individuals to shun frightening entertainment and others to seek it out. Media effects scholarship lends strong support to the uses & grats claim that media affect different people differently.

ASSUMPTION 5: PEOPLE CAN ACCURATELY REPORT THEIR MEDIA USE AND MOTIVATION

If uses & grats was to have any future as a theory, researchers had to find a way to uncover the media that people consumed and the reasons they consumed it. For these purposes, the most obvious way to collect data involved asking people directly and recording their answers. There is now a long tradition in mass communication research that asks people to report the amount of time they devote to different kinds of media and why. The early research on uses & grats can take a good deal of the credit for starting that practice.[15]

The controversial aspect of this measurement strategy is whether or not people are truly capable of discerning the reasons for their media consumption. It may be easy for us to report the reason we watch a local weather forecast, but it might be more difficult to know exactly why we're so willing to kill a few hours each day playing a game like *Candy Crush Saga* on our smartphones.

If Paul were to ask Alex why he spends so much time playing video games, Alex might simply say, "Because I like it." Scholars attempting to arrive at the best scientific explanation for Alex' behavior might question that response. Is it possible, for example, that Alex is playing the games to avoid having to talk with others face-to-face? If so, would he necessarily be aware of that motivation? While some scholars have attempted to show that we can trust people's reports of the reasons for their media consumption,[16] this assumption of the theory continues to be debated. Sometimes assumptions turn out to be wrong.

A TYPOLOGY OF USES AND GRATIFICATIONS

What are the reasons people give for their media consumption? For more than 50 years, uses & grats researchers have compiled various lists of the motives people report. These studies are designed to construct a *typology* of the major reasons why people voluntarily expose themselves to different media. A typology is simply a classification scheme that attempts to sort a large number of specific instances into a more manageable set of categories.

Typology
A classification scheme that attempts to sort a large number of specific instances into a more manageable set of categories.

One of the most comprehensive typologies of media uses and gratifications was proposed by communication scholar Alan Rubin in 1981.[17] Rubin claims that his typology of eight motivations can account for most explanations people give for why they watch television. Notice that each category describes both a reason for TV *use* as well as a potential *gratification* experienced from that use.

1. **Passing time.** Consider the waiting room at the doctor's office. The primary reason for watching TV is to simply pass the time until you're called in for your appointment.
2. **Companionship.** When sports fans get together to watch the big game, some fans are there primarily for the chance to get together with friends. Watching the game is secondary.
3. **Escape.** Instead of focusing on that anxiety-causing term paper due in two weeks, a college student might just turn on the tube to escape the pressure.
4. **Enjoyment.** Many report that the main reason they watch a TV show is that they find the whole experience enjoyable. This might be the most basic motivation to consume any media.
5. **Social interaction.** TV viewing provides a basis for connecting to others. If I make sure to watch the most recent episode of a series like *Game of Thrones,*

I may find that I have more opportunities to start a conversation with someone else who saw the same show.

6. **Relaxation.** After working all day, many people report that they find it relaxing to watch TV. Today, many households have at least one bedroom with a TV. People sometimes report that watching TV relaxes them so much that they have difficulty falling asleep any other way.

7. **Information.** News junkies report that watching TV is all about keeping up with the latest information of the day. If they don't get to watch TV for several days, they report feeling uncomfortable about the information they know they've missed.

8. **Excitement.** Sometimes media consumers are after an intense sense of excitement. This could be one reason why media violence is a staple of TV entertainment. Conflict and violence generate a sense of excitement that few other dramatic devices can match.

When you look at Rubin's typology, it's easy to see that these broad categories may not be mutually exclusive. While some people gratify their need for excitement by watching violence, others, like Alex, look for a competitive online game. Still others might seek a movie with erotic content in order to provide a sense of sexual excitement. Excitement can be subdivided into sexual excitement, competitive excitement, and excitement that arises from a suspenseful story line. But if each of Rubin's eight categories were subdivided into three more, the resulting typology of 24 categories would be unwieldy and inelegant. Remember that *relative simplicity* is a valuable asset for objective theories.

Rubin claims that his typology captures *most* of the explanations people give for their media consumption. There may well be others. When Bradley Greenberg studied uses and gratifications among British children back in 1974, he discovered that many kids reported they watched TV simply because they had developed a *habit* of doing so that was difficult to break.[18] Rubin discussed habitual viewing under the "passing time" category. In a 2002 *Scientific American* cover story entitled "Television Addiction Is No Mere Metaphor," communication researchers Robert Kubey and Mihaly Csikszentmihalyi present hard evidence of TV's habit-forming nature.[19] Today, habitual texting and social media use are common among millennials. Maintaining that habit feels good. Breaking it is agony. Paul may realize that if he asks Alex to simply stop playing video games, his roommate will balk at the request. Alex may have developed a habitual behavior that is no longer volitional.

PARASOCIAL RELATIONSHIPS: USING MEDIA TO HAVE A FANTASY FRIEND

Using media to gratify a habitual urge may not be the only motivation to consider as an additional category for Rubin's typology. Years ago, actor Robert Young played the lead role in the hit TV series *Marcus Welby, M.D.* As the ideal physician who combined kindness with authority and expertise, he attracted millions of weekly viewers who were curious about how Dr. Welby would solve the next medical mystery. As the popularity of the series grew, something strange started to happen—the actor began receiving personal letters from viewers asking him for medical advice. In fact, according to one researcher who wrote a book on the "psychology of fame and celebrity," Robert Young received more than 250,000 such letters during the first five years of the program.[20]

Parasocial relationship
A sense of friendship or emotional attachment that develops between TV viewers and media personalities.

Why did so many viewers come to believe that a Hollywood actor with no medical credentials was a good source of health advice? The answer to that intriguing question is now best understood in terms of what researchers refer to as the *parasocial relationship.* According to Rubin, a parasocial relationship is basically a sense of friendship or emotional attachment that develops between TV viewers and media personalities. This relationship can be measured by asking viewers some basic questions about their involvement with popular characters. Rubin says these relationships are experienced in different ways, including ". . . seeking guidance from a media persona, seeing media personalities as friends, imagining being part of a favorite program's social world, and desiring to meet media performers."[21] While Rubin doesn't suggest that a desire for a parasocial-relationship might count as another category in his typology, it certainly seems to be a candidate.

In his review of research on uses & grats, Rubin does note several studies that utilize the existence of parasocial relationships to predict different effects of media content on viewers.[22] For example, marketing researchers compared the behavior of viewers who have parasocial relationships with the behavior of viewers who don't. When the media personalities appeared in TV or movie scenes with specific product brands, those brands were rated much more positively by viewers who were in parasocial relationships than by viewers who weren't.[23] Studies that use parasocial relationships to make predictions about media effects provide a start for responding to one of the main criticisms of the uses & grats perspective—that it focuses on description instead of prediction.

BEYOND TV: USES & GRATS IN THE AGE OF NEW MEDIA

In our post-television era, parasocial interaction is taking new forms. After the release of the blockbuster movie *Star Wars: The Force Awakens,* hundreds of thousands of fans followed the "Lonely Luke Skywalker" Twitter account. If you've seen the movie, you probably remember the last scene that shows the now aged and bearded Luke Skywalker standing alone in a place where he has been hiding in seclusion for years. Of course, the Twitter feed isn't really run by the fictional Jedi

Master. But by following the feed, *Star Wars* fans might feel a special sense of direct connection. In contrast, fans of Marcus Welby couldn't experience anything like that without getting a personal reply to a letter—something that rarely occurred.

Such parasocial interaction also makes sense of fans' reaction to the sudden death of *Glee* star Cory Monteith in 2013. Weeks after his fatal drug overdose, social media tribute pages with thousands of followers continued to percolate with activity. In fact, Monteith's Twitter followers increased by more than a half million *after* he was gone.[24] Who would start following the account of a dead person? A uses & grats theorist might suggest that following the feed expresses a deep para-social involvement with Monteith. Most fans aren't able to communicate their grief by going to the funeral and hugging family members, but they *are* able to use social media to show they care.

S. Shyam Sundar, founding director of the media effects laboratory at Penn State, believes technologies such as social media challenge the notion that people use media to satisfy needs that arise from within themselves.[25] Instead, he suggests that media technology itself can create gratification opportunities that people then seek. For example, platforms like Twitter enable easy, two-way communication between celebrities and fans, which may stimulate a newfound need for interaction. Likewise, the Internet might create a new gratification to be sought and found through browsing the web—a gratification that dating websites are happy to exploit for financial gain. Whether or not Sundar is right that gratifications may arise from technology rather than ourselves, it seems that the gratification possibilities that emerge with new media aren't quite the same as the ones formulated when TV ruled the mass media world.

CRITIQUE: HEAVY ON DESCRIPTION AND LIGHT ON PREDICTION?

In Chapter 3 you read that a good objective theory explains the past and present and predicts the future. These two criteria are called the "twin objectives of scientific knowledge." One criticism of uses & grats is that its major contribution is a *descriptive* typology of media uses and gratifications. For some, the emphasis on description rather than *explanation* and *prediction* is one of the theory's weak spots.

Jiyeon So, a communication professor at the University of Georgia, tackles the "description–prediction" critique head-on.[26] She notes that uses and gratifications theory was never intended to be merely descriptive; it was originally designed to offer specific predictions about media effects. But for whatever reason, the research on uses & grats has emphasized description. She explains that the theory can be used to predict different media effects by first understanding why people are consuming a particular media message. If other researchers follow her lead, it could set a new course for future research on the theory.

How well does uses & grats measure up against the other criteria mentioned in Chapter 3: *relative simplicity, testability, practical utility,* and *quantitative research?* There's nothing overly complex about the theory. The propositions that people use media to gratify particular needs and that those needs can be succinctly described using eight categories seem *relative simple.* On the other hand, scholars continue to question the extent to which people can accurately report the reasons for their media use.[27] If they can't, then at least one aspect of the theory's *testability* is jeopardized. Depth psychologists from Freud to present-day therapists would suggest that the average media user is probably in one of the worst positions to explain his or her choices. There may also be a logical contradiction between the habit motive for consuming media and the theory's notion that media choices are conscious and deliberate. To the extent that Alex plays video games out of a deeply ingrained habit, he may never think about why he spends his time playing. If that's the case, his failure to reflect creates a problem for testing a theory that takes such reflection for granted.

To their credit, uses & grats scholars aren't content to simply double down on the premise that media audiences are uniformly active and making conscious choices. Rubin modified uses & grats by claiming that activity is actually a variable in the theory.[28] Though some consumers exemplify the highly active audience member described in early versions of the theory, others consume media passively, out of habit, or with little conscious deliberation. Still others fall somewhere in between—or even at different points of the continuum at different times or in different situations. When Alex returns from class and unthinkingly slumps into his chair to play an online video game, he's on the passive end of the continuum. When he makes arrangements with his friends to meet online to play the game together, he's much more active.

As a student of communication theory with insider knowledge of your own communication behavior, you may be in the best position to evaluate the *practical utility* of uses & grats. What implications does the theory have for you? At the very least, you might think of uses & grats as raising your own personal consciousness about the media you consume and the reasons you consume them. By reflecting on your media use, you could come to a new realization of your needs and how you choose to gratify them. And this self-awareness can lead to more satisfying choices in the long run. If Alex realizes his game playing is based on a habitual urge that's threatening his health, he might be more inclined to take the advice of a concerned friend like Paul and seek help to curtail his habit.

Katz' notion in the 1950s that the theory of uses and gratifications could save the entire field of communication turned out to be an extreme exaggeration. Perhaps that was his way of getting scholars to pay attention to a new idea. A view that emphasizes what people do with media instead of what media do to people seemed like a strange theoretical twist. But despite the fact that Katz may have initially overplayed his hand, the theory has fared well. Uses & grats has generated a large body of *quantitative research*. It's also poised to serve as one of the main theories guiding media research well into the twenty-first century.

QUESTIONS TO SHARPEN YOUR FOCUS

1. To what extent can you give an *accurate report* of the media content you consume? Are you always aware of the reasons you choose the media you do? Why or why not?

2. Consider Facebook and other *social networking sites*. Have you heard others express reasons for using Facebook that aren't reflected in the typology proposed by Alan Rubin?

3. Do you think many people have *parasocial relationships* with media personalities? Were the people who grieved the death of the *Glee* star truly comforted by following his Twitter feed? Why or why not?

4. Think of a specific example of how two individuals might use the same *media content* to gratify different needs. How could these individuals experience very different *media effects?*

A SECOND LOOK

Recommended resource: Elihu Katz, Jay G. Blumler, and Michael Gurevitch, "Utilization of Mass Communication by the Individual," in *The Uses of Mass Communications: Current Perspectives on Gratifications Research,* Jay G. Blumler and Elihu Katz (eds.), Sage, Beverly Hills, CA, 1974, pp. 19–32.

Current update and overview: Alan M. Rubin, "Uses-And-Gratifications Perspective on Media Effects," in *Media Effects: Advances in Theory and Research,* 3rd ed., Jennings Bryant and Mary Beth Oliver (eds.), Lawrence Erlbaum, New York, 2009, pp. 165–184.

Parasocial relationships: Alan M. Rubin and Mary M. Step, "Impact of Motivation, Attraction, and Parasocial Interaction on Talk Radio Listening," *Journal of Broadcasting & Electronic Media,* Vol. 44, 2000, pp. 635–654.

Using media as a substitute for face-to-face relationships: Will Miller and Glenn Sparks, *Refrigerator Rights: Creating Connections and Restoring Relationships,* Perigree, New York, 2002.

Validity of self-reports in uses & grats research: Jack M. McLeod and Lee B. Becker, "Testing the Validity of Gratification Measures Through Political Effects Analysis," in *The Uses of Mass Communications,* pp. 137–164.

Related theory: Dolf Zillmann, "Mood Management: Using Entertainment to Full Advantage," *Communication, Social Cognition, and Affect,* Lewis Donohew, Howard E. Sypher, and E. Tory Higgins (eds.), Lawrence Erlbaum, Hillsdale, NJ, 1988, pp. 147–171.

Gender differences in media use: Silvia Knobloch-Westerwick, "Gender Differences in Selective Media Use for Mood Management and Mood Adjustment," *Journal of Broadcasting & Electronic Media,* Vol. 51, 2007, pp. 73–92.

Gratifications in Online Support: Isolde Anderson, "The Uses and Gratifications of Online Care Pages: A Study of CaringBridge," *Health Communication,* Vol. 26, 2011, pp. 546–559.

Policy implications: Harold Mendelsohn, "Some Policy Implications of the Uses and Gratifications Paradigm," in *The Uses of Mass Communications,* pp. 303–318.

Comprehensive critique: Philip Elliott, "Uses and Gratifications Research: A Critique and a Sociological Alternative," in *The Uses of Mass Communications,* pp. 249–268.

Uses & grats is a theory describing needs and interests.
For another theory of motivation, click on Hierarchy of Needs
in Archive under Theory Resources at
www.afirstlook.com.

Cultivation Theory

of George Gerbner

What are the odds that you'll be involved in some kind of violent act within the next seven days? 1 out of 10? 1 out of 100? 1 out of 1,000? 1 out of 10,000?

According to Hungarian-born George Gerbner, the answer you give may have more to do with how much TV you watch than with the actual risk you face in the week to come. Gerbner, who died in 2005, was dean emeritus of the Annenberg School for Communication at the University of Pennsylvania and founder of the Cultural Environment Movement. He claimed that because TV contains so much violence, people who spend the most time in front of the tube develop an exaggerated belief in a *mean and scary world.* The violence they see on the screen can cultivate a social paranoia that counters notions of trustworthy people or safe surroundings.

Like Marshall McLuhan (see Chapter 25), Gerbner regarded television as the dominant force in shaping modern society. But unlike McLuhan, who viewed the medium as the message, Gerbner was convinced that TV's power comes from the symbolic content of the real-life drama shown hour after hour, week after week. At its root, television is society's institutional storyteller, and a society's stories give "a coherent picture of what exists, what is important, what is related to what, and what is right."[1]

Until the advent of broadcast media, the two acceptable storytellers outside the home were schools and faith communities. Today, whether it's viewed on cable or streamed online, television is a key member of the household, with virtually unlimited access to every person in the family. Television dominates the environment of symbols, telling most of the stories, most of the time. Gerbner claimed that people now watch television as they might attend church, "except that most people watch television more religiously."[2]

What do they see in their daily devotions? According to Gerbner, violence is one of the major staples of the TV world. He wrote that violence "is the simplest and cheapest dramatic means to demonstrate who wins in the game of life and the rules by which the game is played."[3] Those who are immersed in the world of TV drama learn these "facts of life" better than occasional viewers do.

Most people who decry violence on television are worried that it affects receptive young viewers by encouraging aggressive *behavior.* Gerbner was more concerned that it affects viewers' *beliefs* about the world around them and the *feelings* connected to those beliefs. If viewers come to believe that the world around them is filled with crime, they're also likely to feel scared about the prospect of engaging in that crime-filled world. Gerbner thought that watching television violence might result in viewers wanting to own guard dogs, double-bolt locks, and home security systems. One study found that those who watch police reality shows are more likely to own a gun.[4] Cultivation theorists are concerned that television violence convinces viewers that it is indeed "a jungle out there."

Gerbner's general expertise in the field of communication was widely acknowledged. He served as editor of the *Journal of Communication,* and for almost two decades he spearheaded an extensive research program that monitored the level of violence on television, classified people according to how much TV they watch, and compiled measures of how viewers perceive the world around them. He was especially interested in how viewers' consumption of TV violence increased their perceptions of risk for crime, and most of his research sought to gather support for that idea.

But cultivation theory isn't limited to TV violence. Other scholars have used it to theorize about how TV affects perceptions of the health risks of smoking, the popularity of various political positions, and appropriate gender roles. The ways that TV might affect views of social reality are probably too many to count. Partly because of Gerbner's credentials and partly because of the intuitive appeal of the theory itself, his cultivation explanation of his research findings remains one of the most popular yet controversial theories of mass communication.

Gerbner introduced the theory of cultivation as part of his "cultural indicators" paradigm. As you'll recall from Fisher's *narrative paradigm* (see Chapter 24), a paradigm is a conceptual framework that calls for people to view events through a common interpretive lens. You might think of Gerbner's framework as a three-pronged plug leading to a TV set, with each of the prongs uniquely equipped to tell us something different about the world of TV.[5] Each of the three prongs is associated with a particular type of analysis that Gerbner considers a critical component in understanding the effects of television on its viewers.

INSTITUTIONAL PROCESS ANALYSIS—THE FIRST PRONG

Institutional process analysis
Scholarship that penetrates behind the scenes of media organizations in an effort to understand what policies or practices might be lurking there.

The first prong of the plug represents scholars' concern for the reasons why media companies produce the messages they do. Gerbner labeled the research addressing this concern *institutional process analysis.* Scholars who do this type of research penetrate behind the scenes of media organizations in an effort to understand what policies or practices might be lurking there. For example, Gerbner believed that one reason there is so much violence on TV is that Hollywood is mainly concerned with how to export its product globally for maximum profit at minimum cost. Since violence speaks in a language that is universally understood, studios adopt policies that call for their shows to include lots of violent content.

It would be difficult for a scholar to discover institutional policy without conducting in-depth interviews with media producers, accountants, and studio executives. When scholars conduct these sorts of interviews, they are engaging in institutional process analysis. Gerbner was fond of promoting his own views about the inner workings of Hollywood. However, it isn't always clear whether those views were based on systematic scholarship. Cultivation theory is far better known for the concerns represented by the second and third prongs of the plug.

MESSAGE SYSTEM ANALYSIS—THE SECOND PRONG

If TV cultivates perceptions of social reality among viewers, it becomes essential to know exactly what messages TV transmits. The only way to know for sure is to undertake careful, systematic study of TV content—*message system analysis*. For Gerbner, that involved employing the method of quantitative *content analysis*, which resulted in numerical reports of exactly what the world of television contained.

While Gerbner designed most of his content analyses to reveal how much violence was on TV and how that violence was depicted, this method can be used to focus on any type of TV content. For example, scholars who thought that TV cultivated perceptions about smoking behavior and appropriate gender roles used content analysis to document the prevalence of smoking and the different roles played by males and females in prime time. Other researchers have examined depictions of marriage and work, attitudes about science, portrayals of the paranormal, treatment of various political views, and ways environmental issues are handled.[6] Before one can examine how certain messages might affect perceptions of social reality, however, it's important to know exactly what those messages contain.

Message system analysis
Scholarship that involves careful, systematic study of TV content, usually employing content analysis as a research method.

An Index of Violence

As the opening paragraphs of the chapter reveal, Gerbner devoted most of his research to studying the cultivating impact of media violence. His content analysis was designed to uncover exactly how violence was depicted on TV. Of course, that required Gerbner to clearly specify what he meant by violence. He defined *dramatic violence* as "the overt expression of physical force (with or without a weapon, against self or others) compelling action against one's will on pain of being hurt and/or killed or threatened to be so victimized as part of the plot."[7]

The definition rules out verbal abuse, idle threats, and pie-in-the-face slapstick. But it includes the physical abuse presented in a cartoon format. Whether it's the roadrunner-chasing coyote flattened by a steamroller in an old *Looney Tunes* short, or *Pokémon's* Pikachu sending Team Rocket blasting off again, Gerbner would label the scene violent. He also counted auto crashes and natural disasters. From an artistic point of view, these events are no accident. The screenwriter inserted the trauma for dramatic effect. Characters die or are maimed just as effectively as if they'd taken a bullet to the chest.

Dramatic violence
The overt expression or serious threat of physical force as part of the plot.

For more than two decades, Gerbner's team of researchers randomly selected a week during the fall season and videotaped every prime-time (8 to 11 p.m.) network show. They also recorded programming for children on Saturday and Sunday (8 a.m. to 2 p.m.). After counting the incidents that fit their description, they gauged the overall level of violence with a formula that included the ratio of programs that scripted violence, the rate of violence in those programs, and the percentage of characters involved in physical harm and killing. One indisputable fact to emerge from Gerbner's analysis is that the cumulative portrayal of violence varies little from year to year. The annual index is both remarkably stable and alarmingly high.

Equal Violence, Unequal Risk

More than half of prime-time programs contain actual bodily harm or threatened violence. *The Big Bang Theory* and *Modern Family* are not typical. Dramas that include violence average five traumatic incidents per viewing hour. Almost all the weekend children's shows major in mayhem. They average 20 cases an hour. By the time the typical TV viewer graduates from high school, he or she has observed 13,000 violent deaths.

On any given week, two-thirds of the major characters are caught up in some kind of violence. Heroes are just as involved as villains, yet there is great inequality as to the age, race, and gender of those on the receiving end of physical force. Old people and children are harmed at a much greater rate than are young or middle-aged adults. In the pecking order of "victimage," African Americans and Hispanics are killed or beaten more than their Caucasian counterparts. Gerbner noted that it's risky to be nonwhite. It's also dangerous to be female. The opening lady-in-distress scene is a favorite dramatic device to galvanize the hero into action. And finally, blue-collar workers "get it in the neck" more often than do white-collar executives.

The symbolic vulnerability of minority-group members is striking, given their gross underrepresentation in TV drama. Gerbner's analysis of the world of television recorded that 50 percent of the characters are white, middle-class males, and women are outnumbered by men 3 to 1. Although one-third of our society is made up of children and teenagers, they appear as only 10 percent of the characters on prime-time shows. Two-thirds of the United States labor force have blue-collar or service jobs, yet that group constitutes a mere 10 percent of the players on television. African Americans and Hispanics are only occasional figures, but seniors are by far the most excluded minority group. Less than 3 percent of all dramatic roles are filled by actors over the age of 65. If insurance companies kept actuarial tables on the life expectancy of television characters, they'd discover that the chance of a poor, black grandma's avoiding harm for the entire hour is almost nil.

In sum, Gerbner's content analyses reveal that people on the margins of American society are put in symbolic double jeopardy. Their existence is understated, but at the same time their vulnerability to violence is overplayed. When written into the script, they are often made visible in order to be victims. Not surprisingly, these are the very people who exhibit the most fear of violence when they turn off the TV.

CULTIVATION ANALYSIS—THE THIRD PRONG

Most devotees of cultivation theory subscribe to the notion that *message system analysis* is a prerequisite to the third prong of the plug: *cultivation analysis*. It's important to recognize the difference between the two. Message system analysis deals with the content of TV; cultivation analysis deals with how TV's content might affect viewers—particularly the viewers who spend lots of time glued to the tube.

It might be helpful to think of cultivation analysis as the prong that carries the most electrical current in the theory. This is the part of the paradigm where most of the action takes place. Gerbner's research associates, Michael Morgan, James Shanahan, and Nancy Signorielli, offer a clear definition of *cultivation:*

Cultivation analysis
Research designed to find support for the notion that those who spend more time watching TV are more likely to see the "real world" through TV's lens.

The concept of "cultivation" thus refers to the independent contribution television viewing makes to audience members' conceptions of social reality. Television viewing cultivates ways of seeing the world—those who spend more time "living" in the world of television are more likely to see the "real world" in terms of the images, values, portrayals and ideologies that emerge through the lens of television.[8]

After watching an episode of *Law & Order: Special Victims Unit,* Em's student Jeremy found the idea of cultivation perfectly plausible when it comes to watching media violence and developing a fear of real-world crime. His description of the episode and his conclusion about cultivation are worth noting:

> In the episode, a child found the dead bodies of both his nanny and his mom. His nanny was killed by someone she met online and his mom was killed by his dad a few days later because she was having an affair and wanted to leave him. At the end of the episode, a detective and the wife of another detective were in a car accident. Of the nine central characters in the episode, three were victims of violent crime and two were perpetrators of violent crime. Two of the four remaining characters were involved in the car crash, so only two people made it out of the episode unscathed. I can see how heavy viewers of such shows would get the idea that the world is mean and scary.

CULTIVATION WORKS LIKE A MAGNETIC OR GRAVITATIONAL FIELD

If Gerbner is right that heavy TV watching influences viewers' beliefs about the world, how can we understand exactly how this happens? It's tempting to think of cultivation as a linear *push* process, where TV content influences viewers much like the cue ball on a billiard table pushes the other balls to new locations upon impact. But cultivation researchers aren't fond of that metaphor. Michael Morgan and his co-authors point out that the cultivation process is much more like the *pull* of a gravitational field.[9]

As a researcher who majors in media effects and has published research on media cultivation,[10] I (Glenn) like to extend the metaphor of gravity to magnetism. Imagine a table of billiard balls that are made of metal, with the cue ball (representing TV) possessing powerful magnetic properties. Regardless of where the other balls (representing individual viewers) are positioned on the table, they will be affected by the magnetic pull of the cue ball and tend to move closer to it. Depending on the initial position of the balls on the table, they won't all move toward the magnetic cue ball at the same angle and at the same speed—but they will all be susceptible to the pull of the magnet to some degree. In the same way, although the magnitude of TV's influence is not the same for every viewer, all are affected by it.

While metaphors like the magnetic cue ball can shed light on a theoretical process like cultivation, some scholars see them as limited in terms of explaining what's really going on. L. J. Shrum, a professor of marketing at HEC Paris, offers insight into the "black box" of the mind so we can better understand how watching TV affects judgments of the world around us. He relies on the *accessibility principle* in explaining TV's cultivating impact.[11] This principle states that when people make judgments about the world around them, they rely on the smallest bits of information that come to mind most quickly—the information that is most accessible.

Accessibility principle
When people make judgments about the world around them, they rely on the smallest bits of information that come to mind most quickly.

For those who consume lots of TV, the most accessible information for making judgments is more likely to come from TV shows than anywhere else. Heavy TV viewing keeps messages from the screen at the top of the mind's vast bin of information. If you're a heavy TV viewer and someone asks you about your odds of being involved in a violent act, the most accessible information about crime that you will use to construct your answer could come from your steady diet of *CSI*.

Gerbner seemed content to leave scholars like Shrum with the task of explaining exactly how the cultivation process works. In the meantime, he was busy spinning out more specific propositions to test. The two main propositions that guided his thinking about cultivation were *mainstreaming* and *resonance*.

MAINSTREAMING: BLURRING, BLENDING, AND BENDING OF ATTITUDES

Mainstreaming
The blurring, blending, and bending process by which heavy TV viewers from disparate groups develop a common outlook through constant exposure to the same images and labels.

Mainstreaming is Gerbner's term to describe the process of "blurring, blending, and bending" that those with heavy viewing habits undergo. He thought that through constant exposure to the same images and labels, heavy viewers develop similar perspectives in a way that doesn't happen with radio. Radio stations segment the audience to the point where programming for left-handed truck drivers who bowl on Friday nights is a distinct possibility. But instead of *narrowcasting* their programs, TV producers *broadcast* in that they seek to "attract the largest possible audience by celebrating the moderation of the mainstream."[12] Television homogenizes its audience so that those with heavy viewing habits share the same orientations, perspectives, and meanings with each other.

Think of the metaphor of the metal billiard balls scattered on the pool table and visualize the magnetic cue ball in the center. Despite the fact that the individual metal balls are located in many different positions on the table, each one is drawn closer to the magnetic cue ball and, in the process, all of the balls become closer to each other—assuming positions on the table that are more alike than before the magnet had its effect. In a similar way, as TV mainstreams people, it pulls those who might initially be different from each other into a common perception of reality that resembles the TV world. We needn't ask how close this common perception of the way the world works is to the mainstream of culture. According to Gerbner, the "television answer" *is* the mainstream.

He illustrated the mainstreaming effect by showing how heavy TV viewers blur economic and political distinctions. TV glorifies the middle class, and those with heavy viewing habits assume that label, no matter what their income. But those with light viewing habits who have blue-collar jobs accurately describe themselves as working-class people.

In like fashion, those with heavy viewing habits label themselves political *moderates.* Most characters in TV dramas frown on political extremism—right or left. This nonextremist ethic is apparently picked up by the constant viewer. It's only from the ranks of sporadic TV users that Gerbner found people who actually label themselves *liberal* or *conservative.*

Social scientists have come to expect political differences between rich and poor, blacks and whites, Catholics and Protestants, city dwellers and farmers. Those distinctions still emerge when sporadic television viewers respond to a survey. But Gerbner reported that traditional differences diminish among those with heavy viewing habits. It's as if the light from the TV washes out any sharp features that would set them apart.

Even though those with heavy viewing habits call themselves moderates, Gerbner and his associates studying cultural indicators noted that their positions on social issues are decidedly conservative. Heavy viewers consistently voice opinions in favor of lower taxes, more police protection, and stronger national defense. They are against big government, abortion, immigration, open-housing legislation, and affirmative action. The *mainstream* is not *middle of the road.* The magnetic cue ball isn't sitting in the middle of the table—it's distinctly skewed to the right.[13]

RESONANCE: THE TV WORLD LOOKS LIKE MY WORLD, SO IT MUST BE TRUE

To understand the resonance process, consider again the billiard metaphor. The balls closest to the magnetic cue ball are like TV viewers whose real-world environment is very much like the world of TV. They might be viewers who live in the inner city and are accustomed to attacks, police chases, and losing friends to violent crime. The balls farthest from the cue ball are like viewers who live in a world that doesn't resemble TV at all. Which of the balls on the table are most affected by the magnetic cue ball? If you remember how magnets behave and you have a clear image of the billiard table, the answer is clear: The closest balls are the ones that will be most affected. In fact, if they are extremely close to the cue ball, they will be pulled in quickly and end up firmly attached. Although Gerbner didn't use this metaphor, I think he would have seen it as illustrative of the *resonance* process. He thought the cultivating power of TV's messages would be especially strong over viewers who perceived that the world depicted on TV was a world very much like their own. He thought of these viewers as ones who get a "double dose" of the same message.[14]

Resonance
The condition that exists when viewers' real-life environment is like the world of TV; these viewers are especially susceptible to TV's cultivating power.

For three years, Em was a volunteer advocate in a low-income housing project. Although he felt relatively safe walking through the project, police and social workers told stories of shootings and stabbings. Even peace-loving residents were no strangers to violence. Em can't recall ever entering an apartment where the TV was turned off. Gerbner would expect that the daily diet of symbolic savagery would reinforce people's experience of doorstep violence, making life even more frightening. The hesitation of most tenants to venture outside their apartments is consistent with his resonance assumption.

RESEARCH ON CULTIVATION ANALYSIS

Cultivation takes time. Gerbner viewed the process as one that unfolds gradually through the steady accumulation of TV's messages. Consequently, he shunned the experimental method many researchers used to study the effects of TV violence on aggressive behavior. According to Gerbner, these experiments couldn't possibly detect the sort of changes he sought to document. Change due to cultivation takes place over months and years; most experiments measure change that takes place over 30 or 60 minutes. That's why the strategy for performing *cultivation analysis* relies on surveys instead of experiments.

Gerbner's basic prediction was that heavy TV viewers would be more likely than light viewers to see the social world as resembling the world depicted on TV. The strategy for testing this notion was simple. Survey respondents were asked two types of questions: one type focused on reports of TV exposure so that Gerbner could distinguish between heavy and light viewers; the second focused on perceptions of social reality that he thought media might cultivate. Once measured, the responses could be correlated to find out if heavy viewers perceive the world as a scarier place than light viewers do.

Based on the data from survey questionnaires on TV viewing, most of Gerbner's work established a self-report of two hours a day as the upper limit of light viewing. He labeled *heavy viewers* as those who watch four hours or more. He also referred to the heavy viewer as the *television type,* a more benign term than *couch potato* with its allusion to either a steady diet of television and potato chips or a vegetable with many eyes. There are more heavy viewers than light viewers, but each group makes up about one-fourth of the general population. People whose viewing habits are in the two- to four-hour midrange make up the other half, but Gerbner wanted to compare people with distinctly different patterns of television exposure.

Heavy viewers
TV viewers who report that they watch at least four hours per day; television types.

THE MAJOR FINDINGS OF CULTIVATION ANALYSIS

Believing that violence is the backbone of TV drama and knowing that people differ in how much TV they watch, Gerbner sought to discover the *cultivation differential*. That's his term for "the difference in the percent giving the 'television answer' within comparable groups of light and heavy viewers."[15] He referred to *cultivation differential* rather than *media effects* because the latter term implies a comparison between *before*-TV exposure and *after*-TV exposure. Gerbner believed there is no before-television condition. Television enters people's lives in infancy. His surveys have revealed some provocative findings:

Cultivation differential
The difference in the percentage giving the "television answer" within comparable groups of light and heavy TV viewers.

1. *Positive correlation between TV viewing and fear of criminal victimization.* In most of the surveys Gerbner conducted, the results reveal a small but statistically significant relationship between TV consumption and fear of becoming the victim of a crime. The question at the start of the chapter is illustrative: Those with light viewing habits predict their weekly odds of being a victim are 1 out of 100; those with heavy viewing habits fear the risk to be 1 out of 10. Actual crime statistics indicate that 1 out of 10,000 is more realistic. Though more women than men are afraid of dark streets, for both sexes the fear of victimization correlates with time spent in front of the tube. People with heavy viewing habits tend to overestimate criminal activity, believing it to be 10 times worse than it really is. In actuality, muggers on the street pose less bodily threat to pedestrians than does injury from cars.

   Because so many cultivation studies have been published, it is possible to compute an overall average effect based on the correlations from all the individual surveys. Such a study is called a *meta-analysis*. One meta-analysis calculated the average correlation over 82 different studies to be consistently small, but positive ($r = +0.09$)—indicating that as TV viewing increases, there is a tendency for fear of victimization to increase as well.[16] Since correlations can range from 0.0 to 1.0, a value of 0.09 is certainly on the small side. But in most of the studies, the correlation was large enough to conclude that the relationship

Meta-analysis
A statistical procedure that blends the results of multiple empirical and independent research studies exploring the same relationship between two variables (e.g., TV viewing and fear of violence).

was not just a chance finding. TV viewing is definitely related to fear of criminal victimization.

2. *Perceived activity of police.* People with heavy viewing habits believe that 5 percent of society is involved in law enforcement. Their video world is populated with police officers, judges, and government agents. People with light viewing habits estimate a more realistic 1 percent. Gerbner's television type assumes that cops draw their guns almost every day, which isn't true.

3. *General mistrust of people.* Those with heavy viewing habits are suspicious of other people's motives. They subscribe to statements that warn people to expect the worst:

"Most people are just looking out for themselves."

"In dealing with others, you can't be too careful."

"Do unto others before they do unto you."

Mean world syndrome
The cynical mindset of general mistrust of others that's subscribed to by heavy TV viewers.

Gerbner called this cynical mindset the *mean world syndrome.* The evidence suggests that the minds of heavy TV viewers are fertile ground for sowing thoughts of danger.

CRITIQUE: HOW STRONG IS THE EVIDENCE IN FAVOR OF THE THEORY?

For most readers of cultivation theory, it makes sense that the dramatic content of television creates a fearful climate. How could the habitual viewer watch so much violence without it having a lasting effect? Yet over the last several decades, communication journals have been filled with the sometimes bitter charges and countercharges of critics and supporters.[17] Opponents have challenged Gerbner's definition of violence, the programs he selected for content analysis, his decision to lump together all types of dramatic programs (action, soap operas, sitcoms, and so on), his assumption that there is always a consistent television answer, his non-random methods of selecting respondents, his simple hours-per-day standard of categorizing viewers as *light* or *heavy,* his multiple-choice technique of measuring their perceived risk of being mugged, his statistical method of analyzing the data, and his interpretation of correlational results.

Perhaps the most daunting issue to haunt cultivation research is how to clearly establish the causal claim that heavy TV viewing leads a person to perceive the world as mean and scary. Because cultivation researchers shun the experimental method in favor of the survey, they are stuck with a method that is incapable of establishing clear evidence of causality. Critics are quick to point out that the correlation between TV viewing and fear of criminal victimization can be interpreted plausibly in more than one way. The correlation could indicate, as Gerbner contended, that TV viewing cultivates or causes fear of crime. But it could make just as much sense to interpret the relationship the other way—fear of crime causes people to watch more TV. After all, most TV shows depict a just world in which the bad guys get caught in the end. Perhaps those most afraid of crime are the ones most motivated to tune in to TV to become assured that justice will ultimately triumph.

With correlational data, the only way to distinguish what causes what is to collect data from the same people on more than one occasion over a longer period of time. *Longitudinal studies* like these can help determine which of the two variables comes before the other. Unfortunately, longitudinal research typically takes many months or years to complete. Scholars who are under pressure to publish for tenure and promotion are not usually attracted to projects that require them to wait around that long to collect data. As a result, cultivation studies of this type are virtually nonexistent. This state of affairs causes some critics to give cultivation theory low marks on the criterion of *testability* that you read about in Chapter 3.

Another possibility is that the relationship between TV viewing and fear of crime is like the relationship between a runny nose and a sore throat. Neither one causes the other—they are both caused by something else. Some critics suggest that, just as the cold virus is a common cause of runny noses *and* sore throats, the neighborhoods people live in could be the common cause of TV viewing *and* fear of crime.[18] People who live in high-crime areas may fear crime for good reason. They also tend to stay inside to avoid victimization. While indoors, they pass the time by watching TV. In contrast, people who live in low-crime areas don't fear crime as much, so they tend to go outside more frequently, which leads to less TV consumption. If researchers ignore where people live—and most cultivation researchers do—they might miss the role played by this variable or others that weren't included in their questionnaires.

Scholars have another reservation about the evidence: Cultivation effects tend to be statistically small. Imagine an entire pie that represents all the fear of crime that is measured in a cultivation questionnaire. The amount of the pie that researchers can attribute to watching TV might be just a single bite. On the other hand, champions of the theory point out that tiny statistical effects can be crucial. Consider the fact that just a few votes can swing a US presidential election, as in the close calls of the 1960 Kennedy-Nixon and 2000 Bush-Gore contests. Or reflect on the fact that a one-degree change in the average temperature of our planet could have catastrophic consequences.

Issues of statistical size aside, Gerbner's defenders would emphasize the *importance* of the issue at hand. Fear of violence is a paralyzing emotion. As Gerbner repeatedly pointed out, worry can make people prisoners in their own homes, change the way they vote, affect how they feel about themselves, and dramatically lower their quality of life. Even if the effect of TV viewing on these factors is relatively small, the consequences at stake make TV's message one we should be concerned about.

But what is TV's message? When Gerbner formulated his theory decades ago, there were only three major networks. The vast offerings of today's cable and streaming menus were unimaginable. Critics contend that Gerbner's original assumption that TV viewers are constantly exposed to the same images and labels is no longer true. While there may not yet be a channel for left-handed truck drivers who bowl on Friday nights, the TV environment seems to be moving in that direction. The choices between such channels as the Food Network, the Golf Channel, and C-SPAN permit a level of viewing selectivity that cultivation theory doesn't acknowledge. Netflix, Hulu, YouTube, and other streaming services only further that trend. If the theory is to continue to exert influence, many critics maintain that it will have to adapt to the new media environment.

Compared to most of the other theories in this text, cultivation theory's "critique" section is much longer. Does this mean it's a bad theory? Not necessarily. Consider the fact that cultivation theory has generated research for almost a half century. Theories that have been around for that long sustain more attacks than ones recently introduced. It's also important to keep in mind that amid all the criticism, few theories in the area of mass communication have generated as many studies. In addition to its tremendous contribution to research, the theory has cultivated at least three generations of scholars to think about media in a particular way. Most theorists would love to have even a fraction of the recognition that cultivation theory has managed to garner.

As for Gerbner, in 1996 he founded the Cultural Environment Movement, a coalition of organizations and social activists who believe it's vitally important who gets to tell the stories within a culture, and whose stories don't get told.[19] They are committed to changing the stories that American television tells and are convinced this will happen only when the public wrests control of the airwaves from media conglomerates. Gerbner underscored the movement's agenda with repeated references to a line from Scottish patriot Andrew Fletcher:

> "If a man were permitted to make all the ballads, he need not care who should make the laws of a nation."[20]

QUESTIONS TO SHARPEN YOUR FOCUS

1. Think of your favorite TV show. Using Gerbner's definition of *dramatic violence,* how much violence is in the show? Why do you think that's the case?

2. According to Gerbner, are you a heavy viewer, a light viewer, or something in between? How do your TV viewing habits influence your beliefs about crime? Politics? Health? Relationships? Anything else?

3. This chapter uses a magnetic cue ball to explain resonance and mainstreaming. Can you think of another illustration to help explain these concepts to someone unfamiliar with cultivation theory?

4. Why do you think cultivation theory has received so much criticism? Which critique of the theory do you find most troubling, and why?

A SECOND LOOK

Recommended resource: Michael Morgan, James Shanahan, and Nancy Signorielli, "Growing Up with Television," in *Media Effects: Advances in Theory & Research,* 3rd ed., Jennings Bryant and Mary Beth Oliver (eds.), Routledge, New York, 2009, pp. 34–49.

Review of the state of the theory: Michael Morgan and James Shanahan, "The State of Cultivation," *Journal of Broadcasting & Electronic Media,* Vol. 54, 2010, pp. 337–355.

Application to new media: Michael Morgan, James Shanahan, and Nancy Signorielli, "Yesterday's New Cultivation, Tomorrow," *Mass Communication and Society,* Vol. 18, 2015, pp. 674–699.

Historical primary sources: Michael Morgan (ed.), *Against the Mainstream: The Selected Works of George Gerbner,* Peter Lang, New York, 2002.

Violence index: George Gerbner, Larry Gross, Marilyn Jackson-Beeck, Suzanne Jeffries-Fox, and Nancy Signorielli, "Cultural Indicators: Violence Profile No. 9," *Journal of Communication,* Vol. 28, No. 3, 1978, pp. 176–207.

Violence update: Amir Hetsroni, "Four Decades of Violent Content on Prime-Time Network Programming: A Longitudinal Meta-Analytic Review," *Journal of Communication,* Vol. 57, No. 4, 2007, pp. 759–784.

Profile of Gerbner: Scott Stossel, "The Man Who Counts the Killings," *Atlantic,* May 1997, pp. 86–104.

Mainstreaming and resonance research: L. J. Shrum and Valerie D. Bischak, "Mainstreaming, Resonance, and Impersonal Impact: Testing Moderators of the Cultivation Effect for Estimates of Crime Risk," *Human Communication Research,* Vol. 27, 2001, pp. 187–215.

Research review and meta-analysis: Michael Morgan and James Shanahan, "Two Decades of Cultivation Research: An Appraisal and a Meta-Analysis," in *Communication Yearbook 20,* Brant Burleson (ed.), Sage, Thousand Oaks, CA, 1997, pp. 1–45.

Computer game violence: Dmitri Williams, "Virtual Cultivation: Online Worlds, Offline Perceptions," *Journal of Communication,* Vol. 56, 2006, pp. 69–87.

Political beliefs and the 2016 US presidential election: Michael Morgan and James Shanahan, "Television and the Cultivation of Authoritarianism: A Return Visit From an Unexpected Friend," *Journal of Communication,* Vol. 67, 2017, pp. 424–444.

Causality with correlational data: Constanze Rossmann and Hans-Bernd Brosius, "The Problem of Causality in Cultivation Research," *Communications,* Vol. 29, 2004, pp. 379–397.

How cultivation works: L. J. Shrum, Jaehoon Lee, James Burroughs, and Aric Rindfleisch, "An Online Process Model of Second-Order Cultivation Effects: How Television Cultivates Materialism and Its Consequences for Life Satisfaction," *Human Communication Research,* Vol. 37, No. 1, 2011, pp. 34–57.

Critique: W. James Potter, "A Critical Analysis of Cultivation Theory," *Journal of Communication,* Vol. 64, 2014, pp. 1015–1036.

To access a chapter that predicts when and how viewers will
imitate TV violence, click on Social Learning Theory
in Archive under Theory Resources at
www.afirstlook.com.

Agenda-Setting Theory

of Maxwell McCombs & Donald Shaw

Like many nations, the United States recognizes that an independent and free press is necessary for democracy. Journalism is also big business, generating more than $60 billion in revenue.[1] But for all the money, cultural status, and legal protection given to it, does news reporting actually make a difference? Does it change how the public thinks about the world? Based on a half century of research, Max McCombs (University of Texas) and Donald Shaw (University of North Carolina) have found that the answer is *yes.*

For decades, the Gallup organization has asked Americans to name the most important problem facing the country. McCombs examined responses collected across 40 years and found that this list represents the most enduring public concerns in the United States: jobs, unemployment, inflation, cost of living, government spending, welfare, foreign relations, war, law and order, health, the environment, education, racial relations, technology.[2]

But there's a problem: Most of us can't pay equal attention to more than a dozen issues. Time and mental energy are scarce resources. Amid the demands of school, work, relationships, and the daily chores of life, we have to choose which issues get some of our precious attention span. Thus, the typical person can only focus on about five issues at any one time.[3] The small set of issues that's most important to you at the moment is your *personal agenda.* Taking the average of those concerns across an entire community, state, or nation is the *public agenda*—the set of issues most salient (in other words, that capture attention) across a group of people at a given time.

Journalists have limited resources, too. Newspapers have a fixed amount of page space, and a televised newscast has a certain number of minutes. Although the Internet loosens some of these constraints, journalists still have limited time and money to research, write, and publish stories and videos. Therefore, news editors must decide what to emphasize, what to report, and what to ignore. The degree of importance that the news media assigns to issues at a given moment is the *media agenda.*

The basic hypothesis of the theory is this: *Over time, the media agenda shapes the public agenda.* Said differently, there's a cause-and-effect relationship between what the news reports and how the public thinks about the world. This powerful ability of the media to shape our perception of reality is *agenda-setting.*

Personal agenda
The list of issues most salient to a single person at a given time.

Media agenda
The list of issues emphasized by the news media at a given time.

Agenda-setting
Over time, the media agenda shapes the public agenda.

McCombs, Shaw, and others have amassed decades of evidence that documents this power of the press. They've found that agenda-setting occurs in three ways, or *levels*. At the first level, the media tell us *which issues to think about*. At the second level, the media tell us *which aspects of those issues are most important*. The third level tells us *how different issues are connected to each other*. As McCombs puts it, "The mass media are teachers whose principal strategy of communication is redundancy."[4]

LEVEL 1: THE MEDIA TELL US WHAT TO THINK ABOUT

To understand the world beyond our personal experience, we turn to the news media. At least, that was McCombs' initial hunch, which came to mind while browsing the front page of the *Los Angeles Times* in early 1967. The front page contained three stories: a local issue, a national issue, and an international issue. The local story got the most page space—a not-so-subtle cue that editors thought the story was very important.[5] McCombs wondered if, over time, the public agenda came to reflect the media agenda, such that "*we* judge as important what the *media* judge as important."[6] And so the basic agenda-setting hypothesis was born.

McCombs wasn't the only one making these observations. Starting with the Kennedy–Nixon contest in 1960, political analyst Theodore White wrote the definitive account of four US presidential elections. In opposition to then-current wisdom that mass communication had limited effects upon its audience, White came to the conclusion that the media shaped those election campaigns:

> The power of the press in America is a primordial one. It sets the agenda of public discussion; and this sweeping political power is unrestrained by any law. It determines what people will talk and think about—an authority that in other nations is reserved for tyrants, priests, parties and mandarins.[7]

Likewise, Pulitzer Prize–winning author Walter Lippmann claimed that the media act as a mediator between "the world outside and the pictures in our heads."[8] What set McCombs and Shaw apart is that they put these hunches to empirical test. During the 1968 U.S. presidential election, their groundbreaking study of undecided voters in Chapel Hill, North Carolina set the course for five subsequent decades of agenda-setting research.

McCombs and Shaw's first task was to measure the *media agenda*. They determined that Chapel Hill residents relied on a mix of nine print and broadcast sources for political news—two Raleigh papers, two Durham papers, *Time* and *Newsweek* magazines, the out-of-state edition of *The New York Times,* and the CBS and NBC evening news. They established *position* and *length* of story as the two main criteria of prominence. For example, in newspapers, the front-page headline story, a three-column story on an inside page, and the lead editorial were all counted as evidence of significant focus on an issue. Prominence in the television news format was defined by placement as one of the first three news items or any discussion that lasted more than 45 seconds. Their analysis revealed five major issues, in order of importance: foreign policy, law and order, fiscal policy, public welfare, and civil rights. This was the media agenda.

With the media agenda measured, their next task was to assess the *public agenda*. McCombs and Shaw asked undecided voters to outline what each one considered the key issue of the campaign, regardless of what the candidates might be saying. The researchers assigned the specific answers to the same broad categories discovered in their analysis of the news media. The rank of the five issues on both lists was nearly identical.[9]

But there's a problem: The initial Chapel Hill study only demonstrated that the media and public agendas are *correlated.* As critics of cultivation theory would remind us (see Chapter 29), that doesn't mean the media agenda *causes* the public agenda. For example, if newspaper and television coverage simply reflects public concerns that already exist, then the public agenda causes the media agenda—the opposite direction from the agenda-setting hypothesis. Alone, McCombs and Shaw's findings were impressive, but equivocal. A true test must be able to show that public priorities lag behind the media agenda.

It took a tightly controlled *experiment* run by Yale researchers to establish a cause-and-effect chain of influence from the media agenda to the public agenda.[10] Political scientists Shanto Iyengar, Mark Peters, and Donald Kinder spliced previously aired news footage into tapes of current network newscasts. For four days straight, three groups of citizens came together to watch the evening news and complete a questionnaire about their own concerns. Each group saw a different version—one emphasized environmental pollution, another had a daily feature on national defense, and a third discussed economic inflation. Viewers who saw the media agendas that focused on pollution and defense elevated those issues on their own lists of concerns—definite confirmation of a cause-and-effect relationship from the media agenda to the public agenda. (As it turned out, inflation was already an important topic for most participants, so there wasn't any room for that issue to move up in importance.) It was the first of many studies to offer strong evidence that the media agenda *causes* which stories are salient in the public agenda—the first level of agenda-setting.

First level of agenda-setting
The media influence which things are salient in the public agenda.

LEVEL 2: THE MEDIA TELL US WHICH ATTRIBUTES OF ISSUES ARE MOST IMPORTANT

The first level of agenda-setting demonstrates that media tell us *what* to think about, but do they also tell us *how* to think about it? For the first two decades of agenda-setting research, the accepted answer was *no.* Scholars thought the news media might emphasize a topic, such as crime or unemployment, and thus people would agree that it's an important issue, but then they'd make up their own minds what they thought about it. And so, for a long time, almost every article about the theory included this mantra: *The media aren't very successful in telling us what to think, but they are stunningly successful in telling us what to think about.*

Then the evidence challenged that claim. By emphasizing certain attributes of issues over others, the media do more than just make topics salient. They also shape how we think about those issues. The second level of agenda-setting is the transfer of salience of a *dominant set of attributes* that the media associate with an attitude object to the specific features of the image projected on the walls of our minds.[11]

Second level of agenda-setting
The media make certain attributes of a media object salient; framing.

Some scholars call this selection process *framing.* James Tankard, one of the leading writers on mass communication theory, defines a media frame as "the central organizing idea for news content that supplies a context and suggests what the issue is through the use of *selection, emphasis, exclusion,* and *elaboration.*"[12] The final four nouns in that sentence not only suggest that the media set the agenda for which issues, events, or candidates are most important, they also influence which characteristics of those things pop into our minds. They make certain attributes salient while downplaying other attributes. Such emphasis often communicates whether we should view the issue as positive or negative.

One of my (Andrew's) students, Colten, found such framing at play in the case of Blue Bell ice cream. If you've ever lived in Texas, you've heard of it. Although

"Your royal command has been obeyed, Highness. Every town crier in the land is crying: 'Old King Cole is a merry ole soul.' Before nightfall we'll have them all believing it."

Cartoon from the *Saturday Review of Literature*, 1970. ©Ed Frascino. Reprinted by permission.

the brand is sold in several other states, Texans particularly value Blue Bell as part of their culinary culture; for example, during his presidency, George W. Bush served it to world leaders after meals at his Texas ranch.[13] But in April 2015, Blue Bell ice cream was contaminated with dangerous listeriosis bacteria. Ten people became sick after eating the treat, and three of them died. It was a public relations disaster for the company, and they immediately recalled all their ice cream from store shelves.[14] Blue Bell didn't return to Texas until December. The ongoing story captured the attention of Texas journalists during those months.

Colten was interested in how second-level agenda-setting happened in these stories, so he collected all national and local media coverage he could find. National outlets framed the crisis in terms of warnings from the federal government's Centers for Disease Control and Prevention. That's obviously a negative frame for Blue Bell. In contrast, local media downplayed those official edicts. Instead, they voiced stories from fans who missed the ice cream, such as the 92-year-old man who felt that taking his potentially contaminated ice cream back to the store "was like saying goodbye to a longtime friend."[15] Colten concluded, "National media framed the story as a public health risk, while the local media rapidly transformed from a narrative of risk to one of a lost cultural icon."[16] Local media portrayed the company and its lethal dessert with a positive frame. Like Colten, I find that disturbing—after all, some people died from eating the product.

The Blue Bell story demonstrates how the media frame issues, sometimes in shocking and nonsensical ways. They frame people, too, especially political figures. In US presidential elections, the frames are often easy to spot. In the 1960s, the media continually reported on the "youthful vigor" of John F. Kennedy but made no mention of his extramarital affairs, which were well known to the White House press corps. Fast-forwarding to 2008, Americans thought the press portrayed Barack Obama more favorably than John McCain, with content analysis of the news validating that perception.[17] In 2012, Obama sought to frame challenger Mitt Romney as a "vulture capitalist" who "avoids taxes" and was "out of touch" with everyday Americans, and the news media picked up on that framing.[18] During the 2016 campaign, journalists framed both candidates in terms of scandal, focusing on Hillary Clinton's secret email server and Donald Trump's lewd remarks about women.

As you think back on those elections, you may dislike some or all of these frames. You might also wish for a world where the media doesn't frame candidates and issues at all. But it's impossible to report stories without emphasizing certain attributes over others. For better or worse, framing isn't optional. In most studies, the voters' agenda mirrors the media's agenda in substance (the first level) and in tone (the second level). For candidates, framing also predicts the outcome of elections.[19]

But object salience and attribute framing aren't the end of the story. The third level of agenda-setting claims the media also teach us how different issues are connected to each other.

LEVEL 3: THE MEDIA TELL US WHICH ISSUES GO TOGETHER

Third level of agenda-setting
The media indicate which issues are connected to each other.

During much of the 2016 election, border control was near the top of the list of the media agenda. Whether a story describes immigrants as "illegal aliens" or "undocumented workers" reveals something about framing (the second level of agenda-setting). The third level of agenda-setting considers the issues mentioned alongside coverage of immigration. Looking back at the list of enduring public issues at the beginning of this chapter, we can see how the media discuss immigration alongside them:

- **Jobs:** Immigrants do work Americans just don't want to do.
- **Government spending:** Can America really afford to build a wall along the southern border?
- **Law and order:** If they broke the law coming here, they'll keeping breaking laws while living here.
- **Education:** Children of immigrants shouldn't be denied admission to college on the basis of their citizenship status.
- **Welfare:** Immigrants come here to mooch off America's social services.
- **Racial relations:** Some people unfairly fear immigrants because of the color of their skin.
- **Foreign relations:** How would Mexico react to changes in border policy?

If a person consumes a diet of media that continually links immigration to law and order, that person might come to see those issues as intertwined. Likewise for someone who reads news stories connecting the issue to racial relations, and then connecting racial relations to education, and so on. The media communicate issues as though they are an interconnected web, with some connections stronger than others. Like framing, these kinds of connections aren't optional. By the content of the story and the placement on the web page, the media send signals about which issues go together. The third level of agenda-setting examines how the media's issue map influences the public's issue map.[20]

BEYOND OPINION: THE BEHAVIORAL EFFECT OF THE MEDIA'S AGENDA

Most of the research studies on agenda-setting have measured the effect of media agendas on public *opinion*. But in his most recent book on agenda setting,[21] McCombs presents several intriguing findings showing that media priorities also influence people's *behavior*.

In one study, Craig Trumbo, a professor of journalism and media communication at Colorado State University, monitored the headlines for stories about the flu virus in 32 different newspapers between 2002 and 2008.[22] He also had access to the regular flu reports issued by the federal government. Those reports showed the number of visits to doctors for flu-like symptoms as well as the actual number of cases of the flu. Common sense would suggest that with more actual flu cases, doctor visits would increase and journalists would be more likely to cover the story. But Trumbo found that even when he took account of the actual flu cases, there was still an agenda-setting effect. The amount of media coverage on the flu during one week predicted the number of doctor visits the next week. There was no evidence of a reverse effect. Patient visits to the doctor for flu symptoms didn't predict later media coverage about the virus. Trumbo's study provides evidence that the agenda-setting effect extends to behavior.

Two other studies also show a clear behavioral effect of the media agenda. In the first, admission applications to the University of Pennsylvania dropped significantly—particularly among women—after heavy news coverage of crime and violence on campus, including several rapes. A second study found a significant drop in the purchase of airline tickets and a corresponding increase in the purchase of flight insurance following news of plane crashes or reports of skyjackers taking control of an airplane.[23]

Savvy marketers can also use agenda-setting effects to promote their business products. In his book *The Ultimate Assist*, John Fortunato explores the long commercial partnership between network television's agenda and the National Basketball Association's.[24] Television dramatically raised the salience of the sport (the first level of agenda-setting) by scheduling games in prime-time viewing slots. It also put basketball's best attributes forward (the second level of agenda-setting) by focusing on star teams and players. From 1970 to 2000, the number of NBA teams and the number of games doubled. The number of fans going to games quadrupled. But the astronomical difference is in the money. In 1970, the NBA earned $10 million in revenue. In 2000 the payout was $2 billion, by 2012 it was $5 billion, and projections for the 2016–17 season were over $8 billion[25]—no small change. McCombs' comment: "Agenda-setting, the theory, also can be agenda-setting, the business plan."[26]

WHO SETS THE AGENDA FOR THE AGENDA-SETTERS?

Agenda-setting research has gathered strong evidence that the media agenda influences the public agenda. But what shapes the media agenda? In today's crowded media environment, that's a tough question to answer. So far, research has identified several sources journalists rely on to decide what counts as news.

- **Other respected news organizations.** When many news sources feature the same story, it's tough for an editor to ignore the trend. For decades, smaller news organizations would look up to *The New York Times* and *The Washington Post* as elite media outlets. If those big papers covered a story, they would, too. That still happens, although one recent agenda-setting study revealed that the influence of those venerable outlets has waned.[27] Sometimes, online sources may exert stronger influence on the elite papers than the other way around. In any event, when one news source influences the agenda of another, that's *intermedia agenda-setting.*[28]

- **Emerging media.** The Internet is a vast sea of blogs, tweets, discussion boards, and online newspapers. News often breaks there and then gets picked up by mainstream sources.

- **Partisan media.** America has a long tradition of political talk radio. The Internet has fueled growth in partisan news sources, such as Daily Kos, Salon, and Huffington Post for liberals, and Townhall, Newsmax, and Breitbart News for conservatives.

- **Candidates and officeholders.** Sometimes these people can single-handedly set the agenda. One of President Trump's first actions in office was to issue an executive order restricting travel to the United States from several countries with Muslim majorities. After that move, the press could talk about little else.

- **Press releases.** Public relations professionals work for government agencies, corporations, and interest groups. They draft press releases and send them to news outlets, who then repackage the information as news.[29]

- **Interest aggregations.** This term refers to clusters of people who demand center stage for their one overriding concern. Whether it's Tea Party activists decrying tax increases or Black Lives Matter groups protesting police misconduct, the media pay attention to those who grab it.

- **Gatekeepers.** Editors function as *gatekeepers* who ultimately determine what gets published. Their preferences may loom large in determining the media agenda.

During the 2016 US presidential campaign, several media outlets covered the problem of *fake news,* or "news articles that are intentionally and verifiably false, and could mislead readers."[30] Chris Vargo (University of Colorado) conducted an intermedia agenda-setting study on how much fake news influences other media agendas.[31] Using an extensive online database that tracked news stories from 2014 to 2016, he and his colleagues examined the extent to which issues emerged on fake news websites over time. He then examined whether those same issues appeared afterward in other types of media, including elite media outlets, mainstream news sources outside the elite, liberal and conservative partisan news, and fact-checking websites. If the same issue emerged in those places right after fake news "reported" it, then it seems that fake news impacted their agenda.

Vargo's results both confirmed and challenged the mainstream media's alarm about fake news during 2016. Disturbingly, fake news appeared to exert at least some influence on the agenda of more credible news organizations. The influence of the fake news agenda was weaker on mainstream media and more pronounced on partisan media (both conservative and liberal). The researchers also found that the amount of fake news had increased in volume over the years. However, this increase in volume did not necessarily lead to an increase in influence. If anything,

Intermedia agenda-setting
One news source influences the agenda of another.

Interest aggregations
Clusters of people who demand center stage for their one overriding concern; pressure groups.

Gatekeepers
Editors and other arbiters of culture who determine what will appear in the mass media.

Fake news
News articles that are intentionally and verifiably false and could mislead readers.

the power of fake news may have slightly declined over the years of the study—after the mainstream media put the problem on their agenda.

One limitation of the study is that it only tracked which issues appeared in which media over time. When mainstream or partisan news sources responded to an issue raised by fake news, they didn't necessarily pass it on as gospel truth. However, as Vargo notes, fake news could hold power even if no one believes it at all:

> Given that many journalists often pay attention to fake news, in part to address it factually . . . it stands to reason that fake news websites may possess an agenda-setting power of their own. That is, they may have the ability to affect the popularity of issues simply by introducing misinformation that journalists must address.[32]

NEED FOR ORIENTATION INFLUENCES AGENDA-SETTING EFFECTS

At this point, perhaps you're feeling like agenda-setting theory thinks of us as entirely passive, just waiting to have our beliefs and behavior blown here and there by media conglomerates. McCombs and Shaw think it's more complex than that. Even in their original Chapel Hill study, they recognized that "people are not automatons waiting to be programmed by the news media."[33] They suspected that some viewers might be more resistant to the media's priorities than others. In follow-up studies, they turned to the *uses and gratifications* approach, which suggests that viewers are selective in the kinds of TV programs they watch (see Chapter 28). The theorists sought to discover exactly what kind of person is most susceptible to the media agenda.

The key factor they've discovered is our *need for orientation*.[34] Some have also called it an *index of curiosity*. But whatever name it goes by, it represents a drive to make sense of the world around us—to orient our understanding of it. In order to do that, we turn to the media for help.

Need for orientation
A drive to understand what's going on in the world, often fueled by relevance and uncertainty.

For some people, need for orientation is an internal drive that motivates them no matter the issue. They're news junkies who consume vast quantities of any journalism they can get their hands on. Most of us are more selective about what issues get our precious time. That's why need for orientation is so important—if we don't have it, we won't turn to the media in the first place, and none of the three levels of agenda-setting will occur. The media can't shape our agenda if we never turn on the TV or visit a news website.

So what leads us to have a need for orientation about a particular issue? McCombs believes both *relevance* and *uncertainty* fire it up. I (Andrew) felt both of these in the wake of the 2017 terrorist attack at Ariana Grande's concert in Manchester, England. I found this story personally *relevant*. As my wife puts it, I have the musical tastes of a 12-year-old girl, so I like some of Grande's music. I also have daughters who are around the age of kids who attended the concert. It seemed relevant because, in some way, I felt like it touched my life.

It also produced *uncertainty* in me. Terrorist attacks seem to occur at random. Though I don't live my life in constant fear of them, I am not naive enough to think I could never be a victim. That the attack seemed to target young children upped my uncertainty—how could anyone do something so cruel to people so innocent? And so, because I felt the story was relevant and it made me feel uncertain, I paid close attention to the media coverage, just as McCombs would predict.

Likewise, Abby's application log illustrates her tendency to focus only on stories that seem personally relevant:

I confess to being an online newsreader who only clicks on links that interest me. I easily bypass information and headlines on my computer that I couldn't avoid when reading a print version of the news. This caught up with me in my class in American politics. Our assignment was to stay informed about worldwide current events by reading *The New York Times*. I chose to read the paper online—to my detriment. I found myself clicking on stories of personal interest and didn't even notice headlines on other issues. My weekly quiz grades let me know that my study agenda didn't match the media agenda.

MELDING AGENDAS INTO COMMUNITIES

McCombs and Shaw's agenda-setting theory has found an appreciative audience among mass communication researchers because it offers two attractive features: It reaffirms the power of the press while maintaining that individuals are free to choose. But how, exactly, do we choose? Approaching today's media landscape is a bit like trying to assemble a meal while at the grocery store. When you walk through the sliding door, a bewildering set of options awaits you. Do you want chicken, beef, fish, or vegetarian? Organic ingredients that cost more or regular stuff that's cheap? Will dessert be fruit or brownies? Blending your food options into a healthy diet doesn't happen automatically.

Choosing your media diet in the 21st century is also tough. More than ever before, there isn't one dominant media agenda that descends from the boardrooms of East Coast media establishments. Multiple media agendas exist and we can choose from among them. Some people ignore mainstream outlets entirely in favor of talk radio, blogs, local news, international news, Twitter feeds, and other sources. And even the biggest news junkie could never devote attention to it all.

McCombs and Shaw suggest we can make sense of the media landscape if we sort outlets into two types. One type is *vertical media*, which try to appeal to a broad, diverse audience. The theorists ask us to picture them "as if shouting from the top of an Egyptian pyramid to a vast audience below." Examples of such vertical media in the United States include the newspaper *USA Today*, *Time* and *Newsweek* magazines, and nightly news broadcasts on ABC, NBC, and CBS. In contrast, *horizontal media* "usually connect us via valued special interest and personal interest communities."[35] These include partisan talk shows, magazines devoted to particular hobbies and industries, and many sources of news on social media. On cable TV, Fox News targets conservatives, and MSNBC targets liberals. They're horizontal media.

Agenda-setting theorists believe we assemble our view of current events from these media and our own experiences. They call this *agendamelding*, or "the social process by which we meld agendas from various sources, including other people, to create pictures of the world that fit our experiences and preferences."[36] It's a *social* process because agendamelding creates communities. People like to spend time with those who think like they do. The association between similarity and liking (see Chapter 9) extends to the media we choose. It's also selective exposure because we're only paying attention to ideas we find agreeable (see Chapter 16).

One recent study examined agendamelding during the 2012 US presidential campaign. The researchers gathered a database of 38 million tweets that mentioned either Democrat Barack Obama or Republican Mitt Romney. Computer analysis

Vertical media
News media that try to reach broad, diverse audiences.

Horizontal media
News media that try to appeal to specific interest communities.

Agendamelding
The social process by which we meld agendas from various sources to create pictures of the world that fit our experiences and preferences.

Tannen's cross-cultural approach to gender differences departs from much of feminist scholarship that claims conversations between men and women reflect men's efforts to dominate women. She assumes that male and female conversational styles are equally valid: "We try to talk to each other honestly, but it seems at times that we are speaking different languages—or at least different genderlects."[5] Although the word *genderlect* is not original with Tannen, the term nicely captures her belief that masculine and feminine styles of discourse are best viewed as two distinct cultural dialects rather than as inferior or superior ways of speaking.

Genderlect
A term suggesting that masculine and feminine styles of discourse are best viewed as two distinct cultural dialects.

Tannen realizes that categorizing people and their communication according to gender is offensive to many women and men. None of us like to be told, "Oh, you're talking just like a (wo)man." Each of us regards himself or herself as a unique individual. But at the risk of reinforcing a simplistic reductionism that claims biology is destiny, Tannen insists there *are* gender differences in the ways we speak.

> Despite these dangers, I am joining the growing dialogue on gender and language because the risk of ignoring differences is greater than the danger of naming them.[6]

WOMEN'S DESIRE FOR CONNECTION VS. MEN'S DESIRE FOR STATUS

Tannen says that, more than anything else, women seek human *connection,* whereas men are concerned mainly with *status.* While women are focused on cultivating a sense that they're *in touch,* men are working hard to preserve their *independence* as they jockey for position on a hierarchy of competitive accomplishment. When they're together, women's longing for *intimacy* threatens men's desire for freedom and sidetracks the masculine quest to be *one up* in all relationships. Empirical evidence for Tannen's assertions emerged back in 1979 in a study published in *Psychological Bulletin,* one of psychology's most prestigious journals. Adelaide Haas, now retired from the communication department at the State University of New York at New Paltz, found that men use more directive speech, talking about sports, money, and business, while women are often more supportive, polite, and expressive, talking about home and family and using more words implying feeling.[7]

Tannen does believe that some men are open to intimacy, just as some women have a concern for power. You'll recall that Baxter and Bakhtin's relational dialectics theory assumes that all people feel a tension between connection and autonomy in their relationships (see Chapter 11). Tannen agrees that many men and women would like to have intimacy *and* independence in every situation if they could, but she doesn't think it's possible. As a result, these differences in priority tend to give men and women differing views of the same situation.

> Girls and women feel it is crucial that they be liked by their peers, a form of involvement that focuses on symmetrical connection. Boys and men feel it is crucial that they be respected by their peers, a form of involvement that focuses on asymmetrical status.[8]

RAPPORT TALK VS. REPORT TALK

Why is Tannen so certain that women focus on connection while men focus on status? Her answer is that she listens to men and women talk. Just as an ethnographer pores over the words of native informants to discover what has meaning within their society, so Tannen scrutinizes the conversation of representative speakers from the feminine culture and the masculine culture to determine their core values. She offers numerous examples of the divergent styles she observes in everyday communication. These linguistic differences give her confidence that the connection–status distinction structures every verbal contact between women and men.

Julia Wood, communication professor emerita at the University of North Carolina and co-author of standpoint theory (see Chapter 32), thinks that Tannen's observations have merit and that the connection–status distinction is evident even in childhood. In her book *Gendered Lives,*[9] Wood draws upon research with children to highlight the different rules that girls and boys learn as they grow up.[10] Understanding those rules provides insight for some of the key differences Tannen believes characterize the genderlect styles that are at the root of miscommunication between men and women. Three of the key rules boys learn are:

Report talk

The typical monologic style of men, which seeks to command attention, convey information, and win arguments.

1. Communicate to assert your ideas, opinions, and identity.
2. Use talk to solve problems or develop a strategy.
3. Speak in a way that attracts attention to yourself.

In contrast to these rules, girls learn to:

Rapport talk

The typical conversational style of women, which seeks to establish connection with others.

1. Use communication to create and maintain relationships.
2. Involve others in conversations and respond to their ideas.
3. Show sensitivity to others and to relationships.

Consider the following five types of talk. Each of these speech forms shows that women value *rapport talk,* while men value *report talk.*

1. Private Speaking vs. Public Speaking

Folk wisdom suggests that women talk more than men do. Tannen cites a version of an old joke that has a wife complaining to her husband, "For the past 10 years you've never told me what you're thinking." Her husband caustically replies, "I didn't want to interrupt you." Tannen grants the validity of the wordy-woman–mute-male stereotype as it applies to a couple that's alone together—In private conversations, women talk more than men do. She also endorses Alice Walker's notion that a woman falls in love with a man because she sees in him "a giant ear."[11] But in the public arena, men vie for ascendancy and speak much more than women do.

James Pennebaker, a psychology professor at the University of Texas at Austin, is skeptical of the wordy-woman stereotype. After recruiting 2,000 men and women to carry voice-activated recorders all day long, he discovered that men and women each speak about 16,000 words a day.[12] This empirical evidence calls into question the supposed gender difference in the quantity of talk, but not necessarily the quality—its tone and intent.

Setting quantity aside, I (Glenn) believe that if Tannen studied the talk of professors at faculty meetings, she'd gather a wealth of data to support her claim that men are more likely to engage in report talk rather than rapport talk. In 30-plus years of attending these meetings, I've witnessed countless examples of men who pontificate in order to hold the floor, make a point, or badger colleagues into reluctant agreement. It's not surprising that the faculty members who usually bristle at these male monologues are women. In most cases, what women say in these meetings shows more concern about building and maintaining community by drawing others into the discussion rather than scoring points. My perception of this difference fits the childhood conversational rules summarized by Julia Wood. Girls learn to involve others in conversations, while boys learn to use communication to assert their own ideas and draw attention to themselves.

2. Telling a Story

Along with theorists Clifford Geertz, Michael Pacanowsky, and Walter Fisher (see Chapters 19 and 24), Tannen recognizes that the stories people tell reveal a great deal about their hopes, needs, and values. Consistent with men's focus on status, Tannen notes that men tell more stories than women do—especially jokes. Telling jokes is a masculine way to negotiate status. Men's humorous stories have a *can-you-top-this?* flavor that holds attention and elevates the storyteller above his audience.

When men aren't trying to be funny, they tell stories in which they are heroes, often acting alone to overcome great obstacles. On the other hand, women tend to express their desire for community by telling stories about others. On the rare occasions when a woman is a character in her own narrative, she usually describes herself as doing something foolish rather than acting in a clever manner. This downplaying of self puts her on the same level with her hearers, thus strengthening her network of support.

3. Listening

A woman listening to a story or an explanation tends to hold eye contact, offer head nods, and react with *yeah, uh-huh, mmmn, right,* or other responses that indicate *I'm listening* or *I'm with you.* For a man concerned with status, that overt style of active listening means *I agree with you,* so he avoids putting himself in that submissive, or *one-down,* stance. Women conclude that men aren't listening, which is not necessarily true.

Cooperative overlap
A supportive interruption often meant to show agreement and solidarity with the speaker.

When a woman who is listening starts to speak before the other person is finished, she usually does so to add a word of agreement, to show support, or to finish a sentence with what she thinks the speaker will say. Tannen labels this *cooperative overlap.* She says that from a woman's perspective, cooperative overlap is a sign of rapport rather than a competitive ploy to control the conversation. She also recognizes that men don't see it that way. Men regard any interruption as a power move to take control of the conversation, because in their world that's how it's done. Those who win the conversational game can take a don't-talk-while-I'm-interrupting-you stance and make it stick. Tannen concludes that these different styles of conversation management are the source of continuing irritation in cross-gender talk. "Whereas women's cooperative overlaps frequently annoy men by seeming to co-opt their topic, men frequently annoy women by usurping or switching the topic."[13]

4. Asking Questions

Tannen thinks that men and women also annoy each other with their different ways of asking questions—or *not* asking them. When we were first married, my wife Cheri and I set out on a trip from Chicago to Muskegon, Michigan, to visit friends. I glanced at a map before the trip—today's GPS was the stuff of science fiction back then—and noted that I needed to take I-94. About an hour into the trip, Cheri encouraged me to stop and ask for directions because the road we were on didn't seem familiar to her. Knowing that we were on I-94, I confidently declined her request. But when I saw signs for Milwaukee, Wisconsin, I was finally persuaded to stop at a gas station. To my horror, I discovered that I-94 went up *both sides* of Lake Michigan. I was driving up the wrong side. Cheri and I can laugh now about our late arrival in Muskegon, but when she tells the story, she always emphasizes my stubborn refusal to stop and ask for directions.

According to Tannen, men don't ask for that kind of help. Every admission of ignorance whittles away at the image of self-sufficiency that is so important to a man. "If self-respect is bought at the cost of a few extra minutes of travel time, it is well worth the price," she explains.[14] In my case, I gained no self-respect at a cost of several hours of travel time. But I'm still not fond of asking others for directions.

Women ask questions to establish a connection with others. Even a five-minute stop at a gas station to check the best route can create a sense of community, however brief. Tannen notes that when women state their opinions, they often tag them with a question at the end of the sentence: "That was a good movie, *don't you think?*" *Tag questions* soften the sting of potential disagreement that might drive people apart. They are also invitations to participate in open, friendly dialogue. But to men, they make the speaker seem wishy-washy.

Tag question

A short question at the end of a declarative statement, often used by women to soften the sting of potential disagreement or invite open, friendly dialogue.

Ever since *You Just Don't Understand* was published, Tannen has entertained questions during television interviews, radio call-in shows, and discussions following lectures. Women almost always seek more information or offer their own experiences that validate her insights. That's now true for men as well. But when the book was riding high on best-seller lists, men would often pose questions that seemed designed to bring her down from her high horse or to establish their own expertise. Even though she understands that public face is crucial to men, she identifies with the words of a wife in a short story: "I'd have been upset about making the mistake—but not about people *knowing*. That part's not a big deal to me." Her husband replied, "Oh, is it ever a big deal to me."[15]

5. Conflict

After his divorce, Rob Reiner decided to direct the film *When Harry Met Sally,* a humorous depiction of the relationship between a man (Billy Crystal) and a woman (Meg Ryan). Nora Ephron wrote the script and, after interviewing Reiner, used him as the inspiration for Harry's character. The film became a classic after its release in 1989, and is listed among Bravo's "100 Funniest Movies." Reiner's divorce provided the grist for an argument between Harry and Sally, in which Harry blows up at their friends Jess and Marie and then storms out of the room. After making an excuse for his behavior, Sally goes to him to try to calm him down.

HARRY: I know, I know, I shouldn't have done it.

SALLY: Harry, you're going to have to try and find a way of not expressing every feeling that you have every moment that you have them.

HARRY: Oh, really?

SALLY: Yes, there are times and places for things.

HARRY: Well the next time you're giving a lecture series on social graces, would you let me know, 'cause I'll sign up.

SALLY: Hey. You don't have to take your anger out on me.

HARRY: Oh, I think I'm entitled to throw a little anger your way. Especially when I'm being told how to live my life by Miss Hospital Corners.

SALLY: What's that supposed to mean?

HARRY: I mean, nothing bothers you. You never get upset about anything.

This scene illustrates Tannen's description of much male-female strife. Since they see life as a contest, many men are more comfortable with conflict and are therefore less likely to hold themselves in check. By trying to placate Harry and excuse his anger toward their friends, Sally responds in what Tannen believes is an equally typical fashion. "To most women, conflict is a threat to connection—to be avoided at all costs."[16]

The dialogue illustrates another feature of conflict between men and women. As often happens, Sally's attempt to avert a similar outburst in the future sparks new conflict with Harry. Tannen says men have an early warning system that's geared to detect signs that they are being told what to do. Harry bristles at the thought that Sally is trying to limit his autonomy, so her efforts backfire.

6. Nonverbal Communication

Curiously, Tannen doesn't extend the connection-status distinction to the ways in which men and women communicate nonverbally. Susan Pease Gadoua, a licensed marriage counselor who writes a regular column for PsychologyToday.com, finds it difficult to analyze the way men and women talk to each other without including the nonverbal component. Based on her years of experience helping married couples, she's learned to anticipate a common scenario when she sees a man and a woman trying to get over a serious fight or navigate a rift in their relationship.

> Each partner has a different way of wanting to resolve the problem: women want to talk things out and perhaps make love later (when they feel more connected); men want to connect by making love and (maybe) talking later.[17]

Gadoua recalls one husband who told her that all of his marital problems would be solved if only he and his wife could go away for a whole weekend and dedicate the entire time to sex. His wife saw this solution as a superficial gesture that wouldn't solve anything. Deborah Tannen might see it as a way for the husband to score in a never-ending game of who's on top. The husband's solution seems like a classic acting out of one of the early rules that boys learn at play—communicate to assert your identity. The wife's solution reflects one of the rules girls learn—connect through conversation. Sadly, Gadoua observes that when women want to connect and men want to have sex, it's often the case that neither activity takes place.

MEN AND WOMEN GROW UP IN DIFFERENT SPEECH COMMUNITIES

Do men and women really live in different worlds? Tannen cites dialogue from Anne Tyler's *The Accidental Tourist,* Ingmar Bergman's *Scenes from a Marriage,* Alice Walker's *The Temple of My Familiar,* Erica Jong's *Fear of Flying,* and Jules Feiffer's *Grown Ups* to support her claim that the different ways women and men talk reflect their separate cultures. If these fictional examples depict an accurate view of the separate worlds of real men and women, it makes sense to find out how and when these worlds formed.

When Tannen witnessed dramatic differences in conversational style between second-grade boys and girls, she concluded that the origins of speaking in genderlect must be traced back to early childhood. Is it plausible to suggest that boys and girls as young as 7 are already segregated and using conversational styles that will follow them into adult life? Many linguists and communication scholars believe the answer to that question is yes. They refer to the segregated groups to which boys and girls belong as *speech communities.*[18]

Speech community
A community of people who share understandings about goals of communication, strategies for enacting those goals, and ways of interpreting communication.

Julia Wood summarized the concept of a *speech community* this way: "[A] speech community exists when people share understandings about goals of communication, strategies for enacting those goals, and ways of interpreting communication."[19] Tannen's conclusion that the second-grade boys and girls she observed were "two different species" certainly matches up with the idea that they were from distinct speech communities. But these communities don't appear out of thin air. To get insight into their origins, we need to look back to the preschool years.

Louise Cherry Wilkinson, professor of education, psychology, and communication sciences at Syracuse University, suggests that separate speech communities begin with the conversations young boys and girls have with their mothers. She reached this conclusion when she studied the interactions between moms and kids during a free-play session. She recruited mothers with a 2-year-old daughter or son to take part, giving no instructions as to what they should talk about. Along with her colleague Michael Lewis, Wilkinson transcribed the interactions that took place and trained coders to analyze the words that were used. The coders didn't know whether they were coding interactions between a mother and daughter or a mother and son.[20]

Wilkinson and Lewis discovered that mothers of girls talked more, asked more questions, used longer sentences, and were more likely to verbally acknowledge their daughters' comments than were mothers of boys. Mothers of boys were more likely to use directives—telling their sons what to do—than were mothers of girls. Wilkinson and Lewis speculated that these sorts of differences could set early expectations in males and females about what type of conversation is most appropriate for them. The findings suggest that the differences Tannen sees between adult male and female speech have their roots in the early socialization of children.

"NOW YOU'RE BEGINNING TO UNDERSTAND"

What if Tannen is right and all conversation between men and women is best understood as cross-cultural communication? Does that mean genderlect can be taught, like French, Swahili, or any other foreign language? Tannen offers a qualified yes. She regards sensitivity training as an effort to teach men how to speak in a feminine voice, while assertiveness training is an effort to teach women how to speak in a masculine voice. But she's aware of our ethnocentric tendency to think it's the other person who needs fixing, so she expresses only guarded hope that men and women will alter their linguistic styles.

Tannen has much more confidence in the benefits of multicultural understanding. She believes that understanding each other's style, and the motives behind it, is the first step in overcoming destructive responses.

> The answer is for both men and women to try to take each other on their own terms rather than applying the standards of one group to the behavior of the other. . . . Understanding style differences for what they are takes the sting out of them.[21]

Tannen suggests that one way to measure whether we are gaining cross-gender insight is a drop in the frequency of the oft-heard lament *You just don't understand.* I can personally testify to the validity of this standard. While I certainly make no claim to

"And do you, Deborah Tannen, think they know what they're talking about?"

©Peter Steiner/The New Yorker Collection/The Cartoon Bank

have arrived at a complete understanding of Cheri or her conversational style, I've only heard her say, "You just don't understand," in the early stages of our 42 years together. She'd say the same about me. It's difficult for a marriage to survive and thrive without partners' gaining insight into each other's conversational style.

ETHICAL REFLECTION: GILLIGAN'S DIFFERENT VOICE

For more than 30 years, Carol Gilligan was a professor of education in the Harvard Graduate School of Education; she is now a professor at New York University. Her book *In a Different Voice* presents a theory of moral development claiming that women tend to think and speak in an ethical voice different from that of men.[22] Gilligan's view of gender differences parallels Tannen's analysis of men as wanting independence and women as desiring human connection. Gilligan is convinced that most men seek autonomy and think of moral maturity in terms of *justice*. She's equally certain that women desire to be linked with others and that they regard their ultimate ethical responsibility as one of *care*.

On the basis of the quantity and quality of feminine relationships, Gilligan contrasts *women who care* with *men who are fair*. Individual rights, equality before the law, fair play, a square deal—all these masculine ethical goals can be pursued without intimate ties to others. Justice is impersonal. But women's moral judgment is more contextual, more immersed in the details of relationships and narratives.[23] Sensitivity to others, loyalty, self-sacrifice, and peacemaking all reflect interpersonal involvement.

Gilligan's work arose in response to the theory of moral development of her Harvard colleague Lawrence Kohlberg, who identified increasing levels of ethical maturity by analyzing responses to hypothetical moral dilemmas.[24] According to his justice-based scoring system, the average young adult female was a full stage behind her male counterpart. Women were rated as less morally mature than men because they were less concerned about abstract concepts like justice, truth, and freedom. Instead, they based their ethical decisions on considerations of compassion, loyalty, and a strong sense of responsibility to prevent pain and alleviate suffering. Their moral reasoning was more likely to reflect Buber's call for genuine I-Thou relationships than Kant's categorical imperative (see Chapters 6 and 14).

Gilligan is comfortable with the idea that men and women speak in different ethical voices. But she's disturbed that when women don't follow the normative path laid out by men, "the conclusion has generally been that something is wrong with women."[25] She points out "the unfair paradox that the very traits that have traditionally defined the 'goodness' of women are those that mark them as deficient in moral development."[26]

Although Gilligan's theory is more descriptive than prescriptive, the underlying assumption is that the way things *are* reflects the way things *ought to be*. Most ethical theorists are bothered by the idea of a double standard—justice from some, care from others. Traditional moral philosophy has never suggested different ethics for different groups. Yet readers of both sexes report that Gilligan's theory resonates with their personal experience.

CRITIQUE: IS TANNEN SOFT ON RESEARCH—AND MEN?

Aha factor
A subjective standard ascribing validity to an idea when it resonates with one's personal experience.

Is male–female conversation really cross-cultural communication? Tannen suggests we use the *aha factor* to test the validity of her two-culture hypothesis:

> If my interpretation is correct, then readers, on hearing my explanation, will exclaim within their heads, "Aha!" Something they have intuitively sensed will be made explicit. . . . When the subject of analysis is human interaction—a process that we engage in, all our lives—each reader can measure interpretation against her/his own experience.[27]

If we agree to this subjective standard of validity, Tannen easily makes her case. For example, in the book *You Just Don't Understand*, she describes how women who verbally share problems with men are often frustrated by the masculine tendency to offer solutions. *(Qualitative linguistic analysis)* According to Tannen, women don't want advice; they're looking for the gift of understanding. When Em first read her book, he had the kind of *aha* reaction that Tannen says validates her theory. He says, "I realized that her words described me. Anytime my wife, Jean, tells me about a problem she's facing, I either turn coldly analytic or dive in and try to fix things for the woman I love. I now know that Jean would rather have me just listen or voice some version of *I feel your pain.*"

Brittany's application log suggests that she's convinced. Perhaps her masculine upbringing explains why she experienced the *aha factor* even before she read about Tannen's theory.

> From ages 4 to 11, I was raised by my single father. During this developmental time in my life, I conversed mainly with Dad, and therefore adopted the kind of *report talk* that Tannen characterizes as primarily male. Whenever we had conflict, we dealt with it right away. Most of my friends were boys and I had difficulties making connections with girls my age.
>
> After my dad eventually remarried and I had a stepmother to talk with, I began to develop friendships with girls in high school. During a conversation one of them said, "You always try to think of a solution rather than just listen." I understand now that I picked up this communication trait from my dad. Whenever we faced conflict in our home, we immediately addressed it and figured out how we should deal with it. As I have developed more relationships with women I feel my genderlect style has moved toward *rapport talk,* which Tannen categorizes as primarily female. Sometimes, though, I'll have a conversation with a close guy friend back home who will say, "You're the only girl I've ever been able to talk with like this."

Apparently, Tannen's analysis of common misunderstandings between men and women has struck a responsive chord in a million other readers. *You Just Don't Understand* was on the best-seller list for most of the 1990s. And in that decade it was rated by hundreds of mental health professionals as the best of 1,000 self-help books.[28] But does a chorus of *ahas* mean Tannen is right? Astrologer and psychic Jeane Dixon might have made 10 predictions, and if only one came true, that's the prophecy people remembered and lauded her for. They forgot that the other nine turned out to be wrong. According to many social scientists, Tannen's "proof" may be like that.

Perhaps using selective data is the only way to support a reductionist claim that women are one way and men are another. Tannen's theme of intimacy versus independence echoes a prominent dialectic discussed in relational dialectics (see Chapter 11). However, Tannen suggests none of the flux, dialogical contradiction, or ongoing complexity of human existence that's central to Baxter and Bakhtin's theory. Tannen's women are programmed within their gendered culture to embrace connection and deny any desire for autonomy. Her men seek autonomy but avoid connection. Neither group feels any sense of contradiction in their own conversation. Saying it's so may eventually make it so—self-fulfilling prophecy is a powerful force. But as stated in the introduction to this section, most gender researchers spot more diversity *within* each gender than *between* them.

Adrianne Kunkel (University of Kansas) and Brant Burleson (Purdue University) directly challenged the different-cultures perspective that's at the heart of Tannen's genderlect theory. According to Tannen's two-culture worldview, verbal support should be highly desired in the world of women but of little value in the competitive world of men. Kunkel and Burleson's empirical research doesn't bear out Tannen's claim. While it's true that women often *do* it better, both sexes place an equally high value on comforting communication:

> Both men and women view highly person-centered comforting messages as most sensitive and effective; both see messages low in person-centeredness as relatively insensitive and ineffective. . . . Both sexes view comforting skills as important in the context of various personal relationships and as substantially more important than instrumentally focused communication skills.[29]

On the basis of this shared meaning, Kunkel and Burleson rejected the different-cultures perspective. They believed it was a myth that had lost its narrative force. Men and women do understand.

A very different critique comes from feminist scholars. For example, German linguist Senta Troemel-Ploetz accuses Tannen of having written a dishonest book that ignores issues of male dominance, control, power, sexism, discrimination, sexual harassment, and verbal insults. "If you leave out power," she says, "you do not understand talk."[30] The two genderlects are anything but equal. "Men are used to dominating women; they do it especially in conversations. . . . Women are trained to please; they have to please also in conversations."[31]

Contrary to Tannen's thesis that mutual understanding will bridge the culture gap between the sexes, Troemel-Ploetz believes that "men understand quite well what women want but they give only when it suits them. In many situations they refuse to give and *women cannot make them give.*"[32] She thinks it's ridiculous to assume that men will give up power voluntarily. To prove her point, she suggests doing a follow-up study on men who read Tannen's best seller. Noting that many women readers of *You Just Don't Understand* give the book to their husbands to peruse, Troemel-Ploetz states that if Tannen's theory is true, a follow-up study should show that these men are now putting down their papers at the breakfast table and talking empathetically with their wives. She doesn't think it will happen.

Why has genderlect styles received so much criticism? Perhaps because it draws from both objective and interpretive approaches yet doesn't satisfy the demands of either camp. It offers *understanding of people,* but doesn't seek to *reform power differences* among them. It's *relatively simple* but may not *explain the data.* Her book's *aesthetic appeal* and *practical utility* made it a bestseller, but that hasn't translated into a *community of agreement* among scholars. Nevertheless, this controversial theory has inspired both *quantitative* and *qualitative* research aimed at supporting or refuting her claims. Whether she's right or wrong, Tannen's work has encouraged people to think systematically about sex differences in communication.

QUESTIONS TO SHARPEN YOUR FOCUS

1. Apart from the topics of nonverbal communication, conflict, questions, listening, storytelling, and public vs. private speaking, can you come up with your own examples of how *rapport talk* is different from *report talk?*

2. What are the practical implications for you if talk with members of the opposite sex is indeed *cross-cultural communication?*

3. What might be the most effective ways for men and women to gain insight into how their *conversational styles* affect their relationships?

4. Tannen's *aha factor* is similar to Carl Rogers' standard of basing our knowledge on personal experience (see Chapter 4). What are the dangers of relying solely on this indicator?

A SECOND LOOK

Recommended resource: Deborah Tannen, *You Just Don't Understand,* Ballantine, New York, 1990.

Conversational style: Deborah Tannen, *That's Not What I Meant!* William Morrow, New York, 1986.

Linguistic microanalysis of conversation: Deborah Tannen, *Conversational Style: Analyzing Talk Among Friends,* Ablex, Norwood, NJ, 1984.

Gender differences in children's talk: Deborah Tannen, "Gender Differences in Topical Coherence: Creating Involvement in Best Friends' Talk," *Discourse Processes,* Vol. 13, 1990, pp. 73–90.

Discourse analysis: Deborah Tannen, *Gender and Discourse,* Oxford University, Oxford, UK, 1994/96.

Gendered language in the workplace: Deborah Tannen, *Talking from 9 to 5: Women and Men at Work—Language, Sex, and Power,* Avon, New York, 1994.

Gendered language in the family: Deborah Tannen, *I Only Say This Because I Love You: Talking in Families,* Ballantine, New York, 2002.

Support of two-culture hypothesis: Anthony Mulac, James Bradac, and Pamela Gibbons, "Empirical Support for the Gender-as-Culture Hypothesis: An Intercultural Analysis of Male/Female Language Differences," *Human Communication Research,* Vol. 27, 2001, pp. 121–152.

Communication scholars' dialogue on two-culture hypothesis: "Reflections on the Different Cultures Hypothesis: A Scholars' Symposium," Sandra Metts (ed.), *Personal Relationships,* Vol. 4, 1997, pp. 201–253.

Critique of two-culture hypothesis: Adrianne Kunkel and Brant Burleson, "Social Support and the Emotional Lives of Men and Women: An Assessment of the Different Cultures Perspective," in *Sex Differences and Similarities in Communication,* Daniel Canary and Kathryn Dindia (eds.), Lawrence Erlbaum, Mahwah, NJ, 1998, pp. 101–125.

Critique centering on power discrepancy: Senta Troemel-Ploetz, "Review Essay: Selling the Apolitical," *Discourse and Society,* Vol. 2, 1991, pp. 489–502.

For a chapter on Carol Gilligan's theory, click on Different Voice
in Archive under Theory Resources in
www.afirstlook.com.

Standpoint Theory

of Sandra Harding & Julia T. Wood

To illustrate the gist of standpoint theory, Sandra Harding (philosopher of science at the University of California, Los Angeles) asks us to imagine looking into a pond and seeing a stick that appears bent.[1] But is it really? If we walk around to a different place, the stick seems straight—which it actually is. Physicists have developed a theory of light refraction that explains why this visual distortion occurs based on our physical location.

In like manner, standpoint theorists believe our view of the world depends on our *social location.* That location is shaped by our demographic characteristics, including sex, race, ethnicity, sexual orientation, and economic status. As Julia Wood puts it, "the social groups within which we are located powerfully shape what we experience and know as well as how we understand and communicate with ourselves, others, and the world."[2] These group memberships lead to different opportunities, working conditions, and degrees of power and influence, so they generate distinctive accounts of nature and social relationships. Standpoint theorists believe that knowledge starting from the social location of marginalized people "can provide a more objective view than the perspective from the lives of the more powerful."[3]

Social location

Our group memberships that shape our experience of the world and our ways of understanding it.

Feminist standpoint theorists focus on the social location of women: "Men are the dominant, privileged, or centered group, and women are a subordinate, disadvantaged, or marginalized group."[4] But they are quick to warn that a social location is not a standpoint. Being female provides a feminine social location. But a feminist *standpoint* is "achieved through critical reflection on power relations and their consequences."[5] A standpoint necessarily opposes the status quo. Although men have a social location, standpoint theorists think it's nonsensical to speak of a male standpoint—men already control the status quo, and the status quo cannot challenge itself.

Standpoint

A perspective achieved through critical reflection on power relations and their consequences that opposes the status quo.

Just as Harding is recognized as the philosopher who has most advanced the standpoint theory of knowledge among feminist scholars,[6] Julia Wood, communication professor emerita at the University of North Carolina at Chapel Hill, has championed and consistently applied standpoint logic within the field of communication. For communication researchers, taking women's location seriously means heeding Wood's call to choose research topics that are responsive to women's concerns:

> Abiding concern with oppression leads many feminist scholars to criticize some of the topics that dominate research on relationships. When four women are battered

to death by intimate partners every day in North America, study of how abusive relationships are created and sustained seems more compelling than research on heterosexual college students' romances. Is it more significant to study friendships among economically comfortable adolescents or social practices that normalize sexual harassment and rape?[7]

As a male researcher who has studied romance and friendship on a private college campus, I am compelled to explore the logic of Harding and Wood's feminist standpoint agenda. But their standpoint epistemology raises other questions. Do all women share a common social location? Or a common standpoint? Why do Harding and Wood believe a feminist standpoint is more objective or less partial than other starting points for inquiry? Would grounding future research in the lives of women compel me to regard every report of feminine experience as equally true? Should we always disregard what men have to say? The rest of this chapter will explore these issues and other questions raised by standpoint theory. The answers to these questions will make more sense if we understand the varied intellectual resources standpoint theorists have drawn upon to inform their analyses.

A FEMINIST STANDPOINT ROOTED IN PHILOSOPHIES

In 1807, German philosopher Georg Hegel analyzed the master–slave relationship to show that what people "know" about themselves, others, and society depends on which group they are in.[8] For example, those in captivity have a decidedly different perspective on the meaning of chains, laws, childbirth, and punishment than do their captors who participate in the same "reality." But since masters are backed by the established structure of their society, they have the power to make their view of the world stick. They are the ones who write the rules and the history books.

Following Hegel's lead, Karl Marx and Friedrich Engels referred to the *proletarian standpoint.* They suggested that the impoverished poor who provide sweat equity are society's *ideal knowers,* as long as they understand the class struggle in which they are involved.[9] Harding notes that standpoint theory "was a project 'straining at the bit' to emerge from feminist social theorists who were familiar with Marxian epistemology."[10] By substituting *women* for *proletariat,* and *gender discrimination* for *class struggle,* early feminist standpoint theorists had a ready-made framework for advocating women's way of knowing.

Contrary to the economic determinism of Marx, George Herbert Mead claimed that culture "gets into individuals" through communication (see Chapter 5). Drawing on this key principle of symbolic interactionism, Wood maintains that gender is a cultural construction rather than a biological characteristic. "More than a variable, gender is a system of meanings that sculpts individuals' standpoints by positioning most males and females in different material, social and symbolic circumstances."[11]

Strains of postmodernism also weave throughout standpoint theory. When Jean-François Lyotard announced an "incredulity toward metanarratives," he included Enlightenment rationality and Western science.[12] Since many feminists regard these two enterprises as dominated by men who refuse to acknowledge their male-centered bias, they embrace a postmodern critique. In reciprocal fashion, postmodernists applaud the standpoint emphasis on knowledge as locally situated, though they push the idea to the point where there is no basis for favoring one perspective over another. As we will see, Harding and Wood reject that kind of absolute relativism.

Harding and Wood have drawn upon these somewhat conflicting intellectual traditions without letting any one of them dictate the shape or substance of their standpoint approach. The resulting theory might seem a bewildering crosshatch of ideas were it not for their repeated emphasis on starting all scholarly inquiry from the lives of women and others who are marginalized. In order to honor this central tenet of standpoint theory and to illustrate the way of knowing that Harding and Wood propose, I've excerpted events and dialogue from Kathryn Stockett's best-selling novel *The Help*.[13] The story was also portrayed in the 2011 movie of the same name that garnered an Oscar nomination for best picture of the year. The title refers to the term that Southern white families used for the African American women who cooked their meals, cleaned their homes, and raised their children.

THE HELP: STORIES FROM THE LIVES OF MARGINALIZED WOMEN

The setting for *The Help* is early 1960s Jackson, Mississippi, before Congress over-turned Jim Crow laws that guaranteed racial segregation. Of the three women who narrate the tale, Skeeter is the one who hails from a family of privilege. She's a young white college grad who double majored in English and journalism and now longs for a career as a serious writer. But she can only find a part-time job ghost-writing a weekly "Miss Myrna" advice column in a local newspaper—a job she finds deeply unfulfilling.

In desperation, Skeeter seeks help from Aibileen, the black maid working for one of Skeeter's friends. Aibileen, the second narrator, has decades of experience serving white families. She is warm, wise, and sought out by other maids in her church who believe her prayers have special power. High on her prayer list is Mae Mobley, her 17th child, the 3-year-old daughter of her current employer.

> Soon as I walk in her nursery, Mae Mobley smile at me, reach out her fat little arms. . . . She laugh, dance a little happy jig waiting on me to get her out. I give her a good hug. I reckon she don't get too many good hugs like this after I go home. Ever so often, I come to work and find her bawling in her crib. . . . You see [her mom] in the Jitney 14 grocery, you never think she go and leave her baby crying in her crib like that. But the help always know.[14]

Those last five words capture the essence of standpoint theory. The looked-down-upon members of society have a clearer vantage point than those with status and power. If you want to know how things work, start your research with the lives of those on the margins. In *The Help*, that means listening to the stories of dirt-poor, African American women.

Listening to Aibileen, Skeeter catches a glimpse of Mississippi life that she's never seen. She's convinced that firsthand accounts of anonymous Southern maids' experiences with their white "families" would make a fascinating book. After much hesitation, and despite the danger, Aibileen agrees to tell her story. She also recruits her best friend Minny to take part in the project.

Minny, the third narrator, has trouble staying employed because she has no trouble saying what's on her mind.[15] After reading about Minny, Skeeter's New York editor calls her "every Southern white woman's nightmare. I adore her."[16]

As I describe the theory, I'll continue to cite passages from *The Help*. But you should understand that some critical scholars would wonder if it's appropriate to demonstrate standpoints by using this book—one authored by a white woman (Stockett) who created a fictional white character (Skeeter) who represents the lives of African American maids. The perspectives of actual poor black women might get overpowered by the voices of these privileged white people. Those racial realities surrounding the film and novel have generated no small amount of controversy. Along with the Association of Black Women Historians, communication professor Rachel Griffin at the University of Utah questions whether the novel, written by a white woman, accurately represents black voices—a fair critique.[17] Octavia Spencer, who won an Academy Award for best supporting actress as the outspoken Minny, disagreed with those who criticized the film's portrayal:

> I don't have a problem with nominating these two earnest, hardworking women, and we've never seen this story told from their perspective. Be that as it may that a white woman wrote the original text . . . the fact is that at least she had the insight to write about women who we've not heard from.[18]

Her co-star Viola Davis concurred, saying her goal as a black actor is to "tell the truth about humanity, and humanity is messy."[19] These debates demonstrate how messy standpoints can be, too—even among those who take the social location of women seriously.

WOMEN AS A MARGINALIZED GROUP

Standpoint theorists see important differences between men and women. Wood uses the relational dialectic of autonomy-connectedness as a case in point (see Chapter 11): "While all humans seem to seek both autonomy and connectedness, the relative amount of each that is preferred appears to differ rather consistently between genders."[20] Men tend to want more autonomy; women tend to want more connection. This difference is evident in each group's communication. The masculine community uses speech to accomplish tasks, assert self, and gain power. The feminine community uses speech to build relationships, include others, and show responsiveness.[21]

Wood does not attribute gender differences to biology, maternal instinct, or women's intuition. To the extent that women are distinct from men, she sees the difference largely as a result of cultural expectations and the treatment that each group receives from the other. For example, otherness in Minny is engendered through segregation rules crafted by white men before she was born—laws that prevent her and other African Americans from using the same public facilities and businesses as Caucasian Americans.[22] That's during the day. At night with her husband it's even worse as he physically abuses her, sometimes just because he enjoys violence.[23]

Minny's experience also reflects the power discrepancies that Harding and Wood say are found in all societies: "A culture is not experienced identically by all members. Cultures are hierarchically ordered so that different groups within them offer dissimilar power, opportunities, and experiences to members."[24] Along these lines, feminist standpoint theorists suggest that women are underadvantaged and, thus, men are overadvantaged—a gender difference that makes a huge difference.

But Harding and Wood are quick to warn against thinking of women as a monolithic group. They point out that not all women share the same social location, nor for that matter do all men. Besides the issue of gender, Harding stresses economic condition, race, and sexual orientation as additional cultural identities that can either draw people to the center of society or push them to the fringes. Thus, an intersection of minority positions creates a highly looked-down-upon location in the social hierarchy. Impoverished African American lesbian women are almost always marginalized. On the other hand, positions of high status and power are overwhelmingly "manned" by wealthy white heterosexual males.

Even more than Harding, Wood is troubled by the tendency of some feminists to talk as if there were an "essence of women," and then to "valorize" that quality. She believes that Carol Gilligan makes this mistake by claiming that women, as opposed to men, speak in an ethical voice of care (see Chapter 31). For Wood, biology is not destiny. She fears that "championing any singular model of womanhood creates a mold into which not all women may comfortably fit."[25] Yet as an unapologetic feminist committed to the equal value of all human life, Wood understands that a sense of solidarity is politically useful if women are to effectively critique a male-centered world.

This awareness of feminine solidarity can be seen in Skeeter's growing realization after publishing her book revealing the experiences of Mississippi maids. "Wasn't that the point of the book? For women to realize, *We are just two people. Not that much separates us.*"[26] To the extent that she and the African American maids have critically reflected on their social location, they're on their way to achieving a feminist standpoint.

"Actually, Lou, I think it was more than just my being in the right place at the right time. I think it was my being the right race, the right religion, the right sex, the right socioeconomic group, having the right accent, the right clothes, going to the right schools . . ."

©Warren Miller/The New Yorker Collection/The Cartoon Bank

KNOWLEDGE FROM NOWHERE VS. LOCAL KNOWLEDGE

Standpoint theorists emphasize the importance of social location because they are convinced that people at the top of the societal hierarchy are the ones privileged to define what it means to be female, male, or anything else in a given culture. As Harding argues, "the social group that gets the chance to define the important problematics, concepts, assumptions, and hypotheses in a field will end up leaving its social fingerprints on the picture of the world that emerges from the results of that field's research process."[27] Such power is starkly portrayed in *The Help* when Aibileen overhears the pronouncement of Hilly—the wife of a Mississippi legislator—who wants to physically ensure the maids know their place:

> "Everybody knows they carry different kinds of diseases than we do. . . . That's exactly why I've designed the Home Help Sanitation Initiative. . . . A bill that requires every white home to have a separate bathroom for the colored help. I've even notified the surgeon general of Mississippi to see if he'll endorse the idea."[28]

Imagine how different a book entitled *Maids* by Hilly would be from one of the same title written from the standpoint of Aibileen or Minny. The texts would surely differ in starting point, method, and conclusion.

Local knowledge

Knowledge situated in time, place, experience, and relative power, as opposed to knowledge from nowhere that's supposedly value-free.

Harding's insistence on *local knowledge* contrasts sharply with the claim of traditional Western science that it can discover "Truth" that is value-free and accessible to any objective observer. In her book *Whose Science? Whose Knowledge?* Harding refers to empiricism's claims of disembodied truths as "views from nowhere." Feminist writer Donna Haraway calls such pronouncements the *God trick,* which Harding describes as "speaking authoritatively about everything in the world from no particular location or human perspective at all."[29] As for the notion of value-free science, Harding characterizes the claim as promoting "a fast gun for hire" and chides detached scientists that "it cannot be value-free to describe such social events as poverty, misery, torture, or cruelty in a value-free way."[30] Even Galileo's statement *Anyone can see through my telescope* has been interpreted by empirical scientists as dismissing concern for any relationship between the knower and the known.

Harding and other standpoint theorists insist there is no possibility of an unbiased perspective that is disinterested, impartial, value-free, or detached from a particular historical situation. The physical and the social sciences are always situated in time and place. She writes that "each person can achieve only a partial view of reality from the perspective of his or her own position in the social hierarchy."[31] Unlike postmodernists, however, she is unwilling to abandon the search for reality. She simply thinks that the search for it should begin from the lives of those in the underclass.

Neither Harding nor Wood claims that the perspectives of women or any other marginalized groups give them a clear view of the way things are. *Situated knowledge—* the only kind they think there is—will always be partial. Standpoint theorists do maintain, however, that "the perspectives of subordinate groups are more complete and thus, better than those of privileged groups in a society."[32] They recognize that this is a controversial claim. US Supreme Court Justice Sonia Sotomayor voiced the same idea in a 2001 lecture on law and multicultural diversity: "I would hope that a wise Latina woman with the richness of her experiences would more often than not reach a better conclusion than a white male who hasn't lived that life."[33] That one remark was the stated reason why many white male senators voted against her confirmation to the US Supreme Court in 2009.

STRONG OBJECTIVITY: LESS PARTIAL VIEWS FROM THE STANDPOINT OF WOMEN

Strong objectivity
The strategy of starting research from the lives of women and other marginalized groups, which upon critical reflection and resistance provides them with a less false view of reality.

Harding uses the term *strong objectivity* to refer to the strategy of starting research from the lives of women and other marginalized groups whose concerns and experience are usually ignored.[34] Her choice of label suggests that knowledge generated from the perspective of dominant groups offers, by contrast, only a *weak* objectivity. To illustrate this claim, she speaks directly of the oppositional viewpoints of slaves and their masters a century ago: "It is absurd to imagine that U.S. slaveowners' views of Africans' and African Americans' lives could outweigh in impartiality, disinterestedness, impersonality, and objectivity their slaves' view of their own and slaveowners' lives."[35]

Why should the standpoints of women and other marginalized groups be less partial, less distorted, or less false than the perspectives of men who are in dominant positions? Wood offers two explanations: "First, people with subordinate status have greater motivation to understand the perspective of more powerful groups than vice versa."[36] Even if the meek don't inherit the earth, they have a special interest in figuring out what makes it turn. Taking the role of the other is a survival skill for those who have little control over their own lives. Lacking this motivation, those who wield power seem to have less reason to wonder how the "other half" views the world.

Wood's second reason for favoring the perspective of groups that are constantly put down is that they have little reason to defend the status quo. Not so for those who have power. She asserts that "groups that are advantaged by the prevailing system have a vested interest in not perceiving social inequities that benefit them at the expense of others."[37]

Robbie, a student in my class, expressed a new realization of the link between a social location of privilege and the tunnel vision that may go with it.

> This is a hard theory to write on. I am an upper-middle-class white male and this theory deals with the marginalized and underappreciated, particularly women. I struggled to think of any way the theory related to me. But then I got it. My social location made it difficult for me to apply the theory. I was born into the dominant culture and have been taught to maintain the status quo. Our opinion is the "right" one because it follows the "rules" (rules that we wrote, by the way). Admittedly, my perspective is probably one of the least objective of all, and what's worse, I have been taught to think that it is objective.

Robbie's words are unusual coming from a privileged white man with much to lose if the status quo is shattered. Most of his contemporaries would resist grappling with the theory. For those with money, status, and power, ignorance of perspectives on the margin is bliss, so it's folly to be wise. Robbie's new insight is perhaps a testimony to the power of feminist standpoint theory to change the world one mind at a time.

Yet Harding would want Robbie and us to understand that being female is no guarantee of *strong objectivity.* Harding and Wood emphasize that a woman's location on the margin of society is a necessary, but not sufficient, condition to attain a feminist standpoint. They believe a feminist standpoint is an *achievement gained through critical reflection* rather than a piece of territory automatically inherited by being a woman.[38] In *The Help,* Aibileen, Minny, and the other maids who told their stories to Skeeter seem to qualify. By the end of the novel, so does Skeeter. She writes:

I see it in their hardworking, lined faces, how much the maids want this book to be published. They are scared, looking at the back door every ten minutes, afraid they'll get caught talking to me. . . . The risk they're taking is proof they want this to get printed and they want it bad.[39]

THEORY TO PRACTICE: COMMUNICATION RESEARCH BASED ON WOMEN'S LIVES

If we want to see a model of communication research that starts from the lives of women, a good place to begin is Julia Wood's in-depth study of caregiving in the United States. Consistent with standpoint theory's insistence that all knowledge is situated in a time and place, the first chapter of Wood's *Who Cares? Women, Care, and Culture* describes her own situation as a white, heterosexual, professional woman who for nine years took on the consuming responsibility of caring for her infirm parents until they died. Her experience squared with her subsequent research findings:

> First, it seems that caring can be healthy and enriching when it is informed, freely chosen, and practiced within a context that recognizes and values caring and those who do it. On the other hand, existing studies also suggest that caring can be quite damaging to caregivers if they are unaware of dangers to their identities, if they have unrealistic expectations of themselves, and/or if caring occurs within contexts that fail to recognize its importance and value.[40]

Wood discovered that gendered communication practices reflect and reinforce our societal expectation that caregiving is women's work. After rejecting his daughter's proposal to hire a part-time nurse, her father mused, "It's funny, Julia. I used to wish I had sons, but now I'm glad I have daughters, because I couldn't ask a son to take this kind of time away from his own work just to take care of me."[41] She heard similar messages that devalued caregiving from male colleagues at her university. While praising Wood for her sacrifice, they reassured a fellow professor that he had taken the proper action by placing his mother in a nursing home: "Well, she surely understood that as busy as you are with your work you couldn't be expected to take on that responsibility."[42]

Wood says these comments reveal the opposing, gender-based privileges and restraints in our society. As illustrated in the book/film *One True Thing,* women are given the freedom to make caregiving a priority but are denied the right to put their work first and still be a "good woman." Men are given the freedom to make their work a priority but are deprived of the right to focus on caregiving and still be a "good man."

Wood suggests that a standpoint approach is practical to the extent that it generates an effective critique of unjust practices. She believes that "our culture itself must be reformed in ways that dissociate caring from its historical affiliations with women and private relationships and redefine it as a centrally important and integral part of our collective public life."[43]

During his presidency, Bill Clinton endorsed a $1,000 tax write-off for families taking care of an incapacitated relative in their homes (an idea Hillary Clinton echoed during her 2016 presidential bid). A male network news commentator dismissed the idea as "more symbolic than significant." The female cohost chided that the symbolic recognition of worth was *quite* significant. She shared Wood's standpoint.

THE STANDPOINT OF BLACK FEMINIST THOUGHT

Consistent with the description of maids' experience in *The Help,* Patricia Hill Collins, an African American sociologist at the University of Maryland, claims that the patterns of "intersecting oppressions" that black women in the United States have experienced put them in a different marginalized social location than is occupied by either white women or black men. "Countless numbers of Black women have ridden buses to their white 'families' where they not only cooked, cleaned, and executed other domestic duties, but where they also nurtured their 'other' children, shrewdly offered guidance to their employers, and frequently became honorary members of their white 'families.'"[44] She refers to this social location as that of an "outsider within," a status that provides a privileged view of white society, yet one in which a black woman will never belong. She agrees with other black feminists that "we have to see clearly that we are a unique group set undeniably apart because of race and sex with a unique set of challenges."[45] That different social location means that black women's way of knowing is different from Harding and Wood's standpoint epistemology.

I'll use Collins' words from her book *Black Feminist Thought* to describe the four ways she says black women collectively validate what they know:[46]

1. *Lived experience as a criterion of meaning.* For most African American women, individuals who have lived through the experience about which they claim to be experts are more believable and credible than those who have merely read or thought about such experiences.

2. *The use of dialogue in assessing knowledge claims.* For ideas to be tested and validated, everyone in the group must participate. To refuse to join in, especially if one really disagrees with what has been said, is seen as "cheating."

3. *The ethic of caring.* Emotion indicates that a speaker believes in the validity of an argument. The sound of what is being said is as important as the words themselves, in what is, in a sense, a dialogue of reason and emotion.

4. *The ethic of personal accountability.* Assessments of an individual's knowledge claims simultaneously evaluate an individual's character, values, and ethics.

Collins doesn't claim that a black feminist standpoint epistemology provides African American women with the best view of how the social world works. She rejects an additive model of oppression that would claim that poor, black, lesbian women are more oppressed than any other marginalized group. But when the same ideas are validated through black feminist thought and from the standpoints of other oppressed groups as well, those ideas become the least partial, most "objective" truths available.

ETHICAL REFLECTION: BENHABIB'S INTERACTIVE UNIVERSALISM

Seyla Benhabib has undertaken a formidable task. Recall that Enlightenment thinkers such as Kant, Locke, and Habermas believed that "reason is a natural disposition of the human mind, which when governed by proper education can discover certain truths."[47] Benhabib, who is a professor of political science and philosophy at Yale University, wants to maintain that a universal ethical standard is a viable possibility.

Muted Group Theory

of Cheris Kramarae

Cheris Kramarae maintains that language is literally a *man*-made construction.

> The language of a particular culture does not serve all its speakers equally, for not all speakers contribute in an equal fashion to its formulation. Women (and members of other subordinate groups) are not as free or as able as men are to say what they wish, when and where they wish, because the words and the norms for their use have been formulated by the dominant group, men.[1]

According to Kramarae and other feminist theorists, women's words are discounted in our society; women's thoughts are devalued. When women try to overcome this inequity, the masculine control of communication places them at a tremendous disadvantage. Man-made language "aids in defining, depreciating and excluding women."[2] Women are thus a muted group.

For many years, Kramarae was a professor of speech communication and sociology at the University of Illinois; she is now a research associate at the Center for the Study of Women in Society at the University of Oregon. She began her research career in 1974 when she conducted a systematic study of the way women were portrayed in cartoons.[3] She found that women were notable mostly by their absence. A quick survey of the cartoon art we've used in this book will show that little has changed since Kramarae's study. Less than half of the 37 cartoons contain female characters, and only 9 of these women speak. All but three of the cartoonists are men.

Kramarae discovered that women in cartoons were usually depicted as emotional, apologetic, or just plain wishy-washy. Compared with the simple, forceful statements voiced by cartoon males, the words assigned to female characters were vague, flowery, and peppered with adjectives like *nice* and *pretty*. Kramarae noted at the time that women who don't appreciate this form of comic put-down are often accused by men of having no sense of humor or simply told to "lighten up." According to Kramarae, this type of male dominance is just one of the many ways that women are rendered inarticulate in our society. For decades, her muted group theory has helped people understand, explain, and alter the muted status of women and other marginalized groups.

MUTED GROUPS: BLACK HOLES IN SOMEONE ELSE'S UNIVERSE

The idea of women as a *muted group* was first proposed by Oxford University social anthropologist Edwin Ardener. In his 1975 article "Belief and the Problem of Women," Ardener noted the strange tendency of many ethnographers to claim to have "cracked the code" of a culture without ever making any direct reference to the half of society made up of women. Field researchers often justified this omission by reporting the difficulty of using women as cultural informants. They claimed that females "giggle when young, snort when old, reject the question, laugh at the topic," and generally make life difficult for scholars trained in the scientific method of inquiry (which has traditionally been dominated by men).[4] Ardener reminded his colleagues how suspicious they'd be of an anthropologist who wrote about the men of a group on the sole basis of talking to the women. It'd be like a visitor trying to understand your school by only talking to students of one sex. Any conclusions drawn from such a study would be partial at best (and completely wrong at worst).

Ardener initially assumed that inattention to women's experience was a problem of gender unique to social anthropology. But along with his Oxford co-worker and wife Shirley Ardener, he began to realize that mutedness is due to the lack of power that besets any group occupying the low end of the totem pole. Mutedness doesn't mean that low-power groups are completely silent.[5] The issue is whether people can say what they want to say, when and where they want to say it. When a group is dominant, that isn't a problem for them. But muted groups must change their language when communicating in the public domain, and thus cannot fully share their true thoughts.[6] As a result, they are often overlooked, muffled, and rendered invisible—"mere black holes in someone else's universe."[7]

Cheris Kramarae believes that men's dominant position in society limits women's access to communication in public spaces. Her extension of the Ardeners'

Muted group
People belonging to low-power groups who must change their language when communicating publicly—thus, their ideas are often overlooked; for example, women.

"I'm used to him finishing my sentences, but now he starts them, too."
©Barbara Smaller/The New Yorker Collection/The Cartoon Bank

initial concept offers insight into why women are muted and what can be done to loosen men's lock on public modes of communication. Kramarae argues that the ever-prevalent *public-private* distinction in language is a convenient way to exaggerate gender differences and pose separate sexual spheres of activity. This is a pitfall into which Deborah Tannen virtually leaps (see Chapter 31). Within the logic of a two-sphere assumption, women speak often in the home—a "small world" of interpersonal communication. But their words appear less often in the "large world" of significant public debate—a place where the words of men resonate.

Elizabeth, a former student who is now a communication professor researching women in the workplace, describes how men's public discourse shapes the meaning of one of her favorite activities:

> I am a passionate knitter. In the dominant communication code, knitting is associated with domestic women. I cannot count the number of times when men have made jokes or comments about me preparing to be a good wife, or looking for a husband, while I am knitting. But I knit because I enjoy it. I love working with my hands and knitting makes a good change from schoolwork. My choice to knit has nothing to do with finding a husband or preparing to be a housewife. Still, even though knitting is an activity that is primarily engaged in by women, it is men who define its meaning.

Kramarae wonders what it would be like if there were a word that pointed to the *connection* of public and private communication. If there were such a word in everyone's speaking vocabulary, its use would establish the idea that both spheres have equal worth and that similarities between women and men are more important than their differences. Since there is no such word in our lexicon, I think of this textbook as a *public* mode of communication. I am male, as are the other two authors of this book. I realize that in the process of trying to present muted group theory with integrity, I may unconsciously put a masculine spin on Kramarae's ideas and the perceptions of women. In an effort to minimize this bias, I will quote extensively from Kramarae and other feminist scholars. Kramarae is just one of many communication professionals who seek to unmask the systematic silencing of a feminine *voice.* I'll also draw freely on the words and experiences of other women to illustrate the communication double bind that Kramarae says is a feminine fact of life. This reliance on personal narrative is consistent with a feminist research agenda that takes women's experiences seriously.

THE MASCULINE POWER TO NAME EXPERIENCE

Kramarae starts with the assumption that "women perceive the world differently from men because of women's and men's different experience and activities rooted in the division of labor."[8] Kramarae rejects Freud's simplistic notion that "anatomy is destiny." She is certain, however, that power discrepancies between the sexes ensure that women will view the world in a way different from men. While individual women vary from each other in many ways, in most cultures, if not all, women's talk is subject to male control and censorship. French existentialist Simone de Beauvoir underscored this common feminine experience when she declared, "'I am woman': on this truth must be based all further discussion."[9]

The problem facing women, according to Kramarae, is that further discussions about how the world works never take place on a level playing field. "Because of their political dominance, the men's system of perception is dominant, impeding the free expression of the women's alternative models of the world."[10]

Note that my phrase *level playing field* is a metaphor drawn from competitive team sports—historically, an experience familiar to more men than women. This is precisely Kramarae's point. As possessors of the public mode of expression, men frame the discussion. If a man wants to contest the point about a tilted playing field, he can argue in the familiar idiom of sports. But a woman who takes issue with the metaphor of competition has to contest it with stereotypically masculine words, phrases, and metaphors.

Mead's symbolic interactionist perspective asserts that the extent of knowing is the extent of naming (see Chapter 5). If this is true, whoever has the ability to make names stick possesses an awesome power. Kramarae notes that men's control of the dominant mode of expression has produced a vast stock of derogatory, gender-specific terms to refer to women's talking—*catty, bitchy, shrill, cackling, gossipy, chitchat, sharp-tongued,* and so forth. There is no corresponding vocabulary to disparage men's conversation.

In case you think this lexical bias is limited to descriptions of speech, consider the variety of terms in the English language to describe sexually promiscuous individuals. By one count, there are 22 gender-related words to label men who are sexually loose—*playboy, stud, rake, gigolo, player, Don Juan, lothario, womanizer,* and so on. There are more than 200 words that label sexually loose women—*slut, whore, hooker, prostitute, trollop, mistress, harlot, Jezebel, hussy, concubine, streetwalker, strumpet, easy lay,* and the like.[11] Since most surveys of sexual activity show that more men than women have multiple sexual partners, there's no doubt that the inordinate number of terms describing women serves the interests of men.

Under the socio-cultural tradition in Chapter 4, we introduced the Sapir-Whorf hypothesis, which claims that language shapes our perception of reality. Kramarae suggests that women are often silenced by not having a publicly recognized vocabulary through which to express their experience. She says that "words constantly ignored may eventually come to be unspoken and perhaps even unthought."[12] After a while, muted women may even come to doubt the validity of their experience and the legitimacy of their feelings.

MEN AS THE GATEKEEPERS OF COMMUNICATION

Even if the public mode of expression contained a rich vocabulary to describe feminine experience, women would still be muted if *their* modes of expression were ignored or ridiculed. As an example of men's control of the public record, Cheris Kramarae cites the facts surrounding her change of name. When she was married in Ohio, the law required her to take the name of her husband. So at the direction of the state, she became *Cheris Rae Kramer.* Later, when it became legal for her to choose her own name, she reordered the sounds and spelling to Cheris Kramarae. Many people questioned Kramarae about whether her name change was either loving or wise. Yet no one asked her husband why he kept *his* name. Kramarae points out that both the law and the conventions of proper etiquette have served men well.

So have the mass media. Cultivation theory researchers (see Chapter 29) tell us that although men outnumber women on prime-time TV, women are more likely to be portrayed as victims of violence. That's no surprise to Kramarae, given who runs mass media corporations. In Chapter 30 (agenda-setting theory), we described *gatekeepers* as the editors, writers, and producers who control what gets published in the mass media. Kramarae observes that most gatekeepers are men—a "good ole boys" cultural establishment that historically has excluded women's art, poetry, plays, film scripts, public address, and scholarly essays. She notes that women were locked out of the publishing business for 500 years. It wasn't until the 1970s and the establishment of women's presses in the Western world that women could exercise ongoing influence through the print medium. Overall, Kramarae sees traditional mainstream mass media as *malestream expression.*

Malestream expression
Traditional mainstream mass media, controlled by men.

Long before Edwin Ardener noted women's absence in anthropological research, Virginia Woolf protested women's nonplace in recorded history. The British novelist detected an incongruity between the way men characterize women in fiction and how women concurrently appear in history books. "Imaginatively she is of the highest importance; practically she is completely insignificant. She pervades poetry from cover to cover; she is all but absent from history."[13]

Feminist writer Dorothy Smith claims that women's absence from history is a result of closed-circuit masculine scholarship.

> Men attend to and treat as significant only what men say. The circle of men whose writing and talk was significant to each other extends backwards in time as far as our records reach. What men were doing was relevant to men, was written by men about men for men. Men listened and listen to what one another said.[14]

Thus, throughout history, women have struggled to publish—simply because they're women. When British author Joanne Rowling wrote the first *Harry Potter* book, her publisher insisted on printing the book using initials rather than her first name, fearing boys wouldn't read a story written by a female author.[15] This is not an isolated incident. Many women have suppressed their feminine identity to satisfy the demands of a male gatekeeper.

To some extent, Kramarae thinks advances in technology create new spaces where women can make their voices heard.[16] The Internet enables many artists to share their work directly through blogs, social media, YouTube, and a stream of other outlets. Computers don't care about the gender of the person who created the content.

Or do they? As we discussed in the critique of agenda-setting theory (see Chapter 30), the Internet doesn't eliminate gatekeeping. Instead, it replaces human publishers with *algorithmic gatekeepers*—computer programs that filter information and decide what you'll see. Tech executive Eli Pariser notes that these programs are likely to "simply reflect the social mores of the culture they're processing."[17] So who is designing these algorithms, and whose culture do they reflect? One recent report indicates that the culture of Silicon Valley tech corporations is dominated by men, with nearly half of the major Silicon Valley corporations having no female executives at all.[18] Kramarae evaluates this reality bluntly: "This is a discouraging situation, for everyone."[19]

Sheryl Sandberg agrees. As a writer, her best-selling book *Lean In* calls for women to pursue positions in corporate leadership. And as Facebook's chief operating officer, she believes technology won't reflect the interests of female users until we have more women in technology fields. She points to Apple's health app as an example. When first released, it enabled users to track many kinds of health information, but not menstrual periods—a dead giveaway that the technology probably wasn't created by women.[20] Although technology may open new spaces for muted groups to speak and network, it also may enable more subtle forms of muting when marginalized groups have little influence on the technology's design.

SPEAKING WOMEN'S TRUTH IN MEN'S TALK: THE PROBLEM OF TRANSLATION

Assuming masculine dominance of public communication to be a current reality, Kramarae concludes that "in order to participate in society women must transform their own models in terms of the received male system of expression."[21] Like speaking a second language, this translation process requires constant effort and usually leaves a woman wondering whether she's said it "just right." One woman writer said men can "tell it straight." Women have to "tell it slant."[22]

Think back again to Mead's symbolic interactionism (see Chapter 5). His theory describes *minding* as an automatic pause before we speak in order to consider how those who are listening might respond. These periods of hesitation grow longer when we feel linguistically impoverished. According to Kramarae, women have to choose their words carefully in a public forum. "What women want to say and can say best cannot be said easily because the language template is not of their own making."[23]

I have gained a new appreciation of the difficulty women face in translating their experiences into man-made language by discussing Kramarae's ideas with three female friends. Marsha, Kathy, and Susan have consciously sought and achieved positions of leadership in professions where women are rarely seen or heard.

Marsha is a litigation attorney who was the first female president of the Hillsborough County Bar Association (Florida) and was chair of a branch of the Federal Reserve Board. Marsha attributes her success to a conscious shifting of gears when she addresses the law.

> I've learned to talk like a man. I consciously lower my voice, speak more slowly, think bigger, and use sports analogies. I care about my appearance, but a woman who is too attractive or too homely has a problem. A man can be drop-dead gorgeous or ugly as sin and get along OK. I've been told that I'm the most feared and respected attorney in the firm, but that's not the person I live with day by day. After work I go home and make reindeer pins out of dog biscuits with my daughters.

Kathy is an ordained minister who works with high school students and young adults. She is the best speaker I've ever heard in a public address class. Working in an organization that traditionally excludes women from up-front speaking roles, Kathy is recognized as a star communicator. Like Marsha, she feels women have little margin for error when they speak in public.

> In order to communicate effectively with men as well as women, I intentionally use illustrations that connect with men more easily. It is important to me to be authentic to who I am as a feminine, petite woman, yet at the same time relate well to men who otherwise might not be inclined to listen or take me seriously. To that end I carefully choose my words to avoid language and imagery that I'd use with an all female audience.

Susan is the academic dean of a professional school within a university. When her former college closed, Susan orchestrated the transfer of her entire program and faculty to another university. She's received the Professional of the Year award in her field. When she first attended her national deans' association, only 8 out of 50 members were women.

> I was very silent. I hated being there. If you didn't communicate by the men's rules you were invisible. The star performers were male and they came on strong. But no

one was listening; everyone was preparing their own response. The meeting oozed one-upmanship. You wouldn't dare say, "Look, I'm having this rough situation I'm dealing with. Have you ever faced this problem?" It was only when some of the women got together for coffee or went shopping that I could be open about my experiences.

Although their status and abilities clearly show that Marsha, Kathy, and Susan are remarkable individuals, their experience as women in male hierarchical structures supports muted group theory. Kramarae says that "men have structured a value system and a language that reflects that value system. Women have had to work through the system organized by men."[24] For women with less skill and self-confidence than Marsha, Kathy, or Susan, that prospect can be daunting.

SPEAKING OUT IN PRIVATE: NETWORKING WITH WOMEN

Susan's relief at the chance to talk freely with other female deans illustrates a central tenet of muted group theory. Kramarae states that "females are likely to find ways to express themselves outside the dominant public modes of expression used by males in both their verbal conventions and their nonverbal behavior."[25]

Kramarae lists a variety of back-channel routes that women use to discuss their experiences—diaries, journals, letters, oral histories, folklore, gossip, chants, art, graffiti, poetry, songs, nonverbal parodies, gynecological handbooks passed between women for centuries, and a "mass of 'noncanonized' writers whose richness and diversity we are only just beginning to comprehend."[26] She labels these outlets the female "sub-version" that runs beneath the surface of male orthodoxy.

Today, Pinterest posts may be the latest version of these back channels. Although the popular, visually oriented social media site is available to men, so far they've shown little interest in it.[27] That wouldn't surprise Kramarae—she notes that men are often oblivious to the shared meanings women communicate through alternative channels. In fact, Kramarae is convinced that "males have more difficulty than females in understanding what members of the other gender mean."[28] She doesn't ascribe men's bewilderment to biological differences between the sexes or to women's attempts to conceal their experience. Rather, she suggests that when men don't have a clue about what women want, think, or feel, it's because they haven't made the effort to find out.

When British author Dale Spender was editor of *Women's Studies International Quarterly,* she offered a further interpretation of men's ignorance. She proposed that many men realize that a commitment to listen to women would necessarily involve a renunciation of their privileged position. "The crucial issue here is that if women cease to be muted, men cease to be so dominant and to some males this may seem unfair because it represents a loss of rights."[29] A man can dodge that equalizing bullet by claiming, "I'll never understand women."

ENRICHING THE LEXICON: A FEMINIST DICTIONARY

Like other forms of critical theory, feminist theory is not content to merely point out asymmetries in power. The ultimate goal of muted group theory is to change the man-made linguistic system that keeps women "in their place." According to Kramarae, reform includes challenging dictionaries that "ignore the words and definitions created by women and which also include many sexist definitions and examples."[30] Traditional dictionaries pose as authoritative guides to proper language use,

Appearance: A woman's appearance is her work uniform. . . . A woman's concern with her appearance is not a result of brainwashing; it is a reaction to necessity. (A Redstockings Sister)

Cuckold: The husband of an unfaithful wife. The wife of an unfaithful husband is just called a wife. (Cheris Kramarae)

Depression: A psychiatric label that . . . hides the social fact of the housewife's loneliness, low self-esteem, and work dissatisfaction. (Ann Oakley)

Doll: A toy playmate given to, or made by children. Some adult males continue their childhood by labeling adult female companions "dolls." (Cheris Kramarae)

Family man: Refers to a man who shows more concern with members of the family than is normal. There is no label *family woman,* since that would be heard as redundancy. (Cheris Kramarae)

Feminist: "I myself have never been able to find out precisely what feminism is: I only know that people call me a feminist whenever I express sentiments that differentiate me from a doormat." (Rebecca West)

Gossip: A way of talking between women in their roles as women, intimate in style, personal and domestic in topic and setting; a female cultural event which springs from and perpetuates the restrictions of the female role, but also gives the comfort of validation. (Deborah Jones)

Guilt: The emotion that stops women from doing what they may need to do to take care of themselves as opposed to everyone else. (Mary Ellen Shanesey)

Herstory: The human story as told by women and about women. . . . (Ann Forfreedom)

Ms.: A form of address being adopted by women who want to be recognized as individuals rather than being identified by their relationship with a man. (Midge Lennert and Norma Wilson)

One of the boys: Means NOT one of the girls. (Cheris Kramarae)

Parenthood: A condition which often brings dramatic changes to new mothers — "loss of job, income, and status; severing of networks and social contacts; and adjustments to being a 'housewife.' Most new fathers do not report similar social dislocations." (Lorna McKee and Margaret O'Brien)

Pornography: Pornography is the theory and rape is the practice. (Andrea Dworkin)

Sexual harassment: Refers to the unwanted imposition of sexual requirements in the context of a relationship of unequal power. (Catharine MacKinnon)

Silence: Is not golden. "There is no agony like bearing an untold story inside you." (Zora Neale Hurston) "In a world where language and naming are power, silence is oppressive, is violence." (Adrienne Rich)

FIGURE 33–1   Excerpts from Kramarae and Treichler's Feminist Dictionary

Source: Cheris Kramarae and Paula Treichler, with assistance from Ann Russo, The Feminist Dictionary 2e, Pandora Press Routledge & Kegan Paul plc, London 1992.

but, because of their reliance on male literary sources, lexicographers systematically exclude words coined by women.

Kramarae and Paula Treichler have compiled a feminist dictionary that offers definitions for women's words that don't appear in *Merriam-Webster's Collegiate Dictionary* and presents alternative feminine readings of words that do. The dictionary "places *women* at the center and rethinks language from that crucially different perspective."[31] Kramarae and Treichler don't claim that all women use words the same way, nor do they believe women constitute a single, unified group. But they include women's definitions of approximately 2,500 words in order to illustrate women's linguistic creativity and to help empower women to change their muted status. Figure 33–1 provides a sample of brief entries and acknowledges their origin.

The Internet also enables women to remake language with new words. One example is *mansplaining.* Although it isn't clear who coined the term, one account states that it became popular in the blogging world around 2008, describing "a man explaining a topic of conversation to a woman who . . . could reasonably be presumed to know about that topic."[32] By 2010, *The New York Times* recognized it as one of its words of the year.[33] Although 2016 presidential candidates Hillary Clinton and Carly Fiorina represented opposing political parties, both appeared in YouTube videos that poke fun at mansplaining.[34] Despite their many differences, each candidate expressed frustration with men who think they know better than women.

SEXUAL HARASSMENT: COINING A TERM TO LABEL EXPERIENCE

Sexual harassment
An unwanted imposition of sexual requirements in the context of a relationship of unequal power.

Perhaps more than any other single entry in the Kramarae and Treichler dictionary, the inclusion of *sexual harassment* illustrates a major achievement of feminist communication scholarship—encoding women's experience into the received language of society. Although stories of unwanted sexual attention on the job are legion, women haven't always had a common term to label what has been an ongoing fact of feminine life.

In 1992, the *Journal of Applied Communication Research* published 30 stories of communication students and professionals who had been sexually embarrassed, humiliated, or traumatized by a person who was in a position of academic power. All but 2 of the 30 accounts came from women. As Kramarae notes, "Sexual harassment is rampant but not random."[35] One woman wrote this account of her attempt to talk to a senior professor who had made an unsolicited sexual advance:

> I was at a disadvantage in our "open talk," because I approached it as a chance to clarify feelings while he used it as an occasion to reinterpret and redefine what was happening in ways that suited his purposes. I told him I didn't feel right "being so friendly" with him. He replied that I was over-reacting and, further, that my small-town southern upbringing was showing. . . . I told him I was concerned that he wasn't being objective about my work, but was praising it because he wanted to be "friends" with me; he twisted this, explaining he was judging my work fairly, BUT that being "friends" did increase his interest in helping me professionally. No matter what I said, he had a response that defined my feelings as inappropriate.[36]

Muted group theory can explain this woman's sense of confusion and lack of power. Her story is as much about a struggle for language as it is a struggle over sexual conduct. As long as the professor can define his actions as "being friendly," the female student's feelings are discounted—even by herself. Had she been equipped with the linguistic tool of "sexual harassment," she could have validated her feelings and labeled the professor's advances as both inappropriate and illegal.

Date rape
Unwanted sexual activity with an acquaintance, friend, or romantic partner.

Communication professor Ann Burnett (North Dakota State University) identifies similar confusion and powerlessness regarding *date rape*—an acute form of sexual harassment often directed at college women. Although students possess a relatively clear understanding of stranger rape, they have difficulty even defining date rape. That confusion is only heightened by *rape myths* common on campuses. ("All guys expect sex on a first date." "Women who dress a certain way are just asking for it.") Burnett notes that although universities offer programs addressing drug and alcohol abuse, fewer programs exist regarding date rape. There's further uncertainty when a woman tries to say no, because men and women often don't agree on what constitutes sexual consent. After a date rape, the lack of clarity makes the victim feel confused and uncertain about what she's experienced. Talking about the incident with friends doesn't always help: "After the rape occurs, both women and male acquaintances blame the victim for not being more 'sensible.' This vicious circle mutes women by making them feel badly for not 'doing enough' to protect themselves, but sadly, the ambiguity arises, what is 'enough'?"[37] This uncertainty favors men—and mutes women—before, during, and after date rape.

According to Kramarae, when *sexual harassment* was first used in a court case in the late 1970s, it was the only legal term defined by women. Although *date rape* and *rape culture* have entered our cultural vocabulary, research like Burnett's indicates that many men don't understand what women mean by these terms. For muted group theorists, the struggle to contest man-made language continues.

CRITIQUE: DO MEN MEAN TO MUTE?

Feminist scholars insist that "the key communication activities of women's experiences—their rituals, vocabularies, metaphors, and stories—are an important part of the data for study."[38] In this chapter I've presented the words of 30 women who give voice to the mutedness they've experienced because they aren't men. Drawing from *qualitative research* by muted group theorists and from many other sources, I could have easily cited hundreds more. It strikes me that ignoring or discounting women's testimony would be the ultimate confirmation of Kramarae's muted group thesis.

The theory has inspired many scholars to take the voices of women and other muted groups seriously. This *community of agreement* runs roughshod over the disciplinary boundaries that often separate scholars in psychology, sociology, education, communication, and other fields. Few other interpretive theories in this book can claim such wide-ranging support and enthusiasm. This diverse set of scholars is united in their conviction that, by understanding the experiences of muted groups, we also achieve new *understanding of people* overall.

Steeped in the critical tradition, muted group theory is exceedingly candid about trying to *clarify values*. Sometimes I've found that students (both male and female) feel uncomfortable with the theory's characterization of men as oppressors and women as the oppressed. Kramarae addresses this issue:

> Some people using the theory have boxed oppression within discrete, binary categories, e.g., women/men; AfricanAmericans/EuroAmericans. A focus only on the categories of women and men, or white and non-white, for example, is simplistic and ignores other forms of struggle. . . .[39]

So, can men be members of a muted group? Kramarae's answer is *yes*, especially if those men identify with another marginalized group, such as the economically disadvantaged or an ethnic minority. Other men may face criticism or hostility when transgressing gender expectations, like by becoming a stay-at-home dad.[40] Thus, Kramarae acknowledges that oppression is more complex than identification with any one group. Yet she also states that "fixing names to the ones we call 'oppressors' may be necessary in order to have clear discussions" about oppressive power differences.[41] How can we name an oppressive group without speaking in terms of demographic categories that are always too broad? The theory's lack of clarity regarding this thorny question may frustrate activists looking for practical answers.

The question of men's motives is also problematic. Deborah Tannen criticizes feminist scholars like Kramarae for assuming that men are trying to control women. By Tannen's account, yes, differences in male and female communication styles sometimes lead to imbalances of power, but she's willing to assume that the problems are caused primarily by men's and women's "different styles." In fact, Tannen cautions that "bad feelings and imputation of bad motives or bad character can come about when there was no intention to dominate."[42]

Kramarae thinks Tannen's apology for men's abuse of power is too simple. She notes that men often ignore or ridicule women's statements about the problems of being heard in a male-dominated society. Rather than blaming *style differences,* Kramarae points to the many ways that our political, educational, religious, legal, and media systems support gender, race, and class hierarchies. Your response to muted group theory may depend on whether you are a beneficiary or a victim of these systems.

For men and women who are willing to hear what Kramarae has to say, the consciousness-raising fostered by muted group theory can prod them to quit using words in a way that preserves inequities of power. The terms *sexual harassment* and *mansplaining* are examples of how women's words can be levered into the public lexicon and *reform society* by giving voice to women's collective experience. Phrases like *glass ceiling* and *date rape* weren't even around when Kramarae and Treichler compiled their feminist dictionary, but now these terms are available to label social and professional injustices that women face. Cheris Kramarae's provocative analysis of how women are a group muted by men continues to shake up traditional patterns of communication between the sexes.

QUESTIONS TO SHARPEN YOUR FOCUS

1. What words do you use with your same-sex friends that you don't use with members of the opposite sex? Does this usage support Kramarae's hypothesis of *male control of the public mode of expression?*

2. In a journal article about *dictionary bias,* Kramarae wrote the sentence "I *vaginated* on that for a while."[43] Can you explain her wordplay in light of the principles of muted group theory? How does the meaning of the sentence change when you replace her provocative term with alternative verbs?

3. Think about the majors offered at your school. Which ones tend to draw more women, and which tend to draw more men? Which seem evenly split between the sexes? What might Kramarae say about these patterns?

4. Do you tend to agree more with Tannen's genderlect perspective or Kramarae's muted group theory? To what extent is your choice influenced by your gender identity?

CONVERSATIONS

View this segment online at www.afirstlook.com.

In my conversation with Cheris Kramarae, she suggests that the creation of university departments of women's studies is an encouraging sign that women aren't doomed to remain muted. When I asked if there should also be a "men's studies" program, her unexpected response not only made me laugh but also underscored the rationale for her theory. Describing her *International Encyclopedia of Women* entry on *witches,* she gives a fascinating account of how the meaning of that word has changed to women's disadvantage. I conclude the interview by asking Kramarae to look back on our conversation to see if I had said or done something that constrained what she said. See if you agree with her assessment.

A SECOND LOOK

Recommended resource: Cheris Kramarae, "Muted Group Theory and Communication: Asking Dangerous Questions," *Women and Language,* Vol. 22, 2005, pp. 55–61.

Comprehensive statement: Cheris Kramarae, *Women and Men Speaking,* Newbury House, Rowley, MA, 1981, pp. v–ix, 1–63.

Original concept of mutedness: Edwin Ardener, "Belief and the Problem of Women" and "The 'Problem' Revisited," in *Perceiving Women,* Shirley Ardener (ed.), Malaby, London, 1975, pp. 1–27.

Dictionary of women's words: Cheris Kramarae and Paula Treichler, *A Feminist Dictionary: Amazons, Bluestockings and Crones,* 2nd ed., Pandora, London, 1992.

Worldwide feminist scholarship: Cheris Kramarae and Dale Spender (eds.), *Routledge International Encyclopedia of Women: Global Women's Issues and Knowledge* (4 vol.), Routledge, New York, 2000.

Sexual harassment: Julia T. Wood (ed.), "Special Section—'Telling Our Stories': Sexual Harassment in the Communication Discipline," *Journal of Applied Communication Research,* Vol. 20, 1992, pp. 349–418.

Date rape and muting: Ann Burnett, Jody L. Mattern, Liliana L. Herakova, David H. Kahl Jr., Cloy Tobola, and Susan E. Bornsen, "Communicating/Muting Date Rape: A Co-Cultural Theoretical Analysis of Communication Factors Related to Rape Culture on a College Campus," *Journal of Applied Communication Research,* Vol. 37, 2009, pp. 465–485.

Social media and muting: Wei Zhang and Cheris Kramarae, "BOLD Ideas for Creative Social Networking: An Invitational Discussion," in *Handbook of Research on Digital Media and Creative Technologies,* Dew Harrison (ed.), IGI Global, Hershey, PA, 2015, p. 418.

Pregnancy, women's health, and muting: LaKesha N. Anderson, "Functions of Support Group Communication for Women with Postpartum Depression: How Support Groups Silence and Encourage Voices of Motherhood," *Journal of Community Psychology,* Vol. 41, 2013, pp. 709–724.

Alternative interpretations of gender differences in discourse: Candace West, Michelle M. Lazar, and Cheris Kramarae, "Gender in Discourse," in *Discourse as Social Interaction,* Vol. 2, Teun van Dijk (ed.), Sage, Thousand Oaks, CA, 1997, pp. 119–143.

Critique: Celia J. Wall and Pat Gannon-Leary, "A Sentence Made by Men: Muted Group Theory Revisited," *European Journal of Women's Studies,* Vol. 6, 1999, pp. 21–29.

To discover scenes from feature films that illustrate Muted Group Theory, click on Suggested Movie Clips under Theory Resources at *www.afirstlook.com.*

When we think of *culture,* most of us picture a place—the South American culture of Brazil, the Middle Eastern culture of Saudi Arabia, or the Far Eastern culture of Japan. But Gerry Philipsen, a University of Washington emeritus professor who specializes in intercultural communication, says that culture is not basically geographical. Nor is it essentially political or a matter of race. Philipsen describes *culture* as "a socially constructed and historically transmitted pattern of symbols, meanings, premises, and rules."[1] At root, culture is a code.

Ethnographers study the speech and nonverbal communication of people in order to crack that code. We've already looked at Mead's reliance on participant observation (see Chapter 5) and Geertz' use of thick description (see Chapter 19) to unravel the complex web of meanings that people share within a society or culture. In like manner, Philipsen spent multiple years conducting two ethnographic studies. The first study revealed what it was like to "speak like a man" in a multi-ethnic, blue-collar Chicago neighborhood he called "Teamsterville." He discovered that men used talk primarily to show solidarity with friends who were part of the neighborhood.[2] The second study identified the communication patterns of a large group of people dispersed around the United States whom he dubbed the "Nacirema" (*American* spelled backward). He regarded the live audience for the television talk show *Donahue*—a forerunner of *Oprah*—as typical members of the Nacirema culture. He and Donal Carbaugh (University of Massachusetts) found that Naciremans felt any appeal to a universal standard of ethical conduct was considered by members of that culture to be an infringement of their right to be individuals.[3]

Philipsen selected these two American subcultures for study in part because he saw their communication practices as so different from one another. Is there a way he could have measured the extent of their discrepancy—or for that matter, the cultural variability of any two countries across the globe? From a study of multinational corporations in more than 50 countries, Dutch researcher Geert Hofstede concluded that there are four crucial dimensions on which to compare cultures.[4]

1. *Power distance*—the extent to which the less powerful members of society accept that power is distributed unequally (Americans—low; Japanese—medium)

2. *Masculinity*—clearly defined gender roles, with male values of success, money, and possessions dominant in society (Americans—high; Japanese—extremely high)

3. *Uncertainty avoidance*—the extent to which people feel threatened by ambiguity and create beliefs and institutions to try to avoid it (Americans—low; Japanese—extremely high)

4. *Individualism*—people look out for themselves and their immediate families as opposed to identifying with a larger group that is responsible for taking care of them in exchange for group loyalty (Americans—extremely high; Japanese—low)

Many researchers agree that Hofstede's distinction between individualism and collectivism is the crucial dimension of cultural variability. The *we-centered* focus of Teamsterville sets it apart from individualistic American society in general, and from the extremely *I-centered* preoccupation of the Nacirema subculture in particular. Cultural anthropologist Edward Hall was the first to label the communication style of collectivistic cultures as *high-context* and the style of individualistic cultures as *low-context*. The designation divides groups of people on the basis of how they interpret messages.

> A high-context communication or message is one in which most of the information is either in the physical context or internalized in the person, while very little is in the coded, explicit part of the message. A low-context communication is just the opposite, i.e., the mass of information is vested in the explicit code.[5]

Hall contrasted American and Japanese cultures to illustrate the differences between collectivistic societies that have a message-*context* orientation and individualistic societies that rely more on message *content*.[6]

Americans believe in straight talk. Assertiveness is saying what you mean; honesty is meaning what you say. Both are highly prized. Perhaps the highest art form of explicit communication is the legal contract. A US lawyer's dream is to prepare a verbal document that allows no room for interpretation. Hall said that Japanese communication is more subtle. Bluntness is regarded as rude; patience and indirection are the marks of a civilized person. What is said is less important than how it is said and who did the saying. Meaning is embedded in the setting and the nonverbal code. In Japan, the highest form of communication competency is empathy—the ability to sense what others are thinking and feeling without their having to spell it out for you.

Co-author Glenn Sparks experienced these distinctions when he—a typical low-context American—worked with high-context Africans in Ethiopia.

> When I was in Ethiopia, I worked daily with various folks at the university. I came to learn that about half the time, a lunch appointment, a promise to have a key for a room at a certain time, or a commitment to make copies of a reading for the class just didn't pan out. But all of these commitments were made with kindness and politeness. Ethiopians were much more attuned to the overall tenor of an interaction than they were to the actual words that were said.[7]

Glenn is a quick study. By reminding himself of the crucial contextual issue that Hall identified, he was able to reduce his frustration. Hopefully, in turn, his Ethiopian hosts gave him a "visitor's pass" for misinterpreting what they had said.

Communication Accommodation Theory

of Howard Giles

I was born, raised, and educated in the Great Lakes region of the United States. During my sophomore year of college, my folks moved from the south side of Chicago to the Deep South, a region where the style of speech was foreign to my ear. When speaking with other college students I met there over summer vacation, I noticed that I started to talk slower, pause longer, maintain less eye contact, and drop the final *g* off of words ending with *-ing* ("Nice *talkin'* with you"). I didn't adopt a southern drawl, but I definitely adjusted my style of speaking to better match that of those I met. As an outsider, I wanted to fit in.

Although I couldn't lose my Chicago twang, one of the guys I met commented on my go-along-to-get-along effort. "You're beginnin' to talk just like us," he said. His smile suggested appreciation rather than scorn. Not so my older sister when I drove her from San Antonio to eastern Alabama the following Christmas. "You sound ridiculous," was her disdainful reaction when she heard me talk to people in restaurants and motels along the way.

Howard Giles had a similar experience growing up in Wales. He noticed that his accent changed depending on where he was: "My distinctive Cardiff accent would shift to a more South Welsh brogue when talking with other spectators at a rugby game, and then to a more Standard English with my peers at college who hailed from the south of England."[1] These observations led to several questions: *What is our motive for changing our style of speech? Do others accurately perceive our intent when we shift our speech style? What does this have to do with membership in cultural groups? What social consequences do we face from these adjustments?* Now a communication professor at the University of California, Santa Barbara, Giles built *communication accommodation theory* (CAT) to answer these kinds of questions.

Giles now refers to his adaptation (and mine) as *accommodation*—changing communication behavior in a way that reduces social distance. Keeping my northern accent would've been *nonaccommodation,* as would any other communication adjustment that maintains or increases social distance. The interplay of group identities with communicative differences forms the core of CAT.

Accommodation
Adjustments to communication that decrease social distance.

Nonaccommodation
Communication behavior that maintains or increases social distance.

423

The early research of Giles and his colleagues centered on interethnic communication, often between two bilingual groups in the same country. In the last three decades, however, CAT researchers have also shown consistent interest in exploring accommodation in an intergenerational context. They broadly define *young* communicators as teenagers to adults in their 40s or even 50s. They define *old* or *elderly* communicators as those 65 and over.[2] To what extent do members of these two groups adjust their communication when talking to someone of the other generation?

Since the vast majority of this book's readers fit in the younger classification, I'll use intergenerational communication to illustrate the main predictions of the theory. That way you'll have a personal stake in understanding the theory's claims. So will I. In the spirit of full disclosure, you should know that for the past 15 years I've qualified as a member of the elder group. Of course, this means that every time I walk into a college classroom it becomes a potential laboratory to explore intergenerational communication. Indeed, all three of the authors of this book are from different generations, so we try to practice competent intergenerational communication every time we talk as colleagues and friends. Whether differences between people are generational, cultural, or from any other source, Giles thinks an understanding of CAT can help members of different groups communicate effectively with each other.

HOW WE ACCOMMODATE (OR HOW WE DON'T)

Social distance
How similar or different we are from another person.

If you look back at the definitions of *accommodation* and *nonaccommodation,* you'll see that they have to do with *social distance*—how similar or different we are from another person. For four decades, Giles and other CAT researchers have explored how we use communication to manage social distance. Here's the gist of what they've discovered so far.

Convergence: Seeking Accommodation

Convergence
A strategy of adapting your communication behavior to become more similar to another person.

Convergence is a strategy by which you adapt your communication behavior to become more similar to someone else. Most of the time, we do it because we want to accommodate the other person. As we've already seen, one way to accommodate is to adjust your speaking style to approximate that of your conversational partner. If you're talking with an 80-year-old man who speaks in short phrases delivered in a gravelly voice, you could abandon smoothly flowing sentences in favor of brief, raspy responses. You wouldn't try to mimic his voice, but you'd try to get closer to its sound and cadence. If the elderly man wants to converge toward your speaking style, he might need to speak with more energy, display greater facial expression, and increase vocal variety.

Another way you could converge toward the elderly gentleman would be to talk in a way that would make it easier for him to grasp what you're saying. If you notice that he's hard of hearing, convergence would involve speaking one notch louder, while clearly enunciating consonants. Or if he seems to have trouble tracking with abstract ideas, you could aid his comprehension by using examples to illustrate what you're saying. For his part, he might help you interpret what he's saying by not assuming you know the political background of the Vietnam War or singer Pat Boone's biggest hits.

An additional way to bridge the generation gap can be through *discourse management*—the sensitive selection of topics to discuss. Giles and Angie Williams

(Cardiff and Vale University Health Board, Wales) elicited college students' retrospective accounts of both satisfying and frustrating intergenerational conversations. They found that young people greatly appreciated elderly folks who could discern what stories the students wanted to hear. For example, one young woman wrote, "She just talked about the history of the team and all that she knew. . . . I stayed and listened to her stories, which were fascinating."[3] They also appreciated elders who sensed when not to pry: "I'm glad she didn't ask anything about Bekki and my relationship. . . . I would have felt awkward."[4]

As Brittany's application log describes, some parties converge to facilitate communication. When they do, mutual appreciation is often a by-product.

> Some family members on my father's side are deaf. Some of my family members who can hear know how to sign and some of those who can't hear are able to read lips. I've learned to sign a bit so I can communicate more effectively with those who can't hear. I also slow my speech down and try to enunciate my words more clearly so they can more easily understand what I'm saying. They've told me that they appreciate my willingness to reach out to them. In the same way, I appreciate their convergence when they sign slower and also lip words so that I can catch what they're saying.

Divergence and Other Forms of Nonaccommodation

Divergence is a communication strategy of accentuating the differences between you and another person. Most of the time, the goal of divergence is nonaccommodation. In interethnic encounters, you might insist on using a language or dialect with which the other is uncomfortable. In terms of speech style, you could diverge by employing a thicker accent, adopting a rate of speaking distinct from that used by the other person, or speaking in either a monotone or with exaggerated animation. Linguistically, divergence could be signaled by a deliberate substitution of words. Giles offers an example where a young speaker flippantly says to an elderly man, "Okay, mate, let's get it together at my place around 3:30 tomorrow." The disdainful elder might reply, "Fine, young man, we'll meet again at 15:30, at your house tomorrow."[5] All of these communication moves are examples of *counteraccommodation*—direct, intentional, and even hostile ways of maximizing the differences between two speakers. Even if divergence isn't that aggressive, it's often unpleasant.

During intergenerational encounters, CAT researchers have found that divergence is the norm and convergence the exception, especially when the two aren't members of the same family. Young people typically characterize the elderly as *closed-minded, out of touch, angry, complaining,* and *negatively stereotyping youth.*[6] The elderly often increase the social distance through the process of *self-handicapping*—a defensive, face-saving strategy that uses age as a reason for not performing well. For example, University of Arizona communication professor Jake Harwood and two colleagues discovered that many of the ways the elderly talk continually remind younger listeners that their grandparents are old.[7]

1. Talk about age: *You're so young. I turn 70 next December.*
2. Talk about health: *They warned of blood clots with my hip replacement surgery.*
3. Don't understand the world today: *Are Snapchat and texting the same?*
4. Patronizing: *You kids today don't know the meaning of hard work.*

Divergence
A communication strategy of accentuating the differences between you and another person.

Counteraccommodation
Direct, intentional, and even hostile ways of maximizing social distance.

Self-handicapping
For the elderly, a face-saving strategy that invokes age as a reason for not performing well.

"Hey, Gramps, is 'deathbed' one word or two?"

©Jack Ziegler/The New Yorker Collection/The Cartoon Bank

5. Painful self-disclosure: *I cried when she said that to me. It still hurts.*

6. Difficulty hearing: *Please speak up and try not to mumble.*

7. Mental confusion: *I can't think of the word. What were we talking about?*

These features consistently make the speakers' age salient (or noticeable) to the listener, and all seven leave a negative impression. Elders might as well tattoo GZR on their forehead.

Giles and his colleagues describe two other strategies that are similar to divergence but a bit more subtle. Most of the time, they still function as nonaccommodation. *Maintenance* is the strategy of persisting in your original communication style regardless of the communication behavior of the other. Giles offers a college student's recollections of a dissatisfying conversation with an elder as a description of maintenance: "He did most of the talking and did not really seem to care about what I said. . . . He appeared to be so closed minded and unreceptive to new ideas."[8] Similarly, an older person is likely to feel woefully underaccommodated if she shares

Maintenance
Persisting in your original communication style regardless of the communication behavior of the other; similar to divergence.

a fear or frustration and then only hears a quick, "I know exactly how you feel," before the younger person changes the topic.[9]

The other strategy that's similar to divergence is *overaccommodation,* which may be well intended, but has the effect of making the recipient feel worse. Giles describes overaccommodation as "demeaning or patronizing talk . . . when excessive concern is paid to vocal clarity or [amplification], message simplification, or repetition"[10] Often characterized as "baby talk," this way of speaking can frustrate the elderly, thus leading to a perception that they are irritable or grumpy. Frequent overaccommodation from caregivers can not only make the recipient feel less competent, it can actually talk them into becoming less competent (see Chapter 5).

If overaccommodating communication is often counterproductive and sometimes harmful, why do younger folks talk that way? For that matter, other than sheer obstinacy, why would *anyone* opt for a divergent strategy rather than one that's convergent? The next section shows that the motivation for these contrasting behaviors often arises from people's concern for their identity.

Overaccommodation
Demeaning or patronizing talk; excessive concern paid to vocal clarity or amplification, message simplification, or repetition; similar to divergence.

DIFFERENT MOTIVATIONS FOR CONVERGENCE AND DIVERGENCE

CAT theorists have always regarded *desire for social approval* as the main motivation for convergence. You meet a person different from you and you'd like him or her to think well of you, respect you, or find you attractive. As one of the theorems of *uncertainty reduction* states, there's a positive relationship between similarity and attraction (see Chapter 9). So you identify with the other person by adjusting what you say and the way you say it in order to appear more similar. As long as you're both acting as unique individuals who are shaping their own personal identities and relationships, representing convergence as a two-step, cause-and-effect relationship seems justified:

Desire for approval (personal identity) → Convergence → Positive response

There are two problems, however. First, this motivational sequence can't explain why we frequently communicate in a divergent way. Second, and most importantly to CAT theorists, the causal chain doesn't take into account the fact that we often act as a representative of a group. Giles and other CAT theorists draw upon *social identity theory,* the work of Henri Tajfel (University of Bristol, UK) and John Turner (Australian National University), to solve that problem.[11]

Social Identity Theory

Perhaps you've been in a social situation where you were the only member of your gender or ethnicity. If so, maybe you felt you needed to be a good ambassador for others like you, or wanted to emphasize the worth and distinctiveness of your identity. When communicators are aware of their group differences, that's *intergroup contact.* Tajfel and Turner believed such intergroup contact is common, and that our *social identity* is based upon it. As Jake Harwood puts it, "We are not random individuals wandering the planet with no connections to others, and our connections to others cannot be understood purely as a function of individual phenomena."[12] We often communicate in ways designed to uphold these group memberships.

As a case in point, if you click on "Meet the Authors" and "Em Griffin" at the bottom of the home page of *www.afirstlook.com,* you'll find that I identify with groups of communication professors, conflict mediators, people of faith, pilots, an

Intergroup contact
When communicators are aware of group affiliations that distinguish them.

Social identity
Group memberships and social categories that we use to define who we are.

extended Griffin family, and those who work for economic justice in the developing world. By accident of birth, I also have at least four other group identifications: I'm an older, white, American male. According to Tajfel and Turner, whenever any of these associations comes to mind in talking with others, my motivation will be to reinforce and defend my ties to those groups. After all, they make up my social identity. And when these groups are salient at the start of an interaction with someone different, CAT claims that my communication will diverge away from my partner's speech rather than converge toward it.

Tajfel and Turner pictured a motivational continuum with *personal identity* on one end of the scale and *social identity* on the other. As long as both parties consider themselves and their conversational partner to be autonomous individuals acting for themselves, the theorists believed the *desire for approval* → *convergence* → *positive response* sequence is what takes place. But if one (or both) of the interactants regards self or other as a representative of a group of people, their communication will likely become divergent because of their need to emphasize their distinctiveness. So when group identity is salient, the two-step, cause-and-effect sequence is quite different:

Need for distinctiveness (social identity) → Divergence → Negative response

Giles and his colleagues believe that this alternative sequence occurs quite frequently. They hold out the possibility that a person could seek approval and distinctiveness within the same conversation when personal and social identities are both salient. For example, consider an interracial friendship where buddies never lose sight of their ethnicity. Or think of a loving marriage in which both husband and wife are keenly aware of their gender roles. Your first look at communication accommodation theory will come into focus more easily, however, if we stick with Tajfel and Turner's either/or conception of one of the two motivations holding sway in a given interaction. To the extent that their theory is accurate, how can we predict whether concerns for personal identity or social identity will kick in? According to Giles, there's no hard-and-fast rule. But a person's *initial orientation* is a somewhat reliable predictor.

Initial Orientation

Initial orientation
Communicators' predisposition to focus on either their individual identity or group identity during a conversation.

Initial orientation is the predisposition a person has to focus on either individual identity or group identity. Predicting which route a person will take is difficult, but the additive presence of five factors increases the odds that a communicator will see the conversation as an intergroup encounter. I'll continue to illustrate these factors by referring to intergenerational communication.

1. Collectivistic cultural context. As noted in the introduction to the intercultural communication section, the distinction between collectivistic and individualistic cultures is probably the crucial dimension of cultural variability. The *we-centered* focus of collectivism emphasizes similarity and mutual concern within the culture—definitely oriented toward social identity. Their communication with out-group members is often divergent. The *I-centered* focus of individualistic cultures valorizes the individual actor—definitely oriented toward individual identity. As for intergenerational relationships, despite the cultural value of respect for elders shared among East Asian cultures, there's strong evidence that Pacific Rim young people and their Western counterparts both regard the elderly as a group apart.[13] Age transcends ethnic culture.

2. Distressing history of interaction. If previous interactions were uncomfortable, competitive, or hostile, both interactants will tend to ascribe that outcome to the other person's social identity. *(Men are like that. The poor are lazy. Presbyterians are God's frozen people.)* If the previous time together was positive, the result is often ascribed to the individual rather than to a group or class to which he or she belongs. *(By the end I felt good knowing that not all older people hate the younger generation. . . . Every other elder I've talked to has made me fear or want to avoid getting old.)*[14]

3. Stereotypes. The more specific and negative the images people have of an out-group, the more likely they are to think of the other in terms of social identity and then resort to divergent communication. This is a big factor in intergenerational communication. The young tend to stereotype the elderly as *irritable, nagging, grouchy, verbose,* and *addled,*[15] while the elderly stereotype "youth today" as *spoiled,* an accusation often introduced with the phrase, *Why, when I was your age. . . .* These rigid group stereotypes make convergent communication across generations a rare and difficult achievement.

4. Norms for treatment of groups. Norms can be defined as "expectations about behavior that members of a community feel should (or should not) occur in particular situations."[16] These expectations can affect whether a member of one group regards a person from another group as an individual or as "one of them." The oft-stated rule to "respect your elders" suggests that the elderly are a group of people who deserve high regard because they've stayed alive, rather than because they have individual worth. The result of that group norm may be young adults showing deference to an elderly person, but *biting their tongue* and *not talking back,* a process that could build resentment toward a group they may join someday.

5. High group-solidarity/high group-dependence. Picture Lucile, a 70-year-old widow living in a small retirement village where residents rely on each other for social, emotional, and even physical well-being. As the organizer of a successful food co-op, she's at the nexus of communication and has a higher status among her neighbors than she's ever had before. When a county health department official in his late 20s questions the co-op's food handling practices, Lucile goes to talk with him in what she considers an us-against-them encounter. Giles would predict that she would have an initial intergroup orientation because of her strong identification with the group and her high dependence on it for relational warmth and a sense of worth.[17]

No single factor determines a person's initial orientation, but if all five factors line up in the direction of social identity, it's almost certain that a communicator will approach a conversation with an intergroup mindset. That seems to be the case in most intergenerational interactions. Giles would note, however, that a person may change orientations during a conversation.

Norms
Expectations about behavior that members of a community feel should (or should not) occur in particular situations.

RECIPIENT EVALUATION OF CONVERGENCE AND DIVERGENCE

So, people converge when they want social approval and diverge when they want to emphasize their distinctiveness. The theory isn't clear on whether our convergence and divergence are always intentional; the best we can say right now is that sometimes they are and sometimes they aren't. But regardless of the speaker's intent, how do receivers interpret that convergence or divergence? The bottom line is this: Giles and his colleagues continue to believe what he wrote about accommodation in his first major article—that listeners regard convergence as positive and divergence as negative. Specifically, converging speakers are viewed as more competent, attractive, warm, and cooperative.[18] Conversely, "divergence is often seen by its recipients as insulting, impolite, or downright hostile."[19] Yet CAT researchers are quick to remind us that all communication adjustments are in the eyes and ears of the beholder. What's ultimately important is not how the communicator converged or diverged, but how the other *perceived* the communicator's behavior.

Objective vs. Subjective Accommodation

Early in his research, Giles realized that there was a disconnect between the communication behavior that he and other neutral researchers observed and what participants heard and saw. He described the gap as the difference between *objective* and *subjective* accommodation. For example, a speaker's accent, rate, pitch, and length of pauses could actually be shifting toward a conversational partner's style of speaking, but the partner might regard it as divergent. In light of this discrepancy, Giles says it is recipients' subjective evaluation that really matters, because that's what will shape their response.

Speakers who seek approval by converging with the other's style of speaking may also misperceive what that style really is. From an objective point of view, what strikes them as the other group's preferred style of communication may woefully miss the mark. For example, a granddad might try to identify with his grandkids by using phrases like *right on, really hep,* or *that's square,* not realizing that these phrases were more typical for teenagers in the late 1960s than for teens today. Giles notes that "one does not converge toward (or diverge from) the *actual* speech of the recipient, but toward (or from) one's *stereotype* about the recipient's speech."[20] If we think we're converging but the other person perceives us as diverging, we probably won't achieve the social approval we desire.

Attribution Theory

Attribution
The perceptual process by which we observe what people do and then try to figure out their intent or disposition.

Our response to others' communication hinges not only on the behavior we perceive, but also on the intention or motive we ascribe to them for speaking that way. Giles draws from *attribution theory* to cast light on how we'll interpret our conversational partners' convergent or divergent behavior. In two different versions of attribution theory, social psychologists Fritz Heider (University of Kansas) and Harold Kelley (UCLA) suggested that we attribute an internal disposition to the behavior we see another enact.[21] As amateur psychologists, our default assumption is that *people who do things like that are like that.* Yet three mitigating factors may come into play: (1) the other's ability, (2) external constraints, and (3) the effort expended.

Suppose you're talking with an elderly man who continually asks you to repeat what you've said. If you know that his hearing is good (high ability) and the room is quiet (no external constraints), yet he's not paying much attention (low effort), you'll attribute his divergent behavior to lack of respect for you. You'll be more understanding if you know he's hard of hearing (low ability). But as one research study shows, you'll still be irritated by his lack of consideration if he freely chooses not to wear a hearing aid (low effort).[22] What if you know he's almost deaf (low ability), the room is noisy (environmental constraint), and he's wearing a hearing aid and still struggling to catch your words (high effort)? You'll probably appreciate the fact that he cares about what you're saying and wants to understand, even if you find the conversation tiring or uncomfortable.

Overall, listeners who interpret convergence as a speaker's desire to break down cultural barriers react quite favorably.[23] That response is at the core of CAT. But because there's a societal constraint or norm that those with less power (workers, patients, students, immigrants) ought to accommodate to the communication practices of those with higher status (bosses, doctors, professors, citizens), upward convergers don't get as much credit as when status is relatively equal. Still, this moderate reaction is much more favorable than the response toward a low-power person who adopts a divergent strategy. As a case in point, consider the anger of many Anglo Americans toward Latino immigrants who "refuse" to become bilingual.

There are benefits and costs to both convergent and divergent strategies. CAT research continues to document the positive interpersonal relationship development that can result from appropriate convergence. The practice also facilitates better comprehension and understanding. But these gains come at the potential risk of offending other in-group members, just as my sister was disgusted by my attempt to talk like a "down-home" southerner. They may feel that converging toward an out-group is diverging from them. And, of course, the one who accommodates may also feel a sense of inauthenticity.

The interpersonal tension created by divergence or maintenance can certainly block the formation of intergroup or intercultural relationships and understanding. But the upside for the communicator is the reaffirmed social identity and solidarity that comes from enacting a divergent strategy. In that sense, divergence can be an accommodation strategy just as much as convergence is, but it's accommodation to the in-group rather than members of the out-group.

APPLYING CAT TO POLICE OFFICER–CITIZEN INTERACTION

My extensive discussion of intergenerational communication may have given you the idea that the scope of CAT is limited to conversations between the young and the elderly. Not so. CAT can be applied to any intercultural or intergroup situation where the differences between people are apparent and significant. Since Giles is a retired chaplain and reserve lieutenant in the Santa Barbara Police Department, he's found it helpful to apply CAT to the interaction between police officers and citizens during routine traffic stops.

At one time or another, most of us have been pulled over by a police officer for a possible driving infraction. Giles describes these encounters as "potentially negatively valenced, emotionally charged interactions" in which our group membership may be particularly salient and the uncertainty of the outcome can cause great anxiety.[24] If you've been stopped by a cop, you know the feeling. What you might not realize is that the event is also fraught with danger for the officer—as one top FBI official remarks, "Every stop can be potentially fatal."[25] Statistics back up that claim, with police officer deaths rising by 10 percent from 2015 to 2016, including an even sharper increase in ambush-style killings.[26] Police officers are trained to stay on guard, a mindset that could affect the quality of communication in police-citizen interaction.

As recent US headlines make clear, tensions in this already stressful interaction may escalate when the issue of race comes into play. Particularly after the deaths of Michael Brown, Freddie Gray, and others, civil rights advocates have claimed that cops often treat blacks more harshly than whites. The goal of one CAT study was "to move beyond casual assumptions to systematically investigate the extent to which the race of interactants might influence the nature of police–civilian communication."[27]

Giles was part of a team of researchers that viewed 313 randomly selected video recordings from police cars during traffic stops in Cincinnati, Ohio. The research team analyzed the verbal and nonverbal interaction of officer and driver in each encounter to determine the extent of convergence or divergence. For officers, approachability, listening to the driver's explanation, and showing respect were the marks of accommodation. Indifference, dismissive behavior, and an air of superiority were scored as nonaccomodative. Drivers who were courteous, apologetic, pleasant, and who showed respect were rated as accommodating. Drivers who were belligerent were regarded as nonaccommodating.

Based on CAT, the Cincinnati study predicted that interracial interactions would be less accommodating than those where the officer and driver were of the same race. Researchers anticipated this outcome because a mixed-race interaction in this high-pressure context would make each party's ethnic-group identity significant for them during the encounter. With that mind-set, they would no longer act as independent agents. They would see themselves as representatives of their race and speak in a way that accentuates their differences.

The videotapes confirmed CAT's prediction for the police. When the cop and driver were the same race, the officer's communication was viewed by objective judges as convergent. When the cop was white and the driver was black, or the cop was black and the driver was white, the officer's communication was judged as divergent. But the videotape evidence did not support the prediction of similar adjustments in the drivers' communication. Although Giles still suggests that "accommodating civilians may be less susceptible to harsh penalties and reprimands from officers,"[28] that's not a guaranteed prescription for avoiding a ticket if a cop pulls you over.

CRITIQUE: ENORMOUS SCOPE AT THE COST OF CLARITY

From a modest beginning as a narrowly conceived theory of social psychology, CAT has morphed into a communication theory of enormous scope. Giles' adoption of *social identity theory of group behavior* and *attribution theory,* which are essential to CAT's explanation of accommodation, demonstrates that his theory hasn't abandoned its social psych roots. It's appropriate, therefore, to evaluate CAT by using the six criteria for good objective theories presented in Chapter 3.

1. Explanation of data. CAT not only describes communication behavior, it explains why it happens. The dual theoretical engines of *desire for approval* and *need to maintain a distinctive social identity* are compelling reasons for two very different communication strategies. Further, Giles and his colleagues offer multiple factors to clarify which motivation will kick in at any given time.

2. Prediction of the future. Giles doesn't shy away from forecasting what will happen in specific situations. As the scope of the theory has expanded, he's found it necessary to alter or qualify many of these predictions, but CAT places its bets ahead of time. As a communication scholar who was first trained in experimental methodology, I find this put-up-or-shut-up approach appealing. I also appreciate Giles' movement toward qualitative methods as he attempts to predict how recipients will interpret communicative adjustments.

3. Relative simplicity. CAT is an extraordinarily complex theory presented in multiple versions that are sometimes offered simultaneously. As Cindy Gallois (University of Queensland, Australia), Tania Ogay (University of Fribourg, Switzerland), and Giles admit in a summary chapter, CAT's "structure and the underlying terminology are not always represented consistently in texts and propositions."[29] Even the meaning of *accommodation* within the theory is slippery. Sometimes the term seems synonymous with convergence (as opposed to divergence), while other times it's used to refer to any adjustment of communication behavior. Giles' 2016 book on the theory's state of the art tries to boil it all down to seven (or maybe eight) propositions,[30] even as the book calls for more detailed theorizing of contexts, nonaccommodation, and other factors.[31] CAT provides complicated answers to rather simple questions.

4. Testable hypotheses. The complexity problem spills over into the possibility of being able to demonstrate that the theory is false. In one candid assessment, Gallois and Giles wrote:

> CAT has become very complex, so that the theory as a whole probably cannot be tested at one time. This means that researchers using CAT must develop mini-theories to suit the contexts in which they work, while at the same time keeping the whole of the theory in mind.[32]

Looking back over four decades of theory development, Giles and his colleagues admit that it's not clear what "the whole of the theory" actually is.[33] If they aren't sure, it's hard for others to know—and that makes it tough to falsify.

5. Quantitative research. Many alterations and additions to Giles' original theory have been made in response to field research that shows communication accommodation is more complicated than originally thought. Studies using surveys and interviews are the norm; experiments are rare. As illustrated by the Cincinnati traffic-stop study, the frequency of responses is tabulated, but figuring out what behavior means depends on how people interpret their own actions. Many scholars appreciate this mix of quantitative and qualitative methodology, and Giles believes it is a strength of the theory.[34]

6. Practical utility. A recent review of published research found that researchers have used CAT to understand communication in many important contexts—the family, the doctor's office, the classroom, the workplace, and many more.[35] Clearly, the theory provides practical insight into many situations where people from different groups or cultures come into contact.

QUESTIONS TO SHARPEN YOUR FOCUS

1. Can you think of a time when you found another's *divergence* in *speech style* delightful or another's *convergence* distressing?

2. To what extent is it possible to interact with another person and not have *age, gender, race, nationality, sexual orientation, religious commitment,* or *political ideology* be *salient* when you know that one or more of these differs from your own?

3. In what way might you *overaccommodate* to the *stereotypical image* you hold of opposite-sex communication behavior?

4. As you read about the actions and reactions of young people cited from *intergenerational research,* with which strategies and responses do you identify? Which do you believe are uncharacteristic of you?

CONVERSATIONS

View this segment online at www.afirstlook.com.

In his interview with Andrew, Howie Giles doesn't just explain how his interest in different accents led to the development of CAT—he adopts those accents. Giles also provides advice informed by CAT: first to Andrew about moving from the northern United States to the South, and then to students who might be pulled over by a cop. You might consider how his advice compares with what other intercultural communication theories would say. To conclude the interview, Andrew asks Giles whether his knowledge of CAT makes him communicate strategically rather than authentically. As a communication theory student, you'll probably empathize with his candid response.

A SECOND LOOK

Recommended resource: Howard Giles and Jordan Soliz, "Communication Accommodation Theory: A Situated Framework for Relational, Family, and Intergroup Dynamics," in *Engaging Theories in Interpersonal Communication: Multiple Perspectives,* 2nd ed., Dawn O. Braithwaite and Paul Schrodt (eds.), Sage, Thousand Oaks, CA, 2015, pp. 161-173.

Original statement of speech accommodation theory: Howard Giles, "Accent Mobility: A Model and Some Data," *Anthropological Linguistics,* Vol. 15, 1973, pp. 87-109.

SAT expanded and renamed CAT: Howard Giles, Anthony Mulac, James Bradac, and Patricia Johnson, "Speech Accommodation Theory: The First Decade and Beyond," in *Communication Yearbook 10,* Margaret L. McLaughlin (ed.), Sage, Newbury Park, CA, 1987, pp. 13-48.

Propositional synthesis: Marko Dragojevic, Jessica Gasiorek, and Howard Giles, "Accommodative Strategies as Core of the Theory," in *Communication Accommodation Theory: Negotiating Personal Relationships and Social Identities Across Contexts,* Howard Giles (ed.), Cambridge University Press, UK, 2016, pp. 36-59.

Social identity theory: Henri Tajfel and John C. Turner, "The Social Identity Theory of Intergroup Behavior," in *The Psychology of Intergroup Relations,* L. Worchel and W. Austin (eds.), Nelson Hall, Chicago, IL, 1986, pp. 7-24.

Importance of social identity: Jake Harwood, "Communication as Social Identity," in *Communication as ... Perspectives on Theory,* Gregory Shepherd, Jeffrey St. John, and Ted Striphas (eds.), Sage, Thousand Oaks, CA, 2006, pp. 84-90.

Intergenerational communication between grandparents and grandchildren: Karen Anderson, Jake Harwood, and Mary Lee Hummert, "The Grandparent-Grandchild Relationship: Implications for Models of Intergenerational Communication," *Human Communication Research,* Vol. 31, 2005, pp. 268-294.

Accommodation in health care: Sina Farzadnia and Howard Giles, "Patient-Provider Interaction: A Communication Accommodation Theory Perspective," *International Journal of Society, Culture & Language,* Vol. 3, 2015, pp. 17-34.

Accommodation in the workplace: Robert M. McCann and Howard Giles, "Communication With People of Different Ages in the Workplace: Thai and American Data," *Human Communication Research,* Vol. 32, 2006, pp. 74-108.

Police-citizen interaction and simplified propositions: Howard Giles, Michael Willemyns, Cindy Gallois, and M. C. Anderson, "Accommodating a New Frontier: The Context of Law Enforcement," in *Social Communication,* Klaus Fiedler (ed.), Psychology Press, New York, 2007, pp. 129–162.

Application to law enforcement: Howard Giles, Charles W. Choi, Travis L. Dixon, "Police-Civilian Encounters," in *The Dynamics of Intergroup Communication,* Howard Giles, Scott A. Reid, and Jake Harwood (eds.), Peter Lang, New York, 2010, pp. 65–75.

To access a different theory of intercultural communication,
click on Anxiety/Uncertainty Management Theory
in Archive under Theory Resources at
www.afirstlook.com.

Face-Negotiation Theory

of Stella Ting-Toomey

Stella Ting-Toomey's face-negotiation theory describes the diverse styles of conflict management used by people from different cultures. As a volunteer mediator at a metropolitan center for conflict resolution, I have a ringside seat to observe these differences. My role as a mediator is to help people in conflict reach a voluntary agreement that satisfies both sides. Most disputants come to the center in a last-ditch effort to avoid the cost and intimidation of a day in court. After failing or refusing to work out their differences on their own, people walk in the door feeling various degrees of anger, hurt, fear, confusion, and shame. The majority of the negotiations end in freely signed and mutually kept agreements. But our model of negotiation doesn't work equally well for everyone. Although the center serves a multiethnic urban area, my colleagues and I have noticed that the number of people of Asian origin seeking conflict mediation is disproportionately small. On rare occasions when Japanese, Vietnamese, Chinese, or Korean parties come to the center, they appear more embarrassed than angry. If they do reach agreement, they seem more relieved the conversation is over than pleased with the solution.

Face
The projected image of one's self in a relational situation.

Stella Ting-Toomey's face-negotiation theory explains and predicts cultural differences in responses to conflict. A communication professor at California State University, Fullerton, Ting-Toomey assumes that people of every culture are always negotiating *face*. The term is a metaphor for our public self-image—the way we want others to see us and treat us. (That's why Facebook is so aptly named.) *Facework* refers to "specific verbal and nonverbal messages that help to maintain and restore face loss, and to uphold and honor face gain."[1] When people tend to use the same type of facework no matter what the dispute, she refers to it as their *conflict style*.

Facework
Specific verbal and nonverbal messages that help to maintain and restore face loss, and to uphold and honor face gain.

Our identity can always be called into question, and the anxiety and uncertainty churned up by conflict make us especially vulnerable. Face-negotiation theory postulates that the facework of people from individualistic cultures like the United States or Germany will be strikingly different from the facework of people from collectivistic cultures like Japan or China. The underlying assumption of Ting-Toomey's face-negotiation theory is that "face is an explanatory mechanism for conflict styles."[2]

Type of Culture → Type of Face Concern → Type of Conflict Style

In the next three sections I'll unpack the meaning of these concepts, which are linked together in the causal chain within the theory.

COLLECTIVISTIC AND INDIVIDUALISTIC CULTURES

Ting-Toomey bases her face-negotiation theory on the distinction between *collectivism* and *individualism*. The most extensive differentiation between the two types of cultures has been made by University of Illinois emeritus psychology professor Harry Triandis. He says the three important distinctions between collectivistic and individualistic cultures are the ways members perceive *self, goals,* and *duty.*[3]

Consider a man named Em. Collectivistic Em might think of himself as a member of the Griffin clan, a Christian, and a college professor. Individualistic Em would probably define himself simply as Em, independent of any group affiliation. Collectivistic Em wouldn't go against group goals, but his individualistic counterpart would naturally pursue his own personal interests. Collectivistic Em would have been socialized to enjoy duty that requires sacrifice in the service of others; individualistic Em would employ the minimax principle to determine a course of action that he would see as enjoyable and personally rewarding (see Chapter 8).

More than two-thirds of the world's people are born into collectivistic cultures, while less than one-third of the population lives in individualistic cultures.[4] To help you draw a clearer mental picture of the distinctions, I'll follow the lead of cross-cultural researchers who cite Japan and the United States as classic examples of collectivistic and individualistic cultures, respectively. Note that it would be equally appropriate to use most countries in Asia, Africa, the Middle East, or Latin America to represent a collectivistic perspective. I could also insert Australia, Germany, Switzerland, or one of the Scandinavian societies as the model of an individualistic approach. It is Ting-Toomey's grouping of national cultures within the collectivistic and individualistic categories that distinguishes her theory of conflict management from a mere listing of the way a country's citizens tend to respond to conflict.

Individualistic culture
Wherein people look out for themselves and their immediate families; *I*-identity; a low-context culture.

Triandis says that the Japanese value collective needs and goals over individual needs and goals. They assume that in the long run, each individual's decision affects everyone in the group. Therefore, a person's behavior is controlled by the norms of the group. This *we*-identity of the Japanese is foreign to the *I*-identity of the American who values individual needs and goals over group needs and goals. The American's behavior is governed by the personal rules of a freewheeling self that is concerned with individual rights rather than group responsibilities. Marching to a different drummer is the rule in the United States, not the exception.

Triandis claims that the strong in-group identity of the Japanese people leads them to perceive others in us–them categories. It is more important for the Japanese to identify an outsider's background and group affiliation than the person's attitudes or feelings—not because they don't care about their guest, but because unique individual differences seem less important than group-based information. People raised in the United States show a different curiosity. They are filled with questions about the interior life of visitors from other cultures. What do they think? What do they feel? What do they plan to do? Americans assume that every person is unique, and they reduce uncertainty by asking questions to the point of cross-examination.

Collectivistic culture
Wherein people identify with a larger group that is responsible for providing care in exchange for group loyalty; we-identity; a high-context culture.

Participants who come to the conflict center are treated as responsible individuals who can make up their own minds about what they want. The mediator encourages antagonists to deal directly with their differences and keeps the conversation focused on the possibility of a final agreement. While the mediator is careful never to pressure clients to reach an accord, the climate of immediacy suggests this is their best chance to put the whole mess behind them in an acceptable way and get on with their lives. The mediator works hard to make sure that the individual rights of both parties are respected.

Whether or not disputants reach an agreement, the mediation approach we take at the conflict center offers a safe place where no one need feel embarrassed—at least no one from an individualistic American culture. As it turns out, the open discussion of conflict, the encouragement to voice specific needs and interests, and the explicit language used to document any agreement all make the process quite uncomfortable for people raised in a high-context culture. No wonder potential clients from collectivistic cultures often stay away or leave dissatisfied.

THE MULTIPLE FACES OF FACE

Although popular Western wisdom regards *face* as an Asian preoccupation, Ting-Toomey and other relational researchers find it to be a universal concern. That's because face is an extension of self-concept: a vulnerable, identity-based resource. As Ting-Toomey notes, most of us blush. It's a telltale sign that we feel awkward, embarrassed, ashamed, or proud—all face-related issues.[5]

Ting-Toomey defines *face* as "the projected image of one's self in a relational situation."[6] Her simple definition draws upon a rich body of research in both the West and the East. In their well-developed theory of politeness, Penelope Brown and Stephen Levinson (Max Planck Institute for Psycholinguistics, the Netherlands) define face as "the public self-image that every member of society wants to claim for himself/herself."[7] Many Western writers regard face as an almost tangible good that can rise or fall like soybean futures on the commodity exchange at the Board of Trade. Taiwanese writer Lin Yutang called face "a psychological image that can be granted and lost and fought for and presented as a gift."[8] The term includes an aristocratic concern for dignity, honor, and status. It also covers the effect of trash talk after a slam dunk on the basketball court—"in your face!"

Ting-Toomey highlights several issues that turn face into a multifaceted object of study. After all, face means different things to different people, depending on their culture. The *face concern* question *Whose face are you trying to save?* may seem ridiculous to most Americans or members of other individualistic cultures. The answer is obvious: *mine*. Yet Ting-Toomey reminds us that in more than two-thirds of the world, face concern focuses on the other person. Even in the midst of conflict, people in these collectivistic cultures pay more attention to maintaining the face of the other party than they do to preserving their own. Their answer to the *face-concern* question would honestly be an altruistic *yours*.

Face concern
Regard for self-face, other-face, or mutual-face.

But self-face and other-face concerns don't exhaust the possibilities. Ting-Toomey describes a third orientation in which there is equal concern for both parties' images, as well as the public image of their relationship. She calls this a *mutual-face* concern, and people who have it would answer the *Whose face . . .* question with *ours*.

Face-restoration
The self-concerned facework strategy used to preserve autonomy and defend against loss of personal freedom.

Self-concerned *face-restoration* is the facework strategy used to stake out a unique place in life, preserve autonomy, and defend against loss of personal freedom. Not surprisingly, face-restoration is the typical face strategy across individualistic cultures. *Face-giving* out of concern for others is the facework strategy used to defend and support another person's need for inclusion. It means taking care not to embarrass or humiliate the other in public. Face-giving is the characteristic face strategy across collectivistic cultures.

Face-giving
The other-concerned facework strategy used to defend and support another person's need for inclusion.

Of course, collectivism and individualism aren't all-or-nothing categories. The difference between other-face and self-face concerns is not absolute. Just as relational dialectics theory says we talk about wanting both connection *and* autonomy in a close relationship (see Chapter 11), so, too, people desire both affiliation and autonomy within their particular society. Those raised in Japan or other Asian countries do have personal wants and needs; Americans and northern Europeans still desire to be part of a larger group. The cultural difference is always a matter of degree.

Yet when push comes to shove, most people from a collectivistic culture tend to privilege other-face or mutual-face over self-face. In like manner, people raised in an individualistic culture are normally more concerned with self-face than with other-face. Matt, a student of Andrew's, highlights these cultural differences.

When I was a senior in high school, my younger sister studied abroad in Poland and our family decided to house a foreign exchange student for the year she was away—a 16-year-old girl from Taiwan. Her name was Wen-I Wu, but with other-face concern, she asked us to call her Joyce because it would be easier for us to say. The main difference I noticed between Joyce and my sister was that even though we lived under the same roof for the entire year, we never had a confrontation.

The first time Joyce really opened up to us she spoke about her diet. In Taiwan she would eat rice and fish practically every meal and she looked like a twig—not an ounce of fat on her. She told us that she had thin-faced friends who came back from their study abroad with round faces because they only ate fast food. We must have frowned because this girl from a collectivistic culture instantly retracted her statement and continually apologized, saying that she didn't believe we had "round" faces.

Contrast this with the dominating bluntness of my individualistic mother who isn't afraid to say exactly what's on her mind. When we were on vacation in Disney World she spotted Joyce taking selfies to post on Facebook while flashing the peace sign—a typical pose for her. "Joyce, we don't do that in America!" my mom stated bluntly, not explaining her conviction that multiple shots of Joyce alone in the photo portrayed a girl who has no friends. It's now been two years since she's been away. I've never again seen a picture of Joyce on Facebook flashing her classic sign of peace.

PREDICTED STYLES OF CONFLICT MANAGEMENT

Avoiding
Responding to conflict by withdrawing from open discussion.

Obliging
Accommodating or giving in to the wishes of another in a conflict situation.

Based on the work of M. Afzalur Rahim, professor of management at Western Kentucky University, Ting-Toomey initially identified five distinct responses to situations where there is an incompatibility of needs, interests, or goals. The five conflict styles are *avoiding (withdrawing), obliging (accommodating), compromising (bargaining), dominating (competing),* and *integrating (problem solving).*[9] Most Western writers refer to the same five styles of conflict management, although they often use the labels that are in parentheses.[10]

Suppose, for example, that you are the leader of a group of students working together on a class research project. Your instructor will assign the same grade to all of you based on the quality of the group's work, and that project evaluation will count for two-thirds of your final grade in the course. As often happens in such cases, one member of the group brings in a shoddy piece of work, and you have only three days before the project is due. You don't know this group member well, but you do know that it will take 72 hours of round-the-clock effort to fix this part of the project. What mode of conflict management will you adopt?

Compromising
Conflict management by negotiating or bargaining; seeking a middle way.

Dominating
Competing to win when people's interests conflict.

Integrating
Problem solving through open discussion; collaboration for a win-win resolution of conflict.

Avoiding: "I would avoid discussing my differences with the group member."

Obliging: "I would give in to the wishes of the group member."

Compromising: "I would use give-and-take so that a compromise could be made."

Dominating: "I would be firm in pursuing my side of the issue."

Integrating: "I would exchange accurate information with the group member to solve the problem together."

Ting-Toomey and a host of collaborators presented this problem to almost a thousand university students in Japan, China, South Korea, Taiwan, and the United States.[11] The men and women were asked to put themselves in the shoes of the student leader. How would they handle conflict with a little-known group member who's a threat to the project's success and their grade in the class? Figure 35–1 displays the predictions of Ting-Toomey's original theory.

- Students from the individualistic culture of the United States would have high self-concern, and, depending on their relative other-face concern, would adopt a dominating or integrating communication style to manage conflict.

- Students from the collectivistic societies of Japan, China, South Korea, and Taiwan would have relatively low self-concern, and, depending on the strength of their other-face concern, would favor a strategy of obliging, compromising, or avoiding in response to conflict.

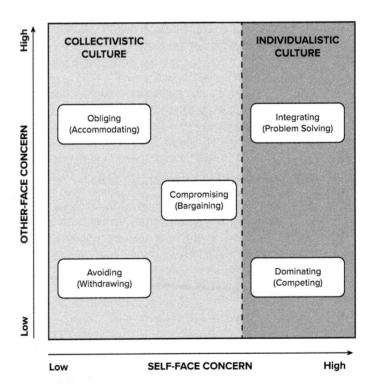

FIGURE 35–1 Five Styles of Conflict Management
Based on Ting-Toomey et al., "Culture, Face Maintenance, and Styles of Handling Interpersonal Conflict: A Study in Five Cultures"

For the most part, the results of the five-culture study supported the basic **culture → face concern → conflict style** theory. But Ting-Toomey and her colleagues were surprised to discover that Asian students were more partial to *integration* than were their American counterparts. This unexpected finding and some recognized procedural flaws in the study motivated Ting-Toomey to join forces with John Oetzel (University of Waikato, New Zealand) in launching a two-decade program of cross-cultural research to refine the theory.[12] Based on what they've learned, face-negotiation theory is now more complex, yet better able to explain and predict conflict behavior around the world. The next two sections describe the theory's alterations and extensions.

SELF-CONSTRUAL: VARIED SELF-IMAGES WITHIN A CULTURE

Self-construal
Self-image; the degree to which people conceive of themselves as relatively autonomous from, or connected to, others.

People aren't cultural clones. Just as cultures vary along a scale anchored by individualistic or collectivistic orientations, so, too, do their members. Ting-Toomey now emphasizes that people *within* a given culture differ on the relative emphasis they place on individual self-sufficiency or group solidarity. She uses the terms *independent* and *interdependent self* to refer to "the degree to which people conceive of themselves as relatively autonomous from, or connected to, others."[13] Ting-Toomey calls this dimension *self-construal,* or the more familiar term *self-image.*[14]

The independent self values *I*-identity and is more self-face oriented, so this concept of self is prevalent within individualistic cultures like the United States. Yet due in part to the ethnic diversity of American society, there are people raised in the US who are highly interdependent. The interdependent self values *we*-identity and emphasizes relational connectedness, and is therefore closely aligned with collectivism. But again, it would be dangerous to stereotype all members of a collectivist society as having the same self-construal. Culture is an overall framework for face concern, but individuals within a culture have different images of self as well as varied views on the degree to which they try to give others face or restore their own face in conflict situations.

The relational reality of self-image differences within two cultures is represented in the following diagram. Each circle (●) stands for the self-construal of a person raised in a collectivistic society that socializes its members to be interdependent and includes everyone in face concerns. Each triangle (▲) stands for the self-construal of a person raised in an individualistic culture that stresses independence and self-reliance. The cultures are obviously different. But the overlap shows that an American might have a self-image more interdependent than that of a person raised in Japan with a relatively high independent self-construal.

Interdependent Self-Image — Collectivistic Culture (Japan) — Individualistic Culture (United States) — Independent Self-Image

Ting-Toomey and Oetzel identify people's self-construal by asking them to respond to surveys about real or imagined conflict situations. Strong agreement with the first two of the following four statements indicates an *independent* self-image. Endorsing the last two shows an *interdependent* self-image.[15]

"It was important for me to be able to act as a free and independent person."

"I tried not to depend on others."

"I sacrificed my self-interest for the benefit of our relationship."

"I was sensitive to the wishes of the other person."

The distinction between collectivistic and individualistic cultures is still important because culture has a strong effect on an individual's self-construal. But that sense of individual identity is one step closer to the person's preferred style of dealing with conflict, so it predicts dispute behavior better than generalized culture does. Therefore, a schematic of the revised theory is now:

$$\text{Type of Culture} \rightarrow \text{Self-Construal} \rightarrow \text{Face Concern} \rightarrow \text{Conflict Style}$$

REFINING THE RELATIONSHIP BETWEEN FACE CONCERN AND CONFLICT STYLE

Since the turn of the century, Ting-Toomey, Oetzel, and many other intercultural researchers have identified three primary conflict styles: *dominance, avoidance,* and *integration.* Each of these terms identifies a conflict style Ting-Toomey explored in her original five-culture study. She and Oetzel now use them as umbrella terms to designate 3 clusters of 11 specific facework strategies.[16]

Dominance

Defend—Stand up for one's opinion; try to persuade the other.

Express emotion—Verbally express one's feelings or emotions.

Aggression—Make a direct or passive effort to hurt the other.

Avoidance

Give in—Accommodate the other's wishes.

Pretend—Act like the conflict doesn't exist.

Third party—Seek an outside party to help resolve the conflict.

Integration

Apologize—Say sorry for past behavior.

Private talk—Avoid public confrontation.

Remain calm—Stay composed during the conflict.

Problem solve—Engage in behaviors to join perspectives together.

Respect—Demonstrate regard for the other by listening.

The three clusters are important because Ting-Toomey and Oetzel claim that the type of face concern people have will best predict the type of facework they'll employ in conflict situations. The theorists say we can expect those most concerned with *self-face* to try to dominate through aggression, emotional expression, or defending. People with an *other-face* concern will attempt to avoid conflict by giving in, pretending they see no conflict, or getting a third party to work it out. Parties with a *mutual-face* concern will favor an integrating strategy of apologizing, private discussion, remaining calm, problem solving, or showing respect. Their basic prediction is:

Self-face   →   **Dominance**
Other-face   →   **Avoidance**
Mutual-face   →   **Integration**

Oetzel and Ting-Toomey conducted a four-nation study to test their revised theory with Chinese, Japanese, German, and American students.[17] About 200 students from each country were asked to think of a conflict they had with a same-sex person from their own culture. With this specific conflict in mind, they responded to a series of scales that measured their face concern and their use of the facework strategies listed above. Figure 35–2 displays what the researchers found.

Each of the 11 facework strategies is superimposed on a rectangle, circle, or oval that represents the type of face concern predicted to foster that kind of conflict management. Dominance strategies are encased in rectangles, avoidance strategies in circles, integrative strategies in ovals. If all of the researchers' claims were validated, the rectangles would be in the lower right-hand corner where self-face is high

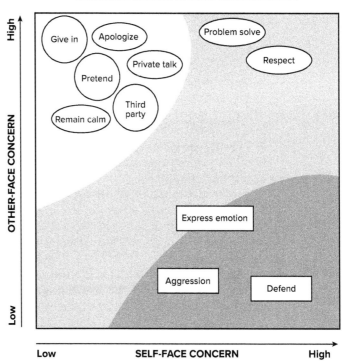

FIGURE 35–2 Comparison of Theory Predictions and Research Results
Based on Oetzel, Garcia, and Ting-Toomey, "An Analysis of the Relationships Among Face Concerns and Facework Behaviors in Perceived Conflict Situations: A Four-Culture Investigation"

"We realize it's a win-win, Jenkins—we're trying to figure out a way to make it a win-lose."
©Matthew Diffee/The New Yorker Collection/The Cartoon Bank

and other-face is low. All the circles would be in the upper left-hand corner where other-face is high and self-face is low. And all the mutual-face ovals would be in the upper right-hand corner where both self-face and mutual face are high. As you can see, the results support much, but not all, of the revised theory.

For the *dominance* tactics, self-face is linked with both defending and aggression, but not emotional expression. Perhaps that lack of association with self-face concern is a result of the survey zeroing in on the respondent clearly describing his or her feelings to the other person rather than displaying emotions nonverbally. As a mediator, I often hear parties deny they're feeling angry, yet their facial expressions, tones of voice, and gestures tell a different story. Note also that aggression isn't linked with high self-face concern; the goal is not to look good but to make the other feel bad.

As predicted, all three of the *avoidance* strategies—giving in, pretending, and seeking third-party help—are associated with high other-face concerns. But what wasn't anticipated is that three of the behaviors presumably fostered by mutual-face concern are shown to be associated with other-face concern alone. Other researchers have had a problem creating survey items that distinguish between other-face and mutual-face, so perhaps this is a measurement glitch rather than a flaw in the theory.[18] Given the complexity of cross-cultural theorizing and research, I regard the study as encouraging support for the revised face-negotiation theory, even though it isn't total confirmation.

APPLICATION: COMPETENT INTERCULTURAL FACEWORK

Ting-Toomey's ultimate goal for her theory goes beyond merely identifying the ways people in different cultures negotiate face or handle conflict. She wants it to help people manage intercultural conflict effectively. Imagine that you are a Japanese student in a US college facing the group research problem brought up earlier. As the appointed leader, you feel it's your uncomfortable duty to talk with the unproductive American member of the group. How would Ting-Toomey recommend you undertake competent intercultural facework? She says there are three requirements.[19]

Knowledge is the most important dimension of facework competence. It's hard to be culturally sensitive unless you have some idea of the ways you might differ from your classmate. Ting-Toomey's theory offers basic insights into collectivistic and individualistic cultures, self-construal, face concerns, and facework styles, all of which could help you understand the American student's perspective, and vice versa. If you've read this chapter carefully, that knowledge will stand you in good stead.

Mindfulness shows a recognition that things are not always what they seem. It's a conscious choice to seek multiple perspectives on the same event. Perhaps the other's inferior work is not due to laziness but is the best he or she can do in this situation. The student might have a learning disability, an emotional problem, a lack of clarity about the assignment, or a desire to merely pass the course. Of course, your initiation of a conversation to discuss the project is also open to multiple interpretations. Ting-Toomey writes:

Mindfulness
Recognizing that things are not always what they seem, and therefore seeking multiple perspectives in conflict situations.

> Mindfulness means being particularly aware of our own assumptions, viewpoints, and ethnocentric tendencies in entering any unfamiliar situation. *Simultaneously,* mindfulness means paying attention to the perspectives and interpretive lenses of *dissimilar others* in viewing an intercultural episode.[20]

When you are mindful, you mentally switch off automatic pilot and process the situation and conversation through the central route of the mind, as ELM suggests (see Chapter 15). But you are also freed up to empathize with the other student and approach the discussion with a fresh or creative mind-set. The result might be a novel solution that takes advantage of your different ways of thinking.

Interaction skill is your ability to communicate appropriately, effectively, and adaptively in a given situation. Perhaps you are studying communication to gain that type of competence. Hopefully your department offers a course in interpersonal or intercultural communication that includes structured exercises, role plays, or simulations. Without hands-on learning and feedback from others on how you're doing, it's hard to improve.

CRITIQUE: PASSING THE OBJECTIVE TEST WITH A GOOD GRADE

Anthropologists and more than a few communication theorists have used ethnography to investigate diverse cultures—a highly interpretive project.[21] Ting-Toomey and Oetzel have gone a different route. They have conducted extensive *quantitative survey research* to craft an objective theory that *predicts* that members of collectivistic cultures will manage conflict differently than members of individualistic societies will. Then they use the constructs of self-construal and face concern to *explain* why that's so. Ting-Toomey has laid out "conflict face-negotiation theory" (which she now calls it) in 24 *testable hypotheses,* which are featured in the recommended resource at the end of this chapter. Most of the hypotheses have proved right, and she adjusts the theory when the research fails to support the others. That makes for a good theory.

Ting-Toomey and Oetzel admit their methodology has shortcomings. One is that all of the survey data that validates the theory is self-reported. There's no actual observation of how people respond in real-life conflict situations. Then there's the issue of sample bias. Almost all the people surveyed are college students from Eastern Asia, Northern Europe, and the United States. The theorists and their colleagues are just beginning to test the theory in Africa, Latin America, and the Middle East. But so far, respondents are still overwhelmingly young adults whom the academic researchers can readily reach and reward. This could be a problem because college students tend to possess more wealth and socioeconomic status than their noncollege peers—and those factors might influence their preferred style of facework.

As presented in the first half of this chapter, face-negotiation theory was a straightforward creation. In order to adjust it to the realities that research revealed, the theory has become more complex. Even after two decades of research, Ting-Toomey continues to explore new variables that might affect *facework.* Given the complex nature of culture, she has made the choice to sacrifice *simplicity* for validity, which makes the theory tougher to grasp.

As a third-party neutral mediator for more than two decades, however, I can attest to the *practical utility* of face-negotiation theory. For example, a few years ago I conducted an extensive conflict mediation between two bitterly divided factions at a Shiite Muslim mosque. Both groups of Pakistani immigrants had accused the other side of immoral and illegal behavior; both groups had filed suit against the other in court. That's how I got involved.

While despairing of being able to help these angry factions agree on anything, I recalled the face-negotiation claim that most members of their collectivistic culture shared a concern for giving face to others—at least within their own expat community. Hoping Ting-Toomey was right, I listened for hints of mutual-face or other-face concern.

Amid the barbs and accusations, I noted a few comments that they feared their fight was affecting the mosque's reputation among their Anglo neighbors. When I explored this concern they agreed they didn't want anyone in their mosque to feel embarrassed—not even their adversaries. I affirmed this concern and focused the discussion on how they could ensure that all members were able to hold their heads up high—to give face to each other. They calmed down and began to work out an agreement stating what each side would do so that they could participate peacefully together in the mosque. Without the insight provided by face-negotiation theory, it wouldn't have happened.

QUESTIONS TO SHARPEN YOUR FOCUS

1. Based on what you know about Afghanistan, is the culture *individualistic* or *collectivistic?* What clues do you have?

2. Do you see yourself as having more of an *independent* or an *interdependent self?* Does this go with the flow of your culture, or are you swimming against the tide?

3. What *face concern* (*self-face, other-face, mutual-face*) does your religious faith, political ideology, or personal set of values embrace? To what extent is the *facework* you do with others consistent with that face concern?

4. What *style of conflict management* would you use with the group member who did poor work? Is your response based on your culture, self-construal, face concern, gender, or status? What other factors affect your response to conflict?

CONVERSATIONS

View this segment online at www.afirstlook.com.

While talking with Stella Ting-Toomey, I raise the embarrassing possibility that students may be bored while watching our discussion. If so, both she and I have some serious facework to do. Ting-Toomey shows how she, a child of a collectivistic culture, might give face to students. She then role-plays how I, the product of an individualistic culture, might save face. Later in the conversation I ask if she's bothered that self-construal has turned out to be a better predictor of conflict style than culture of origin—a potentially face-threatening question. You then get to see Ting-Toomey's real-life facework.

A SECOND LOOK

Recommended resource: Stella Ting-Toomey, "The Matrix of Face: An Updated Face-Negotiation Theory," in *Theorizing About Intercultural Communication,* William Gudykunst (ed.), Sage, Thousand Oaks, CA, 2005, pp. 71–92.

Original theory: Stella Ting-Toomey, "Intercultural Conflict Styles: A Face-Negotiation Theory," in *Theories in Intercultural Communication,* Young Yun Kim and William Gudykunst (eds.), Sage, Newbury Park, CA, 1988, pp. 213–235.

Revision and test of the theory: John Oetzel, Adolfo J. Garcia, and Stella Ting-Toomey, "An Analysis of the Relationships Among Face Concerns and Facework Behaviors in Perceived Conflict Situations: A Four-Culture Investigation,"*International Journal of Conflict Management,* Vol. 19, 2008, pp. 382–403.

Literature review: Stella Ting-Toomey and John Oetzel, "Cross-Cultural Face Concerns and Conflict Styles," in *Handbook of International and Intercultural Communication,* 2nd ed., William Gudykunst and Bella Mody (eds.), Sage, Thousand Oaks, CA, 2002, pp. 143–163.

Collectivistic/individualistic culture: Harry C. Triandis, *Individualism & Collectivism,* Westview, Boulder, CO, 1995.

Theory into practice: Stella Ting-Toomey, "Translating Conflict Face-Negotiation Theory into Practice," in *Handbook of Intercultural Training,* 3rd ed., Dan Landis, Jane Bennett, and Milton Bennett (eds.), Sage, Thousand Oaks, CA, 2004, pp. 217–248.

Face-negotiation in the context of other theories of conflict: Stella Ting-Toomey and Jiro Takai, "Explaining Intercultural Conflict: Promising Approaches and Directions," in *The SAGE Handbook of Conflict Communication: Integrating Theory, Research, and Practice,* John G. Oetzel and Stella Ting-Toomey (eds.), Sage, Thousand Oaks, CA, 2006, pp. 691–723.

A personal account of face: Stella Ting-Toomey, "An Intercultural Journey: The Four Seasons," in *Working at the Interface of Cultures: Eighteen Lives in Social Science,* Michael Bond (ed.), Routledge, New York, 1997, pp. 202–215.

Theorists' research and critique: John Oetzel and Stella Ting-Toomey, "Face Concerns in Interpersonal Conflict: A Cross-Cultural Empirical Test of the Face-Negotiation Theory," *Communication Research,* Vol. 36, 2003, pp. 599–624.

Critique: Gerry Philipsen, "Some Thoughts on How to Approach Finding One's Feet in Unfamiliar Cultural Terrain," *Communication Monographs,* Vol. 77, 2013, pp. 160–168.

Ting-Toomey's response: Stella Ting-Toomey, "Applying Dimensional Values in Understanding Intercultural Communication," *Communication Monographs,* Vol. 77, 2013, pp. 169–180.

Co-Cultural Theory

of Mark Orbe

What do African American men, the LGBTQ community, and people with physical disabilities have in common? According to Mark Orbe, a professor of communication at Western Michigan University, they are members of three different co-cultural groups in the United States that share a similar dilemma. They have less power than members of the *dominant culture,* which is comprised of relatively well-off, white, European American, nondisabled, heterosexual men. When interacting with this privileged group, they are at a distinct disadvantage.

Dominant culture
In the US, the empowered group of relatively welloff, white, European American, nondisabled, heterosexual men.

Orbe uses the term *co-cultural* to refer to marginalized groups of people who are typically labeled as *minority, subcultural, subordinate, inferior,* or *nondominant.* He's chosen this adjective because the term doesn't carry the negative connotations associated with the typical labels. It's a neutral term that designates significant differences from the dominant culture, but with no hint of contempt or condemnation.

There are many varied *co-cultural groups* in the United States, such as women, people of color, the economically disadvantaged, people with physical disabilities, the LGBTQ community, the very old and very young, and religious minorities. Members of these groups are often discounted, dismissed, or disdained by those who occupy a place of privilege in the dominant culture. Although these co-cultural groups are quite diverse, they each face the same problem: When interacting with those in the dominant culture, they have less power, which affects what they say and how they say it.

Co-cultural group
In the US, marginalized groups such as women, people of color, the economically disadvantaged, people with physical disabilities, the LGBTQ community, the very old and very young, and religious minorities.

Orbe sees co-cultural theory as an extension of both standpoint theory and muted group theory—two other theories concerned with unequal power (see Chapters 32 and 33). Recall that muted group theory maintains that women and members of other co-cultural groups aren't free to say what they want because words and customs for their use have been formed by men. Those with less power still have to converse in a "man-made language." Doing so feels awkward, and the language stilted.

Standpoint theory insists that cultural research start with those who are marginalized. That's because they are "outsiders within" the dominant culture, and thus have a less false view of what's really going on. In light of the claims of both theories, Orbe thinks it's important to spend time and effort focusing on *co-cultural communication*—"communication between dominant group and co-cultural group members *from the perspective of co-cultural group members.*"[1] So that's what he's done.

Co-cultural communication
Communication between dominant group and co-cultural group members from the perspective of co-cultural group members.

Orbe has found that, to maneuver within the dominant culture and achieve some degree of success, co-cultural group members will adopt one or more specific communication orientations in their everyday interactions.[2] His co-cultural theory identifies the patterns of what they say and do. As a critical theorist, Orbe is impressed with the linguistic choices oppressed people make—even though the odds are stacked against them.

COMMUNICATION ORIENTATION: WHAT THEY WANT AND WHAT THEY SAY TO GET IT

Orbe claims there are nine communication orientations that different co-cultural group members adopt when trying to survive and thrive within the dominant group culture. *Communication orientation* is the term he uses to describe a co-cultural group member's preferred outcome pursued through the communication approach he or she chooses to achieve that goal. The three-by-three model in Figure 36–1 lays out the framework of co-cultural theory and shows the nine communication orientation possibilities. The three goals heading the columns—*assimilation, accommodation, separation*—describe the preferred outcomes co-cultural members might seek when face-to-face with members of the dominant culture. The three communication approaches labeled on the left side of the model—*nonassertive, assertive, aggressive*—identify the verbal and nonverbal behavior co-cultural members might use to reach their chosen goal. Each intersection of a column and row represents a specific communication orientation.[3]

Communication orientation
The combination of a co-cultural group member's preferred outcome and the communication approach he or she chooses to achieve that goal.

For example, an African American lesbian woman describes the way she interacts with members of the dominant culture:

> A lot of time people have a certain impression of how black people talk, or lesbians are supposed to act. . . . I found if I am just myself . . . they get to see that all African American women are not on welfare [or] heterosexuals dependent on men.[4]

Orbe would say that her practice of communicating openly about herself shows that she's pursuing accommodation in an assertive manner. As you can see in Figure 36–1, the accommodation column intersects with the assertive communication approach row in box 5 at the middle of the grid. Thus, this co-cultural woman has an *Assertive/Accommodation* orientation. What does this mean as opposed to a *Nonassertive/Assimilation* orientation in box 1 or an *Aggressive/Separation* in box 9? To answer that question, we have to dive deeper into the model.

Inside each of the nine communication orientation boxes are shorthand descriptors of *communicative practices*. These practices summarize the specific verbal and nonverbal actions that co-cultural group members take when interacting with members of the dominant culture. The cluster of terms labeling the practices in each box reflects how that orientation plays out in actual types of behavior.

Communicative practices
Recurring verbal and nonverbal actions that co-cultural group members take during their interaction with dominant group members.

The co-cultural theory framework depicted in Figure 36–1 lists 26 communicative practices and shows which communication orientation they illustrate. For your first look at co-cultural theory they will help you picture what's actually said by co-cultural group members with different orientations. As Orbe listened to co-cultural group members talk about their interactions with the dominant culture, these practices strongly influenced his interpretation of the three preferred outcomes, the three communication approaches, and the nine different communication orientations they form.

Nonassertive approach
Communication practices that seem inhibited and nonconfrontational; putting the needs of others before your own.

The three communication approaches he identifies each reflect a certain style of speech and the apparent motivation of the speaker. According to Orbe, a *nonassertive approach* is where "individuals are seemingly inhibited and nonconfrontational

PREFERRED OUTCOME

		Assimilation	Accommodation	Separation
COMMUNICATION APPROACH	Nonassertive	Emphasizing commonalities Developing positive face Censoring self Averting controversy **1**	Increasing visibility Dispelling stereotypes **4**	Avoiding Maintaining personal barriers **7**
	Assertive	Extensive preparation Overcompensating Manipulating stereotypes Bargaining **2**	Communicating self Intragroup networking Utilizing liaisons Educating others **5**	Exemplifying strengths Embracing stereotypes **8**
	Aggressive	Dissociating Mirroring Strategic distancing Ridiculing self **3**	Confronting Gaining advantage **6**	Attacking Sabotaging others **9**

FIGURE 36–1 Nine Communication Orientations in Co-Cultural Theory

Aggressive approach
Communication practices that are seen as hurtfully expressive, self-promoting, and assuming control over the choices of others.

while putting the needs of others before their own."[5] Conversely, an *aggressive approach* is behavior "perceived as hurtfully expressive, self-promoting, and assuming control over the choices of others."[6] The two terms are consistent with the two styles of conflict management in face-negotiation theory that Ting-Toomey labeled *obliging* and *forcing* (see Chapter 35). Orbe pictures the nonassertive and aggressive approaches as anchoring opposite ends of a continuum on which an *assertive approach* falls roughly in between. That's a style of "self-enhancing and expressive behavior that takes into account both self and others' needs."[7]

Assertive approach
Communication practices that include self-enhancing, expressive behavior that takes the needs of self and others into account.

In the next three sections, I'll define the three preferred outcomes and work through the model one box at a time. I'll offer a shorthand description of each communicative practice, paired with a quote from a co-cultural group member as an example. Although there are many co-cultural groups in the United States, I've interspersed comments from African American men, members of the LGBTQ community, and people with physical disabilities because these groups were pivotal in the development of the theory.

ASSIMILATION AS A PREFERRED OUTCOME OF COMMUNICATION

Assimilation
The co-cultural process of fitting into the dominant culture while shedding the speech and nonverbal markers of the co-cultural group.

For co-cultural group members, *assimilation* means fitting into the dominant culture while at the same time shedding the speech and nonverbal markers of their group.[8] In order to participate effectively in mainstream society and reap its benefits, they feel they must become more like its members, or at least visibly support the beliefs and practices of mainstream society. It requires a willingness to "go along to get along."

Assimilation is rarely 100 percent attainable. There is a history, however, of light-skinned African Americans "passing" as white and gay people staying "in the closet" for most of their lives. The constant fear of exposure is just one of the costs of playing the part. Assimilation is hard work.

1. Nonassertive Assimilation. Co-cultural members attempt to meet their own needs as best they can by unobtrusively blending into the dominant society. Some would interpret this communication approach as being kind, wise, or practical. It strikes others as passive or "sucking up to the Man." However the strategy is viewed, it usually serves to reinforce the dominant group's power and take a bite out the co-cultural member's self-esteem.

Emphasizing commonalities—Focusing on similarities; downplaying differences.

> Israeli gay man: "For me, it is important how the straight society sees our society. I prefer . . . gay men who wear jeans and T-shirts."[9]

Developing positive face—Being graciously attentive and considerate.

> African/Native American man: "I find myself even having to approach them differently with a softer tone. I have to go in there and make it seem like it was their [co-worker's] idea."[10]

Censoring self—Remaining silent to inappropriate or offensive comments.

> European American lesbian woman: "I was present in conversations where people stated, 'What do they want, anyway, special rights? And what they do in their bedroom is their business, but why flaunt it?' I found myself . . . biting my tongue to keep silent."[11]

"We no longer shelve gay fiction separately. It's been assimilated."
©William Haefeli/The New Yorker Collection/The Cartoon Bank

Averting controversy—Moving conversation away from risky or dangerous areas.

> Man with a disability: "When I first started working, I wouldn't say anything about my needs. . . . If I had to use the bathroom and they didn't have a handicapped-accessible restroom, I would just try to hold it."[12]

2. Assertive Assimilation. Co-cultural members with this orientation attempt to fit into dominant structures by "playing the game." Their constant drive for success while downplaying cultural differences makes this a difficult approach to sustain, especially if their own co-cultural members refer to them as an "Oreo" or threaten to "out" them.

Extensive preparation—Preparing thoroughly prior to interaction.

> African American man before meeting: "I prepare talking to them [so that] I am much more thorough and pointed."[13]

Overcompensating—Making a conscious and consistent effort to be a "superstar."

> Gay man in corporate office: "I run circles around everyone else so no one will ever be able to say I don't outperform anybody in the building. I can't be just okay."[14]

Manipulating stereotypes—Exploiting the dominant image of the group for personal gain.

> African American man: "I love it when people are intimidated by my presence. Although I wouldn't hurt a fly, white people automatically assume certain things when they see a big black man."[15]

Bargaining—Making covert or overt arrangements to ignore co-cultural differences.

> Gay director of top-secret military research in Israel, speaking to parliament (Knesset) about his sexual orientation: "I did not come to ask for mercy or pity. Let us merge into society."[16]

3. Aggressive Assimilation. This is a single-minded, sometimes belligerent approach to be regarded as part of the dominant group and not as members of a co-cultural group. Fitting into the dominant structure has become so important that others' rights and interests are often ignored.

Dissociating—Trying hard to avoid the typical behavior of one's co-cultural group.

> African American man: "You can't always talk how you want to talk—talking loud or talking Ebonics. . . . You kinda gotta assimilate to White culture—what they see as acceptable."[17]

Mirroring—Adopting dominant communication codes to mask co-cultural identity.

> African/Native American man: "There is that tendency to take up golf and other things like that to say 'okay, I fit in. I'm like one of you guys now.'"[18]

Strategic distancing—Stressing individuality by cutting ties with your own group.

> Gay man: "In order to get this job, I couldn't wear the earring, I couldn't wear the bracelet—I couldn't wear anything that would ever identify me as being a part of the gay community."[19]

*Ridiculing self—*Taking part in discourse demeaning to one's co-cultural group.

> African American man: "A couple of times little comments would be made about black stereotypes—you know, like eating watermelon and fried chicken—and I would laugh right along with them."[20]

ACCOMMODATION AS A PREFERRED OUTCOME OF COMMUNICATION

Accommodation
The co-cultural process of working to change dominant culture rules to take the life experiences of co-cultural members into account.

Rather than following the other guys' rules, as those trying to assimilate do, co-cultural members who seek *accommodation* work at changing the rules to take their own life experiences into account.[21] For example, after decades of advocacy by those who couldn't get the help they needed to live a normal life, Congress passed the Americans with Disabilities Act of 1990, which requires employers to provide accommodations for workers with disabilities without discrimination or penalty.

Accommodation is a two-way street. As Giles' communication accommodation theory suggests, *convergence—*or positive accommodation—is the way we gain approval and appreciation in an intercultural situation (see Chapter 34.) As out-group members adopt their behavior to become more similar to that of the dominant in-group culture, they gain credibility for advocating at least incremental change.

4. Nonassertive Accommodation. By conforming to the norms of the dominant culture, co-cultural members desire to gain acceptance. By suggesting small changes in a nonconfrontational way, they hope to reduce the chance that dominant group members will become defensive or resistant to change.

*Increasing visibility—*Maintaining co-cultural presence within the dominant group.

> African American student on a predominantly white campus: "Sometimes, I feel that we need to be more visible; we need to let students know that we are black, and that isn't a problem."[22]

*Dispelling stereotypes—*Changing images of the group by just being yourself.

> Gay man: "[I make it a practice to] never talk about sex or get too close to children. . . . I'm so cautious because I don't want them to think that these stereotypes fit the typical gay person."[23]

5. Assertive Accommodation. Co-cultural members whose abilities and interpersonal skills are valued work cooperatively within the dominant culture. They openly advocate for the needs of people in both cultures.

*Communicating self—*Interacting with the dominant group in an open, genuine manner.

> Man with a disability: "I'm Aries, I've got hazel eyes, I'm competitive, I'm fun to be around and I also happen to be disabled. And that's just the way life is."[24]

*Intragroup networking—*Talking with co-cultural people with a shared worldview.

> African American man: "I like to talk to people . . . who can relate to me and I can relate to them . . . We have been through some common experiences."[25]

*Utilizing liaisons—*Seeking support from dominant group members you can trust.

> African American man: "The importance of knowing people whom you can call upon is necessary to survive in an oppressive environment."[26]

Educating others—Explaining co-cultural norms and values to the dominant group.

> Person with a disability: "The person with the disability needs to understand their disability, what they need in terms of accommodation and to teach the employer."[27]

6. Aggressive Accommodation. Working within the dominant culture, these co-cultural advocates offer a prophetic voice calling for major transformation of structures and practices that hold co-cultural groups down. They may be regarded as "pushy" or "radical" by members in both cultures, but seem not to care as long as their efforts bring about change that benefits their people. Sometimes that happens, but often there is a negative reaction to their words.

Confronting—Asserting one's "voice" in way that may violate others' rights.

> Man with a disability: "I expect the world to accommodate my wheelchair. I don't mean this from a self-righteous or indignant 'you damn well do it' [attitude]. I'm not angry about it. I had to learn to face the fact that this is what's going on for me and I should not have it held against me."[28]

Gaining advantage—Calling out dominant group oppression to get a response.

> Gay man: "Do we make ourselves so unpleasant that yielding to our demands finally becomes easier than ignoring us?"[29]

SEPARATION AS A PREFERRED OUTCOME OF COMMUNICATION

The co-cultural group members who desire *separation* work to create and maintain an identity distinct from the dominant culture.[30] Their verbal and nonverbal strategy for coping in a world where they will continue to have less power is to promote their own in-group solidarity.

Separation

The co-cultural process of working to create and maintain an identity distinct from the dominant culture and promote in-group solidarity.

Separatist members don't buy the idea that American society is a melting pot where people of different colors, ethnic backgrounds, classes, and sexual orientations all blend together with members of the dominant culture. They have little concern with changing the rules of the dominant culture because they see themselves as realists who have learned that "you can't fight city hall." Separatist speech is akin to what Giles labeled *divergent communication,* and is used to accentuate differences between the two cultures (see Chapter 3).

7. Nonassertive Separation. These co-cultural members have an inherent belief that their lives will be more tolerable when they "stick to their own kind." They avoid being with people from the dominant culture whenever they can. When compelled to interact, they leave as soon as possible. Their communication practices subtly maintain or increase separation.

Avoiding—Staying away from places and situations where interaction is likely.

> African American man: "We're realists. . . . there won't be true integration in the white corporate world or suburbs. . . so we build our own institutions and our own suburbs."[31]

Maintaining personal barriers—Using verbal and nonverbal cues to stay aloof.

> Gay man: "I love to dress flamboyant and fun. Some other men don't appreciate it. One time, I was working and a customer came up to me and told me I was a disgrace to men. . . . I am so used to crazy comments like that I brushed it off my shoulders."[32]

8. Assertive Separation. Co-cultural members with this orientation make a strategic decision to remain separate from an oppressive dominant culture. Their confident communication about the values and accomplishments of their co-cultural group increases the unity within the group and the self-esteem of its members.

Exemplifying strengths—Making the group's strength, success, and contribution known.

> Gay male: "Every chance I get I let my straight co-workers know about gay achievements. My favorite thing is to identify all of the famous people who were gay . . . usually right after they have just talked about how much they like them."[33]

Embracing stereotypes—Putting a positive spin on the dominant group's biases.

> African American man: "Whites are always searching our culture for evidence of our inferiority. . . . They say that normal people wouldn't eat chitins, pigs' feet, or whatever. . . . I eat them with pride! What whites don't understand is that historically blacks have had to make do with what was available—they were able to make great tasting feasts from parts of animals that others simply threw away."[34]

9. Aggressive Separation. This is often employed by a powerful co-cultural group leader when segregation from the dominant culture seems imperative. Leaders can use their personal power to undercut the legitimacy of society's oppression and strengthen the solidarity of the co-cultural group. But by choosing the approach of aggressive separation, co-cultural groups invite massive retaliation from the "powers that be" that they've railed against.

Attacking—Inflicting psychological pain through personal attack.

> African American man recalling student protest: "At one point it got real ugly . . . I mean calling names, threatening lawsuits, personal attacks—you wouldn't believe it."[35]

Sabotaging others—Undermining the benefits of dominant group membership.

> Man in wheelchair's response to repeated nosy questions: "I'll either try to motor away or really get pissed and I'm not beyond rolling over toes, really. I have been in situations where . . . there's no alternative."[36]

PHENOMENOLOGY—TAPPING INTO OTHERS' CONSCIOUS LIVED EXPERIENCE

Phenomenology
A qualitative research method committed to focusing on the conscious experience of a person as she or he relates to the lived world.

When co-cultural members interact with the keepers of the dominant culture, are the three preferred outcomes and the three communication approaches really the defining factors in what they say? How can Orbe be sure that his theoretical framework shown in Figure 36-1 has captured the essence of co-cultural communication? In truth, Orbe is convinced that the goals of co-cultural group members and the different styles of communication they adopt are the key factors because he has great confidence in the research method that revealed them—phenomenology.

Phenomenology is a research commitment to focus "on the conscious experience of a person as she or he relates to the lived world."[37] As a cultural phenomenologist, Orbe began his research with no initial hunches, preconceived ideas, predictions, nor hypotheses that he wanted to support. He notes that, unlike Giles' communication accommodation theory and Ting-Toomey's face-negotiation theory (see

Chapters 34 and 35), he recruited no experimental "subjects," nor did he develop a survey for "respondents" to fill out.

Instead, Orbe enlisted the help of nearly 100 marginalized people from a variety of co-cultural groups and listened to their stories of interactions with people in the dominant culture. He refers to his informants as "co-researchers" because they freely discussed their lived experiences in their own terms, and then explained what these experiences meant to them.[38] Most of their accounts were voiced within a focus group context, so experiences shared early in the session triggered other narratives that might otherwise have been unspoken.

This inductive type of qualitative research is akin to what Baxter did with relationship partners in developing relational dialectics theory and how Deetz partnered with corporate employees to form his critical theory of communication in organizations (see Chapters 11 and 21). For Orbe, it was a three-stage process.[39]

First, Orbe invited his co-researchers to describe their experiences within the dominant culture, recorded everything they said, and later made a word-for-word transcript. Next, Orbe pored over this record, looking for repeated words, phrases, or themes that described and gave meaning to their communication. It was during this second stage that he identified the 26 communicative practices, and also realized that some of the strategies clustered together.

Only then did Orbe try to make sense of the whole, or as he puts it, "Giving "shape to the shapeless."[40] He conducted this phenomenological interpretation by finding meanings that weren't immediately apparent in the first two steps. That's when the overriding themes of preferred outcome and communication approach came together, and the three-by-three framework of the theory was formed.

Through this process, he also identified four other factors that influence how members of co-cultural groups interact with members of the dominant society.[41]

1. Field of experience. This is the sum total of life experiences dealing with "The Man." We learn from our past. If being aggressive with a white Anglo boss has always turned out badly, it may be time to adopt a different style.

2. Situational context. What feels safe depends on the setting. A gay man could hide behind a cloak of heterosexuality when at work or with family at home, yet feel comfortable kissing another guy in a gay bar or at a rock concert.

3. Ability. It's doubtful that a person with a pronounced physical disability can easily assimilate into a nondisabled culture. And despite being humiliated by white members of a dominant culture, some people just don't have the capacity to launch an angry attack or sabotage others.

4. Perceived costs and rewards. All 26 communication strategies have advantages and disadvantages that differ for members within and between co-cultural groups. Recall that social exchange theory suggests this is the crucial issue in all interpersonal interaction (see Chapter 8). With both theories, trying to calculate future costs and rewards of interaction would seem fraught with difficulty unless investments and returns on conversation were measured only in terms of dollars and cents. Of course, ignoring relationships, a sense of self-esteem, and levels of stress might appeal to some powerful members of the dominant group who believe in calculating outcomes in a way that reflects their version of the Golden Rule: "He who has the gold, rules."

Co-cultural group members' preferred outcome, communication approach, and the other four factors above can't be plugged into a formula to predict their responses when they bump into people from the dominant culture. However, Orbe does highlight their importance by weaving them into his summary statement of the theory:

> Situated within a particular *field of experience* that governs their perceptions of the *costs and rewards* associated with, as well as their *capability* to engage in, various communicative practices, co-cultural group members will adopt certain communication orientations—based on their *preferred outcomes* and *communication approaches*—to fit the circumstances of a specific *situation*.[42]

QUANTITATIVE RESEARCH SUPPORTS A QUALITATIVE THEORY

In a highly unusual move, cultural phenomenologist Orbe teamed up with Michigan State University behavioral scientist Maria Knight Lapinski to create self-report scales that measure the two most important dimensions of co-cultural theory.[43] They asked a group of women, and later a mixed-gender group of African Americans, to respond to a variety of statements about their preferred outcome and communication approach when they are the only co-cultural person at a dominant culture gathering. Each of the 35 items reflected one of the three preferred outcomes or three communication approaches Orbe synthesized from his phenomenological research. For example:

> It is usually my goal to "fit in" with members of the majority. (Assimilation)
>
> Members of the majority group should appreciate the unique aspects of the minority group. (Accommodation)
>
> I don't want to be seen as part of the majority group. (Separation)
>
> I sometimes feel inhibited when I interact with members of the majority
>
> group. (Nonassertive)
>
> I make my opinions clear when talking to members of the majority group. (Assertive)
>
> I am outspoken with members of the majority group. (Aggressive)[44]

Co-cultural group members indicated their response to each item on a 5-point scale ranging from "never" to "always."

Lapinski and Orbe first checked to make sure the validity and reliability of their scales met traditional social science standards—which they did. The researchers then ran a sophisticated statistical test to determine that co-cultural group members saw the three preferred outcomes—assimilation, accommodation, separation—as distinct from each other. In like manner, they discovered that their respondents saw communication approach as a single continuum, with nonassertive anchoring one end of the scale, and aggressive the other. An assertive style was in between the two, but closer to aggressive than to nonassertive. For scientific scholars, the results of this quantitative analysis offer assurance that Orbe's qualitative interpretation of what his original co-cultural researchers said was on target.

Another fascinating result was the positive relationship between a co-cultural group member's desired goals and choice of communication style. When asked

I n t e g r a t i o n

By the end of the term, most students have decided which type of theory they favor—objective or interpretive. If you've made your choice, consider four distinct ways you can respond to classmates, instructors, or others who don't share your preference.

1. Reject inferior scholarship. Objective as well as interpretive scholars who take this position believe it's ridiculous to say the other side has something to offer. For example, University of Kentucky emeritus communication professors Robert Bostrom and Lewis Donohew, who searched for objective truth dismissed the work of theorists like Barnett Pearce, Roland Barthes, Kenneth Burke, and Stuart Hall. They claimed the interpretive approach represents "an intellectual nihilism" that leads to "theoretical anarchy and the substitution of pseudo-explanation for scientific explanation."[1] Hall in turn was "deeply suspicious and hostile" to the work of behavioral scientists who focus solely on outward behavior while "consistently translating matters of signification, meaning, language, and symbolization into crude behavioral indicators."[2] You could follow their lead by criticizing the views of misguided others.

2. Respect differences. Princeton University philosophical pragmatist Richard Rorty came down equally hard on objective and interpretive theorists when either group claimed that only their approach had value. He admitted, however, that there *are* irreconcilable differences between the two camps. Both groups are self-sealing language communities that don't—and really can't—talk to each other. The questions posed in one approach have no answers in the other approach. For this reason, Rorty said the debates between the sciences and humanities about human nature, knowledge, and methodology are "not issues to be resolved, only . . . differences to be lived with."[3]

Clinical psychology is a discipline in which this response is common. The behavioral, humanist, and psychoanalytic schools of counseling differ in starting point, method, and conclusion. Most counselors choose to be trained in one approach and then stick to it in their practice. Yet they respect any form of therapy that helps a hurting person get better. Similarly, you could respect any approach that helps people communicate more effectively.

3. Explore the other side. We tend to like what's familiar and not really know what we're missing. You may favor an objective approach because of your interest in interpersonal communication, a field where most theory and research is crafted from a social science perspective. But you might find that taking a course in the qualitative methods of conducting ethnography, discourse analysis, and focus groups could attach faces and feelings to the people behind your statistics. In like manner, if public speaking, debate, and rhetorical criticism are your passion, you might be pleasantly surprised to find that a controlled experiment or survey protocol described in a research design course could confirm or cast doubt on your hunches about what sways an audience.

If you pursue an advanced degree in communication, there's no doubt you'll be asked to narrow your focus. But starting your studies or career track with a narrow focus could cause you to miss out on a variety of ideas and possibilities. Exploring the best of the social sciences and humanities can be enjoyable now and reap unexpected rewards in the future. There will be time to specialize later.

4. Cooperate with colleagues. Cultivation theorist George Gerbner pictured a symbiotic relationship between two worldviews, whereby scientists and artists help each other fulfill a promise that can't be reached by either approach alone.[4] When dealing with communication theory, what would a collaborative relationship between objective and interpretive communication majors look like?

Studying together for exams in courses that investigate both approaches could be a first step. Collaborating on a research project with someone who holds a different worldview is another possibility. Perhaps a creative student in film studies could shoot and edit a video on binge drinking across campus. Another student trained in empirical research could perform a before-and-after study of the alcohol consumption of students who watched the video. Or a social scientist among you could test one of the theories in this book, while an interpretive scholar concentrates on its implications and applied practice. However you might work together, rhetorician Marie Hochmuth Nichols insisted that the sciences and humanities need each other: "The humanities without science are blind, but science without the humanities may be vicious."[5]

Reject. Respect. Explore. Cooperate. Which response do you choose?

Common Threads in Comm Theories

The first four chapters in this book laid the groundwork for understanding the relationship among the wide range of theories you would study. Chapter 1 presented a working definition of both *theory* and *communication.* Chapter 2 introduced the objective-interpretive distinction, and Chapter 3 outlined separate lists of six criteria for evaluating these two types of theories. Chapter 4 mapped out seven distinct traditions of theory within our discipline. Hopefully these integrative tools have helped you compare and contrast the theories throughout the course.

In this final chapter, we present another approach to identifying similarities and differences among the theories, which wouldn't have made sense before you read about them. We identify 10 recurring principles that in one form or another appear in multiple theories. We refer to these as *threads* because each strand weaves in and out of theories that might otherwise seem unrelated.

These threads represent key concepts in other communication courses, so they may be quite familiar. We've decided that in order to qualify as a thread in the tapestry of communication theory, the principle or concept must be a significant feature of at least six different theories covered in the text. The feature could be the engine that drives a theory, a common characteristic of messages, a variable that's related to the process of communication, or the outcome of an interaction.

Each thread is introduced with a shorthand label followed by a summary statement set in boldface. We first illustrate the principle with an exemplar theory that's clearly entwined with that thread, and then describe how other theorists employ this key idea, which is sometimes at odds with how it's used in the exemplar. That's the *contrast* of this compare-and-contrast integration. Consistent with the critique sections that close each theory chapter of the text, each thread discussion ends with Em's cause-for-pause reservation that those who warmly embrace the thread might ponder.

Unraveling these threads isn't intended to exhaust all possibilities—nor to be exhausting. We cite every theory covered in the book at least once, but never more than twice. With one exception, we tie three to five theories into a thread. You or your instructor may think of multiple examples for each thread that we don't mention.

Students tell us that working through the threads helps them make new connections between the theories, and also serves as a comprehensive course review. We hope it does both of these for you.

1. MOTIVATION

Communication is motivated by our basic social need for affiliation, achievement, and control, as well as our strong desire to reduce our uncertainty and anxiety.

Social exchange theory holds that relationships develop based upon the perceived benefits and costs of interaction. Recall that in *social penetration theory,* Altman and Taylor adopt the principle of social exchange to predict when people will become more vulnerable in their depth and breadth of self-disclosure (Ch. 8). The greater the probable outcome (benefits minus costs), the more transparent a person will be. Of course, potential rewards and costs are in the eye of the beholder. As Katz' *uses and gratifications* maintains, people act to gratify their felt needs, but those needs vary from person to person (Ch. 28). It follows, therefore, that the rewards and costs that satisfy those needs can be quite diverse. Despite this range of potential motives, almost every theory you've read about in the book invokes at least one of the five motives named in this thread. We've selected five different theories to illustrate the strong pull that these five different needs exert.

Motivation
Needs and desires that drive or draw us to think, feel, and act as we do.

Need for affiliation. Haythornthwaite's *media multiplexity theory* makes a distinction between weak ties and strong ties in our relationships. She claims that the more types of media both parties use to connect with each other, the stronger and closer their bond will be. Casual relationships based on few channels of communication become deeper as additional media are used, but once strong ties are established, cutting back on the media mix won't necessarily weaken the relationship (Ch. 13).

Need for achievement. Hirokawa and Gouran's *functional perspective on group decision making* assumes that people in problem-solving groups want to achieve a high-quality solution. Any comment that doesn't analyze the problem, set goals, identify alternatives, or evaluate the relative merits of each option is considered a distraction that disrupts the group's effort to achieve their goal (Ch. 17).

Need for control. Hall's *cultural studies* is based on a broad Marxist interpretation of history that claims money is power. Society's haves exercise hegemonic control over have-nots in an effort to maintain the status quo. Corporately controlled media shape the dominant discourse of the day, which frames the interpretation of events (Ch. 27).

Need to reduce uncertainty. Berger's *uncertainty reduction theory* suggests the motive for most communication is to gain knowledge and create understanding in order to increase our ability to predict how future interaction with others will go (Ch. 9). Our desire to reduce uncertainty is especially high when we expect we'll meet again, the other has something we want, or the person is acting in a weird way.

Need to reduce anxiety. Burke's "Definition of Man" suggests that the language of perfection makes us all feel guilty that we aren't better than we are. Guilt is his catchall term to cover every form of anxiety, tension, embarrassment, shame, and disgust intrinsic to the human condition. *Dramatism* claims the only way to get rid of this noxious feeling is through mortification or victimage (Ch. 23).

Cause for pause: If it's true that all of my communication—including this book— is undertaken solely to meet my own personal needs and interests, then it strikes me that I am a totally selfish person. I don't doubt that my desire for affiliation, achievement, and control shapes much of my conversation, as does my desire to reduce my levels of doubt and fear. But there are times when I could (and should) say no to the pull of these needs out of concern for others or a sense of ethical responsibility. To the extent that any theory of motivation suggests I have no choice, I choose to be skeptical.

2. SELF-IMAGE

Communication affects and is affected by our sense of identity, which is strongly shaped within the context of our culture.

Self-image
Identity; a mental picture of who I see myself to be, which is greatly influenced by the way others respond to me.

Mead's ***symbolic interactionism*** claims our concept of self is formed through communication (Ch. 5). By taking the role of the other and seeing how we look to them, we develop our sense of identity. In turn, this looking-glass self shapes how we think and act within the community. According to Aronson and Cooper's revisions of *cognitive dissonance theory,* dissonance negatively impacts our self-image until we find a way to dissipate this distressing feeling (Ch. 16).

Ting-Toomey's *face-negotiation theory* defines face as our public self-image (Ch. 35). She says that people raised in individualistic usually to have an *I-identity* and are concerned with saving face. People born into collectivistic cultures usually have a *we-identity* and are mainly concerned with giving face to others.

Cause for pause: Accepted wisdom in our discipline suggests that most of us have been put down by others and need to find ways to boost our self-esteem. As a counterpoint to this concern, social psychologists have identified a fundamental attribution error—our basic, consistent, perceptual bias that affects our image of self and others.[1] When we have success, we interpret it as the result of our hard work and ability, but when others have that same success, we tend to think of them as lucky. Conversely, when others fail, we consider it their own fault, but when we fail, we blame others or curse the fickle finger of fate. As a corrective to this biased perception, perhaps we should consider giving others the benefit of the doubt while holding ourselves to a more rigorous standard of accountability.

3. CREDIBILITY

Our verbal and nonverbal messages are validated or discounted by others' perception of our competence and character.

Credibility
The intelligence, character, and goodwill that audience members perceive in a message source.

More than 2,000 years ago, ***The Rhetoric*** of Aristotle used the term ethical proof (ethos) to describe the credibility of a speaker, which affects the probability that the speech will be persuasive. Aristotle defined *ethos* as a combination of the speaker's perceived intelligence or competence, character or trustworthiness, and goodwill toward the audience (Ch. 22). Since credibility is in the eye of the beholder, audience perceptions of the speaker's ability, virtue, and concern for their well-being can change while he or she is speaking.

In election studies based on recent versions of McCombs and Shaw's *agenda-setting theory,* researchers not only monitor the frequency of candidate attributes mentioned by the media, but also note the affective tone of these references. The way the media frame a public figure's competence, personality, and morality clearly affects voters' perception of a candidate's credibility and therefore has a major effect on the election (Ch. 30).

Harding and Wood's *standpoint theory* recognizes that women, racial minorities, and others on the margins of society have low credibility in the eyes of those with higher status. The irony of this negative judgment is that the powerless occupy a position that affords them a less false view of social reality than is available to the overprivileged who look down on them (Ch. 32).

Cause for pause: The theories cited in this thread regard perceived credibility as a valuable asset in the communication process. But our focus on the source of a message may cause us to lose sight of the intrinsic value of what's being said. Before embracing the speaker's point of view, we might ask ourselves, "Would I think this was such a good idea if it were presented by someone less popular or attractive?" We might also ask, "Just because an idea is voiced by someone I can't stand, does that mean it's totally wrong and without merit?"

4. EXPECTATION

What we expect to hear or see will affect our perception, interpretation, and response during an interaction.

Expectation

In human interaction, our anticipation of how others will act or react toward us.

Burgoon's *expectancy violations theory* defines expectation as what we anticipate will happen rather than what we might desire (Ch. 7). When our expectations are violated, we react either positively or negatively depending on the violation valence and the communicator's reward valence. And according to Burgoon's subsequent *interaction adaptation theory,* we change our interaction position as a result of our expectations.

Expectation is integral to other interpersonal theories as well. Berger's *uncertainty reduction theory* states that the expectation of future interaction increases our motivation to reduce uncertainty (Ch. 9). This prediction is echoed in Walther's *social information processing theory.* According to his *hyperpersonal perspective* extension of SIP, anticipation of future interaction coupled with an exaggerated sense of similarity results in a self-fulfilling prophecy. The person who is perceived through online communication to be wonderful starts acting that way (Ch. 10).

Gerbner's *cultivation theory* maintains that a steady diet of symbolic violence on television creates an exaggerated fear that the viewer will be physically threatened, mugged, raped, or killed. This expectation causes heavy viewers to have a general mistrust of others, which leads them to urge more restrictions and the use of force against those they fear (Ch. 29).

Cause for pause: Perceptions are interpretations of sensory experiences occurring in the present. Expectations are projections of our perceptions into the future—we anticipate a repeat performance. The two concepts are easy to confuse and tricky to measure. Since we can never know for sure what another person experiences, theories that appeal to the concept of expectation may sound more definitive than they really are.

5. AUDIENCE ADAPTATION

By mindfully creating a person-centered message specific to the situation, we increase the possibility of achieving our communication goals.

Sherif's *social judgment theory* predicts that those who want to influence others should try to figure out their latitudes of acceptance, rejection, and non-commitment on a particular issue. Based on this audience analysis, the persuader can craft a message that falls at the edge of a person's latitude of acceptance—an adaptation that offers the best chance of desired attitude change (Ch. 14). Petty and Cacioppo's *elaboration likelihood model* suggests the persuader first assess whether the target audience is ready and able to think through issue-relevant arguments that support

Audience adaptation
The strategic creation or adjustment of a message in light of the audience characteristics and specific setting.

the advocate's position. If not, the persuader can still achieve a temporary change of attitude by focusing attention on peripheral cues (Ch. 15).

Burke's *dramatism* is concerned with the speaker's ability to successfully identify with the audience. Without identification, there is no persuasion. To the extent that the speaker can establish common ground by demonstrating a similar background, personality, speaking style, and belief and value system, the speech will be successful (Ch. 23).

In an intercultural setting, Giles' *communication accommodation theory* focuses on parties' adjustment of their speech styles. CAT regards convergence of speaking styles as a natural outcome of wanting to be accepted by the other, usually drawing a positive response. Divergence—accentuating differences through manner of speech—occurs when the communicator is concerned with maintaining his or her distinctive group identity (Ch. 34). As each theory in this thread would predict, divergence induces a negative response from the other person.

Cause for pause: All of these theories suggest that for maximum effectiveness, we should consciously adapt our message to the attitudes, actions, or abilities of the audience. That makes sense. There is, however, a danger that in doing so, we'll lose the authenticity of our message or the integrity of our own beliefs. Adjusting becomes pandering when we say whatever others want to hear. Raymond Bauer's article "The Obstinate Audience" suggests an intriguing third possibility—that audience adaptation ends up changing the speaker more than the speaker changing the audience.[2] If so, the counterattitudinal advocacy studies of Festinger's *cognitive dissonance theory* might explain this surprising prediction (Ch. 16).

6. SOCIAL CONSTRUCTION

Persons-in-conversation co-construct their own social realities and are simultaneously shaped by the worlds they create.

This statement of social construction is taken directly from Pearce and Cronen's ***coordinated management of meaning*** (Ch. 6). They see themselves as curious participants in a pluralistic world as opposed to social scientists who they describe as detached observers trying to discover singular Truth. Because CMM claims that people jointly create the social worlds in which they live, the theorists urge us to ask, "What are we doing? What are we making together? How can we make better social worlds?"

Social construction
The communal creation of the social world in which we live.

McPhee's *communicative constitution of organizations* clearly indicates that an organization is what it is because communication has brought it into existence—a particular type of social construction. It's hard to imagine a workplace without four flows of ongoing talk about membership negotiation, self-structuring, activity coordination, and institutional positioning (Ch. 20).

Mead's *symbolic interactionism* denies that there is a real "me" that I can know through introspection. The theory insists that my self-concept is constituted by how others look at me, what they say to me, and how they act toward me. This looking-glass self is socially constructed, especially through the language of significant others in my life (Ch. 5).

McLuhan's *media ecology* describes a more subtle construction process, summarized in his statement that we shape our tools and they in turn shape us (Ch. 25). McLuhan claimed that television and other communication inventions change the sensory environment in which we live. In this massage, the medium is the message, and also the massage.

Cause for pause: The range of theories just cited shows that the idea of social construction is well established in the field of communication. But is there a foundational reality that language can describe, however poorly? As I asked at the end of the chapter on *CMM,* are you willing to give up the notion of a Truth you can count on for a linguistically created social reality that has no existence apart from how it's talked about?

7. SHARED MEANING

Our communication is successful to the extent that we share a common interpretation of the signs we use.

Shared meaning
People's common interpretation or mutual understanding of what a verbal or nonverbal message signifies.

Geertz and Pacanowsky's ***cultural approach to organizations*** describes culture as webs of significance—systems of shared meaning. In light of this definition, Geertz said we should concern ourselves not only with the structures of cultural webs, but also with the process of their spinning—communication. Applying Geertz' ideas to organizations, Pacanowsky focuses on the collective interpretation of stories, metaphors, and rituals (Ch. 19).

Bormann's *symbolic convergence theory* says sharing group fantasies creates symbolic convergence—shared meaning (Ch. 18). In a small-group setting, these dramatized messages can help the speaker and listeners make sense out of a confusing situation or bring clarity to an uncertain future. A composite drama that catches up many groups of people into a common symbolic reality becomes a rhetorical vision.

The road to common understanding is sometimes devious. Barthes' *semiotics* regards the mass media as powerful ideological tools that frame interpretation of events for the benefit of the haves over the have-nots. The media take a denotative sign and use it as a signifier to be paired with a different signified. The result is a new connotative sign that looks like the original sign but has lost its historical meaning (Ch. 26). Its effect is to affirm the status quo.

Cause for pause: The idea that it's people rather than words that *mean* suggests that texts don't interpret themselves. If that's true, shared interpretation is an accomplishment of the audience rather than the intent or clarity of the message. Pushed to an extreme, however, the meaning-in-persons idea implies that what is said or written is wide open for any interpretation, no matter what the communicator intended. As an author, I'm uneasy about this notion. I take words and images

"You'll have to phrase it another way. They have no word for 'fetch.'"

©Drew Dernavich/The New Yorker Collection/The Cartoon Bank

seriously and try to choose them carefully. When I write about a theory, my aim is to create a mutual understanding that's consistent with what I had in mind. To the extent that this takes place, I see communication as successful. Of course, you're then free to respond as you choose.

8. NARRATIVE

We respond favorably to stories and dramatic imagery with which we can identify.

Fisher's *narrative paradigm* claims that people are essentially storytellers. We experience life as a series of ongoing narratives—as conflicts, characters, beginnings, middles, and ends (Ch. 24). Almost all communication is story that we judge by its narrative coherence and narrative fidelity. We continually ponder, does that story hang together? Does it ring true?

Narrative
Story; words and deeds that have sequence and meaning for those who live, create, or interpret them.

Bormann's *symbolic convergence theory* can't predict when a story or other dramatizing message will catch fire among group members. But when it does, the resultant fantasy chain shows that it not only rings true, but also creates symbolic convergence—a common group consciousness and often a greater cohesiveness (Ch. 18).

Gerbner's *cultivation theory* says that television has become the dominant force in our society because it tells most of the stories, most of the time. Because TV stories are filled with symbolic violence, the world they create for heavy viewers is a mean and scary place. These stories cultivate fear by slowly changing viewers' perception of their social environment (Ch. 29).

Tannen observes that the disparity between men's and women's *genderlect styles* can be seen in how they tell a story. As the heroes of their own stories, men try to elevate their status. By telling stories about others, or downplaying their role in their narratives, women seek connection (Ch. 31).

Cause for pause: I believe stories are both fascinating and powerful. Throughout the book we've used extended examples to make theories come alive. But as Warnick reminds us in her commentary on the *narrative paradigm,* there are bad stories that can effectively destroy people or lead them astray. Unless we filter narratives through the values of justice, goodness, and integrity that Fisher and the NCA Credo for Ethical Communication advocate (see Appendix C), we could embrace a lie or perpetuate error. Well-told tales are inherently attractive, but they might not all be good.

9. CONFLICT

Unjust communication stifles needed conflict; healthy communication can make conflict productive.

Deetz' *critical theory of communication in organizations* describes managerial efforts to suppress conflict through discursive closure rather than address legitimate disagreements through open discussion (Ch. 21). He believes that corporations and their stakeholders would be well served by more conflict rather than less when decisions are made. The managerial quest for greater control counters any attempt to establish democracy in the workplace. Opportunities for employees to voice complaints are a chance to let off steam but rarely lead to meaningful participation in the decisions that affect their lives.

Conflict
The struggle between people who are contesting over scarce resources or who perceive that they have incompatible values and goals.

Some theories suggest that conflict must be headed off by proactively talking about the potential problem. A core principle of Petronio's *communication privacy management theory* warns that when co-owners of private information don't effectively negotiate and follow mutually held privacy rules, boundary turbulence is the likely result (Ch. 12).

Cause for pause: As a mediator, I try to facilitate straight talk between parties in conflict. Confronting the problem but not the person is a well-accepted principle of conflict resolution in the West. But, in her *face-negotiation theory,* Ting-Toomey warns that a free and open discussion of conflicting needs and interests within a collectivistic society is counterproductive (Ch. 35). In societies where giving face to others is the cultural norm, straight talk creates great embarrassment. Those of us from individualistic Western cultures need to appreciate and employ subtlety when we're with people from the East.

10. DIALOGUE

Dialogue is transparent conversation that often creates unanticipated relational outcomes due to parties' profound respect for disparate voices.

Drawing upon Bakhtin's conception of dialogue, Baxter's second generation of *relational dialectics theory* describes dialogue as an aesthetic accomplishment that produces fleeting moments of unity through a profound respect for disparate voices (Ch. 11). Baxter stresses that dialogue doesn't bring resolution to the contradictions that parties experience in close relationships. But dialogue and relationship rituals that honor multiple voices provide assurance that living within changing tensions can be exhilarating—never boring.

Dialogue
Transparent conversation that often creates unanticipated relational outcomes due to parties' profound respect for disparate voices.

In *coordinated management of meaning,* Pearce and Cronen adopt Buber's view of dialogue, which is more optimistic than Bakhtin's. Pearce believed that dialogic communication is learnable, teachable, and contagious (Ch. 6). These theorists agree that dialogue can't be produced on demand, but they think we can experience it if we seek and prepare for it. Buber said dialogue takes place only in I–Thou relationships where we regard our partner as the very one we are. We stand our own ground yet are profoundly open to the other.

In *muted group theory,* Kramarae suggests that it's difficult for women to participate as equal partners in a dialogue with men. That's because they have to speak in a man-made, second language in which the rules for use are frequently controlled by males (Ch. 33). Orbe's *co-cultural theory* extends this idea to all groups of marginalized people. He claims the entrenched power disparity between members of co-cultural groups and members of the dominant culture makes dialogue between them almost impossible. Perhaps a communication orientation of *Assertive/Accommodation* can create a conversational space where this kind of open and respectful discussion could occur. Orbe's commitment to cultural phenomenology encouraged his co-researchers to interact in this way in their focus groups (Ch. 36).

Cause for pause: In the communication discipline, *dialogue* is a term that's often used and highly favored, yet advocates—including me—have a tough time describing what it is or how to achieve it. In practice, dialogue is exceedingly rare. Whatever criteria we use, probably less than 1 in 1,000 conversations would qualify as dialogue. That suggests a full-blown theory of relational communication must also take into account legitimate authority, jealousies, boredom, insecurities, interruptions, distractions, time pressures, headaches, and all the other "complications" that make everyday communication less than ideal.

APPENDIX A

Abstracts of Theories

What follows are brief summaries of the 32 theories featured in the book. There's potential danger, of course, in trying to capture the gist of a theory in a few cryptic lines, but we didn't craft the abstracts to convey new concepts. Instead, these capsule statements are designed to jog your memory of ideas already considered. The abstracts are arranged in the same order as the theories in the text. At the end of each summary, we've labeled the communication theory tradition or traditions that undergird each theorist's thought. We hope you'll find the summaries as well as their intellectual roots helpful.

Interpersonal Communication

Mead's symbolic interactionism: Humans act toward people, things, and events on the basis of the meanings they assign to them. Once people define a situation as real, it has very real consequences. Without language there would be no thought, no sense of self, and no socializing presence of society within the individual. (Socio-cultural tradition)

Pearce and Cronen's coordinated management of meaning: Persons-in-conversation co-construct their own social realities and are shaped by the worlds they create. Communication is a two-sided process of making and managing meaning and coordinating our actions. What we say matters because we get what we make. If we get the pattern right, the best possible things will happen. (Socio-cultural and phenomenological traditions)

Burgoon's expectancy violations theory: Violating another person's interpersonal expectations can be a superior strategy to conformity. When the meaning of a violation is ambiguous, communicators with a high reward valence can enhance their attractiveness, credibility, and persuasiveness by doing the unexpected. When the violation valence or reward valence is negative, they should act in a socially appropriate way. (Socio-psychological tradition)

Altman and Taylor's social penetration theory: Interpersonal closeness proceeds in a gradual and orderly fashion from superficial to intimate levels of exchange as a function of anticipated present and future outcomes. Lasting intimacy requires continual and mutual vulnerability through breadth and depth of self-disclosure. (Socio-psychological tradition)

Berger's uncertainty reduction theory: When people meet, their primary concern is to reduce uncertainty about each other and their relationship. As verbal output, nonverbal warmth, self-disclosure, similarity, and shared communication networks increase, uncertainty decreases—and vice versa. Information seeking and reciprocity are positively correlated with uncertainty. (Socio-psychological tradition)

Walther's social information processing theory: Based solely on the information available via online communication, parties who meet online can develop relationships that are just as close as those formed face-to-face—though it takes longer.

Because online senders select, receivers magnify, channels promote, and feedback enhances favorable impressions, online communication may create hyperpersonal relationships. (Socio-psychological tradition)

Baxter and Bakhtin's relational dialectics theory: Interpersonal relationships are created through the interplay of discourses. These discourses occur within the relationship and outside of it. They address the past and the future. Often, discourses struggle with each other—at the same time or at different times. Common discursive struggles include integration–separation, stability–change, and expression–nonexpression. (Socio-cultural and phenomenological traditions)

Petronio's communication privacy management theory: People believe they own and have a right to control their private information; they do so by using personal privacy rules. When others are told, they become co-owners of the information. If co-owners don't effectively negotiate mutually agreeable privacy rules about telling third parties, boundary turbulence is the likely result. (Socio-cultural and cybernetic traditions)

Haythornthwaite's media multiplexity theory: Strong ties use more media to communicate with each other than do weak ties. Communication content differs by tie strength rather than by medium. Which media we use for which ties depends, in part, on group norms. Changes in media availability most strongly influence the quality of weak ties. (Cybernetic and socio-psychological traditions)

Sherif's social judgment theory: The larger the discrepancy between a speaker's position and a listener's point of view, the greater the change in attitude—as long as the message doesn't fall within the hearer's latitude of rejection. High ego-involvement usually indicates a wide latitude of rejection. Messages that fall there may have a boomerang effect. (Socio-psychological tradition)

Petty and Cacioppo's elaboration likelihood model: Message elaboration is the central route of persuasion that produces major positive attitude change. It occurs when unbiased listeners are motivated and able to scrutinize arguments they consider strong. Message-irrelevant factors hold sway on the peripheral path, a more common route that produces fragile shifts in attitude. (Socio-psychological tradition)

Festinger's cognitive dissonance theory: Cognitive dissonance is an aversive drive that causes people to (1) avoid opposing viewpoints, (2) seek reassurance after making a tough decision, and (3) change private beliefs to match public behavior when there is minimal justification for an action. Self-consistency, a sense of personal responsibility, or self-affirmation can explain dissonance reduction. (Socio-psychological tradition)

Group and Public Communication

Hirokawa and Gouran's functional perspective on group decision making: Groups make high-quality decisions when members fulfill four requisite functions: (1) problem analysis, (2) goal setting, (3) identification of alternatives, and (4) evaluation of positive and negative consequences. Most group communication disrupts progress toward accomplishing these functional tasks, but counteractive communication can bring people back to rational inquiry. (Socio-psychological and cybernetic traditions)

Bormann's symbolic convergence theory: Dramatizing messages are group members' expressed interpretations of events other than those in the here-and-now. Message content becomes a group fantasy theme when it spontaneously chains out among members. The sharing of group fantasies creates symbolic convergence—group consciousness and often cohesiveness. Fantasy theme analysis across groups can reveal a rhetorical vision. (Rhetorical and socio-psychological traditions)

Geertz and Pacanowsky's cultural approach to organizations: Humans are animals suspended in webs of significance that they themselves have spun. An organization doesn't have a culture, it is a culture—a unique system of shared meanings. A nonintrusive ethnographic approach interprets stories, rites, and other symbolism to make sense of corporate culture. (Socio-cultural tradition)

McPhee's communicative constitution of organizations: Communication calls organization into being. Such constitutive communication is patterned into four flows: membership negotiation, self-structuring, activity coordination, and institutional positioning. All four flows are necessary for organization to occur, although time and space often separate where each flow appears. (Socio-cultural tradition)

Deetz' critical theory of communication in organizations: The naïve notion that communication is merely the transmission of information perpetuates managerialism, discursive closure, and the corporate colonization of everyday life. Language is the principal medium through which social reality is produced and reproduced. Managers can further a company's health and democratic values by coordinating stakeholder participation in corporate decisions. (Critical and phenomenological traditions)

Aristotle's rhetoric: Rhetoric is the art of discovering all available means of persuasion. A speaker supports the probability of a message by logical, ethical, and emotional proofs. Accurate audience analysis results in effective invention, arrangement, style, delivery, and, presumably, memory. (Rhetorical tradition)

Burke's dramatism: Words are symbolic action, and rhetoric is the search for a scapegoat to take our guilt. Unless we identify with the drama portrayed by a speaker, persuasion won't occur. The dramatistic pentad of act, scene, agent, agency, and purpose is the critic's tool for discovering how a speaker builds such identification. (Rhetorical tradition)

Fisher's narrative paradigm: People are storytelling animals; almost all forms of human communication are fundamentally narrative. Listeners judge a story by whether it hangs together and rings true with the values of an ideal audience. Thus, narrative rationality is a matter of coherence and fidelity. (Rhetorical tradition)

Mass Communication

McLuhan's media ecology: The media must be understood ecologically. Changes in communication technology alter the symbolic environment—the socially constructed, sensory world of meanings. We shaped our tools—the phonetic alphabet, printing press, and telegraph—and they in turn have shaped our perceptions, experiences, attitudes, and behavior. Thus, the medium is the message. (Socio-cultural tradition)

Barthes' semiotics: The significant visual sign systems of a culture affirm the status quo by suggesting that the world as it is today is natural, inevitable, and eternal. Mythmakers do this by co-opting neutral denotative signs to become signifiers without historical grounding in second-order connotative semiotic systems. (Semiotic tradition)

Hall's cultural studies: The mass media function to maintain the ideology of those who already have power. Corporately controlled media provide the dominant discourse of the day, which frames the interpretation of events. Critics should seek not only to interpret culture, but to change it. Media audiences do have the capacity to resist hegemony. (Critical tradition)

Katz' uses and gratifications: The media-effects tradition focuses on what media do to people. Uses & grats focuses on what people do with media. Media consumption is a deliberate choice designed to satisfy particular needs. Media don't have uniform effects on the audience; effects vary according to the individual reasons for media use. (Socio-psychological tradition)

Gerbner's cultivation theory: Television has become society's storyteller. Heavy television viewers see a vast quantity of dramatic violence, which cultivates an exaggerated belief in a mean and scary world. Mainstreaming and resonance are two of the processes that create a homogeneous and fearful populace. (Socio-cultural and socio-psychological traditions)

McCombs and Shaw's agenda-setting theory: The media tell us (1) what to think about, (2) how to think about it, and (3) what issues go together. We especially pay attention to the media agenda when issues are relevant and uncertain. Agendamelding is the social process where we combine multiple agendas to fit our experiences and communities. (Socio-psychological tradition)

Cultural Context

Tannen's genderlect styles: Male–female conversation is cross-cultural communication. Masculine and feminine styles of discourse are best viewed as two distinct cultural dialects rather than as inferior or superior ways of speaking. Men's report talk focuses on status and independence; women's rapport talk seeks human connection. (Semiotic and socio-cultural traditions)

Harding and Wood's standpoint theory: Different locations within the social hierarchy affect what is seen. The standpoints of marginalized people provide less false views of the world than do the privileged perspectives of the powerful. Strong objectivity requires that scientific research start from the lives of women, the poor, the LGBTQ community, and racial minorities. (Critical tradition)

Kramarae's muted group theory: Man-made language aids in defining, depreciating, and excluding women. Because men have primarily shaped language, women frequently struggle to make their voices heard in the public sphere. As women cease to be muted, men will no longer maintain their position of dominance in society. (Critical and phenomenological traditions)

Giles' communication accommodation theory: People in intercultural encounters who see themselves as unique individuals will adjust their speech style and content to mesh with others whose approval they seek. People who want to reinforce a strong group identification will interact with those outside the group in a way that accentuates their differences. (Socio-psychological tradition)

Ting-Toomey's face-negotiation theory: People who have an interdependent self-image in a collectivistic culture are concerned with giving other-face or mutual-face, so they adopt a conflict style of avoiding or integrating. People who have an independent self-image in an individualistic culture are concerned with protecting self-face, so they adopt a conflict style of dominating. (Socio-cultural and socio-psychological traditions)

Orbe's co-cultural theory: African American men, the LGBTQ community, and people with physical disabilities are at a distinct disadvantage when they interact with people in the dominant culture. Phenomenological research reveals they adopt a communication orientation based on their preferred outcome (assimilation, accommodation, or separation) and their communication approach (nonassertive, assertive, or aggressive). (Phenomenological tradition)

APPENDIX B

Feature Films That Illustrate Communication Theories

(With a strong assist from our cinematic colleagues and friends Russ Proctor, Ron Adler, and Darin Garard)

Interpersonal Messages
Arrival (symbolic interactionism)
*Lady Bird** (symbolic interactionism)
Inside Out (symbolic interactionism)
Pygmalion / My Fair Lady (symbolic interactionism)
Nell (symbolic interactionism)
American Teen (symbolic interactionism)
Black Like Me (symbolic interactionism)
The Color Purple (symbolic interactionism)
Mask (symbolic interactionism)
The Perks of Being a Wallflower (symbolic interactionism)
She's All That (symbolic interactionism)
Lars and the Real Girl (CMM)
Arrival (CMM)
Pay It Forward (CMM)
Chocolat (CMM)
Life Is Beautiful (CMM)
Anger Management (CMM)
*Atonement** (expectancy violations)
*Ex Machina** (expectancy violations)
*Almost Famous** (expectancy violations)
*Crash** [2004] (expectancy violations)
Ferris Bueller's Day Off (expectancy violations)
The Sting (expectancy violations)

Relationship Development
*Good Will Hunting** (general)
Annie Hall (general)
*End of the Tour** (social penetration)
The Perks of Being a Wallflower (social penetration)
*Before Sunrise** / Before Sunset** (social penetration)
Get Low (social penetration)
Shrek (social penetration)
*Coming Home** (social penetration)
Waitress (social penetration)
*The Breakfast Club** (social penetration)
Driving Miss Daisy (uncertainty reduction)
My Big Fat Greek Wedding (uncertainty reduction)
*Witness** (uncertainty reduction)
*Knocked Up** (uncertainty reduction)
*Sideways** (uncertainty reduction)
The Chosen [1982] (uncertainty reduction)
*Trust** (SIP)
Catfish (SIP)

The Martian (SIP)
*Her** (SIP)
American Teen (SIP)
You've Got Mail (SIP)
Sleepless in Seattle (SIP)

Relationship Maintenance
Breaking Away (general)
(500) Days of Summer (relational dialectics)
*Children of a Lesser God** (relational dialectics)
*Cyrus** (relational dialectics)
*The Shape of Water** (relational dialectics)
Bend It Like Beckham (relational dialectics)
Like Crazy (relational dialectics)
*The Story of Us** (relational dialectics)
Whale Rider (relational dialectics)
Brave (relational dialectics)
*Dead Man Walking** (CPM)
*End of the Tour** (CPM)
Blue Jasmine (CPM)
*The Darjeeling Limited** (CPM)
Social Network (media multiplexity)
Catfish (media multiplexity)

Influence
Norma Rae (general)
*Dead Man Walking** (social judgment)
Hidden Figures (social judgment)
A Civil Action (social judgment)
Hotel Rwanda (social judgment)
*Schindler's List** (social judgment)
An Inconvenient Truth (ELM)
12 Angry Men (ELM)
*My Cousin Vinny** (ELM)
*Up in the Air** (cognitive dissonance)
Swing Kids (cognitive dissonance)
*Thank You for Smoking** (cognitive dissonance)
*Hell or High Water** (cognitive dissonance)
Casablanca (cognitive dissonance)

Group Communication
O Brother, Where Art Thou? (general)
Dunkirk (functional perspective)
*Argo** (functional perspective)
Apollo 13 (functional perspective)

*Asterisk indicates that movie is rated R.

Flight of the Phoenix (functional perspective)
Poseidon [2006] (functional perspective)
Alien* (functional perspective)
Captain Fantastic* (symbolic convergence)
Guardians of the Galaxy (symbolic convergence)
The Breakfast Club* (symbolic convergence)
Dead Poets Society (symbolic convergence)
Paper Clips (symbolic convergence)

Organizational Communication
Office Space* (general)
Moneyball (cultural approach)
Gung Ho (cultural approach)
Morning Glory (cultural approach)
Outsourced (cultural approach)
Friday Night Lights (cultural approach)
For Love or Money (cultural approach)
Good Morning, Vietnam* (cultural approach)
Up the Down Staircase (cultural approach)
The Firm* (cultural approach)
A Few Good Men* (cultural approach)
The Social Network (CCO)
Erin Brockovich* (critical theory)
The Devil Wears Prada (critical theory)
The Corporation (critical theory)
North Country* (critical theory)
Roger & Me* (critical theory)
The Insider* (critical theory)
Silkwood* (critical theory)

Public Rhetoric
The King's Speech* (general)
Clarence Darrow (general)
Inherit the Wind (general)
Judgment at Nuremberg (general)
Lincoln (rhetoric)
The Great Debaters (rhetoric)
My Cousin Vinny* (rhetoric)
The Verdict* (rhetoric)
Amistad* (rhetoric)
Nixon* (dramatism)
Malcolm X (dramatism)
Julius Caesar (dramatism)
Snow Falling on Cedars (dramatism)
Billy Lynn's Long Halftime Walk* (narrative paradigm)
Mudbound (narrative paradigm)
Stories We Tell* (narrative paradigm)
Lars and the Real Girl (narrative paradigm)
Smoke* (narrative paradigm)
Big Fish (narrative paradigm)
Forrest Gump (narrative paradigm)

Media and Culture
Blade Runner* (media ecology)
Network* (media ecology)
Broadcast News* (media ecology)
Ex Machina* (media ecology)
Amarcord* (semiotics)
Arrival (semiotics)
Stardust Memories (semiotics)
The Seventh Seal* (semiotics)
The Year of Living Dangerously (cultural studies)

The Hunger Games (cultural studies)
Bamboozled* (cultural studies)
Good Night and Good Luck (cultural studies)
Lee Daniels' The Butler (cultural studies)
Blood Diamond* (cultural studies)
Fahrenheit 9/11* (cultural studies)

Media Effects
Network* (general)
The Candidate (general)
Nurse Betty* (uses & grats)
Avalon (cultivation)
Being There (cultivation)
All the President's Men (agenda-setting)
Wag the Dog* (agenda-setting)
Absence of Malice (agenda-setting)
The Post (agenda setting)

Gender and Communication
When Harry Met Sally* (genderlect styles)
The Break-Up (genderlect styles)
Sleepless in Seattle (genderlect styles)
Diner* (genderlect styles)
Steel Magnolias (genderlect styles)
The Help (standpoint)
Slumdog Millionaire* (standpoint)
12 Years a Slave* (standpoint)
The Cider House Rules (standpoint)
Waiting to Exhale* (standpoint)
White Man's Burden* (standpoint)
North Country* (muted group)
The Little Mermaid (muted group)
Maria Full of Grace* (muted group)
Tootsie (muted group)
Legally Blonde (muted group)

Intercultural Communication
A Passage to India (general)
Do the Right Thing* (general)
Tsotsi* (general)
Beasts of the Southern Wild (CAT)
Crash* [2004] (CAT)
Redhook Summer (CAT)
The Right Stuff (CAT)
Zelig (CAT)
Win Win* (face-negotiation)
The Joy Luck Club* (face-negotiation)
42 (face-negotiation)
Iron and Silk (face-negotiation)
Easy A (face-negotiation)
Antz (face-negotiation)
Gung Ho (face-negotiation)
Shall We Dance? [1997] (face-negotiation)
Milk* (co-cultural)
The Big Sick* (co-cultural)
Moonlight* (co-cultural)
Hoop Dreams (co-cultural)
Billy Elliot (co-cultural)
Get Out* (co-cultural)
My Left Foot* (co-cultural)
The Imitation Game (co-cultural)

APPENDIX C

NCA Credo for Ethical Communication

Questions of right and wrong arise whenever people communicate. Ethical communication is fundamental to responsible thinking, decision making, and the development of relationships and communities within and across contexts, cultures, channels, and media. Moreover, ethical communication enhances human worth and dignity by fostering truthfulness, fairness, responsibility, personal integrity, and respect for self and others. We believe that unethical communication threatens the quality of all communication and consequently the well-being of individuals and the society in which we live. Therefore, we, the members of the National Communication Association, endorse and are committed to practicing the following principles of ethical communication.

> **We advocate truthfulness, accuracy, honesty, and reason as essential to the integrity of communication.**

> **We endorse freedom of expression, diversity of perspective, and tolerance of dissent to achieve the informed and responsible decision making fundamental to a civil society.**

> **We strive to understand and respect other communicators before evaluating and responding to their messages.**

> **We promote access to communication resources and opportunities as necessary to fulfill human potential and contribute to the well-being of families, communities, and society.**

> **We promote communication climates of caring and mutual understanding that respect the unique needs and characteristics of individual communicators.**

> **We condemn communication that degrades individuals and humanity through distortion, intimidation, coercion, and violence and through the expression of intolerance and hatred.**

> **We are committed to the courageous expression of personal convictions in pursuit of fairness and justice.**

> **We advocate sharing information, opinions, and feelings when facing significant choices while also respecting privacy and confidentiality.**

> **We accept responsibility for the short- and long-term consequences of our own communication and expect the same of others.**

ENDNOTES

Chapter 1: Launching Your Study of Communication Theory

1 Judee Burgoon, "Expectancy Violations Theory," in *Conversations with Communication Theorists*, 2.0, McGraw-Hill, 2006. (DVD) Band 2; also available at https://www.youtube.com/watch?v=kmnZIxiYHk, accessed December 18, 2017.

2 Ernest Bormann, *Communication Theory*, Sheffield, Salem, WI, 1989, p. 25.

3 Burgoon, *Conversations...*.

4 Fred Casmir, *Building Communication Theories: A Socio/Cultural Approach*, Lawrence Erlbaum, Hillsdale, NJ, 1994, p. 27.

5 Sir Karl Popper, *The Logic of Scientific Discovery*, Hutchinson, London, 1959, p. 59.

6 See "General Semantics of Alfred Korzybski" in the Theory List at www.afirstlook.com.

7 Frank E. X. Dance, "The Concept of Communication," *Journal of Communication*, Vol. 20, 1970, pp. 201–210.

8 Dance, p. 210.

9 Jennifer Daryl Slack, "Communication as Articulation," in *Communication as... Perspectives on Theory*, Gregory Shepherd, Jeffrey St. John, and Ted Striphas (eds.), Sage, Thousand Oaks, CA, 2006, p. 223.

10 Robert T. Craig, "Communication as a Practice," in *Communication as... Perspectives on Theory*, p. 39.

11 For further discussion of Blumer and this statement, see Chapter 5.

12 Wendell Johnson, *People in Quandaries*, Harper, New York, 1946, p. 26.

13 Celeste Condit, "Communication as Relationality," in *Communication as... Perspectives on Theory*, p. 3.

14 Frank E. X. Dance, "Toward a Theory of Human Communication," in *Human Communication Theory: Original Essays*, Holt, Rinehart, and Winston, 1967, p. 289.

Chapter 2: Talk About Theory

1 https://www.youtube.com/watch?v=WuAAXCOUH6Q, accessed October 2, 2017.

2 Ken Wheaton, "Super Bowl Ad Review: The Good, the Bad, the Clydesdales," *Advertising Age*, February 4, 2013, p. 20.

3 http://www.gazette.net/article/20130204/NEWS/130209706/-1/ravens-nope-x2014-clydesdales-eke-out-super-bowl-victory&template=gazette, accessed February 11, 2013.

4 Tony Schwartz, *The Responsive Chord*, Doubleday, New York, 1973, pp. 1–40.

5 C. G. Jung, *The Archetypes and the Collective Unconscious*, 2nd ed., Princeton University, Princeton, NJ, 1981.

6 Michael Osborn, "The Evolution of the Archetypal Sea in Rhetoric and Poetic," *Quarterly Journal of Speech*, Vol. 63, 1977, pp. 347–363.

7 James A. Anderson, *Communication Theory: Epistemological Foundations*, Guilford, New York, 1996, p. 27.

8 Anderson, p. 120.

9 Philosophers call this a question of *ontology*—the study of existence.

10 William Henley, "Invictus," in *The Columbia Anthology of British Poetry*, Carl Woodring and James Shapiro (eds.), Columbia University, New York, 1995, p. 685.

11 Anderson, p. 133.

12 C. S. Lewis, *The Abolition of Man*, Macmillan, New York, 1944, p. 309.

13 Philosophers call this a question of *axiology*—the study of ethical criteria.

14 George C. Homans, *The Nature of Social Science*, Harcourt, New York, 1967, p. 4.

15 William Melody and Robin Mansell, "The Debate over Critical vs. Administrative Research: Circularity or Challenge," *Journal of Communication*, Vol. 33, No. 3, 1983, p. 112.

16 Stan Deetz, "Fundamental Issues in Communication Studies," unpublished paper distributed to students enrolled in his communication theory class.

17 Robert Ivie, "The Social Relevance of Rhetorical Scholarship," *Quarterly Journal of Speech*, Vol. 81, No. 2, 1995, p. 138a.

Chapter 3: Weighing the Words

1 Abraham Kaplan, *The Conduct of Inquiry*, Chandler, San Francisco, CA, 1964, p. 295.

2 James McCroskey, "Validity of the PRCA as an Index of Communication Apprehension," *Communication Monographs*, Vol. 45, 1978, pp. 192–203.

3 Walter Mischel, "Personality Dispositions Revisited and Revised: A View After Three Decades," in *Handbook of Personality: Theory and Research*, Lawrence Pervin (ed.), Guilford, New York, 1990, pp. 111–134.

4 Francis Hylighen, "Occam's Razor," *Principia Cybernetica Web*, http://pespmc1.vub.ac.be/OCCAMRAZ.html, accessed September 16, 2013.

5 http://www.brainyquote.com/quotes/authors/a/albert_einstein.html, accessed September 16, 2013.

6 Karl Popper, *Conjectures and Refutations: The Growth of Scientific Knowledge*, Harper & Row, New York, 1965, pp. 36–37.

7 David Hume, *An Enquiry Concerning Human Understanding*, Tom L. Deauchamp (ed.), Oxford University, London, 1999, p. 211.

8 Donn Byrne, "An Overview (and Underview) of Research and Theory Within the Attraction Paradigm," *Journal of Social and Personal Relationships*, Vol. 14, 1997, pp. 417–431.

9 See Chapter 29: "Cultivation Theory of George Gerbner."

10 Eric Rothenbuhler, "Communication as Ritual," in *Communication as... Perspectives on Theory*, Gregory Shepherd, Jeffrey St. John, and Ted Striphas (eds.), Sage, Thousand Oaks, CA, 2006, p. 19.

11 Klaus Krippendorff, "The Ethics of Constructing Communication," in *Rethinking Communication, Vol. 1: Paradigm Issues*, Brenda Dervin, Lawrence Grossberg, Barbara J. O'Keefe, and Ellen Wartella (eds.), Sage, Newbury Park, CA, 1989, p. 88.

12 William H. Melody and Robin Mansell, "The Debate over Critical vs. Administrative Research: Circularity or Challenge," *Journal of Communication*, Vol. 33, No. 3, 1983, p. 103.

13 Ernest G. Bormann, *Communication Theory*, Sheffield, Salem, WI, 1989, p. 214.

14 Krippendorff, "The Ethics of Constructing Communication," p. 83.

15 Barbara Warnick, "Left in Context: What Is the Critic's Role?" *Quarterly Journal of Speech*, Vol. 78, 1992, pp. 232–237.

16 Edwin Black, "Gettysburg and Silence," *Quarterly Journal of Speech*, Vol. 80, 1994, pp. 21–36.

17 David Zarefsky, "Approaching Lincoln's Second Inaugural Address," in *The Practice of Rhetorical Criticism*, 2nd ed., James R. Andrews (ed.), Longman, New York, 1990, p. 69.

18 John Stewart, "A Postmodern Look at Traditional Communication Postulates," *Western Journal of Speech Communication*, Vol. 55, 1991, p. 374.

19 Kenneth Gergen, *Toward Transformation in Social Knowledge*, Springer-Verlag, New York, 1982, p. 109.

20 Norman K. Denzin and Yvonna S. Lincoln, "Introduction: The Discipline and Practice of Qualitative Research," in *Handbook of Qualitative Research*, 2nd ed., Norman K. Denzin and Yvonna S. Lincoln (eds.), Sage, Thousand Oaks, CA, p. 3.

21 http://rescomp.stanford.edu/~cheshire/EinsteinQuotes.html, accessed September 16, 2013.

22 David J. Garrow, *Bearing the Cross*, William Morrow, New York, 1986, pp. 231–286.

23 Clifford Geertz, "Thick Description: Toward an Interpretive Theory of Culture," in *The Interpretation of Cultures*, Basic Books, New York, 1973, p. 5.

24 Bernie Miklasz, "A Perfect Union: Stan The Man and St. Louis," *St. Louis Post-Dispatch*, January 20, 2013, http://www.stltoday.com/sports/columns/bernie-miklasz/a-perfect-union-stan-the-man-and-st-louis/article_1f42f8b6-a9da-530f-9492-2a767479bd19.html, accessed January 27, 2013.

25 Isabel Briggs Myers, *Introduction to Type*, Consulting Psychologists, Palo Alto, CA, p. 5.

26 Gregory Bateson, *Mind and Nature: A Necessary Unity*, Bantam, New York, 1979, p. 242.

Chapter 4: Mapping the Territory

1 Robert T. Craig, "Communication Theory as a Field," *Communication Theory*, Vol. 9, 1999, p. 122.

2 Ann Margaret Lewis and Helen Keier, "*Star Wars*: The New Essential Guide to Alien Species," Del Rey, New York, 2006.

3 Craig, "Communication Theory as a Field," p. 120.

4 Robert T. Craig, "Communication as a Practical Discipline," in *Rethinking Communication, Vol. 1: Paradigm Issues*, Brenda Dervin, Lawrence Grossberg, Barbara J. O'Keefe, and Ellen Wartella (eds.), Sage, Newbury Park, CA, 1989, pp. 97–122.

5 Craig, "Communication Theory as a Field," p. 130.

6 The identification and titles of the seven traditions are taken from Craig (see note 3). We have altered his order of presentation to match the conceptual plan of Figure 4-1. The boldfaced definitions of communication within each tradition are a paraphrase of, and consistent with, Craig's conception. The selection of a particular research study for each tradition was our decision and reflects the features of the tradition we chose to emphasize.

7 Em Griffin and Glenn G. Sparks, "Friends Forever: A Longitudinal Exploration of Intimacy in Same-Sex Friends and Platonic Pairs," *Journal of Social and Personal Relationships*, Vol. 7, 1990, pp. 29–46.

8 Harold H. Kelley, Ellen Berscheid, Andrew Christensen, John Harvey, Ted Huston, George Levinger, Evie McClintock, Letitia Anne Peplau, and Donald Peterson, *Close Relationships*, W. H. Freeman, New York, 1983, p. 38.

9 Andrew M. Ledbetter, Em Griffin, and Glenn G. Sparks, "Forecasting 'Friends Forever': A Longitudinal Investigation of Sustained Closeness Between Best Friends," *Personal Relationships*, Vol. 14, 2007, pp. 343–350.

10 Norbert Wiener, *The Human Use of Human Beings*, Avon, New York, 1967, p. 23.

11 Malcolm Parks, *Personal Relationships and Personal Networks*, Lawrence Erlbaum, Mahwah, NJ, 2007, pp. 87–96.

12 Cicero, *De Oratore*, E. W. Sutton and H. Rackham (trans.), Harvard University, Cambridge, MA, 1942, p. 25.

13 Aristotle, *On Rhetoric: A Theory of Civic Discourse*, 2nd ed., George A. Kennedy (trans.), Oxford University Press, New York, 2007, 2.4.2.

14 Ibid., 2.4.26.

15 Eugene Garver, *Aristotle's Rhetoric: An Art of Character*, University of Chicago, Chicago, IL, 1994, pp. 104–138.

16 Keith B. Jenkins and Grant Cos, "A Time for Change and a Candidate's Voice: Pragmatism and the Rhetoric of Inclusion in Barack Obama's 2008 Presidential Campaign," *American Behavioral Scientist*, Vol. 54, 2010, p. 194.

17 I. A. Richards, *The Philosophy of Rhetoric*, Oxford University Press, New York, 1936, pp. 11–12.

18 Michael Monsour, "Meanings of Intimacy in Cross- and Same-Sex Friendships," *Journal of Social and Personal Relationships*, Vol. 9, 1992, pp. 277–295.

19 Paul Kay and Willet Kempton, "What Is the Sapir–Whorf Hypothesis?" *American Anthropologist*, Vol. 86, 1984, pp. 65–79.

20 Edward Sapir, "The Status of Linguistics as a Science," in *Selected Writings*, David Mandelbaum (ed.), University of California, Berkeley, CA, 1951 (1929), p. 160.

21 James Carey, *Communication as Culture*, Unwin Hyman, Boston, MA, 1989, p. 23.

22 For an extended discussion of the socio-cultural concept, see Chapter 6: "Coordinated Management of Meaning of W. Barnett Pearce & Vernon Cronen."

23 Patricia M. Sias, Renee Heath, Tara Perry, Deborah Silva, and Bryan Fix, "Narratives of Workplace Friendship Deterioration," *Journal of Social and Personal Relationships*, Vol. 21, 2004, pp. 323–324.

24 Davi Johnston Thornton, "Psych's Comedic Tale of Black–White Friendship and the Lighthearted Affect of 'Post-Race' America," *Critical Studies in Media Communication*, Vol. 28, 2011, p. 427.

25 Ibid., p. 437.

26 Ibid., p. 428.

27 Carl Rogers, "This Is Me," in *On Becoming a Person*, Houghton Mifflin, Boston, MA, 1961, p. 24.

28 William K. Rawlins, *The Compass of Friendship: Narratives, Identities, and Dialogues*, Sage, Thousand Oaks, CA, 2009, p. 72.

29 Ibid., pp. 94–95.

30 Ibid., p. 95.

31 Ibid., p. 72.

32 Robert T. Craig, "The Constitutive Metamodel: A 16-Year Review," *Communication Theory*, Vol. 25, 2015, p. 367.

33 Robert T. Craig and Heidi L. Muller (eds.), *Theorizing Communication: Readings Across Traditions*, Sage, Thousand Oaks, CA, 2007, p. 499. For more information on the pragmatist tradition, see Robert T. Craig, "Pragmatism in the Field of Communication Theory," *Communication Theory*, Vol. 17, 2007, pp. 125–145.

34 Marc Howard Rich, "Spiritual Debate in Communication Theory: Craig's Metamodel Applied," *Journal of Communication and Religion*, Vol. 38, 2015, pp. 134–153.

35 Richard L. Johannesen, "Communication Ethics: Centrality, Trends, and Controversies," in *Communication Yearbook 25*, William B. Gudykunst (ed.), Lawrence Erlbaum, Mahwah, NJ, 2001, pp. 201–235.

36 "NCA Credo for Ethical Communication," National Communication Association, Washington, DC, https://www.natcom.org/sites/default/files/pages/1999_Public_Statements_NCA_Credo_for_Ethical_Communication_November.pdf, accessed September 13, 2017.

37 Craig, "The Constitutive Metamodel," p. 358.

38 Rawlins, pp. 175–184.

39 Craig, "The Constitutive Metamodel," p. 359.

Interpersonal Messages

1. An earlier version of these game metaphors appeared in Em Griffin, *Making Friends*, InterVarsity Press, Downers Grove, IL, 1987, pp. 12–18.

Chapter 5: Symbolic Interactionism

1 George Herbert Mead, *Mind, Self, and Society*, University of Chicago, Chicago, IL, [1934] 1962.

2 The three premises are found in Herbert Blumer, *Symbolic Interactionism*, Prentice-Hall, Englewood Cliffs, NJ, 1969, p. 2. I've

paraphrased the principles for stylistic consistency and to avoid gender-specific language.

3   Gil Musolf, "The Chicago School," in Larry T. Reynolds and Nancy J. Herman-Kinney (eds.), *Handbook of Symbolic Interactionism,* AltaMira, Walnut Creek, CA, 2003, p. 93.

4   Jane Wagner, *The Search for Signs of Intelligent Life in the Universe,* Harper Perennial, New York, 1990, pp. 15, 18.

5   Musolf, pp. 97–98.

6   For a fascinating account of a gorilla that developed these symbolic associations with the word *kitten,* see Francine Patterson, *Koko's Kitten,* Scholastic, New York, 1985. Mead wouldn't have been troubled by the existence of an animal that can communicate hundreds of symbols in American Sign Language. He regarded the symbol-using difference between humans and other primates as one of great magnitude—a quantitative rather than a qualitative distinction.

7   Peter M. Hall, "Structuring Symbolic Interaction: Communication and Power" in *Communication Yearbook 4,* Dan Nimmo (ed.), Transaction, New Brunswick, NJ, 1980, p. 50.

8   Jodi O'Brien (ed.), *The Production of Reality,* 6th ed., Sage, Los Angeles, CA, 2017, p. 79.

9   Douglas Hofstadter, "Changes in Default Words and Images Engendered by Rising Consciousness," in *The Production of Reality,* 3rd ed., Jodi O'Brien and Peter Kollock (eds.), Pine Forge, Thousand Oaks, CA, 2001, p. 158.

10 Mead, p. 43.

11 Peter Kollock and Jodi O'Brien (eds.), *The Production of Reality,* 2nd ed., Pine Forge, Thousand Oaks, CA, 1994, p. 63.

12 Kingsley Davis, "Final Note on a Case of Extreme Isolation," in *The Production of Reality,* 6th ed., pp. 89–94.

13 Oliver Sacks, *Seeing Voices: A Journey Into the World of the Deaf,* Vintage, New York, 2000.

14 Harper Lee, *To Kill a Mockingbird,* Warner, New York, 1982, p. 282.

15 Ralph Waldo Emerson, "Astraea," *The Works of Ralph Waldo Emerson,* Vol. III, Nottingham Society, Philadelphia, PA, n.d., p. 121.

16 David Lundgren, "Social Feedback and Self-Appraisals: Current Status of the Mead–Cooley Hypothesis," *Symbolic Interaction,* Vol. 27, 2004, p. 267.

17 Gregory Shepherd, "Transcendence," in *Communication as . . . Perspectives on Theory,* Gregory Shepherd, Jeffrey St. John, and Ted Striphas (eds.), Sage, Thousand Oaks, CA, 2006, p. 24.

18 Andrew Weigert and Viktor Gecas, "Self," in *Handbook of Symbolic Interactionism,* p. 267.

19 George Herbert Mead, "The Social Self," *Journal of Philosophy, Psychology and Scientific Methods,* Vol. 10, 1913, p. 375.

20 Mead, *Mind, Self, and Society,* p. 174.

21 Thomas Scheff, "A Theory of Genius," in *The Production of Reality,* 5th ed., Jodi O'Brien (ed.), Pine Forge, Thousand Oaks, CA, 2011, p. 137.

22 Shanyang Zhao, "The Digital Self: Through the Looking Glass of Telepresent Others," *Symbolic Interaction,* Vol. 28, 2005, pp. 387–405.

23 Kollock and O'Brien, 2nd ed., p. 63.

24 Michael Katovich and David Mains, "Society," in *Handbook of Symbolic Interactionism,* p. 292.

25 William Shakespeare, *As You Like It,* Act II, Scene VII, line 139, in *The Riverside Shakespeare,* G. Blakemore Evans (ed.), Houghton Mifflin, Boston, MA, 1974, p. 381.

26 Erving Goffman, *The Presentation of Self in Everyday Life,* Doubleday Anchor, Garden City, NY, 1959.

27 Ibid., p. 56.

28 Joan P. Emerson, "Behavior in Private Places: Sustaining Definitions of Reality in Gynecological Examinations," in *The Production of Reality,* 5th ed., pp. 272–285.

29 Jean Mizer, "Cipher in the Snow," *Today's Education,* Vol. 53, November 1964, pp. 8–10.

30 George Bernard Shaw, "Pygmalion," *Selected Plays,* Dodd, Mead, New York, 1948, p. 270.

31 Saul Alinsky, *Reveille for Radicals,* Vintage, New York, 1969 (1946), pp. 77–78.

32 Ronald Arnett, "Emmanuel Levinas: Priority of the Other," in *Ethical Communication: Moral Stances in Human Dialogue I,* Clifford Christians and John Merrill (eds.), University of Missouri, Columbia, MO, 2009, p. 203.

33 Quoted in James H. Olthius, "Face-to Face: Ethical Asymmetry or the Symmetry of Mutuality," in *Knowing the Other-wise,* James H. Olthuis (ed.), Fordham, New York, 1997, p. 139.

34 Arnett, p. 205.

35 Ibid., p. 200.

36 Sheldon Stryker, "From Mead to a Structural Symbolic Interactionism and Beyond," *Annual Review of Sociology,* Vol. 34, 2008, p. 18.

37 Ibid., p. 16.

38 Lundgren, p. 267.

39 Randall Collins, "Toward a Neo-Meadian Sociology of Mind," *Symbolic Interaction,* Vol. 12, 1989, p. 1.

40 Lonnie Athens, "Human Subordination from a Radical Interactionist's Perspective, *Journal for the Theory of Social Behaviour,* Vol. 40, 2010, pp. 339–368.

Chapter 6: Coordinated Management of Meaning (CMM)

1   Kimberly Pearce, *Compassionate Communicating Because Moments Matter: Poetry, Prose, and Practices,* Lulu, 2012, p. 33.

2   Barnett Pearce's discussion with Wheaton College communication theory class at the National Communication Association convention, Chicago, IL, November 2007. See also W. Barnett Pearce, *Interpersonal Communication: Making Social Worlds,* HarperCollins, New York, 1994, pp. 75–76.

3   Personal correspondence with Barnett Pearce.

4   W. Barnett Pearce, "'Listening for the Wisdom in the Public's Whining' or 'Working to Construct Patterns of Public Communication,'" unpublished manuscript.

5   W. Barnett Pearce and Kimberly A. Pearce, "Transcendent Storytelling: Abilities for Systemic Practitioners and Their Clients," *Human Systems: The Journal of Systemic Consultation & Management,* Vol. 9, 1998, pp. 178–179.

6   W. Barnett Pearce, *Interpersonal Communication,* p. 75.

7   W. Barnett Pearce, "A Sailing Guide for Social Constructionists," in *Social Approaches to Human Communication,* Wendy Leeds-Hurwitz (ed.), Guilford, New York, 1995, pp. 88–113.

8   W. Barnett Pearce, *Making Social Worlds: A Communication Perspective,* Blackwell, Malden, MA, 2007, pp. 210–213.

9   Kimberly Pearce, *Compassionate Communicating,* p. 55.

10 Ibid., p. 56.

11 W. Barnett Pearce, "Glossary," *Human Systems: The Journal of Systemic Consultation & Management,* Vol. 15, 2004, p. 9.

12 W. Barnett Pearce, *Communication and the Human Condition,* Southern Illinois University, Carbondale, IL, 1989, p. 40.

13 W. Barnett Pearce, "A Theory of Rule-Structure and Types of Episodes and a Study of Perceived Enmeshment in Undesired Repetitive Patterns ('URPs')," in *Communication Yearbook 3,* Dan Nimmo (ed.), Transaction Books, New Brunswick, NJ, 1979, pp. 225–240.

14 W. Barnett Pearce, Stephen W. Littlejohn, and Alison Alexander, "The Quixotic Quest for Civility: Patterns of Interaction Between the New Christian Right and Secular Humanists," in *Secularization and Fundamentalism Reconsidered,* Jeffrey K. Hadden and Anson Shupe (eds.), Paragon, New York, 1989, pp. 152–177.

15 W. Barnett Pearce, *Communication and the Human Condition,* pp. 32–33.

16 Kimberly Pearce, *Compassionate Communicating,* p. 33.

17 W. Barnett Pearce, "At Home in the Universe with Miracles and Horizons: Reflections on Personal and Social Evolution," in *The Coordinated Management of Meaning: A Festschrift in Honor of*

W. Barnett Pearce, Stephen Littlejohn (ed.), Fairleigh Dickinson University, Madison, NJ, 2013, p. 26.

18 Kimberly Pearce, *Compassionate Communicating*, p. 40.

19 National Communication Association C-Briefs: "Popularity and Value of Communication Major," August 1, 2016; "Total Number of Communication Degree Holders in U.S.," March 1, 2014; "Degrees Conferred, by Discipline, 2009–2010," September 1, 2012; https://www.natcom.org/publication-type/reports-discipline, accessed September 25, 2017.

20 W. Barnett Pearce, "At Home in the Universe," p. 39.

21 Ibid., p. 43; Kimberly Pearce, *Compassionate Communicating*, p. 3.

22 Kimberly Pearce, p. 10.

23 Ibid., pp. 3, 46, 70–71.

24 W. Barnett Pearce, "The Theory and Practice of Transforming Communication," lecture presented to the Hugh Downs School of Human Communication, Arizona State University, Tempe, AZ, April 16, 2008.

25 Tina Fey, *Bossypants*, Little, Brown & Co., New York, 2011, p. 84.

26 W. Barnett Pearce, *Interpersonal Communication*, p. 366.

27 W. Barnett Pearce and Kimberly A. Pearce, "Combining Passions and Abilities: Toward Dialogic Virtuosity," *Southern Communication Journal*, Vol. 65, 2000, p. 172.

28 Kimberly Pearce, "On the Significance of 'The 7th Miracle' for Personal and Social Evolution," in Littlejohn, *Festschrift*, p. 26.

29 W. Barnett Pearce and Stephen W. Littlejohn, *Moral Conflict: When Social Worlds Collide*, Sage, Thousand Oaks, CA, 1997, p. 37.

30 Martin Buber, *I and Thou*, 2nd ed., R. G. Smith (trans.), Scribner's, New York, 1958, pp. 60, 69.

31 Martin Buber, *Between Man and Man*, Macmillan, New York, 1965, p. 204.

32 Ronald Arnett, *Communication and Community*, Southern Illinois University, Carbondale, IL, 1986, p. 37.

33 Robert T. Craig and Heidi L. Muller, "Concluding Remarks," in *Theorizing Communication: Readings Across Traditions*, Robert T. Craig and Heidi L. Muller (eds.), Sage, Thousand Oaks, CA, 2007, pp. 499–500.

34 http://publicdialogue.org; http://www.cmminstitute.net

35 W. Barnett Pearce, "At Home in the Universe," p. 36.

36 J. Kevin Barge and W. Barnett Pearce, "A Reconnaissance of CMM Research," *Human Systems*, Vol. 15, 2004, pp. 13–32.

37 J. Kevin Barge, "Articulating CMM as a Practical Theory," *Human Systems*, Vol. 15, 2004, pp. 193–204.

38 Gabrielle Parker, "CMM: Reports from Users," June 27, 2001, p. 43, http://www.pearceassociates.com/essays/reports_from_users.pdf, accessed March 7, 2013.

39 Kimberly Pearce, *Compassionate Communicating*, pp. 30–45.

Chapter 7: Expectancy Violations Theory

1 Judee K. Burgoon, "A Communication Model of Personal Space Violations: Explication and an Initial Test," *Human Communication Research*, Vol. 4, 1978, pp. 129–142.

2 Ibid., p. 130.

3 Edward T. Hall, *The Hidden Dimension*, Doubleday, Garden City, NY, 1966, p. 1.

4 Judee K. Burgoon and Jerold Hale, "Nonverbal Expectancy Violations: Model Elaboration and Application to Immediacy Behaviors," *Communication Monographs*, Vol. 55, 1988, p. 58.

5 Burgoon, "A Communication Model," p. 141.

6 *Random House Webster's Electronic Dictionary and Thesaurus*, College Edition, WordPerfect, Orem, UT, 1994.

7 Judee K. Burgoon, "Cross-Cultural and Intercultural Applications of Expectancy Violations Theory," in *Intercultural Communication Theory*, Richard Wiseman (ed.), Sage, Thousand Oaks, CA, 1995, pp. 194–214.

8 Judee K. Burgoon and Joseph Walther, "Nonverbal Expectancies and the Evaluative Consequences of Violations," *Human Communication Research*, Vol. 17, 1990, p. 236.

9 Edward Hall, "A System of Notation of Proxemic Behavior," *American Anthropologist*, Vol. 41, 1963, pp. 1003–1026.

10 Cited in Judee K. Burgoon, Valerie Manusov, Paul Mineo, and Jerold Hale, "Effects of Gaze on Hiring, Credibility, Attraction, and Relational Message Interpretation," *Journal of Nonverbal Behavior*, Vol. 9, 1985, p. 133.

11 Douglas Kelley and Judee K. Burgoon, "Understanding Marital Satisfaction and Couple Type as Functions of Relational Expectations," *Human Communication Research*, Vol. 18, 1991, pp. 40–69.

12 Beth A. LePoire and Judee K. Burgoon, "Two Contrasting Explanations of Involvement Violations: Expectancy Violations Theory Versus Discrepancy Arousal Theory," *Human Communication Research*, Vol. 20, 1994, pp. 560–591.

13 Graham Chapman, John Cleese, Terry Gilliam, Eric Idle, Terry Jones, and Michael Palin, *The Complete Monty Python's Flying Circus: All the Words*, Volume One, Pantheon, New York, 1989, p. 40.

14 Judee K. Burgoon, "Nonverbal Violations of Expectations," in *Nonverbal Interaction*, John Wiemann and Randall P. Harrison (eds.), Sage, Beverly Hills, CA, 1983, p. 101.

15 Personal correspondence from Judee Burgoon, January 27, 2017.

16 Burgoon, "Cross-Cultural and Intercultural Applications," p. 209.

17 Judee K. Burgoon, Lesa Stern, and Leesa Dillman, *Interpersonal Adaptation: Dyadic Interaction Patterns*, Cambridge University, Cambridge, UK, 1995.

18 For a chapter-length treatment of Abraham Maslow's hierarchy of needs, go to *www.afirstlook.com* and click on Theory List.

19 Peter A. Andersen, Laura K. Guerrero, David B. Buller, and Peter F. Jorgensen, "An Empirical Comparison of Three Theories of Nonverbal Immediacy Exchange," *Human Communication Research*, Vol. 24, 1998, pp. 501–535.

20 Aimee Miller-Ott and Lynne Kelly, "The Presence of Cell Phones in Romantic Partner Face-to-Face Interactions: An Expectancy Violation Theory Approach," *Southern Communication Journal*, Vol. 80, 2015, pp. 253–270.

Relationship Development

1 Harold H. Kelley, Ellen Berscheid, Andrew Christensen, John Harvey, Ted Huston, George Levinger, Evie McClintock, Letitia Anne Peplau, and Donald Peterson, *Close Relationships*, W. H. Freeman, New York, 1983, p. 38.

2 Keith Davis and Michael Todd, "Friendship and Love Relationships" in *Advances in Descriptive Psychology*, Vol. 2, Keith Davis (ed.), JAI, Greenwich, CT, 1982, pp. 79–122.

3 Carl Rogers, "The Necessary and Sufficient Conditions of Therapeutic Personality Change," *Journal of Consulting Psychology*, Vol. 21, 1957, pp. 95–103.

4 Carl Rogers, "This Is Me," in *On Becoming a Person*, Houghton Mifflin, Boston, MA, 1961, p. 16.

5 Carl Rogers, "The Characteristics of a Helping Relationship," in *On Becoming a Person*, p. 52.

6 See Ron Adler and Russell Proctor II, *Looking Out/Looking In*, 13th ed., Wadsworth, Belmont, CA, 2011; and John Stewart, *Bridges Not Walls*, 11th ed., McGraw-Hill, New York, 2011.

7 Gary S. Becker, *The Economic Approach to Human Behavior*, University of Chicago, Chicago, IL, 1976.

8 http://www.eharmony.com/why, accessed March 12, 2013.

Chapter 8: Social Penetration Theory

1 Dalmas Taylor and Irwin Altman, "Communication in Interpersonal Relationships: Social Penetration Processes," in

Interpersonal Processes: New Directions in Communication Research, Michael Roloff and Gerald Miller (eds.), Sage, Newbury Park, CA, 1987, p. 259.

2   C. Arthur VanLear, "The Formation of Social Relationships: A Longitudinal Study of Social Penetration," *Human Communication Research,* Vol. 13, 1987, pp. 299–322.

3   Denise R. Beike, Nicole R. Brandon, and Holly E. Cole, "Is Sharing Specific Autobiographical Memories a Distinct Form of Self-Disclosure?" *Journal of Experimental Psychology,* Vol. 145, No. 4, 2016, pp. 434–450.

4   Harold H. Kelley and John W. Thibaut, *Interpersonal Relationships,* John Wiley & Sons, New York, 1978.

5   John Stuart Mill, *A System of Logic,* J. W. Parker, London, 1843, Book VI, Chapter XII.

6   J. M. Rist, *Epicurus: An Introduction,* Cambridge University, Cambridge, England, 1972, p. 124.

7   Epicurus, "Leading Doctrines, 8," cited in R. D. Hicks, *Stoic and Epicurean,* Charles Scribner's Sons, New York, 1910, p. 183.

8   Ayn Rand, *The Fountainhead,* Signet, New York, 1971, p. x.

9   Irwin Altman, Anne Vinsel, and Barbara Brown, "Dialectical Conceptions in Social Psychology: An Application to Social Penetration and Privacy Regulation," in *Advances in Experimental Social Psychology,* Vol. 14, Leonard Berkowitz (ed.), Academic Press, New York, 1981, p. 139.

10 Irwin Altman, "Toward a Transactional Perspective: A Personal Journey," in *Environment and Behavior Studies: Emergence of Intellectual Traditions,* Irwin Altman and Kathleen Christensen (eds.), Plenum, New York, 1990, pp. 225–255.

11 Anne Vinsel, Barbara B. Brown, Irwin Altman, and Carolyn Foss, "Privacy Regulation, Territorial Displays, and Effectiveness of Individual Functioning," *Journal of Personality and Social Psychology,* Vol. 39, 1980, pp. 1104–1115.

12 Ibid., p. 1114.

13 Julia T. Wood, "Ethics, Justice, and the 'Private Sphere,'" *Women's Studies in Communication,* Vol. 21, 1998, p. 145.

14 Paul H. Wright, "Self-Referent Motivation and the Intrinsic Quality of Friendship," *Journal of Social and Personal Relationships,* Vol. 1, 1984, pp. 115–130.

15 Richard Conville, *Relational Transitions: The Evolution of Personal Relationships,* Praeger, New York, 1991, pp. 19–40.

16 From John 15:13, *The New American Bible,* J. P. Kennedy & Sons, New York, 1970.

Chapter 9: Uncertainty Reduction Theory

1   Charles R. Berger, "Uncertainty and Information Exchange in Developing Relationships," in *Handbook of Personal Relationships,* Steve Duck (ed.), Wiley, New York, 1988, p. 244.

2   Charles R. Berger and Richard Calabrese, "Some Explorations in Initial Interaction and Beyond: Toward a Developmental Theory of Interpersonal Communication," *Human Communication Research,* Vol. 1, 1975, p. 100.

3   Charles R. Berger, "Beyond Initial Interaction: Uncertainty, Understanding, and the Development of Interpersonal Relationships," in *Language and Social Psychology,* H. Giles and R. St. Clair (eds.), Basil Blackwell, Oxford, UK, 1979, pp. 122–144.

4   Charles R. Berger and William B. Gudykunst, "Uncertainty and Communication," in *Progress in Communication Sciences,* Vol. X, Brenda Dervin and Melvin Voigt (eds.), Ablex, Norwood, NJ, 1991, p. 23.

5   For an excellent introduction to attribution theory, see Kelly Shaver, *An Introduction to Attribution Processes,* Lawrence Erlbaum, Hillsdale, NJ, 1983. Heider's theory is also described in the first two editions of this text (1991, 1994); click on Theory List at *www.afirstlook.com.*

6   Berger and Calabrese, pp. 99–112. The text of the first seven axioms is taken mostly verbatim from Berger and Calabrese, with a few alterations for reader clarity. The text of the eighth axiom is from Berger and Gudykunst.

7   Joseph Cappella, "Mutual Influence in Expressive Behavior: Adult–Adult and Infant–Adult Dyadic Interaction," *Psychological Bulletin,* Vol. 89, 1981, pp. 101–132.

8   Berger and Gudykunst, p. 25.

9   Malcolm Parks and Mara Adelman, "Communication Networks and the Development of Romantic Relationships: An Extension of Uncertainty Reduction Theory," *Human Communication Research,* Vol. 10, 1983, pp. 55–79.

10 Ellen Berscheid and Elaine Walster, *Interpersonal Attraction,* 2ⁿᵈ ed., Addison-Wesley, Reading, MA, 1978, pp. 61–89.

11 Charles R. Berger, *Planning Strategic Interaction,* Lawrence Erlbaum, Mahwah, NJ, 1997, p. 17.

12 Charles R. Berger, "Goals, Plans, and Mutual Understanding in Relationships," in *Individuals in Relationships,* Steve Duck (ed.), Sage, Newbury Park, CA, 1993, p. 34.

13 Charles R. Berger, "Message Production Under Uncertainty," in *Developing Communication Theories,* Gerry Philipsen and Terrance Albrecht (eds.), State University of New York, Albany, NY, 1997, p. 39.

14 Charles R. Berger, "Producing Messages Under Uncertainty," in *Message Production: Advances in Communication Theory,* John O. Greene (ed.), Lawrence Erlbaum, Mahwah, NJ, 1997, p. 222.

15 Personal correspondence from Charles Berger to Em Griffin.

16 Artemio Ramirez Jr., Joseph B. Walther, Judee K. Burgoon, and Michael Sunnafrank, "Information-Seeking Strategies, Uncertainty, and Computer-Mediated Communication: Toward a Conceptual Model," *Human Communication Research,* Vol. 28, 2002, p. 220.

17 Berger, "Message Production Under Uncertainty," p. 39.

18 Charles R. Berger, "Inscrutable Goals, Uncertain Plans, and the Production of Communicative Action," in *Communication and Social Influence Processes,* Charles R. Berger and Michael Burgoon (eds.), Michigan State University, East Lansing, MI, 1995, p. 17.

19 Berger, *Planning Strategic Interaction,* pp. 132–135.

20 Proverbs 15:22, *The Holy Bible: New Revised Standard Version,* Thomas Nelson, Nashville, TN, 1989.

21 Leanne K. Knobloch and Denise H. Solomon, "Measuring the Sources and Content of Relational Uncertainty," *Communication Studies,* Vol. 50, 1999, pp. 261–278.

22 Denise H. Solomon and Leanne K. Knobloch, "A Model of Relational Turbulence: The Role of Intimacy, Relational Uncertainty, and Interference from Partners in Appraisals of Irritations," *Journal of Social and Personal Relationships,* Vol. 21, 2004, pp. 795–816.

23 Leanne K. Knobloch and Jennifer A. Theiss, "An Actor-Partner Interdependence Model of Relational Turbulence: Cognitions and Emotions," *Journal of Social and Personal Relationships,* Vol. 27, 2010, pp. 596–597.

24 Leanne K. Knobloch and Amy L. Delaney, "Themes of Relational Uncertainty and Interference from Partners in Depression," *Health Communication,* 2012, pp. 1–16.

25 Leanne K. Knobloch and Jennifer A. Theiss, "Experiences of U.S. Military Couples During the Post-Deployment Transition: Applying the Relational Turbulence Model," *Journal of Social and Personal Relationships,* Vol. 29, 2012, pp. 423–450.

26 Leanne K. Knobloch and Denise H. Solomon, "Information Seeking Beyond Initial Interaction: Negotiating Relational Uncertainty Within Close Relationships," *Human Communication Research,* Vol. 28, 2002, pp. 243–257.

27 Denise H. Solomon, Leanne K. Knobloch, Jennifer A. Theiss, and Rachel M. McLaren, "Relational Turbulence Theory: Explaining Variation in Subjective Experiences and Communication Within Romantic Relationships," *Human Communication Research,* Vol. 42, 2016, pp. 507–532.

28 Charles R. Berger, "Communicating Under Uncertainty," in *Interpersonal Processes: New Directions in Communication Research,* Michael Roloff and Gerald Miller (eds.), Sage, Newbury Park, CA, 1987, p. 40.

29 Kathy Kellermann and Rodney Reynolds, "When Ignorance Is Bliss: The Role of Motivation to Reduce Uncertainty in Uncertainty Reduction Theory," *Human Communication Research,* Vol. 17, 1990, p. 7.

30 Ibid., p. 71.

31 Michael Sunnafrank, "Predicted Outcome Value During Initial Interaction: A Reformulation of Uncertainty Reduction Theory," *Human Communication Research,* Vol. 13, 1986, pp. 3–33.

32 Walid A. Afifi and Judith L. Weiner, "Toward a Theory of Motivated Information Management," *Communication Theory,* Vol. 14, 2004, pp. 167–190.

33 Charles R. Berger, "Communication Theories and Other Curios," *Communication Monographs,* Vol. 58, 1991, p. 102.

34 Berger, "Communicating Under Uncertainty," p. 58.

Chapter 10: Social Information Processing Theory

1 *The Social Network,* Columbia Pictures, 2010.

2 Andrew Perrin, "Social Media Usage: 2005–2015," *Pew Research Center,* 2015, http://www.pewinternet.org/2015/10/08/social-networking-usage-2005-2015, accessed September 26, 2016.

3 Keith Hampton, Lauren S. Goulet, Cameron Marlow, and Lee Rainie, "Why Most Facebook Users Get More Than They Give," *Pew Internet & American Life Project,* 2012, http://pewinternet.org/Reports/2012/Facebook-users.aspx, accessed October 14, 2016.

4 Amanda Lenhart, "Mobile Access Shifts Social Media Use and Other Online Activities," *Pew Research Center,* 2015, http://www.pewinternet.org/2015/04/09/mobile-access-shifts-social-media-use-and-other-online-activities, accessed October 14, 2016.

5 See Richard Daft, Robert Lengel, and Linda K. Trevino, "Message Equivocality, Media Selection, and Manager Performance: Implications for Information Systems," *MIS Quarterly,* Vol. 11, 1987, pp. 355–365; also Lee Sproull and Sara Kiesler, "Reducing Social Context Cues: Electronic Mail in Organizational Communication," *Managerial Science,* Vol. 32, 1986, pp. 1492–1512.

6 Joseph B. Walther, "Interpersonal Effects in Computer-Mediated Interaction: A Relational Perspective," *Communication Research,* Vol. 19, 1992, pp. 52–90.

7 Albert Mehrabian, *Silent Messages,* Wadsworth, Belmont, CA, pp. 76–77.

8 Judee K. Burgoon, Laura K. Guerrero, and Valerie Manusov, "Nonverbal Signals," in *Handbook of Interpersonal Communication,* 4th ed., Mark L. Knapp and John A. Daly (eds.), Sage, Thousand Oaks, CA, 2011, pp. 239–280.

9 "U.S. Teen Mobile Report: Calling Yesterday, Texting Today, Using Apps Tomorrow," *Nielsenwire,* 2010, http://blog.nielsen.com/nielsenwire/online_mobile/u-s-teen-mobile-report-calling-yesterday-texting-today-using-apps-tomorrow, accessed October 14, 2016.

10 Judy B. Litoff and David C. Smith, "'Will He Get My Letter?' Popular Portrayals of Mail and Morale During World War II," *Journal of Popular Culture,* Vol. 23, 1990, pp. 21–43.

11 Joseph B. Walther, Tracy Loh, and Laura Granka, "The Interchange of Verbal and Nonverbal Cues in Computer-Mediated and Face-to-Face Affinity," *Journal of Language and Social Psychology,* Vol. 24, 2005, pp. 36–65.

12 For a brief synthesis of the impact of nonverbal cues, see Burgoon, Guerrero, and Manusov.

13 The fluid dynamics analogy was suggested by University of Washington communication professor Malcolm Parks at the National Communication Association meeting at Miami Beach, November 2003, on the occasion of Walther receiving the 2002 Woolbert Award.

14 Joseph B. Walther, "Relational Aspects of Computer-Mediated Communication: Experimental Observations Over Time," *Organization Science,* Vol. 6, 1995, pp. 186–202; and Joseph B. Walther, "Time Effects in Computer-Mediated Groups: Past, Present, and Future," in *Distributed Work,* Pamela J. Hinds and Sara Kiesler (eds.), MIT, Cambridge, MA, 2002, pp. 235–257.

15 Jon Swartz, "Time Spent on Facebook, Twitter, YouTube Grows," *USA Today* online, August 1, 2010, http://www.usatoday.com/tech/news/2010-08-02-networking02_ST_N.htm, accessed October 14, 2016.

16 Walther, "Time Effects," p. 248.

17 Andrew M. Ledbetter, "Chronemic Cues and Sex Differences in Relational E-mail: Perceiving Immediacy and Supportive Message Quality," *Social Science Computer Review,* Vol. 26, 2008, pp. 466–482.

18 Joseph B. Walther and Lisa C. Tidwell, "Computer-Mediated Communication: Interpersonal Interaction On-Line," in *Making Connections: Readings in Relational Communication,* 2nd ed., Kathleen M. Galvin and Pamela J. Cooper (eds.), Roxbury, Los Angeles, 2000, p. 326.

19 "New Global Poll Suggests Wide Enthusiasm for Online Dating," *BBC World Service Press,* February 13, 2010, http://www.bbc.co.uk/pressoffice/pressreleases/stories/2010/02_february/13/poll.shtml, accessed October 14, 2016.

20 Joseph Walther, "Symposium on Relationships and the Internet: Interview 1 with Joseph Walther," *Oxford Internet Institute,* December 10, 2011, http://webcast.oii.ox.ac.uk/?view=Webcast&ID=20111210_412, accessed October 14, 2016.

21 Jeff Hancock, "Symposium on Relationships and the Internet: Interview 3 with Jeff Hancock," *Oxford Internet Institute,* December 10, 2011, http://webcast.oii.ox.ac.uk/?view=Webcast&ID=20111210_414, accessed October 14, 2016. The original research report is by Catalina L. Toma, Jeffrey T. Hancock, and Nicole B. Ellison, "Separating Fact from Fiction: Deceptive Self-Presentation in Online Dating Profiles," *Personality and Social Psychology Bulletin,* Vol. 34, 2008, pp. 1023–1036.

22 Joseph B. Walther, "Computer-Mediated Communication: Impersonal, Interpersonal, and Hyperpersonal Interaction," *Communication Research,* Vol. 23, 1996, p. 26.

23 Joseph B. Walther, "Language and Communication Technology: An Introduction to the Special Issue," *Journal of Language and Social Psychology,* Vol. 23, 2004, p. 393.

24 Elaine Hoter, Miri Shonfeld, and Asmaa Ganayim, "Information and Communication Technology (ICT) in the Service of Multiculturalism," *The International Review of Research in Open and Distance Learning,* Vol. 10, 2009, p. 9, http://www.irrodl.org/index.php/irrodl/article/view/601/1207, accessed October 14, 2016.

25 Roger Austin, "ICT and Citizenship in Northern Ireland: A Critique of Experience Since the 1998 Good Friday Agreement," in *Young Citizens in the Digital Age: Political Engagement, Young People and New Media,* Brian D. Loader (ed.), Routledge, New York, 2007, pp. 143–157.

26 Joseph B. Walther, "Computer-Mediated Communication and Virtual Groups: Applications to Interethnic Conflict," *Journal of Applied Communication Research,* Vol. 37, 2009, pp. 225–238.

27 Joseph B. Walther, Brandon Van Der Heide, Sang-Yeon Kim, David Westerman, and Stephanie T. Tong, "The Role of Friends' Appearance and Behavior on Evaluations of Individuals on Facebook: Are We Known by the Company We Keep?" *Human Communication Research,* Vol. 34, 2008, p. 32.

28 David K. Westerman, Brandon Van Der Heide, Katherine A. Klein, and Joseph B. Walther, "How Do People Really Seek Information About Others? Information Seeking Across Internet and Traditional Communication Channels," *Journal of Computer-Mediated Communication,* Vol. 13, 2008, p. 763.

29 Walther, Van Der Heide, Kim, Westerman, and Tong, p. 32.

30 Ibid.

31 Joseph B. Walther, Brandon Van Der Heide, Lauren M. Hamel, and Hillary C. Shulman, "Self-Generated Versus Other-Generated Statements and Impressions in Computer-Mediated

Communication: A Test of Warranting Theory Using Facebook," *Communication Research,* Vol. 36, 2009, pp. 229–253.

32 Harmeet Sawhney, "Strategies for Increasing the Conceptual Yield of New Technologies Research," *Communication Monographs,* Vol. 74, 2007, pp. 395–401.

33 Sherry Turkle, "Connected, but Alone?" TED Talk, April 3, 2012, https://www.youtube.com/watch?v=t7Xr3AsBEK4, accessed September 18, 2017.

34 Ibid.

35 Sherry Turkle, *Reclaiming Conversation: The Power of Talk in a Digital Age,* Penguin, New York, 2015, p. 34.

36 Ibid., pp. 19–58.

37 Ibid., p. 150.

38 Ibid., pp. 198–199.

39 Sara H. Konrath, Edward H. O'Brien, and Courtney Hsing, "Changes in Dispositional Empathy in American College Students Over Time: A Meta-Analysis," *Personality and Social Psychology Review,* Vol. 15, 2011, pp. 180–198.

40 Turkle, p. 170.

41 Ibid., p. 124.

Relationship Maintenance

1 John Stewart, "Interpersonal Communication: Contact Between Persons," *Bridges Not Walls,* 5th ed., John Stewart (ed.), McGraw-Hill, New York, 1990, pp. 13–30.

2 Daniel Canary and Laura Stafford, "Maintaining Relationships through Strategic and Routine Interaction," in *Communication and Relational Maintenance,* Daniel Canary and Laura Stafford (eds.), Academic Press, San Diego, CA, 1994, pp. 3–22.

3 Laura Stafford and Daniel Canary, "Maintenance Strategies and Romantic Relationship Type, Gender and Relational Characteristics," *Journal of Social and Personal Relationships,* Vol. 8, 1991, p. 224.

4 Ibid., pp. 217–242.

5 Andrew M. Ledbetter, "Family Communication Patterns and Relational Maintenance Behavior: Direct and Mediated Associations with Friendship Closeness," *Human Communication Research,* Vol. 35, 2009, pp. 130–147; Scott A. Myers and Natica P. Glover, "Emerging Adults' Use of Relational Maintenance Behaviors with Their Parents," *Communication Research Reports,* Vol. 24, 2007, pp. 257–264.

6 Margaret S. Clark and Judson Mills, "Interpersonal Attraction in Exchange and Communal Relationships," *Journal of Personality and Social Psychology,* Vol. 37, 1979, pp. 12–24.

7 Andrew M. Ledbetter, Heather M. Stassen-Ferrara, and Megan M. Dowd, "Comparing Equity and Self-Expansion Theory Approaches to Relational Maintenance," *Personal Relationships,* Vol. 20, 2013, pp. 38–51.

Chapter 11: Relational Dialectics Theory

1 Leslie A. Baxter, "Relationships as Dialogues," *Personal Relationships,* Vol. 11, 2004, p. 14.

2 Leslie A. Baxter, *Voicing Relationships: A Dialogic Perspective,* Sage, Thousand Oaks, CA, 2011, p. 2.

3 Ibid.

4 Ibid.

5 Ibid., p. 32.

6 Mikhail M. Bakhtin, "The Problem of the Text in Linguistics, Philology, and the Human Sciences: An Experiment in Philosophical Analysis," in *Speech Genres & Other Late Essays,* Caryl Emerson and Michael Holquist (eds.), Vern W. McGee (trans.), University of Texas Press, Austin, TX, 1986, p. 126.

7 Mikhail M. Bakhtin, "The Problem of Speech Genres," in *Speech Genres & Other Late Essays,* Caryl Emerson and Michael Holquist (eds.), Vern W. McGee (trans.), University of Texas Press, Austin, TX, 1986, p. 93.

8 Leslie A. Baxter, "A Dialectical Perspective on Communication Strategies in Relationship Development," in *A Handbook of Personal Relationships,* Steve Duck (ed.), John Wiley & Sons, New York, 1988, p. 259.

9 Meredith M. Harrigan and Aimee E. Miller-Ott, "The Multivocality of Meaning Making: An Exploration of the Discourses College-Aged Daughters Voice in Talk about Their Mothers," *Journal of Family Communication,* Vol. 13, 2013, p. 123.

10 Carolyn Prentice, "Relational Dialectics Among In-Laws," *Journal of Family Communication,* Vol. 9, 2009, p. 76.

11 Ben Sisario, "Prince Died Without a Will, According to Court Documents Filed by His Sister," *The New York Times,* April 26, 2016, http://www.nytimes.com/2016/04/27/arts/music/prince-died-without-a-will-according-to-court-documents.html, accessed May 12, 2016.

12 Maureen P. Keeley and Mark A. Generous, "The Challenges of Final Conversations: Dialectical Tensions During End-of-Life Family Communication," *Southern Communication Journal,* Vol. 80, 2015, pp. 381–382.

13 Dawn O. Braithwaite and Leslie A. Baxter, "'I Do' Again: The Relational Dialectics of Renewing Wedding Vows," *Journal of Social and Personal Relationships,* Vol. 12, 1995, pp. 190–191.

14 Dawn O. Braithwaite and Leslie A. Baxter, "'You're My Parent But You're Not': Dialectical Tensions in Stepchildren's Perceptions About Communicating With the Nonresidential Parent," *Journal of Applied Communication Research,* Vol. 34, 2006, p. 39.

15 Elizabeth A. Suter, Karla Mason Bergen, Karen L. Daas, and Wesley T. Durham, "Lesbian Couples' Management of Public-Private Dialectical Contradictions," *Journal of Social and Personal Relationships,* Vol. 23, 2006, p. 359.

16 Leslie A. Baxter, *Voicing Relationships: A Dialogical Perspective,* Sage, Thousand Oaks, CA, 2011, p. 5.

17 Madeline Berg, "The World's Highest-Paid YouTube Stars 2015," *Forbes,* October 14, 2015, http://www.forbes.com/sites/maddieberg/2015/10/14/the-worlds-highest-paid-youtube-stars-2015/#6973e684542c, accessed May 12, 2016.

18 Leslie A. Baxter, Elizabeth A. Suter, Lindsey J. Thomas, and Leah M. Seurer, "The Dialogic Construction of 'Adoption' in Online Foster Adoption Narratives," *Journal of Family Communication,* Vol. 15, 2015, pp. 193–213.

19 Elizabeth A. Suter, Leslie A. Baxter, Leah M. Seurer, and Lindsey J. Thomas, "Discursive Constructions of the Meaning of 'Family' in Online Narratives of Foster Adoptive Parents," *Communication Monographs,* Vol. 81, 2014, pp. 59–78.

20 Ibid., p. 69.

21 Ibid., p. 71.

22 Ibid., p. 73.

23 Baxter, Suter, Thomas, and Seurer, p. 208.

24 Baxter, "Relationships as Dialogues," p. 12.

25 Ibid., p. 13.

26 Leslie A. Baxter and Dawn O. Braithwaite, "Performing Marriage: The Marriage Renewal Ritual as Cultural Performance," *Southern Communication Journal,* Vol. 67, 2002, pp. 94–109.

27 Baxter, "Relationships as Dialogues," p. 3.

29 Leslie A. Baxter and Lee West, "Couple Perceptions of Their Similarities and Differences: A Dialectical Perspective," *Journal of Social and Personal Relationships,* Vol. 20, 2003, pp. 491–514.

29 Baxter, "Relationships as Dialogues," p. 11.

30 Sissela Bok, *Lying: Moral Choice in Public and Private Life,* Vintage, New York, 1979, p. 48.

31 Ibid., p. 32.

32 Ibid., p. 263.

33 Baxter, "Voicing Relationships," p. 18.

34 Baxter, "Relationships as Dialogues," p. 17.

35 Barbara Montgomery, "Relationship Maintenance Versus Relationship Change: A Dialectical Dilemma," *Journal of Social and Personal Relationships,* Vol. 10, 1993, p. 221.

Chapter 12: Communication Privacy Management Theory

1   Sandra Petronio, "Brief Status Report on Communication Privacy Management Theory," *Journal of Family Communication,* Vol. 13, 2013, pp. 6-14.

2   The rules are paraphrased and abridged from Ashley Duggan and Sandra Petronio, "When Your Child Is in Crisis: Navigating Medical Needs with Issues of Privacy Management," in *Parent and Children Communicating With Society,* Thomas J. Socha (ed.), Routledge, New York, 2009, p. 122; and Sandra Petronio and Jennifer Reierson, "Regulating the Privacy of Confidentiality: Grasping the Complexities through Communication Privacy Management Theory," in *Uncertainty, Information Management, and Disclosure Decisions: Theories and Applications,* Tamara D. Afifi and Walid A. Afifi (eds.), Routledge, New York, 2009, pp. 366-367.

3   Sandra Petronio, *Boundaries of Privacy: Dialectics of Discourse,* State University of New York, Albany, NY, 2002, p. 6.

4   Mary Claire Morr Serewicz and Sandra Petronio, "Communication Privacy Management Theory," in *Explaining Communication: Contemporary Theories and Exemplars,* Bryan Whaley and Wendy Samter (eds.), Lawrence Erlbaum, Mahwah, NJ, 2007, p. 258.

5   Dawn O. Braithwaite, "'Just How Much Did That Wheelchair Cost?' Management of Privacy Boundaries by Persons with Disabilities," *Western Journal of Speech Communication,* Vol. 55, 1991, pp. 258, 266.

6   Serewicz and Petronio, p. 258.

7   Sandra Petronio, Heidi Reeder, Michael Hecht, and Teresa Mon't Ros-Mendoza, "Disclosure of Sexual Abuse by Children and Adolescents," *Journal of Applied Communication Research,* Vol. 24, 1996, pp. 181-199; and Sandra Petronio, Lisa Flores, and Michael Hecht, "Locating the Voice of Logic: Disclosure Discourse of Sexual Abuse," *Western Journal of Communication,* Vol. 61, 1997, pp. 101-113.

8   Maureen Kenny and Adriana McEachern, "Racial, Ethnic, and Cultural Factors of Childhood Sexual Abuse: A Selected Review of the Literature," *Clinical Psychology Review,* Vol. 20, 2000, pp. 905-922.

9   Kathryn Dindia and Mike Allen, "Sex Differences in Self-Disclosure: A Meta-Analysis," *Psychological Bulletin,* Vol. 112, 1992, pp. 106-128.

10 Petronio, Flores, et al., p. 101.

11 Petronio, Reeder, et al., p. 188.

12 Ibid., p. 191.

13 Petronio and Reierson, p. 368.

14 Paige Toller and Chad McBride, "Enacting Privacy Rules and Protecting Disclosure Recipients: Parents' Communication with Children Following the Death of a Family Member," *Journal of Family Communication,* Vol. 13, 2013, pp. 32-45.

15 Duggan and Petronio, p. 124.

16 Petronio and Reierson, pp. 373-374.

17 Ibid., p. 374.

18 Kathryn Greene, Valerian Derlega, Gust Yep, and Sandra Petronio, *Privacy and Disclosure of HIV in Interpersonal Relationships: A Sourcebook for Researchers and Practitioners,* Lawrence Erlbaum, Mahwah, NJ, 2003, pp. 36-83.

19 Mark Leary and Lisa Schreindorfer, "The Stigmatization of HIV and AIDS: Rubbing Salt in the Wound," in *HIV and Social Interaction,* Valerian Derlega and Anita Barbee (eds.), Sage, Thousand Oaks, CA, 1998, pp. 18-19.

20 Petronio and Reierson, pp. 366-367.

21 Petronio, *Boundaries of Privacy,* pp. 177-190.

22 Sandra Petronio, Jack Sargent, Laura Andea, Peggy Reganis, and David Cichocki, "Family and Friends as Healthcare Advocates: Dilemmas of Confidentiality and Privacy," *Journal of Social and Personal Relationships,* Vol. 21, 2004, pp. 33-52.

23 Ibid., p. 49.

24 Frederick Platt and Geoffrey Gordon, *Field Guide to the Difficult Patient Interview,* Lippincott Williams and Wilkins, Philadelphia, PA, 1999, p. 176.

25 Petronio, Sargent, et al., p. 43.

26 Sandra Petronio, "The Moral Imperative of Privacy Management," a handout at the "Negotiating Moralities in Personal Relationships" preconference, National Communication Association Annual Convention, November 2009, Chicago.

27 Sandra Petronio, "Road to Developing Communication Privacy Management Theory: Narrative in Process, Please Stand By," *Journal of Family Communication,* Vol. 4, 2004, p. 200.

28 Duggan and Petronio, p. 124.

29 Petronio, "Brief Status Report," p. 6.

30 Petronio, *Boundaries of Privacy,* pp. 178-182.

31 Petronio, "Road to Developing," p. 193.

32 Petronio, "Brief Status Report," p. 12.

Chapter 13: Media Multiplexity Theory

1   Mark S. Granovetter, "The Strength of Weak Ties," *American Journal of Sociology,* Vol. 78, 1973, p. 1361.

2   Rejection letter from *American Sociological Review,* https://scatter.files.wordpress.com/2014/10/granovetter-rejection.pdf, accessed May 31, 2016. Linked from blog post discussing the rejection: Oleg Komlik, "Mark Granovetter Didn't Win (Yet) the Nobel Prize. Here Is His Rejection Letter, From 1969," Oct. 13, 2014, https://economicsociology.org/2014/10/13/mark-granovetter-didnt-win-yet-%e2%80%aa%e2%80%8enobel-prize-here-is-his-rejection-letter-from-1969/, accessed May 31, 2016.

3   Elliott Green, "What Are the Most-Cited Publications in the Social Sciences (According to Google Scholar)?" *LSE Impact Blog,* May 12, 2016, http://blogs.lse.ac.uk/impactofsocialsciences/2016/05/12/what-are-the-most-cited-publications-in-the-social-sciences-according-to-google-scholar/, accessed May 31, 2016.

4   Caroline Haythornthwaite, "Online Personal Networks: Size, Composition, and Media Use Among Distance Learners," *New Media & Society,* Vol. 2, 2000, p. 195.

5   Caroline Haythornthwaite, "Social Networks and Internet Connectivity Effects," *Information, Communication & Society,* Vol. 8, 2005, p. 130.

6   Nancy K. Baym and Andrew M. Ledbetter, "Tunes that Bind? Predicting Friendship Strength in a Music-Based Social Network," *Information, Communication & Society,* Vol. 12, 2009, pp. 408-427.

7   Artemio Ramirez Jr., Erin M. Sumner, and John Spinda, "The Relational Reconnection Function of Social Network Sites," *New Media & Society,* Vol. 19, 2017, pp. 807-825.

8   John P. Caughlin and Liesel L. Sharabi, "A Communicative Interdependence Perspective of Close Relationships: The Connections Between Mediated and Unmediated Interactions Matter," *Journal of Communication,* Vol. 63, 2013, p. 880.

9   Samuel H. Taylor and Andrew M. Ledbetter, "Extending Media Multiplexity Theory to the Extended Family: Communication Satisfaction and Tie Strength as Moderators of Violations of Media Use Expectations," *New Media & Society,* Vol. 19, 2017, pp. 1369-1387.

10 Haythornthwaite, "Social Networks," p. 137.

11 Andrew M. Ledbetter, "Media Multiplexity Theory: Technology Use and Interpersonal Tie Strength" in *Engaging Theories in Interpersonal Communication: Multiple Perspectives,* 2nd ed., Dawn O. Braithwaite and Paul Schrodt (eds.), Sage, Thousand Oaks, CA, 2015, p. 367.

12 Andrew M. Ledbetter, Samuel H. Taylor, and Joseph P. Mazer, "Enjoyment Fosters Media Use Frequency and Determines Its Relational Outcomes: Toward a Synthesis of Uses and Gratifications Theory and Media Multiplexity Theory," *Computers in Human Behavior,* Vol. 54, 2016, pp. 149-157.

13 See Jennifer Schon, "'Dad Doesn't Text': Examining How Parents' Use of Information Communication Technologies Influences Satisfaction Among Emerging Adult Children," *Emerging Adulthood,* Vol. 2, 2014, pp. 304-312; also Erin K. Ruppel and

Tricia J. Burke, "Complementary Channel Use and the Role of Social Competence," *Journal of Computer-Mediated Communication,* Vol. 20, 2015, pp. 37–51.

14 Nama Budhathoki and Caroline Haythornthwaite, "Motivation for Open Collaboration: Crowd and Community Models and the Case of OpenStreetMap," *American Behavioral Scientist,* Vol. 57, 2012, pp. 548–575.

15 Ledbetter, p. 363.

16 Ledbetter, p. 366.

17 Ramirez, Sumner, and Spinda, pp. 821–822.

18 Paola Tubaro and Lise Mounier, "Sociability and Support in Online Eating Disorder Communities: Evidence from Personal Networks," *Network Science,* Vol. 2, 2014, p. 16.

19 Chih-Hui Lai, Bing She, and Xinyue Ye, "Unpacking the Network Processes and Outcomes of Online and Offline Humanitarian Collaboration," *Communication Research,* 2015. Published online before print.

Influence

1 Irving Janis and Leon Mann, "Effectiveness of Emotional Roleplaying in Modifying Smoking Habits and Attitudes," *Journal of Experiential Research in Personality,* Vol. 1, 1965, pp. 84–90.

2 An earlier version of this description appeared in Em Griffin, "Role Play," in *The Mind Changers,* Tyndale House, Carol Stream, IL, 1976, pp. 79–94.

3 Gerald R. Miller and Michael Burgoon, *New Techniques of Persuasion,* Harper and Row, New York, 1973, p. 57.

Chapter 14, Social Judgment Theory

1 Carolyn Sherif, Muzafer Sherif, and Roger Nebergall, *Attitude and Attitude Change: The Social Judgment-Involvement Approach,* W. B. Saunders, Philadelphia, PA, 1965, p. 222.

2 Daniel J. O'Keefe, "Social Judgment Theory," in *Persuasion: Theory and Research,* Sage, Los Angeles, CA, 2016, pp. 19–34.

3 Maggie Fox, "One in Three Americans Own Guns; Culture a Factor, Study Finds," *NBC News,* June 29, 2015, http://www.nbcnews.com/news/us-news/one-three-americans-own-guns-culture-factor-study-finds-n384031, accessed June 24, 2016.

4 *Lincoln,* DreamWorks, 2012.

5 Sherif, Sherif, and Nebergall, p. 225.

6 Ibid., p. 214.

7 Stephen Bochner and Chester Insko, "Communicator Discrepancy, Source Credibility and Opinion Change," *Journal of Personality and Social Psychology,* Vol. 4, 1966, pp. 614–621.

8 Sandi Smith, Charles Atkin, Dennis Martell, Rebecca Allen, and Larry Hembroff, "A Social Judgment Theory Approach to Conducting Formative Research in a Social Norms Campaign," *Communication Theory,* Vol. 16, 2006, pp.141–152.

9 Immanuel Kant, "On a Supposed Right to Lie from Altruistic Motives," in *Critique of Practical Reason and Other Writings in Moral Philosophy,* Lewis White Beck (trans. and ed.), University of Chicago, Chicago, IL, 1964, p. 346.

10 Immanuel Kant, *Groundwork of the Metaphysics of Morals,* H. J. Paton (trans.), Harper Torchbooks, New York, 1964, p. 88.

11 "Background Checks for Guns," *NRA Institute for Legislative Action,* August 8, 2016, https://www.nraila.org/issues/background-checks-nics, accessed April 7, 2017.

Chapter 15: Elaboration Likelihood Model

1 Richard E. Petty and John T. Cacioppo, *Communication and Persuasion: Central and Peripheral Routes to Attitude Change,* Springer-Verlag, New York, 1986, p. 7.

2 Richard E. Petty and John T. Cacioppo, *Attitudes and Persuasion: Classic and Contemporary Approaches,* Wm. C. Brown, Dubuque, IA, 1981, p. 256.

3 Robert B. Cialdini, *Influence: Science and Practice,* 5th ed., Allyn and Bacon, Boston, MA, 2008.

4 Richard E. Petty and Duane Wegener, "The Elaboration Likelihood Model: Current Status and Controversies," in *Dual-Process Theories in Social Psychology,* Shelly Chaiken and Yaacov Trope (eds.), Guilford, New York, 1999, pp. 44–48.

5 John T. Cacioppo et al., "Dispositional Differences in Cognitive Motivation: The Life and Times of Individuals Varying in Need for Cognition," *Psychological Bulletin,* Vol. 119, 1996, pp. 197–253.

6 "Teen Drinking and Driving," *Centers for Disease Control and Prevention,* October 2012, https://www.cdc.gov/vitalsigns/teen-drinkinganddriving, accessed June 5, 2017.

7 Richard E. Petty and John T. Cacioppo, "The Elaboration Likelihood Model of Persuasion," in *Advances in Experimental Social Psychology,* Vol. 19, Leonard Berkowitz (ed.), Academic Press, Orlando, FL, 1986, p. 129.

8 Louis Penner and Barbara Fritzsche, "Magic Johnson and Reactions to People with AIDS: A Natural Experiment," *Journal of Applied Social Psychology,* Vol. 23, 1993, pp. 1035–1050.

9 Ibid., p. 1048.

10 Quentin Fottrell, "Subway's Jared Fogle, and 10 Other Endorsement Deals Gone Bad," *MarketWatch,* August 19, 2015, http://www.marketwatch.com/story/10-endorsement-deals-gone-bad-2014-08-02, accessed March 18, 2017.

11 Petty and Wegener, pp. 51–52.

12 Younghan Lee and Jakeun Koo, "Can a Celebrity Serve as an Issue-Relevant Argument in the Elaboration Likelihood Model?" *Psychology & Marketing,* Vol. 33, 2016, pp. 195–208.

13 Duane Wegener and Richard E. Petty, "Understanding Effects of Mood Through the Elaboration Likelihood and Flexible Correction Models," in *Theories of Mood and Cognition: A User's Guidebook,* L. L. Martin and G. L. Clore (eds.), Lawrence Erlbaum, Mahwah, NJ, 2001, pp. 177–210.

14 Thomas R. Nilsen, *Ethics of Speech Communication,* Bobbs-Merrill, Indianapolis, IN, 1966, p. 38.

15 Ibid., p. 35.

16 John Milton, *Areopagitica,* John Hales (ed.), with introduction and notes, 3rd ed., revised, Clarendon, Oxford, UK, 1882.

17 John Stuart Mill, *On Liberty,* Gateway, Chicago, IL, 1955.

18 Søren Kierkegaard, *Philosophical Fragments,* Princeton University, Princeton, NJ, 1936, pp. 17–28.

19 Em Griffin, *The Mind Changers,* Tyndale, Carol Stream, IL, 1976, pp. 27–41; and Em Griffin, *Getting Together,* InterVarsity Press, Downers Grove, IL, 1982, pp. 159–167.

20 Paul Mongeau and James Stiff, "Specifying Causal Relationships in the Elaboration Likelihood Model," *Communication Theory,* Vol. 3, 1993, pp. 67–68.

21 In a personal communication with Richard Petty on March 13, 2013, he pointed out that "the ELM is about a myriad of persuasion variables indicating when and why they work." His position is that ELM was never intended to focus on defining strong and weak arguments, nor does it focus on defining high and low credibility or any other message variable.

Chapter 16: Cognitive Dissonance Theory

1 Aesop, "The Fox and the Grapes," in *Aesop, Five Centuries of Illustrated Fables,* Metropolitan Museum of Art, New York, 1964, p. 12.

2 Leon Festinger, *A Theory of Cognitive Dissonance,* Stanford University, Stanford, CA, 1957, p. 4.

3 "Smoke! Smoke! Smoke! (That Cigarette)," Merle Travis, performed by Tex Williams, Capitol Records, 1947.

4 Leon Festinger, "Social Communication and Cognition: A Very Preliminary and Highly Tentative Draft," in *Cognitive Dissonance: Progress on a Pivotal Theory in Social Psychology,* Eddie Harmon-Jones and Judson Mills (eds.), American Psychological Association, Washington, DC, 1999, p. 361.

5   Festinger, *A Theory of Cognitive Dissonance,* pp. 5–6.

6   Ibid., pp. 84–97.

7   Dave D'Alessio and Mike Allen, "Selective Exposure and Dissonance After Decisions," *Psychological Reports,* Vol. 91, 2002, pp. 527–532.

8   Michael A. Tynan, Jonathan R. Polansky, Kori Titus, Renata Atayeva, and Stanton A. Glantz, "Tobacco Use in Top-Grossing Movies – United States, 2010-2016," Centers for Disease Control and Prevention, July 7, 2017, https://www.cdc.gov/mmwr/volumes/66/wr/mm6626a1.htm, accessed September 6, 2017.

9   Dieter Frey, "Recent Research on Selective Exposure to Information," in *Advances in Experimental Social Psychology: Vol. 19,* Leonard Berkowitz (ed.), Academic Press, Orlando, FL, 1986, pp. 41–80.

10 Festinger, *A Theory of Cognitive Dissonance,* pp. 32–47.

11 Alan DeSantis and Susan E. Morgan, "Sometimes a Cigar [Magazine] Is More Than Just a Cigar [Magazine]: Pro-Smoking Arguments in *Cigar Aficionado,* 1992-2000," *Health Communication,* Vol. 15, 2003, p. 460.

12 Festinger, *A Theory of Cognitive Dissonance,* p. 95.

13 Leon Festinger and James Carlsmith, "Cognitive Consequences of Forced Compliance," *Journal of Abnormal and Social Psychology,* Vol. 58, 1959, pp. 203–210.

14 CPI Inflation Calculator, United States Bureau of Labor Statistics, http://data.bls.gov/cgi-bin/cpicalc.pl, accessed January 3, 2017.

15 "Barack Obama Quits Smoking After 30 Years," *The Telegraph,* February 9, 2011, http://www.telegraph.co.uk/news/worldnews/barackobama/8314049/Barack-Obama-quits-smoking-after-30-years.html, accessed January 5, 2017.

16 Amie Parnes, "Obama's Reason to Stop Smoking: His Daughters," *The Hill,* August 22, 2012, http://origin-nyi.thehill.com/video/administration/244859-obamas-reason-to-stop-smoking-his-daughters, accessed January 5, 2017.

17 Elliot Aronson, "The Theory of Cognitive Dissonance: A Current Perspective," in *Advances in Experimental Social Psychology,* Vol. 4, Leonard Berkowitz (ed.), Academic Press, New York, 1969, p. 27.

18 Ibid., pp. 26–27.

19 Joel Cooper, "Unwanted Consequences and the Self: In Search of the Motivation for Dissonance Reduction," in *Cognitive Dissonance,* Harmon-Jones and Mills (eds.), p. 153.

20 Ibid., p. 151.

21 Richard Heslin and Michael Amo, "Detailed Test of the Reinforcement-Dissonance Controversy in the Counterattitudinal Advocacy Situation," *Journal of Personality and Social Psychology,* Vol. 23, 1972, pp. 234–242.

22 Anne E. Kornblut, "But Will They Love Him Tomorrow?" *The New York Times,* Nation, March 19, 2006, sec. 4, p. 1.

23 Jeff Stone and Joel Cooper, "A Self-Standards Model of Cognitive Dissonance," *Journal of Experimental Social Psychology,* Vol. 37, 2001, p. 231.

24 R. B. Zajonc, "Leon Festinger (1919-1989)," *American Psychologist,* Vol. 45, 1990, p. 661.

25 Daryl Bem, "Self-Perception: An Alternative Interpretation of Cognitive Dissonance Phenomena," *Psychological Review,* Vol. 74, 1947, pp. 183–200.

26 Patricia G. Devine, John M. Tauer et al., "Moving Beyond Attitude Change in the Study of Dissonance-Related Processes," in *Cognitive Dissonance,* Harmon-Jones and Mills (eds.), pp. 297–323.

27 Jillian C. Sweeney, Douglas Hausknecht, and Geoffrey N. Soutar, "Cognitive Dissonance After Purchase: A Multidimensional Scale," *Psychology & Marketing,* Vol. 17, 2000, p. 381.

28 Roger A. Elkin and Michael R. Leippe, "Physiological Arousal, Dissonance, and Attitude Change: Evidence for a Dissonance-Arousal Link and a 'Don't Remind Me' Effect," *Journal of Personality and Social Psychology,* Vol. 51, 1986, pp. 55–65.

29 Vincent van Veen, Marie K. Krug, Jonathan W. Schooler, and Cameron S. Carter, "Neural Activity Predicts Attitude Change in Cognitive Dissonance," *Nature Neuroscience,* Vol. 12, 2009, pp. 1469–1474. See also Shinobu Kitayama, Hannah Faye Chua, Steven Tompson, and Shihui Han, "Neural Mechanisms of Dissonance: An fMRI Investigation of Choice Justification," *NeuroImage,* Vol. 69, 2013, pp. 206–212.

Group Communication

1   *Report of the Presidential Commission on the Space Shuttle* Challenger *Disaster* (5 vols.), Government Printing Office, Washington, DC, p. 1414.

2   Irving Janis, *Victims of Groupthink,* Houghton Mifflin, Boston, MA, 1972, p. 9.

3   Irving Janis, *Crucial Decisions: Leadership in Policymaking and Crisis Management,* Free Press, New York, 1989, p. 60.

4   Robert F. Bales, *Interaction Process Analysis,* Addison-Wesley, Reading, MA, 1950; Robert F. Bales, *Personality and Interpersonal Behavior,* Holt, Rinehart, & Winston, New York, 1970.

5   Won-Woo Park, "A Review of Research on Groupthink," *Journal of Behavioral Decision Making,* Vol. 3, 1990, pp. 229–245.

Chapter 17: Functional Perspective on Group Decision Making

1   Some scholars also question the efficacy of communication in group decision making. See Dean E. Hewes, "Small Group Communication May Not Influence Decision Making: An Amplification of Socio-Egocentric Theory," in *Communication and Group Decision Making,* 2nd ed., Randy Hirokawa and Marshall Scott Poole (eds.), Sage, Thousand Oaks, CA, 1996, pp. 179–212 .

2   Randy Hirokawa, "Avoiding Camels: Lessons Learned in the Facilitation of High-Quality Group Decision Making Through Effective Discussion," Van Zelst Lecture in Communication, Northwestern University School of Speech, Evanston, IL, May 24, 1993.

3   Dennis Gouran, "Group Decision Making: An Approach to Integrative Research," in *A Handbook for the Study of Human Communication,* Charles Tardy (ed.), Ablex, Norwood, NJ, 1988, pp. 247–267.

4   Proverbs 15:22, *The Holy Bible: Revised Standard Version,* Thomas Nelson, Nashville, TN, 1946.

5   Dennis Gouran, Randy Hirokawa, Kelly Julian, and Geoff Leatham, "The Evolution and Current Status of the Functional Perspective on Communication in Decision-Making and Problem-Solving Groups," in *Communication Yearbook 16,* Stanley Deetz (ed.), Sage, Newbury Park, CA, 1993, p. 591.

6   Randy Hirokawa and Dirk Scheerhorn, "Communication in Faulty Group Decision-Making," in *Communication and Group Decision Making,* Randy Hirokawa and Marshall Scott Poole (eds.), Sage, Beverly Hills, CA, 1986, p. 69.

7   Hirokawa bases the distinction between rational and political logics on the work of Peter Senge, *The Fifth Discipline,* Doubleday, New York, 1990, p. 60.

8   Dennis Gouran and Randy Hirokawa, "The Role of Communication in Decision-Making Groups: A Functional Perspective" in *Communications in Transition,* Mary Mander (ed.), Praeger, New York, 1983, p. 174.

9   Randy Hirokawa, "Understanding the Relationship Between Group Communication and Group Decision-Making Effectiveness from a Functional Perspective: Why 'It's Not All Bad' Isn't Quite 'Good Enough,'" Thomas M. Scheidel Lecture, University of Washington, Seattle, WA, April 24, 1998.

10 Randy Hirokawa and Poppy McLeod, "Communication, Decision Development, and Decision Quality in Small Groups: An Integration of Two Approaches," paper presented at the annual meeting of the Speech Communication Association, Miami, FL, November 18-21, 1993.

11 Randy Hirokawa, "Functional Approaches to the Study of Group Discussion," *Small Group Research,* Vol. 25, 1994, p. 546.

12 Marc Orlitzky and Randy Hirokawa, "To Err Is Human, To Correct for It Divine: A Meta-Analysis of the Functional Theory of Group Decision-Making Effectiveness," paper presented at the annual meeting of the National Communication Association, Chicago, IL, November 19-23, 1997.

13 See, for example, J. Richard Hackman, "Work Teams in Organizations: An Orienting Framework," in *Groups That Work (and Those That Don't),* J. Richard Hackman (ed.), Jossey-Bass, San Francisco, CA, 1990, pp. 1-14.

14 Ivan Steiner, *Group Process and Productivity,* Academic Press, New York, 1972, p. 9.

15 Randy Hirokawa, "Avoiding Camels," p. 8.

16 Dennis Gouran and Randy Hirokawa, "Counteractive Functions of Communication in Effective Group Decision-Making," in *Communication and Group Decision Making,* p. 82.

17 Gouran, Hirokawa, Julian, and Leatham, pp. 574-579.

18 Robert Craig, "Treatments of Reflective Thought in John Dewey and Hans-Georg Gadamer," paper presented at the 1994 Convention of the International Communication Association, Sydney, Australia, July 11-15, 1994.

19 John Dewey, *How We Think,* Heath, New York, 1910.

20 My analysis of Habermas' discourse ethics has been greatly informed by Theodore Glasser and James Ettema, "Ethics and Eloquence in Journalism: A Study of the Demands of Press Accountability," presented to the Media Ethics Division of the Association for Education in Journalism and Mass Communication, Miami Beach, FL, August 2002.

21 Sonja Foss, Karen Foss, and Robert Trapp, *Contemporary Perspectives on Rhetoric,* Waveland Press, Prospect Heights, IL, 1991, pp. 241-272. (Like all interpreters of Habermas, Foss, Foss, and Trapp refer to his dense writing style. For that reason, all citations in this ethical reflection are from secondary sources. For an overview of Habermas' thinking, see Jane Braaten, *Habermas's Critical Theory of Society,* State University of New York, Albany, NY, 1991. For a primary source, see Jürgen Habermas, "Discourse Ethics: Notes on a Program of Philosophical Justification," Shierry Weber Nicholsen and Christian Lenhardt (trans.), in *Communicative Ethics Controversy,* Seyla Benhabib and Fred Dallmayr (eds.), MIT Press, Cambridge, MA, 1990, pp. 60-110.)

22 Theodore Glasser, "Communicative Ethics and the Aim of Accountability in Journalism," *Social Responsibility: Business, Journalism, Law, Medicine,* Vol. 21, Louis Hodges (ed.), Washington and Lee University, Lexington, VA, 1995, pp. 41-42.

23 Ibid., p. 49.

24 John Cragan and David Wright, "Small Group Communication Research of the 1980s: A Synthesis and Critique," *Communication Studies,* Vol. 41, 1990, pp. 212-236.

25 Cynthia Stohl and Michael Holmes, "A Functional Perspective for Bona Fide Groups," in *Communication Yearbook 16,* Stanley Deetz (ed.), Sage, Newbury Park, CA, 1993, p. 601.

26 Ibid., p. 602.

27 Linda Putnam and Cynthia Stohl, "Bona Fide Groups: A Reconception of Groups in Context," *Communication Studies,* Vol. 41, 1990, pp. 248-265.

28 Dennis Gouran, "Reflections on the Type of Question as a Determinant of the Form of Interaction in Decision-Making and Problem-Solving Discussions," *Communication Quarterly,* Vol. 53, 2003, pp. 111-125.

Chapter 18: Symbolic Convergence Theory

1 Robert Bales, *Personality and Interpersonal Behavior,* Holt, Rinehart, and Winston, 1970.

2 Ernest G. Bormann, John Cragan, and Donald Shields, "Three Decades of Developing, Grounding, and Using Symbolic Convergence Theory (SCT)," *Communication Yearbook 25,* William Gudykunst (ed.), Lawrence Erlbaum, Mahwah, NJ, 2001, pp. 274-276.

3 Ernest G. Bormann, *Small Group Communication: Theory and Practice,* 3rd ed., Harper & Row, New York, 1990, p. 122.

4 Ernest G. Bormann, John Cragan, and Donald Shields, "In Defense of Symbolic Convergence Theory: A Look at the Theory and Its Criticisms After Two Decades," *Communication Theory,* Vol. 4, 1994, p. 280.

5 James O. Olufowote, "Rousing and Redirecting a Sleeping Giant: Symbolic Convergence Theory and Complexities in the Communicative Constitution of Collective Action," *Management Communication Quarterly,* Vol. 19, 2006, p. 455.

6 Ernest G. Bormann and Nancy C. Bormann, *Effective Small Group Communication,* 5th ed., Burgess International, Edina, MN, 1992, p. 124.

7 Ernest G. Bormann, "Fantasy and Rhetorical Vision: The Rhetorical Criticism of Social Reality," *Quarterly Journal of Speech,* Vol. 58, 1972, p. 397.

8 Alan D. DeSantis, "Smoke Screen: An Ethnographic Study of a Cigar Shop's Collective Rationalization," *Health Communication,* Vol. 14, 2002, p. 185.

9 Ernest G. Bormann, "Symbolic Convergence Theory and Communication in Group Decision Making," *Communication and Group Decision Making,* Randy Hirokawa and Marshall Scott Poole (eds.), Sage, Newbury Park, CA, 1986, p. 221.

10 DeSantis, "Smoke Screen," p. 193.

11 Bormann and Bormann, p. 124.

12 Alan D. DeSantis, "A Couple of White Guys Sitting Around Talking: The Collective Rationalization of Cigar Smokers," *Journal of Contemporary Ethnography,* Vol. 32, 2003, p. 462.

13 Olufowote, p. 456.

14 Bormann, "Symbolic Convergence Theory and Communication in Group Decision Making," p. 222.

15 Bormann and Bormann, p. 119.

16 Bormann, Cragan, and Shields, "In Defense," p. 290.

17 John F. Cragan and Donald C. Shields, *Symbolic Theories in Applied Communication Research: Bormann, Burke, and Fisher,* Hampton Press, Cresskill, NJ, 1995, p. 39.

18 Sonja K. Foss, *Rhetorical Criticism: Exploration and Practice,* 4th ed., Waveland, Prospect Heights, IL, 2009, pp. 97-136.

19 Jessi McCabe, "Resisting Alienation: The Social Construction of Internet Communities Supporting Eating Disorders," *Communication Studies,* Vol. 60, 2009, p. 3.

20 Ibid., p. 8.

21 Sanitarium (website), accessed 2004.

22 The Ana Hotline (website), accessed 2004.

23 Blue Dragon Fly (website), accessed 2004.

24 Sanitarium, accessed 2004.

25 Jessi McCabe, p. 11.

26 Pro-Ana Suicide Society (website), accessed 2004.

27 Ibid.

28 Jessi McCabe, p. 13.

29 Bormann, *Small Group Communication,* p. 123; Bormann and Bormann, p. 122.

30 Cragan and Shields, *Symbolic Theories in Applied Communication Research,* pp. 46-47.

31 Ernest G. Bormann, *Communication Theory,* Sheffield, Salem, WI, 1989, p. 254.

32 John Cragan, "Obituary #10694," *Communication, Research and Theory Network,* January 6, 2009, http://www.natcom.org/CRTNET, accessed January 12, 2009.

33 Bormann, Cragan, and Shields, "In Defense," p. 267.

34 Olufowote, pp. 460-461.

35 Borman, Cragan, and Shields, "In Defense," p. 282.

36 Bormann and Bormann, p. 122.

Organizational Communication

1   Gareth Morgan, "Organizations as Machines," in *Images of Organization,* 2nd ed., Sage, Thousand Oaks, CA, 1997, pp. 11-31.

Chapter 19: Cultural Approach to Organizations

1   Clifford Geertz, "Thick Description: Toward an Interpretive Theory of Culture," in *The Interpretation of Cultures,* Basic Books, New York, 1973, p. 5.

2   Michael Pacanowsky and Nick O'Donnell-Trujillo, "Organizational Communication as Cultural Performance," *Communication Monographs,* Vol. 50, 1983, p. 129. (Pacanowsky's early work was co-authored with Nick O'Donnell-Trujillo from the communication department at Southern Methodist University. Because Pacanowsky was the lead author in these articles and Trujillo's scholarship took a critical turn, I refer only to Pacanowsky. For an example of critical ethnography, see Nick Trujillo, "Interpreting November 22: A Critical Ethnography of an Assassination Site," *Quarterly Journal of Speech,* Vol. 79, 1993, pp. 447-466.)

3   Michael Pacanowsky and Nick O'Donnell-Trujillo, "Communication and Organizational Cultures," *Western Journal of Speech Communication,* Vol. 46, 1982, p. 121.

4   Pacanowsky and O'Donnell-Trujillo, "Organizational Communication," p. 146.

5   Ibid., p. 131.

6   Pacanowsky and O'Donnell-Trujillo, "Communication and Organizational Cultures," p. 116.

7   Clifford Geertz, "Deep Play: Notes on the Balinese Cockfight," in *Myth, Symbol, and Culture,* Norton, New York, 1971, p. 29.

8   Geertz, "Thick Description," p. 5.

9   Gareth Morgan, *Images of Organization,* Sage, Newbury Park, CA, 1986, pp. 130-131.

10 Clifford Geertz, "A Life of Learning" (ACLS Occasional Paper No. 45), American Council of Learned Societies, New York, 1999, p. 14.

11 Pacanowsky and O'Donnell-Trujillo, "Communication and Organizational Cultures," p. 127.

12 Jeffrey C. Alexander, "Clifford Geertz and the Strong Program: The Human Sciences and Cultural Sociology," *Cultural Sociology,* Vol. 2, 2008, p. 166.

13 Joseph G. Ponterotto, "Brief Note on the Origins, Evolution, and Meaning of the Qualitative Research Concept 'Thick Description,'" *The Qualitative Report,* Vol. 11, 2006, pp. 538-549.

14 Michael Pacanowsky, "Communication in the Empowering Organization," in *Communication Yearbook 11,* James Anderson (ed.), Sage, Newbury Park, CA, 1988, pp. 357, 362-364. For an update on the culture of W. L. Gore & Associates two decades later, see Alan Deutschman, "The Fabric of Creativity," *Fast Company,* December 2004, pp. 54-62.

15 Ibid., p. 357.

16 Ibid., p. 358.

17 Michael Pacanowsky, "Slouching Towards Chicago," *Quarterly Journal of Speech,* Vol. 74, 1988, p. 454.

18 *Mad Men,* Lionsgate, AMC, 2007, Season 1, Disc 1.

19 Pacanowsky and O'Donnell-Trujillo, "Communication and Organizational Cultures," p. 123.

20 Geertz, "Deep Play," pp. 5, 26.

21 Pacanowsky and O'Donnell-Trujillo, "Organizational Communication," p. 137.

22 Chengxiu Suo, "Culture/Cornerstone Stories: A Window to Detect the Dynamics of Organizational Culture," paper presented at the International Communication Association Annual Meeting 2011, available from *Communication & Mass Media Complete,* Ipswich, MA, accessed February 27, 2017.

23 Attributed to Peter Drucker, https://www.quora.com/Did-Peter-Drucker-actually-say-culture-eats-strategy-for-breakfast-and-if-so-where-when, accessed April 16, 2017.

24 Linda Smircich, "Concepts of Culture and Organizational Analysis," *Administrative Science Quarterly,* Vol. 28, 1983, pp. 339-358.

25 William Gardner, Brian Reithel et al., "Attraction to Organizational Culture Profiles: Effects of Realistic Recruitment and Vertical and Horizontal Individualism-Collectivism," *Management Communication Quarterly,* Vol. 22, 2009, pp. 437-472.

26 Bryan Taylor and Nick Trujillo, "Qualitative Research Methods," in *The New Handbook of Organizational Communication,* Fredric Jablin and Linda L. Putnam (eds.), Sage, Thousand Oaks, CA, 2001, p. 169.

27 Geertz, *The Interpretation of Cultures,* p. 15.

28 Adam Kuper, *Culture: The Anthropologists' Account,* Harvard University, Cambridge, MA, 1999, pp. 112-113.

29 Estelle Jorgensen, "On Thick Description and Narrative Inquiry in Music Education," *Research Studies in Music Education,* Vol. 31, 2009, p. 71.

30 T. M. Luhrmann, "The Touch of the Real," *London Times Literary Supplement,* January 12, 2001, p. 3.

Chapter 20: Communicative Constitution of Organizations

1   Nick Wingfield, "Game Maker Without a Rule Book," *The New York Times,* September 9, 2012, p. BU1.

2   Wendy's Company, "2012 Annual Report," http://ir.wendys.com/phoenix.zhtml?c=67548&p=irol-reportsannual, accessed April 26, 2017.

3   *Valve Handbook for New Employees,* Valve Press, Bellevue, WA, 2012, p. 55.

4   Ibid., p. viii.

5   Ryan S. Bisel, "A Communicative Ontology of Organization? A Description, History, and Critique of CCO Theories for Organization Science," *Management Communication Quarterly,* Vol. 24, 2010, pp. 124-131.

6   Karl Weick, *Sensemaking in Organizations,* Sage, Thousand Oaks, CA, 1995, p. 12.

7   Ibid., p. 12. Weick attributes the story to Graham Wallas, *The Art of Thought,* Harcourt Brace, New York, 1926, p. 106, and repeatedly refers to it as the core idea of retrospective sensemaking.

8   Robert D. McPhee and Pamela Zaug, "The Communicative Constitution of Organizations: A Framework for Explanation," in *Building Theories of Organization: The Constitutive Role of Communication,* Linda L. Putnam and Anne Maydan Nicotera (eds.), Routledge, New York, 2009, p. 29.

9   The largest council for men's Greek organizations is the North American Interfraternity Conference. The National Panhellenic Conference is the counterpart for women's Greek organizations. Statistics were obtained from the websites of these organizations: http://nicindy.org/press/fraternity-statistics and https://www.npcwomen.org/resources/pdf/2015-1620Annual20Report.pdf, accessed April 26, 2017.

10 *Valve Handbook,* p. 6.

11 William Poundstone, "Answers to Google Interview Questions," *The Wall Street Journal online,* December 24, 2011, http://online.wsj.com/article/SB1000142405297020455230457711300370508944.html, accessed April 26, 2017. According to Poundstone, the answer is, "Start both hourglasses at 0 minutes. Flip over the four-minute glass when it runs out (at 4:00); ditto for the seven-minute glass (at 7:00). When the four-minute glass runs out the second time (at 8:00), the seven-minute glass will then have one minute of sand in its lower bulb. Flip the seven-minute glass over again and let the minute of sand run back. When the last grain falls, that will be nine minutes."

12 J. Kevin Barge and David W. Schlueter, "Memorable Messages and Newcomer Socialization," *Western Journal of Communication,* Vol. 68, 2004, pp. 233-256.

13 *Valve Handbook,* p. 16.

14 Ibid.

16   After a 10-year run, the final program aired on December 17, 2012.
17   Winslow, "Comforting the Comfortable," p. 271.
18   Ibid., p. 276.
19   Ibid., p. 280.
20   Ibid., p. 286.
21   Stuart Hall, "Notes on Deconstructing 'The Popular,'" https://www.scribd.com/doc/206586106/Notes-on-Deconstructing-the-Popular-Stuart-Hall, p. 453, accessed October 3, 2017.
22   Meek, "Begging for Change," 2004, https://nga.gov.au/Exhibition/SPACEINVADERS/Default.cfm?IRN=162193&MnuID=3&ViewID=2, accessed July 23, 2017.
23   Grossberg, "History, Politics and Postmodernism," p. 65.
24   James Anderson and Amie Kincaid, "Media Subservience and Satirical Subversiveness: *The Daily Show, The Colbert Report,* The Propaganda Model and the Paradox of Parody," *Critical Studies in Media Communication,* Vol. 30, 2013, pp. 171–188.
25   Ibid.
26   Lawrence R. Frey, "Communication Scholarship, Civic Engagement, and Social Justice Activism," *National Communication Association Spectra,* Vol. 53, No. 1, 2017, p. 12.
27   Lawrence R. Frey, W. Barnett Pearce et al., "Looking for Justice in All the Wrong Places: On a Communication Approach to Social Justice," *Communication Studies,* Vol. 47, 1996, p. 111.
28   Personal correspondence with Larry Frey, May 2017.
29   Mara B. Adelman and Lawrence R. Frey, *The Fragile Community: Living Together with AIDS,* Lawrence Erlbaum, Mahwah, NJ, 1997.
30   Stuart Hall, "On Postmodernism and Articulation: An Interview with Stuart Hall," Lawrence Grossberg (ed.), *Journal of Communication Inquiry,* Vol. 10, No. 2, 1986, p. 45.
31   Stuart Hall, Charles Critcher et al., *Policing the Crisis: Mugging, the State, and Law and Order,* Pelgrave, London, 1978.
32   The comparison was suggested in a book review by Merijn Oudenampsen, PhD candidate at the Dept. of Culture Studies at Tilburg University, the Netherlands, May 22, 2014, https://anthropoliteia.net/2014/05/22/revisiting-policing-the-crisis, accessed July 22, 2017.
33   Clifford Christians, "Normativity as Catalyst," in *Rethinking Communication Theory,* p. 148.
34   Claire Alexander, "Introduction: Stuart Hall and 'Race,'" *Cultural Studies,* Vol. 23, 2009, p. 457.

Media Effects

1   Paul Lazarsfeld, Bernard Berelson, and Hazel Gaudet, *The People's Choice, Duell,* Sloan and Pearce, New York, 1944.
2   A. W. van den Ban, "A Review of the Two-Step Flow of Communication Hypothesis," in *Speech Communication Behavior,* Larry L. Barker and Robert Kiebler (eds.), Prentice-Hall, Englewood Cliffs, NJ, 1971, pp. 193–205.
3   Dolf Zillmann, "Excitation Transfer in Communication-Mediated Aggressive Behavior," *Journal of Experimental Social Psychology,* Vol. 7, 1971, pp. 419–434.
4   Albert Bandura, *Social Learning Theory,* Prentice-Hall, Englewood Cliffs, NJ, 1977.
5   Igor Pantic, Aleksandar Damjanovic, Jovana Todorovic, Dubravka Topalovic, Dragana Bojovic-Jovic, Sinisa Ristic, and Senka Pantic, "Association Between Online Social Networking and Depression in High School Students: Behavioral Physiology Viewpoint," *Psychiatria Danubina,* Vol. 24, 2012, pp. 90–93.
6   Lauren Jelenchick, Jens Eickhoff, and Megan Moreno, "'Facebook Depression?' Social Networking Site Use and Depression in Older Adolescents," *Journal of Adolescent Health,* Vol. 52, 2013, pp. 128–130.
7   Maria Kalpidou, Dan Costin, and Jessica Morris, "The Relationship Between Facebook and the Well-Being of Undergraduate College Students," *Cyberpsychology, Behavior, and Social Networking,* Vol. 14, 2011, pp. 183–189.

Chapter 28: Uses and Gratifications

1   Katie Hunt and Naomi Ng, "Man Dies in Taiwan After 3-Day Online Gaming Binge," *CNN,* January 19, 2015, http://www.cnn.com/2015/01/19/world/taiwan-gamer-death, accessed October 4, 2017.
2   "S Korean Dies After Games Session," *BBC News,* August 10, 2005, http://news.bbc.co.uk/2/hi/technology/4137782.stm, accessed October 4, 2017.
3   Paul and Alex are hypothetical roommates invented for this chapter, but the stories of the men who died playing video games are well-documented, real-life cases.
4   Aliyah Shahid, "Xbox Addict, Chris Staniforth, Killed by Blood Clot After Marathon Gaming Session in England," *New York Daily News,* July 30, 2011, http://www.nydailynews.com/news/world/xbox-addict-chris-staniforth-killed-blood-clot-marathon-gaming-session-england-article-1.162095, accessed October 4, 2017.
5   Elihu Katz, "Mass Communication Research and the Study of Popular Culture: An Editorial Note on a Possible Future for this Journal," *Studies in Public Communication,* Vol. 2, 1959, pp. 1–6.
6   Bernard Berelson, "The State of Communication Research," *Public Opinion Quarterly,* Vol. 23, 1959, pp. 1–6.
7   Paul Lazarsfeld, Bernard Berelson, and Hazel Gaudet, *The People's Choice*, Columbia University Press, New York, 1948.
8   Werner J. Severin and James W. Tankard Jr., *Communication Theories: Origins, Methods, and Uses in the Mass Media,* Longman, New York, 2001, pp. 293–294.
9   The core ideas of the theory detailed here are presented in Alan M. Rubin, "Uses and Gratifications: An Evolving Perspective of Media Effects," in *The Sage Handbook of Media Processes and Effects,* Robin L. Nabi and Mary Beth Oliver (eds.), Sage, Los Angeles, CA, 2009, pp. 147–159.
10 Ziada Ayorech et al., "Personalized Media: A Genetically Informative Investigation of Individual Differences in Online Media Use," *PLOS ONE,* January 23, 2017, http://journals.plos.org/plosone/article?id=10.1371/journal.pone.0168895, accessed October 4, 2017.
11 Elihu Katz, Jay G. Blumler, and Michael Gurevitch, "Utilization of Mass Communication by the Individual," in *The Uses of Mass Communications: Current Perspectives on Gratifications Research,* Jay G. Blumler and Elihu Katz (eds.), Sage, Beverly Hills, CA, 1974, p. 21.
12 Zizi Papacharissi and Alan M. Rubin, "Predictors of Internet Use," *Journal of Broadcasting & Electronic Media,* Vol. 44, 2000, pp. 175–196.
13 Seth Finn, "Origins of Media Exposure: Linking Personality Traits to TV, Radio, Print, and Film Use," *Communication Research,* Vol. 24, 1997, pp. 507–529.
14 Glenn G. Sparks and Cheri W. Sparks, "Violence, Mayhem and Horror," in *Media Entertainment: The Psychology of Its Appeal,* Dolf Zillmann and Peter Vorderer (eds.), Lawrence Erlbaum, Mahwah, NJ, 2000, pp. 73–91.
15 Jay G. Blumler and Denis McQuail, *Television in Politics,* University of Chicago Press, IL, 1969.
16 Jack M. McLeod and Lee B. Becker, "Testing the Validity of Gratification Measures Through Political Effects Analysis," in *The Uses of Mass Communications,* pp. 137–164.
17 Alan M. Rubin, "An Examination of Television Viewing Motives," *Communication Research,* Vol. 8, 1981, pp. 141–165.
18 Bradley S. Greenberg, "Gratifications of Television Viewing and Their Correlates for British Children," in *The Uses of Mass Communications,* pp. 71–92.
19 Robert Kubey and Mihaly Csikszentmihalyi, "Television Addiction Is No Mere Metaphor," *Scientific American,* Vol. 286, 2002, pp. 74–80.

20 David Giles, *Illusions of Immortality: A Psychology of Fame and Celebrity,* Macmillan, London, 2000.

21 Alan M. Rubin, Elizabeth M. Perse, and Robert A. Powell, "Loneliness, Parasocial Interaction, and Local Television News Viewing," *Human Communication Research,* Vol. 12, 1985, pp. 155-180.

22 Alan M. Rubin, "Uses-and-Gratifications Perspective on Media Effects," in *Media Effects: Advances in Theory and Research,* 3rd ed., Jennings Bryant and Mary Beth Oliver (eds.), Lawrence Erlbaum, New York, 2009, pp. 165-184.

23 Johannes Knoll, Holger Schramm, Christiana Schallhorn, and Sabrina Wynistorf, "Good Guy vs. Bad Guy: The Influence of Parasocial Interactions with Media Characters on Brand Placement Effects," *International Journal of Advertising,* Vol. 34, 2015, pp. 720-743.

24 Maane Khatchatourian, "The Memory of Cory Monteith Lives On (and On) Via Social Media," *Variety,* July 31, 2013, http://variety.com/2013/digital/news/the-memory-of-cory-monteith-lives-on-and-on-on-social-media-1200569547, accessed October 4, 2017.

25 S. Shyam Sundar and Anthony M. Limperos, "Uses and Grats 2.0: New Gratifications for New Media," *Journal of Broadcasting & Electronic Media,* Vol. 57, 2013, pp. 504-505.

26 Jiyeon So, "Uses, Gratifications, and Beyond: Toward a Model of Motivated Media Exposure and Its Effects on Risk Perception," *Communication Theory,* Vol. 22, 2012, pp. 116-137.

27 Philip Elliott, "Uses and Gratifications Research: A Critique and a Sociological Alternative," in *The Uses of Mass Communications,* pp. 249-268.

28 Alan Rubin, "Ritualized and Instrumental Television Viewing," *Journal of Communication,* Vol. 34, 1984, pp. 67-77.

Chapter 29: Cultivation Theory

1 George Gerbner and Larry Gross, "Living with Television: The Violence Profile," *Journal of Communication,* Vol. 26, 1976, No. 2, p. 76.

2 Ibid., p. 77.

3 Jerome H. Skolnick, *The Politics of Protest,* Simon and Schuster, New York, 1969, pp. 3-24.

4 R. Lance Holbert, Dhavan V. Shah, and Nojin Kwak, "Fear, Authority, and Justice: Crime-Related TV Viewing and Endorsements of Capital Punishment and Gun Ownership," *Journalism & Mass Communication Quarterly,* Vol. 81, 2004, pp. 343-363.

5 Michael Morgan, James Shanahan, and Nancy Signorielli, "Growing Up with Television," in *Media Effects: Advances in Theory & Research,* 3rd ed., Jennings Bryant and Mary Beth Oliver (eds.), Routledge, New York, 2009, pp. 34-49.

6 Michael Morgan and James Shanahan, "The State of Cultivation," *Journal of Broadcasting & Electronic Media,* Vol. 54, 2010, pp. 337-355.

7 George Gerbner, Larry Gross, Michael Morgan, and Nancy Signorielli, "Charting the Mainstream: Television's Contributions to Political Orientations," *Journal of Communication,* Vol. 32, 1982, p. 103.

8 Morgan, Shanahan, and Signorielli, p. 35.

9 Ibid., p. 38.

10 Glenn Sparks and Robert Ogles, "The Difference Between Fear of Victimization and the Probability of Being Victimized: Implications for Cultivation," *Journal of Broadcasting & Electronic Media,* Vol. 34, 1990, pp. 351-358.

11 L. J. Shrum, "Media Consumption and Perceptions of Social Reality: Effects and Underlying Processes," in *Media Effects: Advances in Theory & Research,* pp. 50-73.

12 Gerbner, Gross, Morgan, and Signorielli, p. 117.

13 For a study that examines cultivation theory and the 2016 US presidential election, see Michael Morgan and James Shanahan, "Television and the Cultivation of Authoritarianism: A Return Visit From an Unexpected Friend," *Journal of Communication,* Vol. 67, 2017, pp. 424-444.

14 George Gerbner, Larry Gross, Michael Morgan, and Nancy Signorielli, "The 'Mainstreaming' of America: Violence Profile No. 11," *Journal of Communication,* Vol. 30, 1980, p. 15.

15 Gerbner, Gross, Morgan, and Signorielli, "Charting the Mainstream," p. 103.

16 Michael Morgan and James Shanahan, "Two Decades of Cultivation Research: An Appraisal and a Meta-Analysis," in *Communication Yearbook 20,* Brant R. Burleson (ed.), Sage, Thousand Oaks, CA, 1997, pp. 1-45.

17 For a recent critique, see W. James Potter, "A Critical Analysis of Cultivation Theory," *Journal of Communication,* Vol. 64, 2014, pp. 1015-1036.

18 Anthony Doob and Glenn Macdonald, "Television Viewing and Fear of Victimization: Is the Relationship Causal?" *Journal of Personality and Social Psychology,* Vol. 37, 1979, pp. 170-179.

19 Visit the archive of the Cultural Environment Movement at http://web.asc.upenn.edu/gerbner/archive.aspx?sectionID=20

20 Morgan and Shanahan, "Two Decades of Cultivation Research," p. 5.

Chapter 30: Agenda-Setting Theory

1 Jesse Holcomb and Amy Mitchell, "Industry Breakdown: Newspapers Still Largest Revenue Segment," Pew Research Center, March 26, 2014, http://www.journalism.org/2014/03/26/industry-breakdown-newspapers-still-largest-revenue-segment, accessed July 3, 2017.

2 The list is adapted from findings of Maxwell McCombs and Jian-Hua Zhu, "Capacity, Diversity, and Volatility of the Public Agenda: Trends from 1954 to 1994," *Public Opinion Quarterly,* Vol. 59, 1995, pp. 495-525.

3 Maxwell McCombs, *Setting the Agenda,* 2nd ed., Polity, Malden, MA, 2014, p. 81.

4 Maxwell McCombs, *Setting the Agenda* (2nd ed.), Polity, Malden, MA, 2014, p. 01.

5 Ibid., p. xi.

6 Maxwell McCombs and Donald Shaw, "A Progress Report on Agenda-Setting Research," paper presented to the Association for Education in Journalism and Mass Communication, Theory and Methodology Division, San Diego, CA, April 18-27, 1974, p. 28.

7 Theodore White, *The Making of the President, 1972,* Bantam, New York, 1973, p. 245.

8 Walter Lippmann, *Public Opinion,* Macmillan, New York, 1922, p. 3.

9 Maxwell McCombs and Donald Shaw, "The Agenda-Setting Function of the Mass Media," *Public Opinion Quarterly,* Vol. 36, 1972, pp. 176-187.

10 Shanto Iyengar, Mark Peters, and Donald Kinder, "Experimental Demonstrations of the 'Not-So-Minimal' Consequences of Television News Programs," *American Political Science Review,* Vol. 76, 1982, pp. 848-858. The experiment reported is only one of a series of studies conducted by Iyengar and Kinder at Yale and the University of Michigan.

11 Maxwell McCombs, "New Frontiers in Agenda Setting: Agendas of Attributes and Frames," *Mass Communication Review,* Vol. 24, 1997, pp. 32-52.

12 James Tankard et al., "Media Frames: Approaches to Conceptualization and Measurement," paper presented at the annual meeting of the Association for Education in Journalism and Mass Communication, Boston, August 1991.

13 Kristen Hays, "DIET: President Bush's Favorite Ice Cream Maker Aims to Maintain Measured Growth," *Tulsa World,* June 24, 2004, http://www.tulsaworld.com/news/diet-president-bush-s-favorite-ice-cream-maker-aims-to/article_e24b9108-b580-5d6f-b939-6f814f7c3549.html, accessed June 30, 2017.

14 "Multistate Outbreak of Listeriosis Linked to Blue Bell Creameries Products (Final Update)," Centers for Disease Control and Prevention, June 10, 2015, https://www.cdc.gov/listeria/outbreaks/ice-cream-03-15/index.html, accessed June 30, 2017.

15 Denise Marquez, "Lubbockite Remains Loyal to Blue Bell Despite Listeria Outbreak," *Lubbock Avalanche-Journal,* April 18, 2015, http://lubbockonline.com/local-news/2015-04-27/lubbockite-remains-loyal-blue-bell-despite-listeria-outbreak, accessed June 30, 2017.

16 Colten Meisner, "'I'd Eat It Now, Straight Up': An Intertextual Analysis of the Media Narrative of the 2015 Blue Bell Creameries Crisis," unpublished manuscript created from his undergraduate honors thesis, "When Product Loss Minimizes Product Harm: The Reframed Narrative of Blue Bell Creameries' 2015 Listeriosis Crisis," Texas Christian University, 2017.

17 Robert M. Entman, "Media Framing Biases and Political Power: Explaining Slant in News of Campaign 2008," *Journalism,* Vol. 11, 2010, pp. 389–408.

18 Sid Bedingfield and Dien Anshari, "Thinking About Romney: Frame Building in a Battleground State in the 2012 Presidential Election," *Journalism & Mass Communication Quarterly,* Vol. 91, 2014, pp. 78–97.

19 Kihan Kim and Maxwell McCombs, "News Story Descriptions and the Public's Opinions of Political Candidates," *Journalism and Mass Communication Quarterly,* Vol. 84, 2007, pp. 299–314.

20 Maxwell E. McCombs, Donald L. Shaw, and David H. Weaver, "New Directions in Agenda-Setting Theory and Research," *Mass Communication and Society,* Vol. 17, 2014, pp. 792–793.

21 McCombs, *Setting the Agenda,* pp. 105–106.

22 Craig Trumbo, "The Effect of Newspaper Coverage of Influenza on the Rate of Physician Visits for Influenza 2002–2008," *Mass Communication and Society,* Vol. 15, 2012, pp. 718–738.

23 McCombs, *Setting the Agenda,* pp. 105–106.

24 John Fortunato, *The Ultimate Assist: The Relationship and Broadcasting Strategies of the NBA and Television Networks,* Hampton, Cresskill, NJ, 2001.

25 Taylor Smith, "NBA Revenue Expected to Hit $8 Billion in 2016–2017," *Today's Fastbreak,* September 8, 2016, https://www.todaysfastbreak.com/nba-news/nba-revenue-expected-to-hit-8-billion-in-2016-2017, accessed July 3, 2017.

26 Maxwell McCombs, *Setting the Agenda,* Polity, Cambridge, UK, 2004, p. 140.

27 Chris J. Vargo and Lei Guo, "Networking, Big Data, and Intermedia Agenda Setting: An Analysis of Traditional, Partisan, and Emerging Online U.S. News," *Journalism & Mass Communication Quarterly,* Vol. 94, 2017, pp. 1031–1055.

28 Maxwell McCombs and Marcus Funk, "Shaping the Agenda of Local Daily Newspapers: A Methodology Merging the Agenda Setting and Community Structure Perspectives," *Mass Communication and Society,* Vol. 14, 2011, pp. 905–919.

29 Young Jun Son and David Weaver, "Another Look at What Moves Public Opinion: Media Agenda Setting and Polls in the 2000 U.S. Election," *International Journal of Public Opinion Research,* Vol. 18, 2006, pp. 174–197.

30 Hunt Allcott and Matthew Gentzkow, "Social Media and Fake News in the 2016 Election," *Journal of Economic Perspectives,* Vol. 31, 2017, p. 213.

31 Chris J. Vargo, Lei Guo, and Michelle A. Amazeen, "The Agenda-Setting Power of Fake News: A Big Data Analysis of the Online Media Landscape from 2014 to 2016," *New Media & Society,* 2017, pp. 3–4, published online before print.

32 Ibid., p. 4.

33 Maxwell McCombs and Tamara Bell, "The Agenda-Setting Role of Mass Communication," in *An Integrated Approach to Communication Theory and Research,* Michael Salwen and Donald Stacks (eds.), Lawrence Erlbaum, Hillsdale, NJ, 1996, p. 100.

34 McCombs, "Setting the Agenda," pp. 63–78.

35 McCombs, Shaw, and Weaver, pp. 793–794.

36 Ibid., p. 794.

37 Chris J. Vargo, Lei Guo, Maxwell McCombs, and Donald L. Shaw, "Network Issue Agendas on Twitter During the 2012 U.S. Presidential Election," *Journal of Communication,* Vol. 64, 2014, pp. 296–316.

38 McCombs, Shaw, and Weaver, p. 800.

39 Clifford Christians, John Ferré, and Mark Fackler, *Good News: Social Ethics and the Press,* Oxford University Press, New York, 1993.

40 Richard Rorty, *Philosophy and the Mirror of Nature,* Princeton University, Princeton, NJ, 1979, p. 373.

41 Christians, Ferré, and Fackler, p. 192.

42 Martin Buber, *I and Thou,* 2nd ed., R. G. Smith (trans.), Scribner's, New York, 1958, pp. 60, 69.

43 Christians, Ferré, and Fackler, pp. 69, 73.

44 Ibid., p. 89.

45 Ibid., pp. 78, 111–113.

46 Clifford Christians and Kaarle Nordenstreng, "Social Responsibility Worldwide," *Journal of Mass Media Ethics,* Vol. 19, 2004, pp. 3–28.

47 Christians, Ferré, and Fackler, p. 92.

48 Michael Barone, "The Surprising Roots of Liberal Nostalgia," *The Wall Street Journal,* June 22, 2011, p. A15.

49 McCombs, Shaw, and Weaver, pp. 788–792.

50 Eli Pariser, "Beware Online 'Filter Bubbles,'" TED Talk, March 2011, https://www.ted.com/talks/eli_pariser_beware_online_filter_bubbles, accessed July 3, 2017. For a book-length treatment of this idea, see Eli Pariser, *The Filter Bubble,* Penguin, New York, 2011.

51 Vargo and Guo, p. 20.

Gender and Communication

1 Judith Vonberg and Laura Smith-Spark, "German Lawmakers Vote to Legalize Same-Sex Marriage; Merkel Votes No," CNN, June 30, 2017, http://www.cnn.com/2017/06/30/europe/germany-gay-marriage-vote/index.html, accessed July 13, 2017.

2 American Psychological Association, "Definitions Related to Sexual Orientation and Gender Diversity in APA Documents," https://www.apa.org/pi/lgbt/resources/sexuality-definitions.pdf, accessed July 13, 2017.

3 Kathryn Dindia, "Men Are from North Dakota, Women Are from South Dakota," paper presented at the National Communication Association convention, November 19–23, 1997.

4 Sandra L. Bem, "Androgyny vs. the Tight Little Lives of Fluffy Women and Chesty Men," *Psychology Today,* Vol. 9, 1975, pp. 58–62.

Chapter 31: Genderlect Styles

1 Deborah Tannen, *You Just Don't Understand,* Ballantine, New York, 1990, p. 42.

2 Deborah Tannen, *Conversational Style: Analyzing Talk Among Friends,* Ablex, Norwood, NJ, 1984.

3 a quote from E. M. Forster's novel *A Passage to India,* appear in Deborah Tannen, *Conversational Style: Analyzing Talk Among Friends,* Ablex, Norwood, NJ, 1984. p. vii

4 Tannen, *You Just Don't Understand,* p. 259.

5 Ibid., p. 279.

6 Ibid., p. 16.

7 Adelaide Haas, "Male and Female Spoken Language Differences: Stereotypes and Evidence," *Psychological Bulletin,* Vol. 86, 1979, pp. 616–626.

8 Tannen, *You Just Don't Understand,* p. 108.

9 Julia Wood, *Gendered Lives,* Cengage, Boston, MA, 2009, pp. 126–128.

10 Daniel Maltz and Ruth Borker, "A Cultural Approach to Male-Female Miscommunication," in *Language and Social Identity,* John Gumperz (ed.), Cambridge University Press, UK, 1982, pp. 196–216.

11 Tannen, *You Just Don't Understand,* p. 48.

12 Nikhil Swaminathan, "Gender Jabber: Do Women Talk More than Men?" *Scientific American,* July 6, 2007, https://www.scientificamerican.com/article/women-talk-more-than-men, accessed July 28, 2017.

13 Tannen, *You Just Don't Understand,* p. 212.

14 Ibid., p. 62.

15 Ibid., p. 72.

16 Ibid., p. 150.

17 Susan Pease Gadoua, "To Connect, Women Want to Talk and Men Want Sex—How Do Straight Couples Reconcile?" *Psychology Today,* February 7, 2010, https://www.psychologytoday.com/blog/contemplating-divorce/201002/connect-women-want-talk-and-men-want-sex-how-do-straight-couples, accessed July 29, 2017.

18 William Labov, *Sociolinguistic Patterns,* University of Pennsylvania Press, Philadelphia, 1972.

19 Wood, p. 126.

20 Louise Cherry and Michael Lewis, "Mothers and Two-Year-Olds: A Study of Sex-Differentiated Aspects of Verbal Interaction," *Developmental Psychology,* Vol. 12, 1976, pp. 276–282.

21 Tannen, *You Just Don't Understand,* pp. 120–121, 298.

22 Carol Gilligan, *In a Different Voice: Psychological Theory and Women's Development,* Harvard University, Cambridge, MA, 1982.

23 Summary statement of Seyla Benhabib, "The Generalized and the Concrete Other: The Kohlberg-Gilligan Controversy and Feminist Theory," in *Feminism as Critique,* Seyla Benhabib and Drucilla Cornell (eds.), University of Minnesota, Minneapolis, 1987, p. 78.

24 Lawrence Kohlberg, *Essays on Moral Development, Volume 1: The Philosophy of Moral Development,* Harper & Row, San Francisco, CA, 1981, p. 12.

25 Gilligan, p. 18.

26 Carol Gilligan, "In a Different Voice: Women's Conceptions of Self and Morality," *Harvard Educational Review,* Vol. 47, 1977, p. 484.

27 Tannen, *Conversational Style,* p. 38.

28 J. W. Santrock, A. M. Minnett, and B. D. Campbell, *The Authoritative Guide to Self-Help Books,* Guilford, New York, 1994.

29 Adrianne W. Kunkel and Brant R. Burleson, "Social Support and the Emotional Lives of Men and Women: An Assessment of the Different Cultures Perspective," in *Sex Differences and Similarities in Communication,* Daniel Canary and Kathryn Dindia (eds.), Lawrence Erlbaum, Mahwah, NJ, 1998, p. 116.

30 Senta Troemel-Ploetz, "Review Essay: Selling the Apolitical," *Discourse & Society,* Vol. 2, 1991, p. 497.

31 Ibid., p. 491.

32 Ibid., p. 495.

Chapter 32: Standpoint Theory

1 Sandra Harding, "Comment on Hekman's 'Truth and Method: Feminist Standpoint Theory Revisited': Whose Standpoint Needs the Regimes of Truth and Reality?" *Signs: Journal of Women in Culture and Society,* Vol. 22, 1997, p. 384.

2 Julia T. Wood, *Communication Theories in Action,* 1st ed., Wadsworth, Belmont, CA, 1997, p. 250.

3 Sandra Harding, *Whose Science? Whose Knowledge? Thinking from Women's Lives,* Cornell University Press, Ithaca, NY, 1991, pp. 269–270.

4 Julia T. Wood, "Feminist Standpoint Theory and Muted Group Theory: Commonalities and Divergences," *Women and Language,* Vol. 28, 2005, p. 62.

5 Ibid.

6 Meenakshi Gigi Durham, "On the Relevance of Standpoint Epistemology to the Practice of Journalism: The Case for 'Strong Objectivity,'" *Communication Theory,* Vol. 8, 1998, p. 117.

7 Julia T. Wood, "Feminist Scholarship and the Study of Relationships," *Journal of Social and Personal Relationships,* Vol. 12, 1995, p. 110.

8 Georg Wilhelm Friedrich Hegel, *The Phenomenology of Mind,* Macmillan, New York, 1910, pp. 182–188.

9 Friedrich Engels, "Socialism: Utopian and Scientific," and "The Origin of the Family, Private Property, and the State," in *The Marx-Engels Reader,* Robert Tucker (ed.), W. W. Norton, New York, 1978, pp. 701–702, 734–736. See also Sandra Harding, "The Instability of the Analytical Categories of Feminist Theory," in *Sex and Scientific Inquiry,* Sandra Harding and Jean O'Barr (eds.), University of Chicago, IL, 1987, p. 292.

10 Harding, "Comment on Hekman's 'Truth and Method,'" p. 389.

11 Wood, "Feminist Scholarship," p. 111.

12 Jean-François Lyotard, *The Postmodern Condition: A Report on Knowledge,* Geoff Bennington and Brian Massumi (trans.), University of Minnesota Press, Minneapolis, 1984, p. xxiv.

13 Kathryn Stockett, *The Help,* Amy Einhorn Books/Putnam, New York, 2009.

14 Ibid., p. 4.

15 Ibid., flyleaf.

16 Ibid., p. 386.

17 Rachel A. Griffin, "Problematic Representations of Strategic Whiteness and 'Post-racial' Pedagogy: A Critical Intercultural Reading of *The Help,*" *Journal of International and Intercultural Communication,* Vol. 8, 2015, pp. 147–166.

18 Interview with Octavia Spencer and Viola Davis on *Tavis Smiley,* PBS, http://www.pbs.org/video/2194955259, accessed July 7, 2017.

19 Ibid.

20 Julia T. Wood, "Engendered Relations: Interaction, Caring, Power and Responsibility in Intimacy," in *Social Context and Relationships,* Steve Duck (ed.), Sage, Newbury Park, CA, 1993, p. 37.

21 Wood, "Feminist Scholarship," p. 112.

22 Stockett, p. 173.

23 Ibid., p. 304.

24 Julia T. Wood, *Communication Theories in Action,* 3rd ed., Wadsworth, Belmont, CA, p. 212. See also Harding, *Whose Science? Whose Knowledge?* p. 59.

25 Julia T. Wood, "Gender and Moral Voice: Moving from Woman's Nature to Standpoint Epistemology," *Women's Studies in Communication,* Vol. 15, 1993, p. 8.

26 Stockett, p. 418.

27 Harding, *Whose Science? Whose Knowledge?* p. 192.

28 Stockett, pp. 8–9.

29 Donna Haraway, "Situated Knowledges: The Science Question in Feminism and the Privilege of Partial Perspective," *Feminist Studies,* Vol. 14, 1988, p. 3; Sandra Harding, "Introduction: Standpoint Theory as a Site of Political, Philosophic, and Scientific Debate," in *The Feminist Standpoint Theory Reader,* Sandra Harding (ed.), Routledge, New York, 2004, p. 4.

30 Harding, *Whose Science? Whose Knowledge?* pp. 159, 58.

31 Ibid., p. 59.

32 Wood, *Communication Theories in Action,* 1st ed., p. 257.

33 Sonia Sotomayor, "Lecture: 'A Latina Judge's Voice,'" *The New York Times,* May 14, 2009, http://www.nytimes.com/2009/05/15/us/politics/15judge.text.html, accessed July 7, 2017.

34 Harding, *Whose Science? Whose Knowledge?* pp. 149–152.

35 Ibid., p. 270.

36 Wood, *Communication Theories in Action,* 1ˢᵗ ed., p. 254.

37 Ibid.

38 Harding, "Introduction," p. 9; Wood, "Feminist Standpoint Theory," pp. 61-64.

39 Stockett, p. 277.

40 Julia T. Wood, *Who Cares? Women, Care, and Culture,* Southern Illinois University Press, Carbondale, 1994, p. 4.

41 Ibid., p. 6.

42 Ibid., pp. 8-9.

43 Ibid., p. 163.

44 Patricia Hill Collins, "Learning from the Outsider Within: The Sociological Significance of Black Feminist Thought," in *The Feminist Standpoint Reader,* p. 103.

45 Pearl Cleage, *Deals with the Devil and Other Reasons to Riot,* Ballantine, New York, 1993, p. 55.

46 The wording of the four criteria of black feminist epistemology and the quotations that accompany them are from Patricia Hill Collins, *Black Feminist Thought: Knowledge, Consciousness, and the Politics of Empowerment,* 2ⁿᵈ ed., Routledge, New York, 2000, pp. 257-266.

47 Seyla Benhabib, *Situating the Self: Gender, Community and Postmodernism in Contemporary Ethics,* Routledge, New York, 1992, p. 4.

48 Ibid., p. 2.

49 Jean-François Lyotard, *The Postmodern Condition.*

50 Benhabib, *Situating the Self,* p. 209.

51 Ibid., p. 229.

52 Ibid., p. 14.

53 Benhabib's critique of Habermas draws on Nancy Fraser, "Rethinking the Public Sphere," in *Justice Interruptus,* Routledge, New York, 1997, pp. 69-98.

54 Benhabib, *Situating the Self,* p. 3.

55 Benhabib, "The Generalized and the Concrete Other: The Kohlberg-Gilligan Controversy, and Feminist Theory," in *Situating the Self,* pp. 148-177.

56 Kathy Davis, "Intersectionality as Buzzword: A Sociology of Science Perspective on What Makes a Feminist Theory Successful," *Feminist Theory,* Vol. 9, 2008, p. 68.

57 Conor Friedersdorf, "A Columbia Professor's Critique of Campus Politics," *The Atlantic,* June 30, 2017, https://www.theatlantic.com/politics/archive/2017/06/a-columbia-professors-critique-of-campus-politics/532335, accessed July 7, 2017.

58 John Michael, "Making a Stand: Standpoint Epistemologies, Political Positions, Proposition 187," *Telos,* Vol. 108, 1996, pp. 93-103.

59 Lynn Worsham, "Romancing the Stones: My Movie Date with Sandra Harding," *Journal of Advanced Composition,* Vol. 15, 1995, p. 568.

Chapter 33: Muted Group Theory

1 Cheris Kramarae, *Women and Men Speaking,* Newbury House, Rowley, MA, 1981, p. 1.

2 Barrie Thorne, Cheris Kramarae, and Nancy Henley (eds.), *Language, Gender and Society,* Newbury House, Rowley, MA, 1983, p. 9.

3 Cheris Kramarae, "Folklinguistics," *Psychology Today,* Vol. 8, June 1974, pp. 82-85.

4 Edwin Ardener, "Belief and the Problem of Women," in *Perceiving Women,* Shirley Ardener (ed.), Malaby Press, London, 1975, p. 2.

5 Shirley Ardener, "The Nature of Women in Society," in *Defining Females,* Halsted, New York, 1978, p. 21.

6 Edwin Ardener, "The 'Problem' Revisited," in *Perceiving Women,* p. 22.

7 Ibid., p. 25.

8 Kramarae, *Women and Men Speaking,* p. 3.

9 Simone de Beauvoir, *The Second Sex,* H. M. Parshley (ed. and trans.), Bantam, New York, 1964, p. xv.

10 Kramarae, *Women and Men Speaking,* p. 3.

11 Julia P. Stanley, "Paradigmatic Women: The Prostitute," in *Papers in Language Variation,* David L. Shores and Carole P. Hines (eds.), University of Alabama, Tuscaloosa, 1977, p. 7.

12 Kramarae, *Women and Men Speaking,* p. 1.

13 Virginia Woolf, *A Room of One's Own,* Hogarth (Penguin edition), 1928, p. 45.

14 Dorothy Smith, "A Peculiar Eclipsing: Women's Exclusion from Man's Culture," *Women's Studies International Quarterly,* Vol. 1, 1978, p. 281.

15 "Biography," J. K. Rowling's website, https://www.jkrowling.com/about, accessed June 5, 2017.

16 Wei Zhang and Cheris Kramarae, "Feminist Invitational Collaboration in a Digital Age: Looking Over Disciplinary and National Borders," *Women and Language,* Vol. 31, 2008, pp. 8-19.

17 Eli Pariser, *The Filter Bubble,* Penguin, New York, 2011, p. 129.

18 "Gender Diversity in Silicon Valley: A Comparison of Silicon Valley Public Companies and Large Public Companies," Fenwick & West LLP, 2014, http://www.fenwick.com/FenwickDocuments/Gender_Diversity_2014.pdf, accessed May 15, 2017.

19 Wei Zhang and Cheris Kramarae, "BOLD Ideas for Creative Social Networking: An Invitational Discussion," in *Handbook of Research on Digital Media and Creative Technologies,* Dew Harrison (ed.), IGI Global, Hershey, PA, 2015, p. 418.

20 Sheryl Sandberg, "Sheryl Sandberg on Why There Should Be More Women in Tech," *Cosmopolitan,* March 12, 2016, http://www.cosmopolitan.com/career/a54355/why-we-need-more-women-in-technology-fields, accessed May 13, 2017.

21 Kramarae, *Women and Men Speaking,* p. 3.

22 Tillie Olsen, *Silences,* Delacorte/Seymour Lawrence, New York, 1978, p. 23.

23 Kramarae, *Women and Men Speaking,* p. 19.

24 Ibid., p. 12.

25 Ibid., p. 4.

26 Cheris Kramarae and Paula Treichler, *A Feminist Dictionary: Amazons, Bluestockings and Crones,* 2ⁿᵈ ed., Pandora, London, 1992, p. 17.

27 Shannon Greenwood, Andrew Perrin, and Maeve Duggan, "Social Media Update 2016," *Pew Research Center,* November 11, 2016, http://www.pewinternet.org/2016/11/11/social-media-update-2016, accessed May 15, 2017.

28 Kramarae and Treichler, p. 4.

29 Dale Spender, *Man Made Language,* Routledge & Kegan, London, 1980, p. 87.

30 Cheris Kramarae, "Punctuating the Dictionary," *International Journal of the Sociology of Language,* Vol. 94, 1992, p. 135.

31 Kramarae and Treichler, p. 4.

32 Sady Doyle, "Mansplaining, Explained," *In These Times,* May 1, 2014, http://inthesetimes.com/article/16552/rebecca_solnit_explains_mansplaining, accessed May 15, 2017.

33 Sam Sifton and Grant Barrett, "The Words of the Year," *The New York Times,* December 18, 2010, http://www.nytimes.com/2010/12/19/weekinreview/19sifton.html, accessed May 15, 2017.

34 For Clinton's take, see "Jimmy Kimmel Mansplains to Hillary Clinton," https://www.youtube.com/watch?v=j2wBpYT6Zlo; for Fiorina's, see "If Men Were Treated Like Women in the Office with Carly Fiorina (Presidential Candidate)," https://www.youtube.com/watch?v=Tq5OQafDVxc, both videos accessed May 15, 2017.

35 Cheris Kramarae, "Harassment and Everyday Life," in *Women Making Meaning: New Feminist Directions in Communication,* Lana Rakow (ed.), Routledge, New York, 1992, p. 102.

36 Julia T. Wood (ed.), "Special Section—'Telling Our Stories': Sexual Harassment in the Communication Discipline," *Journal of Applied Communication Research,* Vol. 20, 1992, pp. 383-384.

37 Ann Burnett, Jody L. Mattern, Liliana L. Herakova, David H. Kahl Jr., Cloy Tobola, and Susan E. Bornsen, "Communicating/

Muting Date Rape: A Co-Cultural Theoretical Analysis of Communication Factors Related to Rape Culture on a College Campus," *Journal of Applied Communication Research,* Vol. 37, 2009, pp. 465–485.

38 Karen A. Foss and Sonja K. Foss, "Incorporating the Feminist Perspective in Communication Scholarship: A Research Commentary," in *Doing Research on Women's Communication: Perspectives on Theory and Method,* Kathryn Carter and Carole Spitzack (eds.), Ablex, Norwood, NJ, 1989, p. 72.

39 Cheris Kramarae, "Muted Group Theory and Communication: Asking Dangerous Questions," in *Women and Language,* Vol. 28, 2005, p. 58.

40 Caryn E. Medved, "Stay-at-Home Fathering as a Feminist Opportunity: Perpetuating, Resisting, and Transforming Gender Relations of Caring and Earning," *Journal of Family Communication,* Vol. 16, 2016, pp. 16–31 (see especially p. 24).

41 Kramarae, 2005, p. 59.

42 Deborah Tannen, *Conversational Style: Analyzing Talk Among Friends,* Ablex, Norwood, NJ, 1984, p. 43.

43 Kramarae, "Punctuating the Dictionary," p. 146.

Intercultural Communication

1 Gerry Philipsen, *Speaking Culturally: Exploration in Social Communication,* State University of New York, Albany, 1992, p. 7.

2 Gerry Philipsen, "Speaking 'Like a Man' in Teamsterville: Cultural Patterns of Role Enactment in an Urban Neighborhood," *Quarterly Journal of Speech,* Vol. 61, 1975, pp. 13–22.

3 Donal Carbaugh, "Communication Rules in *Donahue* Discourse," in *Cultural Communication and Intercultural Contact,* Donal Carbaugh (ed.), Lawrence Erlbaum, Hillsdale, NJ, 1990, pp. 119–149.

4 See chapter on cultural variability in William B. Gudykunst and Stella Ting-Toomey, *Culture and Interpersonal Communication,* Sage, Newbury Park, CA, 1988, pp. 39–59.

5 Edward T. Hall, *Beyond Culture,* Anchor, New York, 1977, p. 91.

6 Ibid., pp. 85–128.

7 Personal correspondence from Gerry Philipsen, August 2, 2009.

Chapter 34: Communication Accommodation Theory

1 Howard Giles, "The Social Origins of CAT," in *Communication Accommodation Theory: Negotiating Personal Relationships and Social Identities Across Contexts,* Howard Giles (ed.), Cambridge University Press, UK, 2016, p. 1.

2 Nikolas Coupland, Justine Coupland, Howard Giles, and Karen Henwood, "Accommodating the Elderly: Invoking and Extending a Theory," *Language and Society,* Vol. 17, 1988, p. 3.

3 Angie Williams and Howard Giles, "Intergenerational Conversations: Young Adults' Retrospective Accounts," *Human Communication Research,* Vol. 23, 1996, p. 237.

4 Ibid., p. 239.

5 Howard Giles, Nikolas Coupland, and Justine Coupland, "Accommodation Theory: Communication, Context, and Consequence," in *Contexts of Accommodation: Developments in Applied Sociolinguistics,* Howard Giles, Justine Coupland, and Nikolas Coupland (eds.), Cambridge University, UK, 1991, p. 10.

6 Howard Giles, Kimberly Noels et al., "Intergenerational Communication Across Cultures: Young People's Perceptions of Conversations with Family Elders, Non-Family Elders and Same-Age Peers," *Journal of Cross-Cultural Gerontology,* Vol. 18, 2003, p. 9.

7 Jake Harwood, Priya Raman, and Miles Hewstone, "The Family and Communication Dynamics of Group Salience," *Journal of Family Communication,* Vol. 6, 2006, pp. 181–200.

8 Williams and Giles, p. 233.

9 Giles, Coupland, and Coupland, p. 46.

10 Ibid., p. 42.

11 Henri Tajfel and John C. Turner, "The Social Identity Theory of Intergroup Behavior," in *The Psychology of Intergroup Relations,* L. Worchel and W. Austin (eds.), Nelson Hall, Chicago, IL, 1986, pp. 7–24.

12 Jake Harwood, "Communication as Social Identity," in *Communication as . . . Perspectives on Theory,* Gregory Shepherd, Jeffrey St. John, and Ted Striphas (eds.), Sage, Thousand Oaks, CA, 2006, p. 89.

13 Giles, Noels et al., p. 24.

14 Williams and Giles, p. 238.

15 Ibid., p. 221.

16 Cynthia Gallois and Victor Callan, "Interethnic Accommodation: The Role of Norms," in *Contexts of Accommodation,* p. 249.

17 Cynthia Gallois, Arlene Franklyn Stokes et al., "Communication Accommodation in Intercultural Encounters," in *Theories in Intercultural Communication,* Young Yun Kim and William B. Gudykunst (eds.), Sage, Newbury Park, CA, 1988, p. 166.

18 Cindy Gallois, Tania Ogay, and Howard Giles, "Communication Accommodation Theory: A Look Back and a Look Ahead," in *Theorizing About Intercultural Communication,* William B. Gudykunst (ed.), Sage, Thousand Oaks, CA, 2005, p. 123.

19 Giles, Coupland, and Coupland, p. 28.

20 Gallois, Ogay, and Giles, p. 126.

21 Fritz Heider, *The Psychology of Interpersonal Relations,* John Wiley, New York, 1958; and Harold Kelley, "The Process of Causal Attribution," *American Psychologist,* Vol. 28, 1973, pp. 107–128.

22 Ellen B. Ryan, Ann P. Anas, and Melissa Vuckovich, "The Effects of Age, Hearing Loss, and Communication Difficulty on First Impressions," *Communication Research Reports,* Vol. 24, 2007, pp. 13–19.

23 Howard Giles, Anthony Mulac, James Bradac, and Patricia Johnson, "Speech Accommodation Theory: The First Decade and Beyond," in *Communication Yearbook 10,* Margaret L. McLaughlin (ed.), Sage, Newbury Park, CA, 1987, p. 26.

24 Howard Giles, Michael Willemyns, Cindy Gallois, and Michelle Chernikoff Anderson, "Accommodating a New Frontier: The Context of Law Enforcement," in *Social Communication,* Klaus Fiedler (ed.), Psychology Press, New York, 2007, p. 130.

25 Michael S. Schmidt and Joseph Goldstein, "Even as Violent Crime Falls, Killing of Officers Rises," *The New York Times,* April 9, 2012, http://www.nytimes.com/2012/04/10/us/defying-trends-killings-of-police-officers-are-on-the-rise.html, accessed April 14, 2017. (Also published on p. A1 of the April 10, 2012 edition, titled "Killing of Police Continues Rising as Violence Falls.")

26 Susan Miller, "Officer Down: Police Deaths Hit a 5-Year High," *USA Today,* December 29, 2016, https://www.usatoday.com/story/news/nation/2016/12/29/officer-down-police-deaths-hit-5-year-high/95984998, accessed April 13, 2017.

27 Travis Dixon, Terry Schell, Howard Giles, and Kristin Drogos, "The Influence of Race in Police–Civilian Interactions: A Content Analysis of Videotaped Interactions Taken During Cincinnati Police Traffic Stops," *Journal of Communication,* Vol. 58, 2008, p. 530.

28 Giles, Willemyns, Gallois, and Anderson, p. 148.

29 Gallois, Ogay, and Giles, p. 134.

30 Marko Dragojevic, Jessica Gasiorek, and Howard Giles, "Accommodative Strategies as Core of the Theory," in *Communication Accommodation Theory,* pp. 50–51.

31 Cindy Gallois, Jessica Gasiorek, Howard Giles, and Jordan Soliz, "Communication Accommodation Theory: Integrations and New Framework Developments," in *Communication Accommodation Theory,* pp. 192–210.

32 Cindy Gallois and Howard Giles, "Accommodating Mutual Influence in Intergroup Encounters," in *Progress in Communication Sciences: Vol. 14,* M. T. Palmer and G. A. Barnett (eds.), Ablex, Stamford, UK, 1998, p. 158.

33 Gallois, Ogay, and Giles, p. 134.

34 Cindy Gallois, Ann Weatherall, and Howard Giles, "CAT and Talk in Action," in *Communication Accommodation Theory,* pp. 105–122.

35 Jordan Soliz and Gretchen Bergquist, "Methods of CAT Inquiry: Quantitative Studies," in *Communication Accommodation Theory,* pp. 60–84.

Chapter 35: Face-Negotiation Theory

1 Stella Ting-Toomey and Atsuko Kurogi, "Facework Competence in Intercultural Conflict: An Updated Face-Negotiation Theory," *International Journal of Intercultural Relations,* Vol. 22, 1998, p. 190.

2 Qin Zhang, Stella Ting-Toomey, and John G. Oetzel, "Linking Emotion to the Conflict Face-Negotiation Theory: A U.S.–China Investigation for the Mediating Effects of Anger, Compassion, and Guilt in Interpersonal Conflict," *Human Communication Research,* Vol. 40, 2014, p. 373.

3 Harry C. Triandis, *Individualism & Collectivism,* Westview, Boulder, CO, 1995, pp. 10–11.

4 Ting-Toomey and Kurogi, p. 190.

5 Ibid., p. 187.

6 Stella Ting-Toomey, "Intercultural Conflict Styles: A Face-Negotiation Theory," in *Theories in Intercultural Communication,* Young Yun Kim and William B. Gudykunst (eds.), Sage, Newbury Park, CA, 1988, p. 215.

7 Penelope Brown and Stephen Levinson, "Universals in Language Usage: Politeness Phenomenon," in *Questions and Politeness: Strategies in Social Interaction,* Esther N. Goody (ed.), Cambridge University Press, UK, 1978, p. 66.

8 Lin Yutang, *My Country and My People,* John Day, Taipei, Republic of China, 1968, p. 199.

9 M. A. Rahim, "A Measure of Styles of Handling Interpersonal Conflict," *Academy of Management Journal,* Vol. 26, 1983, pp. 368–376.

10 Robert Blake and Jane Mouton, *The Managerial Grid,* Gulf, Houston, 1964; Ralph Kilmann and Kenneth Thomas, "Developing a Forced-Choice Measure of Conflict-Handling Behavior: The 'Mode' Instrument," *Educational and Psychological Measurement,* Vol. 37, 1977, pp. 309–325.

11 Stella Ting-Toomey, Ge Gao et al., "Culture, Face Maintenance, and Styles of Handling Interpersonal Conflict: A Study in Five Cultures," *International Journal of Conflict Management,* Vol. 2, 1991, pp. 275–296.

12 Stella Ting-Toomey and Jiro Takai, "Explaining Intercultural Conflict: Promising Approaches and Directions," in *The Sage Handbook of Conflict Communication: Integrating Theory, Research, and Practice,* John G. Oetzel and Stella Ting-Toomey (eds.), Sage, Thousand Oaks, CA, 2006, pp. 701–712.

13 Ting-Toomey and Kurogi, p. 196.

14 Ting-Toomey borrowed this term from psychologists Hazel Markus and Shinobu Kitayama, "Culture and the Self: Implications for Cognition, Emotion, and Motivation," *Psychological Review,* Vol. 2, 1991, pp. 224–253. The term is now used widely within the intercultural communication research community.

15 John Oetzel and Stella Ting-Toomey, "Face Concerns in Interpersonal Conflict: A Cross-Cultural Empirical Test of the Face-Negotiation Theory," *Communication Research,* Vol. 30, 2003, p. 619.

16 John Oetzel, Adolfo J. Garcia, and Stella Ting-Toomey, "An Analysis of the Relationships Among Face Concerns and Facework Behaviors in Perceived Conflict Situations: A Four-Culture Investigation," *International Journal of Conflict Management,* Vol. 19, 2008, pp. 382–403.

17 Ibid.

18 Courtney Vail Fletcher, Masato Nakazawa et al., "Establishing Cross-Cultural Measurement Equivalence of Scales Associated with Face-Negotiation Theory: A Critical Issue in Cross-Cultural Comparisons," *Journal of International and Intercultural Communication,* Vol. 7, 2014, pp. 148–169.

19 Stella Ting-Toomey, "Translating Conflict Face-Negotiation Theory into Practice," *Handbook of Intercultural Training,* 3rd ed., Daniel Landis, Janet M. Bennett, and Milton J. Bennett (eds.) Sage, Thousand Oaks, CA, 2004, pp. 217–248.

20 Stella Ting-Toomey, *Communicating Across Cultures,* Guilford, New York, 1999, p. vii.

21 For examples of ethnography, see anthropologist Clifford Geertz' approach to cross-cultural communication in Chapter 19 of this book, or my chapter on Gerry Philipsen's *speech codes theory* in the archive at *www.afirstlook.com.*

Chapter 36: Co-Cultural Theory

1 Mark P. Orbe, *Constructing Co-Cultural Theory: An Explication of Culture, Power, and Communication,* Sage, Thousand Oaks, CA, 1998, p. 4.

2 Maria Knight Lapinski and Mark P. Orbe, "Evidence for the Construct Validity and Reliability of the Co-Cultural Theory Scales," *Communication Methods and Measures,* Vol. 1, 2007, p. 138.

3 All of the features in the three-by-three model (preferred outcomes, communication approaches, communication orientations, and communicative practices) and their relationships with each other are explained in the first three sources cited in the Second Look bibliography at the end of the chapter.

4 Mark P. Orbe, "Laying the Foundation for Co-Cultural Theory: An Inductive Approach to Studying 'Non-Dominant' Communication Strategies and the Factors that Influence Them," *Communication Studies,* Vol. 47, 1996, p. 168.

5 Orbe, *Constructing Co-Cultural Theory,* p. 104.

6 Ibid., p. 105.

7 Ibid.

8 Mark P. Orbe and Regina E. Spellers, "From the Margins to the Center," in *Theorizing About Intercultural Communication,* William B. Gudykunst (ed.), Sage, Thousand Oaks, CA, 2005, p. 175.

9 Amit Kama, "The Quest for Inclusion: Jewish-Israeli Gay Men's Perceptions of Gays in the Media," *Feminist Media Studies,* Vol. 2, 2002, p. 202.

10 Orbe, "Laying the Foundation," p. 166.

11 Anna L. Spradlin, "The Price of 'Passing': A Lesbian Perspective on Authenticity in Organizations," *Management Communication Quarterly,* Vol. 11, 1998, p. 601.

12 Cebreco, quoted in Orbe, *Constructing Co-Cultural Theory,* p. 88.

13 Orbe, "Laying the Foundation," p. 168.

14 J. D. Woods, *The Corporate Closet,* America Free Press, New York, 1993, p. 210.

15 Orbe, *Constructing Co-Cultural Theory,* p. 65.

16 Amit Kama, "From Terra Incognita to Terra Firma: The Logbook of the Voyage of Gay Men's Community into the Israeli Public Sphere," *Journal of Homosexuality,* Vol. 38, 2000, p. 146.

17 Cerise L. Glenn and Dante L. Johnson, "'What They See as Acceptable:' A Co-Cultural Theoretical Analysis of Black Male Students at a Predominantly White Institution," *Howard Journal of Communications,* Vol. 23, 2012, p. 357.

18 Orbe, "Laying the Foundation," p.165.

19 Ibid.

20 Orbe, *Constructing Co-Cultural Theory,* p. 77.

21 Ibid., p. 91.

22 Orbe, "Laying the Foundation," p. 165.

23 Ibid., p. 167.

24 Dawn O. Braithwaite, "'Just How Much Did That Wheelchair Cost?' Management of Privacy Boundaries by Persons with Disabilities," *Western Journal of Speech Communication,* Vol. 55, 1991, p. 267.

25 Mark P. Orbe, "'Remember, It's Always Whites' Ball': Descriptions of African American Male Communication," *Communication Quarterly,* Vol. 42, 1994, p. 290.

26   Orbe, "Laying the Foundation," p.168.

27   Mark P. Orbe, "Civil Rights Health: A Community-Based Assessment of Kalamazoo County (MI)," Michigan Department of Civil Rights, Lansing, February 5, 2003.

28   Marsha Cohen and Susan Avanzino, "We Are People First: Framing Organizational Assimilation Experiences of the Physically Disabled Using Co-Cultural Theory," *Communication Studies,* Vol. 61, 2010, p. 296.

29   Michael Cunningham, "If You're Queer and You're Not Angry in 1992, You're Not Paying Attention; If You're Straight it May Be Hard to Figure Out What All the Shouting's About," *Mother Jones,* May/June 1992, p. 63.

30   Orbe, *Constructing Co-Cultural Theory,* p. 92.

31   James Ezeilo, quoted in A. Hamilton, "For Middle-Class Blacks, Success Can Mean Turmoil," *The Courier-Journal,* April 26, 1996, p. A4.

32   Sakile K. Camara, Amy Katznelson, Jenny Hildebrandt-Sterling, and Todd Parker, "Heterosexism in Context: Qualitative Interaction Effects of Co-Cultural Responses," *Howard Journal of Communications,* Vol. 23, 2012, p. 324.

33   Orbe, *Constructing Co-Cultural Theory,* p. 60.

34   Ibid., pp. 66–67.

35   Ibid., p. 105.

36   Braithwaite, p. 266.

37   Orbe, *Constructing Co-Cultural Theory,* p. 13.

38   Ibid.

39   Ibid.

40   Ibid., p. 44; quoting Max van Manen, *Researching Lived Experience: Human Science for Action Sensitive Pedagogy,* Left Coast Press, Chicago, 2015 (1990), p. 88.

41   Ibid., pp. 86–108.

42   Ibid., p. 107.

43   Maria Knight Lapinski and Mark P. Orbe, "Evidence for the Construct Validity and Reliability of the Co-Cultural Theory Scales," *Communication Methods and Measures,* Vol. 1, 2007, pp. 137–164.

44   Ibid., pp. 147, 149–150.

45   Orbe, *Constructing Co-Cultural Theory,* p. 124.

Integration

1   Robert Bostrom and Lewis Donohew, "The Case for Empiricism: Clarifying Fundamental Issues in Communication Theory," *Communication Monographs,* Vol. 59, 1992, pp. 109, 127.

2   Stuart Hall, "Ideology and Communication Theory," in *Rethinking Communication,* Vol. 1, Brenda Dervin, Lawrence Grossberg, Barbara O'Keefe, and Ellen Wartella (eds.), Sage, Newbury Park, CA, 1989, pp. 52, 42.

3   Richard Rorty, *Consequences of Pragmatism,* University of Minnesota, Minneapolis, 1982, p. 197.

4   George Gerbner, "The Importance of Being Critical–In One's Own Fashion," *Journal of Communication,* Vol. 33, No. 3, 1983, p. 361.

5   Marie Hochmuth Nichols, *Rhetoric and Criticism,* Louisiana State University, Baton Rouge, 1963, p. 18.

Chapter 37: Common Threads in Comm Theories

1   To access a chapter on Heider's attribution theory that appeared in a previous edition of this text, click on Theory List at www.afirstlook.com.

2   Raymond Bauer, "The Obstinate Audience," *American Psychologist,* Vol. 19, 1964, pp. 319–328.

CREDITS AND ACKNOWLEDGMENTS

Interpersonal Messages

pp. 51–52: Em Griffin, "Game Metaphors" from *Making Friends (& Making Them Count)*, pp. 12–18. Copyright © 1987 Em Griffin. Used by permission of InterVarsity Press, P.O. Box 1400, Downers Grove, IL 60515, www.ivpress.com.

Chapter 6

p. 68: LUUUUTT Model from CMM Institute for Personal and Social Evolution, www.cmminstitute.net. 2017 CMM Institute. All rights reserved. Used by permission.

Chapter 36

p. 451 (*Fig. 36-1*): Orbe, M. P. (1998), "From The Standpoint(s) of Traditionally Muted Groups: Explicating A Co-cultural Communication Theoretical Model." *Communication Theory*, 8: 1–26. Table 2 (adapted). © 1998 International Communication Association. Reproduced with permission of Blackwell Publishing Ltd.

Appendix C

A7: "NCA Credo for Ethical Communication" reprinted by permission of National Communication Association, Washington, DC, www.natcom.org.

INDEX